Next Generation Search Engines:

Advanced Models for Information Retrieval

Christophe Jouis
University Paris Sorbonne Nouvelle and LIP6 (UPMC & CNRS), France

Ismail Biskri
University of Quebec at Trois Rivieres, Canada

Jean–Gabriel Ganascia
LIP6, (UPMC & CNRS), France

Magali Roux
INIST and LIP6, (UPMC & CNRS), France

Information Science
REFERENCE

Managing Director:	Lindsay Johnston
Senior Editorial Director:	Heather A. Probst
Book Production Manager:	Sean Woznicki
Development Manager:	Joel Gamon
Development Editor:	Myla Harty
Acquisitions Editor:	Erika Gallagher
Typesetter:	Nicole Sparano
Cover Design:	Nick Newcomer, Lisandro Gonzalez

Published in the United States of America by
Information Science Reference (an imprint of IGI Global)
701 E. Chocolate Avenue
Hershey PA 17033
Tel: 717-533-8845
Fax: 717-533-8661
E-mail: cust@igi-global.com
Web site: http://www.igi-global.com

Library of Congress Cataloging-in-Publication Data

Next generation search engines: advanced models for information retrieval / Christophe Jouis ... [et al.].
    p. cm.
  Includes bibliographical references and index.
  Summary: "This book is intended for scientists and decision-makers who wish to gain working knowledge about search engines in order to evaluate available solutions and to dialogue with software and data providers"--Provided by publisher.
  ISBN 978-1-4666-0330-1 (hardcover) -- ISBN 978-1-4666-0331-8 (ebook) -- ISBN 978-1-4666-0332-5 (print & perpetual access) 1. Information retrieval. 2. Information retrieval--Research. 3. Information storage and retrieval systems--Research. 4. Search engines. 5. Indexation (Economics) 6. Data mining. 7. User interfaces (Computer systems) 8. Information behavior. I. Jouis, Christophe, 1965-
  ZA3075.N495 2012
  025.042'52--dc23
                        2011044986

British Cataloguing in Publication Data
A Cataloguing in Publication record for this book is available from the British Library.

Editorial Advisory Board

Table of Contents

Section 2
Data Mining for Information Retrieval

Section 3
Interface

Detailed Table of Contents

Section 1
Indexation

Chapter 1

    Abhishek Das, Google Inc., USA
    Ankit Jain, Google Inc., USA

As the World Wide Web has grown, one notes a significant change and improvement in technologies of indexation. In this chapter, the authors describe in detail the key indexing technologies behind today's web-scale search engines. They are used to provide a better understanding of how web indexes are utilized. An overview of the infrastructure needed to support the growth of web search engines to modern scales is also given. Finally, the authors outline the potential future directions for search engines, particularly in real-time and social contexts.

Chapter 2

    Weimao Ke, College of Information Science and Technology, Drexel University, USA

The Web poses great challenges for information retrieval because of its size, dynamics, and heterogeneity. Centralized IR systems are becoming inefficient in the face of continued Web growth and a fully distributed architecture seems to be desirable. Without a centralized information repository and global control, a new distributed architecture can take advantage of distributed computing power and can allow a large number of systems to participate in the decision making for finding relevant information. In this chapter, the author presents a decentralized, organic view of information systems pertaining to searching in large-scale networks. The Clustering Paradox phenomenon is discussed.

Chapter 3

    Magali Roux, Laboratoire d'Informatique de Paris VI, France

Petabytes of data are generated by data-intensive sciences, also known as e-sciences. These data have to be searched to further perform multifarious analyses, including disparate data aggregation, in order to produce new knowledge. To achieve this, e-sciences have developed various strategies, mostly based on metadata, to deal with data complexity and specificities. In this chapter, Nuclear Physics, Geosciences and Biology, which are three seminal domains of e-sciences, are considered with regards to the strategies they have developed to search complex data. Metadata, which are data about data, were given a pivotal role in most of these approaches. The structure and the organization of metadata-based retrieval approaches are discussed.

Chapter 4

Christian Fluhr, GEOL Semantics, France

For several years, normalized vocabulary has provided an unambiguous description of photos for users' queries. One could imagine that indexes are made by professionals that control normalized vocabulary. However, according to the author, this is only an ideal view far from the reality of the actual indexation process. The description of photos is done by photographers who have no knowledge of information retrieval or of normalized vocabulary. Moreover, the description does not take into account aspects such as semantic ambiguities, cross-lingual querying, etc. In this chapter, the author presents an experience in which all these limitations are avoided.

Chapter 5

Hanêne Ghorbel, University of Sfax, Tunisia

Afef Bahri, University of Sfax, Tunisia

Rafik Bouaziz, University of Sfax, Tunisia

To improve the quality of information retrieval systems, a lot of research has been conducted over the last decade, which resulted in the development of Semantic Web techniques. It includes models and languages for the description of Web resources on the one hand and ontologies for describing resources on the other hand. Although ontologies mainly consist of hierarchical descriptions of domain concepts, some domains cannot be precisely and adequately formalized in classic ontology description languages. To overcome those limitations, promising research is being conducted on fuzzy ontologies. In this chapter, the authors propose a definition for a fuzzy ontological model based on fuzzy description logic, along with a methodology for building fuzzy ontologies and platforms.

Section 2
Data Mining for Information Retrieval

Chapter 6

Brahim Djioua, University of Paris-Sorbonne, France

Jean-Pierre Desclés, University of Paris-Sorbonne, France

Motasem Alrahabi, University of Paris-Sorbonne, France

In this chapter, the authors present a new approach for the design of web search engines that uses semantic and discourse annotations according to certain points of view, which has the advantage of focusing on the user interests. The semantic and discourse annotations are provided by means of the contextual exploration method. This method describes the discursive organization of texts by using linguistic knowledge present in the textual context. This knowledge takes the form of lists of linguistic markers and contextual exploration rules of each linguistic marker. The linguistic markers and the contextual exploration rules can help to retrieve relevant information like causality relations, definitions of concepts or quotations, etc., which are difficult to capture with classical methods using keywords.

In this chapter, the authors propose a new descriptive model for semantics dedicated to Information Retrieval. Every object is considered as a concept. Indeed, the model associates concepts to words. It analyzes every word of a document within its context and translates it into a concept, which will be the meaning of the word. The model is evaluated and documents are classified in categories by using their conceptual representations.

In this chapter the authors discuss the electronic discovery (eDiscovery), which consists of the process of collecting and analyzing electronic documents to determine their relevance to a legal matter. At first glance, the large volumes of data needed to be reviewed seem to lend themselves very well to traditional informational retrieval and text mining techniques. However, the noisy and ever-changing aspects of the collections of documents and the particularities of the domain cause the results to be inconsistent using existing tools. Therefore, new tools that take these specific elements into consideration need to be developed. Starting with the history of the collection process of legal documents, the authors then examine how text mining and information retrieval tools are used to deal with the collection process and further propose some research directions to improve it, such as collaborative filtering and cloud computing.

With the tremendous rise in popularity of social media web over the last few years, enterprises are showing more and more interest in the exploitation of opinions and sentiments expressed by the users about their products and services in the content of social media. Indeed, it contains precious and strategic data for product marketing and business intelligence. However, conventional search engines are inadequate for this task, as they are not designed to retrieve these particular kinds of data. Consequently, the field of opinion mining and retrieval is getting increasing amounts of attention. In this chapter, the authors present the Doxa project, a work in progress that aims to build a semantic enterprise search engine with integrated business intelligence technology and state of the art opinion and sentiment extraction, analysis and querying of electronic text in French.

In the Internet era, searching information on the Web has become an essential part of the lives for many people. Research on information retrieval in recent years has mainly focused on addressing issues such as document indexation, document ranking and on providing simple and quick means to search the Web, in an attempt to provide fast and high-quality results to user queries. Despite the great progress made in regard to those aspects and the success of many search engines, people still commonly have difficulties retrieving the information they are seeking, especially when they are unable to formulate an appropriate query or are overwhelmed by results. More needs to be done to include the user into the search process and assist them into the crafting and refinement of their queries and the exploration of the results. This chapter discusses the state-of-the-art research in the field of human-centered Web search.

In this chapter the author illustrates the customization of the web browser from the perspective of users who work at any of the tasks of using, planning, acquiring, searching, analyzing, organizing, storing, programming, distributing, marketing, or otherwise contributing to the transformation and commerce of information. In fact, the browser and its various possible parameterizations seem to be an important factor that allows a user to better meet its task. An analysis of the customization of web browsers for knowledge workers is proposed. It demonstrates that a browser offering the possibility of add-ons is an application that is highly adaptable in meeting the specific requirements of its users.

When using search engines, users tend to input very short and thus often ambiguous queries. Therefore, identifying the correct user's search needs is not always an easy task. In order to solve this issue, the next generation of search engines will assist the users in dealing with large sets of results by offering various post-search tools such as result clustering, which has received a lot of attention recently. It consists of clustering search results into a hierarchical labeled tree so the users can customize their view of search results by navigating through it. In this chapter, the author presents WSC, a high-performance result clustering system, based on a mixed clustering method and a genuine divisive hierarchical clustering algorithm to organize the labels into a hierarchical tree. The author also shows that WSC achieves better performances than current commercial and academic systems.

Chapter 13

To express their needs, users formulate queries that often take the form of keywords submitted to an information retrieval system based either on a Boolean model, on a vector model, or on a probabilistic model. It is often difficult for users to find key words that express their exact needs. In many cases, the users are confronted on the one hand with a lack of knowledge on the subject of interest in their information search and on the other hand with biases that may affect the results. Thus, retrieving relevant documents in just one pass is almost impossible. There is a need to carry out a reformulation of the query either by using completely different keywords, or by expanding the initial query with the addition of new keywords. In this chapter, authors present a semi-automatic method of reformulation of queries based on the combination of two methods of data mining: text classification and maximal association rules.

Chapter 14

In order to provide a more sophisticated and satisfactory answer to informational needs, question answering systems aim to give one or more answers in the form of precise and concise sentences to a question asked by a user in natural language, instead of only a set of documents as a result to a query as in a traditional retrieval information system. Therefore, Question Answering systems rely heavily on natural language processing techniques for syntactic and semantic analysis and for the construction of appropriate answers. This chapter presents the state of the art in the field of question answering, within which the authors cover all types of promising QA systems, techniques and approaches for the next generation of search engines, focusing mainly on systems aimed at the (semantic) web.

This chapter is dedicated to factual question-answering in open domains and in specialty domains. In querying a database, it is expected that factual questions will yield short answers that give precise information. However, with a web environment, topics are not limited and knowledge is not structured. Finding answers requires analyzing texts. In fact, the problem of finding answers to questions consists of, in this context, extracting a piece of information from a text. In this chapter, the author presents question-answering systems that extract answers from web documents in a fixed multilingual collection.

Chapter 16

The recent emergence of mobile handsets as a new means of information exchange has led up to the need for information retrieval systems specialized for mobile users. Lately, a lot of efforts have been put into the development of robust mobile search engines capable of providing attractive and practical services to mobile users, such as tools that provide directions to business locations according to the user location or voice speech search that uses speech recognition technologies. However, the capabilities of current mobile search engines are still limited. In particular, enhancements are made possible by exploiting information about the current context of the users and providing this to search engines to improve the relevance of the results. In this chapter, a context model and an architecture that promote the integration of contextual information are presented through a case study.

Chapter 17

The explosion of information available on the Internet and its heterogeneity has considerably reduced the effectiveness of traditional information retrieval systems. In recent years, much research has been devoted to develop contextual information retrieval technologies. Moreover, from the proliferation of new means of communication and information access, such as mobile devices, have emerged new needs in IR. In this chapter, the authors discuss this specific issue with respect to mobile information retrieval, followed by a presentation of a model of spatio-temporal-based personalization for mobile search, using contextual data such as location and time in order to dynamically select the most appropriate profile from a given situation. Each profile contains user interests learnt according to searches in past individual explorations. They also propose a novel evaluation scenario for mobile search based on diary study entries.

Section 4
Evaluation

In this chapter, the user perspective is highlighted. Some recent challenges in search engine evolution change users' information behavior. The authors identify four major trends in the "user-oriented approach" that focus respectively on strategies and tactics, cognitive and psychological approaches, management, and consumer and marketing approaches. However, the authors note that there is a need to better understand the dynamics and the nature of the interaction between Web searching and users. Also, other aspects such as ethics, cultural issues, growing social networks, etc. need to be considered.

Chapter 19

Nowadays, search engines constitute the main means of classifying, sorting, and delivering information to users over the Internet. As time progresses, advances in Artificial Intelligence will be made and thus new artificial intelligence technologies will be developed to enhance the sophistication of the search engines. This future generation of search engines, called artificial intelligence enabled search engines, will be compelled to play an even more crucial role for information retrieval, but this will not be without any consequences. Through this chapter, the author analyzes the concept of technological singularity, discusses the direct and indirect impacts of the development of new technologies and artificial intelligence, notably regarding search engines, and proposes a four-stage evolution model of search engines.

Chapter 20

The evaluation of information retrieval systems and search engines in development or already on the market is a crucial process for the improvement of the quality of the search results. Quality measures for most evaluations consist of calculating precision and recall using a set of ad-hoc queries and assume that common users examine every result returned by a search engine in the same order they are presented. While this may be true in some contexts, it has been shown that it is not necessarily the case in Web searches, where modern Web search engines present results in various and enriched forms and where the users are typically interested only in a few highly relevant results and examine them as they see fit. Therefore, there is a need for new extended evaluation models for Web search engines. To this end, the author proposes a framework for evaluating the retrieval effectiveness of next-generation search engines.

Preface

NEEDS AND REQUIREMENTS FOR INFORMATION RETRIEVAL

Scientific and economic organizations are confronted with handling an abundance of strategic information in their domain activities. One main challenge is to be able to find the right information quickly and accurately. In order to do so, organizations must master information access: getting relevant query results that are organized, sorted, and actionable.

As noted by Mukhopadhyay and Mukhopadhyay (2004), almost everyone agrees that in the current state of the art on Internet search engine technology, extracting information from the Web is an art itself. Almost all commercial search engines use classical keyword-based methods for information retrieval (IR). That means that they try to match user specified patterns (i.e., queries) to the texts of all documents in their database and then return the documents that contain terms matching the query. Such methods are quite effective for well-controlled collections - such as bibliographic CD-ROMs or handcrafted scientific information repositories. Unfortunately the organization of the Internet has not been rationally supervised, but it has rather spontaneously evolved and, therefore, cannot be treated as a well-controlled collection. It contains a lot of garbage and redundant information and, what is maybe even more important, it does not rely on any underlying semantic structure intended to facilitate navigation.

In addition, some of the current issues result from inappropriate query constructions. The user queries that are usually submitted to search engines are often too general (like "water sources" or "capitals") and this produces millions of returned documents. The results, which are of interest to users, are probably among them, but they cannot be distinguished from the mass; it appears impossible to emphasize them to the human attention. One hundred documents are generally regarded as the maximum amount of information that can be useful to users in such situations.

On the other hand, some documents cannot be retrieved because the specified pattern does not exactly match. This can be caused by flexion in some languages, or by confusion introduced by synonyms and complex idiom structures (e.g., in English the word Mike is often given as an example of this, as it can be used as a male name or as a shortened form for the noun "microphone"). Most search engines have also very poor user interfaces. Computer-aided query constructions are very rare and the presentation of the search results concentrates mostly on individual documents, but it does not provide any general overview of retrieved data, which is crucial when the number of returned documents is huge. A last group of problems comes from the nature of information stored on the Internet. Search tools must not only deal with hypertext documents (in the form of WWW pages) but also with text repositories (message archives, e-books etc.), FTP and Usenet servers and with many sources of non-textual information such as audio, video, and interactive contents.

Recent technological progress in computer science, Web technologies, and constantly evolving information available on the Internet has drastically changed the landscape of search and access to information. Web search has significantly evolved in recent years. In the beginning, web search engines such as Google and Yahoo! were only providing search service over text documents. Aggregated search was one of the first steps to go beyond text search, and was the beginning of a new era for information seeking and retrieval. These days, new web search engines support aggregated search over a number of vertices, and blend different types of documents (e.g., images, videos) in their search results. New search engines employ advanced techniques involving machine learning, computational linguistics and psychology, user interaction and modeling, information visualization, Web engineering, artificial intelligence, distributed systems, social networks, statistical analysis, semantic analysis, and technologies over query sessions.

Documents no longer exist on their own; they are connected to other documents, they are associated with users and their position in a social network, and they can be mapped onto a variety of ontologies. Similarly, retrieval tasks have become more interactive and are solidly embedded in a user's geospatial, social, and historical context. It is conjectured that new breakthroughs in information retrieval will not come from smarter algorithms that better exploit existing information sources, but from new retrieval algorithms that can intelligently use and combine new sources of contextual metadata.

With the rapid growth of web-based applications, such as search engines, Facebook, and Twitter, the development of effective and personalized information retrieval techniques and of user interfaces is essential. The amount of shared information and of social networks has also considerably grown, requiring metadata for new sources of information, like Wikipedia and ODP. These metadata have to provide classification information for a wide range of topics, as well as for social networking sites like Twitter, and Facebook, each of which provides additional preferences, tagging information and social contexts. Due to the explosion of social networks and other metadata sources, it is an opportune time to identify ways to exploit such metadata in IR tasks such as user modeling, query understanding, and personalization, to name a few. Although the use of traditional metadata such as html text, web page titles, and anchor text is fairly well-understood, the use of category information, user behavior data, and geographical information is just beginning to be studied.

OBJECTIVES OF THE BOOK

The main goal of this book is to transfer new research results from the fields of advanced computer sciences and information science to the design of new search engines. The readers will have a better idea of the new trends in applied research. The achievement of relevant, organized, sorted, and workable answers – to name but a few – from a search is becoming a daily need for enterprises and organizations, and, to a greater extent, for anyone. It does not consist of getting access to structural information as in standard databases; nor does it consist of searching information strictly by way of a combination of key words. It goes far beyond that. Whatever its modality, the information sought should be identified by the topics it contains, that is to say by its textual, audio, video or graphical contents. This is not a new issue. However, recent technological advances have completely changed the techniques being used. New Web technologies, the emergence of Intranet systems and the abundance of information on the Internet have created the need for efficient search and information access tools.

TARGET AUDIENCE

This book is intended for scientists and decision-makers who wish to gain working knowledge of searches in order to evaluate available solutions and to dialogue with software and data providers. It also targets intranet or Web server designers, developers and administrators who wish to understand how to integrate search technology into their applications according to their needs. This book is further designed for designers, developers and administrators of databases, groupware applications and document management systems (EDM), as well as directors of libraries or documentation centers who seek a deeper understanding of the tools they use, and how to set up new information systems. Lastly, this book is aimed at all professionals in technology or competitive intelligence and, more generally, the specialists of the information market.

A BRIEF OVERVIEW OF THE ORGANIZATION OF THE BOOK

The book is divided into four sections:

Section 1 is "Indexation". The goal of automatic indexing is to establish an index for a set of documents that has to facilitate future access to documents and to their content. Usually, an index is composed of a list of descriptors, each of them being associated to a list of documents and/or of parts of documents to which it refers. In addition, theses references may be weighted. When searching to answer the users' queries, the system looks for a list of answers, of which an index is as close as possible to the demand. As a consequence, indexation could be seen as a required preliminary to intelligent information retrieval, since it pre-structures textual data according to topic, domain, keyword or center of interest.

Section 2 is "Data Mining for Information Retrieval". Data Mining (i.e., Knowledge Discovery from Data Bases) is the process of automatically extracting meaningful, useful, previously unknown and ultimately comprehensible patterns from large data sets. Data mining is a relatively young and interdisciplinary field that combines methods from statistics and artificial intelligence with database management. With the considerable increase of processing power, storage capacities, and inter-connectivity of computer technology, in particular with the grid computation, data mining is now seen as an increasingly important field by modern business for transforming unprecedented quantities of digital data into new knowledge that provides a significant competitive advantage. This is now a large part of what people refer to as business intelligence strategy. It is currently used in a wide range of profiling practices, such as marketing, surveillance, fraud detection, and scientific discovery. The growing consensus that data mining can bring real added value has led to an explosion in demand for novel data mining technologies.

Section 3 is "Interface". The term "interface" refers to the part of the search engine in which (1) the user formulates his request and (2) the user reads the results. The interface is then seen in four views: Human-centered Web Search, Personalization, Question/Answering, and Mobile Search Engines. "Human-centered Web Search" is understood to be how Web search engines help people to find the information they are seeking. "Personalization" takes keywords from the user as an expression of their information need, but also uses additional information about the user (such as their preferences, community, location or history) to assist in determining the relevance of pages. "Question/Answering" addresses the problem of finding answers to questions posed in natural language; answering is the task which, when given a query in natural language, aims at finding one or more concise answers in the form of sentences or phrases. "Mobile Search Engines" may be defined as the combining of search technologies and knowledge about the user context in his mobile environment into a single framework in order to provide the most appropriate answer for users information needs.

Finally, Section 4 is "Evaluation". Evaluation means two things: (1) tracing the users' behaviors, with a special attention to the concept of "information practice" and other related concepts such as "use", "activity", and "behavior" largely used in the literature but not always strictly defined, the aim being to place the users and their needs at the center of the design process; (2) evaluating the next generation search engines with four main criteria for improving the quality of the search results: index quality, quality of the results, quality of search features, and search engine usability.

Christophe Jouis
University Paris Sorbonne Nouvelle and LIP6 (UPMC & CNRS), France

Ismaïl Biskri
University of Quebec at Trois Rivieres, Canada

Jean-Gabriel Ganascia
LIP6, (UPMC & CNRS), France

Magali Roux
INIST and LIP6, (UPMC & CNRS), France

REFERENCE

Mukhopadhyay, B., & Mukhopadhyay, S. (2004, February 11-13). Data mining techniques for information retrieval. In *Proceedings of the 2nd International Conference of the Convention on Automation of Libraries in Education and Research Institution*, New Delhi, India (p. 506).

Section 1
Indexation

Chapter 1
Indexing the World Wide Web:
The Journey So Far

Abhishek Das
Google Inc., USA

Ankit Jain
Google Inc., USA

ABSTRACT

In this chapter, the authors describe the key indexing components of today's web search engines. As the World Wide Web has grown, the systems and methods for indexing have changed significantly. The authors present the data structures used, the features extracted, the infrastructure needed, and the options available for designing a brand new search engine. Techniques are highlighted that improve relevance of results, discuss trade-offs to best utilize machine resources, and cover distributed processing concepts in this context. In particular, the authors delve into the topics of indexing phrases instead of terms, storage in memory vs. on disk, and data partitioning. Some thoughts on information organization for the newly emerging data-forms conclude the chapter.

INTRODUCTION

The World Wide Web is considered to be the greatest breakthrough in telecommunications after the telephone, radically altering the availability and accessibility to information. Quoting the new media reader from MIT press (Wardrip-Fruin, 2003):

"The World-Wide Web (W3) was developed to be a pool of human knowledge, and human culture, which would allow collaborators in remote sites to share their ideas and all aspects of a common project."

The last two decades have witnessed many significant attempts to make this knowledge "discoverable". These attempts broadly fall into two categories:

DOI: 10.4018/978-1-4666-0330-1.ch001

1. Classification of webpages in hierarchical categories (directory structure), championed by the likes of Yahoo! and Open Directory Project;
2. Full-text index search engines such as Excite, AltaVista, and Google.

The former is an intuitive method of arranging web pages, where subject-matter experts collect and annotate pages for each category, much like books are classified in a library. With the rapid growth of the web, however, the popularity of this method gradually declined. First, the strictly manual editorial process could not cope with the increase in the number of web pages. Second, the user's idea of what sub-tree(s) to seek for a particular topic was expected to be in line with the editors', who were responsible for the classification. We are most familiar with the latter approach today, which presents the user with a keyword search interface and uses a pre-computed web *index* to algorithmically retrieve and rank web pages that satisfy the query. In fact, this is probably the most widely used method for navigating through cyberspace today, primarily because it can scale as the web grows. Even though the indexable web is only a small fraction of the web (Selberg, 1999), the earliest search engines had to handle orders of magnitude more documents than previous information retrieval systems. Around 1995, when the number of static web pages was believed to double every few months, AltaVista reported having crawled and indexed approximately 25 million webpages. In 1997, the total estimated number of pages indexed by all the largest search engines was 200 million pages (Bharat, 1998), which reportedly grew to 800 million pages by 1998 (Lawrence, 1999). Indices of today's search engines are several orders of magnitude larger (Gulli, 2005); Google reported around 25 billion web pages in 2005 (Patterson, 2005), while Cuil indexed 120 billion pages in 2008 (Arrington, 2008). Harnessing together the power of hundreds,

if not thousands, of machines has proven key in addressing this challenge of grand scale.

Using search engines may have become routine nowadays, but they too have followed an evolutionary path (Figure 1). Jerry Yang and David Filo created *Yahoo* in 1994, starting it out as a listing of their favorite web sites along with a description of each page (Yahoo, 2010). Later in 1994, *WebCrawler* was introduced which was the first full-text search engine on the Internet; the entire text of each page was indexed for the first time. Introduced in 1993 by six Stanford University students, *Excite* became functional in December 1995. It used statistical analysis of word relationships to aid in the search process and is part of *AskJeeves* today. *Lycos*, created at CMU by Dr. Michael Mauldin, introduced relevance retrieval, prefix matching, and word proximity in 1994. Though it was the largest of any search engine at the time, indexing over 60 million documents in 1996, it ceased crawling the web for its own index in April 1999. Today it provides access to human-powered results from *LookSmart* for popular queries and crawler-based results from *Yahoo* for others. *Infoseek* went online in 1995 and is now owned by the Walt Disney Internet Group. *AltaVista,* also started in 1995, was the first search engine to allow natural language questions and advanced searching techniques. It also provided multimedia search for photos, music, and videos. In February 2003, *AltaVista* was bought by *Overture*, which itself was acquired by *Yahoo* later in the year. *Inktomi* was started in 1996 at UC Berkeley, and in June of 1999 introduced a directory search engine powered by *concept induction* technology. This technology tries to model human conceptual classification of content, and projects this intelligence across millions of documents. *Yahoo* purchased *Inktomi* in 2003.

AskJeeves launched in 1996 and became famous for being the natural language search engine, that allowed users to search by framing queries in question form and responding with what seemed to be the right answer. In reality, behind the scenes,

Figure 1. History of major Web search engine innovations (1994-2010)

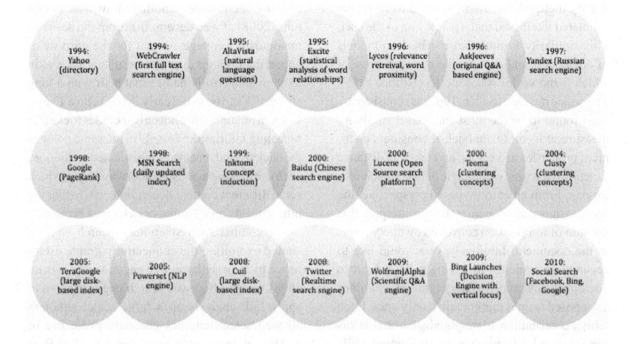

the company had many human editors who monitored search logs and located what seemed to be the best sites to match the most popular queries. 1997 was the first year in which two major non-US search engines launched: *Fast Search & Transfer* (FAST) in Norway and *Yandex* in Russia. *Yandex* is the most popular site in Russia to this day and has over 64% market share (Wikipedia, 2011). In 1999, they acquired *Direct Hit*, which had developed the world's first click popularity search technology, and in 2001, they acquired *Teoma* whose technology was built upon clustering concepts of subject-specific popularity. *Teoma* was founded in 2000 at Rutgers University and was a result of the DiscoWeb project (Davison, 1998). Google, developed by Sergey Brin and Larry Page at Stanford University, launched in 1998 and used inbound links to rank sites. The *MSN Search* and *Open Directory Project* were also started in 1998, of which the former turned into a full-fledged search engine in 2005 and then reincarnated as *Bing* in 2009. The Open Directory, according to its website, "is the largest,

most comprehensive human-edited directory of the Web". Formerly known as *NewHoo*, it was acquired by AOL Time Warner-owned Netscape in November 1998. *Baidu*, China's largest search engine with over 55% market share (Jin, 2011), was formed in 2000, the same year the open source search library, *Lucene*, first released. *Vivisimo* was founded in 2000 by a trio of researchers from CMU to organize numerous search results into several meaningful categories (clusters). They finally became successful in 2004 with the metasearch engine *Clusty*, which got acquired in 2010 by Yippy, Inc. Beginning in 2005, using licensed natural language technology from PARC, *Powerset* started building a natural language search engine to find targeted answers to user questions (as opposed to keyword based search). Microsoft acquired *Powerset* in 2008.

All current search engines rank web pages to identify potential answers to a query. Borrowing from information retrieval, a statistical similarity measure has always been used in practice to assess the closeness of each document (web page) to the user text (query); the underlying principle being that the higher the similarity score, the greater the estimated likelihood that it is relevant to the user. This similarity formulation is based on models of documents and queries, the most effective of which is the vector space model (Salton, 1975). The cosine measure (Salton, 1962) has consistently been found to be the most successful similarity measure in using this model. It considers document properties as vectors, and takes as distance function the cosine of the angle between each vector pair. From an entropy-based perspective, the score assigned to a document can be interpreted as the sum of information conveyed by query terms in the document. Intuitively, one would like to accumulate evidence by giving more weight to documents that match a query term several times as opposed to ones that contain it only once. Each term's contribution is weighted such that terms appearing to be discriminatory are favored while reducing the impact of more common terms. Most similarity measures are a composition of a few statistical values: frequency of a term t in a document d (term frequency or TF), frequency of a term t in a query, number of documents containing a term t (document frequency or DF), number of terms in a document, number of documents in the collection, and number of terms in the collection. Introduction of document-length pivoting (Singhal, 1996) addressed the issue of long documents either containing too many terms, or many instances of the same term.

The explosive growth of the web can primarily be attributed to the decentralization of content publication, with essentially no control of authorship. A huge drawback of this is that web pages are often a mix of facts, rumors, suppositions and even contradictions. In addition, web-page content that is trustworthy to one user may not be so to another. With search engines becoming the primary means to discover web content, however, users could no longer self-select sources they find trustworthy. Thus, a significant challenge for search engines is to assign a user-independent measure of trust

to each website or webpage. Over time, search engines encountered another drawback (Manning, 2008) of web decentralization: the desire to manipulate webpage content for the purpose of appearing high up in search results. This is akin to companies using names that start with a long string of A's to be listed early in the Yellow Pages. Content manipulation not only includes tricks like repeating multiple keywords in the same color as the background, but also sophisticated techniques such as cloaking and using doorway pages, which serve different content depending on whether the http request came from a crawler or a browser.

To combat such spammers, search engines started exploiting the connectivity graph, established by hyperlinks on web pages. Google (Brin, 1998) was the first web search engine known to apply link analysis on a large scale, although all web search engines currently make use of it. They assigned each page a score, called PageRank, which can be interpreted as the fraction of time that a random web surfer will spend on that webpage when following the out-links from each page on the web. Another interpretation is that when a page links to another page, it is effectively casting a vote of confidence. PageRank calculates a page's importance from the votes cast for it. HITS is another technique employing link analysis which scores pages as both hubs and authorities, where a good hub is one that links to many good authorities, and a good authority is one that is linked from many good hubs. It was developed by Jon Kleinberg and formed the basis of Teoma (Kleinberg, 1999).

Search engines aim not only to give quality results but also to produce these results as fast as possible. With several terabytes of data spread over billions of documents in thousands of computers, their systems are enormous in scale. In comparison, the text of all the books held in a small university might occupy only around 100 GB. In order to create such highly available systems, which continually index the growing web and serve queries with sub-second response times, it must optimize all resources: disk, memory, CPU time, as well as disk transfers.

This chapter describes how the index of a web-scale search engine organizes all the information contained in its documents. In the following sections, we will cover the basics of indexing data structures, introduce techniques that improve relevance of results, discuss trade-offs to best utilize the machine resources, and cover distributed processing concepts that allow scaling and updating of the index. In particular, we will delve into the topics of indexing phrases instead of terms, storage in memory vs. on disk, and data partitioning. We will conclude with some thoughts on information organization for the newly emerging data-forms.

ORGANIZING THE WEB

In order to avoid linearly scanning each webpage at query time, an *index* of all possible query terms is prepared in advance. Let's consider the collection of English books in a library. The simplest approach would be to keep track of all words from the English dictionary that appear in each book. On repeating this across all books, we end up with a *term-incidence matrix*, in which each entry tells us if a specific word occurs in a book or not. Figure 2 shows a sample term-incidence matrix. The collection of documents over which a search engine performs retrieval is referred to as a *corpus*. So, for a corpus of 1M documents with 100K distinct words, ~10GB (1M x 100K) will be required to hold the index in matrix form. The corpus itself will require around 4 bytes to encode each distinct word and hence a total of 4 GB (1M x 1000 x 4) storage if each document is 1000 words long on average. Clearly, lot of space is wasted in recording the absence of terms in a document, and hence a much better representation is to record only the occurrences.

The most efficient index structure is an *inverted index*: a collection of lists, one per *term*, recording the documents containing that term. Each item in the list for a term t, also referred to as a *posting*, records the ordinal document identifier d, and its corresponding term frequency (TF): $<d, tf>$. Note that if 4 bytes are used to encode each posting, a term appearing in ~100K documents will result in a posting list of size 100KB to 1MB; though most terms will have much shorter posting lists. We illustrate this in Figure 3 for the same example as in Figure 2.

Figure 2. Term-incidence matrix for a sample of English documents

document identifier

		1	2	3	4	5	6
	the	X	X	X	X	X	X
	to	X		X	X	X	X
term	john		X		X		X
	realize	X		X			X
	algorithm					X	

In our example, all terms in the English dictionary were known before hand. This, however, does not hold true on the web where authors create content in a multitude of languages, along with large variations in grammar and style. Webpages are often found riddled with text in various colors and fonts, as well as images that lead to richer textual content when clicked, thereby providing no clear semantic structure. In addition, the character sequences are encoded using one of many byte-encoding schemes, such as UTF-8 or other vendor-specific standards. Since any visible component of a webpage might reasonably be used as query term, we take a superset of all spoken words. The set also includes numbers, constructs such as IA-32 or X-86, as well as tokens appearing in any URL. This collection of terms in an index is conventionally called a *dictionary* or *lexicon*. Dictionary and posting lists are the central data structures used in a search engine.

Building a Dictionary of Terms

For efficiency purposes, an identifier is used to represent each term in the dictionary, instead of storing them as strings. This mapping is either created on the fly while processing the entire corpus, or is created in two passes. The first pass compiles the dictionary while the second pass constructs the index. In both cases, the first step is to turn each document into a list of tokens and then use linguistic preprocessing to normalize them into indexing terms. This involves simple steps like breaking down sentences on whitespace and eliminating punctuation characters, as well as tricky steps like analyzing uses of the apostrophe for possession and verb contractions. Another common practice is *case-folding* by which all letters are reduced to lower case. This is a good idea in general since it allows the query *(automobile)* to also match instances of '*Automobile*' (which usually occurs at the beginning of a sentence). Another use case is in matching words with diacritics since users often enter queries without the diacritics. Documents also tend to use different forms of the same word, such as *realize*, *realizes*, and *realizing*. *Stemming* is a heuristic process that chops off the ends of words in the hope of collapsing derivationally related words. The most common algorithm used for stemming English words is *Porter's algorithm* (Porter, 1980). Languages other than English may require even more sophisticated techniques for term tokenization (Fung, 1998; Chiang, 1992).

Certain terms, such as '*the*' and '*to*', are extremely common across documents and hence add little value towards matching specific documents to bag-of-words queries. On sorting the dictionary terms by their document frequency (DF), and

Figure 3. Illustration of posting lists for example from Figure 2

Dictionary		Posting Lists	(document identifier, term frequency)			
the	→	1, 9	2, 8	3, 8	4, 5	5, 6	6, 9
to	→	1, 5	3, 1	4, 2	5, 2	6, 6	
john	→	2, 4	4, 1	6, 4			
realize	→	1, 2	3, 1	6, 3			
algorithm	→	5, 3					

then selecting the most frequent terms, allows us to identify all common terms. Posting lists corresponding to such terms tend to be very long too, thereby adding to query processing cost. Removing these frequently occurring words (*stop* words) from the dictionary initially seemed like a good idea since it does little harm and saves considerable storage space. Search engines, however, tend not to discard them since they play an important role in queries framed as phrases. By placing double quotes around a set of words, users ask to consider those words in precisely that order without any change. Eliminating 'the' or 'who' in a query like *(The Who)* will completely alter its meaning and user intent. Later in this chapter, we will discuss how compression techniques overcome the storage cost of posting lists for common words.

Answering the User's Query

Now we look at how retrieval is performed for a typical query using an inverted index. Given a query of three terms, the first step is to find those terms in the dictionary. Following that, the corresponding posting lists are fetched (and transferred to memory if residing on disk). Intersecting the lists on document identifiers then retrieves the relevant documents. A key insight (Cutting & Pedersen, 1997) is to start with the least frequent term since its posting list will be the shortest. Finally, the retrieved set of documents are ranked and re-ordered to present to the user. Given the small corpus size (1M), the above operations can be performed on any machine in well under a second. Understanding the usage of each computing resource is critical since search engines, built over thousands of machines, aim to not only give quality results but to produce these results as fast as possible.

- **Disk space** is typically required to store the inverted posting lists;
- **Disk transfer** is used to fetch inverted lists;

- **Memory** is required for the dictionary and for accumulating documents from the fetched lists; and
- **CPU** time is required for processing inverted lists and re-ordering them.

Performance optimizations of each of these components contribute towards several indexing design decisions. The choice of data structure for posting lists impacts both storage and CPU time. Search engines use both memory and disk to hold the various posting lists. If posting lists are kept in memory, a fixed-length array would be wasteful since common terms occur in many more documents (longer posting lists) compared to others. Singly linked lists and variable length arrays offer two good alternatives. While singly linked lists allow cheap updates such as insertion of documents following a new crawl, variable length arrays win in space requirement by avoiding the overhead for pointers. Variable length arrays also require less CPU time because of their use of contiguous memory, which in addition enables speedup through caching. A potential hybrid scheme is to use a linked list of fixed-length arrays for each term.

When storing posting lists on disk, it is better to store the postings contiguously without explicit pointers. This not only conserves space, but also requires only one disk seek to read most posting lists into memory. Let's consider an alternative in which lists are composed of a sequence of blocks that are linked in some way. Recall that there is a huge variance in size of posting lists; a typical term requires anywhere from 100KB to 1MB, a common term requires many times more, but most terms require less than 1KB for their lists. This places a severe constraint on the size of a fixed-size block, and significantly degrades typical query evaluation time. Apart from demanding additional space for next-block pointers, it also complicates update procedures.

Speeding Up Multi-Term Queries

As mentioned before, a typical query evaluation requires fetching multiple posting lists and intersecting them to quickly find documents that contain all terms. This *intersection* operation is a crucial one in determining query evaluation time. A simple and effective method is the merge algorithm: for a two word query, it maintains pointers into both lists and walks through them together by comparing the ordinal document identifiers. If they are the same, the document is selected and both pointers are advanced; otherwise the one pointing to the smaller identifier advances. Hence the operating time is linear in the size of posting lists, which in turn is bounded by the corpus size.

One way to process posting list intersection in sub-linear time is to use a *skip list* (Pugh, 1990), which augments a posting list with pointers that point to a document further down the list. Skip pointers are effectively shortcuts that allow us to avoid processing parts of the posting list that will not get intersected. Let's first understand how it allows efficient merging. Suppose we've stepped through two lists and both pointers have matched document 8 on each list. After advancing the pointers, list A points to 16 while list B points to 41. At this point we know that documents between 16 and 41 will have no effect on intersection. List A will consider the skip pointer at 16 and check if it skips to a document less than or equal to 41; if it doesn't, following the skip pointer avoids all those comparisons with list B's 41. As more skips are made, processing gets even faster.

A number of variant versions of posting list intersection with skip pointers is possible depending on when exactly the skip pointer is checked (Moffat, 1996). Deciding where to place skip pointers is a bit tricky. More skips imply shorter skip spans, and hence more opportunities to skip. But this also requires lots of comparisons to skip pointers, and plenty of memory gets wasted in storing the skip pointers themselves. On the other hand, though fewer skips require less pointer comparisons, the resulting longer skip spans provide fewer opportunities to skip. A simple heuristic, which has been found to work well in practice, is to use $\sqrt{P}$ evenly spaced skip pointers for a posting list of length P.

Better Understanding of User Intent

When ranking multi-term queries, one of the prominent signals used is the proximity of different terms on a page. The goal is to prefer documents in which query terms appear closest together over the ones in which they are spread apart (Clarke & Cormack, 1997; Buttcher et al., 2006). Proximity of terms is even more critical in the case of phrase queries, where relative position of each query term matters. Rather than simply checking if terms are present in a document, we also need to check that their positions of appearance in the document are compatible with the phrase query being evaluated. This requires working out offsets between words. Posting lists typically add word positions to index entries so that the locations of terms in documents can be checked during query evaluation.

Creating a positional index significantly expands storage requirements. It also slows down query processing since only a tiny fraction of the documents that contain the query terms also contain them as a phrase, thereby needing to skip over the positional information in each non-matched posting. This also results in processing cost often being dominated by common terms since they occur at the start or in the middle of any phrase.

In order to better represent an author's intent in a document and better match a user's intent in their query, there has been significant work done in phrase-based indexing. However, such indexing is potentially expensive. There is no obvious mechanism for accurately identifying which phrases might be used in queries, and the number of candidate phrases is enormous since they grow far more rapidly than the number of distinct terms. For instance, if a dictionary has 200,000 unique terms, and we consider all 1-5 word phrases, the phrase dictionary will be of size greater than $3.2*10^{26}$ – much larger than any existing system can store in memory or manipulate. In order to have a manageable dictionary, only "good" phrases are indexed. A good phrase has terms that often appear together or appear in delimited sections (e.g., titles and headings). Eliminating phrases that are sub-phrases of longer phrases also helps trim the list. Some phrase-based indexers also keep track of phrases that often appear together in order to generate a related-phrases list. This enables a page that mentions '*US President*' to return for a query of *(Barack Obama)*. For phrases composed of rare words, having a phrase index yields little advantage, as processing savings are offset by the need to access a much larger dictionary. A successful strategy is to have an index for word pairs that begin with a common word and combine it with a word-level inverted index.

In practice, Google, through the TeraGoogle project (Patterson, 2004), Yahoo!, through the use of superunits (Kapur, 2004), and startups such as Cuil have shown interest in phrase-based indexing. Table 1 summarizes the advantages and disadvantages of Term- and Phrase-based Indexing.

LAYING OUT THE INDEX

In order to handle the load of a modern search engine, a combination of distribution and replication techniques is required. Distribution refers to splitting the document collection and its index across multiple machines, as well as synthesizing answers for any query from the various collection components. Replication (or mirroring) then involves making enough identical copies of the system so that the required query load can be handled even during single or multiple machine failures.

In this section we discuss the various considerations for optimally dividing data across a distributed system in the most optimal way.

The decision of how to divide the data includes a balancing act between the number of posting lists, the size of each posting list and the penalties involved when multiple posting lists need to accessed at the same machine. Indexing phrases implies having many more (and possibly shorter) posting lists since the number of terms is significantly fewer than the number of phrases. For this section, we will assume the following are constant:

1. Number of phrases in our dictionary
2. Number of documents to be indexed across the system
3. Number of machines

Table 1. Term- vs. phrase-based indexing

	Advantages	Disadvantages
Term-Based Indexing	Limited number of posting lists	Average posting list size is longer
	Simple to implement	Storing positional information bloats index size
		Calculating proximity of multiple terms can be an expensive operation
Phrase-Based Indexing	Better measure of intent	Larger dictionary: More posting lists to manage
	Ability to index related phrases	Breaking user query into phrases correctly is difficult

Document vs. Term Based Partitioning

There are two common ways of distributing index data across a cluster: by document or by term, as illustrated in Figure 4 for the same example as before. Let's discuss the design of each system before examining the advantages and disadvantages of each.

Document Based Partitioning

The simplest distribution regime is to partition the collection and allocate one sub-collection to each of the processors. A local index is built for each sub-collection; when queries arrive, they are passed to every sub-collection and evaluated against every local index. The sets of sub-collection answers are then combined in some way to provide an overall set of answers. An index partitioned by document saves all information relevant to that document on a single machine. The number of posting lists on a machine is thus dependent on the number of unique terms or phrases that appear in the corpus of documents indexed on the given machine. Also, the upper limit on the size of each posting list is the number of documents indexed on the machine. In the example, we have partitioned the

document-space into two indices: the first index contains all information about documents 1, 2 and 3 while the second index contains all information about documents 4, 5, and 6.

The benefit of storing all the posting lists for a given document on a single machine is that intersections, if needed, can be performed locally. For each query, a master index-server dispatches the query to all the workers under it. Each worker server looks up the query (or intersection) on its local index and returns results to the master. In effect, each worker is an independent search engine for the pages that have been indexed and stored in its memory. As the size of the index grows, a hierarchical structure must be created. However, given the expectation of sub-second load times from search engines, the depth of the lookup tree rarely exceeds two.

A document-partitioned index allows for index construction and document insertion more naturally. One of the hosts can be designated to have a dynamic corpus so that it is the only one to rebuild its index. It also allows the search service to be provided even when one or more of the hosts are offline, though the documents indexed on these hosts are no longer seen. Another advantage of a document-partitioned index is that the computationally expensive parts of the process

Figure 4. Illustrating document- vs. phrase-based partitioning for posting lists shown in Figure 3

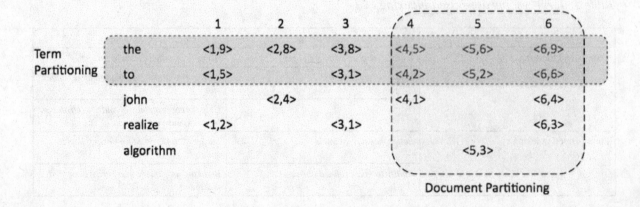

		1	2	3	4	5	6
Term Partitioning	the	<1,9>	<2,8>	<3,8>	<4,5>	<5,6>	<6,9>
	to	<1,5>		<3,1>	<4,2>	<5,2>	<6,6>
	john		<2,4>		<4,1>		<6,4>
	realize	<1,2>		<3,1>			<6,3>
	algorithm					<5,3>	

Document Partitioning

Table 2. Document- vs. term-based partitioning

	Advantages	Disadvantages
Document-Partitioned Index	Posting Lists are Smaller	All machines are contracted for each query
	Easy to manage and scale	Merging results from all machines can be expensive
	Intersections are local to a machine	Network traffic to all machines can be expensive
	Index updates can be done dynamically and one partition at a time	
Term-Partitioned Index	Only a subset of machines are used for each query	Remote intersections can be expensive as entire posting lists need to be copied over network
		Index updates need to be done for entire index

are distributed equally across all of the hosts in the computer cluster.

Term Based Partitioning

The alternative to document based partitioning is term or phrase based partitioning. In a term-partitioned index, the index is split into components by partitioning the dictionary. Each processor has full information about only a subset of the terms. This implies that to handle a query, only the relevant subset of processors needs to respond. Since all postings for a given term are stored on a single machine, posting lists in a term-partitioned index are often significantly longer than their document-partitioned counterparts. Also, unlike the document-partitioned index case, posting lists for different terms that are in the same document can be stored on different machines. Furthermore, each machine can have a different number of posting lists stored on it (depending on machine limits and relative posting list sizes). In the example in Figure 4, we have partitioned the term-space into two indices: the first index contains all information about the terms '*the*' and '*to*' while the second index contains all information about the terms '*john*', '*realize*' and '*algorithm*'.

Since all postings for a given term are stored in one place in a cluster, not all servers need to do work for each query. The master index-server only contacts the relevant worker server(s). This method requires fewer disk seeks and transfer operations during query evaluation than a document-partitioned index because each term's inverted list is stored contiguously on a single machine rather than in fragments across multiple machines. If a cluster is managed efficiently, it can retrieve results to multiple query requests at the same time.

When comparing this index architecture to its document-partitioned counterpart, we observe a few drawbacks. Firstly, intersections cannot always take place locally. If the terms being intersected reside on different machines, one of the posting lists needs to be copied over to the other machine in order to do a local intersection. Usually, the shorter posting list is copied to reduce network traffic. Secondly, the disk transfer operations involve large amounts of data since posting lists are longer. The coordinating machine can easily get overloaded and become a bottleneck, thereby starving the other processors of work. Table 2 summarizes the tradeoffs.

Memory vs. Disk Storage

The next decision we have to make is deciding whether to store the dictionary and index in memory or on disk. It is tempting to store the dictionary in memory because doing so means that a disk access is avoided for every query term. However, if it is large, keeping it in memory reduces the space available for caching of other information and may not be beneficial overall. Fortunately, access to the dictionary is only a small component of query processing; if a B-tree-like structure is used with the leaf nodes on disk and internal nodes in memory, then a term's information can be accessed using just a single disk access, and only a relatively small amount of main memory is permanently consumed. Lastly, recently or frequently accessed query terms can be cached in a separate small table.

Memory Based Index

The two major search engines today, Google and Bing, store the majority of their search engine indices in memory. The benefit of this archi-tecture is that the local lookup time is almost instantaneous. The drawback is that memory is extremely expensive and doesn't scale infinitely. As the size of the web increases, the size of the index increases linearly as does the number of machines needed to hold a copy of this index. At serving time, these search engines employ a scatter-gather approach to find the best results. A master index-server dispatches a query lookup to all the worker machines, and waits for results. The index is usually document-partitioned and each mini-search-engine looks up the relevant results and returns them to the master index-server. As they arrive, the master does a merge-sort of the results received and returns the final result. Since the index is held in memory, the majority of time in this architecture is spent in the data transfers across the network.

While we can imagine an index that is term-partitioned and based in memory, there have been no major search engines that have taken such an approach. This is primarily because posting lists

of many terms on the web are too large to fit in memory.

Disk Based Index

In the last few years, Google (Patterson, 2004), and startups such as Cuil have indicated an interest in disk-based indices wherein data is organized in a way that requires fewer lookups and very few network transfers for each query. In a term-partitioned disk based architecture, the time is spent in disk-seeks and block reads rather than in network transfers and merge-sorts. It is possible to have a disk-based and document partitioned index. No search engine in the recent past has built one with this configuration because each lookup would involve multiple disks seeks on each machine in the cluster.

The big advantage of a disk-based index is that it can scale more cost-efficiently than its memory-based counterpart. Disk is ~100x cheaper than memory while providing significantly larger amounts of storage space. As the number of docu-ments on the web increases, posting lists will get longer in the disk-based index. The increased penalty of traversing longer posting lists is neg-ligible. On the other hand, in the memory-based index, the number of machines needed to support the index increases with the size of the index. Hence, query-processing time is limited by the per-machine lookup time. Once the system starts slowing down (upper limit on performance), the only way to scale further is to duplicate the index across multiple copies of the index and replicate entire clusters. Table 3 summarizes the advantages and disadvantages of these options.

Compressing the Index

From the discussion so far, it is clear that a web-scale index makes storage space a premium re-source for search engines. An attractive solution for conserving space is to use a highly compressed inverted index. However, decompression at query

Table 3. Memory- vs. disk-based indices

	Advantages	Disadvantages
Memory-based Index	*Extremely fast lookup*	*Memory is expensive*
	Works well in document-partitioned case	*Number of machines needed grows as fast as size of index*
Disk-based Index	*Disk is cheap*	*Disk is slow so number of lookups need to be minimized*
	Longer posting lists can be stored contiguously	*Not ideal in document-partitioned case because it involves too many disk seeks*

evaluation time made it an expensive proposition in the past since CPUs were slower. This trend has reversed and decompression algorithms on modern hardware run so fast that the cost of transferring a compressed chunk of data from disk and then decompressing it is usually far less expensive than that of transferring the same chunk of data in uncompressed form. As the ratio of processor speed to disk speed continues to diverge, reducing posting list sizes promises increasingly more performance gains.

Using shorter posting lists has more subtle benefits for a disk-based index. First, it makes it faster to transfer data from disk to memory. More importantly, it reduces disk seek times since the index is smaller. These reductions more than offset the cost of decompressing, thereby reducing the overall query evaluation time. Another beneficial outcome of compression is the increased use of caching. Typically, web queries come with a skewed distribution where certain query terms are more common than others. If the posting list for a frequently used query term is cached, all queries involving that term can be processed entirely in memory and not involve any disk seek. Even for a memory-based index, the cost of decompressing is more than offset by the reduction in memory-to-cache transfers of larger uncompressed data. Since memory is a more expensive resource than disk space, increased speed due to caching has proved to be the primary motivator for using compression in today's search engines (Zhang, 2007).

In the rest of this section, we will discuss simple compression schemes that can not only keep the penalty of decompressing a posting list small, but also cut the storage cost of an inverted index by almost 75%. We begin with the observation that document identifiers for frequent terms are close together. When going over documents one by one, we will easily find terms like 'the' and 'to' in every document, but to search for a term like 'john' we might have to skip a few documents every now and then. The key insight here is that *gaps* between document identifiers in postings are short, requiring a lot less space to encode than say the 20 bits needed in a 1M corpus for document identifier. This is illustrated below using our earlier example. Rarer terms, however, occur only once or twice in a collection and hence their gaps will have the same order of magnitude as the document identifiers. We will need a *variable encoding* representation that uses fewer bits for short gaps but does not reduce the maximum magnitude of a gap.

Original posting lists:
the: $\langle 1, 9 \rangle \langle 2, 8 \rangle \langle 3, 8 \rangle \langle 4, 5 \rangle \langle 5, 6 \rangle \langle 6, 9 \rangle$
to: $\langle 1, 5 \rangle \langle 3, 1 \rangle \langle 4, 2 \rangle \langle 5, 2 \rangle \langle 6, 6 \rangle$
john: $\langle 2, 4 \rangle \langle 4, 1 \rangle \langle 6, 4 \rangle$

With gaps:
the: $\langle 1, 9 \rangle \langle 1, 8 \rangle \langle 1, 8 \rangle \langle 1, 5 \rangle \langle 1, 6 \rangle \langle 1, 9 \rangle$
to: $\langle 1, 5 \rangle \langle 2, 1 \rangle \langle 1, 2 \rangle \langle 1, 2 \rangle \langle 1, 6 \rangle$
john: $\langle 2, 4 \rangle \langle 2, 1 \rangle \langle 2, 4 \rangle$

Variable byte (VB) encoding (Witten, 1999) uses an integral but adaptive number of bytes depending on the size of a gap. The first bit of each byte is a *continuation bit*, which is flipped only in the last byte of the encoded gap. The remaining 7 bits in each byte are used to encode part of the gap. To decode a variable byte code, we read a sequence of bytes until the continuation bit flips. We then extract and concatenate the 7-bit parts to get the magnitude of a gap. Since it reduces the average magnitude of all gaps in a posting list, and is simple to implement, compression techniques benefit greatly from such a transformation. The idea of VB encoding can also be applied to larger or smaller units than bytes, such as 32-bit words and 4-bit *nibbles*. Larger words decrease the amount of bit manipulation necessary at the cost of less effective (or no) compression. Units smaller than bytes achieve even better compression ratios but at the cost of more bit manipulation. In general, variable byte codes offer a good compromise between compression ratio (space) and speed of decompression (time).

If disk space is at a premium, we can get even better compression ratios by using bit-level encoding (Golomb, 1966). These codes, in particular the closely related *g (gamma)* and *d (delta)* codes (Elias, 1975; Rice, 1979), adapt the length of the code on a finer-grained bit level. Each codeword has two parts, a prefix and a suffix. The prefix indicates the binary magnitude of the value and tells the decoder how many bits there are in the suffix part. The suffix indicates the value of the number within the corresponding binary range. In spite of greater compression ratios, these codes are expensive to decode in practice. This is primarily because code boundaries usually lie somewhere in the middle of a machine word, making it necessary to use bit-level operations such as shifts and masks for decoding. As a result, query processing is more time consuming for g and d codes than for variable byte codes.

The choice of coding scheme also affects total fetch-and-decode times, where the byte-wise and word-aligned codes enjoy a clear advantage. Scholer (2002) found that variable byte codes process queries twice as fast as either bit-level compressed indexes or uncompressed indexes, but pay for a 30% penalty in the compression ratio when compared with the best bit-level compression method. Trotman (2003) recommended using VB codes unless disk space is a highly scarce resource. Both studies also show that compressed indexes are superior to uncompressed indexes in disk usage. In a later study (Anh, 2005), variable nibble codes showed 5% to 10% better compression and up to one-third worse effectiveness, in comparison to VB codes. These studies clearly demonstrate that using simple and efficient decompression methods substantially decreases the response time of a system. Use of codes does, however, present problems for index updates. Since it involves decoding the existing list and recoding with new parameters, processing the existing list becomes the dominant cost of the update.

The effectiveness of compression regimes is particularly evident in posting lists for common words, which require only a few bits per posting after compression. Let's consider stop words, for instance. Since these words are likely to occur in almost every document, a vast majority of gaps in their postings can be represented in just a bit or two. Allowing for the corresponding term frequency (TF) value to be stored in at most 10-11 bits (TF of up to ~1000), each posting requires a total of only 12 bits. This is almost a quarter of ~40 bits that would be required if the postings were stored uncompressed. Thus, even though maintaining a list of stop words seemed like an attractive proposition when the index was uncompressed, the additional space savings do not carry over to the size of the compressed index. And even though less frequent terms require longer codes for their gaps, their postings get encoded in a few bits on average since they require shorter codes for their TF values.

For a positional index, word positions account for a bulk of the size in uncompressed form. For instance, it takes almost two bytes to ensure that all positions can be encoded in a document of up to 64K words. This cost can be significantly reduced by representing only the difference in positions, just like we did for document identifiers. These gaps can either be localized to within each document, or can be global across all documents (Zobel, 2006). In the latter case, two sets of codes are used: one that represents the document gaps, and a second to code the position intervals between appearances of a term. While byte-aligned encoding can be used to quickly decode the document identifiers, more efficient interleaved bit-level encoding can be used for the positions. They are decoded in parallel when both components are required during query evaluation. As discussed, for common words compression ratios of 1:4 are easy to achieve without positional information. In a positional index, however, the average per document requirement for common words is much larger because of the comparatively large number of word-gap codes that must be stored.

The compression techniques we describe are *lossless*, that is, all information is preserved. Better compression ratios can be achieved with *lossy compression*, which discards some information. Case folding, stemming, and stop word elimination are forms of lossy compression. Similarly, dimensionality reduction techniques like latent semantic indexing create compact presentations from which we cannot fully restore the original collection. Lossy compression makes sense when the "lost" information is unlikely ever to be used by the search system, for instance postings far down the list in an impact-sorted index (described next) can be discarded.

Ordering by Highest Impact First

To reduce disk transfer costs, it is necessary to avoid fetching the posting lists in their entirety. This is particularly true for common terms for which posting lists are very long. An attractive option is to rearrange the list itself so that only a part of each relevant list is fetched for a typical query. For instance, if only the largest term

frequency values of a posting list contribute to anything useful, it makes sense to store them at the beginning of the list rather than somewhere in the middle of the document-based ordering. Ordering by term frequency also allows for the scanning of many posting lists to be terminated early because smaller term weights do not change the ranking of the highest ranked documents.

Using a frequency-ordered index, a simple query evaluation algorithm would be to fetch each list in turn and process only those values (TF x IDF) that contribute to a threshold S or higher. If disk reads are performed one block at a time, rather than on the basis of entire posting list, this strategy significantly reduces disk traffic without degrading effectiveness. A practical alternative is to use only the first disk block of each list to hold the high impact postings; the remainder of the list can stay sorted in document order. These important first blocks could then all be processed before the remainder of any lists, thereby ensuring that all terms are able to contribute relevant documents. One could also interleave their respective processing; once the first block of each list has been fetched and is available in memory, the list with the highest posting value is selected and its first run of pointers are processed. Attention then switches to the list with the next-highest run, which could either be in a different list or in the same list. So, each list is visited one or more times, depending on the perceived contribution of that term to the query. Since the most significant index information is processed first, query evaluation can be terminated by a time bound rather than a threshold.

So how does this new ordering affect storage requirements? Since the inverted lists are read in blocks rather than in their entirety, contiguous storage is no longer a necessity. Blocks with high-impact information could be clustered on disk, further accelerating query processing. The long lists for common terms will never be fully read, saving a great deal of disk traffic. Query evaluation becomes a matter of processing as many blocks as can be handled within the time that is available. Let's look at an example posting list from (Zobel, 2006) now to understand the impact on compression, shown here as document ordered (<doc id, term frequency>):

$\langle 12, \underline{2} \rangle \langle 17, \underline{2} \rangle \langle 29, \underline{1} \rangle \langle 32, \underline{1} \rangle \langle 40, \underline{6} \rangle \langle 78, \underline{1} \rangle \langle 101, \underline{3} \rangle \langle 106, \underline{1} \rangle$.

When the list is reordered by term frequency, it gets transformed:

$\langle 40, \underline{6} \rangle \langle 101, \underline{3} \rangle \langle 12, \underline{2} \rangle \langle 17, \underline{2} \rangle \langle 29, \underline{1} \rangle \langle 32, \underline{1} \rangle \langle 78, \underline{1} \rangle \langle 106, \underline{1} \rangle$.

The repeated frequency information can then be factored out into a prefix component with a counter that indicates how many documents there are with this same frequency value:

$\langle \underline{6} : 1 : 40 \rangle \langle \underline{3} : 1 : 101 \rangle \langle \underline{2} : 2 : 12, 17 \rangle \langle \underline{1} : 4 : 29, 32, 78, 106 \rangle$.

Not storing the repeated frequencies gives a considerable saving. Finally, if differences of document identifiers are taken, we get the following:

$\langle \underline{6} : 1 : 40 \rangle \langle \underline{3} : 1 : 101 \rangle \langle \underline{2} : 2 : 12, 5 \rangle \langle \underline{1} : 4 : 29, 3, 46, 28 \rangle$.

The document gaps within each equal-frequency segment of the list are now on average larger than when the document identifiers were sorted, thereby requiring more encoding bits/bytes. However, in combination with not storing repeated frequencies, these lists tend to be slightly smaller than document-sorted lists. The disadvantage, however, is that index updates are now more complex.

Since it made sense to order the posting lists by decreasing term frequency, it makes even more sense to order them by their actual impact. Then all that remains is to multiply each posting value by the respective query term weight, and then rank the documents. Storing pre-computed floating-point document scores is not a good idea, however, since they cannot be compressed as well as integers. Also, unlike repeated frequencies, we can no longer cluster exact scores together. In order to retain compression, the impact scores are quantized instead, storing one of a small number of distinct values in the index. The compressed size is still slightly larger compared to document- and frequency-sorted indexes because the average document gaps are bigger.

Managing Multiple Indices

Webpages are created and refreshed at different rates. Therefore, there is no reason to crawl and index pages uniformly. Some pages are inherently ever changing (e.g., a news site like www.cnn.com) while others won't change for years (e.g., my grandmother's static homepage that I designed as a birthday gift 10 years ago). If a search system can learn, over a period of time, the rate of refreshing of a page, it can crawl and index the page only at the optimal rate.

The way we have described search indices so far makes a huge assumption: there will be a single unified index of the entire web. If this assumption were to be held, every single time we re-crawled and re-indexed a small set of fast-changing pages, we would have to re-compress every posting list for the web and push out a new web index. Re-compressing the entire index is not only time consuming, it is downright wasteful. Why can we not have multiple indices -- bucketed by rate of refreshing? We can and that is what is standard industry practice. Three commonly used buckets are:

1. The large, rarely-refreshing pages index
2. The small, ever-refreshing pages index
3. The dynamic real-time/news pages index

At query-time, we do three parallel index lookups and merge the results based on the signals that are retrieved. It is common for the large index to be re-crawled and re-indexed as slow as every month, while the smaller index is refreshed daily, if not weekly. The dynamic, real time/news index is updated on a per-second basis.

Another feature that can be built into such a multi-tiered index structure is a waterfall approach. Pages discovered in one tier can be passed down to the next tier over time. Pages and domains can be moved from the rarely refreshing index to the ever-refreshing index and vice versa as the characteristics of pages change over time. Having such a modular and dynamic system is almost necessary to maintain an up-to-date index of the web.

As pages are re-crawled or re-indexed, older index and crawl file entries can be invalidated. Invalidations are often stored in a bit vector. As a page is re-indexed, the appropriate posting lists must be appropriately updated. There are many ways to update the posting lists but, in general, the per-list updates should be deferred for as long as possible to minimize the number of times each list is accessed. The simplest approach is to process as for the merging strategy and, when a memory limit is reached, then proceed through the whole index, amending each list in turn. Other possibilities are to update a list only when it is fetched in response to a query or to employ a background process that slowly cycles through the in-memory index, continuously updating entries. In practice, these methods are not as efficient as intermittent merge, which processes data on disk sequentially.

Merging is the most efficient strategy for update but has the drawback of requiring significant disk overheads. It allows relatively simple recovery since reconstruction requires only a copy of the index and the new documents. In contrast, incremental update proceeds in place with some space lost due to fragmentation. But recovery in an incremental index may be complex due to the need to track which inverted lists have been modified (Motzkin, 1994).

SCALING THE SYSTEM

Over the last decade, search engines have gone from crawling tens of millions of documents to over a trillion documents (Alpert, 2008). Building an index of this scale can be a daunting task. On top of that serving hundreds of queries per second against such an index only makes the task harder. In mid 2004, the Google search engine processed more than 200 million queries a day against more than 20TB of crawled data, using more than 20,000 computers (Computer School, 2010).

Web search engines use *distributed indexing* algorithms for index construction because the data collections are too large to be efficiently processed on a single machine. The result of the construction process is a distributed index that is partitioned across several machines. As discussed in the previous section this distributed index can be partitioned according to term or according to document.

While having the right infrastructure is not necessary (and search engines before 2004 did not have many of these pieces), they definitely can reduce the pain involved in building such a system. As the dependence on parallel processing increased, the need for an efficient parallel programming paradigm arose: a framework that provided the highest computational efficiency while maximizing programming efficiency (Asanovic, 2008). In this section, we will summarize the features of a distributed file system and a map-shuffle-reduce system used within a web-indexer.

Distributed File System

A search engine index represents only a snapshot of the entire web; a snapshot that is crawled and stored locally. Even if we cared to index all the text documents only on the entire web, this data will need to be stored over hundreds, if not thousands of machines. Assuming that an average webpage requires 25 kilobytes (Tashian, 2009; King, 2008; Ramachandran, 2010), and that there are 100 billion index-worthy webpages (we don't store and index all because many of them are junk or spam), we need 2.5 petabytes of storage. Since we know that the index is at least as big as the initial data, we will need at least 5 petabytes of storage for our entire system. Loading each server with 10 disks of 1 terabyte each will thus require 500 such servers to hold one copy of the web and its index. The requirements grow multifold when we add layers of redundancy to the system.

Search engines are built on top of commodity hardware. In order to manage such large amounts of data across large commodity clusters, a distributed file system that provides efficient remote file access, file transfers, and the ability to carry out concurrent independent operations while being extremely fault tolerant is essential (Silberschatz, 1994). While there are many open source distributed file systems such as (MooseFS) and (GlusterFS), search engine companies such as Google have built their own proprietary distributed file systems (Ghemawat, 2003). The main motivation for a company like Google to develop its own file system is to optimize the operations that are most commonly used in the web-indexing domain. One area where a web indexer differs from a traditional file system user is in the file access pattern. Traditionally, users or systems access 10% of files, 90% of the time (Smith, 1985), and thus caching provides huge performance gains on re-accesses. On the other hand, a web indexer streams through the data once while writing to multiple files in a somewhat random manner. This implies that if a file system optimized for web search indexing can provide efficient random writes (the common operation), it does not need to provide extremely efficient caching.

Once we have an efficient distributed file system, we can develop an indexer that can process data across a cluster and create a single index representing all the underlying data. Many of the indexer functions are data parallel, that is, the same code is run on independent sets of data. However, there are parts of the process that require related pieces of information from all the machines to be combined to create some of the signals (e.g., number of in-links to a given page). We find that there are three programming constructs that are used repeatedly in distributed computing such as building a web index. The next subsection describes such a Map-Shuffle-Reduce framework.

Map-Shuffle-Reduce

While the constructs of map and reduce have been around since the early days of Common Lisp and the idea of shuffling data around a cluster has been done since the beginning of distributed computing, Google was the first company to formally describe a framework (Dean, 2004) that did all this while providing fault tolerance and ease of use. In light of the plethora of literature defining this framework, we present an extremely short treatment of the definitions and focus on their uses in web indexing.

Map: The master node chops up the problem into small chunks and assigns each chunk to a worker. The worker either processes the chunk of data with the mapper and returns the result to the master, or further chops up the input data and assigns it hierarchically. Mappers output key-value pairs, e.g., when extracting anchors from a webpage, the mapper might output <dst_link, src_link> where dst_link is the link found on src_link.

Shuffle: This step is optional. In this step, data is transferred between nodes in order to group key-value pairs from the mapper output to in a way that enables proper reducing, e.g., When extracting anchors (link text), we shuffle the output of the mapper so that all the anchors for a given link end up on the same machine.

Reduce: The master takes the sub-answers and combines them to create the final output, e.g., for the anchor extractor, the reducer re-organizes local data to have all the anchors for a given link be contiguous and outputs them along with a link that summarizes the findings (number of off-domain anchors, number of on-domain anchors, etc.). Additionally, we can output a separate file that has just the summary line and also an offset into the anchor file so that we can seek to it and traverse all the anchors to a given link on demand.

There are many added features and benefits built into such a system. It hides the complexity of a parallel system from the programmer and scales with the size of the problem and available resources. Also, in the case of a crash, recovery is simple: the master simply reschedules the crashed worker's job to another worker.

That said, such a system is not required for many parts of the indexing system. The use of the map-shuffle-reduce framework can be avoided for tasks that have a trivial or non-existent shuffle step. For those tasks, a regular program will perform just as well (given that there is a fault tolerant infrastructure available). It is, in particular, not required for the calculation of signals such as PageRank (iterative graph traversal / matrix multiplication) or document-partitioned indexing (all the data for a given document is available locally and no shuffle is needed). On the other hand, to construct a term-partitioned index, shuffling is a key step. The posting lists from all the worker nodes corresponding to the same term need to be combined into a single posting list.

EXTRACTING FEATURES FOR RANKING

Any modern search engine index spans tens or hundreds of billions of pages, and most queries return hundreds of thousands of results. Since the user cannot parse so many documents, it is a pre-requisite to rank results from most relevant to least relevant. Earlier, we discussed using term frequency as an evidence (or signal) to give more weight to pages that have a term occurring several times over pages containing it only once. Other than such statistical measures, search engines extract several other signals or features from a page to understand the author's true intention, as well as key terms. These signals are then embedded in each posting for a term.

We will highlight a few of these features using results for *(home and garden improvements)* on Google, as illustrated in Figure 5. First note that page structures, such as titles and headings, and URL depth play a major role. Next we see that most terms occur close to each other in the results, highlighting the need for term positions or phrases during indexing. Also important, though not clear from the figure, is the respective position of terms

on pages; users prefer pages that contain terms higher up in the page. Other than these, search engines also learn from patterns across the web and analyze pages for undesirable properties, such as presence of offensive terms, lots of outgoing links, or even bad sentence- or page-structures. The diversity and size of the web also enables systems to determine statistical features such as the average length of a good sentence, ratio of number of outgoing links to number of words on page, ratio of visible keywords to those not visible (meta tags or alt text), etc. Recent search start-ups such as PowerSet, Cuil, and Blekko have attempted to process a page and extract more than term occurrences on a page. PowerSet (Helft, 2007) built an engine that extracted meaning out of sentences and could therefore be made part of a larger question and answer service. Cuil extracted clusters of phrases from each page to evaluate the topics that any page talks about. Blekko (Miller, 2010) extracts entities such as time and locations in order to allow the user to *slashtag*, or filter, results by location, time or other user-defined slashes.

While in a perfect world indexing an author's intent in the form of on-page analysis should be good enough to return good results, there are too many search engine 'bombers' who stuff pages with keywords to fool an engine. In fact, most basic search engine optimization (SEO) firms focus on these on-page features in order to improve rankings for their sites. Hence, off-page signals have increasingly proved to be the difference between a good search engine and a not-so-good one. They allow search engines to determine what other pages say about a given page (anchor text) and whether the linking page itself is reputable (PageRank or HITS). These signals usually require large distributed platforms such as map-shuffle-reduce because they collect the aggregated information about a given page or domain as presented by the rest of the web. The final ranking is thus a blend of static *a priori* ordering that indicates if a page is relevant to queries in general, and a dynamic score which represents the

Figure 5. Importance of basic on-page signals on search results

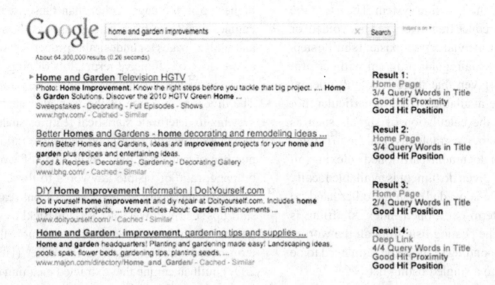

probability that a page is relevant to the current query.

In PageRank, each page is assigned a score that simulates the actions of a random web surfer, who with probability p is equally likely to follow one of the links out of the current page, or with probability 1 − p chooses any other random page to move to. An iterative computation can be used to compute the long-term probability that such a user is visiting any particular page and that probability is then used to set the PageRank. The effect is that pages with many in-links tend to be assigned high PageRank values, especially if the source pages themselves have a high PageRank. On the other hand, pages with low in-link counts, or in- links from only relatively improbable pages, are considered to not hold much authority in answering queries. HITS, as described earlier, scores pages as both hubs and authorities, where a good hub is one that links to many good authorities, and a good authority is one that is linked from many good hubs. Essentially, hubs are useful information aggregations and provide broad categorization of topics, while authorities provide detailed information on a narrower facet of a topic. This is also computed iteratively using matrix computa-

tion based on the connectivity graph. However, instead of pre-computing the hub and authority scores at indexing time, each page is assigned a query specific score at serving time.

Naturally, spammers nowadays invest considerable time and effort in faking PageRank or Hubs and Authorities - this is called link spam. Because spammers will build clusters of web-pages that link to each other in an effort to create the illusion of pages having good structure and good anchor text coming from "other" pages, it is important to have good coverage of pages on the index and a good set of trusted seed pages. Moreover, they filter out links from known link farms and even penalize sites with links to such farms. They rightly figure that webmasters cannot control which sites link to their sites, but they can control which sites they link out to. For this reason, links into a site cannot harm the site, but links from a site can be harmful if they link to penalized sites. To counter this, sites have focused on exchanging, buying, and selling links, often on a massive scale. Over the years there have been many such SEO companies that have tried to aggressively manipulate the effect of optimizations and gaming search engine ranking. Google and other search engines have, on some occasions, banned SEOs and their clients (Kesmodel, 2005; Cutts, 2006) for being too aggressive.

OPEN SOURCE SEARCH ENGINES

For most small enterprises, using a commercial search engine is not always a feasible solution because of the licensing fees, as well as because their focus is on large-scale websites. On the other hand, open source search engines offer an attractive alternative to the proprietary licensed search and discovery software vendors, which in addition come with the benefits of the open source philosophy: no cost, actively maintained software by the community, customizable code to meet individual needs, etc. Nowadays, there are many open source alternatives that can be used, such as Lucene (Nutch, Solr) (Wikipedia, 2011), Sphinx, Zettair, Terrier, Xapian, to list a few. Each of them has different characteristics that must be taken into consideration in order to determine their usefulness (Middleton, 2007).

Lucene is a Java library that adds text indexing and searching capabilities to an application. It currently ranks among the top 15 open source projects (The Open Source Census, 2011) and is one of the top 5 most requested Apache projects (Gritsenko, 2011), with installations at over 4,000 companies. Lucene was originally written by Doug Cutting and was available for download from SourceForge. It joined the Apache Software Foundation's Jakarta family of open source server-side Java products in September of 2001. The Solr search server provides a ready-to-use search platform on top of the Lucene search library, and is the fastest growing Lucene sub-project. It allows for advanced functionalities like query spell checking, "more like this" suggestions, data replication and easy query time relevancy tuning. Combining it with Nutch makes an even more powerful base to build a search application. Nutch is a highly scalable and relatively feature rich crawler, of-

fering features like politeness (obeys robots.txt rules), robustness and scalability. In addition, it helps boost quality by biasing the crawler to fetch "important" pages first, and by extracting links and anchor texts between pages.

FUTURE RESEARCH DIRECTIONS

While core web-search technology has some interesting algorithms, a lot of work over the last few years has gone into building scalable infrastructure, storage, and compression software to support the smooth running of these relatively simple algorithms. We've described the cutting edge for each of these categories earlier in this chapter. In this section, we will describe some of the new frontiers that search is exploring today as well as some areas we believe search will go towards.

Real Time Data and Search

The advent of services such as Twitter and Facebook in the last few years has made it extremely easy for individuals around the world to create information in the form of microposts. For ease of understanding, we will focus on Twitter data in this section. In 140 characters, users can describe where they are, publicize a link to an article they like, or share a fleeting thought. From a search engine perspective, this information is extremely valuable, but as different projects have shown over the last few years, this information has extra importance if it is mined and presented to search engine users in *real time*.

In order to build a real time system, the first prerequisite is access to the raw micropost data. Luckily for the community, Twitter has been extremely good about providing this at affordable prices to anyone who has requested it. Then comes the hard part, dealing with this fire hose of data. At the time of this writing, there are ~90 M tweets being generated daily, i.e., 1040 tweets per second (Rao, 2010). At 140 bytes each, this corresponds to 12.6 GB of tweet-data created in a day. After having dealt with petabytes of data, dealing with corpus of this size is trivial for any search engine today. The question to ponder on is what can we do with each tweet. Let's consider a few ideas:

1. Create a Social Graph: One of the beauties of data creation on services like Twitter is the fact that each user creates a graph of who they are interested in (who they follow) as well as the topics they are interested in (what they tweet about as well as topics in the tweets of the users they follow). The number of followers, too, is a good measure of how well respected that user is. Based on this knowledge, it is possible to create a graph of users as well as the thought leaders for different topic areas. We will refer to a user's influence on his her followers as UserRank and a user's influence on a given topic as UserTopicRank. Startups such as Topsy and Klout have built systems that expose this data.

2. Extract and index the links: Just like a traditional search engine, this would involve parsing each tweet, extracting a URL if present, crawling it and indexing it. The secondary inputs for the indexing stage are similar to those needed for webpage indexing. Instead of having anchor text, we have tweet-text. Instead of PageRank, we have UserRank. Additionally, we can use domain specific data that we have gathered from our web indexing to determine the quality of domains. All of the compression and storage algorithms will work without modification. Google, Microsoft, OneRiot and Topsy are some of the companies that have worked in this direction.

3. Real-Time Related Topics: Related topics help users discover information about current topics better than traditional suggestions. For

instance, on the day of the 2008 presidential debate in Kodak Theater, showing a related topic of 'Kodak Theater' for the query *(Barack Obama)* would be much more meaningful than 'Michelle Obama'. However, a query of *(Byzantine Empire)* would be better served with traditional related topics unless there was a new discovery about it. There has been a lot of work on topic clustering (Kanungo, 2002). Real-time data provides a very different use for these algorithms. By combining co-occurrence and information gain with a time decay factor, it is possible to analyze tweets and derive the related topics in real time are.

4. Sentiment Analysis: There are many teams such as Scout Labs and The Financial Times' Newssift team working on using NLP (Natural Language Processing) techniques to extract sentiment from tweets and other real time sources (Wright, 2009). Whether this adds any value to marketing campaigns or feedback about products and services is yet to be seen.

Social Search and Personalized Web Search

The amount of interaction between users on the World Wide Web has increased exponentially in the last decade. While much of the interaction is still private (on email, chat, etc.), there has recently been a surge in public communications (via Twitter, Facebook, etc.). The services providing such public communication platforms are also enabling third party applications to keep track of these social interactions, through the use of authentication APIs. Only a few companies, so far, have tried to improve user search experience through the use of social networking and related data. We discuss couple of such efforts below.

Over the last few years, Facebook has become the leader in social networking with over 500M users (Zuckerberg, 2010). Facebook users post a wealth of information on the network that can be used to define their online personality. Through static information such as book and movie interests, and dynamic information such as user locations (Facebook Places), status updates and wall posts, a system can learn user preferences. Another feature of significant value is the social circle of a Facebook user, e.g., posts of a user's friends, and of the friends' friends. From a search engine's perspective, learning a user's social interactions can greatly help in personalizing the results for him or her.

Facebook has done two things that are impacting the world of search. First, in September 2009, they opened up the data to any third party service as long as their user authenticates themselves using Facebook Connect (Zuckerberg, 2008). Second, as of September 2010, Facebook has started returning web search results based on the recommendations of those friends who are within two degrees of the user. The full description of this system can be found in their recently granted patent (Lunt, 2004). In light of these recent developments, little has been done with this newly available data.

In February 2011, Google announced that its social search service can help a user discover relevant content from his or her social connections. A signed-in user sees websites, blogs, images and status updates that are shared on his or her social graph (Cassidy, 2011). An immediate observation one can make is that a user's social data is extremely sparse. This is because the average user only has 300-400 friends. This implies that there are very few web search queries for which one can find useful social results. One way to overcome this limitation is by extracting related query terms, which allows for additional social results. A query for *(Lady Gaga)*, for instance, would return friends' statuses that mentioned 'Lady Gaga' but would also return any posts that mentioned songs such as 'Poker Face' or related artists such as 'Rihanna'.

While social data is still relatively new to the web, there have been a few movements to use this data in ways that create value for web search. Klout, a San Francisco based startup, measures the influence of a user on his or her circle of friends and determines their *klout score* (UserRank), as well as the topics they are most influential on (UserTopicRank) (Rao, 2010). In the future, web search engines can use such a signal to determine authority of social data. In October 2010, Bing and Facebook announced the Bing Social Layer (Nadella, 2010) offering the ability to search for people on Facebook and to see related links that a user's friends had liked within Bing's search results.

CONCLUSION

This chapter describes in detail the key indexing technologies behind today's web-scale search engines. We first explained the concept of an inverted index and how it is used to organize the entire web's information. Then we highlighted the key challenges in optimizing query processing time so that results are retrieved as fast as possible. This was followed by a discussion on using phrases over terms for better understanding of user intent in a query, along with its drawbacks for an indexing system. Harnessing together the power of multitudes of machines has been the key to success for today's search engines. Our key focus in this chapter has been to provide a better understanding of how these resources are utilized. We started with discussing the design tradeoffs for distributing data across a cluster of machines, specifically the cost of data transfers and index management. Next, we evaluated the different storage options to hold an index of web scale, specifically highlighting the impact of compression in dramatically shrinking index size and its effect on index updates. We also covered strategies that reorder an index for faster retrieval. This was followed by an overview on the infrastructure needed to support the growth of web search engines to modern scales. Finally, we closed the chapter with potential future directions for search engines, particularly in the real-time and social context. Recent efforts on these new data sources enrich the user's web search experience.

REFERENCES

Alpert, J., & Hajaj, N. (2008). *We knew the web was big...* Retrieved October 13, 2010, from http://googleblog.blogspot.com/ 2008/07/we-knew-web-was-big.html

Anh, V., & Moffat, A. (2005). Inverted index compression using word-aligned binary codes. *Information Retrieval, 8*(1), 151–166. doi:10.1023/B:INRT.0000048490.99518.5c

Arrington, M. (2008). *Cuil exits stealth mode with a massive search engine.* Retrieved October 13, 2010, from http://techcrunch.com/ 2008/07/27/cuill-launches-a-massive-search-engine/

Asanovic, K., Bodik, R., Demmel, J., Keaveny, T., Keutzer, K., & Kubiatowicz, J. ...Yelick, K. (2008). *The Parallel Computing Laboratory at U.C. Berkeley: A research agenda based on the Berkeley View* (Tech. Rep.). Berkeley, CA: UC Berkeley.

Bharat, K., & Broder, A. (1998). A technique for measuring the relative size and overlap of public web search engines. In *Proceedings of the 7th International World Wide Web Conference*, Brisbane, Australia (pp. 379-388).

Brin, S., & Page, L. (1998). The anatomy of a large-scale hypertextual Web search engine. In *Proceedings of the 7th International World Wide Web Conference*, Brisbane, Australia (pp. 107-117).

Büttcher, S., Clarke, C. L. A., & Lushman, B. (2006, August 6-11). Term proximity scoring for ad-hoc retrieval on very large text collections. In *Proceedings of the 29th Annual International ACM SIGIR Conference on Research and Development in Information Retrieval*, Seattle, WA.

Cassidy, M., & Kulick, M. (2011). *An update to Google social search*. Retrieved from March 17, 2011, from http://googleblog.blogspot.com/ 2011/02/update-to-google-social-search.html

Chiang, T., Chang, J., Lin, M., & Su, K. (1992). Statistical models for word segmentation and unknown resolution. In *Proceedings of the Conference on Computational Linguistics and Speech Processing* (pp. 121-146).

Clarke, C. L. A., & Cormack, G. V. (1997, June). Relevance ranking for one-to-three-term queries. In *Proceedings of the 5th Recherche d'Information Assistee par Ordinateur sur Internet*, Montreal, QC, Canada.

Cutting, D. R., & Pedersen, J. O. (1997, June). Space optimizations for total ranking. In *Proceedings of the Computer-Assisted Information Searching on Internet*, Montreal, QC, Canada (pp. 401-412).

Cutts, M. (2006, February 2). *Confirming a penalty*. Retrieved October 13, 2010, from http://www.mattcutts.com/ blog/confirming-a-penalty/

Davison, B. D., Gerasoulis, A., Kleisouris, K., Lu, Y., Seo, H., Wang, W., & Wu, B. (1999, May). DiscoWeb: Applying link analysis to Web search. In *Proceedings of the Eighth International World Wide Web Conference*, Toronto, ON, Canada.

Dean, J., & Ghemawat, S. (2004, December). MapReduce: Simplified data processing on large clusters. In *Proceedings of the Sixth Symposium on Operating System Design and Implementation*, San Francisco, CA. Retrieved October 13, 2010, from http://labs.google.com/ papers/mapreduce.html

Do you know how massive Google is? (2010). *99c Blog*. Retrieved October 13, 2010, from http://www.99cblog.com/ 4739/do-you-know-how-massive-is-google-size-infographic

Elias, P. (1975). Universal code word sets and representations of the integers. *IEEE Transactions on Information Theory, 21*(2), 194–203. doi:10.1109/TIT.1975.1055349

Funt, P. (1998). Extracting key terms from Chinese and Japanese texts. *International Journal of Computer Processing of Oriental Languages*, 99-121.

Ghemawat, S., Gobioff, H., & Leung, S. (2003, October). The Google file system. In *Proceedings of the 19th ACM Symposium on Operating Systems Principles*, Lake George, NY. Retrieved October 13, 2010, from http://labs.google.com/papers/gfs.html

Gluster, F. S. (2010). *Gluster file system*. Retrieved October 13, 2010, from http://www.gluster.org

Golomb, S. W. (1966). Run-length encodings. *IEEE Transactions on Information Theory, 12*(3), 399–401. doi:10.1109/TIT.1966.1053907

Gritsenko, V. (2011). *Daily statistics*. Retrieved March 24, 2011, from The Apache XML Project website: http://people.apache.org/ ~vgritsenko/stats/daily.html

Gulli, A., & Signorini, A. (2005, May 10-14). The indexable web is more than 11.5 billion pages. In *Proceedings of the International World Wide Web Conference*, Chiba, Japan.

Helft, M. (2007, September 2). In a search refinement, a chance to rival. *The New York Times*. Retrieved November 15, 2010, from http://www.nytimes.com/ 2007/02/09/technology/09license.html

Jin, T. (2011, February 15). *China economic watch: Regional GDB, inflation, search market, rate hike*. Retrieved March 17, 2011, from http://www.thechinaperspective.com/ articles/chinaeconomicwatchregionalgdpinflationsearchmarket-ratehike8181/index.html

Kanungo, T., Mount, D., Netanyahu, N., Piatko, C., Silverman, R., & Wu, A. (2002). An efficient k-means clustering algorithm: Analysis and implementation. *IEEE Transactions on Pattern Analysis and Machine Intelligence, 24*, 881–892. doi:10.1109/TPAMI.2002.1017616

Kapur, S., Parikh, J., & Joshi, D. (2004). *U. S. Patent Application No. 20050080795: Systems and methods for search processing using super-units*. Washington, DC: Untied States Patent and Trademark Office.

Kesmodel, D. (2005, September 22). Sites get dropped by search engines after trying to 'optimize' rankings. *Wall Street Journal*. Retrieved October 13, 2010, from http://online.wsj.com/article/SB112714166978744925.html

King, A. (2008). *The average Web page*. Retrieved March 17, 2011, from http://www.optimization-week.com/ reviews/average-web-page/

Kleinberg, J. (1999). Authoritative sources in a hyperlinked environment. *Journal of the ACM, 46*(5), 604–632. doi:10.1145/324133.324140

Lawrence, S., & Giles, C. L. (1999). Accessibility of information on the web. *Nature, 400*, 107–109. doi:10.1038/21987

Lunt, C., Galbreath, N., & Winner, J. (2004). *U. S. Patent No. 10/967,609: Ranking search results based on the frequency of clicks on the search results by members of a social network who are within a predetermined degree of separation*. Washington, DC: United States Patent and Trademark Office.

Manning, C., Raghavan, P., & Schütze, H. (2008). *Introduction to information retrieval.* Cambridge, UK: Cambridge University Press.

Middleton, C., & Baeza-Yates, R. (2007). *A comparison of open source search engines.* Retrieved March 24, 2011, from http://wrg.upf.edu/ WRG/ dctos/Middleton-Baeza.pdf

Miller, C. C. (2010, October 31). A new search engine, where less is more. *The New York Times.* Retrieved November 15, 2010, from http://www. nytimes.com/ 2010/11/01/technology/01search. html

Moffat, A., & Zobel, J. (1996). Self-indexing inverted files for fast text retrieval. *ACM Transactions on Information Systems, 14*(4), 349–379. doi:10.1145/237496.237497

Moose, F. S. (2010). *Moose file system.* Retrieved October 13, 2010, from http://www.moosefs.org

Motzkin, D. (1994). On high performance of updates within an efficient document retrieval system. *Information Processing & Management, 30*(1), 93–118. doi:10.1016/0306-4573(94)90026-4

Nadella, S. (2010, October 13). *New signals in search: The Bing social layer.* Retrieved October 13, 2010 from http://www.bing.com/ community/ blogs/search/archive/2010/10/13/ new-signals-in-search-the-bing-social-layer.aspx

Patterson, A. L. (2004). *U.S. Patent No. 20060031195: Phrase-based searching in an information retrieval system.* Washington, DC: United States Patent and Trademark Office.

Patterson, A. L. (2005). *We wanted something special for our birthday...* Retrieved October 13, 2010, from http://googleblog.blogspot.com/ 2005/09/we-wanted-something-special-for-our. html

Porter, M. F. (1980). An algorithm for suffix stripping. *Program, 14*(3), 130–137. doi:10.1108/ eb046814

Pugh, W. (1990). Skip lists: A probabilistic alternative to balanced trees. *Communications of the ACM, 33*(6), 668–676. doi:10.1145/78973.78977

Ramachandran, S. (2010, May 26). *Web metrics: Size and number of resources.* Retrieved March 17, 2011, from http://code.google.com/ speed/ articles/web-metrics.html

Rao, L. (2010, September 14). *Twitter seeing 90 million tweets per day, 25 percent contain links.* Retrieved October 13, 2010, from http:// techcrunch.com/ 2010/09/14/twitter-seeing-90-million-tweets-per-day

Rao, L. (2010, October 13). *Facebook now has klout.* Retrieved October 13, 2010, from http:// techcrunch.com/ 2010/10/13/facebook-now-has-klout/

Rice, R. F. (1979). *Some practical universal noiseless coding techniques* (Tech. Rep. No. 79-22). Pasadena, CA: Jet Propulsion Laboratory.

Salton, G. (1962). *The use of citations as an aid to automatic content analysis* (Tech. Rep. No. ISR-2, Section III). Cambridge, MA: Harvard Computation Laboratory.

Salton, G., Wong, A., & Wang, C. S. (1975). A vector space model for automatic indexing. *Communications of the ACM, 18*(11), 613–620. doi:10.1145/361219.361220

Scholer, F., Williams, H., Yiannis, J., & Zobel, J. (2002). Compression of inverted indexes for fast query evaluation. In *Proceedings of the 25th Annual International ACM SIGIR Conference on Research and Development in Information Retrieval* (pp. 222-229).

Selberg, E. (1999). *Towards comprehensive Web search* (Unpublished doctoral dissertation). University of Washington, Seattle, WA.

Silberschatz, G. (1994). Distributed file systems. In Silberschatz, A., Galvin, P. B., & Gagne, G. (Eds.), *Operating system concepts*. Reading, MA: Addison-Wesley.

Singhal, A., Buckley, C., & Mitra, M. (1996). Pivoted document length normalization. In *Proceedings of the 19th Annual International ACM SIGIR Conference on Research and Development in Information Retrieval*, Zurich, Switzerland (pp. 21-29).

Smith, A. J. (1985). Disk cache—miss ratio analysis and design considerations. *ACM Transactions on Computer Systems, 3*(3), 161–203. doi:10.1145/3959.3961

Tashian, C. (2009). *Bytes and Pixes (Web Page Sizes)*. Retrieved March 17, 2011, from http://tashian.com/ htmlguide/sizes.html

The Open Source Census. (2011). *Census summary report*. Retrieved March 24, 2011, from https://www.osscensus.org/ summary-report-public.php

Trotman, A. (2003). Compressing inverted files. *Information Retrieval, 6*(1), 5–19. doi:10.1023/A:1022949613039

Wardrip-Fruin, N., & Montfort, N. (Eds.). (2003). *The new media reader (Sec. 54)*. Cambridge, MA: MIT Press.

Wikipedia. (2011). *Lucene*. Retrieved March 16, 2011, from http://en.wikipedia.org/wiki/Lucene

Wikipedia. (2011). *Yandex*. Retrieved March 16, 2011, from http://en.wikipedia.org/ wiki/Yandex

Witten, A. H., Moffat, A., & Bell, T. C. (1999). *Managing gigabytes: Compressing and indexing documents and images* (2nd ed.). San Francisco, CA: Morgan Kaufmann.

Wright, A. (2009, August 23). Mining the Web for feelings, not facts. *The New York Times*. Retrieved October 13, 2010, from http://www.nytimes.com/2009/08/24/technology/internet/24emotion.html

Yahoo. (2010). *The history of Yahoo! How it all started...* Retrieved October 13, 2010, from http://docs.yahoo.com/ info/misc/history.html

Zhang, J., Long, X., & Suel, T. (2007). Performance of compressed inverted list caching in search engines. In *Proceedings of the 17th International Conference on World Wide Web* (pp. 387-396).

Zobel, J., & Moffat, A. (2006). Inverted files for text search engines. *ACM Computing Surveys, 38*(2). doi:10.1145/1132956.1132959

Zuckerberg, M. (2008, December 4). Facebook across the Web. *The Facebook Blog*. Retrieved October 13, 2010, from http://blog.facebook.com/blog.php?post=41735647130

Zuckerberg, M. (2010, July 21). 500 million stories. *The Facebook Blog*. Retrieved October 13, 2010, from http://blog.facebook.com/ blog.php?post=409753352130

KEY TERMS AND DEFINITIONS

Anchor Text: Visible, clickable text in a hyperlink.

Corpus: A collection of documents that are used for indexing.

Delta Encoding: Encoding technique that stores differences in values in a sorted array rather than full values.

Dictionary: A collection of terms used in an index.

Gamma Encoding: Technique used to encode positive integers when the upper bound is unknown.

Intersection: The operation of finding the overlapping elements of two sets. In the context of web search, posting lists are intersected for multi-term queries.

Inverted Index: A collection of posting lists.

Off Page Signals: Features extracted for a term on a given webpage from the contents of other webpages. Example: Presence of a term in anchor text.

On Page Signals: Features extracted for a term on a given webpage from the contents of that page itself. Example: Presence of term in Title.

Posting List: A list of identifiers for documents that contain a given term.

Skip List: An auxiliary data structure to posting lists that enables skipping parts of it during intersection.

Term-Incidence Matrix: A boolean matrix indicating whether or not a given term appears in a given document.

Chapter 2
Decentralized Search and the Clustering Paradox in Large Scale Information Networks

Weimao Ke
College of Information Science and Technology, Drexel University, USA

ABSTRACT

Amid the rapid growth of information today is the increasing challenge for people to navigate its magnitude. Dynamics and heterogeneity of large information spaces such as the Web raise important questions about information retrieval in these environments. Collection of all information in advance and centralization of IR operations are extremely difficult, if not impossible, because systems are dynamic and information is distributed. The chapter discusses some of the key issues facing classic information retrieval models and presents a decentralized, organic view of information systems pertaining to search in large scale networks. It focuses on the impact of network structure on search performance and discusses a phenomenon we refer to as the Clustering Paradox, in which the topology of interconnected systems imposes a scalability limit.

INTRODUCTION

Information distributes in many large networked environments, in which it is rarely possible to collect all information in advance for centralized retrieval operations. The Web, as one of such information spaces, poses great challenges for information retrieval because of its size, dynamics, and heterogeneity. Baeza-Yates et al. (2007) reasoned that centralized IR systems will become inefficient in the face of continued Web growth and a fully distributed architecture is desirable. Today, a web search engine has to have more than one million servers to survive. However, how to

DOI: 10.4018/978-1-4666-0330-1.ch002

coordinate information collection, indexing, and query processing operations among the huge number of computers internally remains a challenging question.

In addition, there are realistic situations in which collection of information in advance is hardly possible, sometimes unnecessary. The deep web, for example, possesses at least half million databases behind their diverse, sometimes complex, interfaces that do not provide information without being properly queried (Mostafa, 2005; He et al., 2007). In other systems, information is not allowed to be collected and indexed for issues such as privacy and copyright. Sometimes, it is useless to store information beforehand because it is transient and might become irrelevant after being gathered.

In these cases, a large number of information collections distributed in a networked environment is inevitable. The traditional notion of knowing where information is and indexing a "known" collection for later retrieval no longer holds (Marchionini, 1995). While an information need may arise from anywhere in the space (from a delegate system, an agent, or a connected peer), relevant information may exist in certain segments but there requires a mechanism to help the two meet each other – by either delivering relevant information to the one who needs it or routing a query (representative of the need) where information can be retrieved. Potentially, intelligent algorithms may be designed to help one travel a *short path* to another in the networked space.

As these information spaces continue to evolve and grow, it has become crucial to study retrieval models that can adapt and scale into the future. While centralized, "one for all" IR systems are unlikely to keep up with the evolving challenges, a decentralized architecture is promising and, due to many additional constraints, is sometimes the only choice (Baeza-Yates et al., 2007). Without a centralized information repository and global control, the new architecture has to take advantage of distributed computing power and allow a large

number of systems to participate in the decision making for finding relevant information.

What is potentially useful in such an information space is that individual systems (e.g., sites, peers, and/or agents) connect to one another and collectively form some global structure. Examples of these network structures include the Web graph of hyperlinks, peer-to-peer networks, and interconnected services/agents in the Semantic Web. Understanding these structures will provide guidance on how decentralized search and retrieval methods can function in networks. Seen in this light, finding relevant information in these information spaces transforms into a problem concerning not only information retrieval but also complex networks (Albert & Barabási, 2002; Kleinberg, 2006).

BACKGROUND

Related challenges for search in distributed settings have been studied in areas of distributed (federated) IR, peer-to-peer networks, multi-agent systems, and complex networks (Callan, 2000; Crespo & Garcia-Molina, 2005; Yu & Singh, 2003; Kleinberg, 2006). In peer-to-peer information retrieval research, for example, problems regarding the applicability of federated IR models in fully distributed environments and scalability of various P2P search models were scrutinized (Zarko & Silvestri, 2007).

While traditional IR and federated IR research provides basic tools for attacking decentralized search problems, the evolving dynamics and heterogeneity of today's networked environments have challenged the sufficiency of existing methods and call for new innovations (Baeza-Yates et al., 2007). Whereas peer-to-peer offers a new type of architecture for application-level questions and techniques to be tested, research on complex networks studies related questions in their basic forms (Albert & Barabási, 2002; Zarko & Silvestri, 2007; Barabási, 2009).

DISTRIBUTED AND P2P INFORMATION RETRIEVAL

Distributed (federated) IR models were shown to be effective for database selection and result fusion given hundreds of distributed, persistent information collections. Their scalability to larger, unstable environments is questionable. A peer-to-peer network, for instance, often involves more than tens of thousands, sometimes millions, of distributed peers who dynamically join and leave the community. Usually there is no global information about available collections; seldom is there centralized control or a central server for mediating (Lua et al., 2005; Doulkeridis et al., 2008).

Recent years have seen growing popularity of peer-to-peer (P2P) networks for large scale information access (Lua et al., 2005). With network topology and placement of content tightly controlled, *structured* peer-to-peer networks have the advantage of search efficiency (Stoica et al., 2001; Ratnasamy et al., 2001; Bender et al., 2005; Luu et al., 2006; Skobeltsyn et al., 2007). However, their ability to handle unreliable peers and transient populations was not sufficiently tested. *Unstructured* overlay systems work in an non-deterministic manner and have received increased popularity for being fault tolerant and adaptive to evolving system dynamics (Lua et al., 2005; Doulkeridis et al., 2008).

As the peer-to-peer paradigm becomes better recognized for IR research, there have been ongoing discussions on the applicability of existing P2P search models for IR, the efficiency and scalability challenges, and the effectiveness of traditional IR models in such environments (Zarko & Silvestri, 2007). Some researchers applied Distributed Hashing Tables (DHTs) techniques to *structured* P2P environments for distributed retrieval and focused on building an efficient indexing structure over peers (Bender et al., 2005; Luu et al., 2006; Skobeltsyn et al., 2007). However, others questioned the sufficiency of DHTs for dealing with high dimensionality of IR in dynamic P2P environments (Bawa et al., 2003; Lua et al., 2005; Lu & Callan, 2006). For information retrieval based on a large feature space, which often requires frequent updates to cope with the transiency of information and participants, it is challenging for distributed hashing to work in a traffic- and space-efficient manner.

Semantic overlay networks (SONs), based on peer segmentation and network clustering, have been widely used for distributed IR operations (Crespo & Garcia-Molina, 2005; Doulkeridis et al., 2008). In SONs, peers containing similar information formed semantic groups for efficient searches (Bawa et al., 2003; Crespo & Garcia-Molina, 2005; Tang et al., 2003; Lu & Callan, 2006; Raftopoulou & Petrakis, 2008). Clustering, sometimes in the form of hierarchical segmentation, was the key idea for bringing similar peers together in a more organized way so that topically relevant peers or information sources can be quickly identified. These techniques were shown in experiments to achieve good retrieval performance.

Research experiments have been conducted on SONs for peers to self-organize and perform clustering to form a hierarchical structure, in which super-peers assumed greater responsibilities for mediating queries. From a complex network standpoint, however, some researchers have questioned the reliability of such an architecture because attacks on super peers (nodes or agents) can lead to a large disconnected structure (Albert & Barabási, 2002; Lua et al., 2005). In addition, as Lu (2007) observed, updating super-peers for changes in distributed collections are traffic intensive and may cause problems in environments where bandwidth is limited.

In P2P research, multi-agent systems were often used to model retrieval problem in large scale, decentralized environments. Some researchers used multi-agent systems to model distributed information retrieval in semantic overlay peer-to-peer networks and focused on federated IR operations such as resource representation, database selection, and result fusion in P2P environments (Zhang et al., 2004; Fischer & Nurzenski, 2005; Bender et al., 2005; Vouros, 2008). Some studied agent learning and adaptation for efficient retrieval in dynamic environments, and emphasized the overall system utility and throughput (Zhang & Lesser, 2006, 2007). Others employed multi-agent techniques to build recommender systems based on agent-user and agent-agent interactions (Birukov et al., 2005).

Regardless of the various applications/technologies used, the central problem remains how we can afford to do search in a rather decentralized environment. Peers (or agents, websites) are computing systems that, with individual capabilities and limits, can interconnect and communicate with one another. In light of complex networks, the major two elements here are *nodes* and *edges*. Whereas *nodes* refer to individual systems, *edges* are the manifestation of their inter-connectivity. This conceptualization, as we will elaborate on later, is key to understanding large scale, decentralized search problems at a basic, fundamental level.

CLUSTERING AND NETWORK CLUSTERING FOR INFORMATION RETRIEVAL

Generally speaking, *clustering* is the process of bringing like entities together (Berry, 2004). Clustering is an important notion for information organization and retrieval. One important statement in IR, known as the Cluster Hypothesis, conjectures that relevant documents are more similar to each other than to non-relevant documents, and hence similar documents tend to be relevant to the same requests (van Rijsbergen, 1973). Further experiments supported that relevant documents tend to appear in the same cluster(s), beneficial to both browsing and searching (Hearst & Pedersen, 1996). Document-level clustering is useful not only in information indexing but also

in user-system interaction for retrieval purposes (Hearst & Pedersen, 1996; Ke et al., 2009).

For information retrieval in distributed environments, one level of clustering, as discussed earlier, involves partitioning of the document-key index across peers. The MINEVAR and ALVIS architectures based on distributed hashing tables (DHTs), for example, demonstrated the utility of *key* clustering for retrieval efficiency in structured P2P networks (Bender et al., 2005; Skobeltsyn et al., 2007). In semi-structured environments such as Freenet, it was shown that clustering of the key space significantly improved search effectiveness (Lua et al., 2005).

Another level of clustering, which is likely more relevant in the distributed IR context, is segmentation or clustering of nodes/peers. As discussed in the previous section, semantic overlay networks (SONs) have been widely adopted for retrieval effectiveness and efficiency (Bawa et al., 2003; Crespo & Garcia-Molina, 2005; Lu, 2007; Doulkeridis et al., 2008). This is what we refer to as *network clustering* because the outcome of peer segmentation is some global structure of network connectivity. *Network clustering* enables similar peers to connect to each other and sometimes allows super peers to coordinate local reconstruction and to update remote connections for efficient query routing.

In distributed environments, *network clustering* is not a centralized operation for grouping entities. Rather, *network clustering* emerges from how individual systems interconnect and represents an approach to understanding the structure and patterns of a networked community. In our approach to network clustering, we use a parameter for a probability distribution to guide interconnectivity of distributed systems. We will discuss this further.

For decentralized IR, particularly in peer-to-peer networks, some have assumed the unitary benefit of clustering and overlooked its potential negative impact on search. How much clustering is enough? How much clustering is too much?

The potential problem of over-clustering (or "too much" clustering) has rarely been scrutinized in IR settings. From a distributed service discovery perspective, Singh et al. (2001) observed that over-clustering degraded network quality for finding quality information and services. They reasoned that this was because too many connections were used up for within group connections, lacking long distance connections that bridged groups. In the following section, we shall summarize our view of the major challenge being introduced and continue the discussion on the impact of network clustering.

A DECENTRALIZED VIEW FOR INFORMATION RETRIEVAL

Finding relevant information in distributed environments is a problem concerning not only information retrieval but also inter-connectivity (networks). We know from the small world phenomenon, common in many real networks that every piece of information is within a short radius from any location in a network. However, relevant information is only a tiny fraction of all densely packed information in the "small world."

If we allow queries to traverse the edges of a network to find relevant information, there has to be some association between the network space and the relevance space in order to orient searches. Random networks could never provide such guidance because edges are so independent of content that they have little semantic meaning (Albert & Barabási, 2002; Boguna, 2009). Fortunately, research has discovered that development of a wide range of networks follows not a random process but some preferential mechanism that captures "meanings" (Barabási, 2009).

Surely, these networks, even with a good departure from randomness, do not automatically ensure efficient search and retrieval of relevant information. To optimize such a network for search, mechanisms should be designed to en-

able more meaningful semantic overlay on top of physical connections. In this chapter, the focus of discussion is on logical networks, in which edges/connections are essentially inter-system references/indices.

Information Network and Semantic Overlay

Let us refer to the type of networks in this discussion as information networks to emphasize the focus on finding relevant information. Practically, information networks include, but are not limited to, peer-to-peer networks for information sharing, the deep web where many large databases reside, and networks formed by information agents. Close examination of these networks reveals some common characteristics illustrated in Figure 1.

As shown in Figure 1, an information network is formed by nodes (e.g., peers, web sites, or agents) through edges, by means of communication/interaction/links. A node has a set of information items or documents, which in turn can be used to define its overall topicality. If we can somehow discover the content of each node and layout the nodes in terms of their topicality, then the information network in Figure 1 can be visualized in the form of Figure m2(a).

Figure 2(a) shows a circle representation of the topical (semantic) space, in which there are two topical clusters of nodes, i.e., cluster 1-3-5-7 and cluster 2-4-6 (visually separated on the topical circle space). Connection-wise, there are local edges (solid lines) within each cluster and long-range ones (dashed lines) between the clusters.

Within-group local connections are useful because they bring "close" (topically similar) nodes together to form segments, which is consistent to their topical separation. This establishes an important association between the topological (network) space and the topical (search) space that potentially guides searches. In terms of Granovetter (1973), these can be seen *strong ties*.

Figure 1. Information Network. Solid lines are local connections and dash lines are remote connections, as illustrated in Figure 2 and discussed in the following text

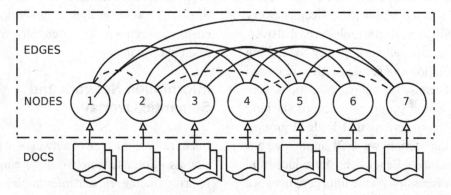

Long-distance connections, shown as dashed lines in Figure 2, bring randomness and *serendipity* to the network. These between-group connections, or *weak ties*, often serve as bridges and are critical for efficient diffusion of information (Granovetter, 1973). When there are too many long-range connections, however, the topological space (interconnectivity) tells little about the topical space. In short, we can hardly rely on topically non-relevant edges in the search for topical relevance. We will provide further explanation on this later.

While the initial network, shown in Figure 2(a), might not be good enough for decentralized search, some overlay can be built upon the physical layer to bring more semantics to the network space. Due to no global control over such

an information network, mechanisms should be designed to guide individual adaptation and network evolution for this purpose. Over the course of network development shown in Figures 2(a), 2(b), and 2(c), for example, semantic overlay is strengthened through the reinforcement of strong ties and re-establishment of some weak ties[1].

Strong Ties vs. Weak Ties

In the organization of networks, *strong ties* and *weak ties* play important roles. According to Granovetter (1973), *strong ties* were widely studied in network models for small, well-defined groups in which individuals have strong neighborhood overlap and are similar to one other. Empha-

Figure 2. Evolving semantic overlay

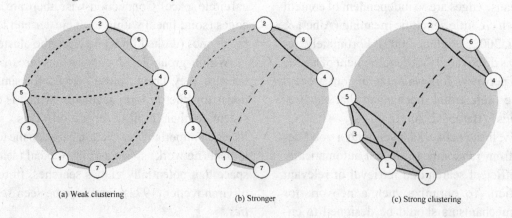

(a) Weak clustering (b) Stronger (c) Strong clustering

sis on *weak ties*, however, shifts the discussion to relations *between* groups and to analysis of "segments of social structure not easily defined in terms of primary groups" (Granovetter, 1973, p. 1360). *Weak ties* often serve as bridges of groups, removal of which will lead to fragmented larger structures. These principles are applicable to the discussion on interconnected computing systems for large scale information retrieval.

To clarify the key notions of tie strength, i.e., the meanings of strong vs. weak ties, we shall define them at three levels, namely, 1) the dyadic meaning in terms of an interaction relationship between two nodes, 2) the topological meaning in terms of a tie's macro-level impact on the network structure, and 3) the topical definition based on pairwise similarity/relevance in the IR context. These three levels will enable us to scrutinize network clustering from multiple perspectives.

Dyadic Meaning of Tie Strength

Granovetter (1973, p. 1361) loosely defined the *strength* of an interpersonal tie as "a combination of the amount of time, the emotional intensity, the intimacy (mutual confiding), and the reciprocal services which characterize the tie." While implications of tie strength are beyond the dyadic characteristics of an interpersonal (or inter-system) relationship, it is still useful to define it on a similar level in the decentralized IR context, in which interactions and trust among distributed nodes (peers/agents) are important aspects. The strength of a tie, on the dyadic level of this research, can thus be defined as a combination of time, mutual trust of two nodes (peers/agents) and the value of help they have offered each other. It can be operationalized as the number of times they interact with each other and rewards exchanged in interactions.

Topological Meaning of Tie Strength

Whereas strong ties are unlikely to be bridges, all bridges are weak ties. Following the "bridge" notion of tie strength, the *weakness* of a tie was referred to as the number of broken paths or changes in average path length due to its removal (Granovetter, 1973). More precisely, it can be defined as a bridge of *degree* n_d, where n_d is the shortest path between its two points if the tie is removed. Besides this, the *betweenness centrality* measure, developed by Anthonisse (1971) and Freeman (1977), can also be used to evaluate node or tie centrality/*weakness*:

$$C_B(v) = \sum_{s \neq v \neq t \in V} \frac{\sigma_{st}(v)}{\sigma_{st}} \tag{1}$$

where $\sigma_{st} = \sigma_{ts}$ is the number of shortest paths from s to t and $\sigma_{st}(v)$ the number of shortest paths from s to t that pass through v (either a tie or a node) in graph V (Brandes, 2001; Girvan & Newman, 2002).

Topical Meaning of Tie Strength

In the IR context, closeness or remoteness of two nodes depends on their topical relevance or similarity. Provided a vector representation, distance can be measured by the angle of two vectors and similarity measured as cosine of the angle (Baeza-Yates & Ribeiro-Neto, 2004). On this level, therefore, the strength of a tie can be seen as the pairwise relevance and operationalized as cosine similarity. Given two nodes represented by vectors $u = [u_1, .., u_t]^T$ and $v = [v_1, .., v_t]^T$, if they form a tie/link, the strength can be calculated using the cosine coefficient. Therefore, tie *weakness* can be equated with pairwise topical distance or angle value: $\angle_{uv} = \arccos\left(c_{uv}\right)$, where c_{uv} is the cosine coefficient of vectors u and v.

$$c_{uv} = \cos(u, v) = \frac{\sum_{i=1}^{t} x_i \_ y_i}{\sqrt{(\sum_{i=1}^{t} x_i^2) \_ (\sum_{i=1}^{t} y_i^2)}} \qquad (2)$$

Here we present three levels of tie strength, namely, the dyadic, topological, and topical meanings of *strong ties* vs. *weak ties*. They are different angles that can be used to scrutinize network clustering and to help us understand the impact of strong ties vs. weak ties, under the direction of network clustering, on search performance.

CLUSTERING PARADOX AND DECENTRALIZED SEARCH

How can we find relevant information items scattered among databases of a large scale information network? Back to the basic problems in the introduction, one main objective of research in this area is to develop improved distributed IR systems that can function and scale in the growing magnitude and distribution of information. By studying network characteristics, we hope to understand what structural patterns are needed to facilitate retrieval among interconnected systems and how we can design an infrastructure for large scale retrieval. We expect to clarify the relationship of critical IR functions to characteristics of distributed environments and identify effective search strategies.

Clustering Paradox

Research on complex networks has studied related problems in their basic forms and demonstrated useful results. It was found that a proper level of network clustering (with strong ties) with some presence of remote connections (weak ties) has to be maintained for efficient searches (Kleinberg, 2000; Watts et al., 2002; Liben-Nowell et al., 2005; Simsek & Jensen, 2008; Boguñá et al., 2009). Clustering reduces the number of "irrelevant" links and aids in creating topical segments useful for orienting searches. With very strong clustering, however, a network tends to be fragmented into local communities with abundant *strong ties* but few *weak ties* to bridge remote parts (Granovetter, 1973; Singh et al., 2001). Although searches might be able to move gradually toward targets, necessary "hops" become unavailable. With weak clustering, on the other hand, there are abundant *weak ties* to bridge distant parts of the network but few *strong ties* to hold local members together to form useful segments. Although searches may "jump" quickly from one end of the network to the other, there is rarely any *guidance* on where they are heading to.

We refer to this phenomenon as the *Clustering Paradox*, in which neither strong clustering nor weak clustering is desirable for searches. In other words, trade-off is required between *strong ties* for search orientation and *weak ties* for efficient traversal. In Granovetter's terms we discussed, whereas *strong ties* deal with local connections within small, well-defined groups, *weak ties* capture between-group relations and serve as bridges of social segments (Granovetter, 1973). The *Clustering Paradox*, seen in light of strong ties and weak ties, has received attention in complex network research but requires closer scrutiny in a decentralized IR context.

Clustering Paradox of Search in Complex Networks

Kleinberg (2000), who pioneered this line of research, studied decentralized search in *small world* using a two dimensional model, in which peers had rich connections with immediate neighbors and sparse associations with remote ones (Kleinberg, 2000). The probability p_r of connecting to a neighbor beyond the immediate neighborhood was proportional to r^{-a}, where r was the search distance (topical separation) between the two in the two-dimensional space and α a constant called *clustering exponent*[2]. It was shown that only when *clustering exponent* $\alpha=2$, search time (i.e., search path length) was optimal and bounded by $c\left(\log N\right)^2$, where N was the network size and c was some constant (Kleinberg, 2000).

The *clustering exponent* α, as shown in Figure 3, describes a correlation between the network (topological) space and the search (topical) space (Kleinberg, 2000; Boguñá et al., 2009). When α is small, connectivity has little dependence on topical closeness – local segments become less visible as the network is built on increased randomness, i.e., with too many *weak ties*. As shown in Figure 4(a), the network is a random graph given a uniform connectivity distribution at $\alpha=0$. Searches will be disoriented as there is no consistent topical clue to rely on for traversal in the "right" direction. When α is large, weak ties (long-distance connections) are rare and strong ties dominate. The network becomes highly segmented. As shown in Figure 4(c), when $\alpha\rightarrow\infty$, the network is very regular (highly clustered) given that it is extremely unlikely for remote pairs to connect. Although searches are well guided and can move gradually toward targets, they are slow without *weak ties* to help them jump from one segment to another. Given a moderate α value, as shown in Figure 4(b), the network becomes a narrowly defined *small world*, in which both local and remote connections present.

In this way, the *clustering exponent* α influences the formation of local clusters and overall network clustering. The impact of $\alpha\in[0,\infty)$ on network clustering is similar to that of a rewiring probability $p\in[1,0]$ in Watts and Strogatz (1998). However, α additionally defines the association of connectivity and topical distance. It was further discovered that optimal value of α for search, in

many synthetic networks previously studied, depends on the dimensionality of the search space. Specifically, when $\alpha=d$ on a d-dimension space, decentralized search is optimal. Increasing (stronger clustering) or decreasing the α value (weaker clustering) from the optima greatly degrades search performance. In either case, there is a rapid increase of search time especially in large scale networks. In other words, search will not be able to scale in a growing network without the desired balance of clustering.

Further studies conducted by various research groups have shown consistent results (Watts et al., 2002; Liben-Nowell et al., 2005; Simsek & Jensen, 2008; Boguñá et al., 2009). Recognizing the small world properties in a wide range of real networks and their abilities of efficient information routing/signalling without global intelligence, Boguñá et al. (2009) described a general mechanism to explain the connection between a network structure and the function for navigation. They theorized the supporting mechanism for search as a hid-

Figure 3. Network clustering: Function of clustering exponent α

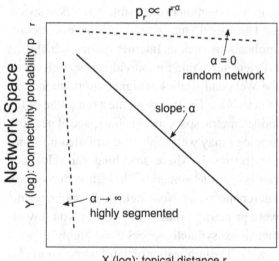

Figure 4. Network Clustering: Impact of Clustering Exponent α. Compare to Watts and Strogatz (1998). (a) a random network, provided no association between connectivity and topical distance at α=0, (b) a small world network when a moderate α value allows the presence of both local and remote connections, and (c) a regular network where nodes only connect to local neighbors at α→∞ (simulated given α=1000). The figures were produced by simulations based on n=24 nodes and k=4 neighbors for each. Topical distance is measured by the angle between two nodes (vectors from the origin/center) in the 1-sphere (circle) representation.

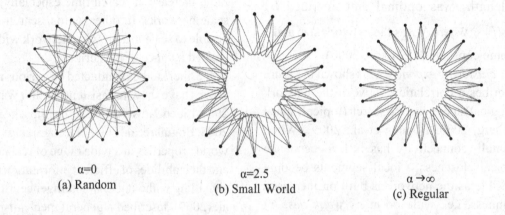

| α=0 | α=2.5 | α →∞ |
| (a) Random | (b) Small World | (c) Regular |

den metric space behind the observable network topology. Experimental simulations revealed that certain characteristics of the correlation between the two spaces – similar to the clustering exponent α in Kleinberg (2000) and the concept of homophily in Simsek and Jensen (2008) – enable efficient search/navigation in the visible networked space.

These works may provide guidance on various applications such as Internet routing scalability, efficient searching for individuals or contents on the Web, and studies of signal/information flow in networks. The theory on the association of the hidden metric space and visible space of network topology may well apply to distributed information retrieval, where searching for relevance can be seen as something hidden under system interconnectivity. Nonetheless, the above results were primarily produced by research on low dimensional synthetic spaces using highly abstract models. The implication of the *clustering paradox* on large scale, decentralized information retrieval has yet to be scrutinized.

Clustering Paradox in Large Scale Information Retrieval

To understand the phenomenon of clustering paradox in the IR context, we have conducted experimental research on decentralized information retrieval in distributed networked environments and focused on the impact of network clustering on search performance. A series of experiments on two benchmark IR collections and various networks of up to 10^5 distributed systems showed that network structure, i.e., how distributed systems connect to one another, was crucial to effective and efficient decentralized IR operations in large information networks (Ke & Mostafa, 2009, 2010; Ke, 2010). Particularly, some balanced level of network clustering well supported search functions in large networks. Too strong clustering and weak clustering undermined information *findability* and search performance – a phenomenon consistent to the *clustering paradox* found in complex network research.

The main experiments were conducted on the ClueWeb09B dataset[3], a recently developed benchmark IR collection that has become popular for large scale experiments. Treating websites as systems serving their individual collections of pages, we enabled the distributed systems to interconnect and self organize into a network structure, with a control parameter α (clustering exponent) to guide network clustering (Ke & Mostafa, 2010; Ke, 2010).

Network clustering was performed without centralized control, in a manner similar to Kleinberg (2000). Specifically, when determining whether to establish a connection with another system from a neighbor pool, each distributed system followed the probability function $p = r^{-a}$, where r was the topical distance (based on a cosine measure of meta-document vectors) between the current system and the other system being considered as a potential neighbor. Considering limited capacities of individual systems, the number of neighbor systems they established connections with was relatively small to the entire network community. For example, in the network of 10,000 systems, each system only maintains a neighbors of roughly 30 member systems (directly connected neighbors).

In the experiments, each query was forwarded from one system to another in a greedy routing manner, until sufficient relevant information was found or the search reached a predefined time limit. With a particular level of network clustering, similarity-based search methods were found to perform very efficiently while maintaining a high level of effectiveness in very large networks (Ke & Mostafa, 2010). For example, searching for single unique documents in 4.4 million pages distributed among 10,000 distributed systems, selectively traversing roughly 100 systems achieved nearly perfect recall and precision, i.e., $P \approx 1$ and $R \approx 1$.

As shown in Figure 5, the superior search performance was supported only by a very specific network clustering level at α=10 in these experiments[4]. Both stronger clustering (larger α) and weaker clustering (smaller α) led to degraded search performance, often with a large increase of search time in large networks.

As we discussed earlier, when network clustering is very strong, there are sufficient *strong ties* to hold local segments and guide searches toward relevant information but few *week ties* for searches to "jump." On the other hand, weak clustering establishes abundant *weak ties* for searches to potentially move fast. However, without sufficient *strong ties*, there is too much randomness in the network and no guidance toward relevance. In either case, information retrieval operations that relied on decentralized methods will be inefficient and ineffective. Some level of network clustering allows for the presence and balance of both strong ties and weak ties, maximizing the likelihood of finding relevant information timely. The inflection points in Figure 5 demonstrate the *clustering paradox* in the IR context. The differences between consecutive network clustering levels in the figure were found to be statistically significant.

Experiments also showed that network clustering was crucial for scalable searches. Given the above network clustering level, search time was found to be a poly-logarithmic function of network size (Ke & Mostafa, 2010; Ke, 2010). Particularly, search time L was found to be proportional to $c \cdot \log^6 (N)$, where c is a constant and observed values of network sizes $N \in [10^2, 10^3, 10^4, 10^5]$. This poly-logarithmic relationship was shown consistent across most of the experiments, with very large effect sizes $R^2 > 0.99$ found in statistical analysis. The implication is that, when an information network continues to grow in magnitude, the increase of search time needed to find information in the network will remain rather moderate. In short, searches are likely scalable given the specific network clustering level.

In addition to the scalability of decentralized searches, the network clustering mechanism required to support the high level of IR performance

Figure 5. Some IR results on the Clustering Paradox. Search time (L) is represented by the number of systems each search traversed to retrieve relevant information. Best performance, i.e., least search time, was achieved at α=10. Details in Ke and Mostafa (2010)

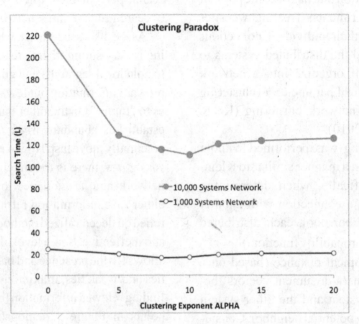

appeared to be scalable as well. Network clustering in the decentralized environment relied on local self-organization of individual systems with preferential neighbors and did not require any global supervision. Experiments showed that clustering time remained almost constant across all network sizes, $N \in \left[10^2, 10^3, 10^4, 10^5\right]$ (Ke & Mostafa, 2010). Additional experiments on finding authoritative relevant documents in the ClueWeb09B collection supported the above findings (Ke, 2010). Another series of experiments conducted on the TREC Genomics 2004 collection produced consistent results (Ke & Mostafa, 2009).

Another important finding is that the *Clustering Paradox* appeared to have a scaling effect on retrieval performance. Although under-clustering or over-clustering only moderately degraded search performance on small networks, it seemed to cause dramatic performance loss for large networks. In other words, little performance disadvantage in small networks might become too big to ignore in large-scale systems. This scaling effect requires closer examination.

These decentralized search experiments, conducted in an information retrieval context, supports findings from previous research on complex networks. The results may provide guidance on how distributed retrieval methods can function and scale into the future while information in our network spaces continues to grow in magnitude.

FUTURE DIRECTIONS

In an open, dynamic information space such as the Web, people, information, and technologies are all mobile and changing entities. The classic view of "knowing" where information is and indexing "known" collections of information for later retrieval is hardly valid in these environments. Finding where relevant repositories are for the *live* retrieval of information is critical. Without global information, new methods have to rely on local intelligence of distributed systems and/or their delegates to collectively construct paths to desired information.

Research in various areas, including IR, peer-to-peer, complex networks, and multi-agent systems, provides guidance on how we can build better systems to deal with this growing dynamicity. We have found that interconnectivity among distributed systems, based on *local* network clustering, is crucial to the scalability of decentralized search methods. The *Clustering Paradox* on decentralized search performance appears to have a scaling effect and deserves special attention for IR operations in large scale networks.

With the magnitude of information and the huge number of computing systems on the Internet, any level of centralization will be doomed to great challenges and potential failure. We believe that the fully decentralized view expressed in this chapter reflects a reality we cannot avoid in information retrieval research. While monolithic search systems continue to struggle with scalability problems of today, the future of search likely requires a better infrastructure where all can participate.

With a focus on the impact of network structure on search performance, recent search experiments produced promising results on finding relevant information in large scale distributed environments. The results and findings, nonetheless, are preliminary and should be interpreted with caution because experiments were conducted under certain assumptions/conditions. We discuss future research directions in light of limitations in current research.

In a dynamic networked information space, all can change and evolve. While users may have different information needs, contents of distributed systems in the network may appear, disappear, and change over time. Information that is relevant, valid and findable now may not be so in the future. How to identify page update and maintain content freshness has been an important topic in web crawler research (Cho & Garcia-Molina,

2003). In a dynamic environment, systems need to interact with others and adapt to changes in the settings. Learning provides an important means for systems to perceive their environment and act accordingly, critical to overall system utility and robustness. In the reported experiments, we assumed that contents in distributed systems were relatively static and a network structure only needed to be built once to reflect the content distribution. Future studies should investigate how a network structure (clustering) can be dynamically maintained when systems/agents come and go with evolving information collections. It is also important to study the dynamics of search traffics and how an entire network can cope with individual system failures. Learning and adaptation will be a key focus in this research direction.

Current large scale IR research primarily relies on automatic simulations based on text queries and pre-established relevance judgment for the evaluation of distributed systems. It is well known in IR that the notion of *relevance* involves multiple dimensions beyond topicality. Relevance often depends on the user's search contexts and can rarely be judged objectively using a pre-established relevance base. Real users and their search contexts should also be involved for research on large scale systems that are highly interactive and user-centric.

Although experiments show promises, much remains to be done before a fully decentralized infrastructure can be designed and implemented to work in a real world environment. One additional important assumption in the reported experiments was that systems/agents were cooperative and trustworthy. However, decentralization in the reality allows for individual participants to do independent decision making and exercise self interests. System behaviors, driven by their own objectives, may become very different from what is ideally expected.

Why would systems participate in decentralized search and contribute their computing power? There have to be benefits and/or incentives that motivate individuals to do so. Ideas can be borrowed from peer-to-peer applications, where individual computer systems share their resources in order to gain access to other resources. Besides incentives, we are yet to study why (and how to make sure) systems would behave in a contributive manner. There have been plenty of examples about free-riders in peer-to-peer networks, who take advantage of existing resources but have very little willingness to contribute. Others may offer contributions only to mislead and boost their own popularity.

Mechanisms have to be built to ensure better behaviors. Methods must also be implemented to detect harmful practices and guide beneficial interactions. Trust plays an important role in all this. Implementation of a decentralized search infrastructure will have to take into account issues of trust among uncooperative, untrustworthy, or malicious systems by drawing on findings and inspirations in distributed trust management.

CONCLUSION

With the rapid growth of digital information, it becomes increasingly challenging for people to navigate its magnitude. It is crucial to study basic principles that support adaptive and scalable retrieval functions in large networked environments such as the Web, where information is distributed among dynamic systems. While centralized, "one for all" IR systems are unlikely to keep up with the evolving challenges, a fully decentralized architecture is promising and, due to many additional constraints, is sometimes the only choice. Without a centralized information repository and global control, the new architecture has to take advantage of distributed computing power and allow a large number of systems to participate in the decision making for finding relevant information.

This chapter addresses one aspect of several scalability challenges facing classic information retrieval models and presents a decentralized,

organic view of information systems pertaining to search in large scale networks. The chapter focuses on the impact of network structure on search performance and discusses a phenomenon we refer to as the *Clustering Paradox*, in which the topology of interconnected systems imposes a scalability limit.

Research involving large scale benchmark collections provides evidence on the *Clustering Paradox* in the IR context. In an increasingly large, distributed environment, decentralized searches for relevant information can continue to function well only when systems interconnect in certain ways. Relying on partial indexes of distributed systems, some level of network clustering enables very efficient and effective discovery of relevant information in large scale networks. For a given network clustering level, search time is well explained by a poly-logarithmic relation to network size (i.e., the number of distributed systems), indicating a high scalability potential for searching in a continuously growing information space.

In addition to the scalability of decentralized searches, the network clustering mechanism that supported very high effectiveness and efficiency of IR operations in large networks was found to be scalable as well. The clustering function requires no "hard engineering" of the entire network but provides an organic way for systems to participate and connect given their opportunities and preferences. This organic mechanism potentially allows for a bottom-up approach to coping with dynamics in a fast growing information network.

REFERENCES

Albert, R., & Barabási, A.-L. (2002). Statistical mechanics of complex networks. *Reviews of Modern Physics, 74*(1), 47–97. doi:10.1103/RevModPhys.74.47

Anthonisse, J. (1971). *The rush in a directed graph* (Tech. Rep. No. BN9/71). Amsterdam, The Netherlands: Stichting Mahtematisch Centrum.

Baeza-Yates, R., & Ribeiro-Neto, B. (2004). *Modern information retrieval*. Reading, MA: Addison-Wesley.

Barabási, A.-L. (2009). Scale-free networks: A decade and beyond. *Science, 325*, 412–413. doi:10.1126/science.1173299

Bawa, M., Manku, G. S., & Raghavan, P. (2003). Sets: search enhanced by topic segmentation. In *Proceedings of the 26th Annual International ACM SIGIR Conference on Research and Development in Information Retrieval* (pp. 306-313). New York, NY: ACM.

Bender, M., Michel, S., Triantafillou, P., Weikum, G., & Zimmer, C. (2005). Improving collection selection with overlap awareness in p2p search engines. In *Proceedings of the 28th Annual International ACM SIGIR Conference on Research and Development in Information Retrieval* (pp. 67-74). New York, NY: ACM.

Berry, M. W. (2004). *Survey of text mining: clustering, classification, and retrieval*. New York, NY: Springer.

Birukov, A., Blanzieri, E., & Giorgini, P. (2005). Implicit: an agent-based recommendation system for web search. In *Proceedings of the Fourth International Joint Conference on Autonomous Agents and Multiagent Systems* (pp. 618-624). New York, NY: ACM.

Boguñá, M., Krioukov, D., & Claffy, K. C. (2009). Navigability of complex networks. *Nature Physics, 5*(1), 74–80. doi:10.1038/nphys1130

Brandes, U. (2001). A faster algorithm for betweenness centrality. *The Journal of Mathematical Sociology, 25*(2), 163–177. doi:10.1080/0022250X.2001.9990249

Callan, J. (2000). Distributed information retrieval. In *Proceedings of the International Conference on Advances in Information Retrieval* (pp. 127-150). New York, NY: Springer.

Cho, J., & Garcia-Molina, H. (2003). Estimating frequency of change. *ACM Transactions on Internet Technology, 3*(3), 256–290. doi:10.1145/857166.857170

Crespo, A., & Garcia-Molina, H. (2005). Semantic overlay networks for p2p systems. In *Proceedings of the Third International Workshop on Agents and Peer-to-Peer Computing* (pp. 1-13). New York, NY: Springer.

Cutting, D. R., Karger, D., Pedersen, J. O., & Tukey, J. W. (1992). Scatter/Gather: A cluster-based approach to browsing large document collections. In *Proceedings of the 15th Annual International ACM SIGIR Conference on Research and Development in Information Retrieval* (pp. 318-329). New York, NY: ACM.

Doulkeridis, C., Norvag, K., & Vazirgiannis, M. (2008). Peer-to-peer similarity search over widely distributed document collections. In *Proceedings of the ACM Workshop on Large-Scale Distributed Systems for Information Retrieval* (pp. 35-42). New York, NY: ACM.

Fischer, G., & Nurzenski, A. (2005). Towards scatter/gather browsing in a hierarchical peer-to-peer network. In *Proceedings of the ACM Workshop on Information Retrieval in Peer-to-Peer Networks* (pp. 25-32). New York, NY: ACM.

Freeman, L. (1977). A set of measuring centrality based on betweenness. *Sociometry, 40*, 35–41. doi:10.2307/3033543

Girvan, M., & Newman, M. E. J. (2002). Community structure in social and biological networks. *Proceedings of the National Academy of Sciences of the United States of America, 99*(12), 7821–7826. doi:10.1073/pnas.122653799

Granovetter, M. S. (1973). The strength of weak ties. *American Journal of Sociology, 78*(6), 1360–1380. doi:10.1086/225469

He, B., Patel, M., Zhang, Z., & Chang, K. C.-C. (2007). Accessing the deep web. *Communications of the ACM, 50*(5), 94–101. doi:10.1145/1230819.1241670

Hearst, M. A., & Pedersen, J. O. (1996). Reexamining the cluster hypothesis: Scatter/Gather on retrieval results. In *Proceedings of the 19th Annual International ACM SIGIR Conference on Research and Development in Information Retrieval* (pp. 76-84). New York, NY: ACM.

Ke, W. (2010). *Scalability of findability: Decentralized search and retrieval in large information networks* (Unpublished master's thesis). School of Information and Library Science, The University of North Carolina, Chapel Hill, NC.

Ke, W., & Mostafa, J. (2009). Strong ties vs. weak ties: Studying the clustering paradox for decentralized search. In *Proceedings of the 7th Workshop on Large-Scale Distributed Systems for Information Retrieval, in conjunction with the 32nd Annual International ACM SIGIR Conference on Research and Development in Information Retrieval*, Boston, MA (pp. 49-56). New York, NY: ACM.

Ke, W., & Mostafa, J. (2010). Scalability of findability: effective and efficient IR operations in large information networks. In *Proceeding of the 33rd International ACM SIGIR Conference on Research and Development in Information Retrieval* (pp. 74-81). New York, NY: ACM.

Ke, W., Sugimoto, C. R., & Mostafa, J. (2009). Dynamicity vs. effectiveness: Studying online clustering for Scatter/Gather. In *Proceedings of the 32th Annual International ACM SIGIR Conference on Research and Development in Information Retrieval*, Boston, MA (pp. 19-26). New York, NY: ACM.

Kleinberg, J. M. (2000). Navigation in a small world. *Nature, 406*(6798). doi:10.1038/35022643

Kleinberg, J. M. (2006). Social networks, incentives, and search. In *Proceedings of the 29th Annual International ACM SIGIR Conference on Research and Development in Information Retrieval* (pp. 210-211). New York, NY: ACM.

Liben-Nowell, D., Novak, J., Kumar, R., Raghavan, P., & Tomkins, A. (2005). Geographic routing in social networks. *Proceedings of the National Academy of Sciences of the United States of America, 102*(33), 11623–11628. doi:10.1073/pnas.0503018102

Lu, J. (2007). Full-text federated search in peer-to-peer networks. *SIGIR Forum, 41*(1), 121–121. doi:10.1145/1273221.1273233

Lu, J., & Callan, J. (2003). Content-based retrieval in hybrid peer-to-peer networks. In *Proceedings of the Twelfth International Conference on Information and Knowledge Management* (pp. 199-206). New York, NY: ACM.

Lu, J., & Callan, J. (2006). User modeling for full-text federated search in peer-to-peer networks. In *Proceedings of the 29th Annual International ACM SIGIR Conference on Research and Development in Information Retrieval* (pp. 332-339). New York, NY: ACM.

Lua, E. K., Crowcroft, J., Pias, M., Sharma, R., & Lim, S. (2005). A survey and comparison of peer-to-peer overlay network schemes. *IEEE Communications Surveys and Tutorials, 7*, 72–93. doi:10.1109/COMST.2005.1610546

Luu, T., Klemm, F., Podnar, I., Rajman, M., & Aberer, K. (2006). Alvis peers: a scalable full-text peer-to-peer retrieval engine. In *Proceedings of the International Workshop on Information Retrieval in Peer-to-Peer Networks* (pp. 41-48). New York, NY: ACM.

Marchionini, G. (1995). *Information seeking in electronic environments*. Cambridge, UK: Cambridge University Press. doi:10.1017/CBO9780511626388

Mostafa, J. (2005). Seeking better web searches. *Scientific American, 292*(2), 66–73. doi:10.1038/scientificamerican0205-66

Raftopoulou, P., & Petrakis, E. G. (2008). A measure for cluster cohesion in semantic overlay networks. In *Proceeding of the ACM Workshop on Large-Scale Distributed Systems for Information Retrieval* (pp. 59-66). New York, NY: ACM.

Ratnasamy, S., Francis, P., Handley, M., Karp, R., & Schenker, S. (2001). A scalable content-addressable network. In *Proceedings of the Conference on Applications, Technologies, Architectures, and Protocols for Computer Communications* (pp. 161-172). New York, NY: ACM.

Simsek, O., & Jensen, D. (2008). Navigating networks by using homophily and degree. *Proceedings of the National Academy of Sciences of the United States of America, 105*(35), 12758–12762. doi:10.1073/pnas.0800497105

Singh, M. P., Yu, B., & Venkatraman, M. (2001). Community-based service location. *Communications of the ACM, 44*(4), 49–54. doi:10.1145/367211.367255

Skobeltsyn, G., Luu, T., Zarko, I. P., Rajman, M., & Aberer, K. (2007). Web text retrieval with a p2p query-driven index. In *Proceedings of the 30th Annual International ACM SIGIR Conference on Research and Development in Information Retrieval* (pp. 679-686). New York, NY: ACM.

Stoica, I., Morris, R., Karger, D., Kaashoek, M. F., & Balakrishnan, H. (2001). Chord: A scalable peer-to-peer lookup service for internet applications. In *Proceedings of the Conference on Applications, Technologies, Architectures, and Protocols for Computer Communications* (pp. 149-160). New York, NY: ACM.

Tang, C., Xu, Z., & Dwarkadas, S. (2003). Peer-to-peer information retrieval using self-organizing semantic overlay networks. In *Proceedings of the Conference on Applications, Technologies, Architectures, and Protocols for Computer Communications* (pp. 175-186). New York, NY: ACM.

Vouros, G. A. (2008). Searching and sharing information in networks of heterogeneous agents. In *Proceedings of the 7th International Joint Conference on Autonomous Agents and Multiagent Systems* (pp. 1525-1528). Richland, SC: International Foundation for Autonomous Agents and Multiagent Systems.

Watts, D. J., Dodds, P. S., & Newman, M. E. J. (2002). Identity and search in social networks. *Science, 296*(5571), 1302–1305. doi:10.1126/science.1070120

Watts, D. J., & Strogatz, S. H. (1998). Collective dynamics of 'small-world' networks. *Nature, 393*(6684). doi:10.1038/30918

Yu, B., & Singh, M. P. (2003). Searching social networks. In *Proceedings of the Second International Joint Conference on Autonomous Agents and Multiagent Systems* (pp. 65-72). New York, NY: ACM.

Zarko, I. P., & Silvestri, F. (2007). The CIKM 2006 workshop on information retrieval in peer-to-peer networks. *SIGIR Forum, 41*(1), 101-103.

Zhang, H., Croft, W. B., Levine, B., & Lesser, V. (2004). A multi-agent approach for peer-to-peer based information retrieval system. In *Proceedings of the Third International Joint Conference on Autonomous Agents and Multiagent Systems* (pp. 456-463). Washington, DC: IEEE Computer Society.

Zhang, H., & Lesser, V. (2006). Multi-agent based peer-to-peer information retrieval systems with concurrent search sessions. In *Proceedings of the Fifth International Joint Conference on Autonomous Agents and Multiagent Systems* (pp. 305-312). New York, NY: ACM.

Zhang, H., & Lesser, V. (2007). A reinforcement learning based distributed search algorithm for hierarchical peer-to-peer information retrieval systems. In *Proceedings of the 6th International Joint Conference on Autonomous Agents and Multiagent Systems* (pp. 1-8). New York, NY: ACM.

ENDNOTES

[1]   Note that semantic overlay is a logical (soft) layer of inter-connectivity. Even if two nodes are physically connected, semantic overlay may maintain a probability function that makes them unlikely to contact each other for search, thus removing the connection *logically*. Logical connections are the focus of this chapter.

[2]   The *clustering exponent* α, sometimes in a slightly different function, is also known as the *homophily exponent* (Watts et al., 2002; Simsek & Jensen, 2008).

[3]   ClueWeb09 was created in early 2009 by the Language Technologies Institute at CMU for IR experiments. It contains multiple crawls of about 1 billion web pages. Category B, or ClueWeb09B, is a subset of 50 million pages from 3 million websites.

[4]   The optimal value of α depends on a variety of other experimental variables. So the value 10 obtained in one set of experiments does not necessarily apply to others.

Chapter 3
Metadata for Search Engines:
What can be Learned from e–Sciences?

Magali Roux
Laboratoire d'Informatique de Paris VI, France

ABSTRACT

E-sciences are data-intensive sciences that make a large use of the Web to share, collect, and process data. In this context, primary scientific data is becoming a new challenging issue as data must be extensively described (1) to account for empiric conditions and results that allow interpretation and/or analyses and (2) to be understandable by computers used for data storage and information retrieval. With this respect, metadata is a focal point whatever it is considered from the point of view of the user to visualize and exploit data as well as this of the search tools to find and retrieve information. Numerous disciplines are concerned with the issues of describing complex observations and addressing pertinent knowledge. In this paper, similarities and differences in data description and exploration strategies among disciplines in e-sciences are examined.

INTRODUCTION

The starting point of information retrieval is the definition of types of data on which searches are conducted as these features will determine the architecture and strategies to bring into use.

Unstructured data consist of texts, pictures, videos, movies, etc., i.e., all documents that do not have any explicit organization and do not tell anything about their subdivisions. Such documents are difficult to exploit unless effective strategies allow encompassing these limitations. Currently, keyword-based approaches are used to perform search in unstructured data and to alleviate these challenges. Document search engines aims at browsing the web by looking for specific terms to address structure and semantic document content. Crawler application programs methodically

DOI: 10.4018/978-1-4666-0330-1.ch003

traverse the web to recover relevant information. Index databases are then created for the purpose of providing fast search results when a query is given (Meng & He, 2009). Current search engines (Apple's Spotlight and Google Desktop) rely upon such traditional indexing techniques requiring large resources.

In contrast, structured data are searched with more sound strategies. In databases, data is stored with its structure and, consequently, retains its own semantics. For a given query, the database management systems (DBMS) returns a very specific data whereas a search engine will only provide links to data ordered by estimated relevance. Nevertheless, such systems are not suitable for complex large data access; in particular, relational database systems do not support multidimensional or hierarchical objects and quite different data models are needed to facilitate data retrieval, modification, mathematical manipulation and visualization.

Actually, valuable information and especially scientific information, is dumped in multiple databases disseminated over multiple sites and is becoming more and more complex. Integrating large, heterogeneous data sources to gain into new knowledge is quite a challenging problem. This is especially the case in scientific disciplines that produce and/or store data on multifarious sites, from multi-campus projects. Heterogeneity is found to be syntactic and semantic, and several approaches are developed to provide the user with a unified data view (Hull, 1997). In the field of distributed databases, virtual integration is achieved by the loose coupling of source data models into a federated scheme that provide information sharing and exchanging (Heimbigner & McLeod, 1985). To improve extensibility, three-tier architecture is introduced to define the concept of mediator (Wiederhold, 1992). The upper layer represents the users and user interfaces, the middle layer contains the mediators that provide uniform interfaces and query accesses to wrappers and, at last, the lower layer contains data sources and wrappers translate

both queries from the mediator level to source databases and results returned from source databases to mediators. Example of non-grid database federation systems include Oracle 10g federated Solution (Poggi & Ruzzi, 2004). Otherwise, the data Grid technology allows the integration of distributed resources on standardized interfaces between infrastructures.

Another problem with scientific data is it continually evolves, containing many new variables across numerous dimensions and levels (as it is the case with biology that deals with many levels, from molecules to Earth ecosystems). In addition, sophisticated data treatments use complex programs that run on special-purpose hardware unlike conventional applications making data management and integration much more complicated for scientific data. These results in specific problems mainly because of specific discipline's concepts and vocabulary that make difficult to tackle relevant information to scientific interpret data sets. Extensibility of integrated systems is a major requirement and the use of widespread metadata greatly facilitates the pairing of new databases. Hybrid approaches, which combine search engine and declarative query languages, have been proposed (Houstis, Lalis, Tsalapata, & Vouton, 1999). In addition to the classical mediator/wrappers architecture, metadata are added as a join piece of information to every object. In these conditions, a search engine can easily seek for datasets whose metadata match a user query.

The size of scientific data continuing to increase dramatically, searching in large scientific files is as important as search on the web and the importance of search in a storage system is comparable to its importance on the Web. Petabytes of data are spread across billions of files and the metadata about these files can be used to locate it without knowing its path name (that corresponds to the URL on the web). Metadata is a key part of the information infrastructure in data management and its general characteristics and functions are abundantly discussed (Shankaranarayanan & Even, 2006).

THE E-SCIENCE ISSUE: SEARCHING THROUGH METADATA

The term of e-science was coined to refer to new system organization policies in data-intensive sciences to provide access to distributed data resources (Hey & Trefethen, 2002). These perspectives were turned to be realistic because the concept of Grid layer and associated tools were developed to permit the transport and mining of distributed digital data sets (Foster, Kesselmann, & Globus, 1997). As a corollary, advances in natural sciences became tightly coupled with advances in computer sciences and the magic mixture that creates e-sciences is the outcome of these relations.

In the Fourth Paradigm (The Fourth Paradigm: Data-Intensive Scientific Discovery, 2009), a posthumous homage to Jim Gray for his vision of data-intensive sciences, several new dimensions including data heterogeneity and mutiscaleness were pointed out as the core concepts of the digital paradigm and accountable for some common concerns among e-sciences.

Until the digital area, scientific data was stored in laboratory notebooks and shared according to domain-specific publishing rules. With the simultaneous occurrence of Internet and large-scale projects, new ways to manage data production, storage and integration were developed (Ailamaki, Kantere, & Dash, 2010), and the role of metadata has gained in importance in data storage and retrieval. For example, metadata catalogs storing attributes for describing experiment contents are used for constructing intelligent search engines and the power of these search engines relies on metadata quality. To quote T. Hey (The Data Deluge: An e-Science Perspective, 2003): "the quality of the search engine so constructed will only be as good as the metadata that it references."

With advents of the web, technology performances and large and widely distributed collaborations, information is stored in numerous interrelated data sources. To have these data interoperable, scientific communities have launched several initiatives for managing scientific datasets efficiently by defining consensual metadata for high-level data descriptions which are of interest in the context of a data intensive computing Grid environment:

- The MetaData Catalog (MCAT) (http://www.sdsc.edu/srb/index.php/MCAT) is a resource discovery repository that categorizes general scientific metadata into four different types of elements: resources, methods, datasets and users. Metadata stored in MCAT can be viewed from any of these four descriptions; for example, the resource-centric view deals with attributes including name, type, and access address, etc. MCAT is tightly coupled to the Storage Resource Broker (SRB) (http://www.sdsc.edu/srb/), which maintains the MCAT metadata catalog of all data using a back-end database; conversely, MCAT cannot be installed and used without SRB server configurations and so, cannot be used as a standalone component
- The Metadata Catalog Service (MCS) (Singh et al., 2003) is another general metadata catalog service providing mechanisms for storing and accessing descriptive metadata attributes. MCS is based on a three levels hierarchical architecture. At the lowest level, physical metadata include information about the characteristics of data on physical storage systems as well as replica location metadata. The next level concerns general metadata attributes that apply to data regardless of the application domain (for example, information about the creator of data content). The upper levels concerns metadata attributes specific

to an application domain and are often defined by metadata ontologies that are developed by application communities. MCS uses a web service model.

- The CCLR Scientific Metadata Model (CSMD) (Sufi, Matthews, & Kleese van Dam, 2003) is a study-data orientated model which capture the high level information pertaining to scientific studies and the data that they produce. It supports indexing at various levels of granularity from the study to investigations, inside the studies to data collections and atomic data objects as well as indexing mechanism using keywords and taxonomic classification.

All these high-level metadata frameworks support domain-specific metadata through user-defined extensions to fulfill customized tasks. Among MCAT/SRB projects, let's mention the US NASA (National Aeronautics and Space Administration) archival information accessed uniformly and securely from all Information Power grid (IPG) systems through MCAT/SRB or the Biomedical Information Research network (BIRN) project in Neuroimaging. In Earth sciences, MCS is one component of the Earth System Grid (ESG) application and ESG scientists successfully use the MCS to discover and query for ESG data files based on metadata attributes. Finally, the CSMD model is used as a template for a variety of other projects; for example, the Engineering and Physical Sciences Research Council (EPSRC) MyGrid project (Sharman et al., 2003).

In the following sections, metadata management is considered from the double point of view of data producers and users and based on cases studies in e-sciences with respect to High Energy Physics, Earth sciences and Life sciences. This study shows a tight organizational pairing between data production and data availability with impacts on search strategies and tools.

CASE STUDY 1: HIGH ENERGY PHYSICS

High Energy Physics (HEP) studies particles and basic forces that shape the Universe. Main experimental approaches are based on particles fragmentation and uses giant infrastructures such as Large Hadron Collider (LHC) at CERN which is the largest superconducting installation in the world, colliding beams of protons at energy of 14 TeV. The creation of new particles produces electrical signals that interact with the detectors. At peak collision energy, LHC produces over one million gigabytes (Gb) of data per second.

Data associated with a single collision of particles is the raw data, called "event", and must be processed to be further used in Physics analysis. In the preparatory phase, simulations were used to design and optimize the detectors. A generator program produced simulated particles events containing information similar to the estimated raw data. Simulations are repeated as much as necessary to achieve expected measurements and even during the real experiments to estimate detector response.

The ATLAS Experiment

Among the four experiments at LHC, ATLAS (A Toroidal LHC Apparatus) is a multi-purpose trial designed for the observation of a wide span of physics signature based on proton-proton (pp) collisions. The ATLAS detector is the biggest never built and in the pp collision mode, it looks at more than 30 to 40 million beams crossing per second, each of them generating up to several physics collisions. The experiment produces about 3 petabytes (Pb) of raw data per year that is clearly overpassing all today's computer capabilities making data management a central challenge in HEP.

Because of the importance of data management, it was considered at the early beginning of the preparatory phase and policies and tools were developed to administer this central issue.

From the engineering side, the design and implementation of the detector, its electronics, its software, and the computing facility corresponding to the technical side of the experiment produce tremendous amount of information and require special data management system. An Equipment Data Management System (EDMS) was developed to manage information on all the life cycle of equipment with LHC projects, including ATLAS experiments. The EDMS portal gives access to different classes of information (location, technology, job to be performed, etc.) and a search engine allows handling engineering and equipment data (Tsyganov, Mallón Amérigo, Petit, Pettersson, & Suwalska, 2008). Recently, this search engine was implemented with the Oracle Text technology (Tsyganov, Petit, & Suwalska, 2009) and was used to index metadata and data, search and view documents. Indexes for metadata are brought up-to-date with the data every ten minutes and indexes optimization is performed every week-end. For operational reasons, temporary files are created while maintenance operations are carried out on the real indexes. The current EDMS platform gives access to more than one million documents and drawings augmented every month of five thousands new documents. In addition, it registers more than one million individual components with one thousand new equipments recorded each month and two millions equipment interventions with more than ten thousands new ones per month.

From the Physics standpoint, the data associated with the particle collision consists in the raw data. As an ATLAS run takes several hours not all the events are stored and a trigger system evaluates beams which present the required features according to a set of criteria imposed to a beam. The ATLAS trigger strategy is based on selection of particles to cover the most important physics topics and results in rejecting 99.9995% of the events that are lost forever! A rate of 200 events per second is considered as acceptable after triggering and the time scale for trigger decision is the time during which detector and beam conditions are constant. For further data processing, the Atlas computing model was developed over a ten years period, well before the real data taking on November 2009 and the first collision at 7TeV obtained on March 2010. Preparative data challenge (DC) workshops were held regularly starting with DC0 to define and validate the AT-LAS data and computing models, and to ensure the correctness of the technical choices:

- The ATLAS Data Challenge 1 (DC1) was run in 2002-2003 to put in place the world-wide production infrastructures. DC1 provided large-scale production system deployment. During DC1, the emergence of the production on the Grid was afforded and a significant fraction of DC1 was performed in the Grid environment over 20 sites. Today, the ATLAS worldwide LHC Computing Grid (LCG) involves the Open Science Grid (OSG) in the Americas and the Enabling Grids for E-sciencE (EGEE) in Europe; it uses software and toolkits developed from different projects including gLite (http://glite.web.cern.ch/glite/), Globus (http://www.globus.org/), Condor (http://www.cs.wisc.edu/condor/) and the Virtual Data Toolkit (http://vdt.cs.wisc.edu/).

- At DC2 held in 2004-2005, the second large scale production ($\sim$ 15 M events) was performed. The prototype of the ATLAS event data model was presented. Different strategies were developed to address prompt data analysis and to process raw data into several different types of datasets, corresponding to different stages of reconstruction. Full use of the grid was achieved although the ATLAS middleware was not fully ready, simulation data was not accessible and physics validation was not possible.

- In 2006, Computing System Commissioning (CSC, formerly DC3) was in charge of testing the data flow from the online data acquisition to the offline processing system and the distribution of raw and processed data to the external computing centers.

Event Data Model

The Event Data Model defines data objects which will be reconstructed for Physics analysis. The first steps start with online calibration and alignment to perform fine-tuning of hardware and software sub-detectors. Further data processing achieves several reduction steps after filtering the interesting events through large amounts of raw data (Figure 1).

- Raw data are events as output by the final stage of High Level Trigger; it arrives in "bytestream" format that corresponds to the format in which data are delivered from the detector. Each file contains events corresponding to a single run using the same trigger conditions although events in each file are neither consecutive nor ordered; the event size for data storage is about 1,5 MB and two copies of each event are made. The role of reconstruction is to derive from raw data the particles parameters and supplementary information for physics analysis.

- The Event Summary Data (ESD) production begins as soon as raw data files and appropriate calibration and conditions data arrive at the Tier-0 centre. ESD production takes a single raw event data file in bytestream format as input and produces a single file of reconstructed events. ESD is the more complete set of reconstructed data and will have data and metadata on cells, clusters and tracks that represent an approximate size of about a 0,5 MB for storage.

Figure 1. Objects of the Event Data Model and reduction steps

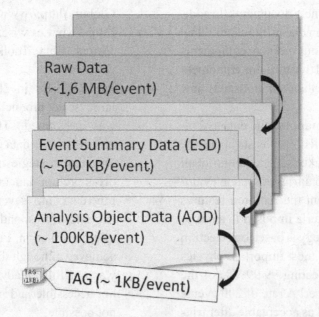

- The production of Analysis Object Data (AOD) from ESD is a lightweight process that captures all the necessary information to perform most analyses. The AOD is the last common, centrally produced format; it will contain information on electrons, clusters and tracks, but will not have the cells; the size of storage is about 100 KB per event. As AOD events are read many times more often than ESD and raw data, they are physically clustered on criteria that reflect more common analysis access patterns.
- TAG sets are event-level metadata and are produced as a keyed list of variables/event to provide direct access for event selection from every data format (AOD/ESD/RAW) event; they list more than 200 keywords/variables per event, which help to characterize a specific physics.
- At least, DPD (Derived Physics Data) is a lightweight data formats produced by individual or groups of users that decide to generate further derived data from ESD and AOD, or even, the primary PDP. These datasets may again be more specialized using the following processes (Figure 4c):
  - Skimming (event selections: keeping only interesting events),
  - Thinning (selecting containers or objects from a container: keeping only interesting objects in events),
  - Slimming (selection of properties of an object: keeping only interesting information in objects).

Data processing time varies from hours for "Prompt Reconstruction" (PR) (Barlow, 2010) to months for reprocessing. Prompt Reconstruction reads the raw data (i.e., bystream format) for reconstructing each collision in quasi-real time and persisting the results; a fraction (~10%) of the bulk data is used to get data quality estimation. The processing of data starts during data acquisition, and is finished shortly after the end of the run, representing a high volume activity. Data reprocessing is performed 1-3 months after acquisition using the same or improved software versions with upgraded calibration and alignments; all levels of processing from high-level trigger to event simulation, reconstruction and analysis, take place within the Athena framework.

ESD and AOD as well as most DPD are stored in POOL/ROOT files and are accessed locally or on the grid through the Athena framework. Typically, an AOD production job takes one or more ESD files in POOL/ROOT format as input, and produces one or more POOL ROOT files containing AOD as output. TAGs can be stored both in POOL/ROOT files or in database and users may access the TAG database via the Event Level Selection Service (ELSSI) web interface.

Data Flow and Storage

In ATLAS, all levels of data processing, from high-level trigger to event simulation, reconstruction and physics analysis, take place within the Athena framework. ATHENA is the ATLAS concrete implementation of the underlying architecture GAUDI. Major design principles are the clear separation of data and algorithms and between transient (in memory) and persistent (on disk) data. The four main services that algorithm objects use are: the Event Data Service (provides storing and retrieving all event related data, lifetime of these data objects is one simple event only), the Detector Data Service (stores information about detector, such as its geometrical and environment parameters), the Histogram Service (typically collect some parameters through all events) and the Message Service (provides reporting about progress and other communication with the world outside). Figure 2(a) (Broklova, 2004) presents the data workflow in Athena; the Transient Data Store (TDS) allows communication among different Athena modules; each algorithm can create

Figure 2. Data Object flow in the Athena framework: (a) data processing, (b) storage flowchart

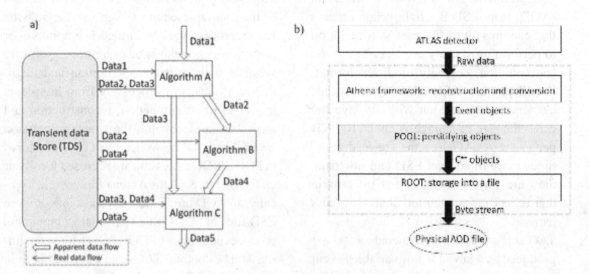

new data objects and save them into the TDS for further retrieval by any other algorithm.

To perform petabytes storage of data and metadata from transient data store on disk to persistent data store on tape, a specific project, the POOL (Pool Of persistent Objects for LHC) project (http://pool.cern.ch), was developed. Figure 2(b) presents the data object storage flowchart, from raw data bytestream to the ROOT file storage system (Kurauskas & Šileikis, 2006) based on a hybrid approach combining C++ object streaming technology for the bulk data and transactional relational database services (RDBMS) for catalogs, collections and metadata. POOL is a middle layer between Athena and ROOT: to write output of reconstruction and achieve persistent data, Athena calls the storage module, POOL metadata are added and objects are stored in ROOT libraries to be further retrieved through the Athena StoreGate (Calafiura, Leggett, Quarrie, Ma, & Rajagopalan, 2003).

The ROOT data format addresses the requirements coming from massive data in HEP and allows quick navigation, storage and retrieving subsets of objects and attributes. ROOT layout includes self-describing, schema-evolvable de-

scription and offers high-performance and highly-scalable object serialization (http://pool.cern.ch/catalog/index.html). In ROOT, one of the key classes is TTree, a class describing a data structure for keeping collections of objects of the same type and accessing them rapidly; per-event information is stored in branches and leaves, branches are subdirectories and leaves represent variables and contain data. An example is provided with coordinates, <dx, dy, dz>; each of the variables can be assigned to one leaf in a tree and written together; when retrieving the data, the variables will be retrieved together. Trees with leaves but not branches can be thought of like tables with rows that represent individual events and columns (leaves) that represent different event quantities.

Tiers Data Infrastructures

The Physicist community involved in the Atlas Experiment is estimated, at least, to be around 2.000 contributors allocated in worldwide campus and universities. Although, the HEP organization is based on virtual resources based on Grid, physical infrastructures allow managing in a strong coordinated manner data processing, storage and access; this physical organization is based on a tiered structure.

The Tier-0 at CERN is responsible for the archiving and distribution of the primary raw data received from the Event Filter. Triggered events are reconstructed at the Tier0, this is first done in a so called "express stream", which calculates some calibration constants. After the calibration loop, which takes maximum 36 hours, the newly calculated constants are used for the bulk reconstruction of physics streams. The derived datasets (ESD, primary AOD and TAG sets) are distributed from the Tier-0 to the Tier-1 facilities. Access to the Tier-0 facility is granted only to restricted people and data is transferred strictly hierarchically from T0 to T1 to T2/T3.

Ten Tier-1 centers are allocated all over the world; they host and provide long-term archiving of a one tenth of the raw data. The Tier-1s perform re-reconstruction of raw data and producing new ESD and AOD; all AOD and TAG as well as some of the raw/ESD data are transferred to Tier-2s. Access to the Tier-1 facilities is restricted to the production managers and the reprocessing people.

Thirty Tier-2 federated centers contribute to data calibration, simulation and analysis depending of their resources. They host the full TAG samples and one third of the current AOD. All members of the ATLAS virtual organization may have access to a given Tier-2 although access to CPU and resources are given to specific working groups in accordance with the ATLAS central administration.

Tiers-3s perform job submission and retrieval on the Grid. The size of Tier-3 resources depends on the local user community size and other factors, such as any specific software development or analysis activity although they are neither centrally planned nor controlled.

Data Access and Discovery Tools

As mentioned, the Athena control framework aims to provide a consistent outlook of writing and registration procedures for any king of data. As scientific data stores grow in volume, the difference between writing and registration is increasing in importance and retrieving relevant data using rapid and efficient procedures, become an important challenge.

File registration is to insert the file ID and PFN (Physical File Name) in a catalog and the ATLAS framework supports the notion of registration wherein one can record an object along with additional metadata that may later be used to select object of interest. A file catalog keeps track of the physical location of the file and is responsible for maintaining a list of physical locations of accessible files together with their unique and immutable ID, translating the logical file reference into its physical representation. This approach is more flexible than hard-coding the location information in the file itself although HEP metadata storage in event data files is often used to address mass data storage issues, notably for in HEP experiments.

In the following sections, metadata-based data access is considered with regards to the file-level or in-file metadata levels.

File-Level Metadata

The POOL File Catalog

In POOL (http://pool.cern.ch/catalog/index.html), the basic content of the File Catalog is the many-to-many mapping of Logical File Name (LFN) to Physical File Names (PFN) and a system generated FileID, based on the universal Globally Unique Identifiers (GUID), to perform definite inter-file reference in an environment where both logical and physical file names may change after data has been written (Figure 3). In addition, the POOL catalog includes user-defined file-level metadata that can be used for querying or extracting partial catalogs that can be shipped to other sites. Most of Pool Catalog applications are Grid aware: a user can access a Grid based catalog and, based on file or collection descriptions, can extract a set of interesting files or catalog fragments into a local XML catalog. After disconnecting from the Grid the user can execute some jobs on the extracted data; once the new data is ready for publishing, the corresponding catalog fragment can be submitted to the Grid based catalog.

The TAG Database and the iELSSI Browser

TAGs are event-level metadata with "pointers" to POOL file-resident event data. TAGs are built from AOD during the reduction process and loaded into the TAG relational database as events attributes. The ATLAS Event Level Selection Service (ELSSI) is a web interface developed to exploit Tags; it allows users to access event-level metadata in TAGs database to quickly identify and select events that are interested for a given analysis. ELSSI was initially built as a browser of TAGs hosted on a CERN server but as ATLAS experiments collect more data and users develop more physics analysis, the hosting topology of TAG datasets becomes heterogeneous; for ex-

ample, several Tier-1 and Tier-2 sites are storing different sets of TAG data that may overlap at the run level. This report has needed to develop a new integrated interactive event level selection service, iELSSI (Zhang, 2011) for dealing with all foreseeable scenarios in data search. The iELSSI design is grounded on two-layer architecture: (1) a parent page that starts with datasets whose TAGS have been uploaded into the Oracle database; (2) an ELSSI page that is created on the fly according to the received requests from the parent page. These improvements avoid managing and updating multiple clones at the same time

The ATLAS Metadata Interface (AMI)

AMI is the Atlas Metadata Interface (http://ami.in2p3.fr/) catalogue although it does neither store low-level file metadata nor information about physical instances of logical files; datasets are listed in the several catalogues. The current source for dataset information accessed with AMI is the Tier 0 management system, the ATLAS production database, the production Task Request system, the ATLAS SVN repository, and other AMI based

Figure 3. POOL file schema catalog (http://pool.cern.ch/catalog/image/XMLschema.txt)

```
<!ELEMENT POOLFILECATALOG (META*, File*) >
<!ELEMENT META EMPTY>
<!ELEMENT File (physical,logical,metadata*)>
<!ATTLIST META name CDATA #REQUIRED>
<!ATTLIST META type CDATA #REQUIRED>
<!ELEMENT physical (pfn)+ >
<!ELEMENT logical (lfn)* >
<!ELEMENT metadata EMPTY >
<!ELEMENT lfn EMPTY >
<!ELEMENT pfn EMPTY >
<!ATTLIST File ID ID #REQUIRED >
<!ATTLIST pfn name ID #REQUIRED >
<!ATTLIST pfn filetype CDATA #IMPLIED >
<!ATTLIST lfn name ID #REQUIRED>
<!ATTLIST metadata att_name CDATA #REQUIRED>
<!ATTLIST metadata att_value CDATA #REQUIRED>
```

applications such as the TAG Collector. Each AMI compliant database, or catalogue has its own relational schema, and contains its own schema description. The self-description contained in each AMI catalogue allows the web interface and the searches to adapt and support schema evolution. Internally AMI refers to the catalogues using two parameters "project" and "processingStep"; in most cases the AMI commands must be given the values of these two parameters in order to make the correct database connection. Queries which use glite grammar can be instructed to send queries in parallel to a set of catalogues.

Other Broad Spectrum Applications

The offline reconstruction framework in Athena and the interface provided by the COOL (Conditions Objects for LHC) technology allow access to the Conditions and Configuration Databases that store all parameters describing run and logging conditions, on the one hand, and the entire data needed hardware and software configuration at the start of the run, on the other hand.

Criteria across broad spectrum of Atlas run conditions can be searched with RunQuery (http://atlas-runquery.cern.ch), a web interface that allows consolidating information scattered around the Atlas databases. Main databases used with RunQuery are the Conditions Database, as well as PVSS (http://www.pvss.com/) detector control information database, Sub-farm output (SFO) database for online-to-offline file information, Tier-0 database for the offline data processing and the trigger configuration database for all data related to the ATLAS trigger.

In-file Metadata

ROOT is data architecture for storage and retrieval of distributed data. It was designed for Physics data and has numerous features including hierarchical, column-oriented data structures, dynamic schema evolution, and support for binary float numbers.

File structure has a file header and then several logical records of variable length that contain different possible data; data objects are always written in consecutive order on the file. Figure 4a and b shows, respectively, the file structure and the column-oriented layout used in ROOT.

AthenaROOTAccess is an alternative to the ATHENA framework; it allows accessing POOL data (ESD / AOD / DPD) directly from ROOT, using the column structure of the file for efficient reading of single attributes. When a specific object is requested, the persistent data is brought to the transient format using the POOL converter, which is invoked automatically on demand. ROOT and AthenaROOTAccess allow access to individual data without reading the entire object.

As previously mentioned, data reduction is performed to select specific datasets for physic analysis. ESD and AOD are used for further data processing (skimming, trimming, and/or slimming, as defined above in the "Event Data Model" section) based on in-file metadata (Figure 3c). Search in-file level metadata is more sophisticated than in file-level ones and strategies are ground on file layout (van Gemmeren & Malon, 2010).

CASE STUDY 2: EARTH SCIENCES

Earth sciences are grounded on two types of data collection, long lasting sampling performed by small-size groups sharing domain interests and skills as it is the case with the study of magmatic processes (Timescales of Magmatic Processes, 2010) and large scale, multi-source data (Rutledge, Alpert, & Ebuisaki, 2006; Hurt, Gauthier, Christensen, & Wyatt, 2009; Boucon et al., 2009) produced in the context of key missions and programs held by government agencies and intergovernmental organizations. These missions and campaigns stand on multi-disciplinary topics regarding Earth observations; including weather, climate, water and related matters; these observations are performed through an intricate network of

Figure 4. (a) Structure of ROOT file, (b) ROOT column organization, (c) in-file metadata-based data reduction

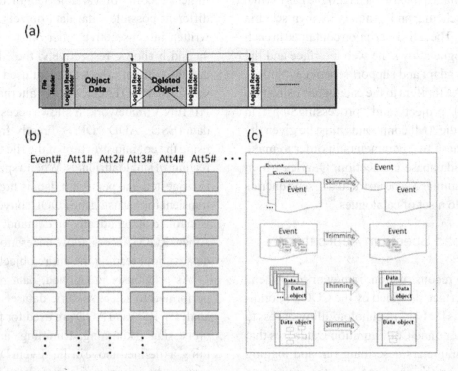

(a)

(b)

(c)

sensors, satellites, airplanes, oceanographic ships, buoys and other instruments. Data produced by Earth observing systems is characterized by large volumes and heterogeneity. Satellite remote sensing that is one of the major data sources produces terabytes of data per day, the overall data volume for a 5 year mission duration being approximated over 1 petabyte and multifarious sensors and devices produce data in different formats. Among applications, areas include environment, urban development, air quality monitoring, soil, civil protection, disaster monitoring, etc and data users are scientists belonging to many research domains not to mention policy makers, students, educators or simple citizens (Figure 5).

To coordinate access to the data, applications, models, and products, large data management systems are needed. One of the world's largest scientific data systems, the NASA's Earth Observing System Data and Information System (EOS-

DIS) stores multi-petabytes of Earth science data in a geographically distributed mass storage system. In Europe, the Ground European Network for Earth Science Interoperations -Digital Repositories (GENESI-DR) - is a centralized discovery service to overcome, not only to data volume issues but also difficulties in discovering and accessing data due to repository multiplicity and differences in data policies and formats. At the international level, the World Meteorological Organization (WMO) facilitates international cooperation on weather topics and up to 189 countries and regions belong to the organization today. Along with WMO activities, programs are underway to co-ordinate and stimulate research, for example, on the composition of the atmosphere and weather forecasting, by collecting data on the atmospheric chemistry.

*Figure 5. Data integration (middle) of **multi-sensory** Earth observations (bottom) and expected societal benefits (upper)*

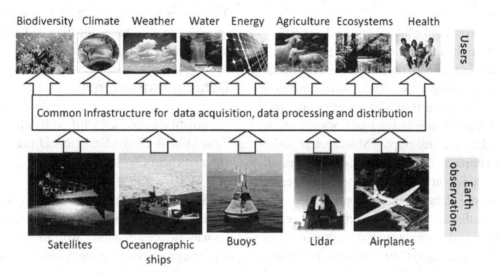

Data Formats and Standards

Earth observations experience a large variety of phenomena, methods and devices to realize an integrated view of digital Earth. Data volume and heterogeneity are the main bottlenecks to overcome and standardization is the favorite highway to address these issues. A quite new, different data model is needed to surmount the volume problem and facilitate rapid retrieval, modification, mathematical manipulation and visualization; some insights are given.

The Network Common Data Form (NetCDF) (http://www.unidata.ucar.edu/software/netcdf/) was developed to support the creation, access, and sharing of array-oriented scientific data. The NetCDF data sets contain dimensions, variables, and attributes, which all have both a name and an ID number by which they are identified. These components can be used together to capture the meaning of data and relations among data fields in an array-oriented dataset. NetCDF is widely used in climate modeling, ocean science, and atmospheric science although it shows limitations. The new NetCDF-4 data model is an ongoing ef-

fort to identify a common subset of NetCDF and the Hierarchical Data Format (HDF) (http://www.hdfgroup.org/). HDF is a self-describing extensible file format using tagged objects that are the part of a data descriptor and tell what kind of data is contained in the corresponding data element. One set of HDF tags supports a hierarchical grouping structure and allows hierarchically organizing data objects. The idea with HDF is to store both a known format description and the data in the same file. HDF5 was designed to address some of the limitations of the older HDF and to represent very complex data objects and a wide variety of metadata and. Thus, HDF5 format is composed of two primary types of objects: groups, i.e., a set of objects together with supporting metadata and datasets, i.e., a multidimensional array of data elements together with supporting metadata; both, group and dataset may have an associated list of attributes. Recently, HDF and NetCDF were merged to achieve gains in performance and interoperability. A domain-specific profile was derived to adapt HDF to Earth Observation (HDF-EOS) (http://hdfeos.org/); HDF-EOS adds geolocation data types that allow data to be queried by Earth coordinates and time. HDF-EOS is the official data format for EOSDIS data production and archive.

In the geospatial context, one of the most active body in the definition of Open Standards is the Open Geospatial Consortium (OGC), Inc.® (http://www.opengeospatial.org), an organization composed by more than 370 commercial, governmental, non-profit and research organizations worldwide. The Geography Markup Language (GML) (Portele, 2007), a XML-based format, was developed at OGC for signifying vector based spatial data. It allows representing and storing spatial and temporal phenomena, reference systems and units in conformance with other standards, including ISO 19103 (units of measure, basic types), ISO 19107 (spatial geometry and topology); ISO 19108 (temporal geometry and topology, temporal reference systems). GML is organized as a hierarchy of classes corresponding to various sets of entities such as features, geometries, topologies etc.

Otherwise, the Sensor Markup Language (SensorML) is a XML language that provides a complete description of an instrument's capabilities and gives the information needed to process and locate measured data. By describing sensors using SensorML, anyone can put sensors or sensor data online for others, to find and use. As networks of sensors become more and more common, users will be able to use real-time sensor data directly from the sensor, without need for intermediate, time-consuming processing at a central data processing center. To enable all possible types of sensors to be detectable, accessible and controllable via the Web in a standardized and open way, the Sensor Web Enablement (SWE) initiative was launched at OGC. A Sensor Interpreter Description (SID) used in the Sensor Web is an extension of the SensorML to describe the sensor protocol of a particular sensor type. The Sensor Observation Service (SOS) (Na & Priest, 2007) provides a standardized web service interface which allows accessing observations in a standard format and interacting with intelligent sensor network for automatic sensor registration and data storage. The Sensor Alert Service (SAS) is a standard web service interface for publishing and subscribing to alerts from sensors.

Data Infrastructures

National Level Data Infrastructure: The NASA Earth Science Data Information System (ESDIS)

NASA is involved in scientific programs to study the Earth system and its response to natural and human-induced changes, with the main goal to improve prediction of climate, weather, and natural hazards. The main initiative is the Earth Observing System (EOS) program that was started in 1990; a set of space-borne instruments was designed by the NASA science teams with international collaborations, to perform accurate, frequent and global measurements of geophysical properties of land, oceans and atmosphere. Due to the importance of data management, NASA has developed the Earth Science Data and Information System (ESDIS) project separately from the projects in charge of the spacecraft and instruments and ESDIS provides access to over 3 terabytes per day through the development of the EOS Data and Information System (EOSDIS) (Figure 6).

All the spacecraft operations and maintenance are conducted by the Earth Science Mission Operations (ESMO) project and flight operations (command and control of spacecraft and instruments) are managed by the Flight Operations Segment (FOS). Spacecrafts transmit instrument science data, spacecraft engineering (housekeeping) data, and instrument engineering (housekeeping) data to ground stations. The first processing (L0) is performed at the EOS Data and Operations System (EDOS), L0 processing consists in reconstructing instrument data by removing all communications artifacts. EDOS is responsible for ingest, archive and distribution of NASA Earth science data to Science Data Processing Segment (SDPS) through the NISN/Ebnet network.

Further processing known as the Science Data Processing Segment (SDPS) is performed at the Science Investigator-led Processing Systems (SIPSs) under the coordination of ESDIS. EOS data have different levels of processing that are well specified; for example, L1A refers to time-referenced data annotated with ancillary information though L4 that is the up-level processing grade refers to the results from analyses of lower-level data (e.g., variables derived from multiple measurements).

The SDPS ingests the data from the processing systems and archives them to the data centers. Special SDPS hardware and software consist in the EOSDIS Core System (ECS) developed to support the high ingest rates of the EOS instruments. ECS is deployed to only three sites (Land Processes DAAC, National Snow and Ice Data Center, and Atmospheres Science Data Center)

Twelve interlinked data centers named Distributed Active Archive Centers (DAACs) are the EOSDSIS key parts of the Science Data Processing Segment and serve a specific Earth system science discipline (Table 1). For example, the Oak Ridge National Laboratory (ORNL) DAAC provides data and information about the dynamics between the biological, geological, and chemical components of Earth's environment. The Alaska Satellite Facility (ASF) is the synthetic aperture radar (SAR) data center specializing in SAR sensors on different airborne platforms.

Among functions of EOSDIS data centers, they must receive EOS level 0 data from the EDOS, contribute to processing and reprocessing of standard data products following instrument team's priorities, provide data and information services to the EOSDIS user community, preserve complete documentation of the EOS data, instrument, calibration, processing history and processing source code.

EOSDIS supports several data format standards that are used by the Earth science community. The primary format of the EOS data products is the Hierarchical Data Format for EOS (HDF-EOS), suitable for remote sensing data. EOSDIS is serving scientific community by managing all data for EOS facilities to 200.000 scientists.

International Level Data Infrastructure: The WMO Information System (WSI)

The World Meteorological Organization (WMO) heads four large programs: the Global Observing System (GOS), the World Hydrological Cycle Observing System (WHCOS), the Global Atmosphere Watch, (GAW) and the World Climate Program (WCP). In addition, WMO is involved in collaborative initiatives including Global Climate Observing System, GCOS; Global Ocean Observing System, GOOS and Global Terrestrial Observing System, GTOS. Actually, data is collected and exchanged by WMO Members from a large variety of devices and instruments, including sixteen satellites, several hundred buoys, thousand of aircrafts, ships and land-based stations For managing and moving all this data, the WMO information system (WIS) was created to be a coordinated, distributed, global infrastructure for the collection and sharing of data and information for all WMO and related international programs (Figure7a).

The WIS project is based on a Service Oriented Architecture (SOA) implemented through communications networks. The WIS compliance specifications focus primarily on network services that occur at interfaces between communicating WIS components. By pointing on interoperability at the interfaces, WIS greatly reduces the complexity otherwise evident across the diverse systems. It also minimizes impacts on any given component system other than at its WIS interfaces; this is very important because the component systems are built and managed independently. A central part of the innovative development is clearly the metadata catalogue that is structured in accordance with the WMO core

Figure 6. The NASA Earth Observing System (EOS) Data and Information System (EOSDIS)

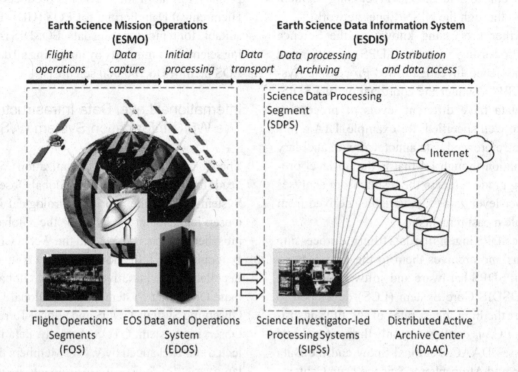

profile (WMO Core Metadata Profile, 2010) developed in conformance with the ISO 19115 geographic information standard; each WMO program is expected to develop and maintain its own "community extension". In operational terms, WIS encompasses three types of centers that must support interoperability with external systems as well as data access via the Internet (Figure 7b).

- *Data Collection or Production Centers* (DCPCs) collect, disseminate, add value to, and archive regional or programme-specific data and products. DCPCs maintain catalogues of their holdings and services, and appropriate parts of these catalogues update the comprehensive catalogue of WIS holdings, hosted by the GISCs.
- *Global Information System Centers* (GISCs) hold and distribute copies of at least 24 hours of WMO data and products intended for global distribution.

- *National Centers* (NCs), which are existing National Meteorological and Hydrological Centers will become WIS NCs. Every WIS NC must supply metadata for their data and products.

Each member country is implementing and operating WIS and so far, WMO Members have proposed 13 candidate GISC's and about 110 candidate DCPC's. To be officially designated as a WIS Centre does demonstrate the capability to implement the WIS compliance specifications procedures and be endorsed by WMO Experts. The first WIS Centers should be operational soon as a total of 126 centers are identified (http://www.wmo.int/pages/prog/www/WIS/centres/index.html). Thereafter, the number of designated WIS Centers is expected to grow to about 300 when fully complete.

Table 1. Panel of EOSDIS data centers, locations and scientific disciplines covered

Data centers	Science Disciplines	Locations
Data Center Location Science Disciplines Alaska Satellite Facility, (ASF)	Synthetic Aperture Radar (SAR) Products, Sea Ice, Polar Processes and Geophysics	Univ. of Alaska, Fairbanks, AK
Crustal Dynamics Data and Information System (CDDIS)	Space Geodesy and Geodetics	NASA Goddard Space Flight Center, Greenbelt, MD
Global Hydrology Resource Center (GHRC)	Hydrologic Cycle, Severe Weather Interactions, Lightning, and Atmospheric Convection	NASA Marshall Space Flight Center, Huntsville, AL
GSFC Earth Sciences (GES) Data and Information Services Center, (DISC)	Global Precipitation, Solar Irradiance, Atmospheric Composition, Atmospheric Dynamics, Global Modeling	NASA Goddard Space Flight Center Greenbelt, MD
Land Processes (LP)	Land Processes, Land Imaging	USGS EROS Data Center, Sioux Falls, SD
Langley Atmospheric Sciences Data Center(ASDC)	Radiation Budget, Clouds, Aerosols, and Tropospheric Chemistry	NASA Langley Research Center Hampton, VA
Level 1 and Atmospheres Archive and Distribution System (LAADS)/MODIS Adaptive Processing System (MODAPS)	MODIS Level 1 and Atmospheric Data Products	NASA Goddard Space Flight Center Greenbelt, MD
National Snow and Ice Data Center (NSIDC)	Snow and Ice, Cryosphere, Climate Interactions and Sea Ice	Univ. of Colorado Boulder, CO
Oak Ridge National Laboratory (ORNL) DAAC	Biogeochemical Dynamics, Ecological Data, and Environmental Processes	Department of Energy Nashville, TN
Ocean Biology Processing Group (OBPG)	Ocean Biology, Sea Surface Temperature, and Biogeochemistry	NASA Goddard Space Flight Center, Greenbelt, MD
Physical Oceanography (PO) DAAC	Sea Surface Temperature, Ocean Winds, Circulation and Currents and Topograpy and Gravity	Jet Propulsion Laboratory (JPL), Pasadena, CA
Socio-Economic Data Applications Center (SEDAC)	Human Interactions, Land Use, Environmental Sustainability, Geospatial Data, Multilateral Environmental Agreements	Columbia University Palisades, NY

Figure 7. The WMO Information System (WIS). (a) WMO and related international programs, data collection and sharing of information (b) The data communication structure (NC: National Centers; GISC: Global Information System Centers; DCPC: Data Collection and Production Centers)

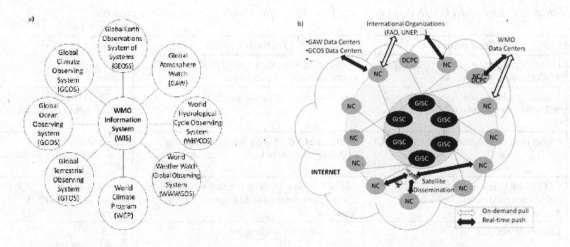

Clearinghouse Architecture and Metadata-based Data Discovery

The clearinghouse concept was developed to address the problem of naming and locating objects in a distributed environment (Oppen & Dalal, 1983). A data clearinghouse is a distributed, Web-based network of three main components: Web client (client tier), clearinghouse gateway (middle tier) and clearinghouse nodes (server tier). It is an example of client-server architecture: the server machines contain metadata and the client (user) request information about the availability of data by visiting the server nodes.

Calling a web site a clearinghouse uses the architectural metaphor to indicate that the site is expected to function as ``a central institution or agency for the collection, maintenance, and distribution of materials, information'' (The American Heritage, 2006). Concretely, the main goal of a data clearinghouse is to provide access to digital data through metadata; a clearinghouse does not collect information but organizes the dissemination of descriptions about available information; it is neither a central repository where data sets are stored nor a set of web sites referencing data; it

is a federated system of compatible data catalogs that can be searched through a common interface.

Metadata is the central feature of the data clearinghouse and each metadata collection is known as a clearinghouse node. Figure 8 shows the typical clearinghouse architecture; metadata points to where data is, so users can go and request it.

The NASA Earth Observing System Clearinghouse (ECHO)

The Earth observing system ClearingHOuse (ECHO) provides a uniform view of NASA's data (http://www.echo.nasa.gov/documents/guides/ECHO_Data_Partner_User_Guide.pdf); it contains more than 2800 data sets held at 12 EOSDIS data centers. ECHO has a metadata catalog whose model is derived primarily from the EOSDIS Core System (ECS). The ECS Data Model is very large and not suited to be displayed legibly in a single diagram. It is logically segmented into eight modules and there are about three hundreds attributes referenced in a data dictionary, which is also used by ECS components to validate metadata. Producers choose attributes to describe their data. Collections are described by a series

Figure 8. Typical data clearinghouse architecture

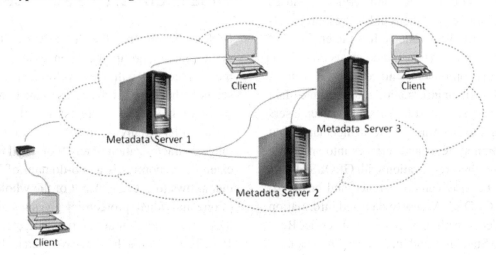

of attributes, including General Description, Data Origin, Spatial Coverage, Temporal Coverage, and Contents. Granules within collections are described by a different set of attributes. These are similar to collection level attributes, except that they are used to describe individual granules within a collection. In addition to the 300 standard attributes, Product Specific Attributes (PSAs) can be included.

Key features of the ECHO concern an easy participation of partners. First, all interactions with it occur using XML as the base message format; ECHO offers a set of standard ways for partners to interface with the system and a metadata exchange approach that accommodates existing partners and technology. Second, an open system approach and publishes domain APIs are used to accommodate independent ECHO clients and an incremental development allows for insight and feedback during the development cycle.

Metadata is stored in an Oracle database with spatial extensions and can be searched through different data catalogs (Topic, Data Center, Campaign and Platform) that give access to a broad collection of NASA Earth Science data. The Warehouse Inventory Search Tool (WIST) allows searching for science data holdings, retrieving high-level descriptions of data sets and detailed descriptions

of the data inventory and submitting orders via ECHO to the appropriate data providers. Datasets can be searched by discipline, categories/attributes or keywords. Thus, users are allowed to explore the list of data sets or granules returned by a search by viewing their temporal coverage, spatial coverage, attributes (metadata), related documents (guide search), and browse images. They could further select data for ordering, choose packaging information, enter ordering information (such as shipping address), place an order, and view order status. WIST is the primary web-based client for discovering and ordering cross-discipline data from all of ECHO's metadata holdings.

The GEOSS Clearinghouse

The Group of Earth Observation (GEO) aims to achieve comprehensive, coordinated and sustained observations of the Earth system. It was launched by the 2002 World Summit on Sustainable Development and by the G8 leading industrialized countries. GEO is constructing the Global Earth Observations System of Systems (GEOSS) on the basis of a 10-Year Implementation Plan for the period 2005 to 2015 (The Global Earth Observation System of Systems, 2005). The GEOSS clearinghouse encompasses many other clearinghouses, catalogs, data directories, and service registries wherein hundreds of thousands of resources relevant to Earth observations. It is the engine that drives the entire system and connects directly to the various components and services; it collects and searches their information and distributes data and services via the GEO Portal to the user. Users can enter into an online web form metadata about observation systems and services into an online web form; their registration with GEOSS allows them to be discovered (searched and browsed) through GEOSS. Access to data and information is provided from the Component and Service Registry; the Standards and Interoperability Registry list Approved Standards and *ad hoc* community practices, methods and techniques. At last, a User Requirement Registry stores requirements by generalized user types (values, quality, etc.); the goal is to match requirements to services according to a common vocabulary of observables under development. Each of the GEOSS Registries and the Clearinghouse expose service interfaces for the ingest of and search for information; in addition, the GEO-wide Web Portal that provides a single, official 'front door', gives access to to the non-registered community resources (Figure 9).

The main scope of GEOSS is "to supplement and not to supplant" program-driven initiatives and observations. This is specially the case when considering individual programs likewise, the Global Atmosphere Watch (GAW) program that collects global, long-term observations of the chemical and physical characteristics of the atmosphere and offers a dedicated interface as those maintained at EMPA (http://gaw.empa.ch/gawsis); in contrast, the GEOSS clearinghouse provides wide scope data. With this respect, specific data centers and programs are critical to rapidly provide much focused information.

CASE STUDY 3: LIFE SCIENCES

Biology has entered the digital era and joined the fascinating group of e-sciences at the turn of the XXIe century with the development of Omics sciences that have given access to the large-scale study of biological systems; in other words, Omics refer to any approach that allow wide-range characterization of any biological trait; for example, genomics is a sub-domain of biology that allows to get a snapshot of the whole genes of one individual, proteomics gives insights into the protein landscape at a global scale, etc. (Figure 10a). These approaches have resulted in dramatic increases in data volumes. Actually, a conventional DNA-microarray contains up to 40.000 genes; if 10 different samples are investigated according to 20 different conditions, a set of 8×10^6 data points is produced by a single experiment. More often, multiple technologies are used to address one particular issue; for example, mass spectrometry (MS) and nuclear magnetic resonance (NMR) might be used for protein characterization and such a variety adds to the data volume problem a heterogeneity issue. However, this technological heterogeneity is though not so critical compared to biological complexity: one human individual is composed of 100.000×10^7 cells, each containing 30.000 genes that could produce about six transcripts each and more than 500.000 functionally different proteins. Last but not least, the network of molecular interactions between two genes (from a source gene to a target gene) is approximated to 360×10^6 putative links that exhibit remarkable robustness and self-organization capabilities. This complexity crosses over the multiple biological levels from molecules to complete organisms (Figure 10b).

This broken landscape turns into nightmare when technological heterogeneity is superimposed to biological heterogeneity. To prevent these is-

Figure 9. The GEOSS infrastructure

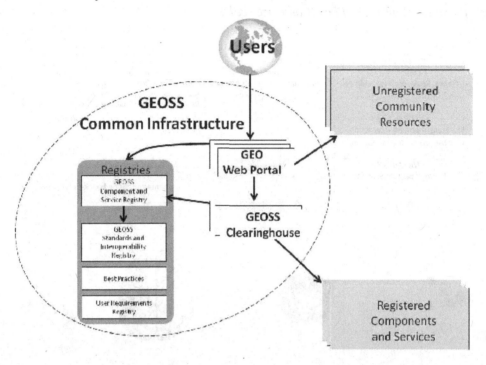

sues, initiatives were developed to achieve standardized representations and controlled vocabularies. Among them, the MGED (Microarray Gene Expression Data Society, http://www.mged.org/) consortium was launched in 1999 to gather biologists, computer people, data experts, etc., to design a common conceptual model for microarrays. As result of this effort, the MAGE-OM (Micro-Array gene Expression Object Model) standard was published on October 2002; since that, numerous implementations of this model were performed.

Although modeling and standardization are not usual practices and habits among biologists, strong expectations from data interoperability have elicited small groups to come out in technology-specific domains to develop relevant data representations and vocabularies.

Minimum Information Guidelines and Metadata Standards in Omics Sciences

The "Minimum Information" Checklists

A "Minimum Information About" guideline is a document that lists, in a verbal format, the necessary information that must be provided in order to describe unambiguously an experiment and to ensure its interpretability. Such checklists consist in metadata about experiments and are functionally related to metadata standards, for example, the Dublin Core (http://dublincore.org/). The idea of having a defined minimum standard of information associated with the experimental approaches was first used in Life Sciences by the macromolecular community that had agreed on the information to be provided before publication.

With the development of multifarious technologies associated to the emergence of Omics sciences, comprehensive annotation about ex-

Figure 10. The premises of digital biology (a) Omics sciences with their corresponding technologies and biological types; (b) biological levels and size scales

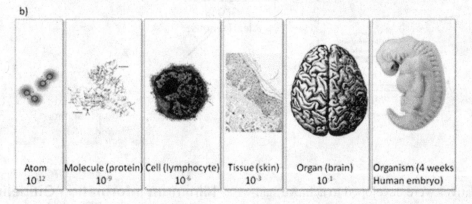

a)

Biological type	Omics	Technology
COMPENENT: Genes, RNAs, proteins, cells etc.	Genomics, Transcriptomics, Proteomics, Cellomics, etc.	DNA sequencing, SNP array, DNA gene expression, Chromatography, Mass Spectrometry, Magnetic Nuclear Resonance, Two Dimensional-gel, ...
INTERACTION: Protein-protein interaction, DNA-protein interaction, etc.	Interactomics	Protein arrays, ChIP-chip with DNA or tiling array, ...
PHENOTYPE: Normal, pathological, etc.	Physiomics	Cell phenotype: Cellular microarray, FACS, ... Whole phenotype: Gene knock-out, RNAi

b)

| Atom
10^{-12} | Molecule (protein)
10^{-9} | Cell (lymphocyte)
10^{-6} | Tissue (skin)
10^{-3} | Organ (brain)
10^{-1} | Organism (4 weeks
Human embryo) |

periments became an authoritative requirement. The following sections illustrate some of more important initiatives.

MIGS/MIMS (Minimum Information About a (Meta)Genome Sequence)

Among the more popular omics approaches, genomics was made famous in 2003 when the International Human Genome Sequencing Consortium announced the successful completion of the Human Genome Project even if numerous genomes - including bacteria genomes - were decrypted before this date. According to long lasting sequencing methods used at the turn of the century, new methods are in progress that would enable human genome sequencing within minutes, turning personalized medicine into reality. In this context, the genome community is aware of developing methods for capturing and exchanging metadata as well as harmonizing metadata collections and analysis efforts. In this context, the main goal of the Genomics Standard Consortium (GSC, http://gensc.org/) is to extend the core information traditionally captured by the International Nucleotide Database Consortium (INSDC, http://www.insdc.org/). As a result, the current guidelines named MIGS/MIMS (Minimum Information About a (Meta-Genome Sequence) (Field et al., 2008) include objective facts about genomic investigations, specific information about the genome sequenced using values selected from controlled vocabularies/ontologies, etc.

MIAME (Minimum Information about Microarray Experiment)

Micro-array experiments give insights on gene activity. Data are more complex than sequence data as they are contextual, e.g., they are meaningful only in the context of a detailed description of the conditions under which they were generated, including the state of the living system under study and the perturbations to which it has been subjected. MIAME (Brazma et al., 2001) rests on the following principles: a detailed annotation of the sample and experimental conditions must be given to allow results reproduction and comparison; the use of terms from controlled languages and ontologies must be preferred to limit the use of natural language, which hampers further automatic treatments. MIAME contains six sections for which information must be provided; these concern the experimental design, the array design, samples, hybridization technics, measurements and the normalization controls. The resulting MIAME document represents the overall consensus of the FGED (Functional Genomics Data Society, http://www.mged.org/) working groups; the standard was adopted by several scientific journals in 2002 and information compliant to the standard must obligatorily be communicated by scientists to the publishers before publication.

MIAPE (Minimum Information about Proteomics Experiment)

MIAPE (Taylor et al., 2007) was developed in the context of the HUman Protein Organization (HUPO) launched in 2002 in Paris. This document contains basic information for describing a proteomic experiment. As protein analysis is complex and uses several technologies, enabling the analysis of different (although frequently overlapping) submodules makes the checklist more complex due to the intricacy of technical methods. These submodules include column chromatography, gel electrophoresis, mass spectrometry, etc.

what required to set up different working groups to customize the core guidelines according to the relevant topics. Thus, draft modules are in progress for column chromatography (MIAPE-CC), gel electrophoresis (MIAPE-GE), mass spectrometry (MIAPE-MS), etc.

The Biosharing Initiative

On 2008, the MIBBI (Taylor, 2008) project was launched to provide a common resource coordinated by community representatives. Currently, thirty-four Minimum Information checklists are under development in very various fields, for example, flow cytometry (MIFlow: Minimum Information for a Flow Cytometry Experiment) or RNA inhibition (MIARE: Minimum Information About a RNAi Experiment), and it would be difficult to the scientists to identify if standards and guidelines exist in their favorite domains without coordination among projects. To achieve these goals, the Biosharing web portal (http://otter.oerc.ox.ac.uk/biosharing/) offers a unique access to minimum information guidelines as well as a vast list of standards including ontologies. Founded by Susanna-Assunta Sansone and Dawn Field, the Biosharing web portal gives access to catalogues, which centralize bioscience data policies, reporting standards and links to other related portals. The Standards catalogue allows selecting standards according to the technology,

Databases and Data Infrastructures

In Life Sciences, information is scattered over thousands of sites and locations. For example, the 2011 NAR (Nucleic Acids Research) Database issue reports 1330 molecular biology databases carefully selected among a huge amount of very diverse initiatives (Galperin & Cochrane, 2011). Information in most of these databases is more relevant with secondary even tertiary data, e.g., data extracted from literature in contrast to raw and normalized data as mentioned.

These databases are classified according to the biological entity of interest; e.g., nucleotide sequence, protein sequence, Human genome, etc. (Table 2).

Among this myriad of databases, only a few big centers provide services to the international community:

- The *National Center for Biotechnology Information* (NCBI, http://www.ncbi.nlm.nih.gov/) in U. S. was established on 1988, as a division of the National Library of Medicine (NLM) at the National Institutes of Health (NIH). NCBI's mission is to provide information technologies to facilitate in the understanding of fundamental processes in health and disease. Although a national resource, the NCBI provides worldwide access for molecular biology information, Among famous databases, MEDLINE is the National Library of Medicine's premier bibliographic database that covers 17 millions of bibliographic references since 1950. Other extensively used databases are, for example, GenBank, a nucleotide and amino acid sequences or UniGene, a collection of ESTs and full-length mRNA sequences. In addition, NCBI provides data repository facilities with Gene Expression Omnibus (GEO) (Edgar, Domrachev, & Lash, 2002), a gene expression and hybridization array storehouse.

- The *European Bioinformatics Institute* (EBI, http://www.ebi.ac.uk/) in U.K., as part of the European Molecular Biology laboratory (EMBL, http://www.embl.org/), is a centre for research and services in bioinformatics that manages databases of biological data including nucleic acid, protein sequences and macromolecular structures; for example, EMBL Nucleotide Sequence Database (also known as EMBL-Bank) (Stoesser et al., 2002) or BioModels (Le Novère et al., 2006), a repository of published computational models. As well, EBI provide access to repositories for gene expression (ArrayExpress) (Brazma et al., 2003) and proteomics (PRIDE) (Vizcaíno et al., 2009) data.

- Until a few years ago, the *Swiss Institute of Bioinformatics* (SIB) with EBI was producing Swiss-Prot (a high-quality resource on protein sequence and functional information manually annotated and reviewed) and TrEMBL, (an automatically annotated database). In parallel, Protein Information Resource (PIR), established in 1984 by the National Biomedical Research Foundation (NBRF), was producing the Protein Sequence Database (PIR-PSD) (Wu et al., 2003). In 2002, the three institutes decided to pool their resources and expertise and formed the Universal Protein Resources (UniProt) Consortium.

Table 2. Top-level categories of biological resources provided by the Nucleic Acids Research Molecular Biology Database Collection

Nucleotide Sequence Databases	Genomics Databases (non-vertebrate)
RNA sequence databases	Microarray Data and other Gene Expression Databases
Protein sequence databases	Proteomics Resources
Structure Databases	Other Molecular Biology Databases
Metabolic and Signaling Pathways	Organelle databases
Human and other Vertebrate Genomes	Plant databases
Human Genes and Diseases	Immunological databases

Otherwise, non-profit societies, organizations and/or foundations aim to organize data resources for the research communities. Among them, let's mention HUPO or FGED previously cited. However, recent database surveys detected prejudicial discrepancies between these resources that motivated the new BioDBcore (Gaudet et al., 2011) initiative launched with the sponsorship of the International Society for Biocuration (http://www. biocurator.org/). The main goal of BioDBcore is to achieve a community-defined, uniform, generic framework to describe key technical metadata in a formalized way as it was experienced with the CASIMIR project (Smedley et al., 2011); for each category, there is a three-tier level criterion to describe database functionalities and aid identification according to relevance (Table 3).

Discovery Tools and Data Integration

With highly distributed information, the main challenge is to select relevant and reliable information among countless resources. In absence of sophisticated database descriptions as mentioned with the CASIMIR project, different levels of data coupling/decoupling are used to encompass these difficulties:

First, a copy of the different resources is made and a datawarehouse is created that contains all the previously selected data; users might further query the datawarehouse without wondering about reliability and significance of the source.

Second, a global schema is used to virtually integrate all the resources of interest in a complete framework; the physical data is not moved and stayed at its initial location and the users query the databases through the common schema; federated databases are grounded on this strategy.

Third, the coupling of resources is based on semantics; any database behave independently with its own schema; nevertheless, a mediator layer is created above the database schemas to map related data elements. Mediator-based federations are using such architecture.

In all three cases, databases must be selected to either be ingested into the datawarehouse or to participate to the federation. Some examples of these approaches are mentioned below:

Ensembl (http://www.ensembl.org/) is a datawarehouse that collects genomic data from different species (horizontal integration) and from different types (vertical integration). In the same group, the *UCSC Genome Browser database* (http://genome.ucsc.edu/) collects data from 237 databases that can be queried for further genome annotation. In contrast, *Biobank Information Management System* (BIMS) (Ölund, Lindqvist, & Litton, 2007) and *DiscoveryLink* at Karolinska Institute are two examples of federated resources. At last, *BioMediator* (http://www.biomediator. org/) at Washington University is an illustration of mediator-based federated databases. It includes a knowledge database that contains the mediator layer and the list of databases, as well as semantic and syntactic adapters.

Otherwise, the *ISA* infrastructure (http://isatab. sourceforge.net/) is a worldwide community effort to gather data and metadata, especially for multiomics, in a consistent way with respect to ongoing standards. An umbrella ISA-TAB (Sansone et al., 2008) model was designed to overlay the technology-specific standards in a metamodelling-like architecture (Terrasse & Roux, 2010). ISA tools (Rocca-Serra et al., 2010) are made available to the community to collect data in a common format; this would precede the onset of a large, standards-based information system as it is the case in Earth sciences.

CONCLUSION

This paper aims to serve as a first guide to enable easier and quicker familiarization with the use of metadata in e-sciences and related challenges for data retrieving.

Among them, a first issue concern data organization as the way data and metadata are produced

Table 3. The CASIMIR Database Description Framework (DDF)

Category	Level 1	Level 2	Level 3
Quality and Consistency	No explicit process for assuring consistency	Process for assuring consistency, automatic curation only	Process for assuring consistency with manual curation
Currency	Closed legacy database or last update more than a year ago	Updates or versions more than once a year	Updates or versions more than once a month
Accessibility	Access via browser only	Access via browser and database reports or database dumps	Access via browser and programmatic access (well defined API, SQL access or web services)
Output formats	HTML or similar to browser only	HTML or similar to browser and sparse standard file formats, e.g., FASTA	HTML or similar to browser and rich standard file formats, e.g., XML, SBML (Systems Biology Markup Language)
Technical documentation	Written text only	Written text and formal structured description, e.g., automatically generated API docs (JavaDoc), DDL (Data Description Language), DTD (Document Type Definition), UML (Unified Modeling Language), etc.	Written text and formal structured description and tutorials or demonstrations on how to use them
Data representation standards	Data coded by local formalism only	Some data coded by a recognized controlled vocabulary, ontology or use of minimal information standards (MIBBI)	General use of both recognized vocabularies or ontologies, and minimal information standards (MIBBI)
Data structure standards	Data structured with local model only	Data structured with formal model, e.g., an XML schema	Use of recognized standard model, e.g., FUGE
User support	User documentation only	User documentation and Email/web form help desk function	User documentation as well as a personal contact help desk function/training
Versioning	No provision	Previous version of database available but no tracking of entities between versions	Previous version of database available and tracking of entities between versions

is tightly coupled to the way data are accessed. Three case studies were considered:

In HEP, data production, diffusion and use are based on a hierarchical architecture with a data production at the top level and distributed users at the bottom; simulation, reconstruction and analysis are best accomplished by a strong computing facility at CERN, referred to Tier -0 Centre, supported by a hierarchical collection of computing centres of various sizes and capabilities distributed throughout the world. This hierarchical organization has impacts on job categorization in part based on the differences in data-access patterns. A typical job is designed to perform some calculation on a specified input dataset and produces some output; organized jobs that are planned in advance perform a homogenous set of tasks and simultaneous requests to the same input dataset are minimized by a proper organization of the production. In contrast, jobs submitted by many users acting more or less independently (known as "chaotic jobs") are encompassing a wide variety of tasks, making data access variable, from predictable and sequential, on the one hand, to completely unpredictable and sparse, on the other hand.

In Earth sciences, data production is program-centered in the context of large-scale collaborations with multiple scientific objectives. This is specially the case with Earth observations programs, large centers collect and store world-wide data in a domain-specific manner to give access to the corresponding community. Data diffusion is based on a star-like organization as shown for the WIS centers (Figures 7a and 7b). This data is of economic value and the application domains extend from biodiversity to health, including climate and agriculture (Figure 5). The clearinghouse concept widely used in Earth sciences is a smart solution to the data property issue, as the clearinghouses allow mainly to locate data and, if relevant, to ask for the conditions of use. Straightforward strategies are used for data retrieval; e.g., in retrieving spatial data by region.

In biology, the data explosion and the availability of powerful desktop tools have contributed to create thousands more data silos. Furthermore, the social network organization of specialized communities has severely worsened this phenomenon; for example, researchers on proteins are affiliated to the HUPO society, researchers on gene transcription are members of the FGED organization, etc. actually, there are limited links between main scientific communities that use to have their own journals, own meetings and own perspectives, own data and own databases. However, addressing complex issues in biology requires integrated, cross-disciplinary approaches. Up to recent time, data producers and users were often the same but the development of platform facilities has provided researchers with high-throughput technologies, including Next Generation Sequencing (NGS) or Mass Spectrometry (MS). Data is yet complicated and inhomogeneous and, when available, infrastructures for data storage and access are more organized in a loose mesh-like style of limited communities. Nevertheless, the new Biosharing initiative that aims to develop catalogs on data standards establishes the premises of a world-wide information system in Big Biology.

A second issue is related to metadata that is the critical clue to discovering scientific datasets. Though searching documents over Internet is made easy using classical web search engine, massive binary datasets are difficult to browse or search and suitable technologies tuned for scientific datasets are required. The Metadata Catalog Service (MCS) and MCAT Metadata Catalog manage metadata for scientific datasets though some disciplines are reluctant to use them because of the domain complexity. In Life Sciences, numerous initiatives were launched to achieve metadata standardization as shown with the MIBBI and Biosharing web portals.

Last but not least, a third issue concerns file-level versus in-file metadata. Separating metadata from data has become an approach, which enables efficient metadata representations and queries without intermixing with large binary numeric data they describe. Nevertheless, in-file metadata might be relevant for metadata that inherently describe the file's production and the sample it contains. Sometimes, metadata might be cached in file for convenience, for example, if the data is needed at multiple stage of further analysis and is unlikely to be changed. Simpler scientific data models can then be used while more auxiliary information can be maintained and accessed easily at the same time.

As scientific data grows in volume, rich metadata and advanced tools would allow users to perform their data discovery efficiently and further developments in e-sciences would parallel data sharing and achieve remarkable added-value. Different initiatives, including SIDR (http://www.sidr-dr.inits.fr), aims to make data sets interoperable and reusable, by putting accent on high quality metadata.

ACKNOWLEDGMENT

My sincere thanks to all the people who have accepted to clarify some aspects considered in the present paper. In HEP, thanks to Andrey Tsyganov for insights in EDMS, to Andreas Hoecker and Joerg Stelzer for precisions on RunQuery, to Solveig Albrand for comments on AMI, to Raffaello Trentadue and Andrea Valassi for enlightenments on the Pool File catalog. In Earth sciences, many thanks to Anthony Dosseto for explanations on domain-specific data collect and databases, to Howard Diamond for precisions on the Global Observing Systems Information Center (GOSIC) and to Philippe Keckut for comments on WMO and ESDIS. Last but not least, many thanks to Susanna-Assunta Sansone in Biology for her continuing efforts that have given rise to a bioscience 'commons' of interoperable tools and data sets.

REFERENCES

Ailamaki, A., Kantere, V., & Dash, D. (2010). Managing scientific data. *Communications of the ACM*, *53*(6), 68–78. doi:10.1145/1743546.1743568

Barlow, N. (2010, October). Prompt processing of LHC collision data with the ATLAS reconstruction. In *Proceedings of the Software International Conferences on Computing in High Energy and Nuclear Physics*, Taipei, Taiwan.

Boucon, D., Moreno, R., Heulet, D., Kopp, P., Duplaa, M., & Larroque, M. (2009). *SERAD (CNES Service for data referencing and archiving) ensuring long-term preservation and adding value to scientific and technical data.* Madrid, Spain: European Space Astronomy Centre (ESAC) ESA, Villafranca del Castillo.

Brazma, A., Hingamp, P., Quackenbush, J., Sherlock, G., Spellman, P., & Stoeckert, C. (2001). Minimum information about a microarray experiment (MIAME)-toward standards for microarray data. *Nature Genetics*, *29*(4), 365–371. doi:10.1038/ng1201-365

Brazma, A., Parkinson, H., Sarkans, U., Shojatalab, M., Vilo, J., & Abeygunawardena, N. (2003). ArrayExpress--a public repository for microarray gene expression data at the EBI. *Nucleic Acids Research*, *31*(1), 68–71. doi:10.1093/nar/gkg091

Broklova, Z. (2004). *Simulations of ATLAS silicon strip detector modules in Athena framework* (Unpublished master's thesis). Charles University, Prague, Czech Republic.

Calafiura, P., Leggett, C. G., Quarrie, D. R., Ma, H., & Rajagopalan, S. (2003). *The StoreGate: a data model for the Atlas software architecture*. La Jolla, CA: Computing in High Energy and Nuclear Physics.

Clearinghhouse. (2006). *The American Heritage Dictionary of the English Language* (4th ed.). New York, NY: Houghton Mifflin.

Cochrane, G. R., & Galperin, M. Y. (2011). The 2011 nucleic acids research database issue and the online molecular biology database collection. *Nucleic Acids Research, 39*(1), 1–6.

Dosseto, A., Turner, S. P., & van Orman, J. A. (2010). *Timescales of magmatic processes.* Oxford, UK: Wiley-Blackwell. doi:10.1002/9781444328509

Edgar, R., Domrachev, M., & Lash, A. E. (2002). Gene expression omnibus: NCBI gene expression and hybridization array data repository. *Nucleic Acids Research, 30*(1), 207–210. doi:10.1093/nar/30.1.207

Field, D., Garrity, G., Gray, T., Morrison, N., Selengut, J., & Sterk, P. (2008). The minimum information about a genome sequence (MIGS) specification. *Nature Biotechnology, 26*(5), 541–547. doi:10.1038/nbt1360

Foster, I., & Kesselman, C. (1997). Globus: A metacomputing infrastructure toolkit. *The International Journal of Supercomputer Applications, 11*(2), 115–128. doi:10.1177/109434209701100205

Gaudet, P., Bairoch, A., Field, D., Sansone, S. A., Taylor, C., & Attwood, T. K. (2011). BioDBCore working group. Towards BioDBcore: a community-defined information specification for biological databases. *Nucleic Acids Research, 39*(1), 7–10. doi:10.1093/nar/gkq1173

Hey, T., Tansley, S., & Tolle, K. (2009). *The fourth paradigm: Data-intensive scientific discovery.* Redmond, WA: Microsoft Research.

Hey, T., & Trefethen, A. (2003). The data deluge: An e-science perspective. In Berman, F., Fox, G., & Hey, A. J. G. (Eds.), *Grid computing – Making the global infrastructure a reality.* New York, NY: Wiley.

Hey, T., & Trefethen, A. E. (2002). The UK e-science core program and the grid. In *Proceedings of the International Conference on Computational Science-Part I* (pp. 3-21).

Hurt, R. L., Gauthier, A., Christensen, L. L., & Wyatt, R. (2009). Astronomy Visuallization Metadata (AVM) in action. In *Proceedings of the American Astronomical Society Meeting* (Serial No. 213).

Kurauskas, V., & Šileikis, M. (2006). *Wrapping persistent ROOT framework objects in an object-oriented mediator system* (Unpublished master's thesis). University of Uppsala, Uppsala, Sweden.

Le Novère, N., Bornstein, B., Broicher, A., Courtot, M., Donizelli, M., & Dharuri, H. (2006). BioModels database: a free, centralized database of curated, published, quantitative kinetic models of biochemical and cellular systems. *Nucleic Acids Research, 34*(1), 689–691. doi:10.1093/nar/gkj092

Na, A., & Priest, M. (2007). *Sensor Observation Service: Version 1.0.0* (Report No. OGC 06-009r6). Wayland, MA: Open Geospatial Consortium. Retrieved from http://portal.opengeospatial.org/ files/?artifact_id=26667

Ölund, G., Lindqvist, P., & Litton, J.-E. (2007). BIMS: An information management system for biobanking in the 21st century international business machines. *IBM Systems Journal, 46*(1), 171–182. doi:10.1147/sj.461.0171

Oppen, D. C., & Dalal, Y. K. (1983). The Clearinghouse: A decentralized agent for locating named objects in a distributed environment. *ACM Transactions on Information Systems, 1*(3), 230–253. doi:10.1145/357436.357439

Portele, C. (2007). *OpenGIS Geography Markup Language (GML) Encoding Standard. Version 3.2.1.* (Report No. OGC 07-036). Retrieved from http://portal.opengeospatial.org/ files/?artifact_id=20509

Rocca-Serra, P., Brandizi, M., Maguire, E., Sklyar, N., Taylor, C., & Begley, K. (2010). ISA software suite: supporting standards-compliant experimental annotation and enabling curation at the community level. *Bioinformatics (Oxford, England)*, *26*(18), 2354–2356. doi:10.1093/bioinformatics/btq415

Rutledge, G. K., Alpert, J., & Ebuisaki, W. (2006). NOMADS: A climate and weather model archive at the National Oceanic and Atmospheric Administration. *Bulletin of the American Meteorological Society*, *87*, 327–341. doi:10.1175/BAMS-87-3-327

Sansone, S. A., Rocca-Serra, P., Brandizi, M., Brazma, A., Field, D., & Fostel, J. (2008). The first RSBI (ISA-TAB) workshop: can a simple format work for complex studies? *OMICS: A Journal of Integrative Biology*, *12*(2), 143–149. doi:10.1089/omi.2008.0019

Shankaranarayanan, G., & Even, A. (2006). The metadata enigma. *Communications of the ACM*, *49*(2), 88–94. doi:10.1145/1113034.1113035

Sharman, N., Alpdemir, N., Ferris, J., Greenwood, M., Li, P., & Wroe, C. (2004, August). *The myGrid information model*. Paper presented at the UK e-Science All Hands Meeting, Nottingham, UK.

Singh, G., Bharathi, S., Chervenak, A., Deelman, E., Kesselman, C., Manohar, M., et al. (2003, November). A metadata catalog service for data intensive applications. In *Proceedings of the ACM/IEEE Conference on Supercomputing*, Phoenix, AZ (p. 33).

Smedley, D., Schofield, P., Chen, C. K., Aidinis, V., Ainali, C., & Bard, J. (2010). Finding and sharing: new approaches to registries of databases and services for the biomedical sciences. *Database*, (n.d.), 2010.

Stoesser, G., Baker, W., van den Broek, A., Camon, E., Garcia-Pastor, M., & Kanz, C. (2002). The EMBL nucleotide sequence database. *Nucleic Acids Research*, *30*(1), 21–26. doi:10.1093/nar/30.1.21

Sufi, B., Matthews, K., & van Dam, K. (2003, September). *An interdisciplinary model for the representation of scientific studies and associated data holdings*. Paper presented at the UK e-Science All Hands Meeting, Nottingham, UK.

Taylor, C. F., Field, D., Sansone, S. A., Aerts, J., Apweiler, R., & Ashburner, M. (2008). Promoting coherent minimum reporting guidelines for biological and biomedical investigations: the MIBBI project. *Nature Biotechnology*, *26*(8), 889–896. doi:10.1038/nbt.1411

Taylor, C. F., Paton, N. W., Lilley, K. S., Binz, P. A., Julian, R. K. Jr, & Jones, A. R. (2007). The minimum information about a proteomics experiment (MIAPE). *Nature Biotechnology*, *25*(8), 887–893. doi:10.1038/nbt1329

Terrasse, M. N., & Roux, M. (2010). Metamodelling architectures for complex data integration in systems biology. *International Journal of Biomedical Engineering and Technology*, *3*(1-2), 22–42. doi:10.1504/IJBET.2010.029650

The Global Earth Observation System of Systems (GEOSS). (2005). *10-year implementation plan*. Retrieved from http://www.earthobservations.org

Tsyganov, S., Mallón Amérigo, S., Petit, T., Pettersson, A., & Suwalska, A. (2008). A search engine for the engineering and equipment or data management system (EDMS) at CERN. *Journal of Physics: Conference Series*, *119*(4), 20–29. doi:10.1088/1742-6596/119/4/042029

Tsyganov, S., Petit, T., & Suwalska, A. (2009). Oracle Text at the CERN engineering and equipment data management system search engine. *Swiss Oracle User Group Newsletter*, *1-2*, 28–35.

Van Gemmeren, P., & Malon, D. (2010, October). Supporting high-performance I/O at the petascale: the event data store for ATLAS at the LHC. In *Proceedings of the IEEE International Conference on Cluster Computing*, Heraklion, Crete, Greece.

Vizcaíno, J. A., Côté, R., Reisinger, F., Foster, J. M., Mueller, M., & Rameseder, J. (2009). A guide to the proteomics identifications database proteomics data repository. *Proteomics, 9*(18), 4276–4283. doi:10.1002/pmic.200900402

World Meteorological Organization. (2010). *Core metadata profile version 1.2. Guidelines on the use of metadata for WIS*. Retrieved from http://www.wmo.int/

Wu, C. H., Yeh, L. S., Huang, H., Arminski, L., Castro-Alvear, J., & Chen, Y. (2003). The protein information resource. *Nucleic Acids Research, 31*(1), 345–347. doi:10.1093/nar/gkg040

Zhang, Q. (2011). *Engineering the ATLAS TAG Browser* (Tech. Rep. No. ATL-SOFT-PROC-2011-034). Retrieved from http://cdsweb.cern.ch/ record/1322654

Chapter 4
Crosslingual Access to Photo Databases

GEOL Semantics, France

ABSTRACT

This paper is about search of photos in photo databases of agencies which sell photos over the Internet. The problem is far from the behavior of photo databases managed by librarians and also far from the corpora generally used for research purposes. The descriptions use mainly single words and it is well known that it is not the best way to have a good search. This increases the problem of semantic ambiguity. This problem of semantic ambiguity is crucial for cross-language querying. On the other hand, users are not aware of documentation techniques and use generally very simple queries but want to get precise answers. This paper gives the experience gained in a 3 year use (2006-2008) of a cross-language access to several of the main international commercial photo databases. The languages used were French, English, and German.

INTRODUCTION

Access to photo database has been studied for several years. Librarians have applied classical indexing using a normalized vocabulary often included into a thesaurus. This permits to have an unambiguous description of the photos but indexing and queries must be done by profession-als that well know the normalized vocabulary and thesaurus. Normalized vocabulary is composed of noun phrases. A lot of them are compounds to avoid ambiguities. In case it is organized into a thesaurus, relations are used to choose the right keyword to eliminate problems of synonymy and homography (Use, used for) and to suggest new keywords (broader term, narrower term, related term) (Wielinga, 2001).

DOI: 10.4018/978-1-4666-0330-1.ch004

With the introduction of natural language processing, there is an increasing interest in the description and search of images through captions and more generally natural language descriptions. The interest in natural language description and query is in the recognition of compounds, of subject verb object relationship and the possibility of semantic disambiguation using these relations. Evaluation of search quality is done inside the ImageClef competition and has a large success among the numerous teams working on natural language access to photo databases and especially crosslingual access to these bases.

If we study the real use of photo description and search on the internet we must say that the situation is far from the ideal view given by the two previous kind of processing. We will focus on professional sites but what will be described can be applied to general public photo database like Flickr.

Several companies are selling photos on internet from various Photo agencies. Even if the majority of photos are described in English a significant number are described in other languages like French, German, Spanish or Italian.

Generally, the description is done by the photographer who has no knowledge of information retrieval and use words (generally single words) for this description. There is no attempt to use a normalized vocabulary. They use nouns but also verbs in infinitive or past participle, adjectives, adverbs … Often compounds are split into single words and syntactic link cannot be restored.

Another problem is due to the fact that many photographers think that the more they put words the more they will sell photos. In fact some words have few relations with the photo.

In some cases, photos have caption that are much more interesting because some syntax is preserved but generally captions are very short descriptions like "man relaxing outdoors". It is much more a precise long noun phrase that really a description.

On a user point of view, the majority of customers in non English speaking countries prefer to interrogate in their mother tongue. But in this context, companies selling photos ask that the crosslingual querying system give approximately the same results by a querying of the multilingual database by any of the possible querying language.

They also want to have the best precision especially by solving semantic ambiguities like crane bird or machine.

There are two different attitudes, the one done by Getty consist in rephrasing the author's keywords into English with taking into account the problem of words with several meanings. This process is very costly. Other agencies try to obtain the same quality with an automatic process based on linguistic processing.

This paper presents the experience gained in helping these last agencies to give their clients a possibility of a cross-language quierying solving also semantic ambiguities without a human rephrasing.

PROBLEMS OF IMAGE DESCRIPTION BY AUTHORS

Have a look on Figure 1 and Figure 2.

We can observe that, except one, all the keywords are single words. It is well known that single words are often ambiguous.

The key words are not only nouns: adjectives can be found: black, red, residential, Caribbean, horizontal, past participles: closed, cropped, displayed, named, parked, pronouns: nobody, adverbs: still.

It is not the case in this example but we have also found verbs in the infinitive form.

The combination of the fact that most words are single words and the used of noun and adjectives can bring a lot of ambiguities. What is black, the car?, the door?, the building?

There is also a merging of metadata corresponding to the conditions of the shot: Horizontal,

Figure 1. An example of image

colour, daylight, side view and a description of the image content: car, door…

There are a lot of redundancies probably to permit access with systems that do not include language processing. For example: (daylight, day) (color, colour) English/US spelling. There is also terms that can be inferred using a thesaurus or an ontology using broader term relationship: (car, vehicle), (building, architecture).

This redundancy is not a handicap because it can help in semantic ambiguity resolution (see the following chapter).

Photographers when they describe their photos do not imagine that they use words that can be interpreted by the computer in a completely different way. It is the case for "plant" that can be interpreted as a vegetal thing or a factory.

Finally, the presence of words that do not correspond to the photo content is often found. We can probably say that for the word "plant".

SEMANTIC AMBIGUITIES

Because the choice of keywords is not generally done by librarians aware of documentation techniques, there are generally a lot of ambiguous words in the photo description. This is increased also because of the fact that single words are generally used.

Thanks to the fact that descriptions contain a large number of keywords with a redundancy and a general use of hyperonyms, simple co occurrence methods can be used to disambiguate words.

Everybody can experiment the fact that adding a hyperonym to an ambiguous word in a Google image query brings generally images of the right meaning (Popescu, 2006). Of course this simple way do not permit to retrieve all images of this meaning but can be enough in the major part of the use cases (ex: query jaguar car, Figure 3 and Figure 4).

The use of a hyperonym has the drawback of elimination of relevant images that contain the ambiguous word but not the hyperonym.

Two ways of solving this problem can be used.

Figure 2. Description of the preceding image

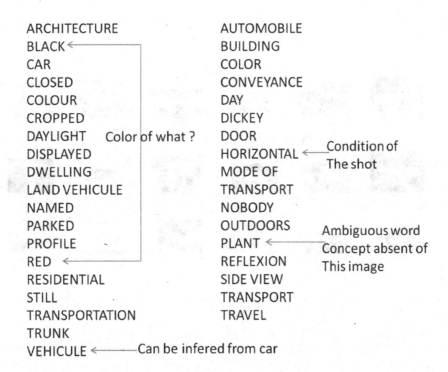

The first one is the manual creation of a complex query for each meaning of an ambiguous word. This is time consuming but can exploit the knowledge of the person in charge of this work and its knowledge the part of speech of each keyword. It must also base its work on the knowledge of keywords used in the database for this ambiguous word.

All possible words and all possible meanings are not used in a particular photo database even if it is a general purpose one. A query of the database using character strings can retrieve all the possible meanings. By examining the keywords given for each meaning one can choose the discriminating words than can be used for the disambiguation query.

Ex: crane and (bird or (flight, flying) or ...)

Learning methods are probably the best way to exploit co occurrences to solve semantic ambiguities. The largest set of image descriptions must be tagged manually with the right meaning. Statistical methods can be used to get discriminant keywords representation of each meaning that can be used if the user gives the meaning he is searching for.

This tagged corpus can be used by categorization methods like SVM (Cristianini, 2004) that can provide a way to add a meaning keyword to a new image.

USER BEHAVIOUR IN QUERYING

Most of the users interrogate using short queries. This habit is probably caused by the fact that search engines give bad results in case of long queries.

Short queries have a lot of drawbacks. The first one is because the lack of context prevents to solve semantically ambiguous words. In fact, with a query like "crane" to know the user's need,

Figure 3. Answer of the query "jaguar car" on Google image

Figure 4. Answer of the query "jaguar cat" on Google image

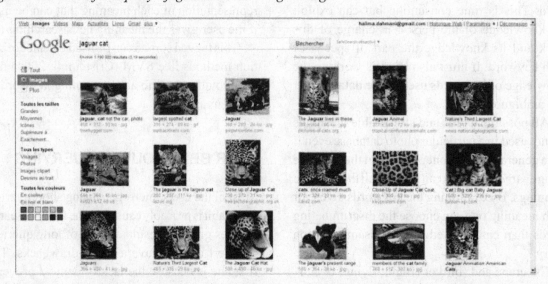

it is necessary to ask him what meaning is behind the word.

But if there is a context like in the query: "crane flying", no question is necessary if the system has learned that "to fly" in the context of crane gives the meaning of bird.

Longer queries can also bring problems when used as a bag of word and not a natural language query. Users have taken the habit with web search engines to consider that a query is a set of single words without syntax. A part of the users continue to use bag of words even with a system that performs a linguistic parsing of the query.

Example of bag of word query: "car woman bag"

Example of syntactic query: "a man walking in a street with an umbrella"

These two kinds of queries are difficult to handle in a unique querying slot. For example if a query contains "orange plate" does the user wants a plate with an orange (bag of word query) or the result of the syntactic parsing, a plate whose color is orange (natural language query).

An easy way to treat this difficulty should be to have separate slots for bag of words queries and natural language queries but it is difficult to get acceptance from the photo agencies. In the following lines are considered only natural language queries.

CROSS-LANGUAGE QUERYING

Implementation of cross-language querying of professional photo databases has been made in several agencies like Jupiter, ImageObsession or Roger-Viollet. Unfortunately the 2009 crisis has stopped activities of many of these agencies.

Nevertheless, the 2-3 years of activity has brought a lot of experience on the difficult problem of cross-language access to photo databases.

The cross-language indexing and querying technology was developed by the start-up New-

Phenix based on the results of the LIC2M laboratory of the French Atomic Energy Agency.

This cross language search engine uses a morphosyntactic parser to generate normalized keywords by processing the textual description of photos. Of course, a really textual description or caption is better than a list of keywords but in most cases, only keywords are available.

This morphosyntactic processing, recognize single words and compounds, recognize idiomatic expressions (a monkey wrench), disambiguate syntaxic ambiguities (train noun, train verb) if there is a context. In case of multiple spelling a normalized form is used (color → colour), all flexional forms are reduce to the dictionary form like infinitive for verbs (builds → build), singular for nouns (birds → bird), normal forms for comparatives (shorter → short). For more flexional languages like German nouns and adjectives are reduced to nominative.

In addition, in German, compounds are composed of concatenated parts. It is useful to permit queries using these parts. A splitting of German compounds into their parts is done by the morphosyntactic parser.

The result of the linguistic parsing is a list of single words, idiomatic expressions that are considered as single words that means that parts cannot be used as querying criterions, compounds are both considered as a whole or each part as a single world.

Ex: query: a men walking in a street with an umbrella

Keywords: man, walk, street, umbrella, man – walk, walk – street, man – umbrella

The weighting function base on the number of photos described by the keyword favors the photo having the compounds as keywords.

Description of a photo is supposed to be monolingual. There is an inverted file for each language. At the indexing phase we can consider that there are as many photo databases as many languages in the system.

For the querying, we consider only natural language queries even of one word. Of course, longer queries are better because the more the query is precise the more accurate is the answer and also, larger is the context; easier is the syntactic and semantic disambiguation.

The morphosyntactic parsing of the query must be identical to the one used during indexing. The reason is easily to understand, to obtain a match, indexing and query normalization must be the same.

The search process is done separately for each language. The first phase is a morphosyntactic processing of the query using the language resource (dictionary, grammar) of the query language. A reformulation tool is used to infer all possible query terms to find but keeping the link with the words used in the query. For a search in the query language, a monolingual reformulation is used producing for example synonyms of each query term.

Figure 5 shows the process on cross language querying for a query in French to search documents in English. The query is: grues volant ou grues qui volent. The result of the morphosyntactic parsing is the two lemmatized words: "grue" and "voler" and the relation subject verb grue ← voler.

From the word "grue" the bilingual dictionary infers all possible translations (they are not all displayed in the example). It is also the same for the word "voler". The translation of "grue" is particular because the ambiguity between bird and machine is in both languages. But in French another meaning (prostitute) is translated in English with different words. On the contrary, "voler" has different translation for the different meaning.

In a particular database only a part of the translation can be found in the photo descriptions. The corresponding translations are eliminated. In our example a translation of "grue", the word "tart" is an insult which is ambiguous with a word which is common and can be found in the photo database. This word is eliminated thanks to the following mechanism. This can append

when using a large general bilingual dictionary. To avoid such situation, a manual cleaning of the bilingual dictionaries is necessary by people having a good knowledge of the database content. It was the case for the system which has been put in use. The problem can be more difficult with more than 2 languages. A feedback from German users has obliged to change translations of the word "black" because one of the translations in German was considered as an insult.

Then if a photo description contains the relation crane − fly (verb), this photo is considered as the best answer and for the query "grues volant", the translation of "grue" is "crane" and the translation of "voler" is to "fly" (verb)

Crane remains ambiguous but for photo descriptions containing either the relation crane − fly (verb) or the co-occurrence of the two words, the probability to get a photo with the "bird" meaning is high.

For a monolingual query, the disambiguation follows the same path. Synonym dictionaries are used to infer other formulation of the query. For example "voler" can infer "vol". the concept of grues volant can be represented either by grue − voler or vol ← grue.

The semantic disambiguation is done in the same way we explained for cross-language queries (Figure 6). If the photo description contains one of the two relations or at least a co-occurrence of the two words "crane" and ("voler" or "vol") the probability to get a photo with the "bird" meaning is high.

This process of translation or monolingual reformulation is done for each language of the database. A comparison is done between the result of the reformulation and the inverted file for this language. The result is an answer for each language in the database. It is then necessary to merge the results. For more information on the crosslingual system, see Fluhr (1998) and Besançon (2004).

If the query is "crane" without context, the only possibility is to ask the user what does it wants bird or leverage machine. In this case the

Figure 5. French to English bilingual reformulation for the query "grue Volant"

French	English	Database lexicon	Best document
	Crane (bird and machine)	crane	crane (bird)
grue	hoist		
	hooker		dependancy relation
	tart		
dependancy relation	fly (verb)	fly(verb)	fly(verb)
voler (verb)	rob	rob	
	steal	steal	
	filch		

only way is to add context words that have been manually elaborated or taken from an ontology or learned from a tagged corpus.

Then when the word meaning of the query is chosen by the user, the system asked for "crane" and ("bird" or "fly" or …) to obtain only photos of a crane (bird).

Figure 7 shows an example of the query "grue" as a bird using manually established rules.

Figure 8 shows the result of "grue" when the user has chosen the meaning "machine."

This disambiguation procedure which oblige to have one of the disambiguation word in the same photo description if it gives answer with a good precision prevent to find relevant photos that have not one of the disambiguation words.

A more general way is used but only in case of long queries. The copresence of a maximum of the query words or of one translation for each query word gives a good chance to have the ambiguous word in the right meaning without the

manual construction of disambiguation word list for each ambiguous word.

Another way is to use a hyperonym taken in a lexical network like wordnet. Adding automatically an hyperonym from wordnet in a search on google image or flicker increase strongly the precision of results (Popescu, 2006).

GROWING DIFFICULTY WITH THE INCREASE OF THE LANGUAGE NUMBER

As described in Chapter 3, semantic ambiguity in one language can be resolved using the co-occurrence of words either in the photo description and/or in the query. The results are not perfect but give the user the satisfaction of finding relevant photos in the answer. The lack of some relevant photos is not a handicap because the user in not aware of the fact he didn't get a full answer.

Figure 6. Cross-language querying

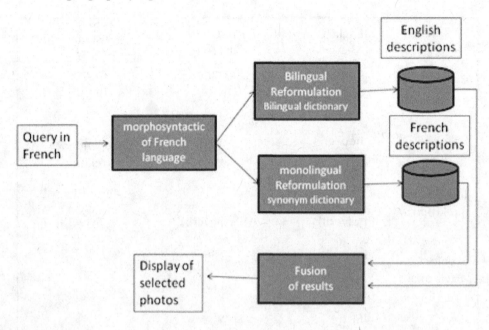

Figure 7. Result of the query "grue" (crane) when the user choose the meaning bird (oiseau) (screenshot of the ©French Jupiter Image web site in 2008)

Figure 8. Result of the query "grue"(crane) when the user choose the meaning machine (engin de chantier) (screenshot of the French ©Jupiter Image web site in 2008)

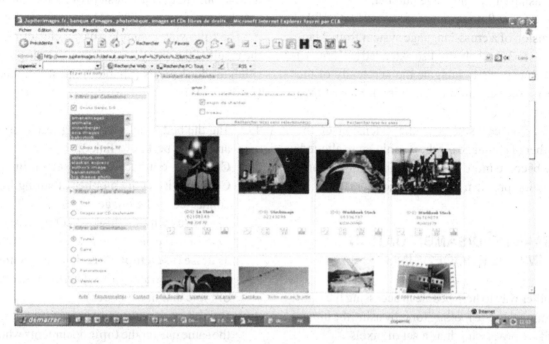

The user is more sensible to the fact that the system gives an incomprehensible answer.

For a cross lingual system the problem of semantic disambiguation is much more difficult especially if the number of languages is more than 2.

For a couple of languages, the problem is similar to the monolingual one. Ambiguities in translation are due to semantic ambiguities in the source language. The word in the source language has different meanings or has different sub-meanings for which the target language uses different words.

The first case can be illustrated by the French "avocat" that gives in English "avocado" and "lawyer". It is really a semantic ambiguity in the sources languages.

The second case concerns words that are not strictly ambiguous in the source language but the target language considers sub-meanings and use different words. An example can be found in the translation of the French word "mouton" which is used for the animal and for the meet while in English two words are used "sheep" and "mutton".

A cross language querying with two languages can use the same tools that are used for monolingual disambiguation. For this disambiguation, systems verify the presence for each meaning of co-occurring words. These co-occurring words are written in humanly made rules or taken from an ontology.

This is not a problem for the photo description because the ambiguous word is in a context of several other words. It is not also a problem for long queries when the ambiguous word is in a context of other words that can disambiguate it.

The problem is when the user uses a single ambiguous word as a query. For an ambiguity which he knows in his own language he can understand that he is asked for "crane" to answer "bird" or "machine". But if the system ask for "mouton" do you want an animal or a meet, the user cannot understand the reason of the question.

The problem is much more difficult with the increasing of the language number.

In Figure 9 you can found the problem of the extension of a cross-language system from 2 languages to 3 (French-English extended to German)

You can easily imagine the perplexity of the user if you ask him if he is asking for a castrated sheep.

As you can see, with the extension of the number of languages, if the meanings are aligned, they become more and more thin and the disambiguation problem has no solutions.

SEMANTIC DISAMBIGUATION BY IMAGE PROCESSING

Another way to help people in accessing the right meaning they are looking for is by using the image itself by processing it as a set of pixels.

Semantic interpretation of images is also an unsolved problem even if some interesting studies can be found (Smeulders, 2000).

A simpler approach consists in performing a clustering of images which are answers of a user query to help the user to choose the right meaning they are looking for.

To obtain the clustering of a set of image, the first phase is to compute a matrix that expresses the distance (or proximity) between each two images. This distance is based on color, texture and shape (Mathieu, 2004).

Based on this matrix a clustering algorithm is used to put photos into clusters of images having a visual proximity.

The following example gives a clustering on the result of the query "sea". The clustering algorithm used is K-SNN (Shared Nearest Neighbor) (Ertöz, 2001).

1. Tag the better links as **strong link** (for example the best 20% links).
2. Compute connectivity of each image. Connectivity is the number of strong links connected to the image.
3. Tag nodes with the highest connectivity as *topic*, and the ones with lowest connectivity as **noise** (use a **topic threshold** and a **noise threshold** parameter to determine the rate of topic and noise nodes).
4. Build clusters with topics images (merge into the same cluster the **topic** documents whose distance is less than a **merging distance** parameter number of strong links).
5. For each non-noise document, if it is strongly linked to a topic document, then add it to the corresponding cluster.

If the user gives a word like "sea" that can be interpreted in several ways, the clustering help him to precise the concept he is looking for (Figure 10).

The four best clusters given on the answer to the query "sea" can be interpreted as: sunset on the sea, sea food, beech with people, beech and

Figure 9. Problem of translation for 3 languages

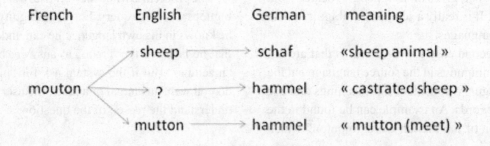

Figure 10. Clustering of an answer of the query "sea" (screenshot of images from © Graphic Obsession in 2007)

sea without people. This is a way to prevent user to be asked about the meaning they are looking for.

EVALUATION

Evaluation campaigns are a useful way to compare technologies and choose the best ones (Fluhr, 2006). For image cross-language retrieval there is a track in CLEF (Cross-Language Evaluation Forum) (Braschler, 2010) named ImageClef (Popescu, 2010). These campaigns follow the evaluation paradigm established by the NIST (National Intitute of Standards) with the TREC campaigns. Descriptions of images are textual and queries are also natural language ones with several words.

This type of image access is probably the situation we can expect in the future but do not represent the actual reality of people accessing commercial image databases.

There are no test databases that can be used to evaluate the real user query accessing photos described by authors using mainly single words.

The technologies described in this paper has been implemented and used by several photo agencies during the 2006-2008 period. Unfortunately, the crisis has stopped this experience both with the disappearance of the agencies and the software company producing the system.

During the period of use a lot of qualitative feedback has been obtained especially from the Jupiter Image company. This paper presents some elements of this feedback.

CONCLUSION

A good photo research access can only be obtained either by a description given by professional librarians or using a text describing the content of the image.

On the user side, in case of image description done by librarians based on a thesaurus, querying must be done using the same thesaurus and Boolean operators. In case of textual description, long queries in natural langue are better than a set of words.

It is difficult to eliminate bad habits and the increasing number of photos and photo authors with the generalization of numerical devices is not in favor of a normalized way for image description. We can expect in the future that people really interested in future search of their photos take the time to perform a textual description. In a remote future we can expect that contextual information will be written by devices as metadata (location, monument, time, etc.) with the content description, produced by image analysis. Nowadays, some research enable to recognize that photos are taken in town or mountain or in wood, some can give the number of persons, some recognize person faces, some recognize objects or animals. A lot of work remains. But this is the only way to avoid the problems listed in this paper. Nevertheless, querying will use a language? The natural language especially mother tongue is the easiest way to interrogate. The problem of query interpretation and semantic disambiguation will remain.

REFERENCES

Besançon, R., Ferret, O., & Fluhr, C. (2004). *Integrating new languages in a multilingual search system based on a deep linguistic analysis*. In C. Peters, P. Clough, J. Gonzalo, G. J. F. Jones, M. Kluck, & B. Magnini (Eds.), *Proceedings of the 5th Workshop of the Cross-Language Evaluation Forum on Multilingual Information Access for Text, Speech and Images* (LNCS 3491, pp. 83-89).

Besançon, R., Hède, P., Moëllic, P.-A., & Fluhr, C. (2004). *Cross-media feedback strategies: Merging text and image information to improve image retrieval*. In C. Peters, P. Clough, J. Gonzalo, G. J. F. Jones, M. Kluck, & B. Magnini (Eds.), *Proceedings of the 5th Workshop of the Cross-Language Evaluation Forum on Multilingual Information Access for Text, Speech and Images* (LNCS 3491, pp. 709-717).

Braschler, M., & Harman, D. (2010, September 20-23). Introduction. In *Proceedings of the Conference on Multilingual and Multimodal Information Access Evaluation*, Padua, Italy.

Cristianini, N., & Shawe-Taylor, J. (2000). *An introduction to support vector machines and other kernel-based learning methods*. Cambridge, UK: Cambridge University Press.

Ertöz, L., Steinbach, M., & Kumar, V. (2001). *Finding topics in collections of documents: A shared nearest neighbor approach*. Paper presented at the Actes de Text Mine Workshop of the 1st SIAM International Conference on Data Mining.

Fluhr, C., & Moellic, P.-A. (2006). *Usage-oriented multimedia information retrieval technological evaluation*. Santa Barbara, CA: MIR.

Fluhr, C., Schmit, D., Ortet, P., Elkateb, F., Gurtner, K., & Radwan, K. (1998). Distributed cross-lingual information retrieval. In Grefenstette, G. (Ed.), *Cross-language information retrieval*. Boston, MA: Kluwer Academic.

Joint, M., Moellic, P.-A., Hede, P., & Adam, P. (2004). PIRIA: a general tool for indexing, search, and retrieval of multimedia content. *Proceedings of the Society for Photo-Instrumentation Engineers, 5298*, 116.

Mathieu, B., Besançon, R., & Fluhr, C. (2004, April 26-28). Multilingual document clusters discovery. In *Proceedings of the 21st International Conference on Computational Linguistics and the 44th Annual Meeting of the Association for Computational Linguistics*, Avignon, France.

Popescu, A., Grefenstette, G., & Moëllic, P.-A. (2006, December 4-5). Using semantic common-sense resources in image retrieval. In *Proceedings of the International Workshop on Semantic Media Adaptation and Personalization*, Athens, Greece (pp. 31-36).

Popescu, A., Tsikrika, T., & Kludas, J. (2010, September 20-23). Overview of the Wikipedia Retrieval Task. In *Proceedings of the Conference on Multilingual and Multimodal Information Access Evaluation*, Padua, Italy.

Smeulders, A., Worring, M., Santini, S., Gupta, A., & Jain, R. (2000). Content-based image retrieval at the end of the early years. *IEEE Transactions on Pattern Analysis and Machine Intelligence, 22*(12). doi:10.1109/34.895972

Wielinga, B., Schreiber, A., Wielemaker, Q., & Sandberg, J. (2001, October 22-23). From thesaurus to ontology. In *Proceedings of the 1st International Conference on Knowledge Capture*, Victoria, BC, Canada.

KEY TERMS AND DEFINITIONS

Bag of words: a set of words. The order in which the element are listed has no influence on the result of the querying process

CLEF (Cross-Language Evaluation Forum): a set of evaluation campaigns on cross-lingual and cross media access. The specialized campaign for cross-lingual image access is IMAGE CLEF.

Crosslingual query: query in one language of a document (or images) described in several languages

Homography: the same character string which has several meanings depending on the context (ex crane (bird) and crane (machine).

Hyperonym: a word which has a larger meaning (ex whisky is an hyperonym of alcool)

Image clustering: Image clustering is a process which takes a large image database and regroups images that are similar. The similarity can be obtained using the word description given by authors or documentalists or using the visual characteristics of the images (color, texture and shape)

Lemma: it is the standard form of a word as they can be found in a dictionary (singular for nouns, infinitive for verbs, for example)

Morphosyntactic analysis: This process takes a natural language text or query, identifies words, disambiguates syntactically ambiguous words and recognizes compounds. The result is a list of normalized words (lemmas) and compounds.

Natural language query: querying with a syntactically correct succession of words according to a human language (French, English…)

Synonymy: In a search process, synonymy concerns different character strings that are semantically equivalent (ex: *U.S.A.* and *USA* but also *colour* and *color* or *truck* and *lorry*)

Chapter 5
Fuzzy Ontologies Building Platform for Semantic Web:
FOB Platform

Hanêne Ghorbel
University of Sfax, Tunisia

Afef Bahri
University of Sfax, Tunisia

Rafik Bouaziz
University of Sfax, Tunisia

ABSTRACT

The unstructured design of Web resources favors human comprehension, but makes difficult the automatic exploitation of the contents of these resources by machines. So, the Semantic Web aims at making the cooperation between human and machine possible, by giving any information a well defined meaning. The first weavings of the Semantic Web are already prepared. Machines become able to treat and understand the data that were accustomed to only visualization, by using ontologies constitute an essential element of the Semantic Web, as they serve as a form of knowledge representation, sharing, and reuse. However, the Web content is subject to imperfection, and crisp ontologies become less suitable to represent concepts with imprecise definitions. To overcome this problem, fuzzy ontologies constitute a promising research orientation. Indeed, the definition of fuzzy ontologies components constitutes an issue that needs to be well treated. It is necessary to have an appropriate methodology of building an operationalization of fuzzy ontological models. This chapter defines a fuzzy ontological model based on fuzzy description logic. This model uses a new approach for the formal description of fuzzy ontologies. This new methodology shows how all the basic components defined for fuzzy ontologies can be constructed.

DOI: 10.4018/978-1-4666-0330-1.ch005

1. INTRODUCTION

In the Semantic Web, the manipulation of Web resources by machine requires the description of these resources. Several languages have been defined for this purpose, as *RDF Schema* (abbreviated as *RDFS*, *RDF(S)*, *RDF-S* or *RDF/S*) which represents an extensible knowledge representation language. *RDFS* provides basic elements for the description of ontologies with *Resource Description Framework* (*RDF*) vocabularies, intended to structure *RDF* resources (Broekstra et al., 2001). We can also use it to describe services and to give an abstract model of a domain through the use of ontologies (Ghorbel et al., 2008). Informally, ontology consists of a hierarchical description of the concepts of a particular domain, along with the instances description of the properties of each concept. The Web content is then annotated by relying on the concepts defined in specific domain ontology. However, ontology description languages become less suitable in all those domains in which the concepts to be defined have not a precise definition. For instance, just consider the case where we would like to build ontology about "Management of Employee's Competences". Then we may encounter the problem of representing ideas like "Hakim acquires the competence – know how to interpret a message – with a good level". As it becomes apparent that such notions are hardly encoded into concepts in ontology, as they involve so-called fuzzy or vague concepts, like "Acquire" and "Level-Acquisition" for which a clear and precise definition is not possible. The problem to deal with imprecise concepts has been addressed several decades ago by Zadeh (1975), who gave birth in the meanwhile to the so-called fuzzy set and fuzzy logic theory. A huge number of real life applications are based on it. Unfortunately, despite the popularity of fuzzy set theory, only a few number of works has been carried out in extending ontology description languages towards the representation of imprecise concepts (Ghorbel et al., 2008). Indeed, fuzzy ontologies

now constitute a promising research orientation, on which we located our work. The definition of fuzzy ontologies components constitutes an issue that need to be well treated. Most of the works realized on fuzzy ontologies suppose that fuzzy ontology components are already defined and they just need to use them. We see that methods used to construct crisp ontologies are insufficient in this context. To use successfully fuzzy ontologies in the Semantic Web, it is necessary to have an appropriate methodology for building and making operational fuzzy ontological models.

So, to help developers to use fuzzy ontologies in order to improve the quality of result in Web information retrieval system, we need to propose a methodology for fuzzy ontologies building, on the one hand, and to create the necessary tools to make them operational, on the other hand.

This chapter goes as follows. We present in Section 2 our motivations and some related works. Section 3 deals with fuzzy ontologies and proposes a definition of a fuzzy ontology model. Section 4 defines the fuzzy ontologies building methodology: *Fuzzy OntoMethodology*. In Section 5, we present our *Fuzzy Ontologies Building Platform*: *FOB Platform*. Finally in Section 6, we conclude and we present some further works.

2. MOTIVATIONS AND RELATED WORK

Motivations

Fuzzy ontology building may be a difficult task, especially if it is done by hand. Some classic ontologies exist, such as *WordNet*[1], exhibiting different kinds of relations between concepts. For some extents, these relations can be mapped to degrees of membership values. For instance, relations such as synonymy and hyponymy (i.e., specialization) yield degrees of membership. Other semantic relations, like "Acquire" (cf., Section 1 – Introduction), can be interpreted in terms of degrees of membership. A degree of membership may reflect the category of the relation that it comes from. Another approach (e.g., Ghorbel et al., 2010) can use corpus analysis and statistical occurrences of terms to establish relations.

Ontologies should be checked and tuned by experts, even if their draft versions are automatically generated. This is necessary not only because of the limitations of the automatic generation process, but also because ontologies are application-dependent and often include pragmatic information. The *Fuzzy OntoMethodology* and the *FOB Platform* are proposed to solve these problems.

RELATED WORK

With the evolution of the Semantic Web, more and more works are interested on the extension of ontologies with fuzzy logic which is considered as a promising and important research direction that needs to be well treated by the Semantic Web Community. In Pereira et al. (2006), a fuzzy relational model for ontologies is introduced. The proposed model is very simple, with no proper semantics generally applicable in other domains. Gottgtroy et al. (2006) focuses on mining knowledge from databases and uses fuzzy rules to refine the resulting ontologies. The problem of this approach consists on the fact that data resources need to be represented in databases while in the Semantic Web, web resources may be presented differently. Equally there is no formal semantics associated to fuzzy ontologies. Moreover, there is an indirectly related research in *Fuzzy OWL* (Stoilos et al., 2006) and *Fuzzy Description Logic* (Straccia, 2006). However, these approaches suppose that the fuzzy knowledge base already exist and do not propose any method to construct it. *Artificial Intelligence* (*AI*) methods of heuristic (Hobbs et al., 2005) or analogical (Kokinov et al., 2003) reasoning present alternative paradigms that have, however, not been connected to a mechanism of automatic real-world knowledge acquisition.

Several Fuzzy Description Logics can be found in the literature (some examples are enumerated in Straccia, 2006), including a fuzzy extension of *OWL* (Stoilos et al., 2006).

The recent work of Yuncheng et al. (2010) is interested on fuzzy ontologies modeling. The authors affirm that most of current knowledge based systems manage impressive amounts of information and especially distributed fuzzy information. In addition, to widely pointed-out integration and maintenance difficulties, another common problem is overwhelming of users with much more information than the strictly necessary for fulfilling a task. This issue has been pointed out with the name of "information overload". The use of context knowledge has been envisioned as an appropriate solution to deal with this information overload matter. So the authors present a *D*istributed *F*uzzy *C*ontext-*D*omain *R*elevance (*DFCDR*) model for representing fuzzy ontologies relevant relations between fuzzy context ontology and distributed fuzzy domain ontologies. In fact, the *DFCDR* model is a distributed fuzzy extension of the *C*ontext-*D*omain *R*elevance (*CDR*) model.

Fuzzy ontologies is an interesting research area and even the *W3C*[2] (*W*orld *W*ide *W*eb *C*onsortium) is interested on it. Unfortunately, before the introduction of fuzzy ontology languages as standards by the *W3C*, new tools need to be developed. The authors of Bobillo et al. (2007, 2008) propose a method and a tool to reduce a fuzzy ontology into a crisp one defined with OWL and reason with it using existing inference engines. They make then possible the use of fuzzy ontologies even though there is no yet a standard used to represent it. *Thanh Tho Quan* proposes in Quan et al. (2004) an automatic framework for generation fuzzy ontologies in the Semantic Web *FOGA* (*F*uzzy *O*ntology *G*eneration fr*A*mework). However, while in crisp ontologies, a multitude of works are realized for crisp ontology building from conceptualization to operationalization there is neither an approach nor a tool that can be used to construct a fuzzy ontology from Web resources.

3. FUZZY ONTOLOGIES

Fuzzy ontologies are an extension of the domain of crisp ontologies for solving the uncertainty problems. To represent formally the fuzzy knowledge, we applied the fuzzy logic and we proposed an appropriate model. The fuzzy logic is based on two fundamentals: fuzzy linguistic variable and membership function.

Fuzzy linguistic variable, proposed by Zadeh (1975). It is non-numeric variable and can be formally defined as follows.

- **Definition 1:** Fuzzy linguistic variable is a 3-tuple (*X*, *T* and *M*), where:
  - *X* is a name of fuzzy linguistic variable, e.g., "age" or "speed".
  - *T* is a set of terms which are the values of the fuzzy linguistic variable, e.g., **T** = {young, middle aged, old} for the linguistic variable "age" or **T** = {fast, middle, slow} for the linguistic variable "speed".
  - **M** is a mapping rule which map every term of **T** to a fuzzy set.

Membership function is a graphical representation of the magnitude of participation of each input. It associates a weighting with each of the inputs that are processed, define functional overlap between inputs, and ultimately determines an output response. The rules use the input membership values as weighting factors to determine their influence on the fuzzy output sets of the final output conclusion. Once the functions are inferred, scaled, and combined, they are defuzzified into a crisp output which drives the system. There are different memberships functions associated with each input and output response. Some features to note are: trapezoidal function, triangular function, l-function and r-function (see. Figure 1).

A fuzzy ontology is an ontology which has besides these crisp components (i.e., crisp concepts and crisp relations), another fuzzy logic founded components (i.e., fuzzy concepts and fuzzy relations). It organizes domain knowledge in terms of crisp concepts, crisp properties, fuzzy concepts, fuzzy properties, crisp semantic relations, fuzzy semantic relations, crisp association, fuzzy association and axioms (Ghorbel et al., 2010). Here, we found 4 new concepts: fuzzy concepts, fuzzy properties, fuzzy semantic relations and fuzzy associations. Let us start with fuzzy concept; we can be defined as follows.

- **Definition 2:** fuzzy concept is a concept which possesses, at least, one fuzzy property.

Let us pass now to the definition of the fuzzy property; we can be defined as follows.

- **Definition 3:** fuzzy property is a property which be represented in the form of fuzzy linguistic variable.

We inspired the definition of a fuzzy property starting from the definition of fuzzy linguistic variable. We present, on Figure 2, an illustrative example of fuzzy concepts and its fuzzy propriety.

We define also the fuzzy semantic relation as follows.

- **Definition 4:** fuzzy semantic relation is a relation which be represented in the form of fuzzy linguistic variable.

For example, the semantic relation of equivalence can be a very strong, strong, middle or weak equivalence relation between two concepts. We can then define, in this context, 3 fuzzy semantic equivalence relations: very strong equivalence, strong equivalence, middle equivalence and weak equivalence.

Finally, we define the fuzzy association as follows.

Figure 1. The membership functions of fuzzy logic

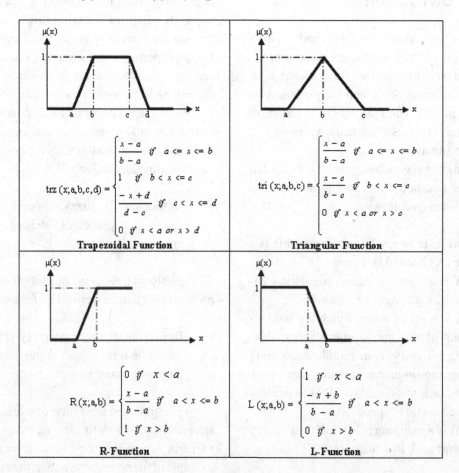

- **Definition 5:** fuzzy association is an association which be represented in the form of a fuzzy linguistic variable.

In the same way, we inspired this definition of a fuzzy association starting from the definition of fuzzy linguistic variable. Shown in Figure 3, an illustrative example of fuzzy association.

Fuzzy ontologies can be resolving many problems in Semantic Web, but it has a complex model. As far as that goes, we must then find the means to ensure their correct building.

4. FUZZY ONTOLOGIES BUILDING METHODOLOGY: FUZZY ONTO METHODOLOGY

Fuzzy ontologies have complex components (fuzzy concepts, fuzzy relations...). Its construction represents a hard work. Therefore a clear method of construction of fuzzy ontologies is essential. In the literature we do not find such a method. But, we can define it while taking as a starting point the methodologies of construction of crisp ontologies. These methodologies can relate to the whole of the process and guide the ontologist in all the steps of construction. It is the case of *Methodology*, elaborated by Gomez-Perez

Figure 2. Example of fuzzy concepts

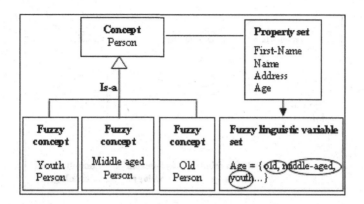

et al. (2004), which covers all the life cycle of ontology (see. Figure 4).

We see that the construction of fuzzy ontologies must pass by the same steps of crisp ontologies construction, but with additional efforts. In this section, we describe our fuzzy ontologies building methodology *Fuzzy OntoMethodology*.

First Step: Conceptualization

The goal of the first step of *Fuzzy OntoMethodology* is to reach a semantic agreement about the meaning of the labels used for naming the concepts. Natural language is usually the best access to the knowledge of a domain. The ontologist must give

a special attention to uncertainties and inaccuracies which can exist in the domain. These uncertainties require more work of analysis so that one can count and understand them.

After having extracted labels, the ontologist has to specify their meaning clearly and therefore to use a relevant semantic theory. We are going to build a differential fuzzy ontology which will turn these terms into notions based on differential semantics. Practically, the ontologist has to be able to express the similarities and differences of each notion with respect to its neighbors: its parent-notion and its siblings-notions. The result is taxonomy of notions, where the meaning of a node is given by the gathering of all similarities

Figure 3. Example for fuzzy association

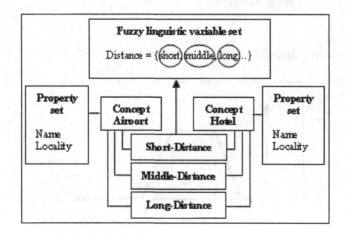

Figure 4. Methodology - A process for building crisp ontologies

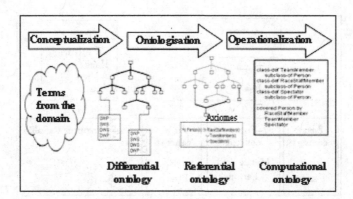

and differences attached to the notions found on the way from the root notion (the more generic) to this node.

We find, in the literature, four principles to render explicit this information (Troncy et al., 2002):

- The similarity with parent principle (or **SWP**): explicit why the notion inherits properties of the one that subsumes it;
- The similarity with siblings principle (or **SWS**): gives a semantic axis, a property – assuming exclusive values – allowing to compare the notion with its siblings;
- The difference with siblings principle (or **DWS**): precise here the property allowing to distinguish the notion from its siblings;
- The difference with parent principle (or **DWP**): explicit the difference allowing distinguishing the notion from its parent.

In the case of a fuzzy ontology, **SWS** and **DWS** principles can be to check using the fuzzy subsets found in its properties:

- For the principle of **SWS**, the ontologist must check that the siblings share same fuzzy property and same linguistic variable (like the case of the linguistic variable "Age" of our example (see Figure 2)).
- For the principle of **DWS**, we can check that the siblings have different functions membership. For our example in Figure 2, we note the following rules:
  ○ The fuzzy concept "Young Person" has a trapezoidal membership function characterized by the points **a = 12**; **b = 18**; **c = 30** and **d = 45** (see Figure 5).

Figure 5. Trapezoidal membership function "Young Person"

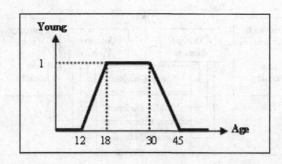

Figure 6. Trapezoidal membership function "Middle Aged Person"

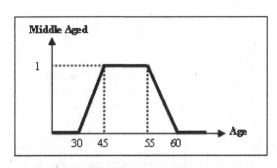

○ The fuzzy concept "Middle Aged Person" has a trapezoidal membership function characterized by the points **a = 30**; **b = 45**; **c = 55** and **d = 60** (see Figure 6).

○ Finally, the fuzzy concept "Old Person" have an L-function of membership characterized by the points **a = 50** and **b = 60** (see Figure 7).

We notice that the conceptualization is a dainty step. For that, we sought to define a demarche to be followed. Indeed, the departure of the ontologist is a fuzzy semantic data bearing text describing uncertainties and the imperfections of the domain. Starting from this text, the ontologist must find the fuzzy differential ontology. To obtain this goal, we propose 4 phases (see Figure 8):

1. Constitution of a fuzzy semantic data corpus describing the domain.

2. Extraction of crisp and fuzzy concepts in *XML*[3] files. This extraction. can be made while being based on a parser.

3. Extraction of the semantic relations in *XML* files. This extraction can be made some is through a parser (e.g., the case of a generalization relation) or through dictionaries (e.g., the case of the synonymy and autonomy relations).

4. Validation of the fuzzy differential ontology structure and recording in the data base.

At the end of this step, the ontologist obtains an abstract description of the crisp (crisp concepts and crisp relations) and the fuzzy (fuzzy concepts and fuzzy relations) components of a differential fuzzy ontology.

Figure 7. L-Function of membership – "Old Person"

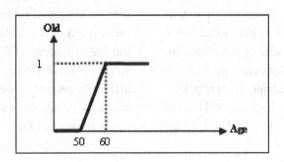

Figure 8. Differential fuzzy ontology construction demarch

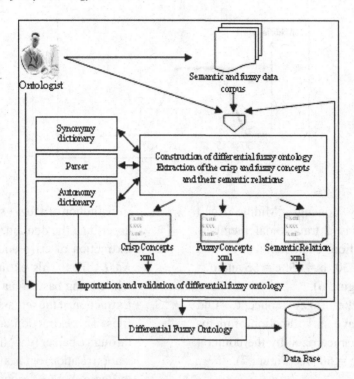

Second Step: Ontologisation

The fuzzy differential ontological tree obtained in the first step allows disambiguating the notions and to clarify their meanings for a domain-specific application. The transition to extensional semantics aims at linking the notions to a set of referents. The notions become concepts behaving as formal primitives and being part of a referential fuzzy ontology. Each concept refers to a set of objects in the domain (its extension). Therefore, we can use set operations (i.e., union, intersection or complementary) in order to obtain new crisp and fuzzy concepts. The comparison of extensions allows defining an extensional inheritance relation between concepts: one is subsumed by another if and only if its extension is included in its parent's extension. The subsumption relations of the differential fuzzy ontology are still true in the referential ontology, but additional nodes may change the tree structure.

Referential semantics allows introducing new defined concepts, but also definitions for existing concepts imported from the differential fuzzy ontology. Also, the ontologist has to precise here the arty and domains of the relations. In addition, the ontologist can add some logical axioms in relation to part-whole reasoning, composition of relations, exhaustive partitions, etc.

In this step, the ontologist must define the appropriate solutions to represent the found uncertainties. He must describe formally, beside the precise concepts and relations, the fuzzy concepts and relations. To solve the problems of representation of referential fuzzy ontology, we proposed a new graphical formalism. We chose the class diagram of *UML* to create this formalism. Our *UML* profile *UML - Fuzzy Ontologies* allows representing correctly the referential fuzzy ontology (Ghorbel et al., 2010) (see Figure 9).

At the end of this step, the ontologist obtains an abstract description of the crisp (crisp concepts

Figure 9. "UML – Fuzzy Ontologies" language concepts

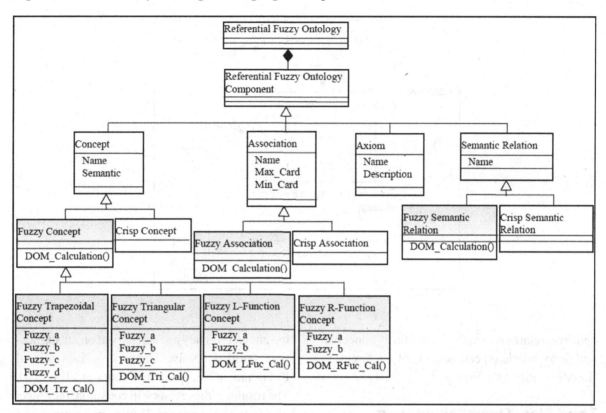

Figure 10. Referential fuzzy ontology construction demarche

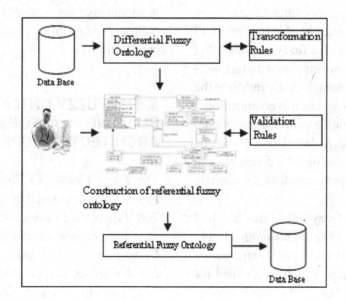

Figure 11. Computationnel fuzzy ontology construction demarch

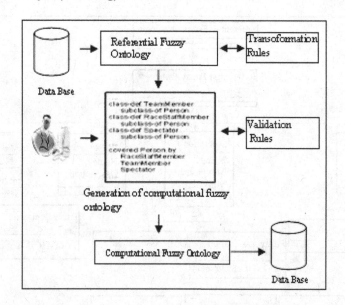

and crisp relations) and the fuzzy (fuzzy concepts and fuzzy relations) components of a referential fuzzy ontology (see Figure 10).

Third Step: Operationalization

In the third and last step of the *Fuzzy OntoMethodology*, the ontologist must use the appropriate tools to ensure the correct operationalization of his fuzzy ontology: this is the computational fuzzy ontology. These tools must be able to support all the fuzzy components of a fuzzy ontology and especially the calculation formulas of the functions of membership. The ontologist must transform the referential fuzzy ontology towards computational fuzzy ontology written in the form of an operational fuzzy ontologies language description. From this computational fuzzy ontology, the ontologist can deduce fuzzy knowledge system dedicated domain (see Figure 11).

We define a new fuzzy ontologies building methodology: *Fuzzy OntoMethodology*. Using this new methodology, we succeed in construction all the basic components which we defined for fuzzy ontologies. The tests of these tools are be-

ing analyzed. They are carried out on an application, entitled "Noise Dangers in Professional Environment" defined in Caubet et al. (2009). The results of these tests will constitute the object of a forthcoming paper. However, we must now think about the implementation of these solutions. We seek to create a framework for the construction and the operationalization of fuzzy ontologies based on our fuzzy ontological model and our methodology *Fuzzy OntoMethodology*. We implement so *FOB Platform* (*Fuzzy Ontologies Building Platform*).

5. THE FUZZY ONTOLOGIES BUILDING PLATFORM ARCHITECTURE SPECIFICATION

The *Fuzzy Ontologies Building Platform* (see Figure 12) is composed by three frameworks: (1) *Text2FuzzyOnto Framework*, (2) *Fuzzy Ontologies Modeler Framework* and (3) *Fuzzy Ontologies Generation Code Framework*. *Text2FuzzyOnto Framework* is responsible of extracting and organizing fuzzy ontological components from

Figure 12. The fuzzy ontologies building platform architecture

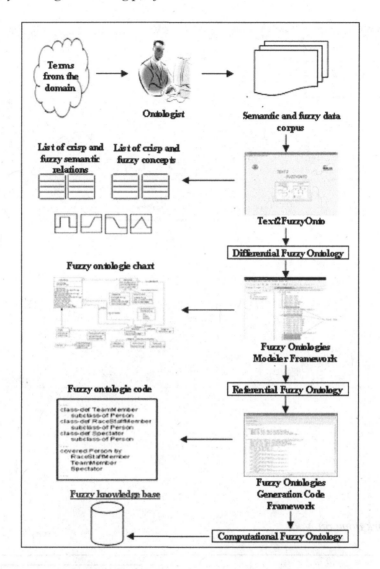

semantic fuzzy data corpus what helps the ontologist at the first step of *Fuzzy OntoMethodology*. With the *Fuzzy Ontologies Modeler Framework*, we interested to developing a support to model fuzzy ontologies which allows the formal representation of fuzzy components while using *UML –Fuzzy Ontologies*. Finally, with *Fuzzy Ontologies Generation Code Framework* we succeed to transform the fuzzy ontology towards an operational fuzzy ontologies language description. The *Fuzzy*

Ontologies Building Platform offers assistance in different fuzzy ontologies building levels.

Text2FuzzyOnto Framework

Text2FuzzyOnto Framework is a tool which allows the extraction and the organization of crisp and fuzzy concepts starting from a fuzzy semantic data corpus (Maalej et al., 2010). It allows also the extraction of the fuzzy semantic relations (i.e.,

Figure 13. Text2FuzzyOnto Framework

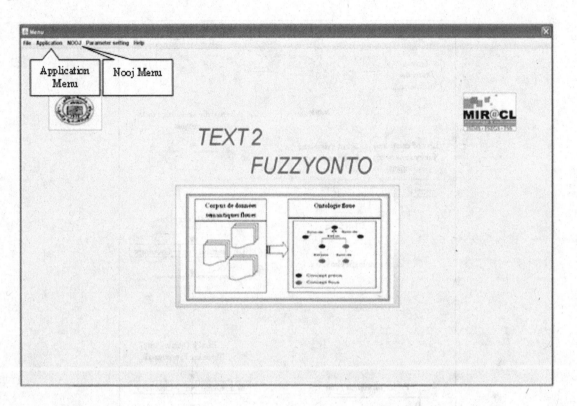

Figure 14. The work done on Nooj

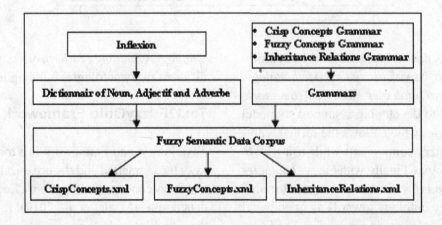

Figure 15. Crisp and fuzzy grammar

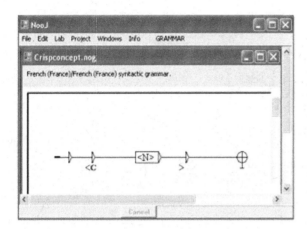

Crisp Concepts Grammar

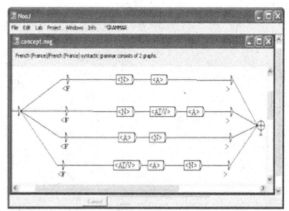

Fuzzy Concepts Grammar

inheritance relations, synonymy and antonymic). Figure 13 shows the interface of this framework.

To carry out the extraction of the crisp and fuzzy concepts, we used the parser *Nooj* (Silberztein et al., 2005). This last includes dictionaries, grammars and a corpus analysis, but it does not treat the semantic part of the words and then makes errors during the words retrieval. To solve this problem, we have then creates our own data dictionary where we associate with each word one and only one grammatical role: noun, adjective or adverb (see Figure 14). Indeed, we can determine the basic criteria (i.e., which represents the entries of the analyzer grammar) of the concepts starting from their definition according to the analyzer language. While being based on these criteria, the analyzer extracts automatically the concepts starting from corpus (see Figure 15). We propose also the safeguard of the crisp and fuzzy concepts listed in *XML* files.

For the inheritance relations, we propose to use the same parser for the same reasons. So, the objects of low level (i.e., specialized classes) specialize in the generic classes. Typically, a class can inherit the properties of several more abstract classes (Koenig et al., 2008). The inheritance relations in fuzzy semantic data corpus can exist

between: (1) the crisp concepts, (2) the fuzzy concepts and (3) a fuzzy concept, like classifies specialized, and a crisp concept, like generic class. Indeed, we never find an inheritance relation between a generic fuzzy concept and a crisp concept specialized, since a specialized class inherits all the properties of the generic class, including its fuzzy properties; a concept which inherits the fuzzy properties can be only fuzzy. These relations can be marked by the keyword "is a". The grammatical structures characterizing the inheritance relations in the fuzzy semantic data corpus are used as a basis to specify the criteria of entry for the grammar of the parser in order to be able to extract these relations (see Figure 16).

Let us pass now to the synonymy and antonymic relations. They are contextual relations, with a definition close to that of *WordNet* (Fellbaum, 1998). X is a synonym of Y if the two terms are semantically identical and X is antonym of Y if the two terms are semantically contrary (Hamon et al., 2001). In our case, the synonymy and antonymic relations of fuzzy ontologies are relations between the crisp or fuzzy concepts. Contrary to the inheritance relations, we do not find structures, like criteria of grammar entry, allowing the

Figure 16. Inheritance relations grammar

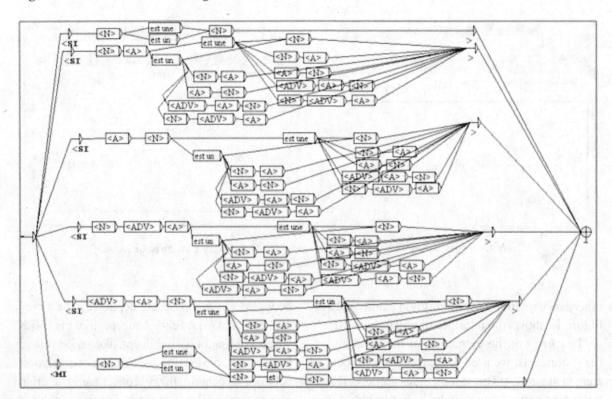

Figure 17. Fuzzy concept membership function interface

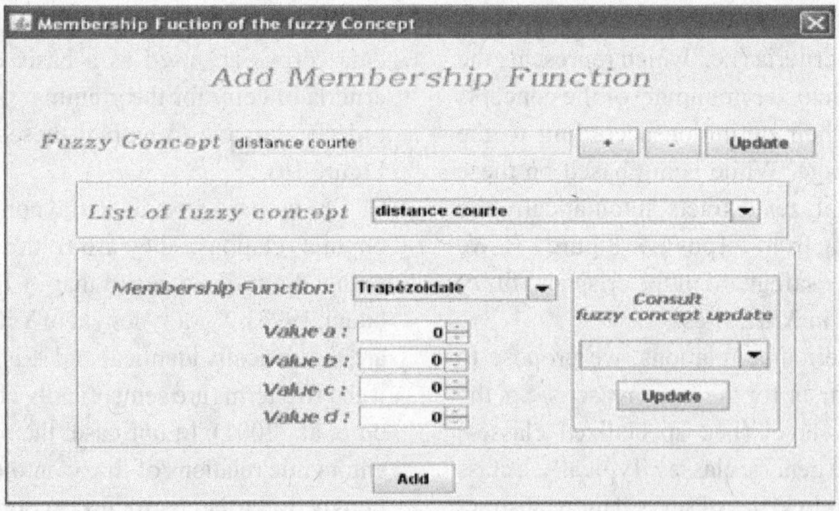

Figure 18. Fuzzy ontologies modeler framework

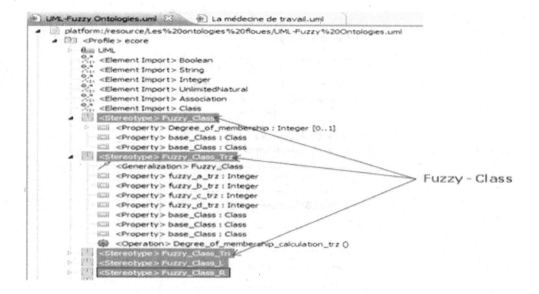

extraction of the synonymous concepts and antonyms starting from corpus. It is not then possible to extract automatically these relations while being based on a parser. We then propose to create a dictionary of the synonyms and a dictionary of the antonyms recorded in **XML** files. These dictionaries include a whole of the names, adjectives and adverbs and their synonyms and antonyms with the weight of the relation since it is about a fuzzy relation. It must continuously be enriched by linguists.

After the analysis of the corpus of data with the parser *Nooj*, the ontologist can import the list of the concepts starting from *XML* files, check these concepts and define the fuzzy concepts linguistic variables (see Figure 17). Finally, the ontologist must constitute the fuzzy semantic relations through the auditing and the checking of these relations.

FUZZY ONTOLOGIES MODELER FRAMEWORK

After the automatic step of fuzzy ontologies components generation starting from fuzzy semantic data corpus through *Text2FuzzyOnto Framework*, we have need now for framework which ensures the validation of fuzzy ontologies and its chart. We then implemented *Fuzzy Ontologies Modeler Framework* which is based on our profile *UML UML - Fuzzy Ontologies* (see Figure 9). Figure 18 shows the interface of this framework.

Fuzzy Ontologies Modeler Framework was carried out using the *EclipseUML* (http://www.eclipseplugincentral.com/displayarticle572.html) tool although we were vis-a-vis several choices such as for example *Fujaba* (http://www.fujaba.de/) and *StarUML* (http://staruml.en.softonic.com/). We succeeded in to extend the **UML** metamodel by stereotypes representatives fuzzy ontologies components (Ghorbel et al., 2010). Our profile was creates, definite and record (see Figure 19).

Finally to validate fuzzy ontologies, us proposers to implement *OCL* (OMG, 2006) constraints

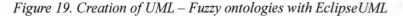

Figure 19. Creation of UML – Fuzzy ontologies with EclipseUML

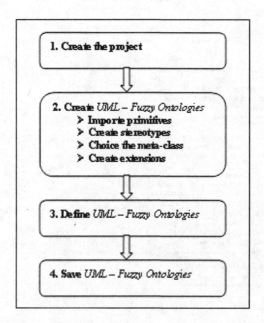

Figure 20. Fuzzy ontologies generation code framework

```
http://www.owl-ontologies.com/Ontology1206007813.owl

☑ Use XML Entities

Source Code

<?xml version="1.0"?>


<!DOCTYPE rdf:RDF [
    <!ENTITY owl "http://www.w3.org/2002/07/owl#" >
    <!ENTITY xsd "http://www.w3.org/2001/XMLSchema#" >
    <!ENTITY rdfs "http://www.w3.org/2000/01/rdf-schema#" >
    <!ENTITY rdf "http://www.w3.org/1999/02/22-rdf-syntax-ns#" >
]>


<rdf:RDF xmlns="http://www.owl-ontologies.com/Ontology1206007813.owl#"
    xml:base="http://www.owl-ontologies.com/Ontology1206007813.owl"
    xmlns:xsd="http://www.w3.org/2001/XMLSchema#"
    xmlns:rdfs="http://www.w3.org/2000/01/rdf-schema#"
    xmlns:rdf="http://www.w3.org/1999/02/22-rdf-syntax-ns#"
    xmlns:owl="http://www.w3.org/2002/07/owl#">
    <owl:Ontology rdf:about=""/>
</rdf:RDF>
```

(*O*bject *C*onstraint *L*anguage). These constraints relate to the three following points:

1. Check the linguistic variables attributes values. For example, for a linguistic variable which has a trapezoidal membership function, the value of the attribute "a" must be lower than the value of the attribute "b". The latter must be itself lower than the value of the attribute "c". Finally, the value of the attribute "c" is lower than the value of the attribute "d".
2. Check the degree of membership values for the fuzzy components. These values must be to belong to the interval [0 ; 1].
3. Check the heritage relations. As we explained before (cf. Section *Text2FuzzyOnto Framework*), it is necessary to prohibit the case of heritage between a generic fuzzy concept and a specialized crisp concept.

Using *Fuzzy Ontologies Medeler Framework*, we obtain a complete and validated fuzzy ontologies.

FUZZY ONTOLOGIES GENERATION CODE FRAMEWORK

The last *FOB Platform* component is *Fuzzy Ontologies Generation Codes Framework* which makes it possible to transform the fuzzy ontology of a simple comprehensible diagram that by the human being towards an exploitable code that is by the human being where still by the machines. Figure 20 shows the interface of this framework.

Fuzzy Ontologies Generation Codes Framework is based on fuzzy ontologies description language. To find the adequate language, we sought first of all in the literature. We found tests which speak on new languages like *Fuzzy OWL* in Calegari et al. (2007). But our idea consists in defining adaptations on language *OWL[4]* without defining new beacons again nor language since

OWL presents a standard world supported by *W3C*.

The definition of the basic fuzzy components ontological model is very dainty. Indeed, it must be complete without to be redundant. To carry out this objective, we studied work of Straccia (2006) and of Stoilos et al. (2006) which treat mainly fuzzy description logic.

The integration of fuzzy logic in the description logic is done primarily by the definition of membership functions associated with the concepts and the relations. For example, the concept "Young-Person" (cf. Figure 5) is defined while being based on the function associated with the linguistic variable "Young". The degree of membership of an authority to the concept "Young-Person" is given by the following trapezoidal formula:

- $\mu(age) = (Age - 12) / (18 - 12)$ if $Age >= 12$ and $Age < 18$
- $\mu(age) = 1$ if $Age >= 18$ and $Age < 30$
- $\mu(age) = (45 - Age) / (45 - 30)$ if $Age >= 30$ and $Age < 45$
- $\mu(age) = 0$ else

We do not use the expression defined in Straccia (2006) for the declaration of "Young-Person". We rather propose the following expression which appears mathematically more rigorous to us:

Young-Person = Person $\cap$ Young (x, s)

With Young (x, s) = {x / $\mu(age_x) >= s$}

s is the threshold of selection (ranging between 0 and 1)

While basing itself on the idea to associate membership functions with the ontological components, we hereafter will define the various components of our fuzzy ontological model.

The ontologies description language *OWL* is based on the concept of class and properties (Ghorbel et al., 2008). Nevertheless, this description is based on an exact logic and cannot be used as such for the description of fuzzy ontologies. We then propose to define a new type of class, entitled "*Fuzzy_Class*", and a series of other types of classes which specialize it. It acts in the same way for the associations: *"Fuzzy_Association"* and its types of specialized associations and the fuzzy semantic relations *"Fuzzy_Semantic_Relation"*. These types are intended for the design of fuzzy ontologies. Our framework must thus ensure the handling of these types.

- **Fuzzy_Class:** it is the root class which represents a generalization of various fuzzy classes. It has *"Degree_of_Membership"* property, which is a calculable property.
- **Fuzzy_Class_Trz:** it is a specialization of the class *"Fuzzy_Class"*. It is used to represent fuzzy concepts which have trapezoidal functions. It has 4 properties *"Fuzzy_a"*, *"Fuzzy_b"*, *"Fuzzy_c"* and *"Fuzzy_d"* which represent respectively the attributes *"a"*, *"b"*, *"c"* and *"d"* of the corresponding membership function.
- **Fuzzy_Class_Tri:** it is a specialization of the class *"Fuzzy_Class"*. It is used to represent fuzzy concepts which have trianguler functions. It has 3 properties *"Fuzzy_a"*, *"Fuzzy_b"*, and *"Fuzzy_c"* which represent respectively the attributes *"a"*, *"b"* and *"c"* of the corresponding membership function.
- **Fuzzy_Class_L:** it is a specialization of the class *"Fuzzy_Class"*. It is used to represent fuzzy concepts which have L-functions. It has 2 properties *"Fuzzy_a"* and *"Fuzzy_b"* to represent respectively the attributes *"a"* and *"b"* of the corresponding membership function.
- **Fuzzy_Class_R:** it is a specialization of the class *"Fuzzy_Class"*. It is used to represent fuzzy concepts which have R-functions. It has 2 properties *"Fuzzy_a"* and *"Fuzzy_b" to represent respectively the attributes "a" and "b"* of the corresponding membership function.
- **Fuzzy_Association_Trz, Fuzzy_Association _Tri, Fuzzy_Association_L,**

Fuzzy_ Association _R: they are specializations of the class *"Fuzzy_ Association"*. They definite and are used in a way completely similar to what was declared for the specialized classes of *Fuzzy_Class*.
- **Fuzzy_Semantic_Relation**

Let us note that the property "Degree_Of_Membership" can be factorization in a generalized class, Fuzzy_Component for example.

The integration of these classes in the description of ontologies allows a correct description of the fuzzy ontologies components. Indeed, it is enough to define each fuzzy ontological component as a subclass of the one of the *"Fuzzy_Class"* defined in the model. For example, the class *"Young-Person"* in our fuzzy ontological model must inherit the two classes:

- The class "Person": since it represents its basic class.
- The class "Fuzzy_Classe_Trz": since it represents the basic class of all the fuzzy concepts which have a function of trapezoidal membership.

After all these steps and work with *FOB Platform*, we obtain our fuzzy ontology in the form of an exploitable *OWL* code by any hardware, software or human agent. There remains only the validation of this code through an *OWL reasoner*. We seek to use an Open Source *OWL reasoner* to make the necessary adaptations, like case of *Pellet* (Clark & Parsia, 2004).

6. CONCLUSION

In this chapter, we are interested in the study of fuzzy ontologies and their construction methodologies. Our contributions consist on the proposal of the method *Fuzzy OntoMethodology* and the implementation of the platform *FOB Platform*. We show how this platform assist ontologist on

Figure 21. Young-Person class source code

```
<? Young-Person class description ?>

<rdfs:Class rdf:ID="Young-Person">
    <rdfs:subClassOf rdf:resource="#Person"/>
     <rdfs:subClassOf rdf:resource="#Fuzzy : Fuzzy_Class_Trz"/>
</rdfs:Class>
<? Fuzzy-Class-Trz class description ?>
<rdf:Description rdf:about="&Fuzzy;Fuzzy_Class_Trz">
  <owl:Restriction>
      <owl:onProperty rdf:resource="&Fuzzy;a"/>
      <owl:hasValue rdf:datatype="&xsd;int">12</owl:hasValue>
  </owl:Restriction>
   <owl:Restriction>
      <owl:onProperty rdf:resource="&Fuzzy;b"/>
      <owl:hasValue rdf:datatype="&xsd;int">18</owl:hasValue>
    </owl:Restriction>
<owl:Restriction>
      <owl:onProperty rdf:resource="&Fuzzy;c"/>
      <owl:hasValue rdf:datatype="&xsd;int">30</owl:hasValue>
  </owl:Restriction>
   <owl:Restriction>
      <owl:onProperty rdf:resource="&Fuzzy;d"/>
       <owl:hasValue rdf:datatype="&xsd;int">45</owl:hasValue>
   </owl:Restriction>
</rdf:Description>
```

fuzzy ontology building and helps him to save time and to improve the quality of his work. The outputs of this platform are *OWL* files which can be saved on fuzzy knowledge bases to be used by search engines in the Semantic Web. These tools allow as to create a new generation of intelligent information research tools.

The tests of these tools are incur of analysis. They are carried out on an application entitled "Noise Danger in Professional Environment" (Caubet et al., 2009). We obtained a percentage of automation of approximately 54%. The results of these tests will constitute the object of a forthcoming paper.

As a future work, we plan to create a prototype of an intelligent search engine basing on fuzzy knowledge bases. This system takes as an input a question (i.e., request user) and it produces as output a correct and intelligent answer. The information sources used for the research of this answer are the systems containing fuzzy knowledge already created by FOB Platform.

REFERENCES

Bobillo, F., Delgado, M., & Gomez-Romero, J. (2007). Optimizing the crisp representation of the fuzzy description logic SROIQ. In P. C. da Costa, C. d'Amato, N. Fanizzi, K. B. Laskey, K. J. Laskey, T. Lukasiewicz, M. Nickles, & M. Pool (Eds.), *Proceedings of the 3rd International Workshop on Uncertainty Reasoning for the Semantic Web* (LNCS 5327, pp. 189-206).

Bobillo, F., & Straccia, S. (2008, May). Towards a crisp representation of fuzzy description logics under Łukasiewicz Semantics. In A. An, S. Matwin, Z. W. Raś, & D. Ślçzak (Eds.), *Proceedings of the 17th International Conference on Foundations of Intelligent Systems* (LNCS 4994, pp. 309-318).

Broekstra, J., Klein, M., Decker, S., Fensel, D., Harmelen, F., & Horrocks, I. (2001). Enabling knowledge representation on the web by extending RDF schema. In *Proceedings of the 10th International Conference on World Wide Web*, Hong Kong (pp. 467-478).

Calegari, S., & Ciucci, D. (2007). Fuzzy ontologies, fuzzy description logic and fuzzy-OWL. In *Proceedings of the 7th International Workshop on Fuzzy Logic and Applications: Applications of Fuzzy Sets Theory*, Camogli, Italy (pp. 118-126).

Caubet, A., & Verger, C. (2009). Dangers du bruit en milieu professionnel. *Réseau pédagogique de l'Université Médicale Virtuelle Francophone*. Retrieved from http://www.med.univrennes1. fr/ wkf/stock/RENNES20090319042208molac-BRUIT_module_7.pdf

Clark & Parsia. (2004). *Pellet OWL 2 reasoner for Java*. Retrieved from http://clarkparsia.com/pellet

Fellbaum, C. (1998). *WordNet: an electronic lexical database (Language, speech and communication)*. Cambridge, MA: MIT Press.

Ghorbel, H., Bahri, A., & Bouaziz, B. (2010). Fuzzy ontologies model for semantic Web. In *Proceedings of the International Conference on Information and Knowledge Management*, St. Maarten, The Netherlands.

Ghorbel, H., Bahri, A., & Bouaziz, R. (2008, March). Les Langages de Description des Ontologies: RDF & OWL. In *Proceedings of the Conference Génie électrique et informatique*, Sousse, Tunisie (pp. 597-606).

Ghorbel, H., Bahri, A., & Bouaziz, R. (2008, December). A framework for fuzzy ontology models. In *Proceedings of the Conference Journées Francophones sur les Ontologies*, Lyon, France (pp. 21-30).

Ghorbel, H., Bahri, A., & Bouaziz, R. (2010, June). *UML – Fuzzy ontologies: Towards a language for the representation of fuzzy ontologies*. Paper presented at the Meeting of Ontose, Hammamet, Tunisie.

Ghorbel, H., Bahri, A., & Bouaziz, R. (2010, July) Fuzzy ontologies building method: Fuzzy ontomethodology. In *Proceedings of the Meeting of the North American Fuzzy Information Processing Society's Conference*, Toronto, ON, Canada (pp. 1-8).

Gomez-Pérez, A., Fernandez-Lopez, M., & Corcho, O. (2004). Ontology development methods and methodologies. *International Journal of Ontological Engineering*, 113-153.

Gottgtroy, P., Kasabov, N., & MacDonell, S. (2006). Evolving ontologies for intelligent decision support. In Sanchez, E. (Ed.), *Fuzzy logic and the semantic Web, capturing intelligence* (pp. 415–440). Amsterdam, The Netherlands: Elsevier. doi:10.1016/S1574-9576(06)80023-7

Hamon, T., & Nazarenko, A. (2001). Exploitation de l'expertise humaine dans un processus de constitution de terminologie. In *Proceedings of the International Conference on Traitement Automatique des Langues Naturelles*, Tours, France (pp. 213-222).

Hobbs, J. R., & Gordon, A. S. (2005). Toward a large-scale formal theory of commonsense psychology for metacognition. In *Proceedings of the AAAI Spring Symposium on Metacognition in Computation*, Stanford, CA (pp. 49-54).

Koenig, P., & Melançon, G. (2008). Dagmap: exploration interactive de relations d'héritage. *Revue d'Intelligence Artificielle*, *22*(1), 353–368. doi:10.3166/ria.22.353-368

Kokinov, B., & French, R. M. (2003). Computational models of analogy making. In Nadel, L. (Ed.), *Encyclopedia of conginitve science* (*Vol. 1*, pp. 113–118). London, UK: Nature Publishing.

Maalej, S., Ghorbel, H., Bahri, A., & Bouaziz, R. (2010). Construction des composants ontologiques flous à partir de corpus de données sémantiques floues. In *Proceedings of Actes du XXVIIIème Congrès INFORSID*, Marseille, France (pp. 361-376).

OMG. (2006). *Documents associated with object constraint language, version 2.0*. Retrieved from http://www.omg.org/ spec/OCL/2.0/

Pereira, R., Ricarte, I., & Gomide, F. (2006). Fuzzy relational ontological model in information search systems. In Sanchez, E. (Ed.), *Fuzzy logic and the semantic Web, capturing intelligence* (pp. 395–412). Amsterdam, The Netherlands: Elsevier. doi:10.1016/S1574-9576(06)80022-5

Quan, T. T. Hui1, S. C., & Cao, T. H. (2004). FOGA: A fuzzy ontology generation framework for scholarly semantic Web. In *Proceedings of the Knowledge Discovery and Ontologies Workshop at ECML/PKDD* (pp. 37-48).

Silberztein, M., & Tutin, A. (2005). Nooj, un outil TAL pour l'enseignement des langues. Application pour l'étude de la morphologie lexicale en FLE. *International Journal of Apprentissage des langues et systèmes d'information et de communication, 8*, 123-134.

Stoilos, G., Simou, N., Stamou, G., & Kollias, S. (2006). Uncertainty and the semantic Web. *International Journal of IEEE Intelligent Systems, 21*(5), 84–87. doi:10.1109/MIS.2006.105

Straccia, U. (2006). A fuzzy description logic for the semantic Web. In Sanchez, E. (Ed.), *Fuzzy logic and the semantic Web, capturing intelligence* (pp. 73–90). Amsterdam, The Netherlands: Elsevier. doi:10.1016/S1574-9576(06)80006-7

Troncy, T., & Isaac, A. (2002, June). *Semantic commitment for designing ontologies: A tool proposal*. Poster presented at the Meeting of the International Semantic Web Conference, Sardinia, Italia.

Yuncheng, J., Yong, T., Ju, W., & Suqin, T. (2010). Representation and reasoning of context-dependant knowledge in distributed fuzzy ontologies. *International Journal of Expert Systems with Applications, 37*(8), 6052–6060. doi:10.1016/j.eswa.2010.02.122

Zadeh, L. (1975). The concept of a linguistic variable and its application to approximate reasoning. *International Journal of Information Science, 4*(4), 301–357.

ENDNOTES

[1] *WordNet* is a lexical resource, developed since more than 25 years, for the English language

[2] *W3C* is an international community that develops standards to ensure the long-term growth of the Web.

[3] *XML*: e*X*tensible *M*arkup *L*anguage is a set of rules for encoding documents in machine-readable form.

[4] *OWL*: *O*ntology *W*eb *L*anguage is a family of knowledge representation languages for authoring ontologies. The languages are characterised by formal semantics and RDF/XML-based serializations for the Semantic Web. OWL is endorsed by the W3C and has attracted academic, medical and commercial interest.

Section 2
Data Mining for Information Retrieval

Chapter 6
Searching and Mining with Semantic Categories

Brahim Djioua
University of Paris-Sorbonne, France

Jean-Pierre Desclés
University of Paris-Sorbonne, France

Motasem Alrahabi
University of Paris-Sorbonne, France

ABSTRACT

A new model is proposed to retrieve information by building automatically a semantic metatext[1] structure for texts that allow searching and extracting discourse and semantic information according to certain linguistic categorizations. This paper presents approaches for searching and mining full text with semantic categories. The model is built up from two engines: The first one, called EXCOM (Djioua et al., 2006; Alrahabi, 2010), is an automatic system for text annotation, related to discourse and semantic maps, which are specification of general linguistic ontologies founded on the Applicative and Cognitive Grammar. The annotation layer uses a linguistic method called Contextual Exploration, which handles the polysemic values of a term in texts. Several 'semantic maps' underlying 'point of views' for text mining guide this automatic annotation process. The second engine uses semantic annotated texts, produced previously in order to create a semantic inverted index, which is able to retrieve relevant documents for queries associated with discourse and semantic categories such as definition, quotation, causality, relations between concepts, etc. (Djioua & Desclés, 2007). This semantic indexation process builds a metatext layer for textual contents. Some data and linguistic rules sets as well as the general architecture that extend third-party software are expressed as supplementary information.

DOI: 10.4018/978-1-4666-0330-1.ch006

INTRODUCTION

Web search needs no introduction. Current existing web search engine systems that index texts generate representations as a set of simple and complex index terms; so that a traditional search engine performs this model for information retrieval. It answers to queries defined in the form of linguistic terms which could be connected by logical operators. In the existing web search systems, it is assumed that the major problem in current retrieval systems is to capture the meaning that a document may have for its users in relation with simple or/and morphological extended keywords. The general project for Semantic Web for Information Retrieval is to extend the current web by semantic representations according to domain ontologies such that queries will return much more meaningful results. This contribution explains how, by using semantic and discourse automatic annotation according to semantic maps, implement a new kind of web search engine. We'll try to explain how linguistic information (especially the discourse and semantic organization of texts) helps to retrieve relevant information, which is difficult to capture in keywords way. A user who's searching relevant information proceeds by guided readings, which give preferential processing to certain textual segments (sentences or paragraphs). The aim of this hypothesis is to reproduce: "what makes naturally a human reader" who underlines certain segments relating to a particular point of view which focuses his or her interest. There are several points of view for text mining of discourse organizations. Indeed, such a user could be interested by the identification of the relations of *causality* by formulating a request such as: *find documents which contain "the causes of the tsunami"*. Another user will search by exploring many texts (specialized encyclopedias, handbooks, articles) the *definitions* of a concept (for example "social class" in sociology, "inflation" in economy, "polysemic" in linguistics...). Yet another user may be interested, by consulting

the past five years old press, to know *connections* and the *meetings* which could take place between two named-entities or by *quotations* of a popular person about a particular topic.

SEMANTIC SEARCH ENGINE OR QUESTION-ANSWERING SYSTEM?

It is always obvious to declare that traditional search engines deal with terms for the index organization and numbers for the quantity of documents indexed and provided to a search. And it is usual to assimilate a system, which identify specific information not provided with keyword queries, as a question-answering system. But in the standard information retrieval paradigm, in which the user provided with a ranked list of references to documents thought to contain information needed, it requires the user to search through the documents to satisfy his needs. Another approach to meting user's information need in a more focused way is to provide specific answers to specific questions. Search engines as information retrieval per excellence, can be thought of allowing users to satisfy information needs. The main limitation of this paradigm is that it requires user's involvement to identify the information they require: they must (1) express their needs by keywords and (2) must read through the documents to find the information they were looking for.

Information retrieval on the Web today makes little use of NLP processing. The perceived value of improved understanding is greatly outweighed by practical difficulty of storing complex linguistic annotations in a scalable indexing and search framework. Linguistics can help to identify automatically textual categorizations, organized as points of view of text mining, which can satisfy user's needs. Our search engine tries to take advantage of both classical IR and QA systems. It acts like a classic search engine in which, a user formulates a query with terms and *semantic categories* and the IR systems answers by providing a list of references for documents containing textual segments (*sentences, paragraphs, ...*), identified as discourse and semantic relations (*causality, definition, quotation, ...*). It is identifiable to QA systems, by providing precise information and the user does not have to explore the document contents to satisfy his targeted needs, but our system does not use any knowledge database and does not process user's queries as natural language expression.

Users often seek specific parts of information like `What did say Sarkozy about Europe?'; the answer to this question may be contained in a newspaper article as an event happened at a particular time or in official declaration he made at Europe Council. But theses documents generally contain a large amount of irrelevant information that a user had to read before accessing to the needed information. It can be straightforward to identify particular pieces of information in documents, which contain structured knowledge. Natural Language Processing can automatically identify the structured information; this is a big part of what our search engine process before indexing. Besides as mentioned by Russel-Rose and Stevenson (2009), standard approaches to text retrieval such as boolean, vector space and probabilistic models, rely on index terms to describe the content documents. These terms are easily obtained from the documents themselves and generally consist of a list of the words contained in those documents. This model called `bag of words' fails when it comes to identify semantic and discourse structured information, which are specific characteristics of natural languages:

1. Words can have several possible meanings – *lexical polysemy*
2. Ideas can be expressed different ways – *semantic relations such as synonymy, paraphrase, polysemy, metaphor*
3. Topics of a document is not determined by words it contains – *negation, modality, ...*

4. Documents contain more semantic information that cannot be identified by simples terms – *definition, direct quotation, causality, ...*

BACKGROUND

Text mining is becoming an increasingly important application of NLP in a variety of domains, including media/publishing, counter terrorism, competitive intelligence and recently in life sciences. Named Entities Recognition is the process by which key concepts such as names of people, places and organizations can be identified within a document. So by then, it is possible to index documents with a fine-grained level which turn allowing precise searching and relation between these entities. The prototypical semantic search engines allowing categorized answers with named entities are ISeek and Hakia. The notion of synonymy is generally handled by using WordNet synsets to enhance indexes. Terms of a query are related to a set of synonyms for each of them and are connected to more documents than if not used synsets.

Some BioNLP systems has been realized as semantic search engines for Medline like Medie, which retrieves relations and their concepts from the whole of Medline as a real time application; and InfoPubMed which combines full parsing and machine learning techniques to recognize different types of interactions (e.g., inhibit, enhance or promote) between genes and proteins, based on ontological information. MEDIE enables the user to perform semantic querying, thus going beyond keyword searching. These systems rely on a combination of deep linguistic knowledge, the richness of annotations obtained from biological resources (ontologies) and efficient parsing technologies (Ananiadou, 2004). InFact (Marchisio et al., 2006) is another IR system, which relies on a new approach to text parameterization that captures many linguistic attributes like syntactic categories (part of speech), syntactical roles (such as subject, objects, verbs, prepositional constraints, modifiers, etc …) and semantic categories (such as people, places, etc…). InFact is already used in the search engine GlobalSecurity. org. The general idea of this model concern the indexation process based on the Subject-Action-Object structure of a sentence. Thus, a query can be expressed in terms of a syntactic schema like "George Bush ◇ * ◇ *", which answers by providing documents containing events relying 'Bush' as subject or as a object.

The most successful experience in the Semantic Web and Information Retrieval is probably the combination of a general framework for text annotation (Gate) and an ontology and knowledge base built for named entities and their relations (KIM). The KIM platform (Kiryakov, 2004) provides infrastructure and services for automatic semantic annotation, indexing, and retrieval of documents. It allows scalable and customizable ontology-based information extraction (IE) as well as annotation and document management, based on GATE platform (Cunningham, 2002). The model used in KIM believes that massive automatic semantic annotation is the prerequisite for the build-up of most of the metadata, needed for the Semantic Web. For each entity, mentioned in the text, KIM provides references (URI) (i) to the most relevant class in the ontology, and (ii) to the specific instance in the knowledge base. As a result of the automatic semantic annotation, metadata is generated and associated with the resource processed. This metadata is not embedded in the processed document, thus allowing different semantic annotation tasks to take place, accordingly resulting in diverse sets of metadata. The couple GATE-KIM is focused to build automatically instances of ontology by named-entities extraction using the pattern language Jape.

Clustering objective is to group similar and unlabeled documents together based on some similarity measure. The goal is to collect all documents that are similar in the same cluster and classify all documents, which are dissimilar in different clusters. For search result clustering, the clustering task is to, given a query, do a search and group the results into clusters.

There are many different algorithms available for clustering and covering them all is beyond the scope of this section, but we can mention for instance K-Means, Fuzy K-Means, Mean-Shift, Dirichlet and Latent Dirichlet Allocation algorithms which are generally implemented by the major part of machine learning frameworks. These algorithms can be divided into top-down and bottom-up (agglomerative) techniques; a good presentation of *web clustering engines* can be explored in (Carpineto et al., 2009).

On the other hand, text categorization aim is to assign documents into pre-defined categories. The general idea is to use a trained model on a set of possible categories and as explained in Monchady (2008):

- First, the algorithm select the most appropriate training documents for each category
- A second step extracts features by using the text of the training documents to build a model
- Once a set of good features have been identified, most of the standard machine learning techniques such as K-Nearest neighbor, decision trees, neural networks, or naïve Bayes classifiers categorize documents with a reasonable accuracy.

Our approach handles another part of text categorization: the discourse organization of texts by focusing on segments (sentences, paragraphs, titles…) expressing semantic categories. Our approach is based on discourse and semantic analysis of texts and does use any statistics model or a specific machine learning technique. It uses two interconnected engines EXCOM-MOCXE in order to, first, automatically annotate textual segments with discourse and semantic organizations by using Contextual Exploration method

(Desclés, 1997) and in a second time index these textual segment within their semantic annotations to provide a new kind of information retrieval by given to a user to perform queries with discourse and semantic categories (Djioua & Desclés, 2007).

SEMANTIC AND DISCOURSE INDEXATION AS A REVERSE ENGINEERING

Semantic and discourse annotation by contextual exploration method can be regarded to some extent as a process of reverse engineering. The author of a certain textual content has an organization of semantic and discourse categories in mind as an expertise which he shares to some extent with co-locutors reading their textual production and other authors writing texts about the same domain. This implicit expertise shapes the metatext of the resulting text. The task of reconstructing the semantic and organization model of the author or even the one shared by different authors can thus be seen as one the reverse engineering.

General Ontologies

An Upper-Ontology is often presented in the form of a hierarchy of entities and of their associated rules (theorems and constraints), which try not to hold account of a particular issue in specific domain. It appears increasingly that more than the domain ontologies, general ontologies are economically relevant.

Recognizing the need for large domain-independent ontologies, diverse group of collaborators from the fields of engineering, philosophy and information science have come to work together to Upper-Ontologies like (1) CyC as an artificial intelligence project that attempts to assemble a comprehensive ontology and database of every-day common sense knowledge, with the goal of enabling AI applications to perform human-like reasoning (Lenat & Guha, 1990), (2) Suggested

Upper Merged Ontology or SUMO as an upper ontology intended as a foundation ontology for a variety of computer information processing systems. It is one candidate for the "standard upper ontology" that IEEE working group 1600.1 is working on; (3) DOLCE designed by N. Guarino and his group which is based on a fundamental distinction between enduring and perduring entities (between what philosophers usually call continuants and occurrents) (Gangemi et al., 2002); (4) GOLD as a linguistic ontology (Farrar & Langendoen, 2003). It gives a formalized account of the most basic categories and relations used in the scientific description of human language. Other sources for inspiration are the lexical and ontological projects that are being developed for computational linguistics, natural language processing and the semantic web. Pustejovsky and his team propose a general framework for the acquisition of semantic relations from corpora guided by theoretical lexicon principles according to the Generative Lexicon model. The principal task in this work is to acquire qualia structures from corpora (Cimiano, 2006).

At present, no Upper-Ontology description became de facto a standard, even if some of them alike NIST2 try to define the outlines of standardization with, for instance, the proposition of a standard for the specific domains like PSL (Process Specification Language) which is a general ontology for describing manufacturing processes that supports automated reasoning.

The general ontology used to describe the organization of the notions of *definition, direct quotation, causality* and other discourse categories used in texts is organized in three layers (Desclés, 2008):

1. Domain ontologies with instantiation of linguistic relations, discursive (quotation, causality, definition) and semantics (whole-part, spatial movement, agentivity) projected on terminologies of a domain.

119

2. The intermediate level presents a certain number of discursive and semantic maps organizing different linguistic categorizations.
3. The high level describes the representation of various categorizations with Semantico-Cognitive Schemes in accordance with the linguistic model of the Applicative and Cognitive Grammar

The second-level concepts of our ontologies organization are structured in semantic maps that are to define networks of concepts. The instances of these concepts are linguistic markers. The relations between concepts, in a semantic map, are relations such as ingredience, whole-part, inclusion, subclass-of, etc. Thus, the point of view of definition is associated with a semantic map presented further in this article. The concepts of semantic maps can be analyzed with the aid of semantic notions described in the third layer, based on the semantic and cognitive concepts of the Applicative and Cognitive Grammar. For instance, if a second-level concept contains spatial and temporal relations then we must use, to describe it, more general concepts (third-level concepts) such as, in time domain: "event", "state", "process", "resulting state", "consequence state", "uttering process", "concomitance", "non concomitance", "temporal reference frame"; or, in space domain: "place", "interior of a place", "exterior of a place", "boundary of a place", "closure of a place", "movement in space", "oriented movement", "movement with teleonomy", "intermediate place in a movement". Other general concepts must be also defined with precision, for instance: "agent who controls a movement", "patient", "instrument", "localizer", "source and target".

Point of View for Text Mining

A user's search relevant information proceeds by guided readings, which gives preferential processing to certain textual segments (sentences or paragraphs). The aim of this hypothesis is to reproduce: "what makes naturally a human reader" who underlines certain segments relating to a particular point of view which focuses his or her attention.

Semantic Maps

The aim of the points of view for text mining is at a focusing reading and a possible annotation of the textual segments which correspond to a research guided in order to extract information from them. Each point of view, as mentioned above, is explicitly indicated by identifiable linguistic markers in the texts. Our hypothesis is that semantic relations leave some discursive traces in textual document. We use the cognitive principle which is based upon the linguistic marks found in the organizing discursive relations in the text. A semantic map, which is comparable to a linguistic ontology, represents the various specifications of the semantic relationship between concepts associated to a "point of view".

Direct Quotation

The term *reported speech* covers a number of forms: direct and indirect speech, free indirect speech, direct speech introduced by *"that"*, etc. We are particularly interested in direct reported speech (quotations). This linguistic act (Figure 1) permits the enunciator to make a commitment for what is said or written by the speaker, without modifying it. As we have already mentioned, we can distinguish two types of linguistic markers: indicators and clues. For us, the indicators of D-RS are typographical signs (in French, Arabic and also in a number of many other languages) that define the scope of the D-RS. These signs are the quotation marks surrounding the clause3, sometimes preceded by a colon (therefore the clause constitutes a syntactically independent sentence) or by the conjunction '*that*'.

Figure 1. This semantic map (SM) is a "linguistic ontology" of grammatical or discursive categories, interlinked by the elements of specification, opposition, application, value attribution, etc. It corresponds to one or more points of view. The values of the SM (the nodes of the graph) are represented in texts by different indicators and clues (node instances) in one language or another, and by the CE rules that are associated to these instances. The fundamental dialogical dipole is between the enunciator (I) and the co-enunciator (YOU). The (I) reports to (YOU) the utterance of a speaker (X), absent from the dialogue. In the same way, the D-RS is centred on the dialogical relation speaker-interlocutor. All the enunciative relations in this SM are under the commitment of the enunciator. Some of them concern the simple I-YOU speech relation, and others concern the D-RS (Alrahabi & Desclés, 2008).

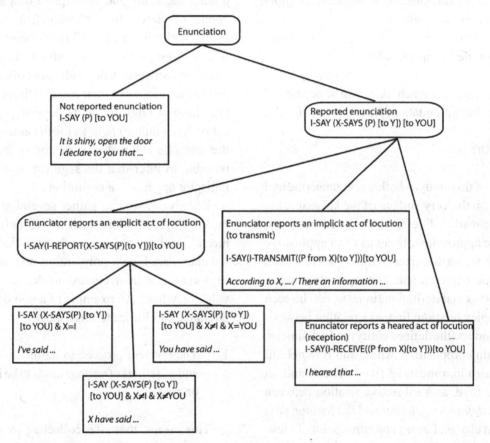

As to the contextual clues for D-RS, they are the declarative linguistic markers that introduce or succeed the citation:

- Verbs (*X denied the facts: "…"*). French examples: *écrire, souligner, avouer, affirmer, critiquer,*
- Nouns (*This is the declaration of X: "…"*): French examples: *déclaration, annonce, slogan, appel…*
- Gerunds (*X affirmed this by adding: "…"*): French examples: *en soulignant, en affirmant, en ajoutant…*
- Adverbials (*According to X: "…"*): French examples: *d'après, selon…*

We note that in French, verbs can be positioned in the middle of the citation ("…, *affirme-t-il,* …").

Definition

The aim of this study is both to circumscribe and analyse, on the very surface of the language, the linguistic marks of definition: this theoretic and linguistic approach will lead us to an applicative approach, trying to extract definitory utterances on a linguistic-based ground. The assumption we try to support is that definition, in texts, can be seen as a complex relation: first, as a relation between a definiendum (the defined entity) and a definiens, the defining proposition, which aim is to delimit the definiendum meaning (its essence); and, at the same time, as a subjective relation between this first *definitory relation* and the *locutor* who takes it in charge. From a cognitive point of view, definition boils down to an assertion concerning the invariant of the defined entity. To define consists in circumscribing properties thought to be distinctive and essential to an entity. In other words, to define consists in mapping the frontier of an entity's invariant, the frontier of its mental representation. Such a modelling of definition leads us to the theory of scientific definition developed by LaLIC laboratory: a scientific definition

should find its expression in a necessary and sufficient condition. Doing so, a definition delimits a frontier, in the intension of a concept, between typical (but non definitory) properties and essential properties. A key distinction also needs to be introduced between proper definitions and facets of definition: while a proper definition deals with the frontier of invariance, facets of definition only express necessary, but not distinctive, properties.

The linguistic approach relies on the Contextual Exploration method, which consists in identifying textual segments that correspond to a semantic "point of view". In our research of linguistic marks with which the definition point of view is expressed in texts, the method introduces a hierarchy between strong indicators of definition and features found in their context: those features (any kind of linguistic units, lexical, grammatical or typographic) help to lift the ambiguity on the semantic value of an indicator, so that it gets possible to infer that the segment in which the indicator appears is a definition.

Intuitively, we can gather several strong indicators of definition, such as "to define", "to mean", "to denote": but even those obvious verbal indicators are highly polysemous and require an exploration of their context to determinate the value they held. An example of a non definitory utterance can illustrate this aspect:

1. The lawyers proceed to define taxes, tolls, and exactions of various kinds to be imposed on trade.

This means, that after collecting strong indicators (mostly verbs, but not exclusively), it is necessary to bring out regularities in their context of apparition that facilitate semantic disambiguation. Different features appear to be very regular: for instance, if the expression "the word xxx" (or any approaching expression) is in the left context of the verbal indicators we've mentioned, the sentence is likely to be a definition:

2. Plato used the word aeon to denote the eternal world of ideas, which he conceived was "behind" the perceived world (...).

3. The verb krstiti in Croatian means "to baptize".

4. The term abstract algebra now refers to the study of all algebraic structures, as distinct from the elementary algebra ordinarily taught to children (...).

Among the important and frequent features, several interpolated clauses help to raise the ambiguity of an indicator: these clauses are often traces left by the definitory work. Among those, we can count rewording clauses and parenthesis ("also called,", "(or)", etc.) and clauses related to signification (", in its literal meaning,", ", in a metaphorical sense,", ", strictly speaking,", "by extension,", "in a philosophical terminology," etc.). These clauses help to disambiguate many identification utterances: indeed, identification utterances (introduced by "is a" or "is the") may not be confused with definitory utterances, though they may be frequent ingredients of definition. In some case, though, some identification utterances may stand for definitions - but definitions in which the definitory work is silent. Beyond these, there are many others features we haven't mentioned: there all are organised in some way around the indicators, on their left or right context. A linguistic work progressively brings out these organisations and formalises them in contextual exploration rules that express discursive and semantic configurations. The linguistic analysis our work has carried out shows that definition is organized by a semantic map of the definition in texts. The semantic of each relation corresponds to intrinsic properties alike functional type, algebraic properties and combination with other relations in the same context.

SEMANTIC ANNOTATION WITH CONTEXTUAL EXPLORATION

In the perspective to build a search engine, the major objective for our annotation system EXCOM, using the Contextual Exploration method, is to explore semantics and discourse organizations of texts, in order to enhance information extraction and retrieval through automatic annotation of textual segments. As mentioned above, most linguistic-oriented annotation systems are based on morphological analysis, part-of-speech tagging, chunking, named entities recognition and dependency structure analysis. The methodology used by Contextual Exploration method, describes the discursive organization of texts exclusively using linguistic knowledge available in the textual context. Linguistic knowledge is structured in form of lists of linguistic marks and declarative rules for the Contextual Exploration from each linguistic mark. The constitution of this linguistic knowledge is independent of a particular domain. Domain knowledge describes the concepts and their sub-concepts of a subject domain with their relationships. The contextual knowledge concerns communicative knowledge as a discursive organization, which deals with the preferences and needs of those who use information in the texts. Linguistic rules for identifying and semantically annotating segments use different strategies defined through rules. Some of these rules use lists of simple patterns coded as regular expressions, others need to identify structures like titles, sections, paragraphs and sentences for extraction purposes. The most relevant rules for EXCOM are those called Contextual Exploration (CE) rules. A CE rule is a complex algorithm based on a prime textual mark (called indicator), and secondary contextual clues intended to confirm or invalidate the semantic value carried by the indicator. The core of EXCOM annotation schema is divided on: (i) textual document; (ii) general metadata like (title, author, edition, etc.) and (iii) semantic annotations in relation with semantic categories for discourse (represented by semantic maps).

An annotation system based on Contextual Exploration system is defined by a quintuple:

<R, M, E, S, T>

- *R* is a set of rules divided essentially on regular grammars and EC rules,
- *M* a set of linguistic markers organized in semantic lists,
- *E* an engine that uses a particular algorithm focused on a primary linguistic marker and secondary markers. It start by identifying the primary marker (called indicator) and by its essence polysemy, the engine mine the context in both directions (left and right) to identify secondary markers, which can confirm or infirm the decision affecting a particular textual segment (a sentence, a paragraph, a title) by a semantic annotation according a semantic map,
- *S* a semantic map which guides the annotation process in the semantic and discourse organization process,
- *T* a set of structured texts. The structures are expressing the physical organization of the text (general metadata, title, section, paragraph and sentence)

The methodology used by the general automatic annotation engine EXCOM (Djioua et al., 2006; Alrahabi, 2010), called Contextual Exploration (Figure 2), describes the discursive organization of texts exclusively using linguistic knowledge present in the textual context. Linguistic knowledge is structured in the form of lists of linguistic marks and declarative rules for the Contextual Exploration of each linguistic mark. The constitution of this linguistic knowledge is independent of a particular domain. Domain knowledge describes the concepts and sub-concepts of a subject domain with their relationships.

Contextual knowledge concerns communicative knowledge as a discursive organization, which deals with the preferences and needs of those who use information in the texts. Linguistic rules define different strategies for identifying and semantically annotating textual segments. Some of these rules use lists of simple patterns coded as regular expressions, others need to identify structures like titles, sections, paragraphs and sentences for extraction purposes.

Excom engine explores the semantic and discursive organisations of text, in order to annotate pertinent segments with semantic tags, considering a given 'point of view': in the present study, the 'point of view' chosen to explore texts is the definition angle. The tags with which texts are enriched are the values given by the semantic map of the exploration point of view. Indeed, Excom is designed in accord with Contextual Exploration. The process only depends on linguistic units found in texts and does not rely on any external Knowledge Base or domain ontology. It does not either proceed to syntactic or morphological analysis. The knowledge implemented in the engine only consists in a list of linguistic indicators or features and in rules that refer to those lists.

Designing Excom rules for the definitory point of view meant encoding the discursive organisations that the linguistic analysis that we briefly described brought out. Lists of indicators had to be collected and the layout of features around the indicators has then been described in contextual exploration rules.

The major characteristic of this work in comparison with other points of view that have been implemented in Excom (quotation, causality, etc.) is that the number of indicators is rather small, while the variety of discursive layouts around these indicators is, on the contrary, rather large. This explains that, for a single indicator, numerous rules were implemented.

Rules as Linguistic Knowledge

Linguistic resources are organized as typed semantic rules (contextual exploration rules, regular

Figure 2. A text mining pipeline from unstructured to annotated text using pre-processing, segmentation and semantic annotation, using linguistic resources (list of markers and contextual exploration rules) and general ontologies (semantic map of definition in this example). Each module enhances text representation with a layer of annotation, which represents explicit linguistic and semantic information attached to text in machine-usable form. Markers and linguistic rules are inferred by human expert using (i) general linguistic, and (ii) corpora mining. However, for the text to be annotated automatically at a higher semantic level, such semantic and discourse knowledge has to be explicitly represented in machine-readable form and processed by an engine based on Contextual Exploration method. The given figure illustrates the output representation of the sentence "The term abstract algebra now refers to the study of all algebraic structures, as distinct from the elementary algebra ordinarily taught to children (...)." with multiple layers of annotation including segmentation, semantic and general ontology related.

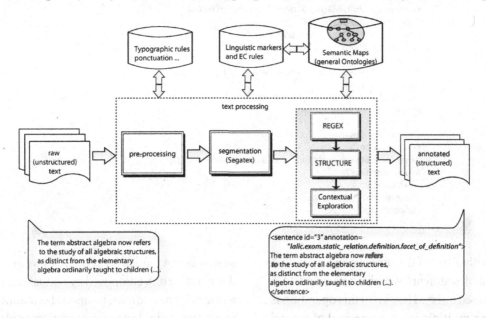

expression rules, etc.) (Figure 3) Semantic rules are intended to capture the discursive organization of a text. Each rule is based on a set of markers lists, which can be used as indicators (to trigger the rule) or as clues (to confirm or refuse the annotation). List can be composed of lexical variations or regular expressions. These lists of linguistic terms are coded as Unicode plain files, while semantic rules are expressed in XML format.

The core of EXCOM annotation model is divided on the following interlinked parts: (1) a textual document representing the structured textual content (2) a general metadata handling (title, author, edition, etc.), and (3) semantic an-

notations in relation with semantic and discourse categories (direct quotation, definition, …) (Figure 4).

SEMANTIC INDEXATION

The strategy used in our retrieval system is divided into two parts: A first step which deals with annotation of the textual documents according to discursive point of view and finally the storage of these annotated documents; in the second step, indexing annotated segments (sentences and paragraphs), in order to provide an answer

Figure 3. Contextual Exploration rule for direct quotation. The CE rule is represented by conditions to satisfy before assigning an annotation to a textual segment. The condition is divided on first a primer indicator which should be identified first on any sentence in the text. Then, by a contextual exploration, the engine tries to identify, on the left of the indicator, a secondary marker (called a clue) to confirm or reject the annotation affectation which is the action defined in the last part of the CE rule. The action in this example is to add a semantic tag (quotation) to the sentence in where the engine satisfied the conditions (annotation_location="0" which express the XPath location from the original sentence).

```xml
<?xml version="1.0" encoding="UTF-8"?>
<excom:rules xmlns:excom="http://www.mocxe.org/excom/ExcomRuleSchema"
xmlns:xsi="htp://www.w3.org/2001/XMLSchema-instance"
si:schemaLocation="http://www.mocxe.org/excom/ExcomRuleSchema
../XML/ExcomRuleSchema.xsd ">
<excom:rule id="DR-D_rule5" name="ConfirmerDiscours"
task="Enunciation" type="ec"
point_of_view="Direct_Quotation">
<excom:conditions>
<excom:ec>
<excom:indicator search_location="sentence" type="regex"
value=":\s"[^"]+""/>
<excom:clue contexte="left" search_location="0" type="list"
value="Confirm"/>
</excom:ec>
</excom:conditions>
<excom:actions>
<excom:annotation annotation_location="0" type="add_tag"
value="assertion"/>
</excom:actions>
</excom:rule>
</excom:rules>
```

not only with a list of documents, but also with the annotated segments which correspond to a semantic based query. The aim of this operation is to build up a multiple index composed of textual segments (sentences, paragraphs, section titles, ...), semantic discursive annotations (relations between concepts, causality, definition, quotation,...) and, when it is possible, named-entities (enamex, locations and timex) representing the arguments of the discursive and semantic relations.-

To answer a question like *"Search quotations of X about Y?"* the search engine can just use linguistic terms such as *"X"* and the morphologic forms of the verb *"to say"* or connect the user to some dedicated web sites for quotations. The notion of quotation is defined by linguistic marks (indicator and clues such as *to indicate, to insist, to declare* ...) organized by writing traces of the author in the text. So instead of organizing the search engine index by terms, our system uses a double structure composed by textual segments in a side and annotations, terms and semantic marks in another side. Index organization explains the relationship between the initial document, constitutive textual segments, discursive annotations, named-entities (enamex, location, timex) and the terms which compose textual segments (sentence, paragraph, image, table and section title). A document is seen, in this organization, as a set of textual segments identified automatically by EXCOM as discursive organization of the text written by an author. Each textual segment is associated with several important pieces of information such as: (1) a set of semantic annotation (discursive mark like *quotation, definition* or *factual meeting*). Each textual segment identifying as relevant for a document can be associated to a set of discursive annotations (defined by index subfields) according

Figure 4. Result of the annotation processing for direct quotation: Ce que confirme sans hésitation un haut fonctionnaire de l'organisation: " L'OMS est au centre même des conflits d'intérêts......".[2]. In the system EXCOM, this annotated file is represented by two interconnected XML files: (1) annotation file which shows two annotations: a confirmation and an assertion relied to textual segments (sentences 49 and 52) and (2) document file with sentences associated to semantic annotations previously described.

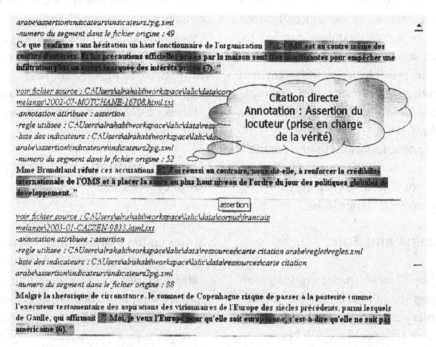

to the semantic point of views used in the annotation engine EXCOM. So a same textual segment can be chosen by the search engine as a response for a query about *causality* and *quotation;* (2a) the document URI for a unique identification on the Internet; (2b) the document title; (3) the full-text content for a relevant answer to users; (4) when possible, named-entities like proper names, organizations and trades to be able to answer *"Who SAYS What?";* (5) location named-entities to be able to answer *"Where X MET Y?";* (6) time named-entities to be able to answer *"When X SAYS Y?"*

The index organization explains the relationship between the initial document, constitutive textual segments, discursive annotations, named-entities (enamex, location, timex) and the terms, which compose textual segments (sentence, paragraph and section title). A document is handled, in this organization, as a set of textual segments identified automatically by EXCOM, as discursive organization of the text written by an author. Each textual segment is associated with several important pieces of information such as:

1. A set of semantic categorization (nodes of semantic maps, discursive mark like *factual meeting, definition* or *direct quotation*). Each textual segment identifying as relevant for a document can be associated to a set of discursive annotations (defined by index sub-fields) according to the semantic point of view used in the annotation engine EXCOM. So that a same textual segment can be chosen by the search engine MOCXE as response for a query about *causality* and *quotation*.

2. Document URI for a unique identification on the Internet.
3. Document title for a pleasant answer.
4. The full-text content for a relevant answer to users. The indexing process used for a textual segment is the same usually used according to the methodology applied by traditional search engines.
5. When it is possible to identify, enamex named-entities like proper names, organizations and trades to be able to answer *"Who SAYS What?"*
6. When it is possible, location named-entities to be able to answer *"Where X MET Y?"*
7. When it is possible, timex named-entities to be able to answer *"When X MET Y?"*

Apache Lucene and Solr

Apache Solr (http://lucene.apache.org/solr) is an industrial-strength, high-performance, thread-safe search server based on Apache Lucene. Solr wraps and extends Lucene. Since Solr became an apache project, it has grown to include many new capabilities and a large and active community committed to adding new features, fixing issues and improving performance. Solr provides many key features that make it a top-of-the-line search server, including faceted searching, hit highlighting, support multiple output formats (XML, JSON) and most important, it is installed as a REST web service, and it comes with an HTTP-based administration interface. Since Solr is a web-based search service, most operations take place by sending HTTP Get and Post requests from a client application to the Solr server.

Indexing in Solr (Figure 5) involves constructing an XML message from pre processed content and sending it as an HTTP Post message. Much like indexing, search is accomplished by sending HTTP requests to Solr that specify the information need of the user. Solr contains a rich query language, which enables users to use terms, phrases, wildcards and a number of other options. In fact, the options seem to grow with every release.

An example of a searching activity for definition of a concept in documents is depicted in Figure 6. Definitions were extracted and categorized in accordance with the semantic map, even though the analysis has not always been able to distinguish subtly inside the big categories: the recognized categories are mainly "definition", opposed to "facet of definition", and, within the "facets of definition", the category of "etymology."

Query Language and Semantic Search API

The system uses a query language which is based at the same time on both linguistic terms (constitutive of textual segments) and discursive semantic categories (*direct quotation, definition,...*). Simple queries can be *"category:direct_quotation"* to search all documents containing *direct quotations*, *"category:quotation and contents:Strauss-Kahn"* to search documents which containing *quotations* and *Strauss-Kahn* as *locutor* or a topic argument or *"category:quotation and locutor:Strauss-Kahn"* specifying the locutor. Advanced queries can be expressed by *(category:quotation and contents:Chomsky) and (category:definition and contents:grammar)* to try to find documents which contains quotations of Chomsky defining the term "grammar".

The search engine can also be reached as a REST web service with HTTP GET request with parameters (http://tamis:8182/?{query}&{start}&{results}&{onto}&{lang}&{schema}) where query is the string parameter using a language as described.

*   **query:** the string query to search according to the Boolean model for the textual content for segments (sentence, paragraph, title) annotated as *definition, direct quotation, meting relation or causality.*

Figure 5. The structure of an index built on French online newspaper with the point of view of direct quotation

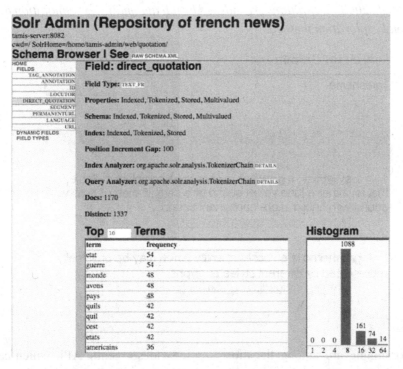

- **start:**the offset of the fist answer, the default value is 0 and the max is calculated by using the rule: the finishing position (start + results) cannot exceed 1000
- **results**: is total answers, the default value is 10 and the total
- **onto:** represents a "point of view", focusing the search on a semantic category
- **lang**: represents the language of contents, the default value is 'fr'
- **schema**: is specifying the format of results (XML by default or JSON)

The Authorization header (we used a basic digest authentication system with a username and password) controls access to the web service. A future development for the web service access is planed with a more controlled process for authentication and authorization by using the two-legged OAuth protocol.

An example of query and results about direct quotation declared by M. Chevènement (Figure 7):

Scalability and Distribution

Our implementation based on Lucene API uses both index distribution (*Sharding*) and index replication techniques. Index distribution enables the search engine quickly and efficiently process queries against a large index. If necessary, index shards can later be merged into a single intact index. Index replication enables to scale and to provide adequate responsiveness to queries against large search volumes.

The question of distributed Text Mining is actually emerging as an important question in the community since corpora chosen for processing became heavier. This situation presents a unique set of challenges and opportunities. A real-world document collections grow in size, distributed

Figure 6. Part of output of MOCXE answering the query 'find in definitions of 'grapheme.'' The answers are retrieved from ExcomMocxe system by identifying definitions inside documents crawled from Google index (Teissedre et al., 2008). Definitions are indexed by full automatic text annotation by using semantic map and contextual exploration method.

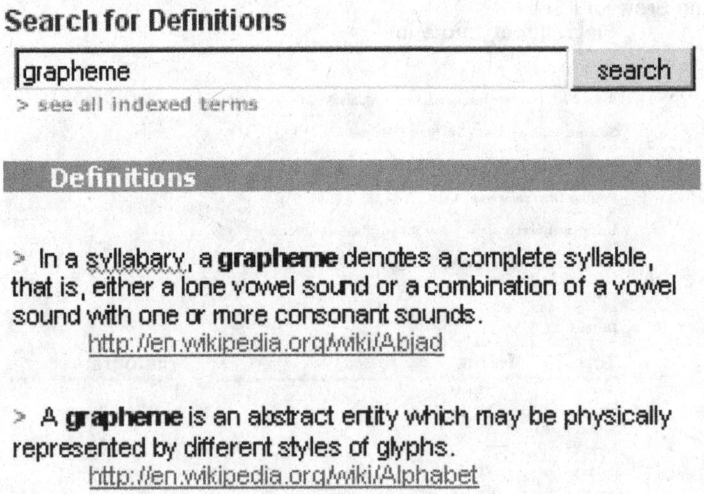

Search for Definitions

| grapheme | search |

> see all indexed terms

Definitions

> In a syllabary, a **grapheme** denotes a complete syllable, that is, either a lone vowel sound or a combination of a vowel sound with one or more consonant sounds.
http://en.wikipedia.org/wiki/Abjad

> A **grapheme** is an abstract entity which may be physically represented by different styles of glyphs.
http://en.wikipedia.org/wiki/Alphabet

methods for text mining are among the most promising approaches to get results in reasonable time. Both semantic and discourse annotation and indexation processes can be easily recast as a sequence of map and reduce steps (Table 1).

Besides of this analyze, free and high-quality open source implementation are now available, like the Apache project Hadoop, which implements the famous Google map/reduce algorithm. The map/reduce phases run independently on different splits of data. Hadoop takes care of splitting and partitioning the data, assigning processors for the map/reduce steps, and finally synchronizing the different phases. The popular architecture that was originally developed by Google to handle documents processing tasks in search engines is based on the map-reduce paradigm. The architecture hides the distributed system details from the programmer and handles all synchronization, parallelization, fault recovery and I/O operations. As a result, the programmer can concentrate on solving the text-processing task. The Hadoop project responds to these recommendations and

provides a gentle API, which can be used efficiently on local clusters or through a cloud computing architecture (using Amazon EC2 for example).

BROWSING AND MINING WITHIN SEMANTIC ANNOTATIONS

Browsing is a central search tactic in categorized content retrieval. Through browsing the user either gains enough knowledge to begin query interactions or already finds a suitable categorized content. Browsing differs from querying in that it allows users to recognize what interests them within the collection rather than needing to formulate a precise query in advance, which is very difficult in a non-structured content. This makes browsing an attractive search strategy, especially for users with little prior knowledge about the expertise domain or collection. When searching on the web, non-professional users may also navigate directly to a website they feel is likely

Figure 7. Result set returned by Solr for a query searching direct quotation of the locutor "Chevène-ment." A document contains both arguments of the quotation relation: the locutor "Chevènement" and the direct quotation expressed between quotes. Semantic annotation ("manière_de_dire_locutor") and textual segment (a paragraph in this case) are also associated to document response. Other general metadata are also collected to each answer (id, url, language, ...)

```
– <response>
   – <lst name="responseHeader">
        <int name="status">0</int>
        <int name="QTime">1</int>
      + <lst name="params"></lst>
      </lst>
   – <result name="response" numFound="12" start="0">
      – <doc>
         – <arr name="annotation">
              <str>enonciation fr.maniere dire locuteur avant</str>
           </arr>
         – <arr name="direct_quotation">
            – <str>
                 " Il faut porter remède à la situation particulière dans laquelle se retrouve l'islam en France du fait de la difficulté qu'il éprouve à s'organiser dans la
                 norme qui est celle des grands cultes, notamment en se dotant d'instances représentatives. "
              </str>
           </arr>
           <str name="id">37e80a14-cd55-436f-b7a5-be3f2e24a25e</str>
           <str name="language">fr</str>
           <str name="locutor">M. Chevènement</str>
           <str name="permanentUrl">2002-01-DOLLE-16026.html.txt.xml</str>
         – <str name="segment">
              Dans le même élan, M. Chevènement justifiait son initiative : " Il faut porter remède à la situation particulière dans laquelle se retrouve l'islam en
              France du fait de la difficulté qu'il éprouve à s'organiser dans la norme qui est celle des grands cultes, notamment en se dotant d'instances
              représentatives. "
           </str>
         – <arr name="tag_annotation">
              <str>maniere_dire_locuteur_avant</str>
           </arr>
           <str name="url">2002-01-DOLLE-16026.html.txt.xml</str>
        </doc>
```

Table 1. The map-reduce functions 'mapper' and 'reducer' for important layers of the annotation and indexation processes. For example, for the task of segmentation, a map function is applied to each un-structured content for each file and generates a list of sentences. The reduce function in this case is built structured textual contents for each file. However, the algorithm is more interesting for the annotation process in where, a mapper handle the annotation process across all sentences of each structured content and the reducer aggregates the results to rebuilt a still structured content by enhanced by semantic annotation. For the indexation process, only the map function is used to parallelize and distribute the parsing and the collect from the annotated contents the necessarily information to inject in the index; the reduce function is represented by the identity.

task	input	mapper	reducer
Segmentation	unstructured	List(String filename, String contents) • List(List(String Sentences))	• Text text
annotation	structured	List(String SentParaSecText, String content) • List(List(int SentParaSecText, List(Annotation an-nots))	• List(Text text, List(Annotation annots))
indexation	structured	List(Text text, List(Annotation annots)) • List(Segment segs)	• Inverted index

to contain desired content or use a search engine to identify a suitable website to browse. Browsing is often used in combination with broad and simple textual queries.

In experience made about image browsing by Markkula and Sormunen (2000), it seems underline that searchers browsed because they wanted to avoid excluding potentially relevant images from the result set by formulating too narrow queries. According to Frost et al. (2000), users have expressed preference for multimode search, by combining both browse and query, since it provide alternate modes of access. Browsing annotated document with semantic and discourse categorizations provide a suitable alternative to a difficult query expression built with the query language described previously. Indexing annotated documents allows presenting to the end-user many criteria for browsing. Our experimentation allows four different angles for exploring a repository of textual content (Figure 8).

The first copy the traditional search by terms associated to the a particular textual segment (sentence, paragraph or title); for example a user can search a particular topic to find in a direct quotation, this is what it is shown when a user asks about a term *'islam'* in direct quotation. The second kind of navigation is defined through the *locutor tag cloud*, which lists all the locutors identified as argument of the direct quotation relation.

The third manner to browse the semantic index is to use the semantic map which depicted here as *annotation tag cloud*, which presents all annotations associated to the textual segments indexed as direct quotation. The last way to browse the semantic repository focuses to answer a question like "X SAYS Y", which X is representing a locutor and Y a topic localized as a term in the direct quotation as it is shown in Figure 9.

Searching by mining semantic categories involves modifications step by step to an initial query. So a user discovers results along his browsing activity on semantic and discourse annotations,

arguments of semantic relations (*locutor* and *topic* for a direct quotation, a *concept* and its *definition* for the point of view of the definition in texts, a *cause* and *effect* for the concern of the causality in texts, …)

FUTURE RESEARCH DIRECTIONS

The notion of relevance plays an extremely important role in Information Retrieval. The concept of relevance, while seemingly intuitive, is nevertheless quite hard to define, and even harder to model in a formal way when we deal with a semantic content indexation process. The intrinsic scoring for textual segments includes boosting weights for annotations assigned from general to specific values. So an annotation related to semantic category localized on the top of the semantic map, will have a boost value lower than another annotation associated to a bottom semantic category. In a near future, we'll test a new formalism for modeling relevance of a document based upon semantic content for queries from the linguistic knowledge of the semantic maps associated to the "point of views." The main distinguishing qualities of this formalism is to handle semantic discursive marks in indexed documents, to use the hierarchic structural organization of the semantic point of view and the associated semantic map and boost the quality for linguistic indicators (defined by linguistic experts) affects the general score for a textual segment.

The most common approach to evaluation within NLP is to compare machine output against human judgment. The only evaluation that we already realized is the comparison of the results of a traditional search engine and a prototype, we build, about the semantic notion of "definition" (Teissedre et al., 2008). A dual comparison was made between the relation *document-terms* in classical indexing process and *document-textual segment-terms* in our indexing methodology. The results between the Google 'define' and our

Figure 8. Graphical interface for semantic navigation through a repository of articles crawler from a French newspaper (le Monde Diplomatique). The repository counts 1176 textual annotated segments with the 'direct-quotation' point of view. Each textual segment is associated to a document (the article crawled). The interface also presents two tag clouds: one for semantic map (represented by all 'direct-quotation' annotations associated to the 1176 textual segments and another for some named entities identified as locators for the relation of direct quotation. Two text area are also available to cross a locutor with a topic contained in the direct quotation.

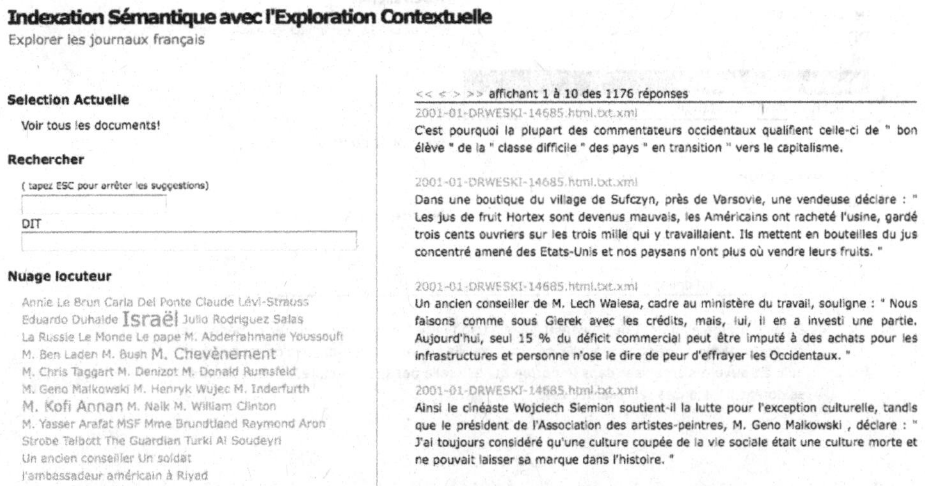

Indexation Sémantique avec l'Exploration Contextuelle

Explorer les journaux français

Selection Actuelle

Voir tous les documents!

Rechercher

(tapez ESC pour arrêter les suggestions)

DIT

Nuage locuteur

Annie Le Brun Carla Del Ponte Claude Lévi-Strauss Eduardo Duhalde Israël Julio Rodriguez Salas La Russie Le Monde Le pape M. Abderrahmane Youssoufi M. Ben Laden M. Bush M. Chevènement M. Chris Taggart M. Denizot M. Donald Rumsfeld M. Geno Malkowski M. Henryk Wujec M. Inderfurth M. Kofi Annan M. Naik M. William Clinton M. Yasser Arafat MSF Mme Brundtland Raymond Aron Strobe Talbott The Guardian Turki Al Soudeyri Un ancien conseiller Un soldat l'ambassadeur américain à Riyad le PDG de Vivendi-Universal le ministre argentin des affaires étrangères le ministre espagnol de l'intérieur le prince héritier une vendeuse

Nuage annotation

assertion_negative_avant attitude_locuteur_eralte_avant definition_locuteur_avant interlocution_appreciation_defavorable_avant interlocution_appreciation_favorable_avant interlocution_org_dialogue_avant interlocution_volonte_avant jugement_enonciateur_avant locuteur_appreciation_defavorable_avant locuteur_appreciation_favorable_avant locuteur_appreciation_neutre_avant maniere_dire_locuteur_avant org_discours_locuteur_avant propos_locuteur_evalue_avant volonte_locuteur_avant

<< < > >> affichant 1 à 10 des 1176 réponses

2001-01-DRWESKI-14685.html.txt.xml
C'est pourquoi la plupart des commentateurs occidentaux qualifient celle-ci de " bon élève " de la " classe difficile " des pays " en transition " vers le capitalisme.

2001-01-DRWESKI-14685.html.txt.xml
Dans une boutique du village de Sufczyn, près de Varsovie, une vendeuse déclare : " Les jus de fruit Hortex sont devenus mauvais, les Américains ont racheté l'usine, gardé trois cents ouvriers sur les trois mille qui y travaillaient. Ils mettent en bouteilles du jus concentré amené des Etats-Unis et nos paysans n'ont plus où vendre leurs fruits. "

2001-01-DRWESKI-14685.html.txt.xml
Un ancien conseiller de M. Lech Walesa, cadre au ministère du travail, souligne : " Nous faisons comme sous Gierek avec les crédits, mais, lui, il en a investi une partie. Aujourd'hui, seul 15 % du déficit commercial peut être imputé à des achats pour les infrastructures et personne n'ose le dire de peur d'effrayer les Occidentaux. "

2001-01-DRWESKI-14685.html.txt.xml
Ainsi le cinéaste Wojciech Siemion soutient-il la lutte pour l'exception culturelle, tandis que le président de l'Association des artistes-peintres, M. Geno Malkowski , déclare : " J'ai toujours considéré qu'une culture coupée de la vie sociale était une culture morte et ne pouvait laisser sa marque dans l'histoire. "

2001-01-DRWESKI-14685.html.txt.xml
Ancien dirigeant de Solidarité, M. Henryk Wujec résume : " La seule chose que veulent les dirigeants de l'Union, c'est la fermeture de la frontière (11). "

2001-01-DRWESKI-14685.html.txt.xml
Une paysanne de la région de Chelm s'écrie : " Et qui viendra acheter nos légumes quand la frontière sera fermée ? Je suis contre. Après tout, les Ruskis [terme populaire englobant les Biélorusses, les Russes et les Ukrainiens] sont plus proches de nous que les Allemands ; nous les comprenons. "

2001-01-JAMAI-14698.html.txt.xml
CONTRE toute attente, le 2 décembre 2000, M. Abderrahmane Youssoufi , socialiste, premier ministre du gouvernement du Maroc, a interdit " définitivement " trois hebdomadaires - Le Journal, Assahifa et Demain - pour avoir rendu publique une lettre que lui avait adressée, en 1974, une des figures emblématiques de la gauche marocaine, Mohammed " Fquih "

2001-03-GUEYRAS-15001.html.txt.xml
Catégorique, il nous a déclaré : " Le président était non seulement d'accord avec le projet de Meghri, mais il en était l'un des défenseurs les plus enthousiastes, allant même jusqu'à proclamer qu'il en était le véritable auteur. "

133

Figure 9. An example of a browsing by choosing a locutor (click on the locutor tag cloud); automatically only the textual segments containing 'Chevènement' as locutor and associated annotations (restricted tag cloud) are shown. Within a text area, a user types a topic available as a term in the textual content of direct quotation (6 textual segment containing 'islam' as a topic). The semantic content browser displays only the answers for this query.

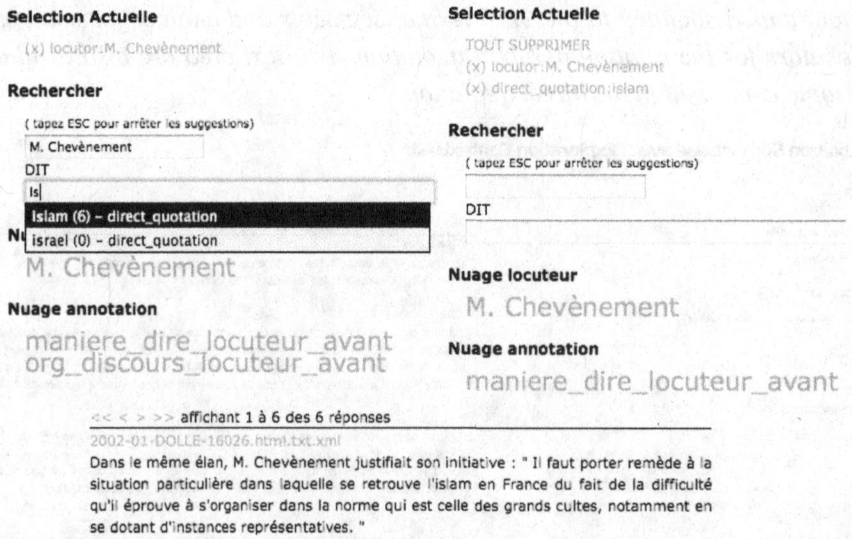

prototype for definition retrieval show that the prototype answers with more textual segments contained in documents indexed with Google but not used by its 'define' meta-term. The growing system we are building for text mining and semantic indexation is going to be confronted a grown size of data regarding to the projects involving EXCOM and MOCXE. To respond to these new challenges, an important evaluation campaign for each point of a view:

1. **Direct quotation** with all archives of '*Le Monde Diplomatique*' and also by using a dual comparison between French and Arabic,
2. **Definition** with all French Wikipedia articles. A first work in English already started.

CONCLUSION

In this chapter, we began by discussing two paradigms; first about limitations of current search technology and proceeded to discuss text mining and NLP and how they could be used to annotate textual documents collections semantically, particularly with regard to discourse and semantic relations occurring within documents. The second paradigm discussed concerns the different processes used in NLP architecture. Some text annotation framework uses either a stratified layers involving morphological and syntactical analysis or learning machine model applied to annotated corpora realized by human experts. The approach described in this chapter underline the importance of using a textual analysis based on forms with a deep linguistic description for semantic categories like direct quotation and definition.

We then explained how semantic and discourse annotations could be used in search engines to overcome some of the problems identified in traditional information retrieval system, like important amount of responses and difficulties to met user's information need.

Finally, we focused our presentation on searching and browsing textual content by using semantic and discourse categories. Our purpose is to underline that this new kind of search engine allow a greater precision in search and can also link some entities (locators) occurring in documents to general ontologies represented by semantic maps. The index organized with semantic annotations allows browsing through different angles, including semantic maps, discourse annotations and named entities.

REFERENCES

Alrahabi, M. (2010). *EXCOM2: Plate-forme d'annotation automatique de catégories sémantiques: Conception, modélisation et réalisation informatique. Applications à la catégorisation des citations en arabe et en français* (Unpublished doctoral dissertation). University of Paris-Sorbonne, Paris, France.

Alrahabi, M., & Desclés, J.-P. (2008, August 25-27). Automatic annotation of direct reported speech in Arabic and French, according to semantic map of enunciative modalities. In *Proceedings of the 6th International Conference on Natural Language Processing*, Gothenburg, Sweden (pp. 41-51).

Ananiadou, S., Kell, D. B., & Tsujii, J. (2006). Text mining and its potential applications in systems biology. *Trends in Biotechnology, 24*(12). doi:10.1016/j.tibtech.2006.10.002

Carpineto, C., Osinski, S., Romano, G., & Weiss, D. (2009). A survey of Web clustering engines. *ACM Computing Surveys, 41*(3). doi:10.1145/1541880.1541884

Cimiano, P. (Ed.). (2006). *Ontology learning and population from text*. New York, NY: Springer.

Cunningham, H., Maynard, D., Bontcheva, K., & Tablan, V. (2002, July). GATE: A framework and graphical development environment for robust NLP tools and applications. In *Proceedings of the 40th Anniversary Meeting of the Association for Computational Linguistics*, Philadelphia, PA.

Desclés, J.-P. (1997). Systèmes d'exploration contextuelle. In Guimier, C. (Ed.), *Co-texte et calcul du sens* (pp. 215–232). Caen, France: Presses Universitaires de Caen.

Desclés, J.-P. (2008). Towards a bridge between cognitive linguistics and formal ontology. In *Proceedings of the Twenty First International Florida Artificial Intelligence Research Society Conference*, Coconut Grove, FL (pp. 18-20).

Djioua, B., & Desclés, J.-P. (2007). Indexing documents by discourse and semantic contents from automatic annotations of texts. In *Proceedings of the International Florida Artificial Intelligence Research Society Conference Special Talk "Automatic Annotation and Information Retrieval: New Perspectives."*

Djioua, B., García Flores, J. J., Blais, A., Desclés, J.-P., Guibert, G., & Jackiewicz, A. …Sauzay, B. (2006). EXCOM: an automatic annotation engine for semantic information. In *Proceedings of the International Florida Artificial Intelligence Research Society Conference* (pp. 285-290).

Frost, C. O., Taylor, B., Noakes, A., Markel, S., Torres, D., & Drabenstott, K. M. (2000). Browse and search patterns in a digital image database. *Information Retrieval, 1*(4), 287–313. doi:10.1023/A:1009979200555

Gangemi, A., Guarino, N., Masolo, C., Oltramari, A., & Schneider, L. (2002). Sweetening ontologies with DOLCE. In *Proceedings of the 13th International Conference on Knowledge Engineering and Knowledge Management. Ontologies and the Semantic Web* (pp. 166-181).

Kiryakov, A., Popov, B., Terziev, I., Manov, D., & Ognyanoff, D. (2004). Semantic annotation, indexing and retrieval. *Journal of Web Semantics: Science. Services and Agents on the World Wide Web*, *2*, 49–79. doi:10.1016/j.websem.2004.07.005

Konchady, M. (2008). *Building search applications. A practical guide to building search applications using open source software*. UK: Mustru.

Lenat, D., & Guha, R. V. (1990). *Building large knowledge-based systems: Representation and inference in the Cyc Project*. Reading, MA: Addison-Wesley.

Marchisio, G., Dhillon, N., Liang, J., Tusk, C., Koperski, K., & Nguyen, T. (2007). A case study in natural language based Web search. In Kao, A., & Poteet, S. R. (Eds.), *Natural language processing and text mining* (pp. 69–90). New York, NY: Springer. doi:10.1007/978-1-84628-754-1_5

Markkula, M., & Sormunen, E. (2000). End-user searching challenges indexing practices in the digital photograph archive. *Information Retrieval*, *1*(4), 259–285. doi:10.1023/A:1009995816485

Russel-Rose, T., & Stevenson, M. (2009). The role of natural language processing in information retrieval: Searching for meaning and structure. In Göker, A., & Davis, J. (Eds.), *Information retrieval, searching in the 21st century* (pp. 215–227). New York, NY: John Wiley & Sons. doi:10.1002/9780470033647.ch10

Teissedre, C., Djioua, B., & Desclés, J.-P. (2008). Automatic retrieval of definitions in texts, in accordance with a general linguistic ontology. In *Proceedings of the 21st International Florida Artificial Intelligence, Research Society Conference* (pp. 518-523).

KEY TERMS AND DEFINITIONS

Discourse: The discourse can be defined as a linguistic unit composed of more than a sentence (Z. Harris), a set of utterances (Foucault) or more recently as the linguistic of text. We consider the discourse analysis as related to the context, which can be modified during enunciation.

Contextual Exploration: A linguistic and computational method which states that semantic information associated to textual segments can be identified by linguistic primary marks (called indicators) and a set of clues that would help to handle their polysemy and indetermination.

Enunciation: The theory of the enunciation refers to a linguistic of I(JE) and YOU(TU), granting two enunciative parameters in the transmission of any message and presenting a dialogic role describable in the analysis of the activity dialog.

Metatext: means in this context, all structured discourse and semantic categories, identified automatically by linguistic rules.

Point of view: A point of view represents the cognitive operations provided by a user when he tries to identify relevant information by guided readings. He gives preferential processing to certain textual segments (sentences, titles or paragraphs).

Semantic category: A semantic organization of text is generally defined in opposition to a physical organization of a text. A semantic category is the information contains by a textual segment and left by the enunciator. For instance, this applicative relation defines the category "direct reported quotation": *SAY (SAYS (dictum) Enunciator) I.*

Semantic map: A linguistic ontology, which is comparable to Upper-Ontologies, used in the Web Semantic

Semantic search engine: A program that provides for users, semantic information build automatically by identifying semantic categories and which can answers queries like: *"Search direct quotations of X about Y?"* and *"Search definitions of a concept Z?"*

ENDNOTES

[1]   Metatext means in this context, all structured discourse and semantic categories, identified automatically by linguistic rules.

[2]   *What confirms without hesitation a senior official of the organization: "The WHO is in the middle of conflicts of interests... "*

Chapter 7
Semantic Models in Information Retrieval

Edmond Lassalle
Oranges Labs, France

Emmanuel Lassalle
Université Paris 7, France

ABSTRACT

Robertson and Spärck Jones pioneered experimental probabilistic models (Binary Independence Model) with both a typology generalizing the Boolean model, a frequency counting to calculate elementary weightings, and their combination into a global probabilistic estimation. However, this model did not consider indexing terms dependencies. An extension to mixture models (e.g., using a 2-Poisson law) made it possible to take into account these dependencies from a macroscopic point of view (BM25), as well as a shallow linguistic processing of co-references. New approaches (language models, for example "bag of words" models, probabilistic dependencies between requests and documents, and consequently Bayesian inference using Dirichlet prior conjugate) furnished new solutions for documents structuring (categorization) and for index smoothing. Presently, in these probabilistic models the main issues have been addressed from a formal point of view only. Thus, linguistic properties are neglected in the indexing language. The authors examine how a linguistic and semantic modeling can be integrated in indexing languages and set up a hybrid model that makes it possible to deal with different information retrieval problems in a unified way.

DOI: 10.4018/978-1-4666-0330-1.ch007

INTRODUCTION: USING SEMANTICS IN INFORMATION RETRIEVAL

Several tasks in IR are based on the common principle of content matching. This is not only apparent with search engines comparing a query with various documents of its database, but also in other major tasks such as document categorization (or clustering) and question/answering (QA). For example, in document categorization the content matching is operated between a document and the descriptive sections of a category system, and the document is then assigned to the best matched category. Another example is making an abridgment of a document: this can be done by splitting the text in sentences and comparing them to the entire text, keeping a few of those that produce the best matches. However, the complexities of these several tasks are different:

- Documents categorization is simpler to achieve than clustering.
- Documents retrieval is easier than question/answering (QA).
- Within the QA task, simplest systems deal with factual information (the height of a monument, the capital of a country) whereas most complex state of the art systems try to answer the questions of why or how.
- Extracting the answer in QA systems requires a filtering mechanism and selecting sentences of the documents so as to make an automatic abridgment. On the other hand, the difficulty of QA lies in mapping the sentence and the question opposed to mapping the sentence and the document in an automatic abridgment. Knowing that a question provides less information than a document, we can imagine the difficulty.

These different tasks are processed by specific implementations that are not reusable from one task to another. If we want to unify the processes for all those tasks in a reusable mechanism, we must define a generic model that allows a wide coverage of all the tasks. The difference in complexity between two similar tasks lies in the fact that one requires a deeper "semantic analysis" than the other, as we can see below:

- If we compare clustering to categorization, the second has the outset of a pre-computed classification nomenclature and predefined comparison criteria for each section. Categorizing a document consists in extracting from the document elements allowing the comparison with those aforementioned criteria. On the other hand, clustering has to build a classification nomenclature beforehand and calculate for each section the characteristics of comparison. This is done by analyzing a referential corpus of documents that corresponds to a prior semantic processing.

- While QA task has to supply one or several concise answers to a composed question, "search engine" task returns a list of documents to a query, in responsibility for the user to view each document and estimate its relevance to her/his query. A QA system may be seen as a search engine coupled with a post-processing system: the question is initially treated as a query by the search engine component; and the contents of documents listed as reply are then parsed to extract salient elements that may be possible answers to the question. The complexity in this case is due to a subsequent a posteriori semantic processing.

If we were able to address the highest semantic analysis we would obtain a generic model and then we would be able to deal with IR problems in a unified way. The difficulty of semantic approaches is due to the high cost of the manual construction of large knowledge databases. Sometimes, for simple semantic tasks, resorting to manual analyses (such as editorial functions) or semi-automatic processing (such as statistical analysis of queries logs and manual revision) will improve the quality of a search engine. Thus, a fully automatic semantic processing has a real interest only if we manage to build automatically large knowledge databases in a reasonable cost.

Exploiting the collaborative knowledge databases available on the Internet is a rather good alternative as far as it is validated by experimental implementations. However, the problem remains when passing to full-scale applications: harmonizing or completing collaborative databases becomes essential to cover the needs of real applications. Ad hoc methods have been developed to merge databases with heterogeneous formats and contents. Yet, because of the explosion of such resources, automatic methods are needed, which leads inevitably to a classic machine learning problem.

Instead of using collaborative databases, economical solutions consist in directly resorting to learning techniques on text corpora dedicated to the applications. The key to these approaches is to define an adequate notion of semantic for information retrieval, which could be inferred from plain text with a good scalability.

CHAPTER ORGANIZATION AND STRUCTURE

In the first section, we will remind the basics of IR. We will see how the inverted file provides a solution for a technical problem (processing a large amount of data and a high number of queries) in IR, but also how it sets conditions on documents and queries processing (description language / query language). This data representation is central to the Boolean model, which combines the inputs of the inverted file by means of logical operators.

In the second section we will make a review of the known state-of-the-art approaches to indexing. We will focus on probabilistic models, where semantic processing underlies but is never clarified. In this new light, we will examine how

to translate a document in an explicit semantic representation.

Considering the fact Boolean model provides an unordered set of documents as an answer, we will see how the transition to probabilistic models, starting with the binary independence model (BIM), makes it possible to sort the returned documents according to their "relevance." We will next see how the problem of defining a descriptors language has been addressed, introducing an approach for automatically indexing documents by a 2-Poisson law modeling of the terms frequencies. After that we will examine other aspects of probabilistic models for information retrieval, taking into account new information on documents (term frequencies, document length) with the Okapi model, and secondly by removing constraints on the query language using language models. Finally, we will see how semantic models allow grouping documents by "topics" and therefore allow searches taking into account the similarities of meaning, without needing the exact terms of the query to appear in the documents.

In the third section of the chapter, we propose our semantic model for which we have defined a notion of "explicit concept". In state-of-the-art models, an index basically corresponds to a word of a document (or an associated keyword) whereas in semantic models it corresponds to a concept. The main issue of semantic models is to analyze every word of a document within its context and translate it into a concept, which is the meaning of the word. Our model addresses this by coupling a shallow linguistic analysis (to tokenize the text in sense units) with a distributional model (to represent the concepts). We begin the section explaining how a linguistic analysis of the documents can contribute to the translation task, and why a shallow linguistic analysis is preferable to deep analyses when coupled to machine learning techniques in processing text corpora. We evaluate our model experimentally in two stages: first we cluster concepts to obtain semantics categories, and then we classify documents in these categories by using conceptual representations of the documents.

1. IR BASICS

1.1. About the Inverted File

The simplest way to design a query/documents system consists in returning the set of all the documents satisfying the query, where the sense of "satisfy" must be clarified. We shall see a more concrete definition in the next sub-section, but for the moment we focus on the global architecture of the system.

We might first think that it is sufficient to compare each query to all the documents of the database and select only those that satisfy the above mentioned criterion of satisfiability: an example of such query/documents system is in Unix systems with the function grep *<regular expression> <files list>*, where:

- The query corresponds to the first argument of the function:*<regular expression>* which describes a set of strings in a syntax facilitating string matching.
- The comparison is the operation allowing identifying in a file a sub-string corresponding to *<regular expression>*.
- The database matches the files given by *<files list>*.

Such a system must be able to process a potentially high number of requests in a short time, which can be achieved only with pre-calculations.

First, the inverted file only appears as a technical solution to this problem, because such a data representation is not necessary in the logical architecture of an IR system.

However, in real large scale applications processing a high number of queries, retrieving documents according to this principle is not viable: the database being millions or even billions

of documents, it would not be realistic to rescan it entirely for every new query, even with high computing capacities. With the inverted file, the system avoids that.

Nevertheless using an inverted file is not neutral in modeling the IR system. It induces several constraints (which we will have to always keep in mind):

- At the level of the representations of the documents (language of descriptors) and
- At the level of the formulations of the queries (query language).

To speed up the search process, lists of documents are computed and stored in advance, each list corresponding to the answer to a given query. If all the queries could be covered by such lists, then we would have a complete system returning a pre-established list to any query. However in most applications, the set of all possible queries is very large-sized, even infinite (for instance if queries are formulated in natural language), so we cannot imagine storing it nor computing it due to the limitations of computing capacities. Therefore, we can only store a limited subset of queries called "elementary queries" and their associated lists.

A new question arises: how do we take into account non-elementary queries for which the associated documents list has not been stored? Ideally, we should be able to compute the lists for non-elementary queries from the basic data. In that case, the computation would be made as follows:

- Identification of the elementary queries necessary to create the non-elementary query,
- Identification of lists related to previously identified elementary queries,
- Construction of a new list from the lists identified in the previous step.

In practice, non-elementary queries cannot all be taken into account. This leads to make the following distinctions:

- Valid queries which can be processed from elementary queries and providing as result a list of documents,
- Valid queries involving an empty list of documents,
- Invalid queries for which there are no elementary queries to make the calculation.

Note: Valid queries leading to an empty list can produce a new non-empty list if the database has meanwhile been enriched with new documents. On the other hand, the invalid queries do not lead to any results in all cases.

1.2. Preponderance of Human Intervention in the Context of a Small Database and Low Computing Power: The Boolean Model

Here we introduce a simple definition of "satisfiability": consider we have some basic terms or keywords that we use in documents description and in queries formulation. We say that a document satisfies an elementary query that is containing only one keyword, if the document is indexed by this keyword (for the moment we do not discuss how the indexation is done). This is the basis of the Boolean model: each keyword is a Boolean variable and each document instantiates all the variables (with value 1 if the keyword is in the document, 0 otherwise). A query is then given as a logical function over the same Boolean variables, basically a combination of the variables with "and", "or" and "no" operators. All the documents satisfying the logical function are returned in response to the query.

Retrieving those documents in the database can be done efficiently with the inverted file. Table 1 and Table 2 illustrate the process.

Table 1. Four documents, indexed by a set of three keywords, stored in a Boolean matrix

	Dog	Cat	Mouse
d1	0	0	1
d2	0	1	1
d3	1	1	1
d4	1	0	0

Table 2. The inverted file is the transpose of that matrix

	d1	d2	d3	d4
Dog	0	0	1	1
Cat	0	1	1	0
Mouse	1	1	1	0

- Boolean operations can be done using their dual set operations on the row of this matrix: "and" is "intersection", "or" is "union" and "not" is "complementation". For example, retrieving the documents satisfying the query "dog or (cat and mouse)" is done by taking the intersection of row 2 and 3 and the union on the result with row 1. That produces the set of documents {d2, d3, d4}.

In the boolean model, while the computation of the answer lists is simple, the task of indexing documents by keywords remains to be done. For instance, this can be manual indexation achieved by a human agent (e.g., a librarian) who describes each document with topic keywords. But this "semantic analysis" of each document cannot be trivially automatized to process a large-scaled database. As for the query, it can be only made of known topic keywords, and only a specialist can achieve a document retrieval, using the appropriate vocabulary. Now we are going to examine another manner of indexing the documents, simply by using the terms they contain.

1.3. The Need for Automation: Increasing Volume and Computing Power

If we take the terms observed in our documents as keywords, it is very easy to create an automatic indexing of the documents. First, documents are represented by a Boolean vector indicating the keywords they contain: this is the bag-of-word model of documents. Keywords are spotted in each document, producing a sparse matrix like the first of the example, and then the inverted file is computed by transposing this matrix. Current computing power is sufficient to handle millions of documents and terms by this method. Although it is the most straightforward method to achieve total automation, it is certainly not the most efficient to retrieve documents for two reasons. First, there is no real semantic processing of the document: synonymy nor polysemy are taken into account, and all the terms of a document are put at the same level while some are more informative than others. Second, the Boolean model returns the unordered set of all the documents satisfying a Boolean combination of keywords.

If the database is huge, this set can also be huge and at some point, it grows too large to be browsed by the user. This means there is a need to organize retrieved documents in a "structured answer" or at least to sort them in order to show at the top of a list documents that best corresponds to the expectations of the user.

For the Boolean model, a collation of output documents may help to structure the answer, but it would remain unrefined or require a heavy calculation to be put on-line: as the model operates in a binary manner, a Boolean collation would prioritize a group of documents with regard to another group, and continue by successive refinement until we obtain a classification tree. But the task of selecting documents within that structure is still left to the user.

Example of collation by Boolean operators:

A query "dog or cat or horse" can lead to the following classification:

- The documents that contain dog and cat and horse
- And among the remaining documents, documents containing dog and cat
- And among the remaining documents, documents containing dog and horse
- And among the remaining documents, documents containing dog
- And among the remaining documents, documents containing cat and horse
- And among the remaining documents, documents containing cat
- And finally documents containing horse

For a fine classification, adding a weighting system allows ordering documents directly, avoiding successive 2-2 comparisons. To achieve this as an extension of the Boolean retrieval model with the bag-of-words document model, we can replace the binary values (presence or absence of a term in the document) by real numbers corresponding to the relatedness of the terms to the document. Each document of the database is then represented by a vector, the components of which correspond to the weights of the terms in the document. Those weights can be calculated in various ways (for example, the TF-IDF weighting uses the frequencies of the terms in the documents and in the corpus) (Salton, 1983) as well as the rank of documents (in a vector space model, similarities can be computed using cosine).

Using all the words of all the documents as an extended indexing language, and new methods for classifying or sorting automatically retrieved documents, allow to set up systems free from the intervention of human experts. Henceforth, a user needs not be a specialist of the query language to achieve a search, nor have skills to sort an unordered set of returned documents returned.

In this chapter, we will focus on probabilistic approaches for classifying and sorting documents.

The next section introduces the state of the art probabilistic models for IR.

2. STATE OF THE ART IN PROBABILISTIC IR

2.1. The BIM Model: First Probabilistic Model for Document Retrieval

As seen above, in the Boolean model the answer to the query is an unordered set of documents. When the database gets bigger, this set can become too big to be analyzed by a human agent. An approach to this problem consists in ranking the documents (with regards to the query). This can be done, for instance, by modeling the ranking in a probabilistic way. The binary independence model (BIM) (Robertson, 1977) is among the first of such probabilistic approaches in IR. Transforming the Boolean model into a probabilistic one (by representing the fact that a document is returned or not with a random variable) is not sufficient to obtain a ranking of the documents, and the key idea of the BIM model is to introduce a random variable named "relevance" which models the fact that a document corresponds or not to a query. In this model it is not only decided whether a document is returned in response, but also how relevant it is with respect to the query.

Concretely, another variable D ranging over all the documents is also added: the relevance is a binary variable R such that, when conditioned on $"D = d"$, it takes value 1 if d is "adequate" to answer the query, and 0 if not. One can notice that, because the relevance is a single variable, it has a rather vague interpretation if not seen as a technical artifice permitting to rank documents: probability $P\left(R = 1 \middle| D = d\right)$ determines d's rank in the answer list. However, in the BIM the score obtained by a document is less important than the final global ranking of the retrieved documents

given the query: at last the user should find by herself/himself what is adequate in the top of an ordered documents list.

The BIM for documents retrieval is set up under two simplifying assumptions:

1. Retrieving a document or not is decided independently from the other documents.
2. The rank of a document is evaluated independently from the others.

Now let us detail the functioning of the BIM. As for the Boolean model, we consider that the documents have already been indexed (automatically or not) by a set of known keywords. We are given a query q, fixed in all the following, which means that the calculations will depend on it. There is no restriction on the query structure (because the relevance notion will hide it), but we can still see it as a logical function on keywords like in the Boolean model. The probability of "being relevant (on the query) with a document d" is denoted by $P\left(R \middle| D = d\right)$. Even though R is a binary variable, we will refer to "the relevance of document d" in this case.

As we do not want the answer to contain too many irrelevant or weakly related documents, not all the documents will be returned in the sorted list, but only a part of them. It is possible to measure the quality of the returned set of documents by estimating the error it introduces. Given a document, we define an "error probability" as:

$$P\left(error \middle| D = d\right) = \begin{cases} P(R|D=d) \text{ if d is not returned} \\ P(notR|D=d) \text{ if d is returned} \end{cases}$$

That means "relevant but not returned" and "returned but not relevant" documents are counted as errors. Then the overall error is given by the sum rule:

$$P\left(error\right) = \sum_d P\left(error \middle| D = d\right) P\left(D = d\right),$$

and is minimized if we minimize the

$P\left(error\middle|D=d\right)$ as much as possible (observe that it can be done independently for all the documents).

One can show that the rule "return d if $P(R\middle|D=d) > P(not\ R\middle|D=d)$" minimize this overall error (Ripley, 1996).

There arises the problem of estimating the probability $P\left(R\middle|D=d\right)$. This will be done by using the two simplifying assumptions above and a new strong hypothesis: the independence of term occurrences in the documents and in the query.

First, Bayes theorem is applied to $P\left(R\middle|D=d\right)$ and $P\left(not\ R\middle|D=d\right)$:

$$\begin{cases} P\left(R\middle|D=d\right)=\dfrac{P\left(D=d\middle|R\right)P\left(R\right)}{P\left(D\right)} \\ and \\ P\left(not\ R\middle|D=d\right)=\dfrac{P\left(D=d\middle|not\ R\right)P\left(not\ R\right)}{P\left(D\right)} \end{cases}$$

- Second, to get rid of the marginal probability of D, we introduce the odds of the same events, which is monotonous in $P\left(R\middle|D=d\right)$ and then conserve the ranking of the documents according this probability. The retrieving rule becomes "return d if $O\left(R,d\right)>1$".

- Third, as we are only interested in ranking retrieved documents, we remove the prior probabilities $P\left(R\right)$ that do not vary with d and obtain a score equivalent to the odds:

$$S\left(d\right)=\frac{P\left(D=d\middle|R\right)}{P\left(D=d\middle|not\ R\right)}.$$

- Fourth, as we have modeled the documents in a Boolean way, we can see D as an joint variable over all Boolean variables associ-

ated to the keywords. Then, we use the hypothesis of independence of term occurrences to decompose the calculation of the resulting joint distribution. At this point, we set the variable D to a given value d.

- The same calculation will be done for all the documents. We write $x_i=1$ if the term is a descriptor of d, and $x_i=0$ otherwise.

- Assuming that the probability that a term t_i appears in any relevant (resp. non-relevant) document is p_i (resp. q_i), we obtain products of independent Bernoulli trials:

$$P\left(D=d\middle|R\right)=\prod_{i=1}^{T}P_i^{x_i}\left(1-p_i\right)^{1-x_i}$$ where T is the number of all keywords/terms we dispose of.

Fifth, passing to the logarithm to simplify a little more, we get:

$$\log\left(P\left(D=d\middle|R\right)\right)=\sum_{i=1}^{T}x_i\log\left(p_i\right)+(1-x_i)\log(p_i)$$

and

$$\log\left(P\left(D=d\middle|not\ R\right)\right)=\sum_{i=1}^{T}x_i\log\left(q_i\right)+(1-x_i)\log(q_i),$$
and then

$$\log\left(S\left(d\right)\right)=\sum_{i=1}^{T}x_i\log\left(\frac{p_{i(1-q_i)}}{q_i\left(1-p_i\right)}\right)+\sum_{i=1}^{T}\log\left(\frac{1-p_i}{1-q_i}\right)$$

- Sixth, in the last formula the second sum does not depend on document d because it contains no variable x_i. The ranking stays unchanged if we remove this constant sum. It remains to estimate the probabilities p_i and q_i so as to calculate the final score. Here comes the main problem of the BIM: it is required to know the relevance of the documents to estimate these probabilities.

Table 3. Counting table giving a frequentist estimation

	Documents containing t_i	Documents not containing t_i	
Relevant Documents	r_i	$n - r_i$	N
Non Relevant Documents	$R_i - r_i$	$N - R_i - n + r_i$	N − n
	R_i	$N - R_i$	N

If we suppose we do, we can give a frequentist estimation by using Table 3.

The estimation of the different probabilities is given as follows:

$$p_i = P\left(t_i \in D | R\right) = \frac{r_i}{n}$$

$$1 - p_i = P\left(t_i \notin D | R\right) = \frac{n - r_i}{n}$$

$$q_i = P\left(t_i \in D | not\, R\right) = \frac{R_i - r_i}{N - n}$$

$$1 - q_i = P(t_i \notin D | not\, R) = \frac{N - R_i - n + r_i}{N - n}$$

Then the final score after removing constant terms is given by:

$$\sum_{i=1}^{T} x_i log\left(\frac{p_{i(1-q_i)}}{q_i\left(1 - p_i\right)}\right) = \sum_{i=1}^{T} x_i w_i$$

where,

$$w_i = log\left(\frac{p_{i(1-q_i)}}{q_i\left(1 - p_i\right)}\right) = log\left(\frac{\frac{r_i}{n - r_i}}{\frac{R_{i-r_i}}{N - R_i - n + r_i}}\right)$$

which amounts to giving a certain weight to every term in the document. During the esti-

mate of these, w_i we may use smoothing methods to avoid zero values, for example:

$$w_i = log\left(\frac{\frac{r_{i+0.5}}{n - r_i + 0.5}}{\frac{R_{i-r_i} + 0.5}{N - R_i - n + r_i + 0.5}}\right)$$

Now the fundamental question is: how do we know in advance the relevance of a document given a query, when relevance is (part of) what we want to determine? We absolutely need some values for p_i and q_i to compute the ranking. There are different approaches to the problem: Croft and Harper (1979) eliminate it by setting all p_i to 0.5 and, by supposing relevant documents are a very small portion of the total database, and they approximate q_i by $\frac{R_i}{N}$, which amounts to saying that we do not have any information about relevance to estimate the probabilities.

An interactive method proposed by Greiff (1998) consists in iteratively asking the preferences of the user to estimate the probabilities p_i and q_i: after a first ranking, the user gives back his preferences, which will help to reorder the documents. This operation is repeated several times. The human partially solve the problem of estimating the probabilities, but the resulting system requires external knowledge and is not fully automatic.

Note that in the BIM model, the estimate of the probabilities is relative to a given query, and can be fully automated only under the simplifying assumptions that eliminate information on the relevance itself.

To end this subsection, let us call back the different assumptions of the BIM, discuss them and see when they become problematic:

1.   Retrieving a document or not is decided independently from the other documents. This does not take into account potential relations

existing between documents. Moreover, the retrieving rule of the BIM requires knowing the relevance in advance (as it is required to estimate the probabilities).

2. The relevance of a document does not depend on that of other documents, so the rank of a document is evaluated independently from the rest. This makes the computation easy, but rather imprecise compared to a hypothetical global ranking. Evaluating the relevance may be improved if we have some prior information on it (for instance, the evaluation can be done iteratively).

3. The documents have a Boolean representation (presence or absence of terms), which induces all the terms have the same importance and leads to same problems encountered by the Boolean model.

4. The relevance is a binary variable. It completely hides the query in ranking and retrieving documents. Thus, there is no restriction on the structure of the query. However, one can define the prior information about relevance as the result of a prior Boolean retrieval with regards to the query (when seeing the BIM as a proper extension of the Boolean Model).

5. The term occurrences are assumed to be independent in the document, which might cause imprecise estimations. To replace this simplifying hypothesis, Rijsbergen suggested modeling the dependencies between terms in a tree-like structure (van Rijsbergen, 1979).

2.2. Automated Indexing via 2-Poisson Modeling

Until now, in the Boolean model and in the BIM, we supposed that the task of indexing the documents was achieved beforehand. We saw it could be easily automated by modeling documents by bags of words, i.e., indexing the documents by all the terms they contain. But in that method, all the

terms have the same importance and there is no treatment of polysemy and synonymy: documents are indexed by terms that are not really representative and they are not indexed by terms that are representative but do not occurred. This hurts the quality of results. In this subsection, we consider a probabilistic indexing method that determines if a given term is a good keyword for a document according to its distribution in the document. The method makes the assumption that term distributions follow a 2-Poisson (Robertson, 1981): this mixture model can capture the fact that there are common words and specific terms in texts, and only specific terms should be considered as good keywords.

Consider a fixed term. The probability that t appears k times in a document can be modeled by a Poisson distribution:

$$P(freq(t, d) = k) = \frac{\lambda^k e^{-\lambda}}{k!}.$$

It has been observed that most common words follow this distribution, but specific words tend to appear grouped and thus to be more frequent in certain documents. We would like to retain t as keyword for a document only if it occurs more frequently in this document than in general. We distinguish two types of documents:

- Documents for which t is representative (that is, frequent). These documents deal with a topic related to t, they are called "elite documents" (and the set of elite documents is called the "elite set" for t and is denoted by E_t).

- Documents for which t is not representative and appears marginally. The probability of occurrence in those two groups are different, and a mixture of Poisson distributions can capture this variability. Then the probability of observing term t k times in any document d is: (see Exhibit 1) with

Exhibit 1.

$$P\big(freq(t,d)=k\big)=P\big(freq(t,d)=k\big|d\in E_t\big)P\big(d\in E_t\big)+P\big(freq(t,d)=k\big|d\notin E_t\big)P\big(d\notin E_t\big)$$

$$P\big(freq(t,d)=k\big)=\pi.\frac{\lambda_1^k e^{-\lambda_1}}{k!}+(1-\pi).\frac{\lambda_2^\lambda e^{-\lambda 2}}{k!}.$$

Exhibit 2.

$$P\big(d\in E_t\big|freq(t,d)=k\big)=\frac{P\big(freq(t,d)=k\big|d\,E_t\big).P\big(d\in E_t\big)}{P\big(freq(t,d)=k\big)}=\frac{\pi.\lambda_1^k.e^{-\lambda_1}}{\pi.\lambda_1^k.e^{-\lambda_1}+(1-\pi)\lambda_2^k e^{-\lambda_2}}$$

$\pi=P\big(d\in E_t\big),$ and where the Poisson parameters are such that: the first Poisson law corresponds to the distribution of t in elite documents and the second to the distribution in common documents.

The next step is to estimate the parameters λ_1 and λ_2 : if both values are close, then term is not specific enough to characterize one topic precisely. If parameters have very different values, t is a specific term and it can be used to index its corresponding elite documents.

With this model Robertson proposes an indexing procedure: "index d by terrm t only if $\beta>0$ where

$$\beta=P\big(d\in E_t\big|freq(t,d)=k\big)+\frac{\lambda_1-\lambda_2}{\sqrt{\lambda_1+\lambda_2}}$$

The probability appearing in calculation can be estimated by applying Bayes theorem: (see Exhibit 2).

The main problem of this method is estimating the Poisson parameters (and mixture weightings), which requires to have a prior knowledge on elite documents for all potential index terms.

This limits the applicability of the method because some human expertise is needed to identify elite documents. If β could be calculated easily, it could be used as a weight for t in document d: indexes would have more or less importance in documents, which should improve the precision of documents retrieval. The next subsection introduces a more applicable method for weighting indexes.

2.3. Okapi Models: Taking into Account Term Frequencies and Document Size

As an extension of the Boolean model, the BIM only takes into account the presence or absence of indexes in documents, but not their frequencies. The previous 2-Poisson model could be suitable for that task, but it is difficult to draw a fully automated weighting method for it. Spärck Jones' Okapi BM25 (Spärck Jones, Walker, & Robertson, 2000) uses term frequencies and document lengths to calculate weights on indexes. The main idea is to take term frequencies relatively to the document's length so as to estimate their importance within the document.

Exhibit 3.

$$P\left(freq\left(t_i,d\right)=tf\,\middle|R\right)=$$

$$P\left(freq\left(t_i,d\right)=tf\,\middle|d\in E_{t_i}\right)P\left(d\in E_{t_i}\,\middle|R\right)+P\left(freq\left(t_i,d\right)=tf\,\middle|d\notin E_{t_i}\right)P\left(d\notin E_{t_i}\,\middle|R\right)$$

$$P\left(freq\left(t_i,d\right)=tf\,\middle|not\ R\right)=$$

$$P\left(freq\left(t_i,d\right)=tf\,\middle|d\in E_{t_i}\right)P\left(d\in E_{t_i}\,\middle|not\ R\right)P\left(freq\left(t_i,d\right)=tf\,\middle|d\notin E_{t_i}\right)P\left(d\notin E_{t_i}\,\middle|not\ R\right)$$

Okapi model is quite similar to the BIM in the sense that documents are ranked on a relevance basis. It defines a family of scoring functions, the parameters of which depend on the importance we give to term frequencies and to document lengths. A setting of these parameters known to be very effective is that of the Okapi BM25.

First, let us recall the weighing scheme of the BIM, based on a prior knowledge of relevance:

$$w_i=\log\left(\frac{P\left(t_i\in d\middle|R\right).P\left(t_i\notin d\middle|not\ R\right)}{P\left(t_i\in d\middle|not\ R\right).P\left(t_i\notin d\middle|R\right)}\right)=\log\left(\frac{p_i\left(1-q_i\right)}{q_i\left(1-p_i\right)}\right)$$

To set up the Okapi model, we first replace term occurrences by term frequencies to obtain an alternative formulation of the weights

$$w_i=\log\left(\frac{P\left(freq\left(t,d\right)=tf\middle|R\right)P\left(freq\left(t,d\right)=0\middle|not\ R\right)}{P\left(freq\left(t,d\right)=tf\middle|not\ R\right)P\left(freq\left(t,d\right)=0\middle|R\right)}\right)$$

We can then reuse the 2-Poisson model for term frequencies. Remind that in this model the mixture coefficients were determined by the marginal probabilities of documents to be in the elite set. Now we suppose that and R are conditionally independent given the binary variable,

$\left\{d\in\dfrac{E_{t_i}}{d}\notin E_{t_i}\right\}$, which allows us to come back to the 2-Poisson distribution. After applying the sum rule, we obtain: (see Exhibit 3)

So we have two different mixtures with coefficients determined by $P\left(d\in E_{t_i}\middle|R\right)$ and $P\left(d\in E_{t_i}\middle|not\ R\right)$.

Substituting it in we obtain:

$$w_i=\log\left(\frac{\left(\alpha\lambda_1^{tf}e^{-\lambda_1}+\left(1-\alpha\right)\lambda_2^{tf}e^{-\lambda_2}\right)\left(\beta e^{-\lambda_1}+\left(1-\beta\right)e^{-\lambda_2}\right)}{\left(\beta\lambda_1^{tf}e^{-\lambda_1}+\left(1-\beta\right)\lambda_2^{tf}e^{-\lambda_2}\right)\left(\alpha e^{-\lambda_1}+\left(1-\alpha\right)e^{-\lambda_2}\right)}\right)$$

with λ_1 and λ_2 being the Poisson distributions parameters of t on the elite and non-elite documents, respectively.

Now there are four parameters per term to estimate, with the same difficulty encountered by the 2-Poisson model. The Okapi model proposes an easy-to-compute approximation of the weights using a formulation that have a similar behavior, specifically:

- It equals 0 if $tf=0$
- It is a increasing function of $tf=0$
- It has a maximum asymptotic value

Exhibit 4.

$$P\left(w_1 \ldots w_n\right) = P\left(w_1\right) P\left(w_2 \middle| w_1\right) \ldots P\left(w_k \middle| w_1 \ldots w_{k-1}\right) \prod_{i=k+1}^{n} P\left(m_i \middle| m_{i-k} \ldots m_{i-1}\right)$$

- It includes a factor of a "basic model" to indicate elitism.

The exact formulation is: $w_i = \dfrac{tf_i\left(k_1 + 1\right)}{k_1 + tf_i} \cdot w_0$ where tf_i is the frequency of term in document, d, k_1 is a constant parameter and the basic function of the model (that why Okapi is a family of scoring functions). The function can be improved by taking into account documents length, which is done by adding a factor expressing the relation between a document's length l_d and the average length. l_{avg}. The importance of this factor score is controlled by a parameter that can vary from 0 to 1 (from "ignored" to "total consideration").

The complete formulation of Okapi weighting is then: $w_i = \dfrac{tf_i\left(k_1 + 1\right)}{k_1\left[\left(1-b\right) + b\dfrac{l_d}{l_{avg}}\right] + tf_i} \cdot w_0$

In Okapi BM25 version, $w_0 = \log\left(\dfrac{N - n_{t_i} + 0.5}{n_{t_i} + 0.5}\right)$ where N is the total number of documents and n_{t_i} the number of documents containing term t, and the other parameters are heuristically determined. Despite this, it is currently one of the most competitive systems according to different benchmarking campaigns (e.g., TREC, http://trec.nist.gov/).

We have seen how probabilistic models evolved to become fully automated (with automatic indexing, retrieval and ranking). The Okapi BM25 is the accomplishment of this evolution; however there are still a lot of improvements to be done. Indeed, the models we presented do not take into account linguistic properties: we already mentioned problems with polysemy and synonymy, but it is a matter of semantics above all. Now, still adopting a probabilistic point of view, we are going to introduce state-of-the art methods that aim at modeling linguistic and semantic properties. We always have to keep in mind that those models must have a good scalability, which eliminates computationally costly models.

2.4. Language Models in IR

In principle, language models make it possible to estimate the coherence of a given sequence of words. The usefulness of such models is the ability to consider linguistic units together instead of making an assumption of independence of terms. With language models, we can both envisage an unrestricted query language (that is, queries in natural language) and go without the notion of relevance in documents retrieval. To avoid using relevance, we try to estimate the probability of having a request given a document, that is to say we assume that the user thinks of an ideal document (e.g., sentences or words it should contain) when he writes his query.

The simplest language models are Markovian. They estimate the joint probability of a sequence of words by assuming those have only local dependencies. The probability of a sequence is then given by (see Exhibit 4) and k is often set to values from 0 to 5 (higher values require too much data to estimate the distributions). Estimating the parameters of these conditional distributions only requires plain text and frequency counting, but it often suffers from sparse data: some sequences can have zero probabilities because they contain a sub-sequence that has not been observed during the estimate. Smoothing techniques are then necessary to address this problem (for instance: Laplace or Good-Turing smoothing, or interpolation).

Markovian models are compatible with a bag-of-words model of documents (set k to 0). In that case, the words order has no importance when calculating the joint probability, and the distribution can be seen as multinomial.

The probability of a document is given by:

$$P\left(d\right) = \frac{L_d!}{tf_{t_1,d}! \, tf_{t_2,d}! \dots tf_{t_M,d}!} P(t_1)^{tf_{t_1,d}} P\left(t_2\right)^{tf_{t_2,d}} \dots P\left(t_M\right)^{tf_{t_M,d}}$$

where $P\left(t_i\right)$ is the marginal probability of term, $\left(t_i\right)$, $f_{t_i,d}$ is the frequency of t_i in document d, $L_d = \sum_{i=1}^{M} tf_{t_i,d}$ is the length of d, and M is the number of different terms within d.

The basic model for using language models in IR is the query likelihood model. In this model, every document is associated to a document template M_d (that captures some of its properties like its length or the term frequencies). Like in previous probabilistic models, the purpose is to sort the documents in accordance with the query: documents are ranked by computing $P\left(d|q\right)$. To calculate this probability we use Bayes theorem: $P\left(d|q\right) = P\left(q|d\right)\dfrac{P\left(d\right)}{P\left(q\right)}$. The marginal $P\left(q\right)$ does not vary with d and it can be ignored for the ranking task. For simplicity, we will take a uniform distribution for the prior $P(d)$ (estimating priors is an entire problem). Only $P\left(q|d\right)$ remains to modeled. The easiest way is to take back the multinomial model of documents. We define the conditional probability as:

$$P\left(q|d\right) = \frac{L_d!}{tf_{t_1,q}! \, tf_{t_2,q}! \dots tf_{t_M,q}!} \prod_{t_i} \in V \; P\left(t_i|M_d\right)^{tf_{t_i,q}}.$$

To obtain a fully functional model, it remains to estimate the conditional. Variants of the query likelihood model can be found in Ponte and Croft's model (Ponte, 1998) and Hiemstra's model (2000).

To summarize, the purpose of language models is to introduce some linguistics properties in IR models. Yet, it only captures local linguistic properties, and all the semantic aspects of language are not taken into account. In the next sub-section, we will examine how the relation between words can be expressed through latent semantic. We will see how latent semantic classes (that produce different term distributions in documents) can improve accuracy in IR tasks.

2.5. Topic Models

The language models above only consider local properties to evaluate text coherence, but they make document retrieval possible without resorting to relevance. However, language is still not fully exploited, and progress can be achieved by exploiting the meaning of words. Here we focus on models that deal with semantics in a macroscopic way: topic models. Some are non-probabilistic (like LSA) (Landauer, 1998), but we only consider probabilistic models which are statistically well founded. The advantage of such models in IR is to be able to predict a query for a document (as in the query likelihood model), even if none of the query words occurs in the document. Below, we describe two generative models well suited for documents retrieval:

2.5.1. Probabilistic Latent Semantic Analysis

Probabilistic Latent Semantic Analysis (PLSA) (Hofmann, 1999) models word distributions in document as being derived from "topics". In this model, a topic induces a multinomial distribution over words (so the word order is ignored), and each word of a document arises from a mixture of topics, which represents the fact that several topics occur in the same document, all likely to produce

Figure 1. PLSA modeling a graphical model the joint probability of words and documents by passing through the topics

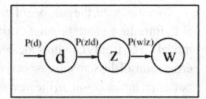
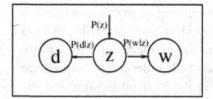

the same word, but with different frequencies. PLSA aims at modeling in a graphical model the joint probability of words and documents by passing through the topics, as illustrated in Figure 1.

Formally, given a set of documents , a set of words and a set of topics , we have (left part of the illustration): $P(w,d) = P(d)P(w|d)$ and $P(w,d) = P(d)P(w|d) = \sum_{z\in Z} P(w|z)P(z|d)$ or equivalently (right part of the illustration): $P(w,d) = \sum_{z\in Z} P(z)P(d|z)P(w|z)$.

As we can see on the plane notation, it is assumed that d and w are conditionally independent given. It is also assumed that the cardinality of is small compared to the number of documents or words. Estimating the probabilities for the latent variables z (that is, the parameters of the distributions) is achieved by maximizing the likelihood, using an Expectation-Maximization (EM) algorithm (Bishop, 2006):

- E-step:

$$P(z|d,w) := \frac{P(z)P(d|z)P(w|z)}{\sum_{z'\in Z} P(z')P(d|z')P(w|z')}$$

- M-step, where *n (d, w)* denotes the number of word w in document *d*:

$$P(w|z) := \sum_{d\in D} n(d,w)P(z|d,w)$$

$$P(d|z) := \sum_{w\in W} n(d,w)P(z|d,w)$$

$$P(z) := \sum_{d\in D}\sum_{w\in W} n(d,w)P(z|d,w)$$

Applying this model in document retrieval is straightforward, we first calculate the probability $P(z|q)$ of a topic given the query, and then the probability $P(d|z)$ of a document given the topic. Using a conditional independence assumption, we can then compute the probability $P(d|z)$ of a document given the query by summing out z. In this method, $P(d|z)$ and $P(w|z)$ are already known, and $P(z|q)$ is estimated using the EM algorithm. Finally, with PLSA's topics we can model the inherent meaning of the words, as we already said, in a macroscopic way. By cons, there is no way to calculate ratios of different topics in a document, so that the number of parameters is proportional to the number of documents, what causes problems of over-learning the corpus.

Latent Dirichlet Allocation

Latent Dirichlet Allocation (LDA) (Blei, 2003) extends PLSA in a more complete Bayesian model. The model is fully generative in the sense that it defines the process of writing a document from the beginning, what cannot be done with PLSA. The key is to add parameters and hyper

Figure 2. Latent Dirichlet Allocation (LDA) extending PLSA

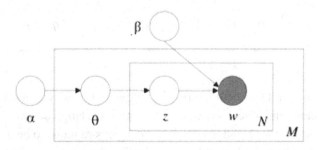

parameters in the graphical model to capture the possibility of different mixtures of topics for a document (that also significantly reduces the number of parameters compared to PLSA), as illustrated in Figure 2.

In this image, represents the number of documents and the number of words in a document. The generative process can then be described basically in three steps. In the model, documents are represented by mixtures over latent topics and topics by distributions over words. The process of generating a document is as follows:

1. The document's size is drawn from a Poisson distribution. $N \sim Poisson(\lambda)$.

2. To the document corresponds a mixture of topics represented by a multinomial over topics, the parameter of which follows a Dirichlet distribution:

    $Parameter\ \theta \sim Dir(\alpha)$

3. After the parameter has been defined, for each N words w_n : a topic is selected as $z_n \sim multinomial(\theta$, then a word w_n is produced with probability $P(w_n|z_n, \beta)$ having a multinomial distribution.

Notice that, w_n is drawn from a multinomial distribution due to its representation as a vector (with component i equals to 1 if w_n is the ith word of a given vocabulary, and 0 if not).

In the model, α and β are hyper-parameters, and θ and z are latent variables such that:

The k-dimensional variable $\theta = (\theta_1, ..., \theta_k)$ follows a Dirichlet distribution which has finite sufficient statistics, and which is the conjugate prior to the multinomial distribution (that allows applying Bayes theorem in good conditions). Let us recall the formulation of Dirichlet distribution:

$$P(\theta|\alpha) = \frac{\Gamma\left(\sum_{i=1}^{k} \alpha_i\right)}{\prod_{i=1}^{k} \Gamma(\alpha_i)} \theta_1^{\alpha_1 - 1} ... \theta_k^{\alpha_k - 1}$$

- The k-dimensional variables $z = (z_1, ..., z_n)$ follow a multinomial with parameter

$$\theta : P\left(z_n^1 = x_1, ..., z_n^k = x_k \middle| \theta\right) = \frac{k!}{x_1! ... x_k!} x_1^{x_1} ... x_k^{x_k}$$

It is assumed that k, that is the number of topics, is known in advance and fixed. Given the settings of α and β, the joint distribution of θ, z, and w (with $z_1 = (z_1, ..., z_N)$ and $w = (w_1, ..., w_N)$) is given by (see Exhibit 5) for the unique i such that $z_n^i = 1$. The fact that there is no order in the calculation comes from a conditional independence assumption, justified by the hypothesis that topics are exchangeable (in the probabilistic sense of

Exhibit 5.

$$P(\theta, z, w \mid \alpha, \beta) = P(\theta \mid \alpha) \prod_{n=1}^{N} P(z_n \mid \theta) P(w_n \mid z_n, \beta) \ \ where \ \ P(z_n \mid \theta) = \theta_i$$

the word) within the document. De Finetti's representation theorem states that exchangeable variables behave like independent and identically distributed variables when conditioned on a certain parameter drawn from a certain distribution. Integrating over θ and summing out z gives the probability of a sequence of words:

$$P(\theta, z, w \mid \alpha, \beta) = P(\theta \mid \alpha) \prod_{n=1}^{N} P(z_n \mid \theta) P(w_n \mid z_n, \beta)$$

Now, the inference of θ and z values given a document cannot be computed in closed form. Because the exact inference is intractable, we have to resort to approximation methods (several methods can be applied e.g., variational Bayes, Gibbs sampling, expectation propagation) (Griffiths, 2004; Minka, 2002). Besides, the estimate of parameters α and β, can be performed by an EM algorithm. Finally, the model can be used in IR the same way PLSA is used.

Before going into our own work, let us conclude this long description of the state of the art in probabilistic models in IR. Probabilistic models have been set up to address major problems in IR, such as ranking/classification in documents retrieval and indexing. Taking into account various properties of documents like term frequencies, size of the documents, language local structure and topics made it possible to automate and improve the accuracy of documents retrieval from the early beginning (indexing) to the final results (ranking/classification). Besides, the probabilistic aspects of those models are that they support well scalability and can be used on very large databases. Finally, we described the evolution of semantic processing from the early problem of choosing

indexes for documents to their classification in topics, via languages models (or text models). Yet, progress remains to be done: it is still possible to refine the semantic aspects of the models, which is our proposal in the next section. By coupling shallow linguistic processing and probabilistic modeling, we will design a model that is both more accurate in semantic processing and scalable on very large databases.

3. SEMANTIC MODELING

In this section, we describe a method to interpret each word of a document (or broader units) as a concept. Context analysis is necessary because a word can potentially be mapped to several senses. Analyzing context requires some yardsticks to compare contexts together, but those yardsticks are not explicitly mentioned in the documents we analyze: they must be acquired in another way. Linguistic analysis is well suited to do that because it provides a priori yardsticks. However, state of the art in linguistic processing is not fully applicable: given that the analysis of only one sentence can take several minutes, we can imagine the difficulty to process large amounts of data such as text corpora to be indexed. Moreover, it is not clear how to take ambiguities into account.

Here we propose a linguistic and semantic probabilistic model that is motivated by computational constraints and applicableness (one has to always consider that the purpose is to fulfill IR tasks). It exploits information redundancy in large amounts of data by statistical analyses.

One can consider that a model (and the computer programs) performs a semantic processing if it deals explicitly with

- Objects representing meaning (i.e., concepts) and
- Relations between these objects (i.e., semantic relations).

However there is no shared definition of the notions of concepts and relations between concepts, given numerous existing and divergent approaches (Lehmann, 1992). As a first approximation, one can distinguish epistemological approaches and more utilitarian approaches where the purpose of semantics is to allow the machine to solve specific problems. We place ourselves in this second perspective, with applications in IR. The availability of large text corpora in this area encourages a statistical approach *a priori*.

Concepts and semantic relations can be fitted out with statistical properties, but that will be a semantic modeling only if objects and relations are made explicit in the calculations. Conversely, statistical models are not semantic models if concepts or semantic relations are not made explicit. This is the case with topics models (LSA, PLSA, LDA) where concepts are latent whereas vectorial (or probabilistic) properties of co-occurrence between documents and index-words reflect underlying semantic properties.

For instance, in formal models a single index can refer to the word "bank" whatever its actual meaning. Then, latent semantic makes it possible to refine the "macroscopic sense" of the word (as "financial institution" or "bank of a river") according to the category of the document. In semantic models the sense of "bank" should be directly inferred rather from its usage at the sentence level.

The differences between categories in formal models and concepts in semantic models concern:

- **Granularity:** in practice there are tens of categories whereas the number of concepts

matches approximately the number of words (hundreds of thousands to millions).

- **Structuring**:(establishing relations between entities, that is categories or concepts): for a low number of categories, structuring leads to a low improvement, whereas structuring concepts in semantic networks makes the process more efficient. The key is to be able to build automatically these large networks.
- **Encapsulation:** document categorization methods from formal models can be applied to concepts to create "semantic domains". In return, this categorization can help to classify the documents.

Introducing concepts and semantic relations in practical applications will require two calculation mechanisms:

- The first one to translate the observed text form in a semantic form, usually in the form of a graph. In an open textual domain where the number of possible sentences is theoretically infinite, a mechanism to analyze patterns is required to deduce the semantic representation from the text form. This must be done by memorizing a limited repository of semantic descriptions.
- The second, related to the application, is a program that takes as input the semantic form and produces results expected by the application (e.g., document retrieval). This second mechanism is specific to the application, and we will discuss that point only within the framework of IR.

Translating textual forms to semantic forms encounters two technical difficulties:

- The repository of semantic descriptions is a knowledge database, the size of which can be very important in some applications. Constructing the knowledge database, adapting it to each application, and maintaining it can be prohibitively expensive if the work is done manually. The challenge is then to use a construction based on automatic learning techniques from text corpora. The first difficulty with this latter approach is the ability to handle large amounts of data coming from a training corpus. The second difficulty relates to the quality of expected results and their adequacy to address the problem.

- The second technical difficulty is the translation of text forms into semantic forms. It usually resorts to a linguistic processing that requires prior constructions of data (lexicons, grammars) and resolving ambiguities when fine-grained results are expected from the processing.

The central issue therefore relates to the choice of a semantic model which is relevant for the applicative component and facilitates the transformation of a text representation into a semantic representation. To make scaling tractable, and to make easy the adjustment of the data to the specificity of each application (wide coverage, varying language levels, specialized vocabulary, terminology ...), a complete automation of the acquisition of linguistic data is preferred.

3.1. Modeling Semantic

Two examples below illustrate the difficulty of automation when using a "traditional" linguistic processing to transform the text into a semantic representation. This will argue in favor of a semantic model specifically designed for IR. In the first case, acquiring semantic and phrase-structured grammar rules from corpora requires to stochastize the production rules and to adapt the Markov model to context-free grammars (Inside-Outside algorithm (Lari & Young, 1990, 1991) is today one of the most advanced, however without reaching an acceptable operational level for our task). In

the second case, lexicalization of grammars can simplify the production rules, but the problem is deferred to lexical description, which involves costly annotations of corpora, and thereby reduces the interest of the approach.

3.2. Phrase Structure Grammars

The most suited method to translate automatically sentences into their semantic representation proceeds by decompositional analysis.

Decompositional analysis assumes that there are units of translation at the level of the vocabulary of the processed language. These units can be only described thoroughly in an exhaustive way; formally it is the triple (V, C, φ) where C is a set of primitive concepts, and φ an application of V in C. The application φ is defined by listing all the values $\varphi(m)$ for each $m \in V$.

For example:

- V={dog, cat, kitten, drink, milk, the}
  C={pet, ingest, liquid, ε denotes an empty concept}
  φ ={(dog, pet), (cat, pet), (drink, ingest), (the, ε), (milk, liquid)}

The word/concept combination is then used to calculate, for each sentence, the semantic representation in the form of:

- A graph whose vertices are elements of C (untyped semantics model)
- A bipartite graph defined by two subsets of vertices, C and T, where T must be introduced for typing relations between primitive concepts (typed semantic model)
- More complex semantic models which allow advanced calculations (as for reasoning). However the semantic graphs of these models can hardly be inferred from the sentences.

The translation of a sentence in its semantic form should reproduce as much as possible the reverse mechanism of what a human does to formulate the sentence. We assume that the formulation of the sentence by a human underlies internally:

- A linguistic construction to return a sentence that can be understandable. The construction is governed by agreed rules (choice of a vocabulary, a syntax, a style, etc.),
- And a construction of the meaning that the sentence must convey.

The observable result is a sequence of words, the translation of which in a semantic form by a machine requires a linguistic knowledge that is missing in the sequence. This knowledge must be set in advance to allow to parse the sequence of words; rules have the same nature as those used by a human being for the linguistic construction previously mentioned.

Translating a sentence into the representation of its meaning thus consists in resuming the former steps of the linguistic construction of the sentence, and at each step applying local construction rules of the (semantic) graph.

3.3. Semantic Phrase Structure Grammars and Example

Let be the grammar $G= \{S, N, V, P\}$ where V is the vocabulary of the previous example,

$N = \{S, GN, GV, DET, N, V\}$ all the non-terminals and

P the set of following rules:

$$R_1 : S \rightarrow GN_1 GV\ GN_2$$

$$[S] = [GV]\left([GN_1],[GN_2]\right)$$

$$R_2 : GN \rightarrow DET\ N$$

$$[GN] = [N]$$

$$R_3 : GV \rightarrow V \cdot$$

$$[GV] = [V]$$

$$R_4 : V \rightarrow drink \cdot$$

$$[V] = ingest \cdot$$

$$R_5 : N \rightarrow dog|cat|kitten$$

$$[N] = pet \cdot$$

$$R_6 : N \rightarrow milk \cdot$$

$$[N] = liquid \cdot$$

$$R_7 : DET \rightarrow the|a \cdot$$

In the construction of the semantic graph, non-terminals correspond to non-instantiated vertices that allow connecting the subgraphs under construction. A bracketed non-terminal denotes an uninstantiated subgraph, associated to this non-terminal by one of its vertices connectable to other subgraphs. Thus [GV] denotes the subgraph to be built, whose top uninstantiated vertex can be linked to other subgraphs.

A semantic rule as $[S] = [GV]\left([GN_1],[GN_2]\right)$ means that the graph [S] will be rewritten into 3 sub-graphs, [GV] $[GN_1]$ and a $[GN_2]$ and that the top vertex GV connects vertices GN_1 et GN_2 into a local tree-like structure $GV\left(GN_1, GN_2\right)$.

A sentence like the *kitten drink(s) the milk* will give rise to a series of rewrites

$$R_1 R_2 R_7 R_5 R_3 R_4 R_2 R_7 R_6$$

and to a construction of the semantic graph:

$$[S] \quad \rightarrow [GV]\big([GN_1],[GN_2]\big)$$

$$\rightarrow [GV]\big([N],[GN_2]\big)$$

$$\rightarrow [GV]\big([N],[GN_2]\big)$$

$$\rightarrow [GV]\big(pet,[GN_2]\big)$$

$$\rightarrow [V]\big(pet,[GN_2]\big)$$

$$\rightarrow ingest\big(pet,[GN_2]\big)$$

$$\rightarrow ingest\big(pet,[N]\big)$$

$$\rightarrow ingest\big(pet,liquid\big)$$

$$\rightarrow ingest\big(pet,[N]\big)$$

3.4. Lexicalized Grammars

In the previous example, the non-terminals were used as markers to construct the syntactic tree and the semantic representation. In a machine learning perspective, an automatic acquisition of grammar rules has to come along with an acquisition of lexical data, consistent with the syntactic model.

The twofold complication of the tasks incites to choose a simpler model. If the syntactic parser has triggered the semantic construction rules, this construction depends at no time on the syntactic structure which is built in parallel. It is therefore possible to use other grammatical formalisms as phrase structure grammars. For example, we will have similar processes of semantic construction based on lexicalized grammars such as TAG (Tree Adjoining Grammar) (Joshi, 2003) or categorial

Box 1. Lexicon:

the\a→	(NP/N) →	[NP]=[N] →
cat\kitten\dog→	N→	[N]=pet→
milk→	N→	[N]=liquid→
drink→	(NP\N)/NP→	[S] = ingest([NP_1], [NP_2])

Box 2. Sentence:

the	*kitten*	*drink(s)*	*the*	*milk*
(NP/N)	N	(NP\S)NP	(NP/N)	N
NP		(NP\S)NP		NP
NP			(NP\S)	
		S		

grammars (Steedman, 1987). Learning will not carry anything in that case but the acquisition of lexical data.(see Box 1 and Box 2)

Categories = {*S, NP, N*}

In the skeleton of derivation:

S $\rightarrow$ N P(NP\S)
  $\rightarrow$ N P(((NP\S)/NP)NP)
  $\rightarrow$ ((NP/N)N)(((NP\S)/NP((NP/N)N))

The last expression $((NP/N)N)(((NP\backslash S/NP)((NP/N)N))$ traces all lexical combinations which are used to construct the semantic structure.

The dependency grammars (Kahane 2001; Mel'čuk, 1997) may be mentioned as another model, easier to implement than the two previous models. For example, if one accepts that as output of the analysis, the dependency graph is a simple tree, it is then possible to cover the context-free grammar rules with only 4 non-terminals (Lee & Choi, 1999). As these non-terminals are formal descriptions of dependencies between words only, they can play the role of a pre-terminal function. The rule to translate a pre-terminal into a word may be related to counting occurrences and co-occurrences within a corpus rather than with the word grammatical category. The small number of nonterminals finally facilitates learning stochastized production rules, by using the Inside Outside algorithm.

3.5. Motivating a Simplified Language Model

In a machine learning perspective, the acquisition of syntactic parsing rules remains an open problem although recent advances have been made on the inference of categorial grammars. To minimize the impact of syntactic analysis, we seek a barer translation mechanism, which would consist in defining a morphism from all sentences to the set of semantic representations. If one considers sentences as elements of the monoid V^* on V, a set with operation of concatenation, semantic forms should be constructed in the monoid C^* on C, a set with a construction operator, $\perp$ remaining to be clarified. The translation of a sentence in a semantic form would be then a morphism from V^* to C^*.

The following constraints must be taken into account when we want to define :

- Ambiguity of the sentences. A classic example "*he looks at the girl on the hill with a telescope*" shows that there are several ways to interpret the meaning of sentences. If the interpretation of semantic forms is unambiguous then an ambiguous sentence must match several semantic forms. So we shall rather deal with an application from V^* to, $\wp\left(C^*\right)$, the power set of set C^* The morphism would then imply a set operation and not the operator $\perp$ defined on C.
- Non-commutativity. The concatenation operation is not commutative in V^* It must also be the case for the operator. $\perp$ Otherwise, if $\perp$ is commutative:

  ○ A permutation of 2 words of a well-formed sentence may mis-form this sentence
  ○ As no syntactic control is available in this simplified language model, the mis-formed sentence will be accepted as is the well-formed one by the translating morphism
  ○ Moreover these two sentences will have the same meaning as $\perp$ is supposed to be commutative
  ○ So the $\perp$ commutativity in the bag-of-words model makes it tolerant to spam indexing. Semantic in this model corresponds to a scalar value and $\perp$ to the multiplication. The semantic of a sentence $m_1 m_2 m_n$ results from the calculation of the following morphism over the semantics of each word:

$$val(m_1 m_2 .. m_n) = val(m_1) \, x \, val(m_2) \, x \, val(m_n).$$

Automatic acquisition of knowledge can be thus facilitated for the following constraints on the semantic model:

- Consideration of the ambiguity of sentences in the semantic representation

  non-commutativity for construction operator $\perp$

On the other hand, as shown in our previous examples, an arbitrary choice of primitive concepts requires a map between V and C and a linguistic analysis of sentences to construct their meaning representation. The linguistic input can be minimized if we define the notion of primitive concept, not in an arbitrary way, but correlated with vocabulary V, which is feasible in the case of a functional modeling.

Figure 3. Example of constructing the triple (V, C, φ)

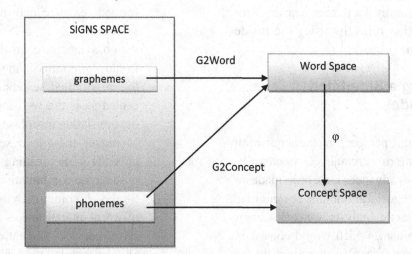

4. EXPLANATORY MODELING VS. FUNCTIONAL MODELING

The difficulty of automation depends on the purpose we have, itself depending on whether we opt for an explanatory modeling or a functional modeling. The first one will attempt to describe concepts and semantic relations independently from any application purpose; the priority is to understand how meaning operates. How to use the model is circumstantial and is described as an afterthought, in a specific way for each particular application, with the validation of the model as purpose.

Functional modeling focuses from the outset on a class of well identified applications, and in this context, it is interested only in properties of the meaning that are useful for this class of applications. These are properties which are used to define the notion of concepts and semantic relations.

In a nutshell, an explanatory modeling describes the functioning of a mechanism at a general operating level, and let any particular application to specify an ad hoc operating mechanism in addition, whereas a functional modeling describes specific mechanisms in a class of applications

and then requires only a minimal adaptation for each application in this class.

R. Shank conceptual dependencies are an example of semantic explanatory modeling (this includes Sowa's model where the linguistic analysis is more complex to implement):

- Primitive concepts are classified into primitive actions (**ATRANS, PTRANS, MTRANS, MOVE, PROPEL, GRASP,** etc.), primitive objects (HAND, MOUTH, HEALTH, etc.), primitive states, etc.
- Under decompositional analysis, the mechanism of general functioning consists in translating any sentence into a representation as a dependency graph whose vertices are the primitive concepts.
- In addition to each application, the *ad hoc* operating mechanism then corresponds to a graph analysis to produce the desired outcome (e.g., graph unification or subsumption for inference problems, graph matching for information retrieval. ...)

An explanatory modeling has the advantage of universality of data representation but the high cost of manual construction of the data remains an obstacle to cover large areas or domains. In addition, learning methods are not economically feasible in the state of the art for this type of modeling.

Functional modeling is useful only if it helps to explain the most relevant properties for automation, which can be included in a computational model in a generic way (compared to an *ad hoc* computing system).

The choice of a functional modeling is therefore essential in the context of machine learning. Therefore primitive concepts and semantic relations will be defined to address Information Retrieval as the class of applications we are interested in.

As already mentioned, it is a question of being able:

- To represent the text content in a semantic form
- To compare the semantic forms (two by two, or by using a common value scale)
- To learn the semantic data from a training corpus of text.

4.1. Word/Concept Duality: the Notion of Signifier/Signified

The simplicity of constructing the triple (V, C, φ) (Figure 3) makes it possible to minimize the complexity of translating text forms into semantic forms. For this reason, but also for a linguistically motivated choice, the notion of primitive concept and the notion of word will be defined respectively as the "signified" and the "signifier" components conveyed by a "signifier/signified" entity (Saussure, 1913). A concept does not exist in vacuum but depends on the words used to express it. The word becomes an abstract notion different from the identifier, a physical form which indicates the word but also the concept.

We have three distinct notions in the model: the signs space, the word space and the concept space.

Signs space is part of the physical medium of communication. This may be a sequence of characters of an alphabet in the case of graphemes or a sequence of speech sounds (or the transcription of these sounds) in the case of phonemes. Sign language is also part of this space.

The role of the signs space is to identify words and concepts in the message conveyed by the sentence. In the case of graphemes, for example, any sequence of characters separated by (blank) spaces is an identifier designating both a word and a concept (which we define as a named-concept, what allows to extend the notion of concept in a probabilistic model). We shall denote by G2Word and by G2Concept the functions transforming a sequence of signs into a sequence of words, and a sequence of signs into a sequence of named-concepts respectively.

A word and a named-concept have the same identifier but will differ on other properties. Computationally, these properties concern interactions between words and words, named-concepts and named-concepts, named-concepts and words, words and named-concepts.

Word/word interactions relate to the linguistic analysis, word/named-concept interactions to the translation of a textual form into a semantic form and named-concept/named-concept interactions to the interpretation of semantic relations. Named-concept/word interactions concerns text generation (e.g., for machine translation) and will not be discussed here.

From an applicative point of view, a sentence is a sequence of signs, the processing of which will produce a sequence of word/named-concept (translations). The analysis of word/word interactions will focus on the sequence of words, extracted from the sequence word/named-concept. The goal of the analysis is to validate correct sentences, but also for inflected languages, to normalize their words into canonical forms (stemming, compounds identification...).

The analysis of word/named-concept interactions takes in input the sequence of words (normalized if necessary) and the sequence of named-concepts both extracted from the initial sequence word/named-concept. Concerning the identifier of named-concepts, the question is to preserve the initially observed forms or replace them by the stemmed forms in the same way as for the words. We opted for the normalized form; the transformation of an inflected form in a stemmed form is a regular syntactic phenomenon, which may ultimately give rise to additional semantic information (as feature annotations). The choice of a normalized identifier can also minimize the statistical bias in the construction of semantic information from learning corpora. The analysis of word/named-concept interactions will produce a semantic representation for the sentence originally expressed. We distinguish the word or concept from the physical medium of communication.

The medium is either the string, or the sequence of speech sounds or their transcripts, or sign language ... and serves as identifiers for word/concept. Words and concepts are functional notions. Words avail sequential consistency of the medium whereas concepts control the coherence between sequences.

4.2. Extended Notion of Concept

We try to define as concept any element which can be the object of a "comparison of sense." For this purpose, we consider the σ-algebra generated by singletons $\{m_i\}$ where the m_i are the elements of the word space. A concept is then defined as a probability function on this σ-algebra. A concept c is a named-concept if there is a sequence g of the signs space and a word m of the words space such as G2Word(g)=m and G2Concept(g)=c.

Any concept is then completely defined by a probability distribution on the word space. The problem is to know how to determine these different probability distributions from a training corpus.

5. COMPUTER IMPLEMENTATION OF SEMANTIC ACQUISITION

A computational modeling will have to comply with both:

- The criteria of what a semantic model is, that is to say, to
  ◦ The representation of a concept
  ◦ The meaning of text content that reflects the context in which the words are used
  ◦ The meaning of text elaboration (descriptive semantics) or more sophisticated representations, such as graphs to allow reasoning (inferential semantics)
- Operating constraints: to be able to automatically build knowledge databases and a portion of the linguistic data by learning from a large amounts of plain text.

The process of automatic construction may be divided into two parts:

- A portion corresponding to the experimental observation of the corpus of words, producing annotated elements that reflect different observing conditions. The hardness of this part is algorithmic, to take into account large amounts of data and cross data (e.g., matrix data).
- A deductive portion where the annotated elements provided by the observation allow the construction of knowledge bases by establishing relations between senses. The methods used for this part are relative to the statistical analysis. It is in this part that the semantic probabilistic modeling becomes important.

If in addition to the experimental part, we want to minimize human intervention in the learning process, a work as manual annotating corpus is also to be avoided. We can still get items properly annotated by varying the conditions of observation. For example:

- An observation of contiguous sequences of words allows the identification of compounds. Because compounds denote a non-compositional meaning, we must consider each compound as a single unit of meaning. In the sequel, we use the terms "lexical item" and "lexical items space" to generalize the notion of word and words space, by appointing a single word token or a compound. Each lexical item can be additionally associated with a named-concept. An analysis at the level of the lexical items allows minimizing the noise when extracting relations between concepts.
- An extraction of relations between senses can be made only by an analysis of co-occurrences, in the absence of corpus annotation. One can nevertheless imagine several types of co-occurrence analyses. For example:
  - Between an element of the document headline and an element of the text body of the same document
  - Between two elements whatever their position within the same document
  - Between two elements within a shifting observation window in the document, etc.

6. IMPLEMENTATION CHOICES: REVISITING BM25 AND PLSA

We consider that we only have corpora without annotations. A knowledge database will be built from each corpus. An initial analysis of contiguous sequences of words in the corpus will help extracting the terminological elements (the compounds) (Lassalle, 2011). These compounds

will be then used on the same corpus to identify the lexical items.

A second step consists in identifying the co-occurrences between lexical items. If structured, a corpus allows varying several types of analysis. However the most used is the analysis within a shifting window. This technique has the advantage of reflecting, in a macroscopic way, the editorial work of a human. Indeed, the order of the sequence is not activated within the window, which makes the learned relations less sensitive to different syntactic structures expressing the same meaning.

Moreover the shift of the window can reflect changes/evolution of meanings along the document.

In all cases, the analysis produces a frequency count of co-occurrences. The result provides for each lexical item the frequencies of its association with all other lexical items of the lexical items space. This result may be then computed in the form of a conditional probability, namely the probability of having a lexical item in a close context knowing that we observed it in the document.

First, the corpus analysis allows defining each named concept by a sequence of words weighted by their frequency (co-occurrence with the named-concept). The representation by frequencies, derived from the experimental observation, is then used to estimate the conditional probability distribution $P(m_i \mid c)$.

An estimate of the conditional probabilities such that the ratio $P(m_i \mid c) = \dfrac{f_i}{\sum_i f_i}$ assumes the independence of words in their different usages. Such an approximation is coarse enough to skew the subsequent calculation of the distributions characterizing named-concepts from unnamed concepts. To better reflect the dependences, we will notice similarities with probabilistic IR models, between observing a frequency distribution and estimating the probability distribution. In this case, each named concept behaves as a document and the set of concepts as the indexed database.

The experiment confirms that the estimate of probabilities $P(m_i \mid C)$ through a TF-IDF calculation gives significantly better results than the ratio $P(m_i \mid c) = \dfrac{f_i}{\sum_i f_i}$. We are now experimenting the BM25 weighting, or a more suitable parameter of the BMxx family, so as to take into account the variability of lengths of co-occurring words sequences.

After normalization, this result can also be interpreted in another way, as a probability distribution over lexical items and thus supply a computable definition of a named-concept.

Finally, it remains to algorithmically define every concept that is not a named-concept. Such concepts correspond mainly to sequences of lexical items (sentences, titles, whole documents, etc.). Translating these sequences into probability distributions is a work related to indexing.

7. MODEL INTEGRATING SEMANTIC AND INDEXING

In the semantic approach, described previously, are considered as concepts: a document, a sentence, a document title, a collection of classified documents... As such, they are modeled as probability functions. These functions are completely defined by their probability distribution on the lexical items.

We have shown that, in our semantic model, a shallow linguistic analysis suffices to easily identify named concepts from words. An analysis of co-occurrences in the text corpus makes it possible to (computationally) describe named concepts as distributions over words.

For unnamed concepts that are identifiable by a sequence of words such as documents and queries, we rely on the sequence to draw a word distribution that characterizes the unnamed concept. The algorithm to compute the distribution has two steps:

- The sequence of words is analyzed and interpreted into a sequence of named concepts
- The interpretation of the sequence of named concepts allows to combine distributions associated to named concepts in a mixture distribution.

Concerning unnamed concepts such as documents (for determining their probability distribution), the behavior of unnamed concepts / named concepts / words is very similar to the aspect model PLSA that we will revisit now. Compared to the PLSA model, with d (document), z (theme) and w (word), our semantic model is constructed from d (document), c (named concept) and m (word). c (resp. m) plays a role equivalent to that of z (resp. w). However, there are differences in the data:

While $P(w \mid z)$ is unknown and must be estimated, $P(m \mid c)$ is determined from experimental observation.

While w is a word observed in d, m is a word that may not appear explicitly in d and corresponds to an element of the application vocabulary. Therefore, while $P(w \mid d)$ is known, $P(m \mid d)$ is derived from an indirect calculation from $(m \mid c)$

The equations of PLSA, however, remain valid in our model. We have:

$$P(d, m) = P(d)P(m \mid d)$$

$$P(m \mid d) = \sum_C P(m \mid c)P(c \mid d)$$

$$P(d \mid m) = \sum_C P(c)P(d \mid c)P(m \mid c)$$

The quantities we are interested in, and that must be estimated are $P(c \mid d)$ and $P(m \mid d)$.

The complete algorithm is given below, with two methods to estimate these probabilities, from a sequence of lexical items and from the probability distributions. Lexical items are relative to what is observable while probability distributions define the concepts appointed by analysis of co-occurrence.

The following principles for calculating concepts stand:

The sequence of lexical items corresponds to a set of unordered pairs (named-concept, coefficient α), rather than a sequence of named-concepts. Coefficient α is determined by calculating

$$m_1 \ldots m_n \rightarrow \left\{ \left(c_1, \alpha_1 \right) \ldots \left(c_n, \alpha_n \right) \right\}$$

determining the weight of the sequence $m_1 \ldots m_n$ usually involves the calculation with Boolean operators. But we will not apply such operators for concepts. The introduction of logical operators would require a complex and unnecessary formalization over probability functions. The direct way is rather to define a mixture law $\left\{ \left(c_1, \alpha_1 \right), \ldots, \left(c_n, \alpha_n \right) \right\} \rightarrow \sum_i \alpha_i c_i$ which requires in the calculation of α_i to have $\alpha_i \geq 0$ and $\sum_i \alpha_i = 1$.

7.1. Bag of Words (or Bag of Lexical Items) Method

The method is based on the calculation of maximum likelihood.

- Initial Data sequence $m_1 m_2 \ldots m_n$ belonging to the training corpus
- Initialization sequence $m_1 m_2 \ldots m_n$ is unduplicated and stored in a set $\{ m_1', m_2', \ldots, m_k' \}$
  To each m_i' of the set $\{ m_1', m_2', \ldots, m_k' \}$ is assigned the coefficient $tf.idf(m_i')$ to eventu-

ally produce a bag of words $\left\{ \left(m_1', p_1 \right), \left(m_2', p_2 \right), \ldots, \left(m_k', p_k \right) \right\}$ with $\sum_i p_i = 1$

Laplace smoothing can be performed if necessary to take into account the elements missing from the set $\{ m_1', m_2', \ldots, m_k' \}$ but also to calculate the KL divergence without zero probabilities

- Iteration to each element m_i' of the set $\{ m_1', m_2', \ldots, m_k' \}$ is associated a named-concept c_i' of distribution $\{ (m_1'', q_1), (m_2'', q_2), \ldots, (m_k'', q_k) \}$. The KL divergence:

$$\beta_i = D_{KL} \left(\left\{ (m_1', P_1), \ldots, (m_k', P_{1k}) \right\} \parallel c_i' \right) = \sum_{j=1}^{N} - p_j \log\left(\frac{q_j^i}{p_j}\right)$$

represents the quantity of information separating the named-concept c_i' and the distribution is computed for the previous bag of words. Its dual value $\pi_i = e^{-\beta_i}$ is the probability of the previous bag of words to be denoted by the named-concept c_i'

Thus we obtain a mixture distribution defined by $\sum_{i=1}^{N} \alpha_i c_i$ where $\alpha_i = \dfrac{\pi_i}{\sum_{j=1}^{N} \pi_j}$

The new distribution derived from this mixture distribution is then assigned to the bag of words for the next iteration

Iteration is repeated until convergence of the new distribution that represents the final concept associated with the sequence $m_1 m_2 \ldots m_n$

The bag of words method is suitable for corpus where the documents are short, where there is little change in focus of discourse in the document. For longer documents, we adopt the following method:

7.2. Analysis Method by Shifting Window

- *Initial Data* sequence $m_1 m_2 \ldots m_n$ belonging to the training corpus
  Probability distributions defining named-concepts we define the size of the shifting window let K with $K < n$

- *Initialization* the sequence $m_1 m_2 \ldots m_n$ is unduplicated and stored in a set $\{m_1', m_2', \ldots, m_k'\}$

- *Iteration* for each k from 1 to $n - K$, on sequence $m_k m_{k+1} \ldots m_{k+K}$, we apply a calculating method similar to the previous of bag of words but without iteration, as follows:

  ○ Unduplicate sequence $m_k m_{k+1} \ldots m_{k+K}$ and define the set $\{m_1'', m_2'', \ldots, m_k''\}$

  ○ Set the bag of words $\left\{ \left(m_1'', p_2''\right), \left(m_2'', p_2''\right), \ldots, \left(m_k'', p_k''\right) \right\}$ for each named-concept c_i' associated with m_i calculate the KL divergence:

$$\beta_i = D_{KL}\left(\left\{(m_1'', P_1''), \ldots, (m_k'', P_k'')\right\} \| c_i\right) = \sum_{j=1}^{N} - p_j'' \log\left(\frac{q_j^i}{p_j''}\right)$$

- *Iteration* for each named-concept c_i, c_i is associated with the sequence $\beta_1^i .. \beta_{n-K}^i$ and the mean $\beta^i = \dfrac{\sum_{j=1}^{n-K} \beta_j^i}{n - K}$

- *Output* from set $\{(c_i, \beta_i)\}$ can be deduced $\{(c_i,_i)\}$ then, as with the previous method, the mixture distribution that defines the concept associated to the sequence $m_1 m_2 \ldots m_n$.

8. CONSTRUCTION OF THE INVERTED FILE IN A SEMANTIC IR MODEL

Any document can henceforth be processed as a concept whose distribution on the space of lexical items was made computable. Any named-concept can then index every document by using the Kullback-Leibler divergence between the document and the named-concept. The value of the divergence is transformed into its dual probability value and it is this last value that will be used as a weight-index of the named-concept.

When the query service is activated and a query (which is also a concept) $q_1 q_2 .. q_n$ is formulated, for performance issues, we will not use any of the above two previous methods to determine the mixture distribution defining the query concept.

A simpler hypothesis is to assume that the mixture distribution is uniform in assigning a coefficient $1 / n$ to each named-concept associated with q_i.

A more advanced method is to assign to each named-concept a coefficient calculated *a priori*. Such a construction is not the object of this paper, also we limit ourselves here to trace the outline. To calculate these coefficients, we must first build a network of implications between named-concept and named-concept (for example *cat→feline*). One possible method for doing this is to conduct an analysis of co-occurrence between named-concepts on the basis of a calculation of KL divergence between named-concepts. This leads to the construction of an automaton and to its stochastization. Its transition matrix can be then made ergodic (Langville & Meyer, 2006). Computing the eigenvector associated with the eigenvalue 1 can finally affect the expected *a priori* coefficients to each named-concept (using the power method to compute eigenvectors).

9. EXPERIMENTATION

There is also a class of unnamed concepts, such as semantic categories, that are not directly observable and only identified by the named concepts they contain. The description of named concepts within a cluster is given as a distribution also, which allows to define the semantic category as a distribution over words resulting from a mixture of the distributions provided by named concepts.

The experimentation was carried out on French newspaper articles (1 Gb of plain text), each article taking the form a short text such as:

"Alassane Ouattara est proclamé vainqueur du second tour, le 2 décembre, par la Commission électorale indépendante. Mais Laurent Gbagbo refuse de quitter le pouvoir. Un coup de force qui hypothèque à nouveau la concrétisation du rêve d'ADO: devenir président."

At first, the corpus is analyzed to extract named concepts, and to describe them as distributions over words.

We now show in two applications how documents are represented as observable but unnamed concepts and how themes can be automatically built as unobservable concepts.

9.1. Disambiguition

The word "avocat" in French is ambiguous and can refer to both "avocado" and "lawyer" in English. The word distribution for the concept "avocat" given bellow reflects this ambiguity without more specific context.

(crevette/shrimp 9.303348e-03)(avocat/avocado_or_lawyer 5.313879e-03)(pamplemousse/grapefruit 5.095467e-03)(roulade de saumon/salmon roulade 4.811111e-03)(procès/trial 4.703822e-03)(justice 4.623396e-03)(salade/salad 4.593557e-03)(coco curry/coconut curry 4.369211e-03)(avis/judgment 4.227039e-03)(garde à vue/custody 4.186575e-03)(mangue/mango 3.934967e-03)(client 3.751331e-03)(défense/defense 3.644256e-03)(magistrat/magistrate 3.524318e-03)(tribunal/court 3.261423e-03)(beignet/donut 3.201281e-03) ...

The following two examples show how disambiguation is processed in context. The analysis by our algorithm of a document d_1 containing "avocat" (avocado or lawyer), "procureur" (prosecutor) and "magistrat" (judge) provides, on one hand, the weight of named concepts.

$P(\textbf{avocat}|d_1) = 3.428038e-01$

$P(\textbf{procureur}|d_1) = 3.263334e-01$

$P(\textbf{magistrat}|d_1) = 3.308628e-01$

On the other hand, the word distribution for d_1 as a concept is:

(justice 8.520301e-03)(république 6.844625e-03)(avocat 6.246524e-03)(magistrat/magistrate 5.510957e-03)(tribunal/court 4.436478e-03)(parquet/prosecution 3.938121e-03)(procureur/attorney 3.792087e-03)(garde à vue/custody 3.613857e-03)(philippe courroye/a french attorney 3.519879e-03)(dossier/record 3.516405e-03)(magistrature/judiciary 3.369131e-03)(juge d instruction/judge 3.294303e-03)(procès/trial 3.286855e-03) ...

For a document d_2 containing "avocat" (avocado or lawyer) and "salade" (salad), the analysis by our algorithm gives:

$P(\textbf{avocat}|d_2) = 5.462394e-01$

$P(\textbf{salade}|d_2) = 4.537607e-01$

And the word distribution of d_2 as a concept is:

(crevette/shrimp 9.811861e-03)(aï/garlic 6.684686e-03)(tomate/tomato 6.358797e-03)(avocat/avocado 5.567631e-03)(lentille/lentil 5.543046e-03)(cervelas/sausage 5.523055e-03)(recette/recipe 5.418542e-03)(chèvre/goat cheese 4.996989e-03)(haricots verts/green beans 4.885013e-03)(vinaigrette 4.625699e-03)(oeuf/egg 4.611595e-03)(melon 4.607437e-03)(miel/honey 4.598647e-03)(gruyère/gruyere cheese 4.182616e-03)(salade 4.090298e-03)(pamplemousse/grape fruit 3.707328e-03)(épinard/spinach 3.622851e-03) ...

9.2. Clustering

We used a K-means algorithm version adapted to the Kullback-Leibler divergence to group concepts into clusters. As Kullback-Leibler divergence does not fulfill triangle inequality and symmetry, which are two properties of distances used in K-means algorithm, the adaptation consists in defining equivalent criterion:

- The equivalent notion for the radius on convergence is entropy
- The seeds are initialized by the most general concepts (those with the highest entropy) and the most far from each other according to Kullback-Leibler divergence.

The number of clusters we obtained is approximately two hundred. After that, newspaper articles are processed as identifiable unnamed concepts, and grouped using clusters previously obtained with named concepts. The lists corresponding to some of the clusters of named concepts (concerning noun phrases in the example) is given below. Named concepts in a same cluster are given in descending order according to relevance in a log-scale (probability for a named concept to be in the cluster).

For the same corpus mentioned above, clusters 1 (French football/soccer players) and cluster 2 (winter sports) show that the analysis with our semantic model provides fine and accurate results, within the same domain (sport). Similarly, clusters 4 and 5 distinguish financial and economic domains, while cluster 3 describes precisely and synthetically tragic events in Russia. Finally clusters 8 and 9 on verbs confirm the relevance of the model even for a grammatical category known for the difficulty of classifying related words/concepts.

Cluster 1

adil rami, florent malouda, matches de suspension, mathieu valbuena, hugo lloris

adil rami, florent malouda, game suspension, mathieu valbuena, hugo lloris

Cluster 2

slalom, ski alpin, première manche, ski, slalom géant, descente, maria riesch, julien lizeroux, skieur, tessa worley, classement général, victoire en coupe, sandrine aubert, skieuse, seconde manche, petit globe, tête du classement, championne olympique, grange, globe de cristal, carlo janka, dossard, benjamin raich, dossard rouge, ingrid, jacquemod, cyprien richard, combiné nordique, premier tracé, troisième victoire, marie marchand, julia mancuso, jason lamy chappuis, ted ligety, tina maze, aubert, second tracé, premier podium, baptiste grange, thomas fanara, grosse faute, viktoria rebensburg, français jean, suissesse, adrien théaux, médaillée de bronze, steve missilier, marcel hirscher, zéro pointé, thomas mermillod, deuxième médaille d or

slalom, downhill skiing, first run, skiing, giant slalom, downhill, maria riesch, lizeroux skier tessa worley, overall, cup victory, sandrine aubert, skier, second round, small globe, head of the rankings, olympic champion, barn, crystal globe, carlo janka, bib, benjamin raich, red bib, ingrid jacquemod, cyprien richard, nordic combined, first stroke, his third victory, marie marchand, julia mancuso, jason lamy chappuis, ted ligety, tina maze, aubert, second trace, first podium, baptist barn, thomas fanara, big mistake, viktoria rebensburg, french jeans, swiss woman, adrien theaux, bronze medalist, steve missilier, marcel hirscher, zero points, thomas mermillod, second gold medal

Cluster 3

anna politkovskaïa, journaliste russe, guerre en tchétchénie, alexandre litvinenko, immeuble à moscou, journaliste d opposition, tuée par balles, iouri tchaïka, boris berezovski, presse russe, tuée par balle, journal russe, journaliste russe d opposition, armée russe en tchétchénie, hall de son immeuble, identité du commanditaire, arrestation de dix, paul klebnikov

anna politkovskaya, russian journalist, war in chechnya, litvinenko, moscow apartment building, opposition journalist killed by bullets, yuri chaika, boris berezovsky, russian press, shot dead, russian newspaper journalist of russian opposition, the russian army in chechnya hall of his apartment building, identity of the sponsor, arrest of ten (?), paul klebnikov

Cluster 4

bénéfice net, perte nette, chiffre d affaires, dépréciation, milliard, milliards de dollars, bénéfice, perte, analyste, premier semestre, euros, milliard de dollars, résultat net, banque d affaires, yen, première banque, société générale, provision, banque américaine, crédit agricole, lynch, morgan stanley, produit net, bons résultats, francs suisses, résultats trimestriels, banque d investissement, directeur financier, banque française, résultat d exploitation, crédit suisse, part de marché, bénéfice d exploitation, résultat opérationnel, clos fin, groupe bancaire, mauvais résultats, deuxième banque, bénéfice par action, éléments exceptionnels, résultats financiers, crise des crédits, pnb, résultats annuels, part du groupe, banques françaises, analystes financiers, bénéfice opérationnel, banque de détail, exercice fiscal

net income, net loss, asset turnover, depreciation, billion, billions dollars, profit, loss, analyst, first semester, euros, billion dollars, net income, investment bank, yen, the first bank, societe generale, bank provision, u.s. bank, crédit agricole, lynch, morgan stanley, net banking, sound results, swiss francs, quarterly results, investment bank, cfo, french bank, other operating income, credit swiss, market share, profit from operations, operating profit, closed end, the banking group, poor

performance, the second largest bank, earnings per share, extraordinary items, financial results, credit crunch, g.n.p, annual earnings, group share, french banks, financial analysts, operating profit, retail banking, fiscal tax

Cluster 5

quatrième trimestre, deuxième trimestre, troisième trimestre, premier trimestre, trimestre, ralentissement, trimestre précédent, prévision, produit intérieur, croissance, récession, progression, recul, dernier trimestre, rebond, contraction, économie américaine, conjoncture, exportation, repli, première estimation, rythme annuel, variation, ralentissement économique, taux de croissance, fourchette, prévision de croissance, commerce extérieur, second semestre, croissance du pib, bond, stagnation, niveau record, mois précédent, prévisions de croissance, institut national, première économie, croissance américaine, production industrielle, mois précédents, déficit commercial, conjoncture économique, glissement annuel, activité industrielle, créations d emploi, bons chiffres, balance commerciale, net ralentissement, département du commerce, chiffres officiels

fourth quarter, second quarter, third quarter, first quarter, quarter slowdown, the previous quarter, forecasting, domestic product, growth, recession, growth, decline, last quarter, rebound, contraction, u.s. economy, economy, export, withdrawal, first estimate, annual rate, variation, slowing economic growth rates range forecast of growth, foreign trade, the second half, g.d.p growth, bond, stagnation, record high the previous month, growth forecasts, national institute, the largest economy, growth u.s. industrial production, previous months, trade deficit, economic, y.o.y, industrial activity, creation of jobs, good figures, trade balance, net slowdown, the commerce department, official figures

Cluster 6

énergies renouvelables, économies d énergie, électricité, énergie, charbon, énergies fossiles, efficacité énergétique, consommation d énergie, chauffage, production d électricité, énergie nucléaire, énergie solaire, gaz naturel, isolation, consommation énergétique, biomasse, panneaux solaires, matériau, extraction, politique énergétique, production d énergie, indépendance énergétique, énergies propres, consommation d électricité, source d énergie, énergie renouvelable, économie d énergie, sources d énergie, énergies alternatives, centrales électriques, combustibles fossiles, géothermie, centrales thermiques, secteurs d activité, chauffage électrique, combustion, chaudière, solutions alternatives, énergie éolienne, facture énergétique, énergie fossile, parc nucléaire, contribution climat, énergies nouvelles, modes de production, production électrique, émissions de carbone, gaz de schiste, croissance verte, technologies vertes

renewable energy, energy savings, electricity, energy, coal, fossil fuels, energy efficiency, energy consumption, heating, electricity generation, nuclear, solar, natural gas, insulation, energy consumption, biomass, solar panels, material, mining, energy policy, energy production, energy independence, clean energy, electricity consumption, energy source, renewable energy, energy saving, energy sources, alternative energy, power plants, fossil fuels, geothermal power plants, sectors activity, electric heating, combustion, boiler, alternative energy, wind energy, energy costs, fossil energy, nuclear power, carbon tax, new energies, modes of production, power generation, carbon emissions, shale gas, green growth, green technology

Cluster 7

nuage de cendres, trafic aérien, espace aérien, volcan islandais, transport aérien, ciel européen, éruption du volcan, éruption d un volcan, paralysie du trafic, espaces aériens, organisation européenne, association internationale nuages de cendres fermeture partielle, éruption volcanique, secteur aérien, nouveau nuage, ciel français, énorme nuage, sommet du glacier, première éruption, fermé dimanche, ciel unique, organisme de contrôle, trafic européen, avions en vol, capitale norvégienne, aérien espagnol, regain d activité, aéroport de dublin, aériennes européennes, nuage volcanique, annulation des vols, volcan merapi, voyage en avion, vitrification, pas de fermeture, institut islandais, européen pendant, john cleese, transport arien, aéroport de yogyakarta, prix du kérosène, aviation marchande, chasseur bombardier, aéroport de reykjavik, agence norvégienne, office météorologique, roxane désiré, commercial international

ash cloud, air traffic, airspace, icelandic volcano, air transport, the european airspace, volcano, eruption of a volcano, paralyzed traffic, airspace, european organization, an international association ash cloud partially closed, volcanic area air new cloud, french airspace, huge cloud on top of the glacier, first eruption, closed sunday, ses, body control, european traffic, airplanes in flight, norwegian capital, spanish airspace, renewed activity, dublin airport, european airspace, volcanic cloud, flight cancellations, merapi volcano, flying, vitrification, no lockout, icelandic institute, european counterpart, john cleese, air transport, yogyakarta airport, price of kerosene, aviation market, fighter bomber, reykjavik airport, norwegian agency, meteorological office, roxane desiré, international trade

Cluster 8

poivrer, saler, assaisonner, mélanger, cuire, incorporer, égoutter, mixer, rajouter, couper, saupoudrer, hacher, remuer, laver, éplucher, émincer, découper, sécher, arroser, peler, préchauffer, émietter, rincer, râper, ciseler, ôter, garnir, enfourner, dorer, parfumer, concasser, badigeonner, mijoter, tremper, épaissir, décorer, napper, mouiller, colorer, caraméliser, enrober, fouetter, bouillir, braiser, griller, déglacer, épépiner, essorer, tartiner, délayer

to pepper, to salt, to favor, to mix, to cook, to incorporate, to drain, to mix, to add, to cut, to sprinkle, to chop, stir, to wash, to peel, to chop, to cut, to dry, to water, to peel, to warm up, to crumble, to wash, to grate, to chop, to remove, to fill, to bake, to brown, to flavor, to chop, to brush something with, to cook, to soak, to thicken, to decorate, to drizzle, to wet, to color and to caramelize, to coat, to whisk, to boil, to braise, to roast, to deglaze, to remove seeds, to dry, to spread, to mix

Cluster 9

réélire, voter, recueillir, emporter, obtenir, devancer, créditer, abstenir, députer, élire, rallier, briguer, totaliser, distancer, départager, officialiser, dépouiller, challenger, talonner, ravir, huer, désister, adouber, recompter, pavoiser, parachuter, encarter, recoller, bourrer, doler, redécouper, ioder, monarchiser, chabler, barguigner, traficoter, tournicoter, bâter, tripatouiller, souquer, resquiller, roustir

to re-elect, to vote, to collect, to win election, to get, to get ahead, to credit, to abstain, mp elect, to rally, to run an election, to totalize votes, outrun, to settle, to officialize an election, to scrutinize, to challenge, to hound a candidate, to win, to boo ...

10. CONCLUSION

After a short presentation of different approaches to linguistic analysis and semantic indexing, we proposed a new model for semantics, which is descriptive and dedicated to Information Retrieval. This model is a result of the experience from our previous work and achievements on linguistic processing applied to Information Retrieval. In a language model approach, a Markov model was implemented for the indexing part. It showed the limits of this approach:

- The difficulty of taking into account the variability in formulating queries
- The difficulty of moving to a Markovian order greater than 1, even by using interpolation techniques

So we gave up the language model as such, considering that concepts must be generalized to any object handled by IR and by assigning a probability function to each concept. This led us to manipulate these probability distributions to resort to existing tools from information theory.

The results of our experiments indicate for us that it is relevant to consider every object in IR as a concept (as it was defined) and to process it in a distributional manner. If our semantic model has been validated at the level of concept pairing, the continuation of our work is to build automatically larger and more fine-grained semantic networks in order to address tasks involving matters of "how and why" such as question-answering.

REFERENCES

Bishop, C. (2006). *Pattern recognition and machine learning*. New York, NY: Springer.

Blei, D. M., Ng, A. Y., & Jordan, M. I. (2003). Latent Dirichlet allocation. *Journal of Machine Learning Research, 3*, 993–1022.

Croft, W. B., & Harper, D. J. (1979). Using probabilistic models of document retrieval without relevance information. *The Journal of Documentation, 35*(4), 285–295. doi:10.1108/eb026683

de Saussure, F. (1913). *Cours de linguistique générale*. Paris, France: Payot.

Greiff, W. R. (1998). A theory of term weighting based on exploratory data analysis. In *Proceedings of the 21st Annual International ACM SIGIR Conference on Research and Development in Information Retrieval* (pp. 11-19).

Griffiths, T. L., & Steyvers, M. (2004). Finding scientific topics. *Proceedings of the National Academy of Sciences of the United States of America, 101*(1), 5228–5235. doi:10.1073/pnas.0307752101

Hiemstra, D. (2000). A probabilistic justification for using tf.idf term weighting in information retrieval. *International Journal on Digital Libraries, 3*(2), 131–139. doi:10.1007/s007999900025

Hofmann, T. (1999). Probabilistic latent semantic analysis. In *Proceedings of the Uncertainty in Artificial Intelligence* (pp. 289-296).

Joshi, A., & Rambow, O. (2003). A formalism for dependency grammar based on tree adjoining grammar. In *Proceedings of the 1st International Conference on Meaning-Text Theory*.

Kahane, S. (2001). Grammaires de dépendance formelles et théorie Sens-Text. In *Proceedings of the Tutoriel Actes Traitement Automatique des Langues Naturelles* (Vol. 2).

Landauer, T., Foltz, P. W., & Laham, D. (1998). Introduction to latent semantic analysis. *Discourse Processes, 25*, 259–284. doi:10.1080/01638539809545028

Langville, A. N., & Meyer, C. D. (2006). *Google's PageRank and beyond: The science of search engine rankings*. Princeton, NJ: Princeton University Press.

Lari, K., & Young, S. J. (1990). The estimation of stochastic context-free grammars using the inside-outside algorithm. *Computer Speech & Language, 4*, 35–56. doi:10.1016/0885-2308(90)90022-X

Lari, K., & Young, S. J. (1991). Applications of stochastic context-free grammars using the inside-outside algorithm. *Computer Speech & Language, 5*, 237–257. doi:10.1016/0885-2308(91)90009-F

Lassalle, E. (2011). Acquisition Automatique de Terminologie à partir de Corpus de Texte. In *Proceedings of the Tutoriel Actes Traitement Automatique des Langues Naturelles*.

Lee, S., & Choi, K.-S. (1999). *A reestimation algorithm for probabilistic dependency grammars*. Cambridge, UK: Cambridge University Press.

Lehmann, F. (Ed.). (1992). *Semantic networks*. Oxford, UK: Pergamon Press.

Manning, C. D., Prabhakar, R., & Hinrich, S. (2008). *Introduction to information retrieval*. Cambridge, UK: Cambridge University Press.

Mel'čuk, I. A. (1997). *Vers une linguistique Sens-Texte. Leçon inaugurale*. Paris, France: Collège de France, Chaire internationale.

Minka, T., & Lafferty, J. (2002). Expectation-propagation for the generative aspect model. In *Proceedings of the 18th Conference on Uncertainty in Artificial Intelligence*.

Ponte, J. M., & Croft, W. B. (1998). A language modeling approach to information retrieval. In *Proceedings of the 21st Annual International ACM SIGIR Conference on Research and Development in Information Retrieval* (pp. 275-281).

Ripley, B. D. (1996). *Pattern recognition and neural networks*. Cambridge, UK: Cambridge University Press.

Robertson, S. E., & Saragoza, H. (2009). The probabilistic relevance framework: BM25 and beyond. *Foundation and Trends in Information Retrieval, 3*(4), 333–389. doi:10.1561/1500000019

Robertson, S. E., & Spärck Jones, K. (1977). Relevance weighting of search terms. *Journal of the American Society for Information Science American Society for Information Science, 27*, 129–146. doi:10.1002/asi.4630270302

Robertson, S. E., van Rijsbergen, C. J., & Porter, M. F. (1981). Probabilistic models of indexing and searching. In *Proceedings of the 3rd Annual ACM Conference on Research and Development in Information Retrieval* (pp. 35-56).

Rozenknop, A. (2009). *Cours de recherche et extraction d'information*. Paris, France: Université de Paris 13. Retrieved from http://www-lipn.univ-paris13.fr/ ~rozenknop/Cours/MICR_REI/

Salton, G., & McGill, M. J. (1983). *Introduction to modern information retrieval*. New York, NY: McGraw-Hill.

Spärck Jones, K., Walker, S., & Robertson, S. E. (2000). A probabilistic model of information retrieval: Development and comparative experiments. *Information Processing & Management: an International Journal, 36*(6), 779-808, 809-840.

Steedman, M. (1987). Combinatory grammars and parasitic gaps. *Natural Language and Linguistic Theory, 5*, 403–439. doi:10.1007/BF00134555

van Rijsbergen, C. J. (1979). *Information retrieval* (2nd ed.). Oxford, UK: Butterworth-Heinemann.

Chapter 8
The Use of Text Mining Techniques in Electronic Discovery for Legal Matters

Michael W. Berry
University of Tennessee, USA

Reed Esau
Catalyst Repository Systems, USA

Bruce Kiefer
Catalyst Repository Systems, USA

ABSTRACT

Electronic discovery (eDiscovery) is the process of collecting and analyzing electronic documents to determine their relevance to a legal matter. Office technology has advanced and eased the requirements necessary to create a document. As such, the volume of data has outgrown the manual processes previously used to make relevance judgments. Methods of text mining and information retrieval have been put to use in eDiscovery to help tame the volume of data; however, the results have been uneven. This chapter looks at the historical bias of the collection process. The authors examine how tools like classifiers, latent semantic analysis, and non-negative matrix factorization deal with nuances of the collection process.

INTRODUCTION

In the United States, litigation has a long history. When two parties are involved in a legal matter, the parties agree to a process of discovery wherein the particular facts of the case are uncovered. Discovery used to be a cordial exchange of legal papers and a few business documents. Today, discovery has moved into the electronic domain where the ease of digital duplication has caused volumes, and therefore costs, of documents to rise. To try and tame both cost and volume, companies and law firms have integrated information technology. When the documents became electronic (either through scanning or no longer being printed), tools from information retrieval and text mining were needed. These tools hold great promise but have had uneven results to date.

DOI: 10.4018/978-1-4666-0330-1.ch008

A BRIEF HISTORY OF LEGAL DISCOVERY

In countries that support discovery in the legal system, paper based discovery generally followed a simple pattern: identify the key people involved (initially referred to as witnesses and later as custodians), identify their support staff, get photocopies of the documents maintained by witnesses or from central filing systems, and send the boxes of documents to the legal team. The legal team would focus on the relevant custodians and thumb through the documents making judgment calls on the likely relevance of expense reports, budgets, and memorandums.

As volumes of documents grew, only larger law firms would continue making photocopies. In time, even those larger firms would be unable to keep up with the demands of photocopying. Without the means, ability, or desire to handle this manual job of photocopying, a market opportunity was created – the legal service provider. Specialists narrowed in on becoming litigation service providers. When a collection of paper-based documents was needed, the litigation service provider would step in and carry out the work that the law firm would not.

As self-motivated agents, the litigation service providers created a business driven by volume. Pricing for manual collections of paper documents were often priced by the page since the underlying cost was a combination of the staff required to handle the collection and the number of photocopies being made. This derivation of a service with revenues generated by volume set a pattern for future business models.

If a company found itself involved in a legal matter, it would often start by hiring a law firm. The law firm would then turn to their legal service providers to assist them in handling the matter. The litigation service provider welcomed advances in office technology that eased the creation of documents. With the gentle hum of the IBM Selectric on a secretary's desk, the litigation

service provider could count on more documents being printed and therefore more documents that needed to be photocopied.

Since the division of labor was cleanly split, law firms were not reviewing paper documents for relevance during collection. They would review the photocopies. Since the litigation service provider did not want to make legal judgments on document relevance, it behooved them to collect as much paper as they could and turn it over to the law firms for further evaluation. Thus a manual culling process carried out by legal experts was necessary. It was often too expensive to send people on repeated trips to make the physical copies of documents and they would collect and photocopy as much as possible. The drive to contain non-legal fees (like photocopying documents on repeated trips to the customer's office) contributed to over-collection.

Information Technology Helps with Document Volume

Eventually, the volume of possibly relevant documents became cumbersome to transport and manage. Forward-looking law firms looked to information technology to help. Information technologists and vendors applied their efforts to litigation support. In 1976, "everything from PC-based database managers such as dBase and InMagic to mainframes such as Control Data's Cyber 2000 were being used to manage portions of litigation support information. Control Data parleyed its mainframe work into Litigation Support Services (now Quorum Legal Services), one of the first companies to perform fee-based automated litigation support services." (Griffin, 1996) Quorum began in 1966 and Kroll OnTrack eventually acquired Quorum in 2004 (Howie, 2009).

As information technology made inroads in litigation support, documents were scanned into images (stored as Tagged Image File Format or TIFFs), allowing hundreds of documents to be stored on floppy disks and whole cases on CD

ROMs. Shnier (2000) recalls working with a joint defense group and several million pages of documents in 1994, "We provided the images on CDs to each JDG member, who kept the CDs at his or her firm, where images were accessed using jukeboxes or disk changers. The firms stored their document databases on their networks, but not the images -- because the systems were very slow when it came to viewing each image. So instead, the firms typically dedicated a stand-alone machine for image viewing."

Many law firms in the US turned to their litigation service provider for help in converting these paper documents into electronic TIFFs. The price was often set to a conversion fee per paper page. A thirty-page report would become thirty TIFFs and might be $0.10 per page, or $3.00 to convert into TIFF. It was a blissful time for litigation service providers. Operational scale could reduce the cost of creating a TIFF.

Of course, TIFFs were just images with the process still requiring people to read the documents and make judgment calls on the relevance of documents. The use of optical character recognition (OCR) provided the TIFF with a corresponding plain text file of the content in the image. Expanding their offerings, service providers could be deployed to handle the manual collection of documents, the photocopying, the scanning, and the OCR. Per page pricing dominated the market. The volume of content rose further with gains in office automation with the typewriter giving way to the early word processor. The word processor and the laser printer greatly increased the number of documents companies could create and increased the volume of documents that would be collected in legal matters.

Early Uses of Information Retrieval

With OCR producing a text version of the scanned image, full text searching was the next evolution, enabling users to find documents using a vocabulary that was relevant to the legal case.

The litigation service provider familiar with collection and scanning generally stopped at this stage, as there was no need for the collection crew to use search. The collection crew did not want to be involved in making a judgment call on relevance. A new market opportunity was created and litigation technology providers stepped in to build software that law firms could use to search their client's documents.

Summation, Concordance, and other vendors saw the demand in litigation support and converted software intended for depositions or library services to fill the growing need of managing corporate documents within the law firm. Each company built a product around the common term-document matrix (Table 1) and provided full text search. Concordance labeled their product the Concordance Information Retrieval System or Concordance IRS. Summation branded their term-document matrix and supporting document preparation tools as Blaze and later iBlaze.

Modest Goals

Simple search provided by companies like Concordance and Summation changed the landscape for legal discovery. In theory, all documents did not have to be reviewed by people. Instead, documents matching responsive terms or custodians could be found and then reviewed. In practice, older patterns of working through documents one by one still persisted alongside the new benefits of search. The parties involved in litigation seek answers to the questions of who, what, when, and where. Search by itself did not answer these questions directly; experienced legal professionals still constructed their own narratives and understandings of the collection. In building their narrative, these professionals still liked to see documents presented in order of date or custodian and not by an information retrieval ranking system. As such, the term-document matrix was a tool to answer Boolean questions roughly equivalent to "Show me all documents owned by Custodian15 where

Table 1. Term-document matrix

Given three simple documents:
1. "The defendant found himself staring at the jury"
2. "The company has never sent an email about discrimination"
3. "I do not understand the question"
The term-document matrix would look like this:

	the	defendant	company	understand	question	...
Doc1	x	x				
Doc2	x		x			
Doc3	x			x	x	

Various ranking systems can replace the simple understanding of existence represented by the X in each cell. Common examples are Term Frequency (TF) and more complex relationships like Document Length and Inverse Document Frequency (IDF).

Stop-words (words too common to index, like "the"), Tokenizers (trying to find word boundaries), and Stemmers (conjugation of verbs, decompounding of complex nouns) influence the choice of words to be indexed.

the document contains the word 'discrimination' and order by date."

Some systems offered primitive TF ranking (Term Frequency ranking counts unique words in a document), others explored TF-IDF (Term Frequency with Inverse Document Frequency is a ranking system used to account for the commonality of a given word in the entire corpus as compared to the current document), but lawyers were more interested in sorting by custodian to understand the parties or by date to construct timelines. As volumes of documents increased, new attention was placed on ranking systems to help find relevant documents, not just documents that matched a simple search query.

Persistence of Early Paradigms

With the diminishing use of paper documents for capturing the creative capital of a corporation, electronic versions replaced their paper counterparts; however, the custodian model persisted. Collecting electronic documents became a process of capturing the digital versions of the former paper documents. To gain confidence in the process, forensically sound collection appeared with litigation service providers once again stepping in. In forensically sound collection, the entire storage media is considered evidence and all of the bits are copied from their source. Creating copies of hard drives altered the pricing model in eDiscovery. Charges were now based on bytes and not pages.

Collecting entire hard drives had two effects: (1) collection was done in custodian batches and (2) relevance of collected information took a back seat to the completeness of collection. Decisions were not being made during collection, instead digital copies were being collected and provided to law firms so the legal assistant could wrangle the documents and load them into a review tool to begin the eDiscovery process.

The rise of WIMP (Windows, Icons, Menus, and Pointers) along with the historical physical process favored the use of the folder as the organizing metaphor for most eDiscovery systems. Even today, folders still dominate most of the UIs (user interface) used in eDiscovery. Along with folders, the idea of a page remains in heavy use. Even though it is hard to understand what a page of electronic mail is or a page of a wiki on an intranet, many firms and vendors still think of volumes of data as number of pages.

These paradigms (custodians, folders, pages) persisted in eDiscovery. Some are comfortable metaphors remaining in wide use while others are neutral. Custodian based collection has likely had the largest interactions with text mining and information retrieval for legal discovery.

USING TEXT MINING AND INFORMATION RETRIEVAL IN EDISCOVERY

Simple search served early needs in legal discovery. The conversion from paper discovery to electronic documents increased the amount of content needing to be reviewed. Coordination with customers and a distributed work force introduced new challenges addressed with Internet technologies. Eventually, the need to organize reviews and understand the content drove new technologies and vendors into the field of eDiscovery.

Using Basic Search

Beginning in 1994, Holland & Hart, a law firm based in Denver, Colorado, broke away from the dominant use of WordPerfect in the practice of law. The firm made an intrepid move to adopt Microsoft Word as the office productivity suite. With the switch to Word, there was still more than a decade of WordPerfect based work product. These documents had been created in terminal emulation software with SCO UNIX and in Microsoft DOS versions of WordPerfect. The documents were locked in a legacy document management system.

The first step taken toward making documents searchable was to unlock the content. After converting the WordPerfect documents to HTML, the metadata from the document management system was collapsed as HTML markup within each document. The resulting HTML representation contained the content and the metadata of each document.

Holland and Hart chose Verity Topic Search to index the thousands of HTML documents. In total, all of the WordPerfect documents represented over a million pages of information. A web interface was written to interact with the Verity search service to provide full text and metadata searching via fielded information. With all of this content, Holland & Hart had built one of the largest HTTP-based intranets in the legal space.

Well before Google became a verb, Holland & Hart was adding "search" to their training lexicon, which proved to be a powerful tool.

The Holland & Hart intranet gradually gave way to extranets allowing key customers access to a growing amount of digital information. According to Shnier (2000), "Now, options exist that allow lawyers to collaborate not only on the same floor, but around the world, via Extranet Web sites. Lawyers in Phoenix and Philadelphia can see new database additions and each other's work instantly. A team member out of town for depositions can see the latest documents or comments by plugging into the hotel room dataport."

Familiarity with basic search at Holland & Hart gave rise to early experiments in eDiscovery. Electronic discovery was in its infancy with paper still outnumbering electronic documents. The dominant process was scanning paper to create TIFFs and adding subjective metadata to a database. Holland & Hart began experimenting with blending structured searches (SQL) with unstructured searches (full text via Verity). As the volume of electronic information grew, specialized providers started appearing, including ASPs, search appliances, and information handlers or processors. A new market opportunity emerged with service providers offering search and review. The chain of vendors was getting larger and more diverse: collection, creating TIFFs or PDFs, and now review products. What started with a photocopying and reviewing a couple of boxes of documents had become a thriving industry.

Using Supervised Models

Supervised learning, a sub-discipline of machine learning which has been applied to information retrieval, takes a subset of labeled documents from a large population of data. The learning is called "supervised" because people manually classify (label) the documents. The data is split into two parts (Figure 1): the training set and the testing set. Using the inputs (features or characteristics) of

Figure 1. Supervised learning

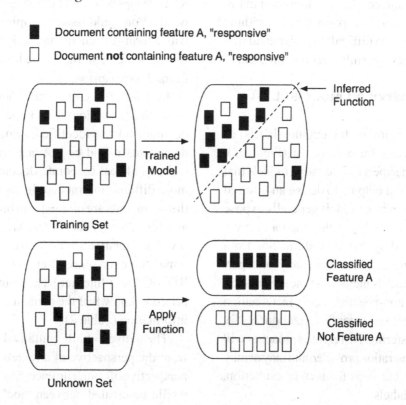

the documents in the training set, plus the outputs (labels) associated with each training instance, a complex function mapping inputs to desired outputs is learned. The quality of this learned function is assessed using the testing set; if the function can produce correct labels for data that it has not been trained on, then the entire population can now be automatically labeled using the learned function. Many types of algorithms exist that can be used for supervised learning.

Herbert Roitblatt, Aric Coady, Andy Kraftsow and team created DolphinSearch in the late 1990s. Based on two US Patents (6,751,628 and 6,189,002), DolphinSearch relied on a supervised learning model using neural networks. The team initially packaged DolphinSearch as the KnowledgeBox using Compaq Alpha hardware (Herper, 2000). With a product and in search of a market, Kraftsow saw opportunity on the Web, but chose not to compete against the contemporary heavy-

weights like AltaVista, Ask Jeeves, or Yahoo. "Kraftsow said the types of broad, ambiguous searches popularized by those engines aren't the best use of DolphinSearch's technology" (Essex, 2005). The market was not favorable and Kraftsow steered the company towards the emerging world of eDiscovery where DolphinSearch gained a loyal customer following.

Strangely, DolphinSearch's neural network toolkit was never used for the more natural purpose of classifying documents. Instead, DolphinSearch continued to focus on improving search results. But, even Kraftsow admitted that, "If you know how to use Boolean logic really well, you can get similar results to what we get" (Essex, 2005). Daticon eventually acquired DolphinSearch and an early experiment with supervised learning in eDiscovery came to a close. Parts of Dolphin-Search live on, but the unfulfilled promise of radical time savings through the vague industry definitions of "Concept Search" tarnished many brands and led to a perception that algorithms were a black-box – so difficult to understand that some lawyers grew fearful of relying on them.

Using Unsupervised Models: LSA

In unsupervised learning, the outputs (labels) of the source material are not known (Figure 2). This differs from supervised learning models that use both inputs and outputs to derive an inferred function. Unsupervised models generally expose characteristics of the data rather than a discrete classification used by the inferred function from supervised learning. There are many unsupervised learning models including Latent Semantic Analysis (LSA), non-negative matrix factorization (NMF), non-negative tensor factorization (NTF), and *k*-means clustering. Different approaches will vary from the illustration provided and may or may not include discrete steps for feature extraction, clustering, and labels.

Latent Semantic Analysis, sometimes Latent Semantic Indexing, is a method of performing matrix factorization on the term-document matrix (Table 1). Generally, LSA uses eigenvalue decomposition with the goal of clarifying polysemy in the collection. "The main idea in latent semantic indexing model is to map each document and query vector into a lower dimensional space which is associated with concepts" (Baeza-Yates, 1999).

The legal market was introduced to LSA through a software company called Engenium. The story of Engenium is similar to Dolphin-Search. Dave Copps and others put together a strategy around licensing LSA (Landauer et al., 2007) and offering it to the legal market and other industries. The resulting product was called Engenium Semetric and was launched with great fanfare. Litigation service providers could license Engenium and add it to their portfolio with other search services. Engenium allowed at least three distinct interactions with their search service. You could explore the concept space that revealed the

relationships being tracked using co-occurrence of words. You could issue a simple search resolved with a term-document matrix. Finally, you could issue a search that likely used the concept space for query expansion.

Idealized use cases were constructed for the use of this technology with hopes that once a key documented was identified, semantically related documents would be just one search away. The makeup of real corporate documents made this more difficult in practice. In most corporations, the documents are divided into binary documents and text documents. Filters are used to extract text from binary documents. Text documents like e-mail, do not require filters. Those familiar with RFC-822 and Internet based e-mail are not surprised to know that the content is mostly routing information (Table 2).

The native e-mails contained too much noise from the perspective of a reviewer and from the perspective of co-occurrence. Strong relationships would be created between "joe" and "example. com" for e-mails like "joe@example.com" and even "joe" and "example" depending on the tokenizer. It was quickly recognized that documents would have to be scrubbed delicately to make the best use of Engenium. Most litigation service providers were left with the difficult task of when and how to scrub the documents. Should the BCC recipients in an e-mail be stripped out before sending the document to Engenium? Should the CC addresses be kept? Should the mail server information be thrown away? What about the Message-ID? It was becoming clear that using LSA inside of eDiscovery with native documents was going to be much harder than using LSA against a reference corpus like Medline.

Since it was the service providers running Engenium, too much time was being spent on making granular decisions about what should be indexed. This was competing with the time needed by the legal professionals to make decisions on relevance. This conflict of time and value became a difficult

Figure 2. Unsupervised learning

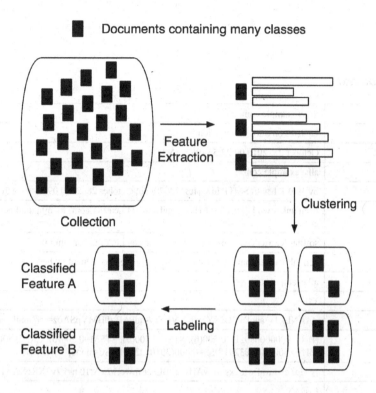

battle for the proponents of Engenium to win. Kroll OnTrack eventually acquired Engenium.

Using Unsupervised Models - NMF

Dealing with the signal versus noise problem when handling native documents in eDiscovery is not a simple process. Much can be gained in finding methods that simplify document scrubbing to compensate for the typical forms of noise found in these documents. The authors have been working on this specific problem using NMF (Non Negative Matrix Factorization) (Lee & Seung, 1999) with other information reduction techniques.

As with the previous example of Engenium, certain models can be sensitive to the noise of the corpus. A large amount of noise in the corpus, such as e-mail headers or signatures (Table 2), can result in seemingly nonsensical themes and inaccurate classification. Latent Semantic

Analysis can produce term relations that aren't often understood including words like "secure" and "channel" in row six and over emphasize the connection between "HR" and "Executive" in the signature block of row eighteen.

One approach to compensate for this noise involves document reduction, distilling each document in a corpus down to a list of *n*-grams (one or more terms in a phrase) each weighted by their frequency in the document. Integrating stop-word filtering can further reduce the noise of common and irrelevant terms. These reduced documents, each represented by the list of weighted *n*-grams (called 'DocVectors' by the authors), offer the flexibility to lend themselves to a number of methods, both supervised and unsupervised. For example, DocVectors can be employed in unsupervised methods for theme extraction using NMF. The DocVectors can be combined to produce a

Table 2. Noisy e-mail text

1	From:	joe@example.com
2	Subject:	Updates on our Conversation
3	Date:	October 28, 2010 09:22:55 -0600 (MDT)
4	To:	all@example.com
5	Received:	by 10.0.1.1 with SMTP id yq4cs113579vdb; October 28, 2010 09:23:01 -0700 (PDT)
6	Received:	from unknown [10.0.1.2] (EHLO mail-qw0-f43.carrier.com) by mta.mail.net over TLS secured channel
7	Received-Spf:	softfail (carrier.com: best guess record for domain of transitioning)
8	Received-Spf:	neutral (carrier.com: 10.0.1.2 is neither permitted nor denied by best guess)
9	X-Beenthere:	all.example.com
10	Mime-Version:	1.0
11	Message-Id:	<AANLkTi=anotW4U2xY2wKVVUFtV-qdPAB=0BMVpSAoz=v@mail.carrier.com>
12	X-Spam:	[F=0.2000000000; B=0.500(0); STSI=0.500(0); STSM=0.500(0); CM=0.500; MH=0.500(2011032918); S=0.200(2010122901); SC=none]
13	X-Analysisout:	[v=1.0 c=1 a=Fwto2xs5-owA:10 a=BLceEmwcHowA:10 a=Pzv3XRqSAA]
14	Precedence:	List
15	List-Id:	<carrier.example.com>
16	Content-Type:	multipart/mixed; boundary=bcaec501c5dcc5cfef049fa178e1
17	Body	All - Please see the Employee Manual for updates regarding suggestions from our last employee meeting.
18	Signature	Thank You Joe Smith HR Executive Example Corporation joe@example.com

synthetic term-document matrix of higher quality than the original matrix.

Using Lee and Seung's (1999, 2001) work, the authors built a prototype using a differential cost function to determine the component matrices from the synthetic DocVector matrix in NMF. NMF is another approach using linear algebra and matrix factorization. NMF and Probablistic Latent Semantic Analysis (PLSA) are closely related. "PLSA avoids the problem of negative values by using nonnegative matrix factorization rather than SVD (singular value decomposition)" (Bellegarda, 2007).

After factorizing using NMF, themes are extracted from the component matrices. Consultants can assist with further refinement of the unsupervised themes. The results have typically been sufficiently comprehensible that they have provided value in several ways: (1) the generated themes allow a corpus to be approached where detailed foreknowledge of the corpus is not required; (2) the themes provide a relatively unbiased summary of subject matter in the corpus, to inform decisions on further exploration of the corpus, or to abandon it as irrelevant; and (3) the themes extracted from NMF can be used as a basis for further classification of documents in the corpus.

Classification of documents in the corpus using NMF features can occur in a number of different ways. A distance calculation (or similarity metric) can be used between the DocVectors from the corpus and each theme. Another approach might be to build a weighted search expression around each theme to search against all documents in the corpus, relying on the search engine's ranking algorithm to determine each document's affinity for a particular theme.

Concept Searching

As more vendors realized the opportunities in eDiscovery, TripleHop (acquired by Oracle), Attenex (acquired by FTI), Syngence, and others joined DolphinSearch and Engenium. A broad market

definition of Concept Search emerged. Concept Search was pitched as "The Next Big Thing in electronic discovery" (Johnson, 2004) with great hopes pinned on the idea of finding semantically related documents. Strict understandings of classifiers, theme extraction, supervised training, and unsupervised learning were not always relevant for the definition of Concept Search in eDiscovery. No matter the underlying technology, the vendors coalesced under the Concept Search banner and tried to find an audience and legitimacy. While some vendors found success others realized that document preparation had the greatest influence on the success of their algorithms, and still others found that a useful UI (user interface) and faceted search could meet the definitions of Concept Searching.

CHALLENGES IN LEGAL ELECTRONIC DISCOVERY

When two sides use the process of discovery for a legal matter, the amount of information is asymmetrical for the parties involved. The defendant has access to their own company's data. They begin by raking relevant custodians and start collection. The custodian-centric collection results in batches of documents instead of a complete corpus. The plaintiffs in a legal dispute have less information. They receive their screened documents from the defendant in batches. Both sides have similar batch models separated by time. In the case of counter suits, the parties play both roles.

For example, the CEO, Director of Engineering, and Lead Developer are all considered principle custodians in a case. With custodian collection, the overlap in personal language magnifies as the CEO generally uses market-facing terms, the Director of Engineering generally uses an operational lexicon, and the Lead Developer speaks about internal project names. The CEO's hard drive is collected first. Documents are extracted and the corpus is started. The next custodian is the Director of Engineering. With these two custodians, the corpus is now 25,000 documents. The CEO and Director use the the product name "Jupiter." The third custodian is the Lead Developer. After her documents are collected, the corpus is now 32,000 documents. When she talks about the product, she uses the internal project name "Zeus."

Both sides use similar tools to assist in different goals. The defendant may be interested in making sure key information is not produced to the other side and they will use basic search terms to look for product names or people names. The defendant may be interested in the quality of the human review and use a supervised learning system to classify documents for quality control. The plaintiff may be interested in unsupervised feature extraction to summarize batches of documents. The plaintiff may use supervised learning to reduce the amount of data for human review or simple search for finding important people.

Batches and Supervised Learning

Most supervised learning models have problems with updating if the corpus changes significantly. Fundamentally, supervised learning uses a training set, which is usually some statistical sample of the larger population. The resulting inferred function is assumed to be valid in the whole population. Classic sampling bias can greatly affect the selection of a training set. Custodian collection increases these concerns by changing the nature of the total population with each new custodian.

Using our example, a training set is created from the corpus after the first two custodians are collected (CEO and Director). The goal of our hypothetical supervised learning model (Figure 1) is to create a classifier that decides if a document is relevant to our case. After experts review the training set, the inferred function identifies documents containing the word Jupiter with relevance to the case. After the Lead Developer's documents are collected, the classifier is used to make decisions about the relevance. Very few documents are

marked relevant because the internal project name for Jupiter is Zeus. She uses Zeus in most of her correspondence and because of this discrepancy the classifier needs to be retrained.

Batches and Unsupervised Learning

Unsupervised tools have mostly been targeted towards a complete corpus. If the corpus changes significantly, the underlying assumptions also change. Under the custodian collection process, each batch brings significantly more information to the corpus. The term relationship information that is trying to be analyzed may require regeneration with each batch. If the unsupervised model uses statistical sampling, the model is affected by changes in the population and may require regeneration or separate systems ensuring the validity of the statistical sample over the new data being received.

For LSA, the term-document matrix is approximated by rank-k partial singular value decomposition (PSVD). The computation time with PSVD is costly. When the corpus changes significantly, new information must be added into the calculation. Current research is looking at ways to avoid the expense of calculating the PSVD with changes in the corpus. Three areas are commonly referenced: folding-in, updating, and folding-up. Kontostathis (2010) suggests that folding-in is "fast and easy" but "generally corrupts orthogonality" of some components, and is "not recommended if collection changes often." She also says that updating is "slower than folding-in, but much more accurate." Finally, she says that folding-up is a hybrid approach where "new documents are folded-in until a threshold is reached, then updated with all new documents." Her research is currently looking at Essential Dimensions of Latent Semantic Indexing (EDLSI) and hybrid approaches with PSVD updates (LSI and LSA can be considered interchangeable). This is promising work, but currently not being offered by vendors servicing the eDiscovery market place. Until useful update models can be applied to PSVD, information will remain incomplete and dated with the custodian batch process. Each PSVD regeneration takes longer as the term-document matrix expands with new content. See Berry et al. (1999) and Zha (1999) for general discussions on the complexity of SVD-updating.

Using an unsupervised model like NMF also suffers update problems when the corpus changes. In this case, two matrices are multiplied together to approximate the term-document matrix. The features and weights found within the factored matrices are presumed to be interesting. Under the custodian collection process, the term-document matrix can change dimensions significantly. New documents expand one dimension of the matrix and different lexicons between custodians change the other dimension of the term-document matrix. The factored matrices would need to change dimensions to represent changes in the term-document matrix. As more custodians are collected the unique terms will decrease significantly, but it could take quite a while before the corpus stabilizes. Heap's Law suggests that the vocabulary of unique words grows at roughly the square root of the corpus and eventually tapers off (Baeza-Yates, 1999).

Berry (2009) has been introducing the idea of using NTF for eDiscovery; however, he has noted that the cost for updating NTF models is unknown and possibly expensive. Balasubramanian et al. (2010) have been working on block coordinate descent methods to improve computation of the factorized tensors, but this is only reducing the cost of computation, it cannot address the update process. For custodian based collection processes, the NTF would need to be recalculated with any significant change in the corpus.

Timeliness of Data

Parties in the legal system could wait until the corpus is complete, but this is not a practical solution. Many court mandated due dates are involved in legal matters and the parties involved cannot wait for the corpus to be complete. Instead, both parties begin work on the key custodians that are likely to be relevant. Both parties start with incomplete data sets. In a recent (2010) high profile merger between two media companies, 120 batches of documents with over 200 custodians were created over 30 days. Some of these batches may have represented just one custodian while other batches aggregated smaller custodians into a batch. Neither side was interested in waiting 30 days for the corpus to be complete. Eventually the corpus grew to 4,000,000 documents.

Systems that require recalculations are difficult to use in the current timelines and processes for eDiscovery. A classifier that misses new information and is retrained creates an operational loop where previously classified documents may have to be run through the new inferred function (Table 3).

RECOMMENDATIONS

Rethinking Custodian Collection

Digital technology has infiltrated much of our lives. Cell phones rarely distinguish work calls from personal calls. Workplace computers access Facebook and share digital photos from our families alongside our proposals for new product offerings and spreadsheets tracking our travel expenses. Collecting documents by making copies of computer hard drives contributes to over-collection and noise for information retrieval in eDiscovery. Rethinking custodian collection could greatly reduce the problems of over-collection.

Creative capital of corporations is exchanged in the front office, not in the back office. These front office systems are often highly decentralized and left as "workgroup" implementations. An example is Microsoft Sharepoint. To effectively find information and share it at the workgroup level, Sharepoint includes text search services.

Table 3. Hypothetical costs of batch updating

Supervised Learning With Classifier						
Batch	Name	Docs	Total	Training Cost [1]	Classifying Cost [2]	Total Cost [3]
1	CEO	12000	12000	18000	6000	24000
2	Dir	13000	25000	37500	12500	50000
3	Lead	7000	32000	48000	16000	64000
Unsupervised Learning With Matrix Regeneration						
Batch	Name	Docs	Total	Matrix Cost [4]	Clustering Cost [5]	Total Cost [6]
1	CEO	12000	12000	15600	6000	21600
2	Dir	13000	25000	32500	12500	45000
3	Lead	7000	32000	41600	16000	57600
Unsupervised Learning With Matrix Update						
Batch	Name	Docs	Total	Matrix Cost [7]	Clustering Cost [8]	Total Cost [9]
1	CEO	12000	12000	15600	6000	21600
2	Dir	13000	25000	22100	12500	34600
3	Lead	7000	32000	11900	16000	27900

In this hypothetical model, different costs were assigned to the Training, Classifying, Matrix, and Clustering Costs. For this table, no update process was considered for supervised learning, although it is feasible. For unsupervised learning, two use cases were considered: full matrix generation and partial updates. For partial updates, a new cost was applied to just the new data and not the total data. The costs are theoretical and used for illustration of the batch update challenges.

1. 1.5 * Total Count, 2. 0.5 * Total Count, 3. Sum of Training Cost + Classifying Cost, 4. 1.3 * Total Count, 5. 0.5 * Total Count

6. Sum of Matrix Cost + Clustering Cost, 7. 1.3 * Docs for initial batch, 1.7 * Docs for batches 2 and 3, 8. 0.5 * Total Count

9. Sum of Matrix Cost + Clustering Cost

This same text search could be used to collect from the network instead of the custodian. Company experts familiar with the projects can help form ad hoc search queries or even contribute to a corporate ontology to help resolve issues with polysemy and synonymy. Similarly, embedded search for e-mail systems could be used to greatly narrow the scope of collection. Special purpose devices like the Google Search Appliance can be layered on top, or simple interfaces to federate search across all of the workgroup systems would be effective in reducing over-collection.

Custodian collection remains an important tool for some legal matters. It will not disappear even if search and other tools help narrow the corpus; however, many litigation matters may not require pure custodian collection. Additionally, as companies increase their adoption of collaborative tools and even social media, the entire idea of custodian collection may become less useful.

Information captured in a corporate wiki won't reside on a custodian's hard drive. The information will be collected from the network and tagged with ownership data. The use of Google Apps or Office Live replaces the need to create content on a personal computer, any network ready device will do. Collecting from these highly distributed resources that are no longer part of the company infrastructure will change the way collection happens (e.g., APIs for Google Apps vs. forensically sound disk images) and further challenge custodian collection.

The Promise of Vast Compute Resources in the Cloud

Cloud computing from Amazon Web Services, Google AppEngine, and others have created options for working with very large sets of data. Tasks that were previously restricted to university clusters or super computers can now be worked with for hundreds of dollars a month.

Harnessing the power of this vast computational resource may decrease the cost of tasks that are currently considered expensive. For example, matrix factorization could be extremely rapid if the SciPy libraries (an open source set of math libraries including n-dimensional array manipulation) could be distributed and coordinated. An algorithm that uses a differential cost function would need to communicate across n-machines to be highly distributed and most implementations rely on the convenience of running in the same physical machine. Creative use of big data tools like Hadoop may also assist the perception of the cost of computationally expensive tasks. Hadoop is an open source version of MapReduce (Dean, 2004) that Google popularized for working with very large sets of data.

FUTURE RESEARCH DIRECTIONS

Even within the realms of custodian collection, there remain opportunities for further applied work. One area includes using the ongoing review process to continuously adjust the rank (and perceived relevance) of the remaining documents. Another possible area is to embrace the custodian batches with isolated sets of summarized data and analyze these sets as stacks of data.

Collaborative Information Seeking

Reviewing of documents in eDiscovery can be seen as a specialized collaborative process. Researchers have been applying information retrieval to the problems of collaboration. During the dot com years, collaborative filtering was the umbrella for this area of research. The goals of collaborative filtering were quickly understood by retail web sites looking to sell more products. These retailers developed highly specialized tools hoping to recommend a relevant product based on the

similarity attributes of the product or the buying habits of other consumers. Recommendation engines have become an area of intense interest as companies try to optimize long tail inventories or simply make another sale. NetFlix awarded one million dollars in 2009 to the winners of their prize. "A good recommendation engine is worth a lot of money. According to a report by industry analyst Forrester, one-third of customers who notice recommendations on an e-commerce site wind up buying something based on them" (Grossman, 2010). Porting a recommendation engine into eDiscovery may not be feasible; however, there may be room to introduce tools that intermingle supervised and unsupervised models to aid in collaboration.

Pickens (2010) describes some features of collaborative information seeking that reorder document ranks using an online, dynamic combination of multiple query results sets over the course of a session, rather than rebuilding classifier models: "In Colum's work (Foley, 2008), the relevance judgments assigned to documents by one user affect (via synchronized influence) the ordering of the not-yet-seen documents in the second user's queue, and vice versa. The Cerchiamo algorithm (Pickens, 2008) looks at unseen, low ranked results from user number one's query history and combines that information with user number one's relevance judgments to present user number two with low-ranked documents that user number one never got a chance to see. At the same time, the system offers dynamically changing (continually-updating) query suggestions back to user number one based in large part on the relevance judgments made by user number two."

This mediated system may be very useful in eDiscovery since it could: overcome the biases of single reviewers without dramatically increasing the costs of review, does not require a full corpus, and adapts to the reviewer's choices rather than relying on fixed training sets. In addition, unlike some inferred functions from classifiers, the ranking choices are relatively easy to explain and if needed, defend in court.

Stacks: Analyzing Batches of Information

Some text mining methods may be better suited for batches and therefore be a better match for the custodian collection process. The authors are experimenting with the idea of using feature extraction via NMF on a custodian level and then stacking the resulting feature matrices together for further analysis. The weights score could be normalized or refined as features reappear across custodian batches. This may prove useful because it allows independent calculations to remain independent and does not require expensive update methods as new documents are added to the corpus. Additionally, the size of the initial matrix is also constrained since it represents one custodian at a time making the factoring a reasonable computation.

Independent tensors may also be well suited to independent analysis via NTF and custodian collection, but the amount of data may be difficult to manage as the corpus grows past 50, 100, or 200 custodians. Using tensors to construct a common timeline would allow certain themes to be mapped to events. The events could be independent of each other via the custodian batch, but annealed into a single timeline as more custodians are collected.

CONCLUSION

In this chapter, we have looked at the world of electronic discovery. Historical collection practices and business practices have influenced modern eDiscovery with large, shifting volumes of content in need of review.

Bringing to bear the traditional tools of text mining, including those for use in theme extraction, classification, and collaborative filtering, proves to be a challenge within the special de-

mands of this domain. Large and noisy document volumes, incremental addition of documents, pressing timelines, tight budgets, as well as court and stakeholder acceptance combine to test the limitations of existing tools.

As a result, opportunities have arisen to develop new tools to meet this challenge, to improve the custodial collection process, to build on emerging technologies such as cloud computing, to reduce the document volumes to those candidate documents most likely to be relevant to a case, and to assist teams of reviewers in efficiently and accurately identifying the most relevant documents to bring to trial.

REFERENCES

Baeza-Yates, R., & Ribeiro-Neto, B. (1999). *Modern information retrieval* (pp. 44–147). Reading, MA: Addison-Wesley.

Balasubramanian, K., Kim, J., Puretskiy, A., Berry, M. W., & Park, H. (2010, May). A fast algorithm for nonnegative tensor factorization using block coordinate descent and an active-set-type method. In *Proceedings of the Text Mining Workshop held in conjunction with the Tenth SIAM International Conference on Data Mining*, Columbus, OH.

Bellegarda, J. R. (2007). *Latent semantic mapping* (p. 27). San Francisco, CA: Morgan & Claypool.

Berry, M. W. (2009). *Exploiting nonnegative tensor factorization for scenario and plot discovery in large document sets*. Retrieved September 1, 2010, from http://www.catalystsecure.com/images/crs/articles/UVA/October/berry-presentation-4up.pdf

Berry, M. W., Drmac, Z., & Jessup, E. (1999). Matrices, vector spaces, and information retrieval. *SIAM Review, 41*, 335–362. doi:10.1137/S0036144598347035

Coady, A. (2002). *U. S. Patent No. 6,751,628: Process and system for sparse vector and matrix representation of document indexing and retrieval.* Washington, DC: United States Patent and Trademark Office.

Dean, J., & Ghemawat, S. (2004). *U. S. Patent No. 7,650,331: System and method for efficient large-scale data processing.* Washington, DC: United States Patent and Trademark Office.

Essex, D. (2005). *Ride dolphin through Web waters.* Retrieved June 27, 2010, from http://www.pcworld.com/ article/16602/ride_dolphin_through_web_waters.html

Foley, C. (2008). *Division of labour and sharing of knowledge for synchronous collaborative information retrieval* (Unpublished doctoral dissertation). Dublin City University School of Computing, Dublin, UK.

Griffith, C. (1996). Summation blaze: Litigation support at the touch of a key. *Corporate Legal Times, 61,* 12.

Grossman, L. (2010). How computers know what we want – before we do. *Time, Inc.* Retrieved May 28, 2010, from http://www.time.com/ time/magazine/article/0,9171,1992403,00.html

Herper, M. (2000). *Dolphin search's knowledge box, trawls networks.* Retrieved June 28, 2010, from http://www.forbes.com/ 2000/10/17/1017dolphin.html

Howie, J., & Potters, M. (2009). Industry consolidation. *Association of Litigation Support Professionals.* Retrieved August 1, 2010, from http://www.howieconsulting.com/ articles/IndustryConsolidation.html

Johnson, L. (2004). *Contextual search capabilities.* Retrieved June 28, 2010, from http://www.litigation-support.org/ viewtopic.php?t=8799

Landauer, T., McNamara, D., Dennis, S., & Kintsch, W. (Eds.). (2007). *Handbook of latent semantic analysis.* Mahwah, NJ: Lawrence Erlbaum.

Lee, D., & Seung, H. S. (1999). Learning the parts of objects by non-negative matrix factorization. *Nature, 401,* 788–791. doi:10.1038/44565

Lee, D. D., & Seung, H. S. (2001). Algorithms for non-negative matrix factorization. In *Proceedings of the Conference on Advances in Neural Information Processing Systems.* Kontostathis, A., Moulding, E., & Spiteri, R. J. (2010, May). EDLSI with PSVD updating. In *Proceedings of the Text Mining Workshop held in conjunction with the Tenth SIAM International Conference on Data Mining,* Columbus, OH.

Pickens, J. (2008). *Communicating about collaboration: Depth of mediation.* Retrieved September 1, 2010, from http://palblog.fxpal.com/ ?p=274

Pickens, J., Golovchinsky, G., Shah, C., Ovarfordt, P., & Back, M. (2008, July 20-24). Algorithmic mediation for collaborative exploratory search. In *Proceedings of the ACM SIGIR Conference on Information Retrieval,* Singapore (pp. 315-322).

Roitblat, H. L. (1999). *U. S. Patent No. 6,189,002: Process and system for retrieval of documents using context-relevant semantic profiles.* Washington, DC: United States Patent and Trademark Office.

Shnier, C. F. (2000). Web-based document repositories. *Law Technology News.* Retrieved August 1, 2010, from http://ltn-archive.hotresponse.com/ august00/litigation_support_p39.html

Zha, H. (1999). On updating problems in latent semantic indexing. *SIAM Journal on Scientific Computing, 21*(2), 782–791. doi:10.1137/S1064827597329266

ADDITIONAL READING

Arkfeld, M. (2010). *Electronic discovery and evidence*. Retrieved September 1, 2010, from http://arkfeld.blogs.com/

Baron, J. R., Braman, R. G., Withers, K. J., Allman, T. Y., Daley, M. J., & Paul, G. L. (Eds.). (2007). *The Sedona conference best practices commentary on the use of search and information retrieval methods in e-discovery*. Phoenix, AZ: The Sedona Conference.

Bhatt, R., Daly, P., Eidelman, J., Tienzo, R., & Toomey, C. (2010). *Catalyst eDiscovery Blog*. Retrieved September 1, 2010, from http://catalystsecure.com/blog/

Brown, T., Lambert, G., & Salazar, L. (2010). *E-Discovery, business goals and best practices*. Retrieved September 1, 2010, from http://www.geeklawblog.com/2010/05/e-discovery-business-goals-and-best.html

Buckwalter, A. J. (Ed.). (2010). *Litigation support today*. Retrieved September 1, 2010, from http://www.litigationsupporttoday.com

Gelbmann, T., & Socha, G. (Eds.). (2010). *The electronic discovery reference model analysis guide*. Retrieved September 1, 2010, from http://edrm.net/ resources/guides/edrm-framework-guides/analysis

Golovchinsky, G. (2010). *On technology and beyond* Retrieved September 1, 2010, from http://palblog.fxpal.com/ ?author=4

Holderman, J. F., & Nolan, N. R. (2010). Seventh circuit electronic discovery pilot program. *United States Courts Southern District of Indiana*. Retrieved September 1, 2010, from http://www.insd.uscourts.gov/ News/7thphase%20one.pdf

Kehoe, M. B., & Bennett, M. L. (Eds.). (2010). *Enterprise search - The business and technology of corporate search*. Retrieved September 1, 2010, from http://www.enterprisesearchblog.com/

Withers, K. (Ed.). (2010). *The Sedona Conference*. Retrieved September 1, 2010, from http://www.thesedonaconference.org/ content/miscFiles/publications_html

Wotipka, J. (Ed.). (2010). *Electronic discovery law – Resources & information*. Retrieved September 1, 2010, from http://www.discoveryresources.org

KEY TERMS AND DEFINITIONS

Collection: The process of gathering data, documents, or evidence to be used in a legal matter

Custodian: In eDiscovery, the owner of a set of documents or data

Discovery: The process of requesting information, documents, or other evidence from opposing parties.

eDiscovery: Electronic Discovery – refers to the process of collecting, analyzing, and reviewing electronic documents during the discovery phase of legal matters.

Review: The process of assessing the relevance of data, documents, or evidence for a legal matter

Chapter 9
Intelligent Semantic Search Engines for Opinion and Sentiment Mining

Mona Sleem-Amer
Pertimm, France

Ivan Bigorgne
Lutin, France

Stéphanie Brizard
Arisem, France

Leeley Daio Pires Dos Santos
EDF, France

Yacine El Bouhairi
Thales, France

Bénédicte Goujon
Thales, France

Stéphane Lorin
Thales, France

Claude Martineau
LIGM, France

Loïs Rigouste
Pertimm, France

Lidia Varga
LIGM, France

ABSTRACT

Over the last years, research and industry players have become increasingly interested in analyzing opinions and sentiments expressed on the social media web for product marketing and business intelligence. In order to adapt to this need search engines not only have to be able to retrieve lists of documents but to directly access, analyze, and interpret topics and opinions. This article covers an intermediate phase of the ongoing industrial research project 'DoXa' aiming at developing a semantic opinion and sentiment mining search engine for the French language. The DoXa search engine enables topic related opinion and sentiment extraction beyond positive and negative polarity using rich linguistic resources. Centering the work on two distinct business use cases, the authors analyze both unstructured Web 2.0 contents (e.g., blogs and forums) and structured questionnaire data sets. The focus is on discovering hidden patterns in the data. To this end, the authors present work in progress on opinion topic relation extraction and visual analytics, linguistic resource construction as well as the combination of OLAP technology with semantic search.

DOI: 10.4018/978-1-4666-0330-1.ch009

INTRODUCTION

As a relatively young sub-field of data mining and computational linguistics, opinion and sentiment mining deals with automatic methods and techniques to extract, analyze and search opinions and sentiments expressed in mostly social media web content (Pang & Lee, 2008).

For companies, knowing what their market thinks and feels about their products and services is vital for their success. Traditionally, this question was addressed by market research using polls and surveys to find out about the customers' opinion. As subjective content is increasingly available in important amounts on the web, search engines seem to be ideal tools for this task. However, existing tools and methods are yet insufficient for capturing them. In this chapter we present our multi-faceted approach to design a semantic enterprise search engine for opinion and sentiment mining.

As opinion mining is a multi-layered task containing in itself independent areas of research and given the fact that this chapter is limited in terms of space and scope, we do not intend to cover all possible aspects of the subject. We made the decision to leave out certain aspects even though they are currently researched actively as an important part of the project (e.g., opinion mining using statistical methods like supervised or unsupervised machine learning) and to concentrate only selected aspects of our opinion search system, including:

- *Relating opinions and topics* – efficient opinion mining does not only extract opinion polarity (e.g., positive/negative) but also topics (e.g., solar cells) or topic features (e.g., the price of solar cells) and the relations between them (e.g., positive opinions about solar cells). While opinion and topic extraction is well covered in literature, works about relating opinions and topics are still sparse. This chapter presents a method of relation extraction and describes the problems encountered.

- *Extracting opinion and topics / building ontologies and dictionaries* – we present a method to create linguistic resources for opinion and topic extraction according to a semantic opinion/sentiment model we developed for the project. Existing applications often limit opinion search to classifying entire web pages or sentences into either positive or negative categories. Our approach is to take into account ambiguity, intensity and negation and refine the binary positive negative scheme to make subjectivity information more relevant for real-life business decision making.

- *Combining OLAP technologies with a search engine* – as search engines usually focus on opinions in individual web documents they often fail to give a measurable overview of the entire document set. However, companies need opinion metrics for benchmarking and decision making. Business intelligence tools like OLAP (online-analytical processing) address this need by enabling multidimensional data storing and benchmark indicator calculation. As these tools could benefit from semantic search engine functionality, we attempt to combine the best of both in one tool.

- *Designing an opinion search user interface* – we have conducted a user needs study for two distinct business use cases and data sets involving companies in the market research (video games) and energy sector. By taking a user centered perspective, we present new strategies for querying, ranking and visualization for opinion search engine interface design. HMI evaluation tests will be conducted in the last phase of the project by the Lutin laboratory. However, these tests are not subject of this chapter.

This chapter is organized as follows: after a literary review on opinion/sentiment search, we present our user needs study used as a reference point for creating a search scenario and build a user interface of which the principal functions are briefly described. The next section focuses on how the different opinion mining components communicate with one another via web services. Then, we zoom in on the main component in charge of linguistic opinion, topic and relation extraction. It holds a strategic position in the system as the semantic annotation extracted from free text will serve as a basis for subsequent modules. Eventually, we present the OLAP analysis module describing how a business intelligence tool can help to interpret subjectivity related information in an opinion and sentiment search engine.

Our goal in this chapter is to present our efforts to build a semantic enterprise search engine with integrated business intelligence technology and state of the art opinion/sentiment, topic and relation extraction. A special focus is on the design of a user-friendly interface in the context of a real-life use case.

BACKGROUND

In literature, the computational analysis of opinions and sentiments in electronic documents is either considered as two separate but closely related research fields called *opinion mining* and *sentiment analysis* or in a broader sense as *subjectivity analysis* (Wiebe & Riloff, 2005; Wilson et al., 2005). There are other terms in use, but up to this date no uniform terminology has been agreed on in literature (Pang & Lee, 2008). The combination of subjectivity mining and information retrieval (IR) is mostly called *opinion retrieval* (Zhang, Yu, & Meng, 2007) or *opinion search* (Miao, Li, & Dai, 2009).

Existing opinion search engines are either web search (e.g., Swotti) or enterprise search applications meaning that they are designed for specific business use cases. The two types of tools have in common that they are limited in terms of thematic scope as opposed to general purpose web search engines like Google or Bing. At the present moment, general public opinion search applications focus on news topics or current events (Grefenstette, Qu, Shanahan, & Evans, 2004) or on product, customer, film, music or literary reviews (Oelke, Hao, Rohrdantz, Keim, Dayal, Haug, & Janetzko, 2009; Chen, Ibekwe-sanjuan, Sanjuan, & Weaver, 2006). Tools can also be limited in terms of content type and format such as blogs (e.g., Opinion Crawl) or Twitter messages (e.g., CrowdEye). In enterprise opinion search the most common type of tool is the e-reputation platform, for marketing and business intelligence purposes (e.g., Radian6, TrendyBuzz, Synthesio, ami news monitor, Alterian). In either type of application, integrating opinion mining functionality into a search engine has various consequences for querying, ranking and result visualization.

Most information retrieval systems build inverted term/document indexes for full-text keyword search (Baeza-Yates & Ribeiro-Neto, 1999). Along the same line, a number of opinion search engines focus on the document (*macro* level) as the information unit for querying and result presentation (Zhang et al., 2007). However, document ranking is generally problematic as it is based on the assumption that one document equals or can be reduced to one opinion, which is insufficient in the case of multiple or controversial opinions (Liu, Hu, & Cheng, 2005). Another approach has therefore been to index and rank on the sentence (*micro*) level (Furuse, Hiroshima, Yamada, & Kataoka, 2007). Wefeelfine.org simply extracts sentences that contain the phrase "I feel" and in a second step, analyzes opinion words contained in these sentences. The sentence level approach represents more accurately individual opinions but fails to detect opinions or sentiments that are expressed in more than one sentence. Wilson, Wiebe, and Hoffmann (2009) take into account the proximity of subjective phrases to topic words in the limits of more than one sentence (*meso* level). Another indexing unit is the blog *post*. Mishne et al. (2007) present a system of sentiment visualization in blog posts using user sentiment tags. The post as information unit is specific to blogs and forums and is therefore not transposable to process other web formats.

In traditional keyword based IR, query results are presented to the user as a list ranked by some sort of relevance criterion to the query. From a visual perspective, different ranking types have been suggested for opinion search. One solution is to create several result lists, one for each polarity, e.g., one list with positive and one list with negative opinions (Swotti). Demartini and Siersdorfer (2010) suggest a single ranking that reflects the correct distribution of opinions in the indexed document set. This ranking method allows the user to read only the items on top of the list but with a distinction between different polarities. Lee, Ferguson, O'Hare, Gurrin, and Smeaton (2010) propose to unite result list items by named entity topics (e.g., Microsoft, Apple). A different approach is to let the user choose between a pre-defined set of different rankings based on boolean existence of subjective keywords such as "easy", "secure", "useful" (e.g., RankSpeed).

Still, single results are often too numerous to be efficiently surveyed by the user (Furuse et al., 2007). There are so many single opinions on any given topic that reading them all sequentially would be an ineffective and costly task. Moreover, ranked result lists are based on the assumption that one result is more meaningful than the other. For market and business intelligence however, overall distribution and evolution of opinions can be more informative than the individual isolated opinion. Therefore, summarizing the results rather than ranking them individually has been suggested for opinion search (Pang & Lee, 2008).

Some existing opinion search application use charts, diagrams and graphs to express summarized opinion metrics visually (e.g., Radian6, Opinion Crawl, TrendyBuzz, Synthesio, ami news moni-

tor). We Feel Fine provides a visual analytics tool for sentiments in blogs by using available user related information (gender, age, country etc.) in social media content. Another type of tool is opinion web directories that classify subjective web documents into pre-determined topic categories (e.g., Epinions).

Visual result summarization can be achieved either by sequential filtering (e.g., RankSpeed, We Feel Fine, Opinion Crawl) or by simultaneous visualization as in temporal sentiment analysis. Fukuhara, Nakagawa, and Nishida (2007) visualize the evolution of opinions and topics in time on two separate graphs. Mishne et al. (2006) present temporal evolution of sentiments in blog posts without any specific topic relation. Generally, temporal sentiment graphs represent rarely more than two to three dimensions. Common dimensions are time, volume (number of indexed units) and polarity (positive, negative) or semantic category (e.g., angry, happy). The difficulty in visualizing more than three dimensions is to present complex data structures while keeping graphics simple and intuitive for the user.

Still, summarizing subjective information bears the risk of losing transparency in how the results have been obtained. There have been several attempts to combine summarization with traditional search engine querying and result lists in order to get the best out of both visualization methods. Gregory, Payne, McColgin, Cramer, and Love (2007) present a visual analytics tool for monitoring opinions in blogs by summarization and in parallel allowing for freely formulated user queries as well. Vechtomova (2010) presents a two stage method of conventional topic-based document retrieval and subsequent re-ranking of the results with different opinion-ranking methods.

DOXA OPINION SEARCH ENGINE PROTOTYPE

Business User Needs Study

The DoXa opinion search engine prototype has been built in several distinct iterative phases each running in parallel to the others. In order to reduce the risk of errors in interface design at an early stage, we identified the user needs of two different companies, called *end-users* in this chapter, wishing to introduce or improve existing opinion search techniques. For this purpose, the LUTIN laboratory conducted a user need analysis with semi-structured interviews. These interviews were guided by two questions:

1. How do the end-users monitor subjectivity at the present time?
2. What is the end-users' representation of the ideal tool to automatically analyze subjectivity?

The study uncovered different yet overlapping goals and needs in terms of opinion mining functionality. The first end-user (a) is a market research company specializing in buzz monitoring on social web sites and currently focuses on the video game market. Their current tool provides a search engine and a dashboard summarizing the product buzz for a video game publisher. However, the tool doesn't yet integrate opinion search and analysis features and relies exclusively on statistical methods to calculate buzz information. Their goal in the project is to find ways for efficiently and intuitively surveying opinions mainly on the video game market. An important demand was to introduce opinion analysis features without radically altering but rather complementing the current interface clients are accustomed to.

The second end-user (b) is an energy producing company wishing to improve the accuracy of their existing opinion detection module. This module is used to analyze customer service emails in order to automatically detect whether the client intends to change energy providers and for what reason. In order to calculate the "churn" score (change and turn), end-user (b) needs improved precision in opinion extraction and to detect the link between a topic and its related opinion as well as a modular processing chain in order to be able to use one task independently from the others.

The results of this study allowed us to define two distinct use cases for monitoring social web sites (end-user a) and structured questionnaire data (end-user b).

Use Case Scenario and Human Machine Interface

The user needs study served as a basis from which we derived a typical search scenario for end-user a) entitled "topic related Web 2.0 opinion monitoring":

In the scenario, the user wishes to monitor opinions on a certain number of video game titles and a number of its competitors on influential gaming blogs. The user may either search by query (e.g., a game title, an editor, a title version etc.) or explore the corpus by navigating in automatically created opinion and topic categories. In the latter mode, the user can filter and narrow down the results by opinions/sentiments and topics zooming in and out on the data. On the same interface, the user also wishes to visualize and compare the opinions evolution in time on his titles and competitors and gain additional insight.

The user scenario has then been the reference point from which we elaborated an interface model and developed a first opinion search engine prototype. In an iterative process, interface design was constantly refined taking into account ongoing end user feedback. The Human-machine-interface (Figure 1) of the prototype includes the following features:

- *Semantic indexation/ranking*: in order to enhance relevance and unlike traditional search engines, we index not only web pages but also - within each web page - small (100 words) overlapping text zones. The text zones are overlapping, in order to keep coherence of meaning and avoid cutting in the middle of topic and related opinions. In the query phase the most relevant text zone for each web page (meso level) is calculated depending on the density of annotated opinion and topic phrases (micro level) and their proximity to the query topic. Finally, the result items (the most relevant text zones in web pages) are ranked by the degree of proximity between the query topic and detected opinions.

- *Temporal opinion / topic graph with topic co-occurrences:* a user query is send simultaneously to both the search engine's index and to the OLAP module (Figure 4) via a web service (Figure 2). The same process is triggered by clicking on a topic facet. As a result a graph visualizes how opinions (on a scale of 5 going from very positive to very negative) on the query topic(s) evolve over time. This feature allows for queries such as: "what are the videos game titles people talk positively about in April?" The user can switch between graphs on different topics. In an updated version of the current HMI, the user will be able to visualize the graph on different document levels. Further planned improvements include visualizing co-occurring topics for each multi-dimensional dot (Figure 1).

- *Faceted search*: due to extensive linguistic extraction on the phrase level described later in this chapter, the user can filter his initial result set by topics and opinion categories (i.e., by extracted semantic categories) via two interactive pie charts (automatic categorization). Both pie charts (opinions and topics) are linked, meaning

that the click on one or more pie chart parts automatically updates and filters the other pie chart as well as the result list. On the future interface, an innovative aspect will be the possibility to visualize opinion and topic facets on different document levels (phrase level, paragraph/text zone level and document level). This feature will allow for zooming in and out on the corpus, thus taking different views on the same data.

- *Query interpretation module:* indexing a video game ontology (OWL) allowed us to build a query interpretation module displaying additional information in the event of a query e.g., the genre, publisher or developer of a video game (not visible in Figure 1).

OVERVIEW OF THE SYSTEM

The whole system comprises two processing chains: the indexing chain analyzes and enriches documents with semantic information in batch mode, before the application is presented to users. The technical framework of interaction is Unstructured Information Management Architecture or UIMA (Ferrucci & Lally, 2004); the search chain involves two servers beside the Human Machine Interface (HMI) and those three components communicate with one another through Web Services.

The first pieces of the UIMA indexing framework were developed in 2005 within the Infom@gic project (Brun et al., 2011). The UIMA framework, born at IBM and today maintained at Apache, provides an open processing bus and a collection processing engine (CPE) to connect together several chain components. The tools plugged in to the platform only interact with one another via a structure circulating on the bus: the common analysis structure (CAS). Project partners Arisem and LIP6 add semantic annotations to the

Figure 2. **Global architecture**

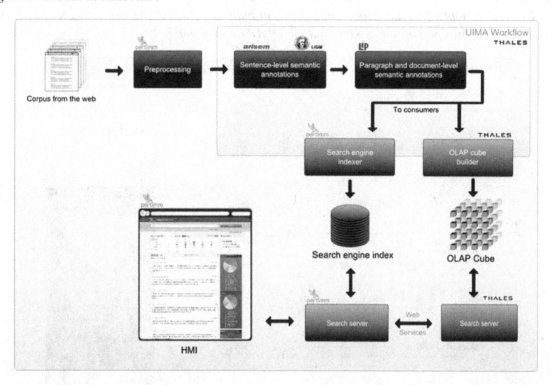

CAS and Pertimm and Thales use them, in addition to the document content and original metadata, to build indexes. This architecture allows the different partners to communicate with each other with minimal constraints. Interoperability issues, and more generally software engineering problems, have been mostly ignored in Natural Language Processing until recently (Leidner, 2003). This state of affairs is evolving because considering interoperability issues seriously makes it easier to process heterogeneous and ill-formed input data, and tackle more and more complex analysis tasks (therefore needing expert components written in different languages using different technologies).

At the other end of the system, the user interacts via the HMI with one search server only. The search engine server thus processes the query in several steps: looking up search results in its own search index, crossing search terms with an ontology to determine which named entities should be send to the OLAP search server, sending

these entities via a web service and displaying the graph returned by the OLAP server. The development of Web Services also is a widespread trend: software as a service, server-based applications, there is a tendency to host programs and data in huge distant datacenters.

Corpus and Pre-processing

We have crawled 21271 blog and forum web pages obtained from RSS feeds monitored by end user a). As web data is typically unstructured and difficult to interpret in its raw state, it had to be "cleaned" before the extraction phase. There have been stages of HTML tag removal, filtering of non-content related text (boilerplate removal), removal of duplicates, spam filtering and hyperlink crawling. The output of this phase is the corpus in an XML format with a text-only version of the web pages and end-user specific metadata.

Figure 1: User interface of the DoXa opinion search engine prototype with a result list (opinions high-lighted in yellow, topics in blue, near search terms in bold), interactive pie charts (aggregation and filtering of results by opinions and topics) and the OLAP module (top half).

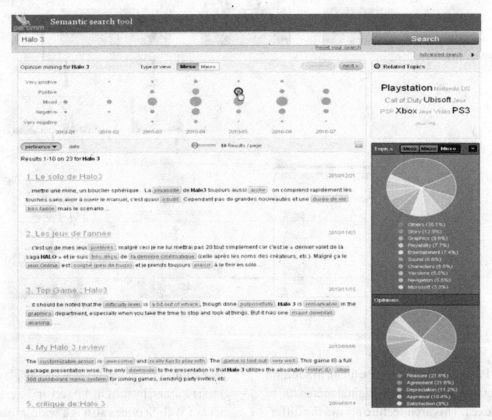

LINGUISTIC APPROACH

In order to efficiently extract opinions and topics, we aim at detecting opinion orientation beyond simple positive or negative polarity. In this section we also focus on detecting relations between opinions and the target of opinions (topics) and the construction of adapted linguistic resources.

Linguistic extraction methods and resources as well as the implementation of the opinion and sentiment semantic model have been developed in collaboration between the Arisem Company and the Laboratoire d'Informatique Gaspard-Monge (LIGM).

Related Work

Subjectivity expressions or opinions and sentiments are words, phrases or sentences expressing opinions, emotions, appraisals or speculations (Wiebe & Cardie, 2005). The DoXa project aims on the one hand at fine automatic extraction of opinions and sentiments in large corpora (Web 2.0), which goes beyond simple positive or negative polarity detection, and on the other hand at detecting relations between opinions and predefined topics which are targets of opinions.

Automatic extraction of opinions and sentiments is quite a difficult task, basically due to the complexity of the linguistic phenomena involved, as well as to the subjectivity underlying their interpretation. Moreover, large and heterogeneous corpora gathering documents from different types of sources (reviews, blogs, coverage of events or exhibitions and client satisfaction surveys, among others) can handle different domains and be written in varied styles, ranging from carefully written newspaper articles to the more spontaneous turn of oral conversations' transcripts.

The symbolic extraction method described here consists in using lexical resources to detect given lexical patterns. This implies developing dictionaries and local grammars, adapted to the end users' needs. Indeed, trying to produce syntactically and semantically comprehensive lexical resources is not enough. It is also necessary to make sure that the resources produced meet the needs of the corpora that are being processed, in order to find a compromise between recall and precision and to avoid noisy extractions.

The linguistic resources developed so far within the scientific community do not grasp all the particularities of the large corpora mentioned earlier. Detailed semantic studies or typologies dealing with opinions and sentiments (ontologies, terminological dictionaries, words lists) usually list vocabulary of a formal kind, without or with few syntactic information, and address only very few domains (psychology, literature): EMOTAIX (Piolat & Bannour, 2009). Sometimes they are not even linked to a specific domain and their implementation on large corpora can lead to multiple interpretations: Wordnet-Affect (Strapparava & Valitutti, 2004), Sentiwordnet (Esuli & Sebastiani, 2006), Appraisal Theory (Martin & White, 2005).

There are also dictionaries where each entry goes with its inflected forms and syntactic codes. To be mentioned are the LADL's and LIGM's (Gross, 1975, 1994) Lexicon-Grammars, as well as the Modyco's dictionaries (Dubois & Dubois-Charlier, 1997) which are organized around syntactic properties so as to facilitate grammatical analysis. However, they lack the specific semantic information necessary for opinion and sentiment extraction.

Some scientific works do combine semantics and syntax such as Mathieu (2006) and Grossmann and Tutin (2004) but do not cover all the semantic fields needed by the DoXa project's end users. The recently published works of Asher, Benamara, and Mathieu (2009) do take into account the cognitive and affective sides of opinions and sentiments but they do not tackle all the syntactic categories that are essential to fine opinion and sentiment extraction.

The positive and negative polarity of opinions and sentiments (semantic orientation) has been studied so far mainly through local adjective-noun combinations (Turney, 2002; Yu & Hatzivassiloglou, 2003; Kamps, Marx, Mokken, & de Rijke, 2004) and with degrees of intensity that are not detailed enough for fine extraction (Harb et al., 2008). Automatic treatment of semantic orientation and intensity still has to be extended to other syntactic categories.

Works dealing with the identification of the target of opinions are rare regarding to those dealing with the identification of opinions. In 2006, Kim and Hovy try to identify the target of opinions by searching the arguments of the verbs or adjectives expressing opinions. In their work, they do not try to relate those targets to predefined topics. The automatic detection of targets of opinion related to a topic was mainly studied on specific corpora dealing with customers comments on products (Popescu & Etzioni 2005; Yi, Nasukawa, Bunescu, & Niblack 2003). The texts of such corpora are entirely dedicated to the expression of opinions on a product or its features. Thus, for the association of a product feature and an opinion (Hi & Liu, 2004) search the closest description of a target from an opinion expression. Such method may be adapted to corpora dedicated to one product and its features, but we want to propose an approach available even on corpora that are more general (dealing with several similar products, or with a company and its competitors). In 2008, Stoyanov and Cardie present a study about the search for the topic element that is also the target of a subjectivity expression, from general texts. Their aim was to identify which topic element (TOPIC SPAN) among many on a target description (TARGET SPAN) was the target of the subjectivity. They observe that such problem was more difficult to solve in the case of opinions not associated with a sentiment (as in "Al thinks that…") whereas in DoXa focus is on opinion combined with sentiment.

DoXa Model and Method

The linguistic resources developed (dictionaries and grammars) are based on a semantic model which is specific to the DoXa project in order to meet the end users' industrial needs in terms of analysis' objectives. This semantic model is part of the overall DoXa Model that connects different methods and levels of processing for opinion and sentiment extraction.

The DoXa Model results from collaboration between Arisem, LIGM, LIMSI/CNRS and Thales Communications France. It is based on the fusion of an opinion and sentiment semantic component and an aggregative component. The semantic model consists of opinion and sentiment categories as well as a set of features linked to semantic categories and lexical forms. The aggregative model relies on operators and aggregation-based heuristics (Detyniecki, 2002; Eude, 1998), as well as on machine learning and fuzzy sets theory (Zadeh, 1965; Dubois & Prade, 1979).

In this project, the linguistic approach aims at implementing the DoXa semantic model in lexical resources. The resulting linguistic resources were used in the first place to validate or modify the opinion and sentiment semantic categories that had been chosen. The results generated by symbolic approach at sentence level (micro level) are used as seeds to feed a chain of treatments.

The aggregative model can synthesize local annotations generated at sentence (micro) level up to paragraph (meso) and text (macro) levels. The model aims at summing up whole texts'

evaluative content through subjectivity segments' characterization and fine aggregation. It can also deal with and make decisions on ambiguous, imprecise, contrasted, not to say contradictory segments such as *"je suis ni content ni mécontent"* (*"I'm neither satisfied nor dissatisfied"*), *"je suis à la fois en colère et déçu" ("I'm both angry and disappointed"*) or on sets of associated annotations that appear in the same text, e.g., *"je ne suis pas en colère" ("I'm not angry")* and *"je suis triste et sidéré" ("I'm sad and flabbergasted"*).

The DoXa Opinion and Sentiment Model

The model's semantic component relies on a set of opinion and sentiment semantic categories that are organized around three main axes: polarity axis, intensity axis and a cognitive/affective axis. Defining a set of opinion and sentiments categories for processing needs is quite a difficult task for theoretical reasons as well as for implementation issues. Within the frame of our work, we understand opinions as judgments of value (as opposed to judgments of fact or judgments of reality) on a concrete or abstract entity which can be an object, an idea, a project, a fact, an event, a situation or a person. This entity is the target of the opinion. According to Kerbrat-Orecchioni (1980), judgments of value can be expressed affectively – the enunciator is affectively involved towards the object being appraised – or appreciatively – the enunciator is intellectually involved towards the appraised object. Judgments can be expressed both affectively and appreciatively at the same time. Working from the point of view of NLP and corpus linguistics and having to deal with result issues, we adopted an empiric and iterative approach to progress. Following the study of the literature dealing more particularly with the theory of emotions – model relying on primary or basic emotions -, Yvette Yannick Mathieu's work on sentiment verb classification and the Appraisal Theory (Martin & White), we defined a preliminary set of semantic categories. We consolidated this set by analyzing the DoXa project's corpora and deducted a typology meant to cover sentiments – affective axis – and opinions and judgments – cognitive axis.

We thus stated on a first set of semantic categories which we gave human annotators for evaluation on a corpus of video games blog posts. The observations made by the annotators caused us to simplify the model, by gathering the categories initially defined and thus reducing their number. Following that experiment, we decided to freeze the model and submit it to linguists for implementation.

The DoXa semantic component consists of 17 opinion (cognition) and sentiment (affect) categories mentioned in Table 1. The polarity is implicit and borne by the semantic categories themselves: for example *Satisfaction* (positive) or *Dissatisfaction* (negative). So as to meet the end users' even more specific needs, one category relating to customer relationship management was added: *Expectation*. Intensity (int), Negation (neg) and Ambiguity (amb) traits are attached to the semantic categories. Moreover, it has been decided to use connotation traits (meliorative and pejorative) so as to characterize vocabulary whose semantic orientation is highly dependent on domain but does not refer to any opinion and sentiment category, such as "monopoly" which is systematically understood negatively in relation with end-user b) for instance.

Implementation of the Opinion and Sentiment Model

Implementing DoXa's semantic model requires the development of linguistic resources covering a great number of opinion and sentiment semantic categories, going beyond the usual three polarity values (positive, negative and neutral) and taking into account intensity values. The designed dictionaries and grammars also address all kinds of syntactic categories. Another challenge is for

these linguistic resources to be operational on large corpora which gather different types of texts (articles, mails, posts), written in different styles. To our knowledge, such linguistic resources meeting all those needs have not been designed so far.

One of the drawbacks of existing dictionaries is that semantically they only cover very partially the DoXa model's semantic fields. Moreover, from a syntactic point of view, they tend to tackle only one or two types of grammatical categories (adjectives or verbs, adjectives and nouns) and do not address all syntactic categories likely to express opinions and sentiments. Finally, the entries that are semantically classified are not or very rarely enriched with their syntactic proprieties, though essential to automatic processing. DoXa's semantic model thus invites us to go beyond linguistic resources designed so far. At first, our aim was to produce lexicons which would be operational on all kinds of corpus. This thus meant they had to be relatively small but also rich enough to ensure fine extraction. For this purpose we used existing word lists (EMOTAIX, CRISCO's synonym dictionaries, Arisem's lexicons, LIGM's lexicon-grammar tables). However, even if those lexicons had been carefully designed, they were finally not easily re-usable to meet the needs of DoXa's end users. Simply merging all data bases was no solution either because the resulting resources could only very partially fit the semantic model. Indeed, opinion and sentiment definition varies greatly according to the domain, the theories applied and the inevitable subjectivity of annotators and lexicographers.

This explains why merged lists had to be recoded following DoXa's semantic model. For instance, we did not keep in our lists non-psychological nouns that can sometimes be used in French to express opinions and sentiments, such as *acidité (acidity)*, *aigreur (sourness* vs. *bitterness)* or *allergie (allergy)*. When possible, we transferred them to dictionaries dedicated to phrases where their context of apparition could

Table 1. Semantic categories (DoXa model)

Semantic categories' paragon label	Semantic categories' content
Sadness	Sadness/Despair/Resignation
Contempt	Contempt/Disdain/Loathing/Disgust/Hatred
Boredom	Boredom
Anger	Anger/Annoyance/Irritation/Exasperation
Displeasure	Displeasure/Disappointment
NegSurprise	Negative surprise
Fear	Fear/Concern
Satisfaction	Satisfaction/Contentment
Dissatisfaction	Dissatisfaction/Discontent
Pleasure	Pleasure/Enjoyment/Joy/Happiness/Exhilaration
PosSurprise	Positive surprise
Appeasement	Relief/Appeasement
Depreciation	Depreciation/Disinterest
Disagreement	Disapproval/Disagreement
Discomfort	Discomfort/Confusion
Appraisal	Evaluation/Appraisal/Interest
Agreement	Approval/Agreement
Expectation	Expectation/Request/Recommandation/Suggestion
PejConnot	Pejorative connotation
MelConnot	Meliorative connotation

be defined more precisely: e.g., venin (*venom*) -> *cracher son venin* (*to spit venom*).

Development Environments

The opinion and sentiment semantic model is being used for automatic subjectivity annotation. The linguistic resources have been developed under two different and complementary environments: Unitex and HST. Unitex is the only robust open source multi-platform software (Paumier, 2008) supporting DELA-format dictionaries (Courtois, 1990) and local grammars (using DELAs) which also offers built-in concordancing functionalities. Arisem's HST (High Speed Transducer) supports the same linguistic resources formats as Unitex, as well proprietary ones and standards such as OWL and SKOS which supplement Unitex' annotation features. The use of both environments for linguistic resources development has been

guided by industrial as well as research needs. HST embarks the opinion and sentiment linguistic resources as well as the domain-specific ontologies and thesauri (for topic extraction) and is integrated in the DoXa UIMA (Unstructured Information Management Applications) chain of treatments. Since HST supports linguistic resources formats that cannot be used as such in Unitex, an HST-to-Unitex compatibility module has been developed by LIGM so that the research community can have open source access to the linguistic resources developed.

Lexical Dictionaries and Local Grammars

The knowledge modelized in the different resources (domain-specific ontologies and thesauri, opinion and sentiment dictionaries or local grammars) is not only semantically categorized or domain-oriented. The resources also include syntactic and morpho-syntactic information so as to resolve ambiguities, e.g., *console* > noun (*video game console*) or *console* > verb (*to console someone for*).

Opinion and sentiment detection depends on the syntactic categories used and also on their position within the sentence. Among the methods used to develop the resources there are on the one hand Lexicon-Grammars (Gross, 1975, 1994) and on the other hand local grammars (Gross, 1995). Lexicon-Grammars aim at a comprehensive description of natural languages, not only for French but also for many other languages, and consider elementary sentences, and not words, as the basic syntactic units to which grammatical information is attached. Local grammars are mostly formalized as finite-state graphs, representing and structuring complex linguistic patterns.

Separate dictionaries have been developed according to the opinion and sentiment semantic categories and also by syntactic categories: nouns ("*peur*" / "*fear*"), adjectives ("*affolé*"/ "*frightened*"), verbs ("*angoisser*" / "*to worry*"), adverbs ("*excessivement*" / "*excessively*") or phrases ("*frissonner de peur*" / "*shiver with fear*").

We took into account intensity modifiers as well: adjectives ("*extraordinaire*" / "*extraordinary*"), connectors ("*Ce jeu est bon marché* **mais** *nul*" / "*This game is cheap* **but** *worthless*"), adverbs ("*terriblement*" / "*terribly*"), comparative structures (**le moins** *cher sur le marché*) or prefixes/suffixes ("*rich***issime**" / "*fabulously rich*", "**hyper***puissant*" / "**hyper***powerful*"). Intensity is treated through local grammars, intensity values ranging from 1 to 10. The intrinsic intensity of basic lexical segments and of modifiers is assigned manually, for instance: *beau* int3 (*beautiful*), *magnifique* int5 (*gorgeous*), *sublime* int7 (*sublime*). According to the intrinsic intensity of each element, a resulting intensity value is calculated for lexical combinations: *absolument excellent*{cat_Satisfaction|int8) (2+6) (*absolutely excellent*{cat_Satisfaction|int8) (2+6)).

One same lexical entry can belong to several opinion and sentiment semantic categories with different intensity values: *monstrueusement*> cat_Contempt|int4|amb, cat_Displeasure|int4|amb, cat_Satisfaction>int7|amb (*awfully*). The example given just above shows that an ambiguity trait is automatically added to entries which belong to categories whose semantic orientations are opposed. It means that such entries can be understood either positively, either negatively depending on the context in which they are used.

Negation is treated through local grammars which modify the semantic orientation of subjectivity segments as well as their intensity. The annotation of negation is addressed differently according to the semantic categories involved. For categories with an existing antonym in the model, annotations are converted in this same antonym category, whereas for semantic categories without antonym, the annotation is enriched with the *neg* attribute.

beau> cat_Satisfaction|int3 (*beautiful*), *pas beau*> cat_Dissatisfaction|int3 (*not beautiful*), *pas très beau*> cat_Dissatisfaction|int2 (*not very beautiful*).

en colère> cat_Anger|int3 (*angry*), *pas en colère*> cat_Anger|int3|neg (*not angry*), *pas très en colère*> cat_Anger|int2|neg (*not very angry*).

The following semantic categories have no antonym equivalent: *Boredom, Contempt, Discomfort, Displeasure, Fear, Pleasure, Sadness.* Assimilated categories such as *MejConnot, Pejconnot* or *Attente* have no antonym either. The semantic categories with antonym equivalents are: *Agreement/Disagreement, Appraisal/Depreciation, Satisfaction//Dissatisfaction,, PosSurprise/ NegSurprise.*

We also resort to local grammars to detect phrases with variable parts, such as verbal inflected forms, possessive adjectives or pronouns between others: *<rire> à gorge déployée* ->cat_Pleasure|int8 (*<roar> with laughter* -> cat_Pleasure|int8), *pas en <croire> <+DETPOSS>*

yeux -> cat_PosSurprise|int5 (*not* <*believe*> <*+DETPOSS*> *eyes* -> cat_PosSurprise|int5).

The domain-specific ontologies and thesauri (OWL, SKOS) modelize domain-specific concepts (*first person shooter, game play*, etc.) and named entities (Martineau et al., 2007) such as organizations, products or brands among others (*Nintendo, X-Box 360, Super Mario Bros,* etc.*),* as well as semantic relations between named entities (*leads, is developed by*, etc.).

As a basis for the development of our resources, we used word lists, synonym dictionaries and vocabulary from domain-specific corpora (video games, energy sector).

Relation Extraction between Opinions and Sentiments and Topic

Linguistic knowledge can be used to detect subjectivity in a corpus, or can also be used to detect related information: the author of the opinion, the target of the opinion, or the date when (and location where) the opinion was expressed. The identification of relations between opinions and topics in a large sense is specifically addressed in the DoXa project. Explicit relations between an opinion and an element of a topic are studied, but also implicit relations, when the opinion is suggested by the description of a situation related to the topic.

To detect the topic elements that are targets of explicit opinions, the first task consists in identifying all textual forms of a topic (like energy or video games topics). Two problems are posed. The first one is to identify *a priori* all the elements related to the topic that may be target of opinions. For instance, in the energy company satisfaction survey, the quality of the contact with the customers is very important, and such abstract element (attitude) has to be defined in the topic description. The second problem deals with the identification of all the lexical forms that can be associated to each element of the topic. Classically, a topic is defined by very specific terms or named entities

(as in a thesaurus). But, each element of a topic can be pointed out with terms that cannot be defined in a specific lexicon or ontology: generic terms ("relation" for "relation clientèle" (*"relationship"* for *"customer relationship"*), "la personne" for "le technicien" (*"the person"* for *"the engineer"*) in a corpus related to energy services), anaphoric terms (pronouns). The target of an opinion can be related to the topic, but not directly to an element described in the topic: "*j'adore l'humour noir des darklings*" (*"I love the darklings' black humour"*) in a video game corpus, "*très satisfait du caractère public du service rendu*" (*"very satisfied with the public character of the service provided"*) in an energy sector corpus.

In order to identify only topics that are targets of opinions, specific grammars were developed. Without such grammars, the analysis of the sentence "*quand on a un problème X est là*" (*"when we have a problem, X is here for us"*) may produce a relation between the topic element X and the Depreciation opinion expressed with "problème" (*"problem"*). Local grammars use the syntactic category of the words expressing the opinion and the topic, in order to be more precise. For example, when an opinion is expressed by an adjective close to a name expressing a topic, the topic element is the target of the opinion, like in "*jeu super*" or "*super jeu*" (*"great game"*). We have also taken into account in those grammars the pronouns that may refer to a topic element. When the topic element has to be just before a verb (subject), we added pronouns such as "*il, ça, ce, c', elles…*" (*"he, it, they"*, etc.). It allows the detection of "*c'est super*" (*"it's great"*) that expresses a relation between an opinion and an element that can be related to the topic. To identify the element designated by "c'" (*"it"*) here, a complementary program is used to search for the referent. The grammar which aims at identifying explicit relations between topics and opinions is organized into six sub-grammars, that are dedicated to the annotation of the following cases:

- "j'adore Transformers" (*"I adore Transformers"*), « Transformers me plaît » (*"I like Transformers"*): the opinions are expressed by the verbs, and the target is the subject or the direct object as appropriate;
- "il est super ce jeu" (*"this game is great"*): here, a state verb is followed by an evaluative adjective, followed by a thematic noun phrase which is the target of the opinion;
- "je le trouve super" (*"I find it great"*): a neutral verb of opinion is followed by an evaluative adjective, and the target of the opinion is the direct object;
- "super jeux", "jeux super" (both are translated by *"great games"*): it manages the cooccurrences of an evaluative adjective and a topic element which is the opinion target) ;
- "Transformers a des qualités" (*"Transformers has qualities"*): in this case, the opinion is expressed by a noun which is the direct object related to a verb expressing a possession, and the target of the opinion is the subject).
- "ce jeu semble super" (refer to Figure 3).

This sub-grammar is based on the occurrence of a state verb, followed by an evaluative adjective (combining the features cl_DoXaOpinion and A –for adjective) or an evaluative noun phrase (combining cl_DoXaOpinion and N- for noun), and preceded by a topic element (with the tag cl_DoXaTopic) or a pronoun potentially related to the topic. The state verb is managed by a sub-grammar named graphe_etre.grf, which detects the variations: "me semble" (*"seems to me"*), "doit être" (*"must be"*), "a vraiment l'air" (*"really seems"*)). This sub-grammar detects and annotates the following examples: "il est super" (*"it is great"*), "j'en suis satisfaite" (*"I'm satisfied with that"*), "leur prix me semble correct" (*"their prices seems to be correct"*).

To express an opinion on a general topic, we can be explicit as in *"je suis satisfaite"* (*"I am satisfied"*), or we can describe a positive or a negative situation *"on manque d'informations"* (*"There's a lack of information"*). In the energy corpus, most of the opinions are expressed indirectly, through the description of situations or facts related to the topic and known to be positive (*"ils sont à l'écoute du client"* / *"they're attentive to the customers"*, *"Je n'ai aucun problème"* / *"I don't have any problem"*) or negative (*"c'est trop cher"* / *"it's too expensive"*). We have tried to include such ways of expressing opinions and sentiments in our grammars. Here the opinion and the topic are strongly linked, so we have proposed to create resources specific to end-user b) for both Satisfaction and Dissatisfaction categories. The current grammar that manages implicit opinions

Figure 3.. A HST sub-grammar for detecting targets of opinions

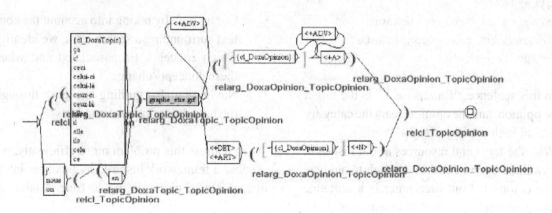

and their relations with topic is divided into five sub-grammars. The building of grammars allowing the identification of such implicit opinions related to the topic is complex, because there are a lot of situations and facts that can more or less express opinions. Also, sometimes a similar situation *"pas de contact"* (*"no contact"*) can be related to dissatisfaction (*"Nous ne sommes pas suffisamment contactés" "They don't contact us enough")* or to satisfaction (*"Je n'ai pas de contacts avec la (société) X parce que ca marche"* / *"I have no contact with (company) X because it works well"*).

To illustrate the results obtained with such grammars, here are the annotations produced by the analysis of the following text, containing an extract of the energy corpus answering a satisfaction question: *"l'Entreprise X est compétente"* (*"the X Company is competent").*

```
<SemTag value="relcl_TopicOpinion"
text="l'Entreprise X est compétente"
offset="0" length="30"/>
<SemTag value="relarg_DoXaTopic_Topi-
cOpinion" text=Entreprise X" off-
set="2" length="13"/>
<SemTag value="cat_Appraisal|int3"
text="compétente" offset="20"
length="10">
<SemTag value="cl_DoXaOpinion"/></
SemTag>
<SemTag value="AppraisalAdj"
text="compétente" offset="20"
length="10"/>
<SemTag value="relarg_DoXaOpinion_
TopicOpinion" text="compétente" off-
set="20" length="10"/>
```

In this sentence, "Entreprise X" is the target of the opinion, and the opinion bears the category Appraisal with the intensity 3.

With the tools and resources at our disposal, the symbolic approach is not enough to analyze segments too far from each other in a sentence or in a text portion, but it is essential to have

sufficiently precise data to feed the whole DoXa chain of treatments. Partial evaluation of the model at micro-level proved the semantic model's implementability. Since the project is still running, evaluation campaigns will be organized later on the whole management of evaluative segments as well as on their annotation at all text levels (document, paragraphs, or portions of paragraphs).

DoXa evaluation will address only the macro and meso levels because of cost and complexity reasons. Two models for evaluation are being developed for the DoXa project (Paroubek et al., 2010). One model will be used for fine-grained opinion mining analysis and the other one, more general, will be used for evaluation. The coexistence of the two models within the same project finds its justification in project management considerations. Having two models enables to start with the evaluation activities early in the project lifetime and we will thus be able to benefit from the evaluation feedback within the timeframe of the project.

SEARCH ENGINES AND TEXT OLAP

At the end of the linguistic extraction phase, new metadata has been created. This metadata needs to be further analyzed in order to enhance the search engine's opinion monitoring functionality. One way to make this possible is to offer the user guided contextual navigation:

- Contextual: by taking into account the context surrounding a search term, we identify which concepts are associated and when these concepts change
- Navigation: by guiding the user through the navigation in these concepts.

To address this problem more efficiently, we propose a framework inspired by business intelligence tools, particularly On-Line Analytical

Processing (OLAP) and multidimensional databases to associate OLAP with a search engine.

With OLAP, we define numerical indicators that can easily be aggregated by functions such as sums, means or counts, when values are computed along different analysis dimensions (such as dates, topics or web sites). Using this technology, it is possible to navigate in multidimensional data while getting results on a general level or on more detailed levels. It is also possible to present information through different formats (tables, graphs, dashboards…) and to have very fast response times (a maximum of information is pre-calculated or can easily be calculated). Moreover, OLAP engines are based on a very powerful language (MDX – multidimensional expression) enabling them to create more complex queries than with SQL for relational databases.

The Text OLAP approach extends OLAP systems to store and process not only numerical data but also textual data and textual indicators (lists of key words for instance). Research works on this subject have been done on modeling textual cubes, populating cubes with results from Text Mining tools, calculation of textual aggregates and data visualization. Most of these studies propose to extend the multidimensional "star schema" model to take into consideration textual data and documents with a "textual dimension" and "analysis dimensions": "textual dimension" can store ontologies, annotated expressions and eventually text corpus, and the "analysis dimensions" qualify the documents (date, sources, authors, opinion…). Quantitative measures such as the number of documents and expression frequencies are also stored. Unlike quantitative indicators, textual measures are non additive and their calculation cannot be done with aggregation operators used by existing OLAP. Lin, Ding, Han, Zhu, and Zhao (2008), Zhang, Zhai, Han, Srivastava, and Oza (2009), Ravat, Teste, and Tournier (2007), and Bringay, Laurent, Poncelet, Roche, and Teisseire (2010) propose textual aggregation operators at the different levels of multidimensional cubes.

Textual Indicators and Aggregates

Our Text OLAP solution implements different textual indicators. These measures are used to select and show the most relevant topics relative to a query. The aggregation functions developed are based on frequencies or relative frequencies, using classic indicators (number of texts or number of topics in the documents). Another indicator is based on TF-IDF (Term Frequency – Inverse Document Frequency). This statistical measure gives a weight to each topic regarding its frequency in a text and minimizing the importance of the ones that are very common in the whole set of documents. For each topic t and each cell

$$c : tf_c(t) = \frac{n_c(t)}{n_c}$$ with $n_c(t)$ the number of oc-

currences of this topic in documents corresponding to this cell and n_c the number of words in

these documents; and $idf_c(t) = \log \dfrac{d_c}{d_c(t) + 1}$

with $d_c(t)$ the number of documents citing this topic in this cell and d_c the total number of documents in this cell. This function is based on an indicator named "Top-Keyword" (Ravat et al., 2007).

DoXa Text OLAP Framework

The different bricks of the DoXa project processing chain include automatic extraction of annotations concerning topics and opinions from corpus of textual documents using predefined ontologies. We are developing a Text OLAP framework to store and analyze the data obtained through the knowledge extraction tools. This framework proposes an interface with the search engine, based on web services, using multidimensional analysis to give additional results. The general architecture of the solution is described.

Multidimensional Data Model: Cube with Textual and Analysis Dimensions

In the first place, we create a textual dimension that contains the annotations relative to the topics and opinions, which is added to the other dimensions like "Time" or "Web sites". And we design a classic OLAP cube with all the dimensions, textual dimension and analysis dimensions, and numerical indicators (number of documents, number of topics…). This way, we use the power of the OLAP server to quickly calculate the aggregates along the dimensions selected.

Implementation of Text OLAP Features

Secondly, we try to identify a subset of relevant annotations along the different analysis dimensions. To do this, we use the aggregation functions described earlier.

- For each cell, corresponding to elements along each of the dimensions, we apply the aggregation function (frequencies or TF-IDF) on the textual dimension;
- Every annotation gets a value as a result of the aggregation function;
- We rank the annotations in descending order;
- We filter the data to keep only the most relevant information that is the annotations with the highest results of the aggregation function.

Besides, thanks to OLAP systems structure, it is possible to analyze this information along other dimensions. For instance, one can follow the evolution along time of the connections between topics, or the differences of these relations depending on the sources or the opinion expressed.

The results are then formatted to be displayed by a third client. Existing OLAP cube visualiza-tion tools are designed to display and navigate in quantitative data. These features are not adapted to show textual information. DoXa Text OLAP Cube Viewer ensures interactive navigation possibilities in a textual cube. Along the dimensions, analysts can also see cells presenting textual aggregates.

Combined Search Engine / OLAP Interface

Using the different results obtained with OLAP and Text OLAP technologies, a communication interface with the search engine gives additional information to enhance the answers to queries, proposing a global understanding of a subject. The search engine interface integrates a three-dimensional graph showing the temporal evolution of opinion orientation and the 'buzz' (number of opinions) for one or more topics. Opinion levels are reflected on a scale of 5 categories ranging from very negative to very positive (Figure 4). Each graph shows one topic, but the user can switch between graphs on different topics.

When the user types a query that relates to one or more topics (e.g., "Halo 3" or "Splinter Cell"), the engine relays this information to the OLAP module which sends back the data relative to the topics crossing it with the time periods, the opinions and the number of documents, so that the search engine can show this information in the form of a graph on the interface. Further results are being obtained through interactivity with this graph: selecting one point generates another query on the OLAP engine bringing more information to the user than his first query.

The two modules interact through web services. The information concerning the query expressed by the user is sent to the OLAP module, which sends back a specific result to the search engine. This result is then displayed along with the classic results of web search.

Figure 4. Dot chart to monitor the temporal evolution of opinions on a topic ("Halo3"). A dot shows three data dimensions: number of opinions, polarity (negative, positive) and time. Co-occurrent topics may be visualized for each dot in the next prototype version.

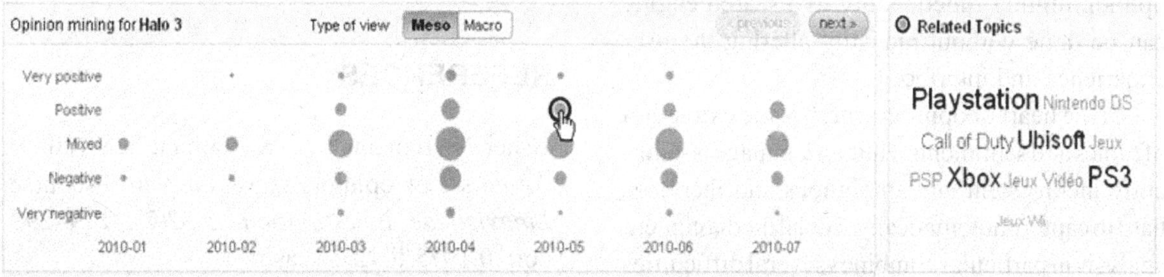

FUTURE RESEARCH DIRECTIONS

The linguistic resources developed for the DoXa project aim at a robust and fine extraction of opinions and sentiments, to be processed by statistical treatments. In a very near future, it is planned to adapt the LIGM's Lexicon-Grammar tables corresponding to the DoXa project semantic categories for better coverage of the studied corpora, as well as more precise extractions. We also intend to develop modular linguistic resources adapted to other domains. On the relations between opinions and topic, one perspective deals with the model of the elements of a domain that may be targets of opinions, in order to develop grammars for implicit relations with a relevant coverage.

The current ranking mechanism only considers three proximity levels: topic to opinion expressions within a distance of a few words (micro level), 100 words (meso level) and the same document (macro level). This rather simple algorithm needs further improvement particularly by taking into account advances in topic-opinion relation detection described in the "Linguistic Extraction" section. Moreover, the prototype is limited to document retrieval. In the next version of the demonstrator, we plan to visualize results on the sentence and paragraph level in order to improve usability as opinions will come out clearer. The further development of our boilerplate removal module is planned to enhance relevance and extraction accuracy.

Works presented here have been implemented in a relational OLAP architecture. Another perspective is to improve the relevance of the analysis by defining and implementing new textual indicators (for example by mixing relevance and position in documents) and new types of information visualization based on stream graphs or tag clouds.

CONCLUSION

The ever growing research area of opinion and sentiment analysis and search has many different aspects and challenges to face ranging from subjectivity extraction to analysis, search and interface design. To this day, there is no single tool that is completely functional and satisfactory in all of these aspects. Even though the DoXa project is still in progress and results therefore are not conclusive, we have been able to show ways of addressing the complex problem of opinion/topic mining and search. We showed ways to combine an enterprise search engine with symbolical linguistic extraction methods and a business intelligence tool. Each of the different tools bring their own advantages and informational viewpoints into the equation. By staying close to the business user needs in design and development of our interface, usability in real-life scenarios can be maintained.

As multidimensional data analysis adds complexity to the system, the search interface needs to stay intuitive and simple. We have shown that adding opinion mining functionality to a search engine can be done without radically altering the user experience and interface.

At the heart of opinion search is the extraction of topics and sentiments. Human language is inherently inconsistent and ambiguous and therefore hard to capture automatically. Social media content analysis in particular combines several difficulties such as approximate spelling or page structure. This problem can't be successfully addressed by one-sidedly focusing on either document or sentence classification. We have presented methods to combine topic and subjectivity extraction on both the document and the sentence level.

The efficiency of opinion search on the phrase and sentence level strongly relies on the availability, quality and coverage of the underlying semantic model and linguistic resources. While previous work made important progress in topic and sentiment detection, little research has been done so far to detect the link between them. However, the capacity of the system to relate the discussed topic to the corresponding opinion is vital for successful opinion search. We have presented innovative symbolical methods to address the extraction of opinion-topic relations based on rich linguistic resources and a semantic opinion/sentiment model.

Our goal in this chapter was to present our approach for the extraction, analysis and querying of opinionated electronic text in the French language. Important aspects like statistical extraction methods and evaluation aspects had to be left out of this chapter, but continue to be actively researched in the DoXa project.

ACKNOWLEDGMENT

Thanks to all research and industry partners of the DoXa project, especially to Catherine Goutas (Thales, France), DoXa project manager and to Baptiste Gaillard (Thales, France), technical integration coordinator.

REFERENCES

Asher, N., Benamara, F., & Mathieu, Y. Y. (2009). Appraisal of opinion expressions in discourse. *Lingvisticae Investigationes, 32*(2), 279–292. doi:10.1075/li.32.2.10ash

Baeza-Yates, R. A., & Ribeiro-Neto, B. (1999). *Modern information retrieval.* Boston, MA: Addison-Wesley.

Bringay, S., Laurent, A., Poncelet, P., Roche, M., & Teisseire, M. (2010). Bien cube, les données textuelles peuvent s'agréger! In S. B. Yahia & J.-M. Petit (Eds.), *10èmes journées d'extraction et gestion des connaissances* (pp. 585-596). Hammamet, Tunisia: Cépaduès-Éditions.

Brun, C., Campedel, M., Dessaigne, N., Gaillard, B., Guillemin-Lanne, S., & Hoogstoel, P. (2011). L'analyse sémantique au profit de la nouvelle génération de moteurs de recherche multimédia. In Campedel, M., & Hoogstoel, P. (Eds.), *Sémantique et multimodalité en analyse de l'information.* Paris, France: Hermès.

Chen, C., Ibekwe-sanjuan, F., Sanjuan, E., & Weaver, C. (2006). Visual analysis of conflicting opinions. In *Proceedings of the IEEE Symposium on Visual Analytics Science and Technology* (pp. 59-66).

Courtois, B. (1990). Un système de dictionnaires électroniques pour les mots simples du français. *Langue Française, 87*(1), 11–22. doi:10.3406/lfr.1990.6323

Demartini, G., & Siersdorfer, S. (2010). Dear search engine: what's your opinion about...? In *Proceedings of the 3rd International Semantic Search Workshop* (pp. 1-7). New York, NY: ACM.

Detyniecki, M. (2002). *Mathematical aggregation operators and their application to video querying* (Unpublished doctoral dissertation). Université Pierre et Marie Curie, Paris, France.

Dubois, D., & Prade, H. (1979). Fuzzy real algebra: Some results. *Fuzzy Sets and Systems*, *2*(4), 327–348. doi:10.1016/0165-0114(79)90005-8

Dubois, J., & Dubois-Charlier, F. (1997). *Les verbes français. Expressions*. Paris, France: Larousse-Bordas.

Esuli, A., & Sebastiani, F. (2006). SENTIWORD-NET: a publicly available lexical resource for opinion mining. In *Proceedings of the 5th Conference on Language Resources and Evaluation*, Genoa, Italy (pp. 417-422).

Eude, V. (1998). *Modélisation de données imprécises et incomplètes dans le domaine du renseignement militaire* (Unpublished doctoral dissertation). Université Pierre et Marie Curie, Paris, France.

Ferrucci, D., & Lally, A. (2004). UIMA: an architectural approach to unstructured information processing in the corporate research environment. *Natural Language Engineering Archive*, *10*(3-4), 327–348. doi:10.1017/S1351324904003523

Fukuhara, T., Nakagawa, H., & Nishida, T. (2007). Understanding sentiment of people from news articles: Temporal sentiment analysis of social events. In *Proceedings of the International Conference on Weblogs and Social Media*, Boulder, CO. Menlo Park, CA: AAAI Press.

Furuse, O., Hiroshima, N., Yamada, S., & Kataoka, R. (2007). Opinion sentence search engine on open-domain blog. In *Proceedings of the 20th International Joint Conference on Artificial Intelligence* (pp. 2760-2765). San Francisco, CA: Morgan Kaufmann.

Grefenstette, G., Qu, Y., Shanahan, J. G., & Evans, D. A. (2004). Coupling niche browsers and affect analysis for an opinion mining. In *Proceedings of the Recherche d'Informations Assistée par Ordinateur conference* (pp. 186 -194).

Gregory, M. L., Payne, D., Mccolgin, D., Cramer, N., & Love, D. (2007). Visual analysis of weblog content. In *Proceedings of the International Conference on Weblogs and Social Media*, Boulder, CO. Menlo Park, CA: AAAI Press.

Gross, M. (1975). Méthodes en syntaxe: régime des constructions complétives. In Schwartz, L. (Ed.), *Actualités scientifiques et industrielles* (*Vol. 1*). Paris, France: Hermann.

Gross, M. (1994). Constructing lexicon-grammars. In Atkins, B. T. S., & Zampolli, A. (Eds.), *Computational approaches to the lexicon* (pp. 213–263). Oxford, UK: Oxford University Press.

Gross, M. (1995). Une grammaire locale de l'expression des sentiments. *Langue Française*, *105*(1), 70–87. doi:10.3406/lfr.1995.5294

Grossmann, F., & Tutin, A. (2004). Joie profonde, affreuse tristesse, parfait bonheur. Sur la predicativité des adjectifs intensifiant certains noms d'émotion. *Cahiers de lexicologie: Revue internationale de lexicologie et lexicographie*, (86), 179-196.

Harb, A., Dray, G., Plantié, M., Poncelet, P., Roche, M., & Trousset, F. (2008). Détection d'opinion: Apprenons les bons adjectifs! In *Proceedings of Informatique des Organisations et Systèmes d'Information et de Décision*, Fontainebleau, France (pp. 59-66).

Hu, M., & Liu, B. (2004). Mining opinion features in customer reviews. In *Proceedings of the 19th National Conference on Artificial Intelligence* (pp. 755-760). Menlo Park, CA: AAAI Press.

Kamps, J., Marx, M., Mokken, R., & de Rijke, M. (2004). Using WordNet to measure semantic orientation of adjectives. In *Proceedings of the 4th International Conference on Language Resources and Evaluation*, Biarritz, France (pp. 174-181).

Kerbrat-Orecchioni, C. (1980). *L'Énonciation - De la subjectivité dans le langage*. Paris, France: Armand Colin.

Kim, S., & Hovy, E. (2006). Extracting opinions, opinion holders, and topics expressed in online news media text. In *Proceedings of the Coling-ACL Workshop on Sentiment and Subjectivity in Text*, Sydney, Australia (pp. 1-8).

Lee, H., Ferguson, P., O'Hare, N., Gurrin, C., & Smeaton, A. F. (2010). Integrating interactivity into visualizing sentiment analysis of blogs. In *Proceedings of the First International Workshop on Intelligent Visual Interfaces for Text Analysis*, Honk Kong, China (pp. 17-20). New York, NY: ACM.

Leidner, J. L. (2003). Current issues in software engineering for natural language processing. In *Proceedings of the HLT-NAACL Workshop on Software Engineering and Architecture of Language Technology Systems*, Edmonton, AB, Canada (pp. 45-50).

Lin, C. X., Ding, B., Han, J., Zhu, F., & Zhao, B. (2008). Text cube: Computing IR measures for multidimensional text database analysis. In *Proceedings of the IEEE International Conference on Data Mining* (pp. 905-910). Washington, DC: IEEE Computer Society.

Liu, B., Hu, M., & Cheng, J. (2005). Opinion observer: analyzing and comparing opinions on the Web. In *Proceedings of the 14th International Conference on World Wide Web*, Chiba, Japan (pp. 342-351). New York, NY: ACM.

Martin, J. R., & White, P. R. R. (2005). *The language of evaluation: appraisal in English*. Basingstoke, UK: Palgrave Macmillan.

Mathieu, Y. Y. (2006). A computational semantic lexicon of French verbs of emotion. In J. G. Shanahan, Y. Qu, & J. Wiebe (Eds.), *Computing attitude and affect in text: Vol. 20. Theory and applications* (pp. 109-124). Berlin, Germany: Springer-Verlag.

Miao, Q., Li, Q., & Dai, R. (2009). AMAZING: A sentiment mining and retrieval system. *Expert Systems with Applications*, *36*(3), 7192–7198. doi:10.1016/j.eswa.2008.09.035

Mishne, G., Balog, K., Rijke, M., & Ernsting, B. (2007). MoodViews: Tracking and searching mood-annotated blog posts. In *Proceedings of the International Conference on Weblogs and Social Media*, Boulder, CO (pp. 323-324). Menlo Park, CA: AAAI Press.

Oelke, D., Hao, M., Rohrdantz, C., Keim, D., Dayal, U., Haug, L.-E., & Janetzko, H. (2009). Visual opinion analysis of customer feedback data. In *Proceedings of the IEEE Symposium on Visual Analytics Science and Technology*, Atlantic City, NJ (pp. 187-194). Washington, DC: IEEE Computer Society.

Pang, B., & Lee, L. (2008). Opinion mining and sentiment analysis. *Foundations and Trends in Information Retrieval*, *2*(1-2), 1–135. doi:10.1561/1500000011

Paroubek, P., Pak, A., & Mostefa, D. (2010). Annotations for opinion mining evaluation in the industrial context of the DoXa project. In *Proceedings of the Language Resources and Evaluation Conference*, Malta.

Paumier, S. (2008). *Unitex manual*. Retrieved December 9, 2010, from http://www-igm.univ-mlv.fr/ ~unitex/index.php?page=4

Piolat, A., & Bannour, R. (2009). EMOTAIX: un scénario de Tropes pour l'identification automatisée du lexique émotionnel et affectif. *L'Année Psychologique*, *109*(4), 655–698. doi:10.4074/S0003503309004047

Ploux, S., & Manguin, J.-L. (1998). *Le dictionnaire électronique des synonymes du CRISCO*. Retrieved November 9, 2010, from http://www.crisco.unicaen.fr/ cgi-bin/cherches.cgi

Popescu, A.-M., & Etzioni, O. (2005). Extracting product features and opinions from reviews. In *Proceedings of the Conference on Human Language Technology and Empirical Methods in Natural Language Processing*, Vancouver, BC, Canada (pp. 339-346). Stroudsburg, PA: ACL.

Ravat, F., Teste, O., & Tournier, R. (2007). OLAP aggregation function for textual data warehouse. In *Proceedings of the 9th International Conference on Enterprise Information Systems* (pp. 151-156).

Stoyanov, V., & Cardie, C. (2008). Topic identification for fine-grained opinion analysis. In *Proceedings of the 22nd International Conference on Computational Linguistics* (pp. 817-824). Stroudsburg, PA: ACL.

Strapparava, C., & Valitutti, A. (2004). WordNet-Affect: an affective extension of WordNet. In *Proceedings of the 4th International Conference on Language Resources and Evaluation*, Lisboa, Portugal (pp. 1083-1086).

Tseng, F., & Chou, A. (2004). The concept of document warehousing and its applications on managing enterprise business intelligence. In *Proceedings of Pacific Asia Conference on Information Systems*, Shanghai, China.

Turney, P. D. (2002). Thumbs up or thumbs down? Semantic orientation applied to unsupervised classification of reviews. In *Proceedings of the 40th Annual Meeting on Association for Computational Linguistics*, Philadelphia, PA.

Vechtomova, O. (2010). Facet-based opinion retrieval from blogs. *Information Processing & Management, 46*(1), 71–88. doi:10.1016/j.ipm.2009.06.005

Wiebe, J., & Cardie, C. (2005). Annotating expressions of opinions and emotions in language. *Language Resources and Evaluation, 39*(2-3), 165–210. doi:10.1007/s10579-005-7880-9

Wiebe, J., & Riloff, E. (2005). Creating subjective and objective sentence classifiers from unannotated texts. In A. Gelbukh (Eds.), *Proceedings of the 6th International Conference on Computational Linguistics and Intelligent Text Processing* (LNCS 3406, pp. 486-497).

Wilson, T., Hoffmann, P., Somasundaran, S., Kessler, J., Wiebe, J., Choi, Y., et al. (2005). OpinionFinder. In *Proceedings of the Human Language Technology Conference Conference on Empirical Methods in Natural Language Processing on Interactive Demonstrations*, Vancouver, BC, Canada (pp. 34-35).

Wilson, T., Wiebe, J., & Hoffmann, P. (2009). Recognizing contextual polarity: An exploration of features for phrase-level sentiment analysis. *Computational Linguistics, 35*(3), 399–433. doi:10.1162/coli.08-012-R1-06-90

Yi, J., Nasukawa, T., Bunescu, R., & Niblack, W. (2003). Sentiment analyzer: Extracting sentiments about a given topic using natural language processing techniques. In *Proceedings of the IEEE International Conference on Data Mining*, Melbourne, FL. Washington, DC: IEEE Computer Society.

Yu, H., & Hatzivassiloglou, V. (2003). Towards answering opinion questions: Separating facts from opinions and identifying the polarity of opinion sentences. In *Proceedings of the Conference on Empirical Methods in Natural Language Process*, Sapporo, Japan (pp. 129-136).

Zadeh, L. (1965). Fuzzy sets. *Information and Control, 8*(3), 338–353. doi:10.1016/S0019-9958(65)90241-X

Zhang, D., Zhai, C., Han, J., Srivastava, A., & Oza, N. (2009). Topic modeling for OLAP on multidimensional text databases: topic cube and its applications. *Statistical Analysis and Data Mining, 2*(5-6), 378–395. doi:10.1002/sam.10059

Zhang, W., Yu, C., & Meng, W. (2007). Opinion retrieval from blogs. In *Proceedings of the Sixteenth ACM Conference on Conference on Information and Knowledge Management*, Lisbon, Portugal. New York, NY: ACM.

KEY TERMS AND DEFINITIONS

Enterprise Search: Unlike public web search, enterprise search systems mainly index and search a company's private data. Typically those contents come from various sources such as email, file systems, databases as well as selected websites of interest.

Faceted Search: An advanced search feature allowing to automatically categorize the result items of a user query into dynamic facets. These facets can then be used to further refine the query and to easily "browse" (search without a planned search strategy) the available data.

Interoperability: The ability of various software components to exchange data and to work along the same processing chain.

Linguistic Approach: Consists in extracting information automatically from electronic corpora through linguistic resources that are either lexical dictionaries or local grammars. Dictionary list entries that bear semantic and morpho-syntactic information (inflected form or gender for instance). Local grammars, mostly represented by finite-state graphs, describe words or lexical patterns in context.

On-Line Analytical Processing (OLAP): OLAP is an approach to answer multi-dimensional queries and is widely used in business industries as a decision tool. Classical OLAP tools are based on the building of easy to navigate data cubes: in a cube, along different analysis dimensions (as: time, company structure, product taxonomy…), a set of numerical indicators are pre-calculated (as quantities, values, amounts…). Dimensions are built with hierarchies that allow general or detailed views of the data depending on the need.

Text OLAP: The Text OLAP approach extends OLAP systems to store and process not only numerical data but also textual data and textual indicators (lists of interesting words for instance).

Topic: In this chapter we use the term 'topic' for the target entity that an opinion can be expressed upon, e.g., a product, a service or a named entity.

Topic-Opinion Relation Extraction: Consists in detecting the relation between opinion and sentiment expressions and predefined topic elements that are targets of the opinion expressed, regardless of who expresses the opinion.

APPENDIX

Useful Websites

1. http://www.swotti.com
    2. http://www.opinioncrawl.com
    3. http://www.crowdeye.com
    4. http://www.radian6.com
    5. http://www.trendybuzz.com
    6. http://synthesio.com
    7. http://www.amisw.com
    8. http://socialmedia.alterian.com

Section 3
Interface

Chapter 10
Human–Centred Web Search

Orland Hoeber
Memorial University of Newfoundland, Canada

ABSTRACT

People commonly experience difficulties when searching the Web, arising from an incomplete knowledge regarding their information needs, an inability to formulate accurate queries, and a low tolerance for considering the relevance of the search results. While simple and easy to use interfaces have made Web search universally accessible, they provide little assistance for people to overcome the difficulties they experience when their information needs are more complex than simple fact-verification. In human-centred Web search, the purpose of the search engine expands from a simple information retrieval engine to a decision support system. People are empowered to take an active role in the search process, with the search engine supporting them in developing a deeper understanding of their information needs, assisting them in crafting and refining their queries, and aiding them in evaluating and exploring the search results. In this chapter, recent research in this domain is outlined and discussed.

INTRODUCTION

Search has become a critical element of modern, computationally augmented life. In the past, people would spend a little bit of time organizing the information in their lives, and then browse it when they needed to find something. As we move toward having technology become a part of almost every aspect of our lives, the amount of informa-tion that must be managed is becoming larger and larger. In many cases, the Web is being used as the universal platform for making this informa-tion available. With so much information at our disposal, browsing is no longer feasible and our only alternative is to search. We search the Web, our email, our contacts lists, our calendars, our computers, our mobile devices. Search has become a daily, if not hourly, activity for many people. As such, researchers need to begin considering not only what would be appropriate techniques

DOI: 10.4018/978-1-4666-0330-1.ch010

and interfaces for searching for documents on the Web, but also for finding information within more specific domains and settings.

In recent years, a large portion of the research and development in the domain of information retrieval has focused on the "back-end" aspect of search. Herein, much research has addressed issues related to the indexing of documents (Baeza-Yates & Ribeiro-Neto, 2011; Rasmussen, 2003), file systems for managing indexes at the scale of the Web (Ghemawat, Gobioff, & Leung, 2003), and algorithms to match and rank documents to queries (Brin & Page, 1998). To a large degree, the growth of companies such as Google and Yahoo! has been due to their ability to efficiently index the billions of documents on the Web, and deploy an infrastructure that allows them to respond to end-user queries in fractions of a second. Of course, the quality of the search result ranking is also an important element of their success.

Because of the popularity and success of these companies, many people consider Web search to be a solved problem. However, there is still a great deal more that can be done to enhance not only how Web search engines work (the focus of this book), but also how Web search engines help people to find the information they are seeking (the focus of this chapter). The key distinction to be made when considering the human element of Web search is that the primary focus changes from the documents being searched to the support that can be provided to the people who are doing the searching (Hoeber, 2008).

Unfortunately, there has been very little progress in terms of Web search engines' support for the fundamental search tasks that people need to perform. The interface for extracting searchers' information needs remains a simple text field. The ranked set of documents that are matched to the query continues to be represented in a simple list of document titles, snippets, and URLs. While improving these interfaces to more adequately support the primary search tasks of query specification and search results evaluation is a good

starting point, a more thoughtful consideration of the types of things people really need (or want) to do within the context of Web search is required.

In this chapter, we explore some of the recent research trends that address the needs of searchers beyond providing a simple query field and search results list. We take a human-centred computing perspective on this topic, wherein the primary focus is on the design, development, and evaluation of computing systems that consider and support human activities (Sebe, 2010). We start with discussions on Web searcher behaviour and what can be done to support their needs, and then provide an overview of a number of specific approaches that have shown promise. Techniques for evaluating such interfaces are discussed, along with a vision for future research directions within this domain.

SEARCHER BEHAVIOUR

Even with the simple and easy-to-use interfaces provided by the top Web search companies, people commonly have difficulties searching the Web. Numerous studies have been conducted in recent years that attempt to characterize the behaviour of Web searchers (Jansen, Booth, & Spink, 2007; Jansen & Pooch, 2001; Jansen & Spink, 2006; Silverstein, Henzinger, Marais, & Moricz, 1999; Spink, Wolfram, Jansen, & Saracevic, 2001). Two things that most of these studies agree on are that people who search the Web use very short queries; and they don't consider many search results. Indeed, most Web search queries are between one and three terms in length, and few people venture past the third page of the search results.

In order to craft a query, all that is provided in terms of guidance from the search engine interface is a text box in which to type the query. But what if the searcher doesn't know what to type? Or what if the searcher types the wrong thing? There have been some recent additions to the top search engines to suggest common queries as a searcher begins typing their query, and even to provide the search results for these queries in real-time. While this can be a useful feature when searching for a common topic, it can also have a narrowing effect by directing searchers toward formulations of their query that, while common, are not accurate representations of the information they are seeking.

Once a searcher is able to craft a query, the search results are provided in a list-based representation, requiring the searcher to consider each for relevance one-by-one. What if the searcher doesn't know enough about what they are searching for to be able to tell the good documents from the bad? The only option is to begin clicking on documents that appear to be relevant. In the best-case scenario, many of the top search results will be relevant and the searcher will be able to resolve their information needs quickly and easily. However, if this is not the case, searchers can quickly become frustrated by the need to evaluate many non-relevant documents (Field, Allan, & Jones, 2010). In such situations, their only recourse is to attempt to craft a better query, try using a different Web search engine, or give up on the search task.

People may be able to resolve very focused searches and simple fact-verification tasks using just a few words in their query, and considering just a few documents in the search results. However, when their task is to find information on a topic that is ambiguous or vague, or in which they have very little prior knowledge, people have great difficulty crafting an accurate query and subsequently evaluating the search results. As a result, the task at hand becomes more of an exploratory process, wherein the searcher may need to perform multiple queries and evaluate many documents as they gain knowledge on their search topic. Unfortunately, the top search engines provide little support for such exploratory search tasks, requiring the users to do all the work to craft and modify their queries and to evaluate and explore within the search results.

Part of the difficulty with the current generation of Web search engines is that they have focused on making their interfaces extremely simple to learn

and use. The result is that by providing a simple interface, people use it in a simple manner. Anyone who wants to do something more complex needs to learn the query language or special features of the search engine, which are often hidden away or difficult to use. While this may be something that an expert searcher is willing to do, within the current incarnation of simple Web search engine interfaces, the general public does not want to invest the time required to learn how to write their queries *properly* or use the *power tools* of the search engine (Spink et al., 2001). However, we believe that there are opportunities for integrating easy-to-learn features within Web search interfaces that enhance the abilities of searchers to be productive and effective in their search tasks.

SUPPORTING SEARCHER NEEDS

If it is our goal to provide better support for searchers, it is important for us to give some thought to why people conduct searches in the first place. People resort to conducting searches when they don't know something. Why then do most search interfaces assume that people will be able to describe what they are looking for only by typing into a textbox? And why do they assume that people will be able to decide the relevance of a document based only on its title and a few lines of text?

In a human-centred approach to search, the focus is on supporting people at the core of their search activities. By giving more attention and support to the human elements of search, we can devise new techniques that strike a balance between providing simple and easy-to-use interfaces, and powerful features that support key activities associated with the search tasks. The key premise here is that people will be willing to learn to use a more complex Web search interface if it is able to provide value-added services that they need.

Fundamentally, there are two elements of search that the interface must support. First, the interface must allow searchers to craft their initial queries, and subsequently refine these queries into accurate descriptions of their information needs. When people conduct searches, they have a vague idea or an incomplete mental model of the information they are seeking. Somehow, they need to communicate this to the search engine. Secondly, the interface must support searchers as they evaluate and explore the search results. When provided with a collection of search results, searchers must draw upon their knowledge of the topic and related concepts, as they seek documents that are relevant to their information needs. Along the way, they may gain some new insights that allow them to further re-formulate their queries, producing new sets of search results, which they can continue to explore.

Before we can make improvements to search interfaces, we need to have a better understanding of how people articulate their search needs, and how they make decisions regarding what is relevant and what is not. While some researchers have made some progress in this area (cf. Jansen et al., 2007; Bhavnani & Bates, 2002; White, Kules, Drucker, & Schraefel, 2006), further work is needed to more fully understand searcher needs.

Taking a human-centred approach to search allows us to transition from an information retrieval focus to a decision support focus (Yao, 2002). In information retrieval, the primary elements of concern are the documents being searched and the queries that need to be matched to documents. The end result is an ordered list of search results. Whether the searcher is able to craft a query or evaluate the search results list isn't a consideration. In decision support, the primary interest is in the users and in providing tools that will help them to make decisions and choices. By taking a decision support perspective on search, we can imagine tools that help searchers to inform the search engine of what they are seeking, as well as tools to assist them in deciding which documents are more likely to be relevant to their goals.

By considering the searcher as a fundamentally important aspect of conducting a search, next-generation Web search interfaces can support them in taking an active role in the search process, and empower them to take control of their search activities. The searcher moves away from just being the person who typed in the query, to a source of supplemental information that will help the search engine to understand more about their reason for searching, and to ultimately finding the documents that are relevant to their information needs.

In this new, active role in the search process, searchers are able to craft and refine queries. They are supported in browsing, filtering, investigating, and exploring search results sets. They are able to analyze, understand, organize, and save retrieved documents. Fundamentally, this moves the focus from the documents being searched to the tasks that people need to perform in conducting a search (Hoeber, 2008).

In the remainder of this section, we will outline a number of systems that have been developed that take steps in the direction of human-centred Web search.

Clustering

In order to cluster Web search results, systems such as Carrot2 (Osiński & Weiss, 2005) use artificial intelligence and machine learning techniques to automatically discover groups of similar documents. The clusters are presented to the searcher in a tree structure alongside the search results (Figure 1). Searchers can scan the cluster names to identify some aspect of the search results they wish to explore further. Clicking on one of these (e.g., "Knowledge Discovery") will filter the search results so that searchers do not need to consider all the search results in the list. In this example, such a filtering operation would reduce the number of search results that need to be considered from 100 to 11.

While Carrot2 only provides one level of clustering within the search results set, other

Figure 1. The Carrot2 clustering interface automatically groups similar documents in the search results, allowing the searcher to navigate the tree of clusters to filter the search results. (© 2010, Stanisław Osiński & Dawid Weiss. Used with permission.)

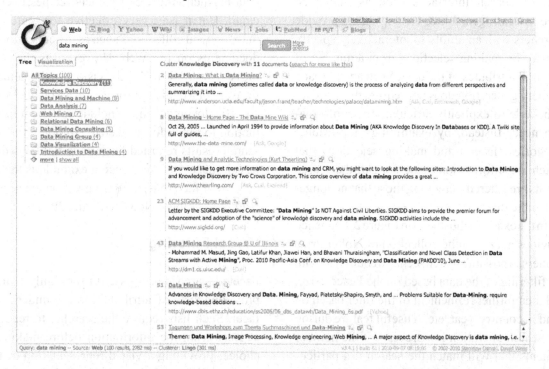

systems such as Yippy (2010) use a hierarchical clustering algorithm. In these cases, some of the larger clusters may include sub-clusters, which can be expanded and explored within the tree structure. This approach provides a finer-grained level of detail with respect to the clusters, at the expense of requiring additional work to understand and navigate the hierarchy.

Some of the early work on clustering Web search results focused on the ability to generate the clusters in near-real time (Zamir & Etzioni, 1999). Since then, others have made advancements with respect to providing accurate and descriptive names for the clusters (Kules, Kustanowitz, & Shneiderman, 2006), and enhancing the clustering interfaces (Carrot Search, 2010).

Clustering the search results can be very useful when the searchers' information needs include ambiguous topics. The clusters allow searchers to identify those aspects of the search results set that are relevant to their search goals, and to reject and ignore those that are not. The fundamental benefit here is that the relevance decision can be made on the entire cluster, rather than on a per-document basis. Further, the names of the clusters may also give searchers clues as to how to further refine their queries.

The main drawbacks to clustering Web search results include difficulties with comparing documents within different clusters and choosing descriptive names for the clusters. In addition, since preference is often given to the larger clusters that are provided at the top of the tree structure, it may be possible for there to be a very small cluster at the bottom of the tree that includes the most relevant documents, but is missed by the searcher.

Faceted Search

Faceted search interfaces such as Flamenco (Yee, Swearingen, Li, & Hearst, 2003) provide searchers with an ability to interactively specify a query by making selections from a number of different attributes of the data. Such an approach to query generation does not require the searcher to be able to explicitly articulate their information need. Instead, by examining the attribute categories (facets) and making selections that match the information being sought, the search results are filtered, removing those that no longer match the query.

In the example illustrated in Figure 2, Flamenco provides access to the collection of Nobel Prize winners. A possible search scenario could start with the filtering of the data based on the Peace Prize, and then further refinement of the filter based on gender, country, year, etc. A useful feature during this search operation is a preview of the number of items that will match the search if a particular attribute is selected (the number included in brackets after each attribute label). Such a search interface is especially beneficial for situations when searchers are more interested in exploring a data set, rather than performing a targeted and specific keyword search. Exploratory interfaces allow the searcher to get a sense of the breadth of information that might be available on a topic (e.g., Nobel Prize Winners), and can be useful when the searcher does not know where to start with a keyword search. Complex filters (which are essentially dynamic queries) can be constructed with just a few clicks of the mouse. However, the default connective in the construction of such queries is a conjunction. As such, it is difficult to construct disjunctive sub-queries that allow the data to be filtered such that multiple attributes on a given facet are satisfied.

Faceted search interfaces are only feasible when there is a well-constructed set of meta-data available for the collection being searched, and when the attribute categories are meaningful to the searcher. As such, a search interface such as Flamenco is useful for exploring well-structured datasets such as movies, products, recipes, or even email. But it isn't very effective for searching more general collections such as the collection of documents on the Web. However, as the Web moves toward fulfilling the vision for the Semantic Web, ontological information associated with specific documents may include sufficient information to allow for a faceted exploration of the search results returned from an initial keyword-based query. One such recent example is the inclusion of facet-based filtering within the search feature of Google News (Google, 2010).

Visual Filtering

Faceted search interfaces tend to be highly textual, providing lists of attribute choices under each facet. Such lists require the searcher to read, or at least scan, the information before making a choice. Providing a visual representation of the facets may allow the searcher to understand their meaning more quickly, and make appropriate selections with less cognitive effort.

VisGets (Dörk, Carpendale, Collins, & Williamson, 2008) is an example of such an approach, favouring visual representations of the attributes in each facet over textual lists (Figure 3). Within this interface, searchers are able to quickly learn the distribution of the search results within the various facets (indicated by the size of the histogram in the time region, the size of the icons within the location region, and the size of the font within the tags region). As with faceted search, the system supports interactive filtering based on selections within the visual facets.

A further enhancement that is made possible by the visual nature of the interface is the use of interactive highlighting across multiple coordinated views (Baldonado, Woodruff, & Kuchinsky, 2000). When the searcher focuses on a particular search result, it is visually highlighted in the search results list; simultaneously, its corresponding

Figure 2. Flamenco allows the searcher to interactively select features of the search results set from among pre-defined categories. Such selections filter the search results, leaving only those that match the specified criteria. (© 2010, Marti Hearst. Used with permission.)

information across the facets is also highlighted. This feature enables searchers to use the results list as a mechanism for exploring the facets, enhancing their ability to refine the visual query even further.

Such a visual filtering mechanism suffers from many of the same problems as faceted search, including the requirement of a robust set of meta-data for the collection being searched, and the ability to only construct conjunctive queries. However, as more structured information becomes available within Web search results, such visual interfaces may provide a valuable approach to both exploring and filtering search results. Further, the application of such an approach to search domains beyond the Web (e.g., email, corporate Intranets) may be valuable given the availability of meta-data associated with such collections.

Visualization

Other visual approaches to supporting Web search activities are also possible. The benefit of visualization is that by providing graphical representations of data or concepts associated with Web search tasks, cognitive activities are promoted that allow searchers to gain insight into the underlying features or aspects of the data that were previously hidden due to the highly textual nature of the activity. Visualization provides a link between the mind of the searcher and the data being processed within the computer system via human vision (Ware, 2004). The ultimate goal is to amplify the cognitive abilities of the searcher (Card, Mackinlay, & Shneiderman, 1999), allowing them to be more effective and efficient in their Web search tasks.

Visual search interfaces such as HotMap Web Search (Hoeber, Brooks, Schroeder, & Yang,

Figure 3. VisGets provides a visual representation of various facets (e.g., time, location, and tags) that can be used to not only filter the search results, but also to identify which facet attributes correspond to a particular search result. (© 2010, Marian Dörk. Used with permission.)

2008; HotMap, 2010) use information visualization techniques to provide the searcher with additional information regarding their current query and the corresponding set of search results. They take advantage of our ability to quickly and easily process visual attributes such as colour, shape, and size. The goal of such systems is to visually encode information that might be useful to the searchers, so that they can see patterns or interesting features, rather than having to read this information.

In the example illustrated in Figure 4, the standard list-based representation of Web search results is enhanced with three visual features. A WordBars histogram illustrates the relative frequency of the terms that appear within the search results list. A visual indication of the query term frequency is provided for each search result. A HotMap representation of the query term frequency within the search results shows at a zoomed out level of detail how a large number of search results are using the query terms.

Each of these features within HotMap Web Search support a high degree of interactivity. Within the WordBars histogram, searchers can select terms that they recognize as relevant to their search tasks, causing the search results to be re-sorted based on the use of these terms. Further, searchers can readily identify their query terms within the histogram by the use of the red font colour. These terms can be removed from their queries or other terms added by clicking on the minus or plus icons. Together, these features allow searchers to first identify potentially relevant terms, see how these terms are being used within the search results sets, and then modify their queries as desired to produce new sets of search results and associated visual representations.

Within the search results list, searchers can readily identify how often their specific query

Figure 4. Visual representations of Web search information allow the searcher not only to see relevant information, but also support interactivity. In HotMap Web Search, a searcher can see the relative frequency of the top terms in the search results list, as well as the frequency of the query terms within individual search results. These can be used to not only interactively re-rank the search results, but also to refine the query. (© 2010, Orland Hoeber. Used with permission.)

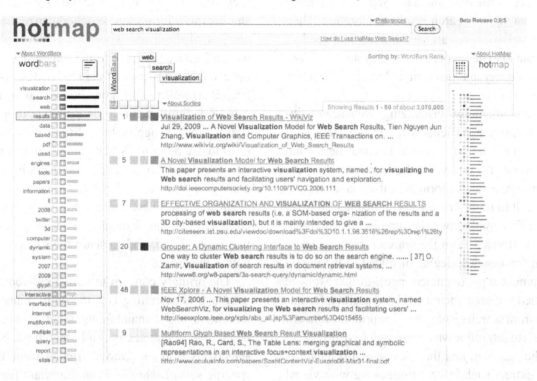

terms are being used within the individual search results based on the intensity of the heat-scale colour encoding. Although similar to the approach used in TileBars (Hearst, 1995), the visual representation shows the frequency over all the information that is available for the document (i.e., title, snippet, and URL). Searchers can use this to re-rank the search results based on how often the documents use their query terms, by clicking on the query term labels. Doing so allows the searchers to indicate to the system that they hold one of the query terms as being more important to their information-seeking goals than the others.

When scrolling within the search results list, the box placed over the HotMap representation moves to show the searchers where the search results that are currently being viewed exist within the currently loaded collection. In addition, they can use this zoomed-out representation of the search results to readily identify how the query terms are being used within the collections. If they identify a location of interest (e.g., where a pair of query terms are being used with similar frequency), they can click on the location, resulting in an automatic scrolling of the search results list to this location and a highlighting of the corresponding search result.

While studies of the specific features of this work showed great promise in helping searchers to more readily and reliably resolve their information needs (Hoeber & Yang, 2008, 2009), the main drawback is that the system is rather visually complex, especially in comparison to the simple interfaces used by the top search engines. However, it is this additional visual complexity that provides the searcher with the power to refine their query and explore the search results in a visual and interactive manner. These additions to the list-based representation were designed to be as lightweight as possible, yet still providing support for the fundamental search tasks of query refinement and search results exploration. They are available for searchers to use when needed, but can also be ignored when they are confident in their query and just want to look at the top few search results.

Fundamentally, visualizing Web search information is a difficult task because there isn't much information available beyond the textual features of the query and the search results. Furthermore, textual information itself is inherently difficult to represent in a visual manner (Wise et al., 1995). While there is some information that can be derived from the search results set (e.g., term frequencies, degree of match to the query, document type, document age), further work is needed to extract meaningful and useful information from search results sets. The primary concern here is to determine what information is truly useful to the searcher, and then devise algorithms that can extract such information, along with visual approaches that can show this information to the searcher in a way they can understand and use to enhance their search experience.

Collaborative Search

Collaborative search tools such as SearchTogether (Morris & Horvitz, 2007) allow multiple searchers who are interested in similar topics to share their search activities and what they have found with their family, friends, and colleagues. As illustrated in Figure 5, searchers are not only able to initiate their own new queries, but they can also see what queries their friends are submitting. As the searcher finds documents that are relevant to the collective information need, these can be saved along with comments regarding the benefit or relevance. In addition, the searcher can inspect their friends'

queries, review the documents they have found, and add additional notes about each.

The end result of such a collaborative approach to searching is that people can easily see what their friends are looking for, and vice versa. By sharing this information, searchers can reduce the amount of duplicate work that is done. When working on a common information need, searchers can take advantage of the knowledge of their friends, as well as learn from their mistakes. They can work simultaneously on the same problem, sharing their progress in real-time without the need to use other tools (e.g., email, instant messaging) to coordinate their work. In addition, the history of documents that were found to be relevant and useful is stored along with searcher comments, making it much easier to re-visit what they have found, and to share their discoveries within the group.

The primary concern in such a collaborative approach to searching is common to many collaborative tools: maintaining security. Further, being able to manage multiple search goals and selectively add or remove friends from these specific sets of searches is an important feature. Even with these drawbacks, such approaches may prove to be very useful within research or educational domains.

Personalized Search

Personalized Web search interfaces attempt to take advantage of the prior interest a searcher has shown in a particular topic to make their future searches on a similar topic more effective. A number of different approaches have been developed to attempt to capture such prior interest based on various sources of information, including query logs (Chen & Huang, 2009), documents found on the searcher's computer (Chirita, Firan, & Nejdl, 2006), Web browsing histories (Sugiyama, Hatano, & Yoshikawa, 2004), and the click histories from previous searches (Speretta & Gauch, 2005). The end result in many of these

Figure 5. SearchTogether allows searchers to work collaboratively to resolve their information needs, sharing with one another their queries (left screenshot) as well as the documents they have found (right screenshot). (© 2007, Meredith Ringel Morris. Used with permission.)

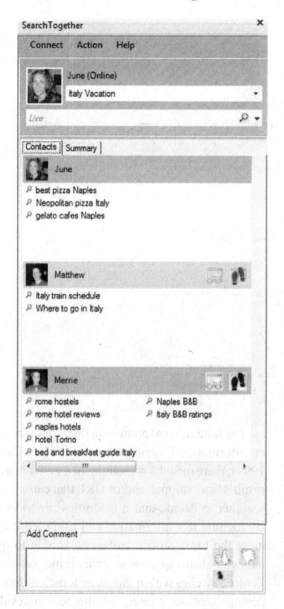

Figure 6. Web search personalization using miSearch allows the searcher to maintain multiple distinct search topics. As the searcher views documents that appear to be relevant, the system dynamically learns the searcher's interests and uses this to re-rank subsequent search results. (© 2009, Orland Hoeber. Used with permission.)

personalization approaches is a re-ranking of the search results, moving those that are most similar to the searchers' prior interests near the top of the search results lists.

A common difficulty in personalized Web search is that a given searcher will often have numerous diverse topics that are of interest to them, producing a monolithic interest profile that contains a significant amount of noise when used to personalize a specific set of search results. An interesting approach to this problem is that which is employed in miSearch (Hoeber & Massie, 2009): allow the searchers to explicitly define distinct search topics, then implicitly learn their interests based on the search results they find relevant when conducting searches within these topics (Figure 6).

The fundamental premise in this work is based on information foraging theory (Pirolli & Card, 1999); there must be something in a given search result's title, snippet, and/or URL that caused the searcher to decide that it is worthwhile to visit. By logging this information and using it to augment the topic profile, miSearch is able to dynamically learn what the searcher is interested in. Future searches within this same topic produce a personalized re-ordering of the search results based on the similarity of the documents to the topic profile.

Experiments with miSearch have found that clicking on as few as two relevant documents can result in significant improvements in the order of the documents in the search results list. However, there are some problems with miSearch that are common to most personalization methods, including topic creep (the changing of a searcher's use and understanding of a topic over time) and robustness (ability to deal with the accidental selection of an irrelevant document).

An interesting area for further enhancements of personalized approaches to Web search is the addition of visual indications of the underlying personalization model (Hoeber & Liu, 2010). One of the drawbacks to dynamically re-ordering the search results is that searchers are uncertain or confused as to why the personalization system thought a particular document was more relevant than another. Adding visual features to the interface can help explain to the searcher the features about the current topic that the system has learned. Further, these features can be made interactive, allowing the searcher to select those that they feel are most relevant to their current search (causing a subsequent re-ranking of the search results) or even the complete removal of specific aspects of the topic profile.

Re-Finding

Re-finding information, such as previously viewed Web pages, can be a somewhat difficult task. If the users know the specific details of the information they need (be it a file on their computer, an email message, or a Web page), they can simply navigate to it. However, what can be done when the users do not remember enough details about the Web page they wish to re-find? Often, they resort to searching the Web, with varying degrees of success.

When attempting to re-finding Web pages, users often have only vague information about when the page was found and what they were doing at the time. This makes crafting a query to re-find a Web page a rather difficult task. Browse-Line (Hoeber & Gorner, 2009) was designed to support this re-finding task by providing a visual representation of the temporal aspect of a user's browsing activities (Figure 7).

This system can be used to visually search prior browsing patterns and identify activities and approximate times in which the page may have been viewed. For example, a user may have visited the page as part of a search activity (represented by a short but wide stack of page views), during the extended use of some Web-based service such as a social networking site (represented by a tall but narrow stack of page views), or by following a link from an external application (represented by a single page view). By visually identifying the type of activities users were performing when they viewed the page they are seeking, they can zoom to a particular location within their browsing history and inspect the specific pages that were viewed. Additional domain filtering operations further enhance the ability of the user to re-find the page they are seeking.

Common Theme

The common theme among all of these search interfaces is the ability for the searcher to interact within the search process, enhancing their ability to specify and refine their query, evaluate and explore the search results, or both. In many cases this interaction occurs explicitly, providing searchers with added interface features that allow them to actively participate in the search activity. This is in contrast to the user experience paradigm that is promoted in most traditional search interfaces, wherein the interaction is limited to typing in a query, looking at the search results, and clicking on those that look like they might be relevant.

In these approaches to human-centred search, the interaction expected from the searcher supports the cognitive activity of sense-making. When conducting a search on a topic that is more complex than a simple fact-verification activity, the goal is often to look for more than just the single document that will fulfill the information need. In many cases, such a single document may not even exist. Instead, searchers want to gain an understanding

Figure 7. By providing a visual representation of the timeline of page views, BrowseLine allows users to narrow down the browsing history based on the type of activity they were performing at the time the page was viewed. (© 2009, Orland Hoeber. Used with permission.)

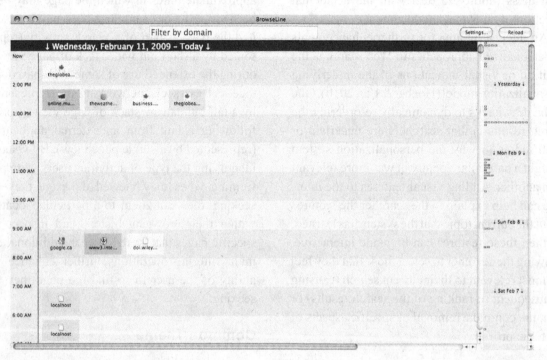

of the topic. They can do this by exploring the search results in an interactive manner, gaining more knowledge about the relationships between the documents and their relevance to the search topic than if they were just entering individual queries and browsing static lists of search results.

Within human-centred Web search interfaces, these interactive features allow searchers to actively participate in the search process. The interaction may be in the process of providing more information about what it is they are searching for, or making choices regarding groups of documents that appear relevant or aspects of the query that are important. It may be in the form of evaluating and manipulating the order of search results. Or it may be through an exploratory process wherein searchers experiment with their queries and the organization of the search results as they seek to make sense of the information they are finding. Ultimately, the goal in the design of human-

centred Web search systems is to provide better tools for searching when the user doesn't know enough about what they are seeking for the task to be considered a simple fact-verification activity.

EVALUATING NOVEL WEB SEARCH INTERFACES

All of the approaches described in this paper include novel and potentially complex interface features that searchers must become comfortable with and be able to use effectively. As such, it is important to evaluate such interfaces to ensure that they indeed providing the benefit to the searcher for which they are designed.

Traditional methods for evaluating information retrieval systems focus on the use of test collections, completely removing the human element from the evaluation of the algorithm under consideration. Testing is done under conditions that assume perfect queries and perfect relevance judgments of documents. Metrics such as precision and recall are used to determine the effectiveness of the algorithm to identify as many relevant documents from the collection as possible, while excluding as many non-relevant documents as possible. Due to the size of the Web, applying such traditional evaluation approaches to Web search introduces a number of difficulties. However, most of the concerns at this level of evaluation are with the underlying algorithms that produce the ranked lists of search results.

By contrast, the concern within human-centred Web search is to evaluate whether the search engine can learn about searchers' information needs, and whether the resulting lists of search results can be manipulated and enhanced to better support the discovery of knowledge. As such, the focus in evaluating such interfaces is through user evaluations. Numerous evaluation methods and procedures have been proposed within the domain of human-computer interaction, including the use of inspection methods (Neilsen, 1994; Neilsen & Mack, 1994), laboratory studies (Barnum, 2001), field trials (Plaisant, 2004), and longitudinal studies (Hoeber, Schroeder, & Brooks, 2009). Conducting such evaluations with interactive Web search interfaces can be challenging due to the knowledge-centric nature of the activities participants are expected to perform with the systems under evaluation.

Recently, a stepped evaluation and refinement model (Figure 8) has been proposed which suggests that various evaluation methods can be used together in a structured way, improving and refining the Web search interface prototype along the way based on knowledge that is learned with each round of evaluation (Hoeber, 2009). Within this model, inspection methods are first used to provide expert analyses of the interface features within simulated settings. Once a sufficiently refined prototype is developed based on the results of these inspections, laboratory studies can be

conducted to measure empirical evidence of the value of the features under controlled conditions. Based on what is learned at this level of evaluation, further enhancements can be made to the interface and subsequent laboratory studies can be conducted to validate the features. Once the researcher has gained confidence in the value and quality of the system, field trials can be conducted to measure subjective evidence from a small group of searchers over a short period of time, or longitudinal studies may be conducted that measure empirical evidence from a large group of searchers over a long period of time. Both of these final stages of evaluation are conducted under real-world search settings, providing the most accurate evidence we can gather regarding the value of the proposed approaches for supporting the searcher's activities.

How this evaluation model can be applied to a specific human-centred Web search interface depends on the specific features and design of such an interface. While the inspection methods are relatively straightforward to apply and can be used as a quality-control check on the interface design, if the interface is highly visual, detailed inspection methods that consider how the data is visually encoded may be useful (Zuk, Schlesier, Neumann, Hancock, & Carpendale, 2006). When conducting laboratory studies on a research prototype, special attention should be given to choosing the types of search tasks to be performed, and in deciding when such tasks should be considered complete. In making these decisions, one should carefully consider what benefit the proposed interface is meant to provide to the searcher, and design the evaluation tasks such that these benefits can be measured. In some cases, it may be better to have each participant in the study conduct the same query; in other cases having participants use the interface for their own queries may provide more realistic results (Spink, 2002). Both quantitative (e.g., time to task completion, error rate, precision) and qualitative (e.g., ease of use, satisfaction, perceived usefulness) should be mea-

Figure 8. By following this stepped evaluation and refinement model, a preliminary research prototype can be evaluated and refined in unison. (© 2009, Orland Hoeber. Used with permission.)

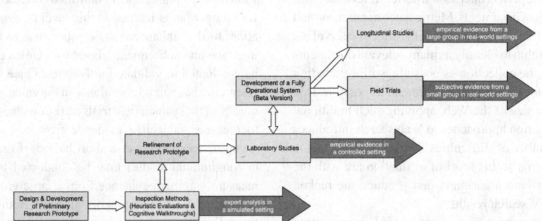

sured in comparison to some baseline search interface.

Field trials and longitudinal studies may be conducted once the interface is sufficiently refined and bug-free. In both types of evaluations, the goal is to collect data on real users conducting real search tasks in real search settings. Field trials are useful when the goal is to carefully observe and discover how the interface is being used in a real-world setting. Since field trials are normally conducted with the researcher present, they can provide a rich source of qualitative information regarding the system under investigation, especially when coupled with focus group discussions (Mazza & Berré, 2007). If the goal is to discover how searchers are able to use the system under investigation over long periods of time, longitudinal studies may be used. Since it is not feasible to observe the participants in such studies, regular questionnaires, such as those based on the technology acceptance model (Davis, 1989) can allow for the collection of data related to the perceived usefulness and ease of use of the system. For both of these types of evaluations, it is difficult to measure the performance of the participants quantitatively. Instead, qualitative measures carry much more weight, with satisfaction being an important indicator of success (Plaisant, 2004).

When designing and conducting such studies, it is important to keep in mind that human-centred Web search systems are designed to support the specific activities and tasks a searcher needs to perform in order to fulfill their information need. Commonly, the goals are much more complex than simple fact-verification (i.e., finding a single document that provides the answer that is being sought). Instead, the searcher may be interested in exploring the search results, comparing multiple documents, refining their queries, and gaining knowledge on a complex topic. The measurements of the success or value of the interface may become very complex if the study is not designed carefully.

FUTURE RESEARCH DIRECTIONS

There are numerous interesting research directions for human-centred Web search. These can be divided along two streams: those that support the searcher activities of specifying to the search engine what they need and then resolving that information need; and those that extend the search paradigm from finding documents on the Web to finding information within other Web-related domains.

Further research is needed to devise new methods for supporting people throughout the search process. The study of such methods is necessary to not only measure the value of such approaches, but also to further understand the cognitive activities associated with searching the Web. New interfaces that support query specification and query refinement will enhance the searcher's ability to specify to the search engine what it is that they are seeking (even if they have difficulty articulating this information need). New interfaces that support search results evaluation and exploration will allow the searcher to browse and filter the search results, investigate and analyze what they have found, and understand and organize the knowledge they have gained. Further support for saving and subsequent re-finding of information will enable the searcher to easily return to previously discovered information without having to go through this whole search process again. Ultimately, the goal here is to enhance the searcher's activities through information visualization, interactivity, machine learning, searcher-centric interface designs, and various other methods that will allow searchers to become better at searching.

In addition to devising novel interfaces that address specific Web search needs, another potentially fruitful avenue for research is to combine some of the features of existing interfaces that have been designed to support the human element of search. For example, more research on providing visual representations of Web search clusters may allow searchers to more easily understand the relationships between clusters. Or personalization may be combined with faceted search in order to learn a searcher's interests and make suggestions for facets that they may wish to explore. Developing a framework in which multiple different interactive features that support the searcher's activities can be "plugged together" may also prove useful for evaluating the impact of various features on a searcher's impressions of interface clutter and system complexity.

Although much of what has been discussed in this paper is related to searching the Web for documents, there are many more types of information available that people need to find on the Web. For example, it is common for searchers to focus their intents on only images or video. In other cases, searchers may wish to find information stored within their Web-based applications (e.g., file sharing, email, calendar, contacts), within their social networking applications (e.g., to find friends or interests), or within the blogosphere or twittersphere (e.g., to find topical and current information). For each of these, it is important to take advantage of whatever domain-specific information can be used to enhance the search process, and to keep in mind that the type of information need and the degree to which a searcher wishes to fulfill this need may be very different depending on the type and source of information. For example, consider the differences between searching for documents versus searching for images. Further study on these differences will allow researchers to make informed decisions regarding the tools they design and develop for such search activities.

CONCLUSION

As the amount of information in our lives continues to grow, search engines are becoming the primary tool we use to find information. As people become more accustomed to searching for the information they need, they will begin to demand more powerful tools to support their search activities. One aspect that will have a significant impact on the utility of search engines in the future will be the support they provide for the human-centric activities of search. The design and development of these next-generation search tools will have a significant impact on how we search the Web not only for documents, but also for the multitude of other information it stores.

In this chapter, we have provided researchers with a motivation for considering the human element of Web search, and outlined a number of different approaches to human-centred Web search. We have discussed the need for conducting user evaluations of such systems, and provided an outline of some future directions for research. In discussing information retrieval systems prior to the explosion of content on the Web, Marchionini (1992) stated that "Much research and development is required to produce interfaces that allow end users to be productive amid such complexity, and that protect them from information overload." This statement remains as true today as when it was first written.

REFERENCES

Baeza-Yates, R., & Ribeiro-Neto, B. (2011). *Modern information retrieval: The concepts and terminology behind search* (2nd ed.). Reading, MA: Addison-Wesley.

Baldonado, M. Q. W., Woodruff, A., & Kuchinsky, A. (2000). Guidelines for using multiple views in information visualization. In *Proceedings of the ACM Advanced Visual Interfaces Conference* (pp. 110-119). New York, NY: ACM

Barnum, C. M. (2001). *Usability testing and research*. London, UK: Longman.

Bhavnani, S. K., & Bates, M. J. (2002). Separating the knowledge layers: Cognitive analysis of search knowledge through hierarchical goal decompositions. *Proceedings of the American Society for Information Science and Technology*, *39*(1), 204–213. doi:10.1002/meet.1450390122

Brin, S., & Page, L. (1998). The anatomy of a large-scale hypertextual web search engine. In *Proceedings of the Seventh International World Wide Web Conference* (pp. 107-117). New York, NY: ACM

Card, S. K., Mackinlay, J. D., & Shneiderman, B. (1999). *Readings in information visualization: Using vision to think*. San Francisco, CA: Morgan Kaufmann.

Carrot Search. (2010). *Circle: Interactive cluster visualization*. Retrieved September 22, 2010 from http://carrotsearch.com/ circles-overview.html

Chen, X., & Huang, L. (2009). The research of personalized search engine based on users' access interest. In *Proceedings of the Asia-Pacific Conference on Computational Intelligence and Industrial Applications* (pp. 337-340). Washington, DC: IEEE Computer Society.

Chirita, P. A., Firan, C., & Nejdl, W. (2006). Summarizing local context to personalize global Web search. In *Proceedings of the ACM Conference on Information and Knowledge Management* (pp. 287-296). New York, NY: ACM

Davis, F. D. (1989). Perceived usefulness, perceived ease of use, and user acceptance of information technology. *Management Information Systems Quarterly*, *13*(3), 319–340. doi:10.2307/249008

Dörk, M., Carpendale, S., Collins, C., & Williamson, C. (2008). VisGets: Coordinated visualizations of Web-based information exploration and discovery. *IEEE Transactions on Visualization and Computer Graphics*, *14*(6), 1205–1212. doi:10.1109/TVCG.2008.175

Field, H., Allan, J., & Jones, R. (2010). Predicting searcher frustration. In *Proceedings of the ACM SIGIR Conference on Research and Development in Information Retrieval* (pp. 34-41). New York, NY: ACM.

Ghemawat, S., Gobioff, H., & Leung, S.-T. (2003). The Google file system. In *Proceedings of the ACM Symposium on Operating System Principles* (pp. 29-43). New York, NY: ACM.

Google. (2010). *Google news*. Retrieved September 22, 2010, from http://news.google.com

Hearst, M. (1995). TileBars: Visualization of term distribution information in full text information access. In *Proceedings of the ACM Conference on Human Factors in Computing Systems* (pp. 59-66). New York, NY: ACM.

Hoeber, O. (2008). Web information retrieval support systems: The future of Web search. In *Proceedings of the IEEE/WIC/ACM International Conference on Web Intelligence – Workshops (International Workshop on Web Information Retrieval Support Systems)* (pp. 29-32). Washington, DC: IEEE Computer Society.

Hoeber, O. (2009). User evaluation methods for visual Web search interfaces. In *Proceedings of the International Conference on Information Visualization* (pp. 139-145). Washington, DC: IEEE Computer Society.

Hoeber, O., Brooks, M., Schroeder, D., & Yang, X. D. (2008). TheHotMap.com: Enabling flexible interaction in next-generation Web search interfaces. In *Proceedings of the IEEE/WIC/ACM International Conference on Web Intelligence* (pp. 730-734). Washington, DC: IEEE Computer Society.

Hoeber, O., & Gorner, J. (2009). BrowseLine: 2D timeline visualization of web browsing histories. In *Proceedings of the International Conference on Information Visualization* (pp. 156-161). Washington, DC: IEEE Computer Society.

Hoeber, O., & Liu, H. (2010). Comparing tag clouds, term histograms, and term lists for enhancing personalized Web search. In *Proceedings of the IEEE/WIC/ACM International Conference on Web Intelligence – Workshops (International Workshop on Web Information Retrieval Support Systems)* (pp. 309-313). Washington, DC: IEEE Computer Society.

Hoeber, O., & Massie, C. (2009). Automatic topic learning for personalized re-ordering of Web search results. In *Proceedings of the Atlantic Web Intelligence Conference* (pp. 105-116). Berlin, Germany: Springer-Verlag.

Hoeber, O., Schroeder, D., & Brooks, M. (2009). Real-world user evaluations of a visual and interactive Web search interface. In *Proceedings of the International Conference on Information Visualization* (pp. 119-126). Washington, DC: IEEE Computer Society.

Hoeber, O., & Yang, X. D. (2008). Evaluating WordBars in exploratory Web search scenarios. *Information Processing & Management, 44*(2), 485–510. doi:10.1016/j.ipm.2007.07.003

Hoeber, O., & Yang, X. D. (2009). HotMap: Supporting visual explorations of Web search results. *Journal of the American Society for Information Science and Technology, 60*(1), 90–110. doi:10.1002/asi.20957

HotMap. (2010). *HotMap Web search: An interactive and visual way to explore your search results!* Retrieved September 23, 2010, from http://www.thehotmap.com

Jansen, B. J., Booth, D. L., & Spink, A. (2007). Determining the user intent of Web search engine queries. In *Proceedings of the International World Wide Web Conference* (pp. 1149-1150). New York, NY: ACM.

Jansen, B. J., & Pooch, U. (2001). A review of Web searching studies and a framework for future research. *Journal of the American Society for Information Science and Technology, 52*(3), 235–246. doi:10.1002/1097-4571(2000)9999:9999<::AID-ASI1607>3.0.CO;2-F

Jansen, B. J., & Spink, A. (2006). How are we searching the World Wide Web? A comparison of nine search engine transaction logs. *Information Processing & Management, 42*(1), 248–263. doi:10.1016/j.ipm.2004.10.007

Kules, B., Kustanowitz, J., & Shneiderman, B. (2006). Categorizing Web search results into meaningful and stable categories using fast-feature techniques. In *Proceedings of the ACM/IEEE-CS Joint Conference on Digital Libraries* (pp. 210-219). New York, NY: ACM.

Marchionini, G. (1992). Interfaces for end-user information seeking. *Journal of the American Society for Information Science American Society for Information Science, 43*(2), 156–163. doi:10.1002/(SICI)1097-4571(199203)43:2<156::AID-ASI8>3.0.CO;2-U

Mazza, R., & Berré, A. (2007). Focus group methodology for evaluating information visualization techniques and tools. In *Proceedings of the International Conference on Information Visualization* (pp. 74-80). Washington, DC: IEEE Computer Society.

Morris, M. R., & Horvitz, E. (2007). SearchTogether: An interface for collaborative Web search. In *Proceedings of the ACM Symposium on User Interface Software and Technology* (pp. 3-12). New York, NY: ACM.

Neilsen, J. (1994). Enhancing the explanatory power of usability heuristics. In *Proceedings of the ACM Conference on Human Factors in Computing Systems* (pp. 152-158). New York, NY: ACM.

Neilsen, J., & Mack, R. L. (1994). *Usability inspection methods*. New York, NY: John Wiley & Sons.

Osiński, S., & Weiss, D. (2005). A concept-driven algorithm for clustering search results. *IEEE Transactions on Intelligent Systems, 20*(3), 48–54. doi:10.1109/MIS.2005.38

Pirolli, P., & Card, S. (1999). Information foraging. *Psychological Review, 106*(4), 643–675. doi:10.1037/0033-295X.106.4.643

Plaisant, C. (2004). The challenge of information visualization evaluation. In *Proceedings of the Working Conference on Advanced Visual Interfaces* (pp. 109-116). New York, NY: ACM.

Rasmussen, E. M. (2003). Indexing and retrieval for the Web. *Annual Review of Information Science & Technology, 37*(1), 91–124. doi:10.1002/aris.1440370104

Sebe, N. (2010). Human-centered computing. In Nakashima, H., Aghajan, H., & Augusto, J. C. (Eds.), *Handbook of ambient intelligence and smart environments* (pp. 349–370). New York, NY: Springer. doi:10.1007/978-0-387-93808-0_13

Silverstein, C., Henzinger, M., Marais, H., & Moricz, M. (1999). Analysis of a very large web search engine query log. *SIGIR Forum, 33*(1), 6–12. doi:10.1145/331403.331405

Speretta, M., & Gauch, S. (2005). Personalized search based on user search histories. In *Proceedings of the IEEE/WIC/ACM International Conference on Web Intelligence* (pp. 622-628). Washington, DC: IEEE Computer Society.

Spink, A. (2002). A user-centered approach to evaluating human interaction with Web search engines: an exploratory study. *Information Processing & Management, 38*(3), 401–426. doi:10.1016/S0306-4573(01)00036-X

Spink, A., Wolfram, D., Jansen, B. J., & Saracevic, T. (2001). Searching the web: the public and their queries. *Journal of the American Society for Information Science and Technology, 52*(3), 226–234. doi:10.1002/1097-4571(2000)9999:9999<::AID-ASI1591>3.0.CO;2-R

Sugiyama, K., Hatano, K., & Yoshikawa, M. (2004). Adaptive Web search based on user profile construction without any effort from users. In *Proceedings of the World Wide Web Conference* (pp. 675-684). Washington, DC: IEEE Computer Society.

Ware, C. (2004). *Information visualization: Perception for design* (2nd ed.). San Francisco, CA: Morgan Kaufmann.

White, R. W., Kules, B., Drucker, S. M., & Schraefel, M. C. (2006). Supporting exploratory search. *Communications of the ACM, 49*(4), 37–39.

Wise, J. A., Thomas, J. J., Pennock, K., Lantrip, D., Pottier, M., Schur, A., et al. (1995). Visualizing the non-visual: Spatial analysis and interaction with information from text documents. In *Proceedings of IEEE Symposium on Information Visualization* (pp. 51-58). Washington, DC: IEEE Computer Society.

Yao, Y. (2002). Information retrieval support systems. In *Proceedings of the IEEE International Conference on Fuzzy Systems* (pp. 1092-1097). Washington, DC: IEEE Computer Society.

Yee, K.-P., Swearingen, K., Li, K., & Hearst, M. (2003). Faceted metadata for image search and browsing. In *Proceedings for the ACM Conference on Human Factors in Computing Systems* (pp. 401-408). New York, NY: ACM.

Yippy, Inc. (2010). *Yippy – Welcome to the cloud.* Retrieved September 23, 2010, from http://search.yippy.com

Zamir, O., & Etzioni, O. (1999). Grouper: A dynamic clustering interface to Web search results. In *Proceedings of the World Wide Web Conference* (pp. 1361-1374). Washington, DC: IEEE Computer Society.

Zuk, T., Schlesier, L., Neumann, P., Hancock, M., & Carpendale, S. (2006). Heuristics for information visualization evaluation. In *Proceedings of the AVI Workshop on Beyond Time and Errors: Novel Evaluation Methods for Information Visualization* (pp. 1-6). New York, NY: ACM.

ADDITIONAL READING

Brusilovsky, P., Kobsa, A., & Nejdl, W. (2007). *The adaptive Web: methods and strategies of web personalization.* Berlin, Germany: Springer-Verlag.

Carpineto, C., Osiński, S., Romano, G., & Weiss, D. (2009). A survey of Web clustering engines. *ACM Computing Surveys, 41*(3), 17. doi:10.1145/1541880.1541884

Fisher, K. E., Erdelez, S., & McKechnie, L. (2005). *Theories of information behavior.* Medford, NJ: Information Today.

Hearst, M. (1999). User interfaces and visualization. In Baeza-Yates, R., & Ribeiro-Neto, B. (Eds.), *Modern information retrieval* (pp. 257–324). Reading, MA: Addison-Wesley.

Hearst, M. (2006). Clustering versus faceted categories for information exploration. *Communications of the ACM, 49*(4), 59–61. doi:10.1145/1121949.1121983

Hearst, M. (2009). *Search user interfaces.* Cambridge, UK: Cambridge University Press.

Hoeber, O., & Yang, X. D. (2010). Supporting Web search with visualization. In Yao, J.-T. (Ed.), *Web-based support systems* (pp. 183–214). London, UK: Springer. doi:10.1007/978-1-84882-628-1_10

Kobayashi, M., & Takeda, K. (2000). Information retrieval on the Web. *ACM Computing Surveys, 32*(2), 114–173. doi:10.1145/358923.358934

Kuo, B. Y.-L., Hentrich, T., Good, B. M., & Wilkinson, M. D. (2007). Tag clouds for summarizing Web search results. In *Proceedings of the International World Wide Web Conference* (pp. 1203-1204). Washington, DC: IEEE Computer Society.

Marchionini, G., & White, R. W. (2009). Information seeking support systems. *IEEE Computer, 42*(3), 30–32. doi:10.1109/MC.2009.88

National Institute of Standards and Technology. (2011). *Text retrieval conference (TREC) home page*. Retrieved March 22, 2011, from http://trec.nist.gov

Shneiderman, B., & Plaisant, C. (2010). *Designing the user interface* (5th ed.). Reading, MA: Addison-Wesley.

Teevan, J. (2008). How people recall, recognize, and reuse search results. *ACM Transactions on Information Systems*, *26*(4), 19. doi:10.1145/1402256.1402258

Tufte, E. (1990). *Envisioning information*. Cheshire, CT: Graphics Press.

Tunkelang, D. (2009). *Faceted search*. San Rafael, CA: Morgan & Claypool.

Ware, C. (2008). *Visual thinking for design*. Burlington, MA: Morgan Kaufmann.

White, R. W., & Roth, R. A. (2009). *Exploratory search: Beyond the query-response paradigm*. San Rafael, CA: Morgan & Claypool.

Wilson, M. L., Kules, B., Schraefel, M. C., & Shneiderman, B. (2010). From keyword search to exploration: Designing future search interfaces for the Web. *Foundations and Trends in Web Science*, *2*(1), 1–97. doi:10.1561/1800000003

Chapter 11
Extensions of Web Browsers Useful to Knowledge Workers

Sarah Vert
Centre Virtuel de la Connaissance sur l'Europe (CVCE), Luxembourg

ABSTRACT

This chapter focuses on the Internet working environment of Knowledge Workers through the customization of the Web browser on their computer. Given that a Web browser is designed to be used by anyone browsing the Internet, its initial configuration must meet generic needs such as reading a Web page, searching for information, and bookmarking. In the absence of a universal solution that meets the specific needs of each user, browser developers offer additional programs known as extensions, or add-ons. Among the various browsers that can be modified with add-ons, Mozilla's Firefox is perhaps the one that first springs to mind; indeed, Mozilla has built the Firefox brand around these extensions. Using this example, and also considering the browsers Google Chrome, Internet Explorer, Opera and Safari, the author will attempt to demonstrate the potential of Web browsers in terms of the resources they can offer when they are customizable and available within the working environment of a Knowledge Worker.

INTRODUCTION

In this chapter, Web browser customization will be illustrated from the perspective of the Internet working environment of Knowledge Workers on a laptop or desktop computer. The term 'Knowledge Worker' is taken to mean 'someone who works at any of the tasks of planning, acquiring, searching, analyzing, organizing, storing, programming, distributing, marketing, or otherwise contributing to the transformation and commerce of information and those (often the same people) who work at using the knowledge so produced' (TechTarget, 1999). This definition therefore covers a wide range of professionals including university researchers, students and information

DOI: 10.4018/978-1-4666-0330-1.ch011

specialists such as information science engineers, knowledge managers and information officers. The Internet has become a prime resource for them (Doyle & Hammond, 2006). as well as one of their many working environments (Germain, 2010). It can provide them with a host of quality sources and cloud computing applications via a single interface: the Internet browser.

Given that such applications are designed to be used by anyone browsing the Internet, their initial configuration must meet generic needs such as reading a Web page, searching for information, and bookmarking. In the absence of a universal solution (Microsoft, 2011)[1] that meets the specific needs of a target audience (Collaud 2007),[2] browser developers offer additional programs known as extensions, or add-ons.[3] Even though the five most used Web browsers in the world (StatCounter, 2011) — Internet Explorer, Firefox, Google Chrome, Safari and Opera — now all offer an official add-ons gallery for their users, this is a fairly recent development. [4] As we will see, Mozilla's Firefox browser offers the largest number of quality add-ons that can serve the needs of Knowledge Workers, but how long will this continue to be the case, given the stiff competition from the add-ons galleries of Google Chrome, Safari, Opera and Internet Explorer, which are developing rapidly through the addition of extensions that mostly experienced initial success with Firefox? We have therefore decided to illustrate our ideas by presenting the add-ons that are most suitable for the purposes of Knowledge Workers for all five Web browser leaders. [5] The add-ons selected were chosen according to various criteria.[6] We began by choosing extensions that feature in at least one of the official galleries of the browsers analyzed[7] and can be tested. This meant that only free add-ons or those with a 'freemium' version not requiring any programming knowledge were selected. The add-ons also had to meet specific requirements of Knowledge Workers which are not covered, or only partly so, by the basic features of the browser for which

they were designed. These include improving the user-friendliness of the browser to provide quicker access to information; refining search results; analyzing the information retrieved while browsing; and collecting and managing sources and documents effectively. Finally, where several add-ons offered equivalent feature(s), we have favored those developed by public and private research entities over those developed by individuals. Through these examples, we will attempt to demonstrate the potential of Web browsers in terms of the resources they can offer when they are customizable and available within the working environment of a Knowledge Worker. To this end, we will only present the most noteworthy, well-developed add-ons. As most add-ons offer several features, we have chosen to present them according to the feature that offers the most potential for Knowledge Workers. However, for particularly comprehensive add-ons, we have occasionally highlighted several relevant features. We have organized the add-ons according to three main activities: searching, collecting and managing. In order to demonstrate the degree of customization available for the browsers considered in this chapter, add-ons similar to the main extensions selected will also be mentioned. To provide an overview of all the selected add-ons according to the above criteria, tables have been inserted in which the add-ons are summarized according to their main features and also by browser [8] and by similarity.

1. SEARCHING FOR INFORMATION

For those wishing to access information quickly, it can be useful to be able to customize the Web browser on their computer to make it more user-friendly. This involves being familiar with the browser's basic features and its search interfaces. An informed choice can then be made as to which extensions it may be helpful to install in order to reduce the number of clicks required and/or search queries that need to be entered. Features offered by such extensions enable users to add further search engines to the browser, to customize the results pages of online search engines, to refine searches by using keywords, and also to perform an automatic analysis of information during browsing or to categorize the elements of a Web page automatically in order to extract them.

1.1. Making Browsing Easier

A number of basic features and extensions (or add-ons) serve the aim of enhancing the user-friendliness of the browser and making browsing easier. Some automate tasks or provide quick access to favorite sites or to the page requested; others prevent confusion between tabs or reduce information noise.

1.1.1. Automated Browsing

It is possible to program pages to open on start-up of the browser. Different options are available for the various browsers. Unfortunately, they generally cannot be used simultaneously (for further details, please consult the summary table at the end of this section). Three basic features have been identified as being particularly useful for Knowledge Workers: opening identical pages each day, opening the most recent session and opening the start-up dialogue box. Only Opera provides a dialogue box allowing users to select the tab(s) they wish to open on start-up of the browser, offering a choice between the homepage, a saved session, the most recent session or 'Start with Speed Dial' (a page listing the sites consulted most frequently by the user). As Opera enables users to save several sessions, it is possible to create as many as necessary to facilitate daily and/or weekly searches. Saved sessions can be opened independently of each other at any point during browsing. Firefox offers the add-on **Morning Coffee** that allows users to program certain tabs to open on certain days.

To avoid having to re-enter long search queries, **Déjàclick** is an extension that saves search sequences and can play them back with a single click when required. Once the played sequence has finished, the updated search results are displayed. The sequence is saved as a bookmark. This is only available for Firefox.

1.1.2. Quick Access to Favorite Sites

With the exception of Safari, the browsers analyzed here all offer the option of 'pinning' the tabs of favorite sites. This improves users' access to the sites that they consult most frequently: when a new tab or a new window is opened, the browser offers to open these sites. All that remains for the user is to select the site required. **Speed Dial** is incorporated into Opera. Add-on available for Firefox.

1.1.3. Quick Access to Requested Page

Some basic features, if they are activated and used correctly, can enable users to access the page requested more quickly. A new tab or new window can be made active as soon as it is opened, and a tab can also be easily duplicated by right-clicking on it. The most practical feature is automatically displaying on a single page the information contained on several pages. This feature can be manually activated in Safari; to make it automatic, the **AutoPagerize** add-on needs to be installed. For Firefox and Google Chrome, the equivalent add-on is **AutoPager**.

1.1.4. Find one's Way Around Tabs More Easily

To browse more quickly between different search results and avoid getting lost on the way, all open tabs can be viewed at once by shrinking each tab to the size of the site icon. This is an automatic basic feature for Google Chrome, IE8, IE9 and

Opera. The **FaviconizeTab** extension can be added to Firefox.

The five Web browser leaders all allow users to preview open tabs by positioning the cursor over them. The information displayed differs from one browser to another. The minimum level of information provided is the page title. This can be combined with the URL of the page (IE8 – IE9) or with a thumbnail of the site (basic feature for Opera, **Tab Scope** add-on for Firefox) and/or the logo (for pinned tabs in IE9).

The browsers also offer the possibility of creating groups of tabs by theme, although the aim of this basic feature differs from one browser to another. IE9 applies color codes to the tabs to illustrate the browsing process more clearly. Firefox allows themed groups of tabs to be separated from the current browsing page, enabling users to switch between different themed groups from the same window, while ensuring that favorite sites are merely a click away in the pinned tabs (known in Firefox as 'App Tabs'). IE9 and Opera help users to compare content by offering them the option of aligning several tabs side by side. All the browsers allow open tabs to be saved in a bookmark folder, whose content can be opened at any moment in the active window or in a new window.

1.1.5. Reduce Information Noise

The basic feature (Table 1) to block pop-up windows is available for each of the five Web browser leaders. Only Safari, with its Reader Mode, enables users to display just the text contained on the pages consulted, and therefore to filter advertisements found on these pages. For automatic advertisement filtering, the **Adblock** extension (whose name differs from one official add-ons gallery to another) can be used. The other browsers also offer the possibility of removing any non-text element from the pages consulted, for example by using the add-on **Read It Later** (Firefox and Google Chrome) or **CleanPage** (IE8 – IE9, Opera).

1.2. Adding Search Engines to the Browser

Users wishing to add online search engines to their browser need to familiarize themselves with the browser's query interfaces and how they operate. The basic features of all five browsers allow users to customize their query interfaces by installing search engines chosen from a selection, but it is possible to go even further by adding search engines from the browser's official add-ons gallery. Given that all specialists and knowledge workers will have their preferred search engines, and that most companies that develop online search engines provide official extensions for them in the various add-ons galleries, we have chosen not to list all the search engine add-ons available. However, we considered it worthwhile presenting an add-on that enables users to integrate search engines which do not have their own extension.

1.2.1. Understand and Customize the Query Interfaces of Search Engines in the Browser

By default, a Web browser includes various search interfaces to enable users to perform queries, either using online search engines such as Google, Yahoo! and Bing, or locally in their history or favorites. These interfaces can be customized by adding extensions.

For the browsers that we are considering here, we have listed up to nine query interfaces: the search bar, address bar, search toolbar, search bookmarklets, context menu, sidebar, multi-functional bar, main page and taskbar. Some of these search interfaces work by entering queries; others simply by highlighting the search element. It should be noted that a search engine added to the search bar can often also be used in the context menu and sidebar; the browser history and favorites can be consulted in different places (main page, address bar, sidebar or multi-functional bar); entering a search query can be aided by

Table 1. Basic browser features and extensions available to facilitate browsing

	Firefox 3.6*- 4.0 addons.mozilla. org	Chrome 10 chrome.google. com/extensions	Safari 5 extensions.apple. com	IE8 - IE9 www.ieaddons. com	Opera 11 addons.opera. com
Automated browsing					
Program page opening on browser start-up					
• *Identical each day*	Basic feature	Basic feature	Basic feature	—	Basic feature
• *Varies depending on the day*	Morning Coffee shaneliesegang. com/projects/cof-fee.php Firefox 4.0b7 - 4.0*	—	—	—	Basic feature
• *Open the most recent pages viewed*	Basic feature	Basic feature Cannot be used in conjunction with the programmed opening of identi-cal pages each day	—	Basic feature, manually acti-vated	Basic feature
Play back a search sequence	DéjàClick www.DejaClick. com Firefox 3.5 - 4.0*	—	—	—	—
Quick access to favorite sites					
Pin the tabs of favorite sites	Basic feature	Basic feature	—	Basic feature of IE9	Basic feature
Open a new page offering access to favorite sites	Speed Dial speeddial.uworks. net Firefox 2.0 - 4.0*	Basic feature	Basic feature	Basic feature that can be activated	Basic feature Speed Dial used
Quick access to requested page					
Make the new tab or new window active when opened	Basic feature that can be activated	Basic feature	Basic feature	Basic feature of IE9	Basic feature
Easily duplicate a tab	—	Basic feature	—	Basic feature of IE9	Basic feature
Display on a single page the information contained on several pages					
• *automatically*	AutoPager www.teesoft.info Firefox 1.5 - 4.0*	AutoPager www.teesoft.info	AutoPagerize From swdyh	—	—
• *manually*	—	—	Basic feature	—	—
Find way around tabs more easily					
Reduce tabs to the size of their logo	FaviconizeTab espion.just-size. jp/archives/06/ 308085916.html Firefox 4.0b12-4.0*	Basic feature	—	Basic feature	Basic feature

Continued on following page

Table 1. Continued

	Firefox 3.6*- 4.0 addons.mozilla. org	Chrome 10 chrome.google. com/extensions	Safari 5 extensions.apple. com	IE8 - IE9 www.ieaddons. com	Opera 11 addons.opera. com
Preview open tabs by positioning the cursor over them					
• *Page title*	Basic feature	Basic feature	Basic feature	Basic feature	Basic feature
• *Page title and URL*	—	—	—	Basic feature	—
• *Thumbnail with page title*	Tab Scope www.xuldev.org/ tabscope Firefox 3.6 - 4.0*	—	—	—	Basic feature
• *Thumbnail or logo with page title*	—	—	—	Basic feature of IE9, only for 'application tabs'	—
Create groups of tabs by theme					
• *Apply color codes to related tabs*	—	—	—	Basic feature of IE9	—
• *Separate themed groups of tabs from the current browsing page so that only one window needs to be open*	Basic feature	—	—	—	—
• *Align several tabs alongside each other more easily to consult them at the same time*	—	—	—	Basic feature of IE9	Basic feature
• *Save all open tabs in a bookmark folder / open all the tabs contained in a bookmark folder*	Basic feature	Basic feature	Basic feature	Basic feature	Basic feature
Reduce information noise					
Block pop-up windows	Basic feature	Basic feature	Basic feature	Basic feature	Basic feature
Filter advertisements					
• *automatically*	Adblock Plus adblockplus.org Firefox 3.5 - 4.2a1pre	Adblock Plus for Google Chrome™ (Beta) adblockplus.org	AdBlock Safari AdBlock	Simple Adblock simple-adblock. com IE8 - IE9	NoAds Fixed
• *manually*	—	—	Basic feature	—	—

auto-completion if the selected search engine so allows; various additional search engines can be used independently of the search bar by highlighting and right-clicking, simply right-clicking, or via the toolbar or the sidebar. For further details on the basic features of the five browser leaders with regard to their search interfaces, please consult Table 2.

Table 2. Interfaces of search engines in the browser and possibilities for customization

	Firefox 3.6*- 4.0 addons.mozilla.org	Chrome 10 chrome.google. com/extensions	Safari 5 extensions. apple.com	IE8 - IE9 www.ieaddons.com	Opera 11 addons.opera.com
Search bar					
Select the search engines to use in the browser	Basic feature	Basic feature	Basic feature	Basic feature IE8 - IE9	Basic feature
Add search engines not covered by an add-on to the search bar	Add to Search Bar firefox.maltekraus. de/extensions/add-. to-search-bar Firefox 3.6*- 4.0*	—	—	—	—
Search by auto-completion / suggestion if permitted by the selected search engine	Basic feature	Basic feature of the multi-functional bar ('omnibox')	Basic feature	Basic feature	Basic feature
Address bar					
Search by auto-completion / suggestion if permitted by the selected search engine	Basic feature	Basic feature of the multi-functional bar ('omnibox')	—	Basic feature of the IE9 multi-functional bar ('One Box')	—
Search in browser history and / or bookmarks while entering text	Basic feature	Basic feature	Basic feature	Basic feature	Basic feature
Context menu					
Interact with search engines integrated into the search bar by highlighting and right-clicking	Basic feature	Basic feature	Basic feature	Basic feature	Basic feature
Interact with additional search engines included in the add-on	Hyperwords www.hyperwords. net Firefox 3.6*- 4.0*	Hyperwords www.hyperwords. net	Hyperwords www. hyperwords.net Beta version	No example in this chapter	Look It Up
Sidebar					
Add search engines	Yoono www.yoono.com 3.0 - 4.0*	Yoono www.yoono.com	No example in this chapter	No example in this chapter	No example in this chapter
Multi-functional bar					
Tab, search field and address bar	—	—		Basic feature of IE9 Tab whose title can be used as a search field / address bar and whose page displays the results	
Address bar and search field	Basic feature	Basic feature		Basic feature of IE9	Basic feature

Continued on following page

Table 2. Continued

	Firefox 3.6*- 4.0 addons.mozilla.org	Chrome 10 chrome.google. com/extensions	Safari 5 extensions. apple.com	IE8 - IE9 www.ieaddons.com	Opera 11 addons.opera.com
Search bookmarklet					
Add search engines in the form of bookmarklets for quick access	Basic feature	Basic feature	Basic feature	Basic feature	Basic feature
Search toolbar					
Add search engines in the form of search toolbars	Google toolbars www.google.com	Google toolbars www.google.com	Google toolbars www.google.com	Google toolbars www.google.com	Google toolbars www.google.com
Taskbar					
Add search engines	Zotero www.zotero.org 3.6 - 4.0*	Zotero www.zotero.org/ support/standalone Plugin for Stand-alone Zotero	Zotero www.zotero.org/ support/standalone Plugin for Stand-alone Zotero	Zotero www.zotero.org/ support/standalone Plugin for Stand-alone Zotero forthcoming	No example in this chapter
Search browser history	Basic feature	—	—	Basic feature	—
Main page					
Search browser history	Basic feature	Basic feature	Basic feature	Basic feature	Basic feature
Search in bookmarks	Basic feature	Basic feature	Basic feature	-	Basic feature
Search in add-ons	Basic feature	Basic feature	Basic feature	Basic feature	Basic feature
Search in downloads history	Basic feature In pop-up windows	Basic feature	—	—	Basic feature
Search notes	—	—	—	—	Basic feature

1.2.2. Add Search Engines Not Covered by an Add-on to the Search Bar

A number of online search engines are available as extensions, allowing users to integrate them into the search bar of their browser or to access them by right-clicking after selecting the information they wish to search for. Some examples include Wikipedia, Flickr, LinkedIn and SnappyWords Visual Dictionary. However, they do not all exist as extensions. Firefox offers the solution of installing the **Add to Search Bar** add-on; this enables users to add a wide range of search engines discovered during browsing to the browser search bar. The

operation is very straightforward: the user simply needs to position the cursor in the search field of the search engine to be added and right-click to select *Add to Search Bar*. One exception identified when testing this extension was search engines in a Flash environment. This add-on is especially useful for those wishing to integrate a customized search engine created using tools such as Google Custom Search.

1.3. Customizing Results Pages

Customizing results pages using add-ons can make the retrieved information visible more quickly for more focused browsing. This is made possible by installing add-ons which enable a maximum of relevant information to be displayed at one time. These extensions can take various forms: some improve the search results of one search engine by interspersing the results list with results from other search engines; some display the results of other search engines alongside the results obtained from a given search engine; and others allow users to preview the information hidden behind a link.

1.3.1. Improve Search Engine Results by Automatically Interspersing Results from Other Search Engines

To optimize a search for information, the results from a search engine can be improved by adding the results from other search engines, an option offered by the add-ons Surf Canyon, SearchGBY and StumbleUpon.

Surf Canyon is an add-on that is compatible with the search results of Bing, Google, Yahoo! and Craigslist. A search performed with one of these search engines will discreetly intersperse the results list with results from the other three search engines. Other search engines can be added to these four, including the real-time search engines OneRiot and Twitter, and it is also possible to favor sources such as encyclopedias or news sites. The options of this extension include the possibility of listing up to ten sites that the user would like to bring forward in the search results. It is also possible to list ten sites that the user does not want to see in the search results. An Opera extension that offers similar features to Surf Canyon is **SearchGBY**. This tool only operates with the search engines Google, Yahoo! and Bing.

Whenever pages tagged on the social bookmarking network Delicious appear in the results pages of search engines Google, Yahoo!, Bing, Ask and AOL, the **StumbleUpon** add-on displays the tags of these pages. In so doing, it adds a layer of human preference to the results pages of these search engines, without interfering in how the pages are ranked. Displaying the tags of pages

indexed by Delicious users offers a more precise idea of what these pages are about, providing direct access to this new type of thematic directory from the search engine results page. Users can therefore directly access the most recent pages tagged and can take their research further by viewing other tags that have been attributed to these pages by Delicious users.

1.3.2. Display Results from Other Search Engines alongside the Results Obtained from a Given Search Engine

If users are to save time when searching for information, it is important for them to have quick access to their favored information sources. To this end, it is possible to display the results of several search engines in parallel after entering the search query just once. The results displayed can come from online search engines but also from personal online accounts or even locally stored directories. This can be very practical for obtaining a quick overview of a subject and making sure that the search is performed on all the quality sources from the user's various working environments. We have chosen to mention the extensions The Search Sidebar and Feedly as they complement each other effectively.

The Search Sidebar is an extension that allows users to search both the Web and their online accounts by entering a search equation into the search engines Google, Yahoo! or Bing. The results from The Search Sidebar are displayed in a sidebar to the right of the results from the search engine used. The Search Sidebar can be customized by selecting the sources to be consulted from a long list. Consultable public sources currently include CNN, Twitter, Wikipedia, YouTube, Amazon, VideoSurf, Google Books™, Digg, the New York Times, the Wall Street Journal, Reddit, Scribd, MTV, eBay, Last.fm, Instructables, Delicious, Forbes, TIME Magazine, Docstoc, the Huffington Post, Google Scholar™, Google Groups™, WIRED, The Economist, Life Photos,

RecipePuppy, Hacker News, the UK Telegraph, TechCrunch, Globe and Mail, Flickr, MySpace, Truveo, Stack Overflow, Quora, Crunchbase and iTunes. The Search Sidebar can also search in the user's online accounts (Gmail, Facebook, LinkedIn, Google Docs™, Google History™ and Dropbox). This feature is particularly practical for those who use online accounts specifically to collect content with high information value for their area of expertise.

It is also possible to perform a search from the search engines Google, Bing or Yahoo! that also searches the content of the RSS feed aggregator Google Reader. If an RSS news item saved in Google Reader corresponds to the search request, this is brought up in a pop-up window on the search engine results page. The add-on that offers this feature is called **Feedly** (the user's Google Reader session needs to be open).

1.3.3. Preview the Information behind a Link

Some search engines offer the possibility of adding thumbnails to the results page to give users a clearer idea of whether or not it is worth clicking on a link. It is also possible to preview the content of a page by displaying it in a pop-up window when the cursor is positioned over the link.

For example, the **SearchPreview** extension adds thumbnails of the pages likely to be consulted on the left of the search results pages in the search engines Google, Yahoo! and Bing. This gives the user a clearer idea of the type of site hosting the information. It should be noted that this feature is integrated into the SearchGBV add-on presented above.

VideoSurf Videos at a Glance enables users to summarize the content of a video in the search results of the major search engines (Google, YouTube, Twitter, AOL, Bing, OneRiot, Reddit, Digg, etc.).

The most comprehensive add-on for previewing the information behind a link simply by positioning the cursor over it is **Interclue**. This allows users to browse all the links on a Web page quickly without having to open them one by one. The cursor simply needs to be positioned over a link for the information hidden behind the link to be displayed. Icons instantly appear to the right to give initial information such as the file type if the link directs to a non-HTML page (PDF, MS Office documents, Open Office documents, audio files, video files, text files, style sheets, JavaScript files, images, scripts, executable files, RSS/Atom, calendar, etc.) or the logo of the site, if it has one.

The second tier of information is obtained by positioning the mouse over one of the icons displayed. For links directing to HTML pages, Interclue displays the main block of text and thumbnails of images in a pop-up window. To display an image in real format, the user simply needs to click on it. To reduce information noise, Interclue's options include the possibility of setting a minimum size for images to be displayed in the pop-up. Additional information such as statistics or metadata is often added to the page. This information is taken from third-party sources such as Delicious or Digg, and gives an even clearer idea of the page content. For audio and video files, Interclue allows users to play the piece or sequence directly in the pop-up. For PDF files, Interclue displays only the file size and publication date, information which is useful for gauging whether the document is recent and how long it will take to download the file. In the same way as the 404-Error add-on, if the URL directs to a 404 error page, Interclue automatically redirects to the Google cache, giving the user access to the most recent archived version of the page.

The only feature missing from Interclue is the possibility of reading the full addresses of shortened URLs. This is made possible with the add-ons **Bit.ly Preview** (Firefox), **Preview and Short Url Tool** (Google Chrome), **Power Twitter** (IE8 – IE9) and **Unshorten** (Opera).

1.4. Refining Searches

As explained in Section 1.2, the basic configuration of the browsers analyzed here offers users the possibility of performing a search by right-clicking on the active search engine(s) in their context menu after highlighting a term, phrase or sentence. Further solutions for refining searches are offered by add-ons that suggest keywords or documents on the same subject.

1.4.1. Refine a Search by Interacting with all the Words on an HTML Page

Hyperwords is an extension that boosts the basic features of Firefox, Google Chrome and Safari by searching for additional information via the context menu. It includes around 100 search engines (page info, converter, share price, social, people, online shopping, images and videos, maps, blogs, academic, medical, download, technology, the world, translator, etc.) and 20 dictionaries, which can be searched separately or at the same time at a click. The options offer the possibility of refining the search by choosing only those sites considered useful. The equivalent add-on for searching via a context menu in Opera is **Look It Up**, an extension with far fewer search engines and dictionaries.

1.4.2. Refine a Search using Keywords

The **Google Semantics** add-on allows users to generate synonyms. After running a Google search, this extension suggests synonyms below the Google search field so that users can perform a new search using a synonym if the results obtained are not satisfactory.

It is also possible to generate a tag cloud using add-ons. The extension that we have selected for this function is **Search Cloudlet**. It generates a tag cloud for the search results from Google, Twitter and Yahoo!, with varying font size depending on the number of occurrences of the keyword in the pages found. To refine the search request, users can click on keywords to add or remove them. Other tabs also highlight the most relevant sites or top-level domains to limit the search to a particular area (such as .com, .org or .uk). Search Cloudlet also offers tag clouds for Google News, Google Blogs, Google Scholar, Google Shopping and Yahoo! News. Search Cloudlet can be incorporated into the Twitter search engine and also into Twitter user profiles. The latter feature can be useful for finding out the latest discussion subjects of a Twitter account-holder.

1.4.3. Refine a Search with Document Suggestions on the Same Subject

Various add-ons exist to automatically generate suggestions of documents on the same subject without leaving the current page. These include LinkSensor and SimilarWeb.

LinkSensor performs an on-the-fly semantic analysis of blog posts to identify the key concepts of the text analyzed. When the mouse is positioned over a highlighted word, a pop-up window appears suggesting other articles in the blog associated with the word, or articles in the Yahoo! search engine. This is a very useful tool for exploring the content of blogs.

SimilarWeb mainly displays its suggestions in the browser sidebar and in the results of the Bing, Google and Yahoo! search engines. The suggestions generated by SimilarWeb are particularly useful when the page content is an indexable article (HTML or PDF). If this is the case, it can make suggestions in the sidebar of similar pages and sites of reference on the subject. The suggested sites are categorized, which helps users target the sites to be consulted and continue with their research. This add-on can also provide users with an idea of what is currently being said on the subject on micro-blogging sites. Finally, SimilarWeb can also search in users' browsing history and favorites.

The **Search Everywhere** add-on also caught our attention. It includes a search engine that allows users to find content linked to the page being consulted. The Search Everywhere search engine is located in the taskbar. Only available for Firefox.

1.5. Automatically Analyzing Information while Browsing

For Knowledge Workers, the basic features of browsers are not enough to make a quick judgment of the relevance and value of the information consulted while browsing. As seen above, the five browser leaders only allow users to perform a search by right-clicking on the active search engine in their context menu after highlighting a term, phrase or sentence. There are, however, various more or less sophisticated extensions that Knowledge Workers can use in their daily tasks to perform an initial automatic analysis of information. We have chosen eight examples that seem to be the most user-friendly and to offer the most effective basic features. It should be noted that six of them, Gazopa Similar Image Search, TinEye Reverse Image Search, Cydral Image Search Engine, ClearForest Gnosis, ImTranslator and SenseBot — Search Results Summarizer, are trial versions ('freemium') for paid software with more advanced features. Scholarometer and OpinionCloud are the result of university research.

1.5.1 Automatic Graphic Recognition

GazoPa Similar Image Search is an image search engine that offers a quick and easy way of finding images that are similar in terms of color and/or shape. Users simply need to position the cursor over an image on a Web page, right-click and select *Search Image on Gazopa*.

TinEye is a reverse image search engine. It provides the user with information about where an image comes from, how it is used, and whether modified or higher resolution versions of the image exist. Users simply need to position the cursor over an image on a Web page, right-click and select *Search Image on TinEye*.

To search for similar or identical images using keywords or images selected while browsing, users can install the official extension of the image search engine **Cydral**, available for Google Chrome and Firefox.

1.5.2. Recognize Named Entities and Targeted Searches

ClearForest Gnosis is a content analysis tool. It analyzes pages and instantly underlines key information in the text such as people, organizations, companies, products, places and URLs. By right-clicking on one of the themes identified in the ClearForest Gnosis sidebar, users can instantly run a search in Google, Google Maps, Reuters, Technorati and Wikipedia to refine their search. For information on the relative use of each term, the terms can be displayed alphabetically or in increasing order of frequency, or expressed as a percentage. ClearForest Gnosis can currently analyze pages from CNN, Google Finance, Wikipedia, Forbes, the International Herald Tribune, the Los Angeles Times, MSNBC, the New York Times, the Wall Street Journal, USA Today, the Washington Post, Yahoo! News and BBC News. Websites can be added to this list by clicking on the button on the sidebar or by going to the ClearForest Gnosis options.

1.5.3. Recognize Keywords Contained on a Page

To detect the presence and density of keywords on a page, tools designed for developers and search engine optimization specialists can be used. An example is **SeoQuake**, available for Firefox, Google Chrome and Safari. It is very easy to use: with one click, users obtain a table presenting the density of the keywords on the page, expressed as a percentage. SeoQuake can provide data for single keywords or key phrases of two, three or four words. The add-on can also generate a tag cloud which can be clicked on to provide details for a given keyword. This latter feature is useful for contextualizing a particular keyword, as it shows clearly the density of key phrases of up to four words associated with the term in the text.

1.5.4. Analyze the Opinions Posted in Online Comments using a Tag Cloud and Percentages of Opinions

We saw above with the add-on VideoSurf Video at a Glance that it is possible to summarize videos with a series of images, providing users with an initial idea of their content. It is also possible to analyze the opinions of people who have consulted these videos, rather than simply reading the comments posted. The add-on that offers this option is **OpinionCloud**, the fruit of a university project (Bauhaus-Universität Weimar) that aimed to analyze the opinions of the general public. The add-on can be used for YouTube and Flickr. The analysis generates a tag cloud, with green tags for positive opinions and red tags for negative opinions. The proportion of positive and negative opinions is also provided, expressed as a percentage. This add-on is particularly helpful for users wanting to know whether it is worth consulting a video; it conveys more than the 'Like'/'Dislike' functions or the number of consultations. With a scope limited to just two popular sites, this add-on can monitor opinions on products, brands, people, subjects, etc.

1.5.5. Summarize Text

Sensebot is a semantic search engine (beta) that summarizes the results of the search engines Google, Yahoo! and Bing using text mining. It can be used to understand a concept or to give an overview of a subject. It is available through the Firefox extension **SenseBot Summarizer**, which is incorporated into the results pages of Google, Yahoo! and Bing. It can be used in two ways:

- By clicking on the **Summary** button located at the top or bottom of the results page of the search engine, a summary text of the results is generated and displayed on the same page. Unlike the extension, the SenseBot search engine can analyze up to ten pages and generate a summary.
- SenseBot Summarizer can also generate a summary of the text on a given Web page by right-clicking. A window opens containing a summary of the text on the current page or of a highlighted section. If the text is too short to be summarized, SenseBot Summarizer will notify the user.

For Google Chrome, the unofficial add-on from the site tldr.it — **Summarize any article, I fetch. You read** — is a tool for summarizing HTML pages, PDFs and RSS feeds. Users simply need to click on the bookmarklet to summarize the current page, with a choice of three summary sizes: short, medium or long. The time required to move from one size to the other is minimal. It should be noted that this add-on does not use technologies to change the wording of the text; it merely extracts sentences from the beginning, middle and end of the original to create a summary.

1.5.6. Perform a Bibliometric Analysis

Scholarometer is an extension available in beta version that makes it easier to analyze citations and helps users assess the factors that determine the quality of publications by an author, such as the author's h-index. It not only offers search functions but also allows the user to annotate, share and export (in formats BIB, RIS, CSV, XLS, ENW and BibJSON) bibliographical data from an author via Google Scholar. Scholarometer is developed by Indiana University Bloomington.

1.5.7. Translate

The basic translation feature offered by Google Chrome makes this browser the leader in performing an on-the-fly translation as soon as a page is opened. In order to offer this feature, Google has integrated the Google Translate tool, which offers 57 languages, into its Web browser. This tool is also available as a website, a bookmarklet for all browsers, a translation kit (Google Translator Toolkit), etc. Google Translate is also incorporated into the **Google toolbar**. It is available for Internet Explorer and Firefox. The Google Translate application programming interface (API) is used in several translation add-ons. Some operate by highlighting the text, right-clicking and selecting the translation direction. This is the case for Firefox's **gTranslate** and Opera's **Easy Translate**. Others operate more quickly. With **Hyperwords**, highlighting the text provides instant access to the translation direction. In their basic features, Internet Explorer and Opera offer a translation tool that allows users to rework the text in a dedicated interface. **Bing Translator** is used by Internet Explorer, and **Yahoo! Babel Fish** by Opera. For Firefox there is **ImTranslator**, a real-time online translator that provides translations for 1 640 language pairs. It includes a voice synthesis application that enables users to listen to the selected text (a basic feature with Opera and Safari). The ImTranslator spell checker offers a high-quality spell-checking service. Its multilingual dictionary provides translations of words, sentences and idiomatic expressions. The virtual keyboard supports multilingual text input.

1.6. Automatically Categorizing and Extracting the Elements on a Web Page

Automatic data extraction can be a time-saving tool, preventing the need for several 'copy/paste' operations and potential manipulation errors. We have selected the extensions developed by the company OutWit Technologies for their ease of use. This company has developed a platform known as OutWit, which is composed of a kernel containing a library of recognition data and extraction features, around which an unlimited number of new extensions, known as outfits, can be developed by anyone. At the current time, OutWit Technologies has developed three semantic Web browsers from its OutWit platform, each available as a Firefox extension: OutWit Hub, OutWit Doc and OutWit Images.

We have also selected the extension Chartlet, for its feature of data extraction at regular intervals.

1.6.1. Data Extraction

OutWit Hub is a tool for collecting and structuring the data on a Web page in just a few clicks. It starts by gathering the various non-structured data on the Web page visited according to type (links, documents, images, emails, data in a table, text, words, RSS feeds, source code, etc.), then extracts and structures these data by type in a table that can be modified and exported, for example to a word-processing application or analysis tools.

Unlike Outwit Hub, the **Chartlet** add-on extracts data on the Web at regular intervals so that graphs can be kept up-to-date. This extension also enables users to keep a history of the values gathered, displayed in tables.

1.6.2. Document Extraction

OutWit Docs is a tool that analyzes every Web page visited and gathers all document types (PDF, DOC, RTF, etc.), spreadsheets (XLS, ODS, etc.) and presentations (PPT, SWF, etc.), so that they can be downloaded to a hard disk. The collected documents can be saved in one operation. It is also possible to rename files in batches so that they are named consistently.

1.6.3. Image Extraction

Similarly to OutWit Docs, **OutWit Images** makes it possible to find all the images on a Web page visited so that they can be viewed on a full-screen slideshow, stored on the hard disk, or sent as links by email.

2. COLLECTING AND MANAGING SOURCES AND DOCUMENTS

Once Knowledge Workers have found the information they are looking for, they generally need to store it so that they can access it easily if they wish to analyze their corpus of material and improve their knowledge in a certain area. For effective collection and management of the sources and documents found while browsing, add-ons have been developed to manage bookmarks, to capture and manage electronic documents and to monitor selected electronic sources. Most of these add-ons also have further uses — some allow users to access collected sources and documents from different computers, or even from different browsers or electronic devices.

2.1. Managing Bookmarks

Since the emergence of smartphones, browser developers have proposed solutions to help users synchronize their bookmarks, or favorites, on all their portable Web devices, as long as they use the same browser on all their devices. The same also applies for developers who have created a version of their browser for tablet computers. However, long before these two developments, users sought ways to access their bookmarks remotely from various devices, to ensure that their personal directory of favorite websites was just a click away. Xmark has long been the reference for synchronizing bookmarks on several workstations and different browsers, alongside Delicious, the solution for sharing bookmarks to create a

customized social directory. More recent tools offer solutions for reading pages that cannot be read straight away at a later date. Reading documents on smartphones or tablet computers can fit more easily into the nomadic lifestyle of some Knowledge Workers, who see their time spent on business trips as an opportunity to catch up with reading. In 2010, new features were added to the existing tools. Diigo, previously a social bookmark for highlighting, marking and annotating Web pages to share them with other users, has become a genuine collaborative platform for managing documents and working on small-scale projects, or at least projects that do not require sources to be referenced in academic fashion (this latter feature is offered by Zotero in its version 2.0 for Firefox).

2.1.1. Synchronize Bookmarks on Several Workstations and Different Browsers

Xmarks is an online bookmark manager available via an add-on. It allows users to back up their bookmarks and synchronize them between several computers and also between different browsers. It also offers the possibility of loading tabs that have been left open on one workstation onto another, regardless of the compatible browser used. Xmarks is available for Firefox, Chrome, Safari and Internet Explorer. A further feature allows users to save and restore favorites, as it automatically makes a backup copy each time a bookmark is changed. Moreover, each bookmark saved is associated with a summary, tags and the number of times it has been saved by other Xmarks users. All this information appears in the Google results pages if this feature is activated.

2.1.2. File Pages to Read Later

Read It Later makes it possible to postpone reading Web pages by saving them with a single click in a Read It Later folder that is stored alongside the user's favorites. This prevents pages from being lost, and also avoids time being wasted filing pages that may not be worth bookmarking. Read It Later avoids users accumulating a large number of poorly filed bookmarks. It also offers the option of filing pages to read later by using keywords. It is then possible to perform a keyword, title or website search of the pages in the reading list, or to display them by chronological or reverse chronological order of the date on which they were saved. Searching pages that have already been read is also possible by selecting the *Read Archive* list.

To enjoy all the features of this extension, users are advised to open a Read It Later account (http://readitlaterlist.com) so that they are free to consult their reading lists from all their computers, smartphones (Android, iPhone) and other synchronized devices (iPod, iPad). This also makes it possible to consult the listed pages even in offline mode, after first downloading and saving them to a dedicated folder on the workstation.

Pages can be downloaded in optimized text-only view to make reading on small devices easier. This removes images and formatting. Pages can also be downloaded in Web mode; in other words, as they appear online at the moment they were saved. The two modes can be used together.

The Read It Later button can be incorporated into Google Reader, and the pages listed in Read It Later can be shared by email and on online accounts such as Connotea, Delicious, Diigo, Digg, Evernote, Facebook, FriendFeed, Google Reader, LinkedIn, MySpace and Twitter.

The Read It Later add-on is the solution for Firefox and Google Chrome. For the other browsers, three Read It Later bookmarklets (Read It Later, Mark as Read and Reading List) can be installed from the user's online account.

2.1.3. Create a Customized Social Directory

Delicious is an online social bookmark available as an add-on that allows users to synchronize the results of searches on the Web interface and share these results with other users if they wish to do so. **Pearltrees** is a visual social bookmark in the form of a pearl map that enables users to organize and share any pages of interest with other users, and to discover other pages in the process. Users can follow the activity of other Pearltrees users with similar interests to enhance their searches. Pearltrees can be integrated into a website or blog and can be shared on Facebook, Twitter or other sites. Pearltrees is available as an add-on that enables users to save any bookmarks that they wish to share in their Pearltrees account.

2.1.4. Social Bookmarks for Collaborative Work

Diigo is primarily an online social bookmarking tool whose extension allows users to add notes, captures and annotations to their bookmarks. URL links, captures and notes can be shared by email, on Twitter and Facebook accounts and via discussion groups created using the Diigo online application. Messages can be sent to several discussion groups at the same time, and even to Delicious. The saved information can be consulted on an iPhone, iPad, Android device or any other platform offering Internet access. Diigo functions not only as a notebook where users can store their fortunate discoveries ('serendipity') but also as a solution for short-term collaborative projects in which sources do not need to be cited in academic fashion. For more academically-oriented projects, a useful tool is **Zotero**, a social bookmark mainly aimed at researchers but open to everyone. A number of specialists use this network to share and exchange their research sources via their home page, their public library and their themed groups. The Zotero 2.0* extension for Firefox enables users to manage their groups and to collect and share bibliographical references (with or without notes, attachments and tags). The solution offered by Zotero is more suitable for long-term projects. Zotero users are not at risk of losing any data because the tool does not store merely URL links or clipped content but the original document in its entirety and in its original format (HTML, PDF, DOC, etc.). This add-on is also a valuable personal knowledge management tool, as we will see in further detail in Section 2.2.3.

2.2. Managing Captured Electronic Documents

It can be useful to capture documents consulted while browsing to make sure that they can be accessed quickly if necessary. It is not unusual for a document found online to disappear from one day to the next, for it to become lost among the documents saved on the user's computer, or for the user to need to access it remotely. The basic browser features *Save as* and *Copy/Paste* do not allow effective management of captured electronic documents; however, a number of add-ons are available to meet this need. We have selected three which complement each other particularly well: FireShot for organizing screenshots; Evernote for creating personal notebooks; and Zotero for managing documents and their multimedia bibliographical references.

2.2.1. Capture, Edit, Annotate and Organize Screenshots of Web Pages

FireShot captures, edits, annotates and organizes screenshots of Web pages. Unlike the Print Screen key, FireShot captures Web pages in their entirety. It provides a much more comprehensive series of tools for editing and annotating than those offered by online notebooks or social bookmarks. Its features allow users to modify screenshots rapidly by inserting text and graphical annotations. They are also very useful for quickly

making comments on the content captured. The screenshots (with or without annotations) can be saved on the hard disk (in PNG, GIF, JPEG or BMP format), printed, copied to the clipboard, sent by email or sent to an external editor to be processed at a later date. The screenshots can be hosted by a server so that they can be accessed from different computers.

2.2.2. Create a Personal Online Notebook — Clip Content

To optimize the full information potential of serendipitous discoveries, it can be useful to be able to store them quickly in a personal online notebook. Being able to collect information and store it in a single location can help users develop their thoughts and ideas. For this feature we have chosen to present Evernote, whose freemium and fee-paying versions offer more possibilities than those of Diigo.

Evernote is a note-taking platform with add-ons for Web browsers and also applications for computers or smartphones. The browser add-on is called **Evernote — Clipper Web Evernote**. It enables users to compile folders of notes by saving captured Web content — Web pages, photos and screenshots — and also offers the option of making text or audio notes. Evernote saves all Web captures with the URL address, so that the source of the information is noted and its context is retained. Keywords can be added to every element captured. All captures are automatically saved and indexed by the Evernote search engine, which makes it possible to search for indexed documents in folders of notes by keyword, title and place. Evernote is even able to perform text searches in images containing printed or handwritten text. Users can access their notes offline regardless of the browser used by installing Evernote on all their computers and smartphones.

Once they have successfully structured their initial thoughts, users can find it useful to save selected sources using an application which manages documents and multimedia bibliographical references. This can help them to cite their sources correctly and above all to keep a copy of the original documents consulted.

2.2.3. Manage Documents and Multimedia Bibliographical References with the Option of Sharing and Retrieving Bibliographical References with Notes, Tags and Keywords

Although it may seem contradictory to use a notebook and social bookmarking tool in conjunction with a tool for managing documents and multimedia references, this approach can actually be highly effective. Working in this way ensures that the document management tool does not become a general repository for all documents found, regardless of their quality; it is used solely for storing selected notes, documents and references that will actually serve in writing a text or research paper. **Zotero** is a tool for managing documents and multimedia bibliographical references that is available as a Firefox add-on and a desktop application. The Firefox add-on is integrated into the browser toolbar. It helps users get the best out of their research finds — both paper and digital — in their browser. It makes it easier to take notes on the Internet and to capture and annotate electronic documents (Web pages, blog posts, articles, PDFs, links, etc.). Documents in the Zotero library are managed by folders, bibliographical metadata and keywords. Zotero offers two search interfaces, one simple and one advanced. The two interfaces enable users to search both in all the fields filled out for the various types of bibliographical notice, and also within the text of saved documents. To help users search among documents saved in their library, Zotero also offers to generate a tag cloud using the tags associated with the saved documents. A narrowing search can be performed on this tag cloud — the user successively selects the tags that best describe the documents searched

for. At each stage of this search, Zotero lists the documents containing the keywords selected and reduces the size of the cloud accordingly. With an online Zotero account, users can synchronize references and notes on several computers. The documents related to these references and notes are saved either on the Zotero server (free up to a maximum of 100 MB) or on a WEBDAV server. If documents are not saved remotely, they can only be accessed from the computer on which they have been saved.

Unlike other extensions with similar features, Zotero can automatically collect the bibliographical data contained on the Web pages consulted and retrieve the bibliographical references available in the online catalogs of some bookshops (such as Amazon) or libraries (Flickr, YouTube, Library of Congress, etc.) when they are consulted. It also allows users to import local documents and automatically retrieve bibliographical references by DOI (Digital Object Identifier), PMID (PubMed Identifier) and ISSN (International Standard Serial Number) via the sites with which it is compatible. It supports seven import formats (MODS, MAB2, MARC, RDF, RIS, Refer/BibIX and BibTeX) and export formats (RDF, MODS, Refer/BibIX, RIS, Unqualified Dublin Core RDF, Wikipedia Citation Templates and BibTeX). Zotero can also generate bibliographies in predefined or custom styles, or create bibliographical reports and chronologies of bibliographical references. Manual creation of bibliographical information is also made easier. Zotero offers 33 templates: newspaper, magazine, journal, conference or encyclopedia article; book, book chapter, document, legal act, case, hearing, podcast, blog post, patent, map, email, radio or TV program, audio or video recording, dictionary entry, film, illustration, interview, letter, manuscript, forum message, instant message, presentation, computer program, draft law or bill, report and thesis.

Other important points to note:

- This extension has an open software architecture that authorizes the addition of new styles of bibliographical reference and new collectors. It is also possible to add extensions that improve or add new features. For example, the Zotero Scholar Citations add-on to Zotero enables users to obtain any number of quotations from Google Scholar.

- There are Zotero plug-ins for the most popular word-processing software (Word, LibreOffice, OpenOffice and NeoOffice). They can generate bibliographical references in predefined styles.

2.3. Monitoring Electronic Sources

Internet content syndication is a time-saving measure that avoids the need to visit sources regularly to check updates. It tells the browser to inform the user automatically of any changes that have occurred to the monitored Web pages. The basic solution provided by Web browsers for content syndication is not sufficient: grouping together and reading RSS feeds in a dedicated folder in the bookmarks or the personal bar is not very convenient or reliable, and does not exclude the possibility that the user will miss out on an important piece of information. Among the extensions available for content syndication, we have chosen to present two RSS feed readers: Feedly and Yoono. This is for purely ergonomic reasons — the first is preferable for reading long content such as blog posts or newspaper articles, whereas the second is more suitable for news from social networks. In addition to these two readers, we will present a Web page monitoring tool, SiteDelta. Monitoring tools serve two purposes: they alert the user of any changes made to a monitored Web page, and automatically save a copy of the page when a change is detected. Finally, two extensions enable users to judge the popularity and influence of articles published on social networks (Le Duff, 2006): Social Media

Monitoring to monitor conversations on Twitter, and PostRank to add a popularity filter to RSS feeds.

2.3.1. Generate a Digital Review of RSS Feeds

Feedly is an online RSS feed reader that takes the form of a digital magazine. The page layout of this digital magazine can be set according to various criteria: title only, title and summary, image or video grid, or entire content. As well as the summary view of the feeds, it is also possible to see just the latest news or the most read items. Users of Feedly services require a Google account to log in and also need to install the extension in their browser. Feedly allows transparent syncing with Google Reader feeds. Any change made to the organization of Feedly's RSS feeds will also be made to Google Reader, and vice versa. Feedly organizes RSS feeds by thematic tabs. It is possible to import new sources directly from Feedly by entering the URL of a Web page or the address of an RSS feed. Feedly also suggests relevant sources on a given theme if asked.

2.3.2. Generating News Feeds for People Followed on Social Networks

Yoono is primarily known as an extension that allows users to follow all the activities taking place on their social networks (Facebook, Twitter, MySpace, LinkedIn, YouTube, Flickr and Friend-Feed) and instant messaging services (Aim, Live Messenger, Yahoo! Messenger and Google Talk) in a single place in the browser sidebar, while being able to browse the Web at the same time.

Yoono can generate separate news feeds for each social network or group all the news from different social networks in a single feed. Each feed has a search engine to make it easier to search for information. For those who find the sidebar too narrow to follow their activities, parallel timelines for the various news feeds can be generated in a tab. Yoono is a very practical tool for keeping up to date and chatting in real time with experts followed on sites such as Facebook, FriendFeed, LinkedIn or Twitter, and is also a quick way of sharing a link, a page, a video or an image from the browser window using a simple drag-and-drop operation. To refine a search, users can run a request with Yoono by simply highlighting a word or the search expression and clicking; the add-on can also recommend sites containing information similar to the site being consulted, if asked. Yoono displays search results by category: similar sites, Wikipedia, videos, photos, similar products, and Google Search. Yoono can also perform real-time searches by integrating the OneRiot search engine into its interface. For those who do not use Firefox and/or Google Chrome as their browser, it is possible to install a desktop version of Yoono.

2.3.3. Monitor Web Pages

Only Firefox and Google Chrome offer Web page monitoring agents in their add-ons galleries. We have chosen to present **Site Delta**, the extension available for Firefox, because it is more comprehensive than **Page Monitor**, the add-on available for Google Chrome.

SiteDelta alerts users of any changes made to a monitored Web page by means of a sound signal or a pop-up window that appears at the bottom right of the screen. The default settings for analyzing pages are fairly advanced. Depending on the criteria selected, SiteDelta can display deleted text, added or removed images or images whose filename has been changed. SiteDelta can ignore changes between small and capital letters and changes made to numbers. The modified pages can be archived. When users visit Web pages registered with SiteDelta for monitoring, the add-on can automatically check whether changes have been made to the given page during browsing, and highlight any changes made since the previous visit. The frequency with which pages are monitored can be left to SiteDelta to deter-

mine or can be selected from four possibilities: every week, every day, every hour, or customized as every *n* minutes. To make the page analysis clearer, users can choose colors to identify the different changes that have occurred on the monitored page — text that has been added, removed or moved — or to select areas on the page to be monitored or ignored. Specific settings for each page to be monitored can be added to SiteDelta's default settings. This add-on therefore gives users a high degree of flexibility to set different alerts for each page monitored. The only negative point is that the notifications can only be made on one computer; this can prove problematic for users working on several computers or devices.

2.3.4. Monitor Conversations on Twitter

Social Media Monitoring is an add-on that only works with Google Chrome. It allows users to monitor Twitter conversations on the basis of the popularity of a word, according to a clearly defined geographical area and timeframe. Users enter their alert criteria depending on the number of tweets they wish to be alerted of per minute. They can also set a specific geographical area. These criteria are then used to alert the user if a subject on Twitter generates more discussion than usual, thereby providing real-time information on news, rumors or other events, depending on the type of information followed by the user on Twitter.

2.3.5. Add a Popularity Filter to RSS Feeds

PostRank is an add-on for Google Chrome and Safari to help users who are short of time or those wishing to follow the latest trends capturing the public imagination on a given subject in real time. The extension works in conjunction with the RSS feed aggregator Google Reader. It allows readers to view the most-read articles quickly, giving them a score from 1 to 10 (10 signifying

Table 3. Summary table of the add-ons used to search for information, displayed according to purpose and browser

	Firefox 3.6*- 4.0 addons.mozilla.org	Chrome 10 chrome.google. com/extensions	Safari 5 extensions.apple. com	IE8 - IE9 www.ieaddons.com	Opera 11 addons.opera.com
1.3. Customizing results pages					
A. Improve search engine results by interspersing results from other search engines					
	Firefox Google Assistant by Surf Canyon www.surfcanyon. com Firefox 2.0 - 4.0*	**Surf Canyon** www.surfcanyon. com	—	**Surf Canyon** www.surfcanyon. com	**SearchGBY** searchgby.com
	StumbleUpon www.stumbleupon. com Firefox 1.0 - 4.0*	**StumbleUpon** www.stumbleupon. com	**StumbleUpon** www.stumbleupon. com	**StumbleUpon** www.stumbleupon. com	**StumbleUpon** www.stumbleupon. com
B. Display results from other search engines alongside the results from a given search engine					
• *Search the Web and online accounts*					
	Search Tabs - get Facebook, Gmail™++ on Google www.webmynd.com Firefox 3.0 - 4.0*	**The Search Side-bar** www.webmynd.com	**The Search Side-bar** www.webmynd.com	—	—
	Feedly www.feedly.com 3.0 - 4.0*	**Feedly** www.feedly.com	**Feedly** www.feedly.com	—	—
C. Preview the information behind a link					
• *Add thumbnails of sites to search results*					
	SearchPreview searchpreview.de Firefox 1.5 - 4.0*	**SearchPreview** searchpreview.de	**SearchPreview** From Felix Cloutier	—	**SearchPreview** searchpreview.de
• *Summarize the content of a video in the search results by a series of thumbnails*					
	VideoSurf Videos at a Glance www.videosurf.com Firefox 3.5b4pre - 4.0*	**VideoSurf Videos at a Glance** www.videosurf.com	—	—	—
• *Skim the information by positioning the cursor over the link*					
Display the type and size of files on a page Display the URLs hidden behind text	**Interclue** interclue.com Firefox 3.0 - 4.0*	**Interclue** interclue.com In planning stage	**Ultimate Status Bar** / **Interclue** interclue.com In planning stage	**Interclue** interclue.com In planning stage	**Interclue** interclue.com In planning stage
Display images	**Interclue** interclue.com Firefox 3.0 - 4.0*	**Interclue** interclue.com In planning stage	**Interclue** interclue.com In planning stage	**Interclue** interclue.com In planning stage	**Image Preview Popup** / **Interclue** interclue.com In planning stage

Continued on following page

Table 3. Continued

	Firefox 3.6*- 4.0 addons.mozilla.org	Chrome 10 chrome.google. com/extensions	Safari 5 extensions.apple. com	IE8 - IE9 www.ieaddons.com	Opera 11 addons.opera.com
View the full address of shortened URLs	**Bit.ly Preview** bit.ly/pages/tools Firefox 1.5 - 3.6*	**Preview And Short Url Tool**	**Power Twitter** From The Start Project	—	**Unshorten**
Play videos and sound	**Interclue** interclue.com Firefox 3.0 - 4.0*	**Interclue** interclue.com In planning stage	**Interclue** interclue.com In planning stage	**Interclue** interclue.com In planning stage	**Interclue** interclue.com In planning stage
1.4. Refining searches using keywords					
A. Interact with all the words on an HTML page					
	Hyperwords www.hyperwords. net Firefox 3.6 - 4.0*	**Hyperwords** www.hyperwords. net	www.hyperwords. net Beta version	—	—
B. Generate synonyms					
	Google Semantics www.indianic.com Firefox 1.5 - 3.6*	—	—	—	—
C. Generate a tag cloud					
	Search Cloudlet www.getcloudlet. com Firefox 2.0 - 4.0*	**Search Cloudlet** www.getcloudlet. com	—	**Search Cloudlet** www.getcloudlet. com	—
D. Generate document suggestions on the same subject					
	LinkSensor www.linksensor. com Firefox 3 - 3.6*	—	—	—	—
	SimilarWeb www.similarsites. com Firefox 3.0 - 4.0*	**SimilarWeb** www.similarsites. com	—	—	—
	Search Every-where notes.komarix.org/ labels/firefox.html Firefox 1.5 - 4.0*	—	—	—	—
1.5. Automatically analyzing information while browsing					
A. Automatic graphic recognition					
• Search for images that are similar in terms of color and/or shape					
	GazoPa Similar Image Search www.gazopa.com Firefox 1.5 - 3.6*	**ChromeEye** From Steven2358	**BackTrack** GazoPa and TinEye	—	—
• Search for information about an image, find an identical image or its different versions					
	TinEye Reverse Image Search www.tineye.com Firefox 1.5 - 4.0*	**TinEye Reverse Image Search** www.tineye.com	**TinEye Reverse Image Search** www.tineye.com		**TinEye Search**

Continued on following page

Table 3. Continued

	Firefox 3.6*- 4.0 addons.mozilla.org	Chrome 10 chrome.google. com/extensions	Safari 5 extensions.apple. com	IE8 - IE9 www.ieaddons.com	Opera 11 addons.opera.com
• Search for similar or identical images using a keyword or image					
	Cydral Image Search Engine www.cydral.fr Firefox 2.0 - 4.0*	Cydral Image Search Engine www.cydral.fr	—	—	—
B. Recognize named entities and targeted searches					
	ClearForest Gnosis www.opencalais. com Firefox 3 - 4.0*	Twitter PNL Swarm blog.tomayac.com	—	—	—
C. Recognize keywords contained on a page					
	SeoQuake www.seoquake.com Firefox 3.5 - 4.0*	SeoQuake www.seoquake.com	SeoQuake www.seoquake.com	—	—
D. Analyze the opinions in comments on the sites Flickr and YouTube					
	OpinionCloud www.webis.de Firefox 3.0 - 3.6*	OpinionCloud www.webis.de		—	—
E. Summarize					
	SenseBot — Search Results Summarizer www.sensebot.net Firefox 1.5 - 6.*	Summarize any article, I fetch. You read. From Yoshua Wuyts	—	—	—
F. Perform a bibliometric analysis					
	Scholarometer scholarometer. indiana.edu Firefox 3.5 - 4.0*	Scholarometer scholarometer. indiana.edu	—	—	—
G. Machine translation					
• Page					
On opening	Google Toolbar	Basic feature Google Translate used	—	Google Toolbar	—
After opening	Google Translate button	Basic feature Google Translate used	Google Translate button	Google Translate button	Google Translate button
• Expression, keywords					
° Highlight + Right-click + Select					
Translation can be reworked in a dedi-cated interface	ImTranslator imtranslator.net Firefox 1.0 - 4.0* Freemium	Bubble Translate code.google.com/p/ bubble-translate	—	Basic feature of IE9 Bing Translator used	Basic feature Yahoo! Babel Fish used

Continued on following page

261

Table 3. Continued

	Firefox 3.6*- 4.0 addons.mozilla.org	Chrome 10 chrome.google. com/extensions	Safari 5 extensions.apple. com	IE8 - IE9 www.ieaddons.com	Opera 11 addons.opera.com
Examples of add-ons based on Google Translate	**gTranslate** code.google.com/p/ gtranslate Firefox 3.0 - 4.0*	**Bubble Translate** code.google.com/p/ bubble-translate	**Translate** From Side Tree Software	**Google Translate** **translate.google. com**	**Easy Translate** Based on Google Translate
○ Highlight + Select					
Translated text re-places original text	**Hyperwords** www.hyperwords. net Firefox 3.6 - 4.0*	**Hyperwords** www.hyperwords. net	**Hyperwords** www. hyperwords.net Beta version	—	—
1.6. Automatically categorizing and extracting the elements on a Web page					
A. Data extraction					
• Go to the page					
	Outwit Hub www.outwit.com Firefox 3.5 - 4.0* Freemium	—	—	—	—
• Program the extraction at regular intervals					
	Chartlet 1.4.1 www.chartlet.net Firefox 3.5 - 4.0*	—	—	—	—
B. Document extraction					
	Outwit Doc www.outwit.com Firefox 3.5 - 4.0*	—	—	—	—
C. Image extraction					
	Outwit Images www.outwit.com Firefox 3.5 - 4.0*	—	—	—	—

maximum popularity). PostRank adds to Google Reader the option of only displaying the articles that have received the highest scores: *All* (1.0+), *Good* (2.7+), *Great* (5.4+) or *Best* (7.6+). Other articles become transparent so as to free up the field of vision for the most important information as chosen by the most people.

3. SUMMARY TABLES

Table 3 and Table 4 give examples for add-ons used to search for information and to collect and

manage the sources and documents found, displayed according to purpose and browser.

CONCLUSION

Our analysis of the customization of Web browsers for Knowledge Workers has demonstrated that a browser offering the possibility of add-ons is an application that is highly adaptable in meeting the specific requirements of its users. With its numerous extensions, Firefox has proved to be the most customizable and comprehensive of

Table 4. Summary table of the add-ons used to collect and manage the sources and documents found, displayed according to purpose and browser

	Firefox 3.6*- 4.0 addons.mozilla.org	Chrome 10 chrome.google. com/extensions	Safari 5 extensions. apple.com	IE8 - IE9 www.ieaddons.com	Opera 11 addons.opera.com
2.1. Managing bookmarks					
A. Synchronize bookmarks on several machines connected to the Internet					
• regularly consulted sites and pages as favorites					
Synchronize bookmarks on several workstations with the same browser	**Basic feature**	**Basic feature**	—	—	**Basic feature**
Synchronize bookmarks on several workstations and different browsers	**Xmark Sync.** www.xmarks.com 3.0 - 4.0*	**Xmark Sync.** www.xmarks.com	**Xmark Sync.** www.xmarks.com	**Xmark** www.xmarks.com	—
• File pages to read later					
	Read it Later readitlaterlist.com 3.5 - 4.0*	**Read it Later** readitlaterlist.com	**Read it Later** readitlaterlist.com Bookmarklets	**Read it Later** readitlaterlist.com Bookmarklets	**Read it Later** readitlaterlist.com Bookmarklets
B. Examples of official social bookmarking add-ons					
• Create a customized social directory					
Share bookmarks with tags	**Delicious bookmarks** www.delicious.com 3.0 - 4.0b3pre	**Delicious bookmarks** www.delicious.com	**Delicious Safari** From Paulo César Machado Jeveaux	**Share with Delicious** www.delicious.com	**Delicious Extension**
Visual social bookmark in the form of a pearl map	**Pearltrees** www.pearltrees.com 2.0 - 4.0*	**Pearltrees** www.pearltrees.com	—	—	—
• For small-scale collaborative projects					
Share bookmarks with notes, tags, captures and annotations	**Diigo** www.diigo.com 3.5 - 4.0*	**Diigo** www.diigo.com	**Diigo Web Highlighter** www.diigo.com	**Diigo bookmark search** www.diigo.com	—
• For large-scale collaborative projects					
Social bookmark for bibliographical references with the possibility of adding notes, keywords and attachments — Annotate HTML attachments	**Zotero** www.zotero.org 3.6 - 4.0*	**Zotero** www.zotero.org/ support/standalone Plugin for Standalone Zotero	**Zotero** www.zotero.org/ support/standalone Plugin for Standalone Zotero	**Zotero** www.zotero.org/support/standalone Plugin for Standalone Zotero forthcoming	—
2.2. Managing captured documents					
A. Capture, edit, annotate and organize screenshots of Web pages					
	FireShot screenshot-program. com/fireshot 2.0 - 4.0*	**FireShot** screenshot-program. com/fireshot	—	**FireShot** screenshot-program. com/fireshot	—

Continued on following page

Table 4. Continued

	Firefox 3.6*- 4.0 addons.mozilla.org	Chrome 10 chrome.google. com/extensions	Safari 5 extensions. apple.com	IE8 - IE9 www.ieaddons.com	Opera 11 addons.opera.com
B. Clip content - Create a notebook					
	Evernote — Clipper Web Evernote www.evernote.com 3.0 - 4.0*	**Clip to Evernote** www.evernote.com	—	**Evernote accelerator** www.evernote.com	—
C. Manage documents and multimedia bibliographical references with the option of sharing and retrieving bibliographical references with notes, tags and keywords — Annotate HTML attachments					
	Zotero www.zotero.org 3.6 - 4.0*	**Zotero** www.zotero.org/ support/standalone Plugin for Stand-alone Zotero	**Zotero** www.zotero.org/ support/standalone Plugin for Stand-alone Zotero	**Zotero** www.zotero.org/sup-port/standalone Plugin for Stand-alone Zotero forth-coming	—
2.3. Monitoring electronic sources					
A. RSS feed aggregator					
	Basic feature	—	**Basic feature**	**Basic feature**	**Basic feature**
B. Generate a digital review of RSS feeds					
	Feedly www.feedly.com 3.0 - 4.0*	**Feedly** www.feedly.com	**Feedly** www.feedly.com	—	—
C. Generate news feeds for people followed on social networks					
	Yoono www.yoono.com 3.0 - 4.0*	**Yoono** www.yoono.com	—	—	—
D. Web page monitoring agent					
	SiteDelta sitedelta.schierla.de 3.0 - 4.0*	**Page Monitor from Max Shaw-abkeh**	—	—	—
E. Monitor conversations on Twitter					
	—	**Social Media Monitoring** From GTUGNA Team SMM code.google.com/p/ chrome-social-media-monitoring	—	—	—
F. Add a popularity filter to RSS feeds					
	PostRank Extension labs.postrank. com/gr	**PostRank Extension** labs.postrank. com/gr	**PostRank Extension** labs.postrank. com/gr	—	—

the five browser market leaders in this respect. It enables Knowledge Workers to make the most of the information available online more quickly and in different ways: firstly by improving browser usability; and secondly by adding tools that enhance its basic features, avoiding the need for additional applications to perform basic information analysis, and enabling the effective capture and management of material found while browsing. The selection and customization of a Web browser can therefore have a positive effect on the work of Knowledge Workers. [9]

It is therefore essential for companies and their personnel to be able to identify and use new tools and also to be capable of adapting them to their needs (Noël, 2008) and potentially even to the needs of their clients, to achieve greater efficiency. This example of Web browser customization should be seen as a strong argument for any companies and IT departments [10] that have not already done so to include in their IT charter the possibility of allowing employees to choose their own browser(s) so that they can adapt the tools to their requirements. All Knowledge Workers should be free to choose their browser(s), being fully informed of the options available, and should have the resources required to customize it/them. [11]

Even if Knowledge Workers as defined in the introduction to this chapter are highly unlikely to respond to the question 'What is a Web browser?' with the answer 'Google', training in browser use is nonetheless important, just as it is for other software applications ("Choosing a Web browser," 2009). It can provide users — in the broad sense of the term — with basic knowledge, and can also ensure that this knowledge is updated to keep step with new developments. Such training can also be seen as an investment to guarantee the security of the company's IT network. Users should be made aware of the fact that installing extensions and failing to update them can cause browser problems such as conflicting add-ons and browser malfunction (browser running slowly or

crashing), and may even lay their computer, and the company network, open to viruses.

As with any free software, the use of add-ons can have its problems. There is no guarantee that the add-ons will be maintained over time. Something that starts off as a time-saving measure can become a hindrance if, for example, the information and sources stored are lost or unable to be exported. Only companies with the necessary resources can remedy this sort of problem by creating their own extensions to meet in-house requirements. Other companies, if they use the Firefox browser, can easily create a collection of extensions using the **Add-on Collector** (Mozilla, 2011) in order to offer their users a selection of add-ons considered useful, sustainable and potentially secure.

Our comparative study demonstrates that many challenges lie in store for Web browser developers if they are to provide more effective solutions to meet the requirements of users whose IT working environment is increasingly Web-based (this phenomenon is known as 'webization'). [12] It seems likely that Web browsers will be increasingly required to integrate business processes. [13] Web developers will have to continue their efforts to facilitate the implementation of official and nonofficial extensions and online applications. [14] One avenue for development that could set them apart from the crowd might be to offer native integration, without the need for extensions, of a standardized process for searching for information [15] that would satisfy as many users as possible and would incorporate tag management. [16]

It seems inevitable that Web browser users will experience major changes in the coming years in terms of how this type of application can be used and the choices available to them. In order to work on the Internet from all their Web-enabled devices, users will favor optimized solutions — Web browsers for desktop and laptop computers which offer a light and ergonomic version for smartphones, tablet computers and other multimedia readers connected to the Internet [17] — enabling easy and secure synchronization of their data (bookmarks, identifiers, passwords, history, open tabs, preferences, add-ons, etc.) between their various Web-enabled devices.[18] The browser war is not over yet, with or without add-ons.

REFERENCES

Apple Inc. (2010a, June 7). *Apple Releases Safari 5*. Retrieved April 4, 2011, from http://www.apple.com/uk/pr/library/2010/06/07safari.html

Apple Inc. (2010b). *What is Safari?* Retrieved September 20, 2010, from http://www.apple.com/safari/what-is.html

Choosing a web browser. (2009, December 3). *Pandia Search Engine News*. Retrieved March 28, 2011, from http://www.pandia.com/sew/2335-choosing-a-web-browser.html?utm_source=feedburner&utm_medium=feed&utm_campaign=Feed%3A+pandia%2Fvfbc+%28Pandia+Search+Engine+News%29&utm_content=Google+Reader

Collaud, G. (2007, September 3). Firefox campus edition. *Le blog du Centre NTE*. Retrieved January 13, 2011, from http://nte.unifr.ch/blog/2007/09/03/firefox-campus-edition

Doyle, T., & Hammond, J. L. (2006). Net cred: evaluating the internet as a research source. *RSR. Reference Services Review, 34*(1), 56–70. doi:10.1108/00907320610648761

Drucker, P. F. (1999a). *L'Avenir du management*. Paris, France: Ed. Village mondial.

Drucker, P. F. (1999b). *Management challenges for the 21st century*. Oxford, UK: Butterworth-Heinemann.

Duff, T. (2006, April 25). A New IE Add-on Site. *IEBlog*. Retrieved April 4, 2011, from http://blogs.msdn.com/b/ie/archive/2006/04/25/583369.aspx

Flock Inc. (2010, September 17). Flock Browser — About Us. *Flock*. Retrieved September 20, 2010, from http://beta.flock.com/about

Germain, M. (2010). Usager numérique et entreprise 2.0. In L. Calderan, B. Hidoine, & J. Millet (Eds.), *L'usager numérique: séminaire INRIA, 27 septembre-1er octobre 2010, Anglet*, Sciences et techniques de l'information (pp. 89-115). Paris, France: ADBS éditions.

Google Inc. (2010, January 25). Extensions, bookmark sync and more for Google Chrome. *The Official Google Blog*. Retrieved April 4, 2011, from http://googleblog.blogspot.com/2010/01/extensions-bookmark-sync-and-more-for.html

Institut national des techniques de la documentation (Paris, France). (2004). Recherche d'information. In A. Boulogne (Ed.), *Vocabulaire de la documentation* (3rd ed.). Paris, France: ADBS éditions. Retrieved September 1, 2010, from http://www.adbs.fr/recherche-d-information-18313.htm?RH=OUTILS_VOC

Le Deuff, O. (2006, November 23). Autorité et pertinence vs popularité et influence: réseaux sociaux sur Internet et mutations institutionnelles (Popularity takes the place of authority, whereas influence replaces relevance). *HAL: Hyper Articles en Ligne*. Retrieved April 3, 2011, from http://hal.archives-ouvertes.fr/sic_00122603

Microsoft. (2011, April). Téléchargements des différentes versions d'Internet Explorer 8, Internet Explorer 9, Internet Explorer 7, Internet Explorer 6. *Windows Internet Explorer*. Retrieved March 30, 2011, from http://www.microsoft.com/france/windows/internet-explorer/telechargement-versions-internet-explorer.aspx

Mozilla. (2004, November 9). Mozilla Firefox 1.0 Release Notes. *Mozilla Firefox*. Retrieved April 4, 2011, from http://www.mozilla.com/en-US/firefox/releases/1.0.html

Mozilla. (2011, April 7). Add-on collector. *Add-ons for Firefox*. Retrieved April 7, 2011, from https://addons.mozilla.org/en-US/firefox/addon/11950

Noël, E. (2008). Veille et nouveaux outils d'information. In J. Dinet (Ed.), *Usages, usagers et compétences informationnelles au 21e siècle, Traité des Sciences et Techniques de l'Information* (pp. 257-284). Paris, France: Hermès science publications; Lavoisier

Opera Software ASA. (2010, December 16). Are you ready for Opera 11? *Opera Software*. Retrieved April 4, 2011, from http://www.opera.com/press/releases/2010/12/16

Opera Software ASA. (2011). Opera business solutions: TV & device OEMs. *Opera Software*. Retrieved April 12, 2011, from http://www.opera.com/business/devices

Owens, T. (2007, August 30). Firefox Campus edition preloaded with Zotero. *Zotero: The Next-Generation Research Tool*. Retrieved January 13, 2011, from http://www.zotero.org/blog/firefox-campus-edition-preloaded-with-zotero

Rosenblatt, S. (2010, June 16). New Flock divorces Firefox, snuggles up to. *cnet Downloads*. Retrieved September 20, 2010, from http://download.cnet.com/8301-2007_4-20007842-12.html

StatCounter. (2011, March 21). Top 12 browser versions on Mar 11. *StatCounter Global Stats*. Retrieved March 21, 2011, from http://gs.statcounter.com/#browser_version-ww-monthly-201103-201103-bar

TechTarget. (1999, February 24). What is knowledge worker? - Definition from Whatis.com. *SearchCRM.com*. Retrieved April 7, 2011, from http://searchcrm.techtarget.com/definition/knowledge-worker

ADDITIONAL READING

Anderruthy, J.-N. (2009). *Les outils de collecte d'information. Techniques de veille et e-réputation: comment exploiter les outils Internet* (pp. 159–214). St Herblain, France: Editions ENI.

B, J.-C. (2009, July 17). Meilleures extensions pour Internet Explorer 6, 7 et IE8: Extensions Internet Explorer. *GNT: Génération Nouvelles Technologies*. Retrieved March 4, 2011, from http://www.generation-nt.com/extensions-ie-ie8-internet-explorer-navigateur-addon-add-on-extension-plugin-article-755601-1.html

Barthole, C. (2009). Firefox, le couteau suisse du veilleur. *Netsources*, (81), 12-14.

Brosseau, F. (2009, March). Firefox & Google quand l'union fait la force. *Linux Pratique Essentiel*, (6), 66-72. Retrieved from http://www.ed-diamond.com/feuille_lpe6/index.html

Centre Virtuel de la Connaissance sur l'Europe. (2009, October 15). *Keynote de Gino Roncaglia (Università della Tuscia)*. L'histoire contemporaine à l'ère digitale — Symposium DHLU, Luxembourg. Retrieved from http://www.ena.lu/lhistoire_contemporaine_lere_digitale_symposium_dhlu_2009_luxembourg_octobre_2009_keynote_gino_roncaglia_universita_tuscia-1-36863

Cocheteau, J.-M. (2009). *Tout sur les meilleures extensions pour Firefox et IE*. Paris, France: Dunod.

Cohen, D. J. (2007, May). History and the changing landscape of information: Zotero: Social and semantic computing for historical scholarship. *American Historical Association: the professional association for all historians*. Retrieved September 17, 2010, from http://www.historians.org/Perspectives/issues/2007/0705/0705tec2.cfm

Denel, M. (2009, December 19). 11 Addons Firefox pour la Veille. *GreyHat: Intelligence Economique, Veille et Web 2.0, Sécurité Informatique, Sécurité de l'Information et Renseignement*. Retrieved August 5, 2010, from http://greyhat.over-blog.com/article-addons-firefox-pour-la-veille-41430863-comments.html#anchorComment

Deschamps, C. (2009). *Le nouveau management de l'information: la gestion des connaissances au coeur de l'entreprise 2.0*. Limoges, France: FYP éditions.

Firefox addon summarizes Google search results. (2008, May 19). *Pandia Search Engine News*. Retrieved April 13, 2011, from http://www.pandia.com/sew/665-summary.html

5 Firefox extensions that will change the way you search. (2006, October 12). *Pandia Search Engine News*. Retrieved September 16, 2010, from http://www.pandia.com/sew/291-top-5-extensions.html

Firefox plug-in personalises search results. (2008, May 8). *Pandia Search Engine News*. Retrieved April 1, 2011, from http://www.pandia.com/sew/661-surfcanyon.html

Gallezot, G., & Le Deuff, O. (2009). Chercheurs 2.0? *Les cahiers du numérique, 5*(2), 15-31.

Hanson, V. L., Richards, J. T., & Swart, C. (2008). Browser augmentation. In S. Harper & Y. Yesilada (Eds.), *Web accessibility* (Human-Computer Interaction Series) (pp. 215-229). London, UK: Springer. Retrieved from http://dx.doi.org/10.1007/978-1-84800-050-6_13

Jdrey, A. (2010, February 2). Mes 10 extensions Chrome au quotidien. *Demain la veille*. Retrieved February 11, 2010, from http://www.demainlaveille.fr/2010/02/02/mes-10-extensions-chrome-au-quotidien/?utm_source=feedburner&utm_medium=feed&utm_campaign=Feed%3A+DemainLaVeille+%28Demain+la+veille%29

Larkin, E. (2010, March 18). Add-on collector keeps your favorite Firefox extensions together to save or share. *PCWorld*. Retrieved May 13, 2010, from http://www.pcworld.com/article/191361/addon_collector_keeps_your_favorite_firefox_extensions_together_to_save_or_share.html

Lombard-Donnet, J. (2005). Firefox pour la veille. *IT Ligentia*. Retrieved May 15, 2010, from http://www.itligentia.com/wp-content/fichiers/firefox-pour-la%20veille-2.pdf

Malaison, C. (2010, August 8). Entreprise 2.0: la gouvernance pour vaincre l'incompétence.... *émergenceweb.com: communication interactive & technologie*. Retrieved September 7, 2010, from http://emergenceweb.com/blog/2010/08/entreprise-2-0-la-gouvernance-pour-vaincre-lincompetence

Marchesson, D. (2009, March 18). Firefox 3 et ses 50 meilleures extensions. *eclaireur.net: Web-Design & Entrepreneur 2.0*. Retrieved September 15, 2009, from http://www.eclaireur.net/firefox/navigateur-firefox-telecharger-50-extensions/

Mediati, N. (2010, July 27). Browser Blowout 2010. *PCWorld*. Retrieved August 19, 2010, from http://www.pcworld.com/article/200963-3/browser_blowout_2010.html

Mesguich, V., & Thomas, A. (2010). *Net recherche 2010: le guide pratique pour mieux trouver l'information utile et surveiller le web*. Sciences et techniques de l'information (4th ed.). Paris, France: ADBS éditions.

Mohib, N. (2009). La recherche d'information sous le regard des sciences humaines. *Distances et savoirs, 7*(3), 507-511.

Monnier, M., & Ruscher, S. (2010a, April 4). Les meilleures extensions Firefox et Google Chrome. *clubic.com*. Retrieved March 3, 2011, from http://www.clubic.com/article-333418-1-meilleures-extensions-firefox-google-chrome.html

Monnier, M., & Ruscher, S. (2010b, August 14). Safari: 10 extensions à découvrir sous Mac et Windows! *clubic.com*. Retrieved August 22, 2010, from http://www.clubic.com/navigateur-internet/safari/article-357210-1-safari-extensions-decouvrir-mac-windows.html

Portal, J.-M., & Rangin, M. (2010, September 9). Les meilleures extensions pour votre navigateur. *Micro Hebdo*, (647), p. 26-29.

Reinders, S. (2009, August 12). 25 extensions Firefox pour les étudiants et les chercheurs. *Pedago-Tic*. Retrieved September 15, 2009, from http://www.pedago-tic.be/2009/08/25-extensions-firefox-pour-les-etudiants-et-les-chercheurs

Varghese, B. (2008, August 23). Top twenty Firefox add-ons that make Firefox the researcher's browser of choice. *RES IPSA BLOG*. Retrieved September 15, 2010, from http://resipsablog.com/2008/08/23/become-an-efficient-researcher-top-twenty-firefox-add-ons-that-make-firefox-the-researchers-browser-of-choice

KEY TERMS AND DEFINITIONS

Add-on: an optional program, also known as an extension that can be added to some software to provide additional features. In this chapter, the add-ons meet specific requirements that are not covered by the browser's basic features.

Automatic analysis: operation that automatically displays the information contained in a document using statistical, linguistic and semantic methods.

Corpus: compilation of documents for the purposes of analysis.

Document: information medium.

Information: data stored on a medium with the aim of passing on knowledge.

Knowledge: sum of assimilated experience and information.

Source: origin of a piece of information (URL, author, publisher, producer, etc.).

Web browser: application that makes it possible to use hyperlinks, to display and bookmark Web pages and to search for and consult documents.

ENDNOTES

[1] Microsoft offers customized versions of its Internet Explorer browser, but these are simply versions which are optimized for a given website. Examples include IE8 optimized for MSN or for 01Net.

[2] In 2007, Mozilla launched Firefox Campus Edition, an optimized version of its browser aimed at students. This was not as successful as expected, and was consequently abandoned.

[3] For example, the creators of the Flock browser specifically designed their application for social network users.

'Flock is a browser. The people here at Flock are committed to building a browser unlike anything you've ever experienced before — because we start by focusing on user needs. We take pride in solving for common behaviors on the Web that seem clunky today, and will seem ridiculous tomorrow. We're taking you there.

We're focused on keeping you close and better connected to the people, places and things you love, more informed about the topics that turn you on, and smiling about the way it all comes together. We love nothing more than hearing from users who didn't know they were experiencing 'conventional browser fatigue' until they've downloaded Flock..and voila. Their lives get that much better.

We're big fans of the many interesting and innovative sites and services that continue to emerge to keep our online lives interesting.

We also share a common vision that your browser should do much more than just get you to where you want to go. It should make sure you don't miss out on things that are important to you and help you break down any barrier to easily share, publish, discover and communicate, so that you can enjoy the web to the fullest extent possible' (Flock Inc., 2010).

However, a social network user does not only surf on social networks. The developers of Flock were particularly shrewd, as were the creators of RockMelt. They both made it possible to implement Chrome extensions in their interface, by choosing to develop their browser using code from the open-source browser Chromium. It should be noted that previous versions of Flock dating from before its June 2010 beta version were based on Firefox (Rosenblatt, 2010).

Other browsers designed for a specific target audience have similarly been unable to overlook the question of extensions: examples include Songbird, for music lovers, and Kirix Strata, for data analysts.

4   Before 2010, only Firefox and Internet Explorer (IE) had an official add-ons gallery. Among the various browsers that can be modified with add-ons, Mozilla's Firefox is perhaps the one that first springs to mind. Indeed, Mozilla has built the Firefox brand around these extensions since it released its first version on November 4, 2004 (Mozilla, 2004). With regard to Internet Explorer, it appears that its official add-ons gallery was brought out sometime around April 25, 2006, during the finalization of its version 7. (Duff, 2006). The first version of the IE browser dates back to August 1995. Google launched its Google Chrome browser on December 11, 2008. The launch of the official Chrome add-ons gallery dates from the release of version 4 on January 25, 2010 (Google Inc., 2010). Apple launched Safari on June 23,

2003. Seven years later, on June 7, 2010, its version 5 was released with an official add-ons gallery (Apple Inc., 2010). Since 1996, Opera Software ASA has released 11 versions of its Opera browser. The most recent dates from December 16, 2010, the same date that its official add-ons gallery was launched (Opera Software ASA, 2010).

5   The add-ons presented in this chapter were analyzed between March 7 and 31, 2011, during which time the final versions of Internet Explorer 9 (IE9), Chrome 10 and Firefox 4 were released (respectively on March 14, 18 and 22, 2011). At this time, Safari was at its version 5 and Opera at its version 11.

6   Given that the customization of a browser is based on the user's own requirements, the selection of add-ons presented in this chapter cannot meet the needs of all Knowledge Workers. There are as many possible configurations as there are users. It is up to individual users to customize their browser as they see fit.

7   The official add-ons galleries consulted for the various browsers are as follows:
- Firefox: addons.mozilla.org
- Google Chrome: chrome.google.com/extensions
- Internet Explorer: ieaddons.com
- Opera: addons.opera.com
- Safari: extensions.apple.com

8   At the time of writing, the add-ons presented here for Firefox 3.6 — the most recent finalized version released before version 4 — are not all compatible with Firefox 4. For reasons of clarity, we have chosen to indicate the compatibility of the add-ons only in the summary tables. Data collected on March 27, 2011. By the time you read these pages, it is highly likely that any non-compatible add-ons presented will have been made compatible, given their previous success. In future, the non-compatibility of add-ons from one version to another should be no

more than a bad memory. The five leaders in Web browsing currently use standard technologies (HTML5, CSS and JavaScript), in particular to make the implementation of add-ons more straightforward. The main advantage for developers in using standard technologies to create add-ons is to eliminate compatibility problems for users upgrading to a new version of the browser for which the add-ons were developed; moreover, they also allow add-ons to be implemented more easily within different browsers that comply with the same standards. This issue had long been a source of difficulties for the developers of extensions, preventing them from bringing their add-ons to as wide an audience as possible.

In order for these tables to be as useful as possible, we have also chosen to mention the basic features and add-ons available for the two most recent versions of Internet Explorer, seeing as the very latest version, IE9, can only be used with the most recent Microsoft operating systems (Vista and Windows 7), whereas IE8 operates under Windows XP, Vista and Windows 7. The tables also include data for browsers Chrome 10, Opera 11 and Safari 5.

9 In the late 1990s, Peter Drucker stated that the challenge facing managers in the 21st century would be to improve the productivity of the field of knowledge and Knowledge Workers (according to Drucker's broader definition of the term) by around 50%, as was the case for industry and manual workers in the 20th century. But he explained that improving their productivity would require both Knowledge Workers and the company they work for to adopt a new approach (Drucker, 1999).

10 Again according to Peter Drucker, the key to managing Knowledge Workers is not so much managing them as individuals but rather guiding them, so that their strengths

and knowledge can become productive (Drucker, 1999).

11 Among the six main factors that determine the productivity of Knowledge Workers, Peter Drucker emphasized the importance of allowing them to be responsible for their own productivity by determining the tasks that they needed to accomplish, and therefore providing them with autonomy. Another integral factor of Knowledge Workers' activities was identified as continuous learning and continuous teaching (Drucker, 1999).

12 'Au sein des différentes formes d'organisation du travail, la webisation est aussi à l'origine de quatre autres mécanismes complémentaires qualifiés de façon respective de glocalisation, d'entreprise étendue, d'approche One Net et le Cloud Computing.' ['Within the various forms in which work can be organized, webization is also at the root of four other complementary mechanisms, termed respectively as glocalization, extended enterprise, One Net approach and Cloud Computing.'] (Germain, 2010, p. 90).

13 Web browser developers seem to be heading in this direction, offering more and more application software integrated into the basic features of their browser(s), in particular via resource- and/or data-sharing systems using cloud computing; for example, Opera Unit for Opera, Google Cloud Print for Google Chrome, Bonjour for Safari and Windows Live Mesh for IE.

14 No Web browser designed for desktop and laptop computers is currently fully compatible with all the add-ons available in the various official add-ons galleries. However, two examples caught our attention, one of which is the solution offered by the Lunascape browser. Lunascape is a browser whose main feature is the fact that it uses the three main Web browser engines (also known as rendering engines): Trident (IE), Gecko (Firefox) and Webkit (Google

Chrome, Safari, Chromium, RockMelt, Flock). This means that it is possible to access the best of the main Web browsers — features, performance and speed — from Lunascape, without needing to use several browsers. Lunascape incorporates IE and Firefox add-ons, which operate only if the open tab uses the appropriate Web browser engine. It is possible to change the Web browser engine of a Web page with a single click, or to display the page simultaneously in three tabs, each tab working with a different Web browser engine.

Given that the Google Chrome source code is based on that of the open-source browser Chromium, Google Chrome extensions can be integrated into all browsers whose source code is based on Chromium source code. This is the case, for example, for the browsers RockMelt and Flock.

[15] 'Ensemble des méthodes, procédures et techniques permettant, en fonction de critères de recherche propres à l'usager, de sélectionner l'information dans un ou plusieurs fonds de documents plus ou moins structurés. Toute recherche d'information suppose trois phases successives: a) une recherche bibliographique des références de documents pertinents ; b) une recherche documentaire, c'est-à-dire une recherche bibliographique complétée par la recherche (l'acquisition) des documents eux-mêmes ; c) et enfin le repérage de l'information dans les documents sélectionnés (recherche de l'information).' ['All the methods, procedures and techniques that enable users to select information, according to their own search criteria, from one or more collection(s) of documents that are more or less structured. Any search for information implies three successive stages: a) a bibliographical search for the references of relevant documents; b) documentary research; in other words, a bibliographical

search including the search for (acquisition of) documents themselves; c) the identification of information in the selected documents (search for information).'] (« Institut national des techniques de la documentation, » 2004).

[16] For all Web users who use online applications (bookmarks, social bookmarks, RSS feed aggregators, notebooks, blogs) which allow content to be tagged, it is becoming increasingly important to be able to search their various online accounts simultaneously by means of the tags that they have used to index the content that they have selected. This ensures that they make the best use of their selected sources and information before starting to write their texts or research papers.

[17] The following are examples of browsers available in light versions for smartphones: Chrome Mobile for Chrome, Firefox Mobile for Firefox, and Internet Explorer Mobile for Internet Explorer. Apple has been able to use the same version of its Safari browser for its various devices: the iPad, iPhone and iPod touch. 'The first browser to deliver the "real" Internet to a mobile device, Safari renders pages on iPad, iPhone, and iPod touch just as you see them on your computer' (Apple Inc., 2010). Opera Software goes even further by offering versions of its Opera browser for smartphones (Opera Mobile), tablet computers (Opera Mini) and televisions (Opera Widgets™). It also offers Opera Devices SDK, which 'enables solutions targeted at the full connected digital life, uniting devices with a common browser and presentation engine and ensuring that additional functionality will work seamlessly' (Opera Software ASA, 2011). Lunascape Corporation offers iLunascape, a version of its Lunascape browser for iPhone and iPad.

[18] To date, Mozilla, Google, Opera Software, Apple and Microsoft all offer a synchronization solution for users working with their

browser(s) on different Web-based devices. Depending on the solution used, the data that can be synchronized may differ. Users have the option of selecting the type of data that they wish to be synchronized on remote servers and also on their different devices. For example, Mozilla has implemented its Sync add-on for Firefox version 4. Sync enables users to synchronize bookmarks, identifiers, passwords, preferences, search history and open tabs. Holders of a Google account using the Google Chrome browser can synchronize the following data: automatic fill-in, favorites, extensions, applications, preferences, identifiers, passwords and themes. They can also consult their favorites from any browser as long as they are logged into their Google account. Opera Software offers a similar solution with its Opera Link extension, which is linked to an online account where bookmarks, notes and Speed Dial entries can be consulted. The Opera Link extension offers users their customized search bar, their bookmarks and their Speed Dial entries if they are logged in to the extension on their Opera and Opera Mini/Mobile browsers. The Opera Link extension does not currently allow users to synchronize their browser history using Opera Mini/Mobile. To synchronize bookmarks on various Web-based devices, Apple has created the MobileMe extension. Microsoft offers the Windows Live Mesh 2011 application, which requires users to be working with Windows 7, Windows Vista or Windows Server 2008.

Chapter 12
Next Generation Search Engine for the Result Clustering Technology

Lin-Chih Chen
National Dong Hwa University, Taiwan

ABSTRACT

Result clustering has recently attracted a lot of attention to provide the users with a succinct overview of relevant search results than traditional search engines. This chapter proposes a mixed clustering method to organize all returned search results into a hierarchical tree structure. The clustering method accomplishes two main tasks, one is label construction and the other is tree building. This chapter uses precision to measure the quality of clustering results. According to the results of experiments, the author preliminarily concluded that the performance of the system is better than many other well-known commercial and academic systems. This chapter makes several contributions. First, it presents a high performance system based on the clustering method. Second, it develops a divisive hierarchical clustering algorithm to organize all returned snippets into hierarchical tree structure. Third, it performs a wide range of experimental analyses to show that almost all commercial systems are significantly better than most current academic systems.

DOI: 10.4018/978-1-4666-0330-1.ch012

INTRODUCTION

Traditional search engines provide an interface to accept the queries and use the index technique to generate a list of URLs to the Web pages containing the query. The goal of search engines is to help the users fulfill their information need with minimal effort. What makes this goal challenging is that most users always tend to input very short queries. According to the literatures (Jansen, Spink, Bateman, & Saracevic, 1998; Silverstein, Henzinger, Marais, & Moricz, 1998; Spink, Wolfram, Jansen, & Saracevic, 2001), the average length of a user query is 2.3 words. In such short queries, it is a difficult task to find users' search needs, especially for ambiguous queries. Next generation search engines will solve this problem by focusing on users' search needs rather than the search query, and by offering various post-search tools to help the users in dealing with large sets of somewhat imprecise results. Such tools include query suggestions or refinements (e.g., Google AdWords and Yahoo Search Marketing), mapping of search results against a predetermined taxonomy (e.g., Open Directory Project and Yahoo Directory), and the result clustering (e.g., Clusty and Lingo3G). All these tools are based in full or in part on the analysis of search results.

Result clustering has recently attracted a lot of attention to provide the users with a succinct overview of relevant results. Many commercial metasearch engines with the feature of result clustering, such as Kartoo, Lingo3G, Excite, MetaCrawler, WebCrawler, Dogpile, Mamma, and Clusty, have been successfully implemented. Their effectiveness have been recognized by (Sherman, 2004, 2005), which conferred the best metasearch engines award to Dogpile, Mamma, and Clusty during 2001 to 2004. The big three search engines (Google, Yahoo, and Bing) also seem to be interested in this technology because it has been called the future of PageRank (Beal, 2004; Mook, 2005).

Result clustering was introduced in a primitive form by Northernlight and then made widely popular by Clusty (formerly Vivisimo). The problem solved by this technology consists of clustering the search results returned by a metasearch engine into hierarchical tree that is labeled with variable-length sentences. The labels assigned to the tree should capture the topic of search results contained in their associated labels. Hierarchical tree structure provides a complementary view to the search results. Users can customize their view of search results by simply navigating hierarchical tree. This navigational approach is especially useful for informative, polysemous, and poor queries (Broder, 2002).

There are three main challenges with this technology: (1) generating good descriptive labels to clusters; (2) clustering the search results into hierarchical tree; (3) clustering must be performed on-the-fly. Traditional data mining approaches are not concerned with the feature of result clustering, but in return they are often very good at grouping documents (Prado & Ferneda, 2007). Unfortunately, regardless of how good the document grouping is, users are not likely to use a clustering system if their labels are poor. Moreover, the search results are presented in hierarchical tree that can help the users to fulfill their search needs. Finally, the processing time is also a major issue of this technology because users expect fast response times.

A common method used by this technology is to cluster partial Web pages, called snippets, rather than entire Web pages. The snippet usually contains the URL, the title, and the fragment of search results summarized by remote search engines. The snippet is considerably smaller than whole Web page, thereby drastically reducing the computational cost of clustering. This is very important because it would be unacceptably costly to download whole Web page and make the labeled clustering from them.

In this chapter, we adopt a mixed clustering method to implement a high-performance result clustering system, called WSC. The output of our system consists of the regular search results and the clustering results. For the regular search results, we use a well-known information retrieval metric, called mean reciprocal rank, to rearrange the search results of major search engines, such as Google, Yahoo, Bing, into our metasearch results. For the clustering results, we first adopt a two-round label construction technique, which involves a suffix tree clustering method and a two-pass hash mechanism, to generate all meaningful labels; and then, we develop a divisive hierarchical clustering algorithm to organize the labels into a hierarchical tree.

The main contributions of this chapter are threefold. First, we present a detailed system design to readers to achieve superior performance than current commercial and academic systems. Our preliminary system (http://cayley.sytes. net/wsc) is shown in Figure 1 and offers a web interface similar to Clusty, which is the most well-known result clustering system. According to the results of experimental analysis, we preliminarily concluded that the performance of our system is better than current commercial and academic systems. Second, the main advantages of our divisive hierarchical clustering algorithm are: (1) the labels are organized into hierarchical tree structure rather than flat structure; (2) a child cluster can be assigned to multiple parent clusters; (3) the most operations of our divisive hierarchical clustering algorithm are only required to do the bitwise operation; thus, the algorithm's speed is relatively fast. Third, we also perform a widely range of experiments to verify that almost all current commercial systems are significantly better than most current academic systems.

The rest of this chapter is organized as follows. In this next section, we briefly discuss the related work about current academic clustering engines. First, the detail of the clustering engine is described. I discuss the results of experimental analysis, and then I conclude this chapter.

RELATED WORK

Academic literature offers various methods to build different result clustering systems. In the simplest case, the labels are shown as a simple bag of words and the labels are organized into flat structure. In more sophisticated case, the labels are shown as variable-length sentences and the labels are organized into hierarchical tree structure. According to the form and structure on the labels, the result clustering methods can be classified into four cases: "single words & flat", "sentences & flat", "single words & hierarchical", and "sentences & hierarchical".

In the first case, "single words & flat", this is a simplest case for the result clustering. Scatter/Gather (Hearst & Pedersen, 1996) used a non-hierarchical partitioning algorithm, Buckshot and Fractionation (Cutting, Karger, Pedersen, & Tukey, 1992), to cluster all returned snippets in linear time based on the cosine similarity between snippets. Retriever (Joshi & Jiang, 2002) used a robust relational fuzzy clustering algorithm to organize the search results into a few clusters. WebCat (Giannotti, Nanni, Pedreschi, & Samaritani, 2003) applied a transactional K-Means algorithm to organize the clusters into flat structure. EigenCluster (Cheng, Kannan, Vempala, & Wang, 2006) employed a divide and merge algorithm, which involves a spectral clustering (efficient with sparse term-document matrices) and a dynamic programming (for merging nodes of the tree resulting from the divide stage), to cluster the snippets.

In the second case, "sentences & flat", the labels are labeled with variable-length sentences but the labels are organized into flat structure. Grouper (Zamir & Etzioni, 1999) was one of the early systems belonging to this case. Although it uses sentences as the name of labels, but such sentences are drawn as contiguous portions of snippets by a suffix tree clustering algorithm. Carrot2-STC (Weiss & Stefanowski, 2003) was an open source implementation of Grouper. SRC

Figure 1. The clustering results of Clusty (left) and WSC (right) in response to the user's query is "mobile phone" (accessed date 2010/03/27)

(a) Clusty   (b) WSC

(Zeng, He, Chen, Ma, & Ma, 2004) applied a regression model on five different measures to extract all candidate sentences. Carrot2-Lingo (Osinski & Weiss, 2005) used a singular value decomposition technique on the term-document matrix to find all possible sentences. Amongst these systems, only Carrot2-STC and Carrot2-Lingo are available online.

In the third case, "single words & hierarchical", the labels are organized into hierarchical tree structure but the labels are labeled with single words. FIHC (Fung, Wang, & Ester, 2003) applied a frequent itemset-based hierarchical clustering approach to construct the labels and organize it into hierarchical tree structure. A frequent itemset is a set of words that occur together in some minimum fraction of snippets in a cluster. CREDO (Carpineto & Romano, 2004) used a formal concept analysis on single words to build a lattice of

clusters later presented to users as a navigation tree. It works in two phases. In the first phase, only the titles of input snippets are taken into account to generate the most general labels. In the second phase, the concept lattice-based method is recursively applied to lower levels using a broader input of both titles and snippets. Amongst these systems, only CREDO is available online.

In the fourth case, "sentences & hierarchical", this is the most interesting case for result clustering. Lassi (Maarek, Fagin, Ben-Shaul, & Pelleg, 2000) used traditional agglomerative hierarchical clustering algorithm to cluster the snippets. Instead of single words, the pairs of words with strong correlation of appearance in the input snippets are used (such pairs are said to share a lexical affinity). An index of lexical affinities discovered in input is later reused for labeling the discovered clusters. Highlight (Wu,

Shankar, & Chen, 2003) first uses the concept terms, a series of noun phrases that appear in snippets, to generate the labels. Then, it analyzed the relationships between higher and lower level terms by a probability of co-occurrence analysis technique (Wu, Rakthin, & Li, 2002) to organize the labels into hierarchical tree. WICE (Zhang & Dong, 2004) applied a semantic hierarchical online clustering algorithm to handle the problem of data locality. The algorithm uses a suffix array for extracting contiguous sentences from snippets, and organizes the labels into hierarchical tree by singular value decomposition. WhatsOnTheWeb (Giacomo, Didimo, Grilli, & Liotta, 2007) used a topology-driven approach to present the clustering results on a graph whose vertices are the sentences in snippets, and whose edges denote the relationships between sentences. The hierarchical tree is obtained by using classical graph-clustering algorithms. SnakeT (Ferragina & Guli, 2008) first extracts the gapped sentences from snippets as labels. It then adopts two special knowledge bases to rank the labels. Finally, it builds a parent cluster if two child clusters converge on a substring among their labels. In this chapter, we propose a result clustering system belonging to this case. In the next section, we will describe the detail of our proposed system.

SYSTEM ARCHITECTURE

In this section, we describe the architecture of our proposed system as shown in Figure 2. Our system involves the following four main procedures: "Metasearch Ranking", "Label Construction for the First Round", "Label Construction for the Second Round", and "Build a Hierarchical Tree Structure". In the "Metasearch Ranking" procedure, we use a metasearch technique to integrate different search results from different search engines into regular search results of our system. The regular search results are not only the output of this procedure but also the input of

the next procedure. In the next procedure, "Label Construction for the First Round", we first apply a series of snippet cleaning techniques, such as Porter stemming, stop words, sentence boundaries, and non-words tokens, to convert the snippets (output by the "Metasearch Ranking" procedure) into a series of meaningful sentence tokens that are the input of our mixed clustering method. Then, we perform "Construct suffix tree" and "Trace suffix tree" steps to generate the base clusters for the first round. In the "Label Construction for the Second Round" procedure, we adopt a two-pass hash mechanism to generate the base clusters for the second round. In the "Build a Hierarchical Tree Structure" procedure, we use a divisive hierarchical algorithm to organize the base clusters for the second round into hierarchical tree. Brief descriptions of the above-mentioned four procedures are given in the following four subsections.

METASEARCH RANKING

The input of our system is a set of snippets associated with the search query. The snippet usually contains the title, the URL, and the fragment of search results summarized by remote search engines.

In this procedure, we first develop a "Web Crawler", a search program that sends the search query to several search engines simultaneously, to fetch many relevant Web pages from several search engines. Currently, we select three search engines (Google, Yahoo, Bing) as the sources of our system. We then utilize a perl compatible regular expressions (PCRE) library (Hazel, 2009), a powerful program library to parse regular Web page, to identify the parts of title, URL, and fragment. At the end of these two tasks, we can get the input of our system. Finally, we use a well-known information retrieval metric, called Mean Reciprocal Rank (MRR) (Baeza-Yates & Ribeiro-Neto, 1999), to integrate different search results returned from different search engines into

Figure 2. The system architecture of our proposed system

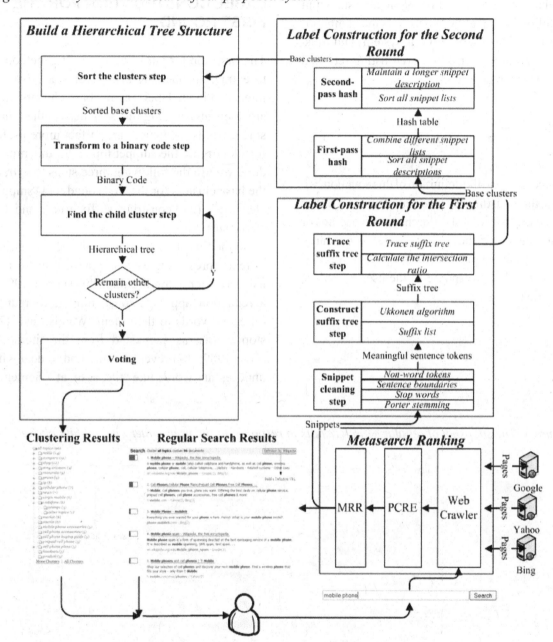

regular search results of our system as shown in the following equation, where |e| is the number of search engines used (3 in our system) and rank$_i$ is the ranking order of a search listing returned from a search engine i.

$$MRR = \frac{1}{|e|} \sum_{i=1}^{|e|} \frac{1}{rank_i} \qquad (1)$$

According to the definition of this equation, we know that a listing has a larger weight if it either wins more votes from different search engines or is ranking high in the listings of at least one search engine. Figure 3 presents the snapshot of regular search results in response to the user's query is "mobile phone".

LABEL CONSTRUCTION FOR THE FIRST ROUND

The first step for our result clustering method is to extract all meaningful base clusters. We are interested in the labels (called base clusters) that are long and intelligible sentences rather than single words. Sentences are in fact more useful for identifying the snippet topics. In this procedure, we use the following three steps to extract the base clusters for the first round: (1) "snippet cleaning", (2) "construct suffix tree", and (3) "trace suffix tree".

In the first step, "snippet cleaning", the string of text representing each snippet is transformed using a Porter stemming algorithm (Porter, 1997), a reduction approach to stemming, to reduce inflected words to their stem. We also use 421 stop words, as suggested from the literature (Fox, 1989), to prevent our method to deal with unnecessary words like "the, a, in, at". Sentence

Figure 3. The snapshot of regular search results in response to the user's query is "mobile phone"

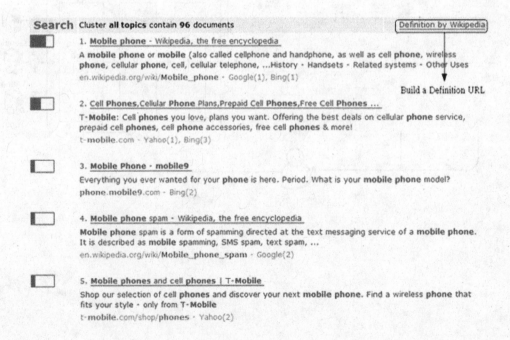

boundaries, stop words, and non-word tokens (such as numbers, HTML tags, and most punctuation characters) are marked. At end of this step, all cleaning snippets should be forming a series of meaningful sentence tokens. We call a sentence using Porter's stemming algorithm is a meaningful sentence token if the stop words or non-word tokens does not appear in this sentence.

In the second step, "construct suffix tree", we use the suffix tree data structure (Gusfield, 1997) for a set of strings and Ukkonen's linear-time suffix tree construction algorithm (Ukkonen, 1995) to generate the suffix tree for all meaningful sentence tokens. The suffix tree of a collection of meaningful sentence tokens is a compact trie containing all the suffixes of all the strings in the collection. The suffix tree for a set of strings "X Y Z" (X, Y, Z are strings) is a tree whose edges are labeled with strings such that each suffix list of "X Y Z" corresponds to exactly one path from the tree's root to a leaf. Each node of suffix tree represents a group of snippets and the label of node represents the common phrase shared by snippets.

Then, we adopt Ukkonen's online suffix tree construction algorithm (Ukkonen, 1995) for

building a suffix tree because it can be easily applied to multiple strings (Goto, Kurokawa, & Yasunaga, 2007). Figure 4 is the suffix tree for three meaningful sentence tokens.

To generate the base clusters for the first round, we use the third step, "trace suffix tree", to trace the suffix tree. In this step, we first calculate the intersection ratio with respect to the total number of snippets in the child node and the parent node for each edge of the suffix tree. For example, the intersection ratio of the edge "mous" is 0.66 (2/3), where the total number of snippets in the child node is 2 (S1, S2) and the total number of snippets in the parent node is 3 (S1, S2, S3).

We then define that the concatenation of strings along the path from the root node to a child node v is a base cluster for the first round if and only if the total number of snippets in v is larger than 1 and the intersection ratios for all edges in this path are all larger than a threshold value. In this example, we assume the threshold value equal to 0.6; thus, the base clusters for the first round are "mous", "cat eat", "eat chees", and "chees".

Figure 4. The suffix tree for three meaningful sentence tokens

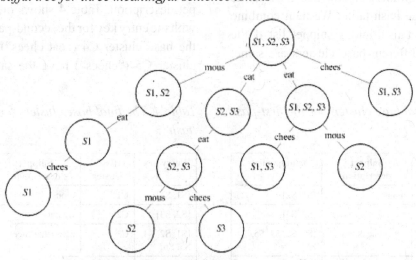

Original Snippets = {S1: mouse eat cheese, S2: eat eat mouse, S3: cat eat cheese}
Meaningful Sentence Tokens = {S1: mous eat chees, S2: cat eat mous, S3: cat eat chees}

Table 1. An example of the final base clusters for the first round

Base cluster	Snippet description	Snippet list
C1	mous	[S1, S2]
C2	cat eat	[S2, S3]
C3	eat cottag chees	[S1, S4, S6]
C4	eat chees	[S1, S3]
C5	chees	[S1, S3]
C6	cottag chees eat	[S2, S5]

Table 2. One hash table with the entry key for the first-pass hash

Entry key	Base cluster	Snippet description	Snippet list
mous	C1	mous	[S1, S2]
cat eat	C2	cat eat	[S2, S3]
chees cottag eat	C3, C6	eat cottag chees, cottag chees eat	[S1, S4, S6], [S2, S5]
chees eat	C4	eat chees	[S1, S3]
chees	C5	chees	[S1, S3]

LABEL CONSTRUCTION FOR THE SECOND ROUND

In this procedure, we use a two-pass hash mechanism to generate the base clusters for the second round. In the first-pass hash, we combine the snippets of different base clusters into a base cluster if such different base clusters have the same words but their permutations are different. That is, if we have two base clusters, "X Y Z" and "Y X Z", then we combine the snippets of these two base clusters into "X Y Z". For example, we assume that Table 1 is the final base clusters for the first round.

In the first-pass hash, we first sort the words of snippet description by alphabetical order as the entry key of one hash table. We then combine different snippet lists into a snippet list if the entry keys of different base clusters are same.

Table 2 shows this table with the entry key for the first-pass hash. Since the base clusters C3 ("eat cottag chees") and C6 ("cottag chees eat") have the same entry key ("chees cottag eat"); thus, we combine the snippet lists of C3 and C6 into C3 and the snippet list of C3 is [S1, S2, S4, S5, S6]. Table 3 shows the final base clusters for the first-pass hash.

In the second-pass hash, we then use the snippet list as the entry key of other hash table. A cluster should be removed if the entry key of this cluster is same as another cluster and the snippet description of this cluster is a subset of another one. We maintain the cluster with a longer snippet description because the longer snippet description has a more rich description than the shorter snippet description. Table 4 shows other hash table with the entry key for the second-pass hash. Since the base cluster C4 ("eat chees") and the base cluster C5 ("chees") have the same entry key

Table 3. The final base clusters for the first-pass hash

Base cluster	Snippet description	Snippet list
C1	mous	[S1, S2]
C2	cat eat	[S2, S3]
C3	eat cottag chees	[S1, S2, S4, S5, S6]
C4	eat chees	[S1, S3]
C5	chees	[S1, S3]

Table 4. The final base clusters for the first-pass hash

Entry key	Base cluster	Snippet description	Snippet list
[S1, S2]	C1	mous	[S1, S2]
[S2, S3]	C2	cat eat	[S2, S3]
[S1, S2, S4, S5, S6]	C3	eat cottag chees	[S1, S2, S4, S5, S6]
[S1, S3]	C4, C5	eat chees, chees	[S1, S3]

Table 5. The final base clusters for the second round

Base cluster	Snippet description	Snippet list
C1	mous	[S1, S2]
C2	cat eat	[S2, S3]
C3	eat cottag chees	[S1, S2, S4, S5, S6]
C4	eat chees	[S1, S3]

("[S1, S3]"), we thus remove C5 because this cluster with a shorter snippet description. Table 5 shows the final base clusters for the second-pass hash.

BUILD A HIERARCHICAL TREE STRUCTURE

In this procedure, we develop a divisive hierarchical clustering algorithm to organize the base clusters for the second round into hierarchical tree structure rather than flat structure. Our divisive hierarchical clustering algorithm involves three steps: (1) "sort the clusters"; (2) "transform to a binary code"; (3) "find the child cluster".

The main task of the first step ("sort the clusters") is sorting all base clusters in descending order by the number of snippets they contain.

Table 6. An example of the base clusters for our divisive hierarchical clustering algorithm

Base cluster	Snippet list	Number of snippets
BC1	[S1, S3, S5, S9, S10, S12, S15]	7
BC2	[S1, S2]	2
BC3	[S1, S3, S5]	3
BC4	[S1, S5, S9, S15]	4
BC5	[S1, S3]	2
BC6	[S1, S2, S3, S5, S9, S15]	6

For example, in Table 6, we assume that the base cluster BC1 has the following snippet list [S1, S3, S5, S9, S10, S12, S15] and the number of snippets of this base cluster is 7. Other base clusters are also shown in Table 6. In this step, we sort all base clusters in descending order by the number of snippets they contain as shown in Table 7.

The main task of the second step ("transform to a binary code") is to transform the snippet list of the base cluster into the binary code. We define that a bit i in the binary code should be encoded as 1 if the base cluster contains the snippet Si. For example, in the cluster BC5 (Table 8), it contains the snippets S1 and S3; that is, in the first (the most significant bit) and third bits are encoded as 1, thus, the binary code for BC5 is 101000000000000.

Table 7. All sorted base clusters based on the number of snippets

Base cluster	Snippet list	Number of snippets
BC1	[S1, S3, S5, S9, S10, S12, S15]	7
BC6	[S1, S2, S3, S5, S9, S15]	6
BC4	[S1, S5, S9, S15]	4
BC3	[S1, S3, S5]	3
BC2	[S1, S2]	2
BC5	[S1, S3]	2

Table 8. The results of binary code for all sorted base clusters

Base cluster	Snippet list	Binary code
BC1	[S1, S3, S5, S9, S10, S12, S15]	101010001101001
BC6	[S1, S2, S3, S5, S9, S15]	111010001000001
BC4	[S1, S5, S9, S15]	100010001000001
BC3	[S1, S3, S5]	101010000000000
BC2	[S1, S2]	110000000000000
BC5	[S1, S3]	101000000000000

Table 8 also shows the results of binary code for other sorted base clusters.

The core step of our divisive hierarchical clustering algorithm is the third step ("find the child cluster"). The main task of this step is finding all child clusters for each cluster. We define that a parent cluster BCj has one child cluster BCk if the snippet list of BCk is a subset of BCj and the snippet list of BCk is not a subset of its sibling clusters. For example, in Figure 5, BC1 has two child clusters, BC4 and BC3, because the snippet lists of BC4 ([S1, S5, S9, S15]) and BC3 ([S1, S3, S5]) both are a subset of BC1 ([S1, S3, S5, S9, S10, S12, S15]), and the snippet list of BC3 is not a subset of its sibling cluster BC4. Although the snippet list of BC5 ([S1, S3]) is a subset of BC1, but the snippet list of BC5 is a subset of its

sibling cluster BC3. Thus, BC5 cannot be a child cluster of BC1.

The subset operation can be easily done by a bitwise logical AND operation. We call that BCk is a subset of BCj if "(the binary code of BCk) AND (the binary code of BCj)" is equal to the binary code of BCk. For example, BC4 is a subset of BC1 because "the binary code of BC4 (100010001000001) AND the binary code of BC1 (101010001101001)" is equal to the binary code of BC4.

In each iteration of Figure 5, the parent cluster is not only holds all child clusters, but also holds a special child cluster ("other topics"). The binary code of "other topics" is done by the following bitwise operations: "(the binary code of the parent cluster) XOR (the binary code of the

Figure 5. All iterations of the third step

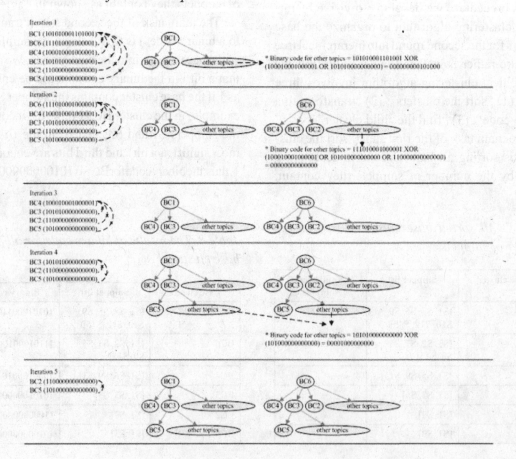

kth child cluster OR the binary code of the mth child cluster)", where k and m both are the child clusters. For example, in iteration 1 of Figure 5, the parent cluster BC1 has three child clusters (BC4, BC3, "other topics"). The binary code of "other topics" is done by "101010001101001 XOR (100010001000001 OR 101010000000000) = 000000000101000". Figure 5 also shows other iterations of the third step.

According to the final results of the third step, we then convert the representation of binary code into the representation of snippet list as shown Figure 6. Note that the snippet list of "other topics" of BC6 is a null set because its binary code is 000000000000000.

Finally, we use a voting technique to present the actual word not the stem word to users. That is, if two actual words, "ABCx" and "ABCy", with a same stem word "ABC" have appeared in one cluster and "ABCx" has won the most votes (snippets) in this cluster, then "ABCx" should be presented to users. For example, two actual words, "cottage" and "cottages", with a same stem word "cottag" have appeared in one cluster and "cottage" has won the most snippets in this cluster; thus, "cottage" should be presented to users. The right part of Figure 1 is our clustering results.

EXPERIMENT ANALYSIS

In this section, we evaluate the performance of our proposed system against other existing online systems, including Carrot2-STC, Carrot2-Lingo, CREDO, Highlight, WhatsOnTheWeb, SnakeT. All systems are described previously.

For the test data set, we selected the 18 most searched queries in 2009 on Google (2010) and Yahoo (2009) that belonging to many different topics ("american idol", "britney spears", "facebook", "farrah fawcett", "glee", "hi5", "hulu", "kim kardashian", "lady gaga", "megan fox", "michael jackson", "naruto", "nascar", "natasha richardson", "paranormal activity", "runescape", "twitter", "wwe"), and asked to forty undergraduate students (21 males and 19 females) and seven graduate students (5 males and 2 females) from National Dong Hwa University.

For each of the 18 queries, forty-seven human evaluators computed the precision at the first K labels associated to the top-level labels generated by different experiments. Precision at top K is defined as (Chen, 2010; Feng, Wang, Yu, Yang, & Yan, 2009; Ferragina & Guli, 2008; Shen, Sun, Yang, & Chen, 2006; Wan, 2009; Zeng et al., 2004), where M@K is the number of labels that have been

Figure 6. A hierarchical tree structure with the snippet list

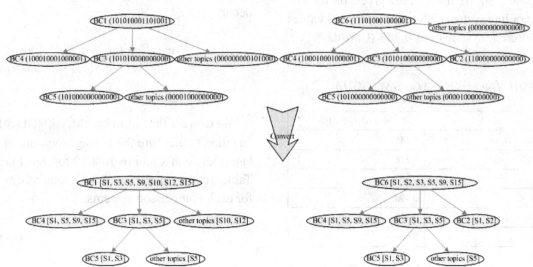

Table 9. Average PR@K for different systems

	Average PR@3	Average PR@5	Average PR@7	Average PR@10
Carrot2-STC	0.706	0.625	0.570	0.491
Carrot2-Lingo	0.723	0.640	0.566	0.497
CREDO	0.653	0.578	0.507	0.451
Highlight	0.412	0.315	0.206	0.131
WhatsOnTheWeb	0.642	0.576	0.489	0.409
SnakeT	0.742	0.673	0.615	0.548
WSC	0.852	0.827	0.817	0.814

manually tagged relevant among the K top-level labels computed by different experiments.

$$PR@K = \frac{M@K}{K} \qquad (2)$$

If a label l has been manually tagged as "ambiguous", we judge l relevant if the majority of its child labels are relevant. We note that the list of queries has been randomly partitioned among the evaluators, in a balanced way. We believe that PR@K, specialized in the top-level labels, reflects the natural user behavior of considering these top-level labels as the most important for hierarchical navigation. We use PR@3, PR@5, PR@7, and PR@10 since lazy users do not like browsing a lot of information.

Table 9 shows the average precision for different online systems. The average PR@3 values for different systems are 0.706 (Carrot2-STC),

0.723 (Carrot2-Lingo), 0.653 (CREDO), 0.412 (Highlight), 0.642 (WhatsOnTheWeb), 0.742 (SnakeT), and 0.852 (WSC), respectively. Moreover, in Table 9, we also extend this analysis to other analyses PR@5, PR@7, and PR@10. According to the results of Table 9, our system has the highest PR@K score.

Then, we use a distance metric, called Normalized Google Distance (NGD) (Cilibrasi & Vitányi, 2007), to automatically evaluate the similarity information between terms from the large corpus of data, such as Google search engine. NGD gives computers the ability to quantify the meaning of terms. It is defined as follows, where M is the total number of webpages searched by Google; f(x) and f(y) are the number of webpages for the search terms x and y, respectively; and f(x,y) is the number of webpages on which both x and y occur.

$$NGD(x,y) = \frac{\max\{\log f(x), \log f(y)\} - \log f(x,y)}{\log M - \min\{\log f(x), \log f(y)\}} \qquad (3)$$

We then use the following "Mean(NGD@10)" equation to measure the average measure of distance between x and its first 10 top-level labels. Table 10 shown the result of Mean(NGD@10) for each comparison systems.

Table 10. The result of Mean(NGD@10)

	Mean(NGD@10)
Carrot2-STC	0.345
Carrot2-Lingo	0.328
CREDO	0.366
Highlight	0.496
WhatsOnTheWeb	0.404
SnakeT	0.304
WSC	0.191

$$Mean(NGD @ 10) = \frac{1}{10} \sum_{y=1}^{10} NGD(x,y)$$

(4)

According to the results of precision and NGD, we preliminarily concluded that the performance of our system is better than current academic systems. That is, in this chapter, we present a detailed system design to readers to achieve superior performance than current academic systems.

CONCLUSION AND FUTURE WORK

In this chapter, we have presented an integrated system with the regular search results and the clustering results. According to the results of experiments, we concluded that using our mixed clustering method to cluster the snippets can give significant performance gains.

Our mixed clustering method consists of two main tasks running in a background mode, one is the label construction, and the other is hierarchical tree building. In the label construction task, we adopt a two-round label construction technique, which involves a suffix tree clustering method and a two-pass hash mechanism, to generate all meaningful labels. In the hierarchical tree building task, we develop a divisive hierarchical clustering algorithm to organize the labels into hierarchical tree.

The main contributions of this chapter are the following twofold. First, we presented a detailed system design to readers to achieve superior performance than current academic systems. Second, the main advantages of our divisive hierarchical clustering algorithm are: (1) the labels are organized into hierarchical tree structure rather than flat structure; (2) a child cluster can be assigned to multiple parent clusters; (3) the most operations of our algorithm are only required to do the bitwise operations, thus the speed of our algorithm is relatively fast.

ACKNOWLEDGEMENT

We would like to thank anonymous reviewers of the chapter for their constructive comments which help us to improve the chapter in several ways. This work was supported in part by National Science Council, Taiwan under Grant NSC 99-2221-E-259-023.

REFERENCES

Baeza-Yates, R., & Ribeiro-Neto, B. (1999). *Modern information retrieval*. Reading, MA: Addison-Wesley.

Beal, A. (2004). *Web 2.0 - Exclusive demonstration of clustering from Google*. Retrieved December 9, 2009, from http://www.searchenginelowdown. com/ 2004/10/web-20-exclusive-demonstration-of.html

Broder, A. (2002). A taxonomy of Web search. *ACM SIGIR Forum*, *36*(2), 3–10. doi:10.1145/792550.792552

Carpineto, C., & Romano, G. (2004). Exploiting the potential of concept lattices for information retrieval with CREDO. *Journal of Universal Computer Science*, *10*(8), 985–1013.

Chen, L.-C. (2010). Using a two-stage technique to design a keyword suggestion system. *Information Research: An International Electronic Journal*, *15*(1). Retrieved from http://informationr.net/ ir/15-1/paper425.html.

Cheng, D., Kannan, R., Vempala, S., & Wang, G. (2006). A divide-and-merge methodology for clustering. *ACM Transactions on Database Systems*, *31*(4), 1499–1525. doi:10.1145/1189769.1189779

Cilibrasi, R. L., & Vitányi, P. M. B. (2007). The Google similarity distance. *IEEE Transactions on Knowledge and Data Engineering*, *19*(3), 370–383. doi:10.1109/TKDE.2007.48

Cutting, D. R., Karger, D. R., Pedersen, J. O., & Tukey, J. W. (1992, June 21-24). Scatter/Gather: A cluster-based approach to browsing large document collections. In *Proceedings of the 15th Annual International ACM SIGIR Conference on Research and Development in Information Retrieval*, Copenhagen, Denmark.

Feng, S., Wang, D., Yu, G., Yang, C., & Yan, N. (2009). Sentiment clustering: A novel method to explore in the blogosphere. In Q. Li, L. Feng, J. Pei, S. X. Wang, X. Zhou, & Q.-M. Zhu (Eds.), *Proceedings of the Joint International Conference on Advances in Data and Web Management* (LNCS 5446, pp. 332-344).

Ferragina, P., & Guli, A. (2008). A personalized search engine based on Web-snippet hierarchical clustering. *Software, Practice & Experience, 38*(1), 189–225. doi:10.1002/spe.829

Fox, C. (1989). A stop list for general text. *ACM SIGIR Forum, 24*(1-2), 19–35. doi:10.1145/378881.378888

Fung, B. C. M., Wang, K., & Ester, M. (2003, May 1-3). Hierarchical document clustering using frequent itemsets. In *Proceedings of the Third SIAM International Conference on Data Mining*, San Francisco, CA.

Giacomo, E. D., Didimo, W., Grilli, L., & Liotta, G. (2007). Graph visualization techniques for Web clustering engines. *IEEE Transactions on Visualization and Computer Graphics, 13*(2), 294–304. doi:10.1109/TVCG.2007.40

Giannotti, F., Nanni, M., Pedreschi, D., & Samaritani, F. (2003, June 24-27). WebCat: Automatic categorization of Web search results. In *Proceedings of the 11th Italian Symposium on Advanced Database Systems*, Cosenza, Italy.

Google. (2010). *Google: Zeitgeist 2009*. Retrieved July 1, 2010, from http://www.google.com/ intl/ en_us/press/zeitgeist2009/overview.html

Goto, N., Kurokawa, K., & Yasunaga, T. (2007). Analysis of invariant sequences in 266 complete genomes. *Gene, 401*(1-2), 172–180. doi:10.1016/j. gene.2007.07.017

Gusfield, D. (1997). *Algorithms on strings, trees and sequences: Computer science and computational biology*. Cambridge, UK: Cambridge University Press. doi:10.1017/CBO9780511574931

Hazel, P. (2009). *PCRE - Perl Compatible Regular Expressions*. Retrieved July 1, 2010, from http://www.pcre.org/

Hearst, M. A., & Pedersen, J. O. (1996, August 18-22). Reexamining the cluster hypothesis: Scatter/gather on retrieval results. In *Proceedings of the 19th Annual International ACM SIGIR Conference on Research and Development in Information Retrieval*, Zurich, Switzerland.

Jansen, M. B. J., Spink, A., Bateman, J., & Saracevic, T. (1998). Real life information retrieval: A study of user queries on the Web. *ACM SIGIR Forum, 32*(1), 5–17. doi:10.1145/281250.281253

Joshi, A., & Jiang, Z. (2002). Retriever improving web search engine results using clustering. In Gangopadhyay, A. (Ed.), *Managing business with electronic commerce: Issues and trends*. Hershey, PA: Idea Group.

Maarek, Y. S., Fagin, R., Ben-Shaul, I. Z., & Pelleg, D. (2000). *Ephemeral document clustering for Web applications (No. RJ 10186)*. Armonk, NY: IBM.

Mook, N. (2005). *Microsoft tests search clustering*. Retrieved April 2, 2010, from http://www.eweek.com/ c/a/Windows/Microsoft-Tests-Search-Clustering/

Osinski, S., & Weiss, D. (2005). A concept-driven algorithm for clustering search results. *IEEE Intelligent Systems, 20*(3), 48–54. doi:10.1109/MIS.2005.38

Porter, M. F. (1997). *Readings in information retrieval: An algorithm for suffix stripping*. San Francisco, CA: Morgan Kaufmann.

Prado, H. A. d., & Ferneda, E. (2007). *Emerging technologies of text mining: Techniques and applications*. Hershey, PA: Idea Group. doi:10.4018/978-1-59904-373-9

Shen, D., Sun, J.-T., Yang, Q., & Chen, Z. (2006, December 18-22). Latent friend mining from blog data. In *Proceedings of the Sixth International Conference on Data Mining*, Hong Kong.

Sherman, C. (2004). *4th Annual Search Engine Awards*. Retrieved April 2, 2010, from http://searchenginewatch.com/ 3309841

Sherman, C. (2005). *Metacrawlers and metasearch engines - Search Engine Watch (SEW)*. Retrieved April 2, 2010, from http://searchenginewatch.com/ 2156241

Silverstein, C., Henzinger, M., Marais, H., & Moricz, M. (1998). *Analysis of a very large AltaVista query log*. Retrieved July 1, 2010, from http://www.hpl.hp.com/ techreports/Compaq-DEC/SRC-TN-1998-014.pdf

Spink, A., Wolfram, D., Jansen, M. B. J., & Saracevic, T. (2001). Searching the Web: The public and their queries. *Journal of the American Society for Information Science and Technology, 52*(3), 226–234. doi:10.1002/1097-4571(2000)9999:9999<::AID-ASI1591>3.0.CO;2-R

Ukkonen, E. (1995). On-line construction of suffix trees. *Algorithmica, 14*(3), 249–260. doi:10.1007/BF01206331

Wan, X. (2009). Combining content and context similarities for image retrieval. In M. Boughanem, C. Berrut, J. Mothe, & C. Soule-Dupuy (Eds.), *Proceedings of the 31st European Conference on Advances in Information Retrieval* (LNCS 5478, pp. 749-754).

Weiss, D., & Stefanowski, J. (2003, June 2-5). Web search results clustering in Poish: Experimental evaluation of Carrot. In *Proceedings of the New Trends in Intelligent Information Processing and Web Mining Conference*, Zakopane, Poland.

Wu, Y.-F. B., Rakthin, C., & Li, C. (2002, August 9-11). Summarizing search results with automatic tables of contents. In *Proceedings of the 8th Americas Conference on Information Systems*.

Wu, Y.-F. B., Shankar, L., & Chen, X. (2003, November 2-8). Finding more useful information faster from Web search results. In *Proceedings of the ACM CIKM International Conference on Information and Knowledge Management*, New Orleans, LA.

Yahoo. (2009). *Yahoo! Year in Review 2009 - Top 10 searches*. Retrieved July 1, 2010, from http://yearinreview.yahoo.com/ 2009/top10

Zamir, O., & Etzioni, O. (1999). Grouper: A dynamic clustering interface to Web search results. *Computer Networks, 31*(11-16), 1361-1374.

Zeng, H.-J., He, Q.-C., Chen, Z., Ma, W.-Y., & Ma, J. (2004, July 25-29). Learning to cluster Web search results. In *Proceedings of the 27th Annual International ACM SIGIR Conference on Research and Development in Information Retrieval*, Sheffield, UK.

Zhang, D., & Dong, Y. (2004). Semantic, hierarchical, online clustering of Web search results. In J. X. Yu, X. Lin, H. Lu, & Y. Zhang (Eds.), *Proceedings of the 6th Asia-Pacific Conference on Advanced Web Technologies and Applications* (LNCS 3007, pp. 69-78).

KEY TERMS AND DEFINITIONS

Meaningful Sentence Token: A sentence using Porter's stemming algorithm is a meaningful sentence token if the stop words or non-word tokens does not appear in this sentence.

MRR: Mean Reciprocal Rank.

PCRE: Perl Compatible Regular Expressions.

Porter Stemming Algorithm: An algorithm to reduce inflected words to their stem.

Snippet: It usually contains the title, the URL, and the fragment of search results summarized by remote search engines.

Suffix Tree: A compact trie containing all the suffixes of all the strings in the collection.

Web Crawler: A search program to fetch many relevant Web pages from several search engines simultaneously.

Chapter 13
Using Association Rules for Query Reformulation

Ismaïl Biskri
University of Quebec at Trois-Rivieres, Canada

Louis Rompré
University of Quebec at Montreal, Canada

ABSTRACT

In this paper the authors will present research on the combination of two methods of data mining: text classification and maximal association rules. Text classification has been the focus of interest of many researchers for a long time. However, the results take the form of lists of words (classes) that people often do not know what to do with. The use of maximal association rules induced a number of advantages: (1) the detection of dependencies and correlations between the relevant units of information (words) of different classes, (2) the extraction of hidden knowledge, often relevant, from a large volume of data. The authors will show how this combination can improve the process of information retrieval.

INTRODUCTION

The ever increasing importance of internet penetration and the growing size of electronic documents has made information retrieval a major scientific discipline in computer science, all while access to relevant information has become difficult, having become an informational tide that is occasionally reduced to nothing more than noise.

Information retrieval consists of selecting the documents or segments of text likely to respond to the needs of a user from a document database. This operation is carried out by way of digital tools that are sometimes associated with linguistic tools in order to refine the granularity of the results given certain points of view (Desclés & Djioua, 2009) or logical tools in question-answer format, or even tools proper to Semantic Web. However, we knowingly omit a presentation of the contributions of these linguistic methods, logical methods, and Semantic Web, due to a concern for

DOI: 10.4018/978-1-4666-0330-1.ch013

not weighing down the writing in this chapter, since we are primarily interested in the numerical side.

Formally, there are three main elements that stand out with regards to information retrieval:

1. The group of documents.
2. The information needs of the users.
3. The relevance of the documents or segments of text that an information retrieval system returns given the needs expressed by the user.

The last two aspects necessarily rely on the user. Not only does the user define their needs, but they also validate the relevance of the documents returned. To express their needs, a user formulates a query that often (but not always) takes the form of key words submitted to an information retrieval system based either on a Boolean model, a vector model, or a probabilistic model (Boughanem & Savoy, 2008). However, it is often difficult for a user to find key words that allow them to express their exact needs. In many cases, the user is confronted by a lack of knowledge on the subject of interest in their information search on the one hand, and on the other hand, by results that may be biased, as is the case with search engines on the Web. Thus, retrieving relevant documents from the first search is almost impossible. Therefore, there is a need to carry out a reformulation of the query either by using completely different key words, or by expanding the initial query with the addition of new key words (El Amrani et al., 2004).

In the case of expanding the query, two variants are possible:

1. The first is manual. The user chooses terms that are judged relevant in the documents that are also judged relevant in order to strengthen the query. This strategy is simple and computationally costs the least. However, it does not allow for a general view of the group of documents returned by the retrieval system considering their large numbers, and given

that it is not humanly possible. Quite often, the user only consults the first few documents, and only judges these few.

2. The second is semi-automatic. The terms added to the initial query are chosen by the user from a thesaurus (which may be constructed manually) or from similarity classes of documents and co-occurrences of terms obtained following a classification applied to a group of documents, obtained following the initial request as in clustering engines. A process of classifying textual data from web sites can help the user of a search engine to better identify the target site or to better formulate a query. Indeed, the lexical units which co-occur with the keywords submitted to the search engine can provide more details concerning the documents to which access is desired. However, the interpretation of similarity classes is a nontrivial exercise. The classes of similarity are usually presented as lists of words that occur together. These lists are often very large and their vocabulary is very noisy.

In this chapter we will show how maximal association rules can improve the semi-automatic reformulation of a query in order to access target documents more quickly.

MAXIMAL ASSOCIATION RULES

A brief survey of the literature on data mining (Amir & Aumann, 2005) teaches us that association rules allow for a representation of regularities in the co-occurrence of data (in the general sense of the term) in transactions, regardless of their nature. Thus, data that regularly appear together are structured in so-called association rules. An association rule is expressed as $X \Rightarrow Y$. This is read as follows: each time that X is encountered in a transaction, so is Y. There are also ways to measure the quality of these association rules: the measure of Support and the measure of Confidence.

The concept of association rule emerges mainly from the late 60 (Hajek et al., 1966) with the introduction of the concept of the support and the confidence. Interest in this concept was revived in the 90s through the work of Agrawal (Agrawal et al., 1993; Agrawal & Srikant, 1994) on the extraction of association rules in a database containing business transactions.

Curently, work is being done on how best to judge the relevance of association rules, as well as the quality of their interpretation (Vaillant & Meyer, 2006; Lallich & Teytaud, 2003; Cherfi & Toussaint, 2002), and their integration into information retrieval systems (Diop & Lo, 2007) and into classification processes for text mining (Cherfi & Napoli, 2005; Serp et al., 2008).

To illustrate association rules, consider the definition of the principal elements in the following example:

- Three transactions to regroup the data that co-occurs: T1:{A, 1, K}; T2:{M, L, 2}; T3:{A, 1, 2}
- Two sets to categorize the data: E1:{A, M, K, L}; E2:{1, 2}
- X and Y: two separate sets of information units: X:{A}; Y:{1}. $X \subseteq E1$ and $Y \subseteq E2$.

For a transaction Ti and a set of information units X, it is said that Ti supports X if $X \subseteq Ti$. The <u>Support of X</u>, noted as S(X), represents the number of transactions Ti such that $X \subseteq Ti$. In the case of transactions T1, T2 and T3, $S(X) = S(A) = 2$.

The Support of the association rule $X \Rightarrow Y$ is the number of transactions that contain X and Y. In the case of our example $S(X \Rightarrow Y) = S(A \Rightarrow 1) = 2$.

The Confidence of the association rule $X \Rightarrow Y$, noted as $C(X \Rightarrow Y)$, corresponds to the support of this association rule divided by the Support of X otherwise stated as $C(X \Rightarrow Y) = S(X \Rightarrow Y)/S(X)$.

In the case of our example, $C(X \Rightarrow Y) = C(A \Rightarrow 1) = 1$.

Despite their potential, association rules cannot be established in the case of less frequent associations. Thus, certain associations are ignored since they are not frequent. For example, if the word *printer* often appears with the word *paper* and less frequently with the word *ink*, it is very probable that the association between *printer* and *paper* will be retained to the detriment of the association between *printer, paper* and *ink*. In fact, the confidence criterion associated to the relationship between *printer, paper* and *ink* would be too low.

The maximal association rules, noted as $X \xrightarrow{max} Y$, compensate for this limitation. They are dedicated to the following general principle: each time that X appears alone, Y also appears. Note that X is reputed to appear alone if and only if for a transaction Ti and a category set Ej ($X \subseteq$ Ej), Ti $\cap$ Ej = X. In this case, X is maximal in Ti with regards to Ej and Ti M-Supports X. Note the M-Support of X by Smax(X), which thus represents the number of transactions Ti that M-Support X.

In the transaction T1, X is not alone with regards to E1 since T1 $\cap$ E1 = {A, K}. On the other hand, in the transaction T3, X is alone since T3 $\cap$ E1 = {A}.

The <u>M-support</u> of the maximal association $X \xrightarrow{max} Y$ noted as Smax($X \xrightarrow{max} Y$) represents the number of transactions that M-support X and support Y.

In the case of our example, only the transaction T3 M-supports X while T1 and T3 support Y. Consequently Smax ($A \xrightarrow{max} 1$) = 1.

The <u>M-confidence</u> noted as Cmax($X \xrightarrow{max} Y$) represents the number of transactions that M-support $X \xrightarrow{max} Y$ relative to the set of transaction that M-support $X \xrightarrow{max} E2$. The M-confidence of the rule $X \xrightarrow{max} Y$ is thus calculated by the formula Cmax($X \xrightarrow{max} Y$) = Smax($X \xrightarrow{max} Y$)/ Smax($X \xrightarrow{max} E2$).

In the association $A \xrightarrow{\text{max}} 1$, the M-Confidence is found to be equal to 0.5.

Finally, it should be noted that we must define the minimum thresholds for the M-support of a maximal association, as well as for its M-Confidence.

REFORMULATING A QUERY FOR A SEARCH ENGINE

We now describe the main elements of our Project, which is currently in progress. Although the project is still in its early stage, we have already designed and developed several components. Let us now have a look at the overall processing strategy which is organised in four main phases.

Phase 1: An original query is formulated and submitted to a standard search engine, such as Google. This original query is most probably sub-optimal, because of the reasons we mentioned. But that is exactly our starting point: we only expect the user to have a relatively good idea of what she is looking for, not too vague but not too precise either. In fact, we expect this original query to subsume the exact information she is hoping to find on the Web. In a subsequent step, the user will be given the opportunity to reconsider her query in the light of the search results returned for her original query. These search results are typically Web sites containing textual information. Of course, there is the possibility that the number of Web sites returned by the search engine will be very large. The user can set (in an arbitrary manner in the present state of our work) the maximum number of web sites to consider.

Phase 2: We consider that each Web site represents a text segment (domain of information). Thus, a set of Web sites forms a set of text segments which, taken altogether, can be looked at as a corpus. We then submit this corpus to the GRAMEXCO software (see next section) that will help us identify segments sharing lexical regularities. Assuming that such similarities correspond to content similarities between the Web sites, then related web sites will tend to be grouped in the same classes. In other words, the classes produced by the GRAMEXCO will tend to contain web pages about the same topic and, by the same token, will identify the lexical units that tend to co-occur within these topics. And this is where we have a first gain with respect to the original query: GRAMEXCO's results will provide a list of candidate query terms that are related to the user's original query and that will help her reformulate a new, more precise. The classes of Web pages obtained at the end of this phase are considered as contextual information, relative to the user's original query, that will allow her to reformulate her query (if necessary).

Phase 3: Words in classes of co-occurring words can act as carrier of more selective or complementary sense when compared with the keywords used in the original query. For instance, such words will be more selective when the original keywords are polysemous or when they have multiples usages in different domains; these new words will be complementary when they broaden the subset of the WWW implied by the original query. Now, *which of these new words should be picked by the user to reformulate her query?* It is at this stage that the process of extracting association rules comes up, the aim being to offer the user a tool to select the words that associate (as the most likely depending of the M-support and the M-confidence) with the keywords of the original query. The user will not have to go through all classes of words, which is a non-trivial task.

At that point the user can formulate an updated query from which she will obtain, through the processing already presented in phase #1 and #2 and #3, another bunch of classes containing similar Web pages, co-occurring words and maximal association rules. Again, at the end of this step, the user may discover new words that could guide her in a more precise reformulation of her query (Figure 1). It entirely up to the user to determine when the query reformulation iterative process will end.

IDENTIFICATION OF MAXIMAL ASSOCIATION RULES IN SIMILARITY CLASSES

The GRAMEXCO (n-GRAMs in the EXtraction of knowledge COnnaissance) is our software tool that has been developed for the numerical classification of multimedia documents (Rompré et al., 2008), particularly text documents. The numerical classification takes place by way of a numerical classifier.

The unit of information considered in GRAMEXCO is the n-gram of characters, the value of n being configurable.

The main objective is to provide the same processing chain, regardless of the corpus language, but with easily legible layouts in the presentation of the results. Recall that the use of n-grams of characters is not recent. It was first used in work by Damashek (1995) on text analysis and work by Greffenstette (1995) on language identification. The interest in n-grams today has been extended to the domains of images (Laouamer et al., 2006), and musicology, particularly in locating refrains (Patel & Mundur, 2005). A character n-gram is defined here as a sequence of n characters: bigrams for n=2, trigrams for n=3, quadrigrams for n=4, etc. For example, in the word *informatique* the trigrams are: *inf, nfo, for, orm, rma, mat, ati, tiq, iqu, que*. We justify our choice of n-gram of characters as the unit of information by: (1) The

cutting into sequences of n consecutive characters is possible in most languages. It is necessary that any approach can be adapted to several languages because of the "multilingual" nature of the web ; (2) The necessary tolerance for a certain ratio of deformation or flexion of lexical units. The functioning of GRAMEXCO is not entirely automatic. The choice of certain parameters is made by the user according to their own objectives. GRAMEXCO takes a raw (non indexed) text as input in UTF format. There are then three first main steps where the user can customize certain processes.

1. The first step consists of building a list of information units and information domains (parts of texts to be compared for similarity). From the two operations carried out simultaneously, we retrieve an output matrix with a list of the frequency of appearance of each information unit in each information domain. The information units may be in the form of bigrams, trigrams, quadrigrams, etc. Obtaining information domains passes through the process of text segmentation which may be done in words, phrases, paragraphs, documents, web sites or simply in sections of text delimited by a character or a string of characters. The choice of the size of the n-gram and the type of textual segment is determined by the user according to the goals of their analysis.

2. The second step consists of reducing the size of the matrix. This operation is indispensable given the important cost in resources that an overly large matrix would represent.

Thus, during this step, a list of n-grams undergoes some trimming that corresponds to:

*   The elimination of n-grams whose frequency is lower than a certain threshold or above another threshold,
*   The elimination of specific n-grams selected from a list (for example, n-grams

Figure 1. From the user's original query to a satisfying query

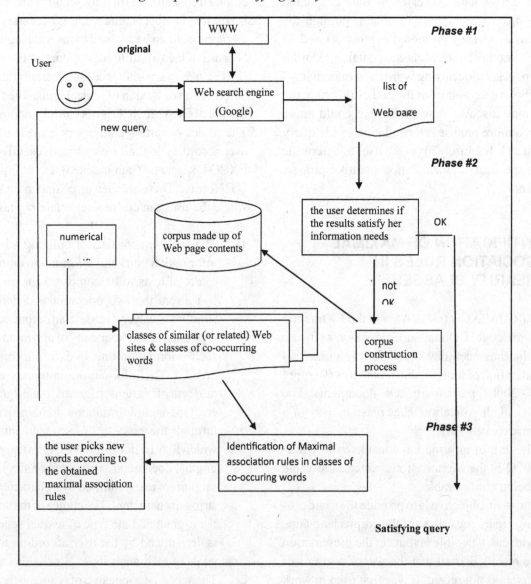

containing spaces or n-grams containing non-alphabetic characters),

- The elimination of certain n-grams considered as functional, such as suffixes.

3. In the third step, the classification process takes place. The classifier used here is the neural network ART (Meunier et al., 1997). The choice of classifier is not dictated by particular performance reasons since this is not our objective. We could have just as

easily chosen another classifier that would have admittedly yielded different results. Such variations continue to be the focus of research such as was presented in Turenne (2000).

At the end of this step, segments considered as similar by the classifier are regrouped into similarity classes. Furthermore, the lexicon of these segments forms the vocabulary of the classes to which they belong.

Whether the goal is lexical disambiguation, or searching for "conceptual" relationships, or information retrieval, etc., the interpretation of similarity classes is not a trivial task. Similarity classes are generally presented as lists of words that co-occur. These lists are quite frequently lengthy and despite organizational attempts, their vocabulary remains rather noisy.

The extraction process of maximal association rules proves to be one of the most interesting for permitting the discovery of lexical associations relevant to making an informed decision. The classes obtained at the end of the classification operation will be the transactions of the process that will allow the extraction of maximal association rules. Finally, in order for the process to be carried out, it must be supervised by the user who will have to first determine the word for which the most probable associations will be found.

To illustrate this step, let us posit the following scenario that will allow us to discover maximal association rules $X \xrightarrow{max} Y$ based on the results of a classification.

The input of the classification is a text in which the vocabulary represents a category set E1: {x, a, b, c, d, e, f}. The classification outputs classes with their respective lexicon: C1: {x, a, b, c}, C2: {a, c, d}, C3: {x, e, f, d}.

If the classes represent the transactions, the vocabulary of the input text represents a set E1 for categorizing the textual data (the vocabulary) in which set X is chosen.

This being established, the extraction process of maximal association rules is carried out in three steps:

Step 1: choice of set X: it is the user who chooses the lexicon from a list of elements of E1 that will represent X. Let us assume for explanatory purposes that X = {x}.

Step 2: identification of set Y and set E2: the identification of the category set E2 in which Y would be a subset largely depends on the set X selected and on the classes of which X is a subset.

In the case of our illustration, X is included in C1 and in C3. Y may therefore be a subset either of {a, b, c} or of {e, f, d}. In other words, Y may represent one of the following subsets: {a}, {b}, {c}, {a, b}, {a, c}, {b, c}, {a, b, c}, {e}, {f}, {d}, {e, f}, {e, d}. {f, d}, {e, f, d}.

The measures of M-Support and of M-Confidence will be calculated with regards to these different possible values of Y. An iterative process would allow for testing the set of these possibilities. We may, however, limit the number of iterations in order to avoid an overly prohibitive computational cost, for example, by fixing (via parameter) the cardinality of subset Y.

Let us suppose that Y = {a, c}; in order to construct E2, the respective categories of elements a and c must first be established. These are obtained by uniting classes that contain a (or c, respectively). Consequently, E2 = category(Y) = category{a, c} would be obtained by intersecting category(a) with category(c). Thus:

$$category(a) = \{a, b, c\} \, \grave{E} \, \{a, c, d\} = \{a, b, c, d\}$$

and

$$category(c) = \{a, b, c\} \, \grave{E} \, \{a, c, d\} = \{a, b, c, d\}$$

therefore:

E2 =

$$category(Y) = category(a,c) = category(a) \, Ç \, category(c) = \{a, b, c, d\}$$

Step 3: once the sets E1, E2, X and Y as well as the transactions have been clearly identified, the calculation of the measures may be made.

Consider the association $x \xrightarrow{\text{max}} a,c$. Using the classes C1: {x, a, b, c}, C2: {a, c, d}, C3: {x, e, f, d} as transactions, and E2 = {a, b, c, d}, it follows that M-support equals 1, since only Class 1 contains X= {x} and Y= {a, c}, and an M-confidence of 0.5 since two classes contain X while only one contains X and Y.

EXPERIMENTS

The whole of the theory presented here was implemented in C#. The results of the analyses are stored in XML databases. Furthermore, in the short term, we hope to graft a more practical visualisation module that would permit the one-step capture of the set of associations of a given lexical unit.

The following experiments were applied to four corpora (three of them are extracted from web sites). Two corpora are in French and two are in Arabic. The first corpus is a collection of interviews with directors of small and medium Quebecois businesses in order to learn about their perspectives on the notion of *risk*. The second corpus addresses the history of the reign of *King Hassan II* of Morocco. The third corpus (in Arabic) addresses the *Organisation of the Petroleum Exporting Countries* (OPEC). Finally, the fourth and final corpus (in Arabic) summarizes the biography of the American President, *Barack Obama*. The domains are sufficiently different to draw conclusions on the efficacy of the methodology. Note: we limit ourselves to show just maximal associations and scores of each association (M-support and M-Confidence). We assume that the reader is sufficiently familiar with the methods of classification and we do not need to show classes of similarities.

Experiment 1: the corpus, as mentioned, addresses the perspective of directors of small and medium Quebecois businesses with regards to the notion of *risk*. One of the constraints during the interviews was the obligation put on the directors to use the word *risk* when they deemed it necessary. In our experiments, this aspect is crucial since we need to know which words are associated to *risk* in the discourse of the directors.

Thus, despite the presence of noisy data such as, for example, *Pause* and *X*, which were intentionally inserted into the text for ethical reasons (*X* represents the name of people who were questioned) and to represent silences (*Pause*), interesting results were still obtained. For example:

- **Risk** $\xrightarrow{\text{max}}$ **Project** is an association that is found in 10 classes (M-support = 10) with a confidence of 100%.
- **Risk** $\xrightarrow{\text{max}}$ **Management** *Project* is an association that we find in 7 classes (M-support = 7) with a confidence of 70%. In other words, 30% of the time, it is possible to find the word *Risk* in classes where *Management* and *Project* did not occur together.
- **Risk** $\xrightarrow{\text{max}}$ **Management** is an association that we find in 7 classes (M-support = 7) with a confidence of 70%.
- **Risk** $\xrightarrow{\text{max}}$ **Product** is an association that we find in 5 classes (M-support = 5) with a confidence of 50%.

Table 1 summarizes the results obtained.

Experiment 2: For the second experiment, we chose a short 4-page text about the reign of *King Hassan II*. For this experiment, we intentionally chose to consider the cardinality of set Y equal to 1. For X = {*Hassan*}, we obtained the results summarized in Table 2.

Table 1. Results of the 1ˢᵗ experiment

X	Y	M-Support	M-Confidence
Risk	Decision, Product	2	20%
	Year	2	20%
	Markets, Price	2	20%
	Science	3	30%
	Interview, Studies	3	30%
	Function	4	40%
	Manner, Level	5	50%
	Product	5	50%
	Question	6	60%
	Interview, Risk	6	60%
	Level, X	7	70%
	Management	7	70%
	Management, Project	7	70%
	Project, Risks	8	80%
	X	10	100%
	Pause	10	100%
	Project, X	10	100%
	Pause, X	10	100%
	Project	10	100%

Table 2. Results of the 2ⁿᵈ experiment

X	Y	M-Support	M-Confidence
Hassan	Doctor	1	7.69%
	Professor	1	7.69%
	Spain	1	7.69%
	Tunisia	1	7.69%
	Spanish	2	15.38%
	Journalist	3	23.08%
	History	3	23.08%
	Prepare	3	23,08%
	Title	4	30,77%
	France	5	38.46%
	Politics	6	46.15%
	Year	7	53,85%
	King	8	61.54%
	Morocco	8	61.54%
	II	13	100%

Table 3. Results of the 3ʳᵈ experiment

X	Y	M-Support	M-Confidence
OPEC	Mechanisms	1	9,09%
	Paris, Countries	1	9,09%
	Creation, prices	2	18,18%
	Petroleum	3	27,27%
	Countries, members	3	27,27%
	Prices	3	27,27%
	Organisation, prices	3	27,27%
	Creation	3	27,27%
	Members	4	36,36%
	Summit	4	36,36%
	World	4	36,36%
	Organisation, country	4	36,36%
	Organisation	6	54,55%
	Countries	7	63,64%
	In	9	81,82%

Note that, for example, the association *Hassan* $\xrightarrow{\text{max}}$ *II* is very strong. Its confidence is 100%. Likewise for the associations *Hassan* $\xrightarrow{\text{max}}$ *Morocco* and *Hassan* $\xrightarrow{\text{max}}$ *King*. Although their confidence is only 61.54%, this is sufficiently high to consider the two associations as maximal.

Experiment 3: For the third experiment, we chose an Arabic text regarding the *Organisation of the Petroleum Exporting Countries* (OPEC), the goal being to evaluate the validity of the method with regards to the Arabic language. For the purposes of the experiment, we chose X = {OPEC}. Table 3 provides a summary of the results (a translation of the Arabic words is provided).

The results obtained indeed show the tight relationship between the acronym *OPEC* and the two words *Organisation* and *Countries*. However, there is an association with a relatively high M-support and M-confidence that relates *OPEC* to the function word *in*. We consider this association as being noise that may be eliminated if a post-process is added to suppress associations with function words.

Experiment 4: The corpus studied here is a short biography of President *Barack Obama*. The text is written in Arabic. Upon reading Table 4, it can be noted that in the text, *Obama* is strongly associated (M-confidence = 100%) to *Barack* even if the M-support is only 3. It is also noted that in terms of important values for M-confidence, *Obama* is strongly associated to the word pairs *origins, African* and *states, united*. However, there is a weak association of *Obama* with the function words *like* and *of* with an M-confidence of 66.67%. Once more, this type of noise can be eliminated with the addition of a post-process that would suppress the undesired associations.

In general, the results of our experiments seem interesting. The configuration of the classification

Table 4. Results of the 4th experiment

X	Y	M-Support	M-Confiance
Obama	candidate, last	1	33,33%
	arms	1	33,33%
	president life	1	33,33%
	Washington, American	1	33,33%
	like	2	66,67%
	of	2	66,67%
	states, united	2	66,67%
	origins, African	2	66,67%
	Barack	3	100,00%

results seems, in fact, to discourage users who found themselves helpless in the face of "voluminous word lists". The downstream use of the numerical classification of an extraction process of maximal association rules may help to better read the results of a classification.

In each experiment, the main topic of each document is represented in the extracted association rules, since the first keyword used. We can conclude, in general, that the maximum extraction rules capture all the main topics of the documents.

Maximal association rules are clues that can help the user to reformulate his query. The M-support and the M-confidence indicate lexical proximity in the documents, but also in the language used and in the areas covered by the textual content of the documents.

Initially, the query is limited to a single keyword: *risk, Hassan, OPEC,* or *Obama.* Now, to improve its results, the user can reformulate her queries by adding new keywords from those associated with them. For this, the user takes into account the M-support and the M-Confidence. But, of course, associations, M-support and M-confidence are only clues. The most important is that the user no longer has to go through all possible classes.

CONCLUSION

Information Retrieval is a relatively mature discipline. Much work has been presented to the scientific community (TREC, SIGIR, etc.). However, the difficulties in carrying out this work and the computational costs make it necessary to continue research in this domain.

In this chapter, we hope to have highlighted certain difficulties encountered in the information retrieval process. The goal was not to create an exhaustive list of these difficulties, but rather to demonstrate that possible elegant, user-oriented solutions exist. These solutions must be adapted to the information retrieval contexts: searching the Web, large documents, multilingualism, new users, etc.

Textual classification allows the identification of similar documents (where in the case of the internet, documents are web pages). It also allows us to highlight lexical co-occurrences, in particular, terms that co-occur with key words in a query. A user may then consider these terms to better tailor their query to their needs. However, the size of vocabularies makes the user's task an arduous one.

The process of extracting maximal association rules allows us to identify co-occurrences in classes, but also to attribute a score according to their relevance. These associations are clues to the disposition of the users that may thus reformulate their queries in an informed manner.

REFERENCES

Agrawal, R., Imielinski, T., & Swami, A. (1993). Mining association rules between sets of items in large databases. In *Proceedings of the ACM SIGMOD International Conference on Management of Data*, Washington, DC (pp. 207-216).

Agrawal, R., & Srikant, R. (1994). Fast algorithms for mining association rules in large databases. In *Proceedings of the 20th International Conference on Very Large Data Bases*, Santiago, Chile (pp. 487-499).

Amir, A., & Aumann, Y. (2005). *Maximal association rules: a tool for mining association in text*. Boston, MA: Kluwer Academic.

Boughanem, M., & Savoy, J. (2008). *Recherche d'information: états des lieux et perspectives*. Paris, France: Éditions Hermès/Lavoisier.

Cherfi, H., & Napoli, A. (2005). Deux méthodologies de classification de règles d'association pour la fouille de textes. In *Revue des nouvelles technologies de l'information*.

Cherfi, H., & Toussaint, Y. (2002). Adéquation d'indices statistiques à l'interprétation de règles d'association. In *Proceedings of Actes des 6èmes Journées internationales d'Analyse statistique des Données Textuelles*, Saint-Malo, France.

Damashek, M. (1995). Gauging similarity with n-grams: Language-independent categorization of text. *Science, 267*, 843–848. doi:10.1126/science.267.5199.843

Desclés, J. P., & Djioua, B. (2009). La recherche d'information par accès aux contenus sémantiques. In Desclés, J.-P. (Ed.), *Annotations automatiques et recherche d'informations. Le Priol Florence, Hermes: Traite IC2 -- serie Cognition et Traitement de l'information*.

Diop, C. T., & Lo, M. (2007). Intégration de règles d'association pour améliorer la recherche d'informations XML. In *Proceedings of Actes de la Quatrième conférence francophone en Recherche d'Information et Applications*, Saint-Étienne, France.

El Amrani, M. Y., Delisle, S., & Biskri, I. (2004). Agents personnels d'aide à la recherche sur le Web. In *Proceedings of Actes de la 11ème conférence de Traitement automatique des langues naturelles*. Rabat, Morocco: GEWEB.

Greffenstette, G. (1995). Comparing two language identification schemes. In *Proceedings of Actes des 3èmes Journées internationales d'Analyse statistique des Données Textuelles*, Rome, Italy.

Hajek, P., Havel, I., & Chytil, M. (1966). The GUHA method of automatic hypotheses determination. *Computing, 1*(4), 293–308. doi:10.1007/BF02345483

Lallich, S., & Teytaud, O. (2003). Évaluation et validation de l'intérêt des règles d'association. In *Revue des nouvelles Technologies de l'information*.

Laouamer, L., Biskri, I., & Houmadi, B. (2005). Towards an automatic classification of images: Approach by the n-grams. In *Proceedings of the World Multiconference on Systemics, Cybernetics and Informatics*, Orlando, FL.

Meunier, J. G., Biskri, I., Nault, G., & Nyongwa, M. (1997). Exploration de classifieurs connexionnistes pour l'analyse terminologique. In *Proceedings of Actes de la conférence Recherche d'Informations Assistée par Ordinateur*, Montréal, QC, Canada.

Patel, N., & Mundur, P. (2005). An N-gram based approach to finding the repeating patterns in musical. In *Proceedings of the European Conference on Internet and Multimedia Systems and Applications*, Grindelwald, Switzerland.

Rompré, L., Biskri, I., & Meunier, F. (2008). Text classification: A preferred tool for audio file classification. In *Proceedings of the 6th ACS/IEEE International Conference on Computer Systems and Applications*, Doha, Qatar (pp. 834-839).

Turenne, N. (2000). *Apprentissage statistique pour l'extraction de concepts à partir de textes (Application au filtrage d'informations textuelles)* (Unpublished doctoral dissertation). Université Louis-Pasteur, Strasbourg, France.

Vaillant, B., & Meyer, P. (2006). Mesurer l'intérêt des règles d'association. *Revue des Nouvelles Technologies de l'Information (Extraction et gestion des connaissances: État et perspectives)*.

KEY TERMS AND DEFINITIONS

GRAMEXCO: Our software for the classification of textual documents.

Maximal Association rules: A maximal association rule is represented by an association between two distinct sets of words, which according to a specific score, co-occurr regularly together. **Multilinguism:** Multilingualism is the ability of a computational method to deal with several different languages.

N-grams of characters: An n-gram of characters is a sequence of n successive characters.

Textual classification: The textual classification is the formal method, which groups together, in classes of similarities, similar documents. It also captures, in texts, patterns of co-occurrence of units of information.

To reformulate a query: Action that involves the use of new keywords in an information retrieval process.

Unit of information: A unit of information allows representing a text as a vector system. In our paper, the unit of information selected, is the n-gram of characters.

Chapter 14
Question Answering

Ivan Habernal
University of West Bohemia, Czech Republic

Miloslav Konopík
University of West Bohemia, Czech Republic

Ondřej Rohlík
University of West Bohemia, Czech Republic

ABSTRACT

Question Answering is an area of information retrieval with the added challenge of applying sophisticated techniques to identify the complex syntactic and semantic relationships present in text in order to provide a more sophisticated and satisfactory response to the user's information needs. For this reason, the authors see question answering as the next step beyond standard information retrieval. In this chapter state of the art question answering is covered focusing on providing an overview of systems, techniques and approaches that are likely to be employed in the next generations of search engines. Special attention is paid to question answering using the World Wide Web as the data source and to question answering exploiting the possibilities of Semantic Web. Considerations about the current issues and prospects for promising future research are also provided.

INTRODUCTION

This chapter is dedicated to question answering (QA). We start with the motivation section where we explain the benefits of QA over the traditional keyword-based search. We also discuss the implications of the changing electronic market with particular attention to the boom of Internet-capable portable devices. Later we also present the commercial considerations of QA systems.

The main part of this chapter sketches the landscape of the state-of-the-art QA systems – both research prototypes and commercial products. We cover all types of QA systems and describe systems of different scopes (open and closed domain systems) as well as of different levels of semantic processing (deep and shallow systems). We address various techniques used across all the systems with the emphasis on natural language processing and various statistical methods.

The objective of this chapter is to cover the technologies that are likely to be applied in the

DOI: 10.4018/978-1-4666-0330-1.ch014

next generation search engines. For this reason we focus on two areas – open-domain QA systems operating on unstructured text data (Web) and QA in the context of the semantic web.

Towards the end of this chapter we identify the problems and challenges that emerge as the current hot topics in the research community and/or have been reported as serious issues from the commercial sector.

OVERVIEW AND BACKGROUND

Question answering (QA) addresses the problem of finding answers to questions posed in natural language.

Traditionally the QA system is expected to provide one concise answer to the user's query. For the question "When did Thomas Jefferson die?" the ideal answer might be "July 4, 1826" with "Thomas Jefferson died on the Fourth of July, 1826" being another possibility. The exact way an answer is presented depends on the context and the application.

More formally, question answering is the task which when given a query in natural language, aims at finding one or more concise answers in the form of sentences or phrases. Due to its high requirements in terms of precision and conciseness, question answering is often seen as a sub-discipline of information retrieval (IR). Compared to IR, QA poses the added challenge of applying techniques developed in the field of natural language processing (NLP), such as the identification of the complex syntactic and semantic relationships present in the text.

QA systems even move a step further in natural language understanding with respect to standard IR systems (which have typical representatives in Web search engines) because they generally do not respond to a question but to a query in a form of a set of words where syntactic structure is ignored. Moreover, Web search engines do not return an answer, but rather a set of documents which are considered relevant to the query, i.e., which it is hoped will be useful to the user. Still, IR technology remains a fundamental building block of QA, in particular for those QA systems that use Web as their data collection (Quarteroni, 2007).

Motivation For Question Answering

Question answering (QA) is beneficial to users since it may offer to user experience which is better than that of traditional search engines – both in terms of relevance of provided information (single well targeted answer rather then larger amount of information that user has to further process) and of quality of user interface (user only say or write one single sentence with no need to specify various options).

In case of delivering relevant information, QA systems benefit from advanced techniques for analysis of user queries which are capable of aggregation of partial results using mathematical operations, advanced comparisons, processing of temporal information and others. Moreover QA systems operating on Semantic Web can answer queries very precisely by transformation of questions to set of conditions used to generate logic query to knowledge base.

To highlight the benefits for user experience let us demonstrate the usability of QA systems vis-à-vis traditional keyword-based search engines with the following Web search example.

First, consider a scenario where the answer to a question is sought by a regular Internet user using a desktop computer. For many factual questions it is easy to find the answer very quickly using a conventional keyword-based search engine such as Google™. In this case the user is presented with the search engine result page (SERP) where the query keywords are highlighted. By simply scrolling down the page and skimming the text close to keywords the user may often get the feeling of what is the right answer. Such a feeling is usually confirmed by random or deliberate clicks to a few top-ranked pages and assessment of the credibility of the presented information. This operation may take anywhere from as little as a few seconds to as long as a few minutes depending on whether the SERP provides enough trusted and/or easy to spot results.

Second, consider a user without access to a desktop computer. Instead let us assume a user of a phone or a personal digital assistant (PDA). The SERP as displayed on such a device shows much less information compared to a desktop device, which makes skimming the page cumbersome. Additionally, such devices are usually much slower then desktop computers, often harder to operate, and their lower bandwidth makes opening a few additional pages to confirm the credibility of an answer a rather painful experience. Arguably such users would appreciate a single sentence answer comprising just a few dozen bytes.

Users of cell phones with no Internet connection capability are left with SMS messaging only and have virtually no other option than to rely on single sentence answers. An extreme case would be users that prefer or must (e.g., due to impaired vision) make a regular phone call to a speech-based QA system.

With the current prevalence of the Internet connection capable mobile devices, the feature of being user-friendly (Budiu & Hielsen, 2009) is becoming a more and more important aspect of the web search experience. We truly believe that user-friendliness of QA will be an essential competitive advantage of many future search engines.

Terms and Definitions

Question answering (QA) is the task which, given a query in natural language, aims at finding one or more concise answers in the form of sentences or phrases (Quarteroni, 2007).

QA is situated at the confluence of a large number of related areas (Maybury, 2004) including information retrieval (Gaizauskas, Hepple, & Greenwood 2004), natural language processing (Ravin, Prager, & Harabagiu 2001; de Rijke &

Figure 1. Classification of question answering systems

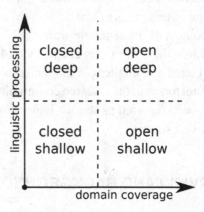

Webber 2003), information extraction, and knowledge representation and reasoning (Harabagiu & Chaudhri 2002).

QA requires much more complex natural language processing techniques than other types of IR systems such as document retrieval. Natural language QA systems are thus often regarded as the next step beyond traditional Web search engines.

In general, QA systems are categorized according to two criteria – the nature of data on which they operate and the level of semantic processing involved. These two criteria are orthogonal to each other (Figure 1).

In terms of the information source on which QA systems operate they are divided into closed-domain and open-domain.

Closed-domain QA deals with *questions within a specific domain* and can be seen as an easier task because natural language processing can exploit domain-specific knowledge frequently formalized in ontologies.

Open-domain QA, often called ODQA (Hori et al., 2003), appeared in the late 90's and soon became the standard in QA. In ODQA, the range of possible questions is not constrained; hence a much heavier challenge is placed on systems, as it is impossible to pre-compile all of the possible semantic structures appearing in a text (Quarteroni, 2007).

Recent research has moved away *from closed-domain* systems tailored to specific domains which (thanks to the possibility of using well-tuned but task specific question analysis techniques) do not offer enough scientific challenge, *towards open-domain* systems that can only rely on general knowledge which are very popular among researchers today.

In terms of methods and techniques the systems are divided by the level of understanding of the question into shallow and deep methods.

Shallow methods use local features for natural language processing. Local features are features that do not require sophisticated manipulating with context or building complex parsing structures. They include e.g., locating interesting snippets of text, detecting predefined patterns, matching with a set of templates or computing similarity to a defined set of questions. The shallow methods usually combine more local features together with the help of simple but robust statistics. The advantage of shallow methods is their robustness and reliability at the cost of failing to understand more complicated questions.

Deep methods on the contrary use more sophisticated linguistic processing to extract and construct the answer. They usually use context dependent analysis that may provide deeper insight into the user question but due to their high complexity they may fail more often than shallow methods.

The technical aspects of these standard approaches are discussed in detail in the next sections along with their various combinations, extensions and applications.

Forum for QA and Evaluation Framework

Before 1999 there was no dedicated forum to exchange ideas, positions and results in QA. Authors published their findings at various IR and NLP conferences and in journals, but it was only with the TREC-QA campaigns where researchers found their platform.

The Text REtrieval Conference (TREC) organizes competitive tasks and comprehensive evaluation for natural language systems. From 1999 to 2007 TREC offered a QA track in which the task was to answer specific questions over a closed corpus. Apart from becoming a competition platform among QA systems it also has had a big impact on motivating their development. By defining new tasks for each year it also de facto formed the direction of research in QA.

Each year, TREC provided large-scale evaluation on increasingly difficult QA tasks, comparing systems from a growing community of research groups against a common metric, and raising the standards for the state of the art in QA (Bilotti, 2004).

The progress of the TREC conferences is well covederd in Dang et al. (2007). Since its inception in TREC-8 in 1999, the QA track has steadily expanded both the type and difficulty of the questions asked. The first editions of the track focused on factoid questions. Whereas in TREC8, followed by TREC9 and 10, the QA system had to return the top 5 answers to the question, in TREC11 the response was limited to only one exact answer. In the following years (TREC12 and TREC13), the answer could be formulated as a string not exceeding 250 bytes. Moreover, systems competing in the TREC tasks must take into account other practical issues, as noted in (Harabagiu et al., 2003). These are *a large document collection* consisting of thousands of documents, *answer redundancy* because more sources can contain an answer for a certain question and *supplemental information needs*, when a document contains only a piece of the required answer.

The task in the TREC 2003 QA track contained list and definition questions in addition to factoid questions (Voorhees, 2003). A list question required different answer instances that satisfy the information need to be found in multiple documents, such as *List the names of whisky brands*. A definition question asks for explanatory information about a particular person or thing. Later the test sequence of questions was augmented with an explicit *"Other"* question, interpreted as *Tell me other interesting things about this as I don't know enough to ask directly*.

In TREC 2004, the target of questions could be a person, organization, or thing. Events were added as possible targets in TREC 2005, requiring that answers must be temporally correct. In TREC 2006, that requirement for sensitivity to temporal dependencies was made explicit in the distinction between locally and globally correct answers, so that answers for questions phrased in the present tense must not only be supported by the supporting document (locally correct), but must also be the most up-to-date answer in the document collection (globally correct).

The main task in the TREC 2007 QA track repeated the question series format, but with a significant change in the genre of the document collection. Instead of just news agency articles, the document collection contained also blog articles. Mining blogs for answers introduced significant new challenges in at least two aspects that are very important for real-world QA systems: 1) being able to handle language that is not well-formed and 2) dealing with discourse structures that are more informal and less reliable than newswire. Based on its successful application in TREC 2006 (Dang et al., 2007), the nugget pyramid evaluation method became the official evaluation method for the *"Other"* questions in TREC 2007.

The primary goal of the TREC 2007 main task (and what distinguished it from previous TREC QA tasks) was the introduction of blog text to encourage research in natural language processing (NLP) techniques that would handle ill-formed language and discourse structures. However, because most of the TREC 2007 questions requested factual information, they did not specifically test systems' abilities to process blog text and as a consequence answers still came predominantly from the newswire documents in the collection.

Because blogs naturally contain a large amount of opinions, it was decided by the organizers that the QA task for 2008 should focus on questions that ask about people's opinions and that there would be no factoid questions in later years (Dang et al., 2007).

Hence the TREC 2007 was the last QA track to date. In later years the focus shifted from QA towards (1) opinion seeking in the blogosphere with a larger collection of blogs and a much longer timespan allowing the temporal and chronological aspects of blogging to be investigated (Ounis et al., 2008) and (2) entity-related search on Web data where the entity is a person, product, or organization with a homepage where the homepage is considered to be the representative of that entity on the web (Balog et al., 2010).

The evaluation of QA system abilities has moved towards more complicated tasks, incorporating procedural questions, geographic reasoning (Santos & Cabral, 2010), multilingual documents (Penas et al., 2010) or speech processing (Comas & Turmo, 2009). Since the previous TREC tasks were oriented mostly towards newswire collections, the CLEF2009 forum decided to study whether the current state-of-the-art QA systems, mostly fine-tuned to the previous tasks, are able to adapt to a new domain and to move the QA field to more realistic scenarios. Furthermore, the CLEF 2009 firstly offered a multilingual fully-aligned question/answer corpus in eight languages (Bulgarian, English, French, German, Italian, Portuguese, Romanian, and Spanish) to allow a comparison among systems working in different languages. The corpus contains five types of questions: factoid, definition, reason, purpose and procedure. Detailed descriptions of the tasks and evaluation of the results can be found in Penas et al. (2010).

In TREC tasks, the standard measure for evaluating the performance of a QA system is the *mean reciprocal rank* (MRR). MRR is computed as follows: after putting the question into the QA system, a list of candidate answers is returned. The reciprocal rank for a given query q is $1/p(a)$, where *p(a)* is the position of the first correct answer within the returned list. If there is no such answer, the reciprocal rank is zero. The whole system is then measured as the mean of reciprocal ranks computed for each query.

Despite the overall positive effect of TREC to QA some criticized (De Boni 2004) the evaluation of the TREC-QA track pointing out the lack of a proper definition of the correct answer – even in the case of factoid questions. For example, *What river is called Big Muddy?* For which the only accepted answer was Mississippi, although Mississippi River could also be considered as acceptable.

Another evaluation method may be used if a particular QA system requires a complete list of correct answers. In such cases, the concepts of *precision* (P), *recall* (R) and *F-measure* (F) are used as it is common in IR. Let C be the number of correctly returned answers, N the total number of answers and T the number of all correct answers that should have been returned. Given precision $P = \dfrac{C}{N}$ and recall $R = \dfrac{C}{T}$ the F-measure is computed as $F = \dfrac{2PR}{P + R}$ The general $F\beta$ measure can be expressed as $F\beta = \dfrac{\left(1 + \beta^2\right)PR}{\beta^2 PR}$ In TREC2003, the Beta value was 5, indicating that recall was considered five times more important than precision (Voorhees, 2003).

STATE-OF-THE-ART QUESTION ANSWERING

In this section we provide overview of currently available technology used in QA. First we describe general architecture of current QA systems, later we also discuss niche areas. Special attention is paid to systems operating on text data in open domain because these are the most common, the most advanced and also the most appealing for

commercial sector. For these reasons they are the key candidate technology to be employed in the next generation of search engines which is the focal point of this book.

General Architecture of QA Systems

For a better understanding of the capabilities of a particular QA system, it is necessary to explore the types of questions it can handle. Generally, the two basic categories are *factoid* and *non-factoid questions* (sometimes simply called *why-questions*). Typical examples of factoid questions are "What currency is used in Ireland?", "When Thomas Jefferson died?" or "Who was the president of the United States in 1961?" These questions (simple, but not necessarily) can be answered by a short answer, e.g., date, name, location, etc. (so-called *named entity*) or by a list of named entities. On the other hand, non-factoid questions may ask for reason, manner, method or definition and thus they require a more detailed explanation in the answer, e.g., a sentence or a paragraph.

Recently, attention to QA systems dealing with why-questions has risen. Although this type of question is not very frequent (e.g., 4.7% in the collection described by Hovy, 2002), the research in this field is challenging since existing systems are not able to cope with this task using methods for factoid questions (Maybury, 2006). Moreover, advanced NLP techniques are essential for non-factoid question processing, both for understanding the question and answer extraction and formulation. Whereas factoid questions ask for a single piece of information and thus the answer is likely to be found in the documents explicitly, non-factoid question processing may involve semantic analysis and reasoning. The work of Verberne (2010) contains an extensive discussion about the issues of why-questions.

Moldovan et al. (2003) proposed a classification of questions and the appropriate QA systems into five classes according to their complexity.

Figure 2. Basic architecture of QA systems

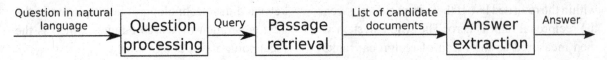

- **Class 1:** covers the already mentioned factoid questions. The answer is presented directly in the retrieved text, it can be its morphological variant, or it can be extracted after simple keyword manipulation.
- **Class 2:** QA system capabilities enable simple reasoning mechanism, such as semantic alternations or world knowledge axioms. These additional capabilities are necessary to answer questions that do not have a direct answer in the data collection.
- **Class 3:** in the proposed classification covers QA systems which are able to fuse the answer from different documents.
- **Class 4:** represents the interactive QA systems.
- **Class 5:** covers QA systems capable of analogical reasoning or speculative question answering.

Although this formal QA system classification has not been widely accepted (most of QA systems presented in literature do not use this classification), it shows various levels of complexity and issues one has to face during QA system design and development. According to this classification, factoid questions were represented by only 67.5% in TREC8, TREC9 and TREC10, as described in Moldovan et al. (2003). Over 27% were covered by questions of class 2 (requiring simple reasoning).

Regardless of the above mentioned query classification, most QA systems are built using a similar architecture. It provides a simple one-way dataflow and consists of three main modules: *question classification* (or question processing, query construction, etc.), *passage retrieval* (document retrieval) and *answer extraction* (answer formulation, Figure 2).

Some QA systems use finer module subdivision (i.e., 10 independent modules in Moldovan et al. (2003) or 5 modules in Moriceau and Tannier (2010) but the basic structure remains. This modularity allows switching among particular implementations of certain parts of the system, as done for example with the passage retrieval module, where many systems use various off-the-shelf IR applications. The one-way data flow is also not mandated. Again Moldovan et al. (2003) tested architecture with feedbacks, resulting in a performance boost.

Question Processing

Generally, the purpose of this part of a QA system is to process the user questions expressed in natural language and transform it to any form which is suitable for the passage retrieval (PR) and answer extraction (AE) components. Although this step heavily depends on the target language and on particular semantic representation of the query, many QA systems use similar approach. Traditionally, two main outputs are produced by the question extraction component: the *expected answer type* and the *query*. The expected answer type describes what kind of information is being sought. The query usually contains question keywords used to retrieve documents with potential answers.

This step usually involves many NLP techniques for preprocessing, such as *tokenization, POS* (part-of-speech) tagging, *NER* (named entity recognition) or *syntactic parsing*. Some QA systems often attempt to extract the semantics from a sentence (Jurafsky & Martin, 2008) following the traditional human-computer dialogue best practices. In contrast, many QA systems do not require the full semantics (Verberne et al., 2010), work only with a so-called *bag of words* and convert the question into a query by simply removing stop words and punctuation. A purely syntactic approach to question processing is used e.g., in Moriceau and Tannier (2010) which uses a robust parser for English and French.

Question Classification

Although *question classification* and *expected answer extraction* slightly differ in their meaning, it usually describes the same task in most QA systems. Usually, its purpose is to determine the type of information which is required by the user. The expected answer type can be used not only as a constraint in limiting returned results in passage retrieval, but it is also important for answer extraction modules. For example, the question *"Where was Ernest Hemingway born?"* may be classified as *place, state* or *city*, depending on the granularity of question types, as described below.

The question types may be a simple set (e.g., date, person, location, list, etc.) or they can be formed into a more complicated *taxonomy*. Only 5 types of question are considered by Moriceau and Tannier (2010), which are factoid (typically who, when, where questions), definition (e.g., "What is"), boolean (yes or no answer), complex question (why or how) and list. A more detailed classification, which involves also the question semantics rather than a simple question type, is introduced in (Quarteroni & Manandhar, 2008) where an 11 question type taxonomy was designed, consisting of e.g., human, geographical expression, organization, or temporal expression types for factoid questions and e.g., list of items, definition/description, or procedure for non-factoid questions. In Buscaldi et al. (2010), a three-level taxonomy is proposed. On the first level, there are four main types: name, definition, date and quantity. On the second and the third level the types are more fine-grained, e.g., person, title, location, or acronym extend the name type on the second level, location is further divided to country or city on the third level.

Although named entity taxonomy is mostly flat (set of classes), hierarchical taxonomies allow more flexibility in matching answer type since an entity can be answered by its descendant entity (e.g., answer type *city* can be a valid for question type *place*, given such taxonomy). There is not a strong agreement whether richer taxonomy leads to less accuracy as claimed by e.g., Kurata et al. (2004) or not as shown by Laurent et al. (2005) with named entity topology consisting of 86 classes. In any case, answer type ambiguity due to overlapping types is an important issue. It can be handled either by allowing multiple type association or by applying the most specific type that covers all possible options (Verberne, 2010).

Assigning an input question to a question class can be viewed as an ordinary classification problem. Thus, many QA systems use standard machine learning algorithms for this task. In Zhang and Lee (2003) Support Vector Machines (SVM) were used with lexical, syntactical and semantic features. The SNoW model was used by Li and Roth (2006). Other features suitable for question classification were examined by Quarteroni and Manandhar (2008), including combination of bag-of-words, bigrams, trigrams, so-called bag-of-Named Entities and POS n-grams. A neural network-based classifier was used by Comas and Turmo (2009) where a rich set of lexical, syntactic and semantic features was fed to a multi-class perceptron classifier.

In contrast to the machine learning approach, answer types are also often identified using patterns or heuristics. For example, Harabagiu et al. (2003) use a list of hard-coded rules to determine the required answer type from the output of syntactic parsing over the input question. Another pattern-based classifier, where the patterns are derived by analysis of the CLEF QA test set, is presented in Buscaldi et al. (2010). These patterns are formed in a three level hierarchy and they are based on simple regular expression. Other similar approaches, e.g., Voorhees (2001b) search for specific pronouns and trigger words in order to extract the answer type.

Query Formulation

As mentioned previously, one of the main tasks of a question processing module is to produce a query which will be fed as input to a search engine. A query can be viewed as a set of keywords or phrases which describe the user's information needs. In a traditional information retrieval system, keywords are more or less lexically related to the expected content of the returned documents (Manning et al., 2008). When dealing with a natural language question, there can be a wider stylistic gap between the input and the document containing an answer, especially when answering why-questions (as pointed out by Soricut & Brill, 2006). Therefore, more attention must be paid to query formulation in order to improve the precision and recall of the passage retrieval system. The simplest approach, yet seldom used, e.g., in Verberne et al. (2010) and Correa et al. (2009), is to tokenize the input question and to remove stop-words and punctuation. For example, the question *"When was Franz Kafka born?"* would be transformed into *"{Franz, Kafka, born}"*. Of course, this naive approach is far from being usable for questions which have an answer expressed using synonyms or for morphologically rich languages, where the answer can use the same words but their morphological categories differ. Another reason for using query reformulation is that the search engine yields better results if the query is formulated lexically similar to the answer and there is an exact match of phrases (Soricut & Brill, 2006).

To deal with this issue, *query expansion*, *query reformulation* or *query transformation* techniques are used. As noted in the previous section, many QA systems use syntactic parsing and the semantics or the question keywords are extracted subsequently. To achieve a higher recall, the query can be enriched with morphological or semantic alternations of the keywords. This can include e.g., keyword, lemma (using a morphological analyser) or keyword synonyms (using for example WordNet). This approach is used by Molodovan et al. (2003). For example, the previously mentioned question could be extended to *"{Franz, Kafka, born, give birth, deliver, bear}"* using a simple synonym dictionary.

The query reformulation technique is based on identifying various ways of expressing answer context given a natural language question (Kosseim & Yousefi, 2008). It uses an assumption that the query can be expressed by a pattern, that could be formulated into a potential answer in the retrieved documents. For example, the question *"When Franz Kafka died?"* would be transformed into *"Franz Kafka died in <year>"* (expecting an year instance within the resulting text) using a kind of source pattern saying: *transform 'when <person> died?' into '<person> died in <year>'*. One of the best results in the TREC10 task by Soubbotin and Soubbotin (2001) was achieved by hand-written reformulation patterns. On the other hand, Brill et al. (2001) used simple automatic permutations of the keywords for the same task, still getting reasonable results. This was mainly because of a large document collection, in which the answer can be found more than once and in various forms. Despite the fact that pattern-based query reformulation techniques can yield good performance when tailored to a specific language and domain, their main drawback is the high manual-development effort and a lack of portability.

Although many QA systems use some sort of pattern for query reformulation, more advanced NLP techniques were also involved. A full semantic representation of the question and the answer was tried by Mollá (2009). Their system creates a graph-based logical form and the question answering is based on matching this graph-based representation. Nevertheless, producing such a representation is a very error-prone task. Thus, semantic features are often reduced to named entities, as e.g., in Kosseim and Yousefi (2008). Full semantic question understanding using syntax parsing and syntax patterns are also very popular in QA systems, as e.g., in Bouma (2006) and Hartrumpf (2005), among others. For example of syntax processing see Section "Lightweight Syntactic Processing" later in this chapter.

A pure statistical approach to query formulation was introduced by Soricut and Brill (2006). They observed that question reformulation does not have a positive impact when answering non-factoid questions, mostly due to the many possible ways of expressing the answer. For question transformation, they proposed a chunking technique based on co-occurrence statistics. Having a corpus of FAQ (frequently asked questions), they trained a statistical chunker on the answer set of the corpus in order to learn 2 and 3-word collocations. The difference between their chunker and a segmentation using a parser is that the phrases obtained from the chunker are not necessarily syntactic constituents. An example of chunking taken from Soricut and Brill (2006): *"How do herbal medications differ from conventional drugs?"* is segmented into these chunks *{"How do", "herbal medications", "differ from", "conventional", "drugs"}*.

Passage Retrieval

The basic assumption of QA systems operating on unstructured data is that the required answer is presented in a particular set of documents. The scale of such a set can vary from hundreds of documents (e.g., for intranets or closed-domain QA systems) up to the whole Web. For indexing and searching within such a quantity of documents, standard IR techniques are adopted by many QA systems. A comprehensive introduction to IR applications in QA as well as a detailed explanation of many state-of-the-art algorithms can be found in Manning et al. (2008).

The simplest approaches to passage retrieval over the Web use existing commercial search engines, such as Google™, Yahoo™ or MSN-Search™. A significant advantage of such an approach is that these engines mostly use cutting edge technologies for indexing and retrieval and also they have a large part of the indexable Web available. Systems using passage retrieval based on commercial search engines are described e.g., in Quarteroni and Manandhar (2008), Soricut and Brill (2006), Ifteen et al. (2010), and Tannier and Moriceau (2010).

On the other hand, question answering is a specialized task which differs from traditional IR in many aspects (among other things, in looking for keywords to obtain relevant passages instead of directly searching for an answer). Furthermore, major search engine companies make their profits through advertisements on their search pages and they do not offer any API of their services (i.e., the AJAX Search API from Google is not a standard web-service based API). To avoid these limitations, some QA systems adapt open-source search engines or commercial standalone search engine libraries. For example Apache Lucene (http://lucene.apache.org/) is used in Moriceau and Tannier (2010) Gloeckner and Pelzer (2009), and as a baseline in Buscaldi et al. (2010), or Lemur (http://www.lemurproject.org/) in Verberne et al. (2011).

When adapting a search engine, attention must be paid to proper selection of objects for indexing (words, paragraphs, etc.). As mentioned first in Harabagiu et al. (2003), three forms of indexing can be performed in QA systems. *Term or word-based indexing*, in its advanced form, includes multi-word term identifiers, document identifiers, and morphological, syntactic or semantic variants of the term, as used in Ferret et al. (2001). *Conceptual indexing* involves a conceptual taxonomy that is built from the document collection and linked to the word-based index (Harabagiu et al., 2003). *Paragraph indexing* is based on the observation that the possible answer is likely to be located in the paragraph surrounding the keywords. It was implemented e.g., in Harabagiu et al. (2000b).

For the searching procedure over the index, many passage retrieval components use the standard Boolean model (e.g., Manning et al., 2008), Vector Space Model (e.g., Manning et al., 2008), or Okapi BM25 (Beaulieu et al., 1997). From 11 participants in CLEF 2009, two competing systems used the Boolean model, whereas the rest mainly used VSM or Okapi (Penas et al., 2009). Unfortunately, the report does not show any apparent influence of the chosen model on the overall performance.

An extension of a traditional passage retrieval model towards QA specific information retrieval is presented in Buscaldi et al. (2010). They present a passage retrieval system based on an n-gram model (clustered keyword positional distance model). In this system, an n-gram is a sequence of n adjacent terms extracted from a sentence or a question. The system is based on the premise that in a large document collection, question n-grams should appear more frequently near the possible answer. The answer coverage was compared with traditional IR methods (using Lucene and IR-n) (Llopis & Vicedo, 2002), obtaining a 20% improvement on the CLEF 2005 test set.

The IR component may also be adapted to a specialized application. For example, to overcome possible drawbacks which can appear when dealing with automatic transcripts such as in CLEF 2009 QAST task (Comas & Turmo, 2009), an IR engine relying on phonetic similarity can be employed as in Comas and Turmo (2009). It uses pattern matching algorithms to search for small sequences of phonemes (the keyword) in a larger sequence (the documents) using a measure of sound similarity.

Ranking

The list of documents or passages returned by an IR module is often sorted by IR score which is computed by the used retrieval model. How-ever, the document with the highest score is not necessarily the document containing the desired answer. This is obviously due to the IR approach to passage retrieval itself. As mentioned before, strictly speaking, the traditional IR engines are not intended for question answering. Therefore, further *ranking* or *re-ranking* of the obtained passages is essential (note that the term *ranking* is used both in IR and QA fields; in the rest of this section we will use this term in the QA context). Another reason for splitting the answer finding process into two parts, IR and ranking, is that IR operate on the whole document collections (which is mostly usually very large) and serves as a filter for selecting appropriate answer candidates that are subsequently subject to ranking. Since the document set retrieved by the IR module is then limited, ranking can involve more heavy-weight algorithms e.g., for NLP.

Whereas passage retrieval often uses existing off-the-shelf engines and algorithms, ranking modules are mostly application dependent. However, there are some common directions of research in candidate ranking, such as syntactic or semantic patterns, machine learning techniques, classifiers, etc.

A pattern based re-ranking approach is presented in Kosseim and Yousefi (2008). In this work, the patterns are based on syntax and semantics and using the initial hand-crafted set of patterns, more patterns are generated automatically. After retrieving the top 200 candidates, the re-ranking is performed by measuring the similarity between semantic concept relations in the question and semantic concept relations in the candidate answers. The main drawbacks of this approach are that (1) the system requires a large collection in order to learn the patterns automatically and (2) it yields sufficient results only for factoid question because corresponding answers are expressed by a simpler pattern than is the case for non-factoid (why, how) questions. Furthermore, the system was developed and tested on the same type of corpus (TREC11) thus the performance result is likely to be much lower when adapted to different domain.

The hand-crafted syntactic rules are the core of another system introduced in Moriceau and Tannier (2010). The set of 100 top documents is processed by a syntactic parser. Subsequently, about 40 rewriting rules are applied to obtain syntactic relations. Ranking is based on 9 complex heuristic rules which have been determined empirically. However, as conceded by the authors, this purely syntactic approach has some substantial disadvantages, such as the assumption that the documents are syntactically correct, or poor system speed (30 s per question) due to comprehensive parsing. This makes it unusable for practical deployment.

A ranking method based on machine learning is presented in Verberne et al. (2011). The authors aim at finding an optimal ranking function, having a set of features and various machine learning techniques (the problem is described as *learning-to-rank*). In QA systems, the list of answers can be considered as a list of items described by a set of features and a class label, which determines the relevance of the item. The relevance is a binary function (the answer is either relevant or irrelevant) and the goal is to rank the correct answers higher than the incorrect answers. Generally, the learning-to-rank can be viewed as supervised learning. The ranking function is trained using the given examples in the training stage to apply the ordered ranking in the testing stage.

As for all machine learning applications, the choice of features is difficult also in QA ranking. In Verberne et al. (2009), and later used in Verberne et al. (2011), a set of 37 features is used by the ranking module. The first feature is the score returned by the IR engine. Further, syntactic features (such as subject, verb), WordNet expansion features, cue phrase features, document structure features and WordNet relatedness features are used. As machine learning algorithms, naive Bayess, support vector machines, support vector regression, logistic regression, ranking SVM, SVMmap and genetic

algorithm were tested. Although the results are very promising and machine learning methods seem to handle well with imbalanced data, the authors conclude that their chosen features are only suboptimal for distinguishing correct from incorrect answers. A similar approach, based on learning-to-rank and features, can be found e.g., in Higashinaka and Isozaki (2008). Their set of features is very large, consisting of 399 features in total. The features are: casual expression features (using automatically created patterns for casual expression from the EDR Japanese corpus), content similarity features (e.g., question candidate cosine similarity, question-document relevance, etc.) and casual relation feature. As in the previously mentioned system, the SVM ranking was used. Both above mentioned systems are focused on why-questions.

Answer Extraction

The task of the answer extraction (AE) module is to obtain the desired answer from the best-scored answer candidates and to present the proper formulation back to the user. The expression of the answer depends mostly on the question type. Since factoid questions ask for a simple fact (e.g., date, name, or other named entity), the answer containing only the named entity may be sufficient. In most cases, it depends on the QA system designer to decide whether the answer to a factoid question is expressed as one precise fact or as a whole sentence. Let us note that a limitation to one exact answer was a crucial requirement e.g., in TREC11 task. On the other hand, answers to non-factoid (why, how) question can be hard to express using a simple few-words answer and thus it is necessary to return a sentence or a whole paragraph that explains the complex answer to satisfy the user needs. Details about answer presentation are discussed later in this section.

Besides the ordered list of candidate answers, the input to the AE component includes the expected answer type and other constraints estimated during the question processing step. This usually includes the answer target (e.g., a named entity type from a given taxonomy).

As in the question processing and ranking modules, the answer extraction approaches based on patterns or heuristics are used very often. Named entity recognition, POS tagging, parsing and other NLP techniques are also used very often as an answer preprocessing step. An example of a pattern matching approach is described in Roussinov et al. (2008) or Moldovan et al. (2003), where the patterns are hand-crafted. After filtering the retrieved passages regarding the expected answer type, the method assumes that the answer is presented in the document in a few exact forms and it can be extracted using templates and regular expressions (see e.g., a template example in Query formulation section). A combination of plain heuristics and similarity computing is presented in Quarteroni and Manandhar (2008). For certain question types (e.g., time, money), class-specific rules are applied. For most factoid and non-factoid questions a bag-of-words similiarity is computed. This measure represents a number of matches between the keywords in the query and in the answer. Such simple score can also include features such as distance between keywords (Moldovan et al., 2003) or the occurrence of the candidate answer within an apposition (Pasca & Harabagiu, 2001). A similar method, based on count of unique question keywords (and their variants or alternations, respectively) in the documents, served as a baseline in Harabagiu et al. (2003). Furthermore, four different types of similarity were proposed by Quarteroni and Manandhar (2008): (1) bigram similarity, which matches the common bigrams, (2) chunk similarity, where chunks produced by a shallow parser are measured, (3) head NP-VP-PP similarity, where the metric is based on a matching group consisting of a noun phrase (NP), verb phrase (VP) and prepositional phrase (PP), and (4) WordNet similarity, where the metrics exploit the WordNet lexical database and word-level distance from Jiang and Conrath

(1997). Similar five distances (word matching, WordNet matching, mismatch words, dispersion, and cluster words) were presented in Ittycheriah et al. (2001) and used as an answer selection using maxiumum entropy. Buscaldi et al. (2010) proposed another approach for choosing the best answer from top 'n' candidates, based on voting, where the candidates are compared by means of a partial string match.

Apparently, the pattern based approaches suffer from the necessity to create the patterns by a knowledge engineer manually. Thus, machine learning techniques were explored in order to eliminate the need of this effort and improve the ability to cover previously unseen questions. AE methods using simple machine learning techniques were discussed in Harabagiu et al. (2000b) and later in Harabagiu et al. (2003). The method is based on seven features and it learns a comparision function between candidate answers. These features share similar foundations with the previously described similarity distances. Instead of direct similarity computing, these features are used for training a classifier, using a labeled training corpus. As a classifier, perceptron was used by Harabagiu et al. (2003).

A statistical model, based on the idea of a noisy channel, was presented in Soricut and Brill (2006). This model consists of three modules, as shown in Figure 3. The first module, *answer generation model*, proposes an answer A according to an answer generation probability distribution. The *answer/question translation model* further transform the answer A into the question Q according to conditional probability $p(A \mid Q)$. On the other hand, the task of *answer extraction module* is to find the answer which maximizes its probability given a question.

To compute mapping between answers and questions, the correspondence between terms was used (called alignment). In Soricut and Brill (2006), the model was trained on a question-answer corpus and the probabilities were computed

Figure 3. A noisy-channel model for answer extraction, as proposed by Soricut and Brill (2006)

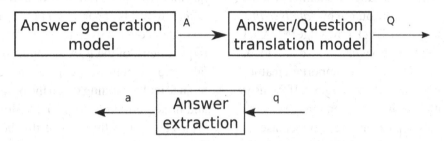

using the expectation-minimization (EM) algorithm.

Answer Formulation

In non-dialogue based QA systems, the last step of the query life-cycle is the *answer formulation* and its presentation back to the user. This task involves many other aspects, such as answer credibility evaluation, proper answer formulation, and also so-called Web 2.0 services, such as user feedback, answer voting, etc. The answer presentation is probably one of the most crucial parts in commercial systems to satisfy user needs. It should assure the user that the system does understand the question properly and it should return appropriate formulation of the answer, given e.g., the question type.

As mentioned before, answers to factoid questions are often formulated only by a single word or other named entity. This limitation was also required in past TREC competitions. Furthermore, a concise answer is advantageous e.g., for devices with limited resources (bandwidth and screen size) such as smart phones. On the other hand, such a plain answer may not sufficient from the information credibility point of view and hence it should be supported by some additional information to ensure the user that his question was well understood and that the data source can be trusted.

A simple method of providing a background for the answer is by presenting links to the top *n* documents which the answer was extracted from. The QA system can either provide the links to the

documents or it can show snippets which contain e.g., keywords or the whole desired answer in a context. This approach is very similar to the one which is offered by current commercial search engines and it is also used e.g., in Quarteroni and Manandhar (2008) or Wenyin et al. (2009).

An extension of this approach can be found in QA systems, which use an advanced semantic processing of the question and the answer candidate documents. They are then able to formulate the answer as a complete sentence instead of a simple named entity. Apparently, the whole-sentence formulation has a positive impact on user satisfaction due to confirmation that the system understood the question properly (Kosseim et al., 2003).

Since the non-factoid question can be hard to answer by a named entity, the presented results mostly range from a single sentence to a whole paragraph.

Additional Supporting Information

Commercial QA systems, such as TrueKnowledge™ (http://www.trueknowledge.com) or WolframAlpha™ (http://www.wolframalpha.com), rely on a structured knowledge base instead of on textual data collection. Whereas QA systems operating on text data (typically Web) can only find their answers in textual form and present them as text, systems operating on proprietary datasets are able to enrich the answer with many additional explanations, e.g., graphics, formulas, or pictures. Furthermore, some systems can explain their inferring mechanism, e.g., which facts from its database were used or demonstrate their reasoning process (for example, look at the output of *"analyse this question"* function on TrueKnowledge™). A set of possible related questions can be also provided.

User feedback is also a very important feature of successful commercial QA systems. If the user is satisfied with the given answer, many systems allows voting for such an answer (to increase its score). A QA system should be able to handle the searching failure, e.g., it does understand the question but it is not able to find an answer. It must be clear to the user, that this is not an issue related to the question and thus its reformulation does not yield any better results (Imiliensi & Signorini, 2009).

Interactive QA: The Dialogue Approach

The lifecycle of a question/answer in traditional QA systems consists of a single step. After posing the question, the system returns either one precise answer or a list of documents, depending on the particular implementation. Due to the lack of any user feedback, the system must be able to understand the question properly and to serve the most precise answer. Hence, huge natural language question ambiguity is one of the issues that must be solved. To improve the results of QA systems, the whole process can be thus modelled as a dialogue, where in each following step the users' intentions are further clarified in order to obtain the answer to the right question. This variant of QA systems is called Interactive Question Answering (IQA).

Inspired by human information-seeking dialogue, Quarteroni and Manandhar (2008) summarized the main issues that must be faced in IQA. These are e.g., *ellipsis*, when a dialogue participant omits a part of the sentence which is obvious from the previous context, *anaphoric reference*, where an entity is not clearly formulated in the sentence but it is referenced from the dialogue context, *grounding and clarification*, when the systems puts the context into a clarification

question to ensure the dialogue direction, and *turn taking*, which is apparently not very relevant in a textual dialogue. Given these possible issues, the requirements of the IQA dialogue manager must take into account e.g., context maintenance, utterance understanding given the previous context and mixed initiative, and so on. However, these issues are not in the core of this book. Instead, they relate to human-computer interaction and we invite the reader to consult e.g., Ahrenberg et al. (1990) for detailed description of discourse representation and discourse management.

Harabagiu et al. (2005) found that the quality of the IQA dialogue can be significantly improved when the system is able to predict a range of possible questions asked by the user. Their system, based on a framework called *predictive questioning*, uses a large question-answer database and it is used to propose a suggested question to the user. The suggested questions are selected according to the most salient aspects of the topic using 7 different similarity metrics. Hickl et al. (2004) proposed question decomposition in a complex scenario environment in order to increase the performance of IQA. An ontology-based approach towards IQA is presented by Magnini et al. (2009). In this work, the ontology is used for capturing aspects of interaction, such as constraints, question, context, etc.

Cross-language Question Answering Systems

Since 90's attempts to extend the knowledge base by incorporating documents from more than one language are regularly reported resulting in dedicated track within the TREC.

For translation two approaches are commonly used. They are based either on lexical resources (e.g., dictionaries, aligned word nets) or on machine translation (e.g., example–based translation). Role of machine translation was studied in Larosa et al. (2005) concluding that extending the document collection by a new language improves the answering of only some domains of factual question. In contrary (and quite surprisingly) experiments documented in Li and Croft (2001) indicate that techniques (templates for question type recognition, NER for query formulation and heuristics for ranking) developed for question answering in English are also effective in Chinese thus demonstrating the techniques to be language neutral.

Considering machine translation the following three traditional approaches to cross language QA are used:

- Translating the queries into the target language,
- Translating the document collection into the source language or
- Translating the queries and the documents into an intermediate representation (inter–lingua).

When dealing with huge amounts of data, as is the case for QA systems using Web as document collection, the only feasible approach today, is translating the question into the language of the document collection and the related issue of back-translating the answer into the language of the user.

Attention to cross-language aspects resulted in the development of a cross-language QA framework for both closed and open domains. The proposed framework (Sacaleanu & Neumann, 2006) handles explicitly two aspects common to QA systems addressed – cross-linguality (which is the original and prime objective of the framework) and credibility (which is a general issue for all QA systems even those bound to a single language).

Recently an interesting experiment comparing QA in various languages was reported (Penas et al., 2010). This experiment differs from all the above in that here the prime goal is not to use documents in one language to answer questions posed in other language. Instead, systems competing in this experiment were working in different languages and were evaluated with the same questions over the same document collection manually translated into 8 different languages. It should be noted however, that the experiment was not aimed to provide simple concise answer to a question but rather to provide a single paragraph where the answer should be found by user himself. Evaluation of confidence in the answer was also considered by allowing the system to leave some questions unanswered which was scored as better then providing answer which is wrong. Organizers of the comparison identified many points for further improvement of their experiment promising more constructive conclusions in its future runs (Penas et al., 2010). In particular the organizers need to introduce inter-annotator agreement measure, to sanitize the parallel corpus (although information should the same in all languages, in fact it is not always such) and user model has to be improved (neither lawyer nor ordinary people would ask questions in the test collection) to find a trade-off between researach and user centered development.

QUESTION ANSWERING IN THE SEMANTIC WEB ENVIRONMENT

In this section we provide an overview of the currently available technology used in QA systems exploiting the Semantic Web opportunities. First we describe a general architecture of such engines and later we examine particular implementation details. The Semantic Web is the second key element towards which the QA community is looking in the hope of new breakthroughs in understanding the information on the Web and thereby the ability to deliver the most relevant answers. Semantic Web technology thus forms the second element upon which the next generation search engines are likely to be built.

The *Semantic Web* vision is one in which the Web content is enriched with the semantic markup to allow machines to understand the meaning – or *semantics* – of information on the World Wide

Web (Antoniou & Harmelen, 2008). In this vision every piece of information is tagged (marked) and has a relation to an *ontology*. Automatic question answering engines can thus profit from such additional semantic information. Finding an answer to questions becomes a simpler matter if one can describe what is sought as a logic formula using the extra information stored in ontologies and semantic markup.

Semantic web tools use many technologies to process the Web content and various logic query languages to extract information – e.g., SPARQL (Prud'hommeaux & Seaborne, 2008) and SeRQL (Broeskstra & Kampman, 2008). However, as the acronyms of the languages indicate, they are much more related to SQL than to a natural language. Hence the core task of question answering in the semantic web environment is to transform the question asked in the natural language to a logic language that can be used in the semantic web environment. In recent years many QA systems designs and prototypes have responded to this challenge. They usually share a common scheme which is presented in the following paragraphs.

In summary the differences and similarities between QA systems for semantic web and QA systems for the general web (described earlier) are the following. The preprocessing and query classification phases and answer formulation are very similar while the methods for retrieving the answers are different. In systems for semantic web no information retrieval is performed. Instead, the *knowledge base* is queried with a language that resembles SQL for databases. The construction of the query (in traditional QA systems called the Query Formulation) is also different. Here the *ontology* is primarily used to find the transformation of the input in the form of natural language question to the output in the form of a logic language to query the knowledge base. Many other principles however remain the same in both systems – notably synonyms, lemmas, syntactic analysis and semantic analysis.

These systems may resemble the QA systems used for querying databases (NLDBI – Natural Language DataBase Interface) however they are in fact very different. QA systems for semantic web make use of the ontology and the whole semantic web framework in order to minimize the amount of work required to tailor the system to a specific domain. The portability of these systems is much higher then in the case of QA systems for databases.

Majority of QA systems exploiting the semantic web share some common features.

- They are closed domain systems – they operate on one or more installed domains.
- They are easy to port – the systems can be easily (at least in theory) installed on a different previously unknown domain with minimal effort needed.
- They use learning – the systems learn from the ontology and also from user feedback.
- They use lightweight linguistic processing of the query – see section "Lightweight Syntactic Processing".
- Some of them also use a dialogue to clarify ambiguous relations.

The systems use two different knowledge sources for query analysis:

- Knowledge of the natural language properties which are language specific and domain independent
- Knowledge of the ontology which is domain specific and language independent.

The *knowledge of the natural language properties* means that systems know how to process the natural language. It contains the knowledge of morphology (part-of-speech tagging, lemmatization, stemming, ...), about the structure of a sentence (syntactic analysis, verb phrase chunking, ...) and the knowledge about the construction of a question meaning representation (general principles of semantic analysis).

The *knowledge of the ontology* allows the system to work with the semantics of the queries (semantic analysis). As we explained in the section "Elements of the Semantic Web" the ontology defines the meaning of concepts and the relations between concepts. We also noted that the ontology can be divided vertically according to levels and that the lowest level is too specific to be shared among domains. This makes these kinds of QA systems domain specific (and thus closed-domain). On the other hand, the ontology describes the semantics of the domain in such a way that QA systems can learn the rules for semantic analysis of questions automatically (see later in the section "System Architecture").

Elements of the Semantic Web

In this section a short description of the semantic web is provided. The purpose of this section is to ease the understanding of the following sections. This section focuses on the essence of the semantic web and abstains from description of every detail. For exhaustive technical details, refer to http://www.w3.org/standards/semanticweb/.

The purpose of the semantic web is to allow the content of the web to be understood and manipulated by computers. This will allow various tasks such as advanced information retrieval, knowledge aggregation and inference, information security control and so on to be automatically performed – including question answering.

In the semantic web the information (the knowledge) is stored in *triplets*. A triplet is a compound of a subject, a predicate and an object. A triplet represents a *relation* (predicate) between a subject and an object. For example *[Beijing, isLocatedIn, China]*. The subjects and objects in triplets are called *concepts*. For more information about conceptual modeling, please see Chen, Akoka, Kangassalu, and Thalheim (1999). All triplets are stored in a place called the *knowledge base*.

The *ontology* is a vehicle to describe the semantics of concepts and relations. The semantics is described by means of relations between concepts and relations themselves. A special type of a relation is the one called *isA* relation. This relation defines the taxonomy that is a relation between general and specific concepts or relations. For example, consider the following part of an ontology definition: *city isA municipality* and *municipality isA populated-place* etc. The ontology may also specify that a city can be located in a state. In terms of our example ontology a relation called *locatedIn* may be defined between a *city* and *state* concepts. The principle we just have shown for concepts also applies to relations. For example, relation *locatedIn* is defined as *locatedIn isA geographicRelation*.

The ontology is sometimes divided into upper, middle and lower ontologies. The *upper ontology* (top-level ontology or foundation ontology) defines the most abstract concepts that can be shared by everyone. There are many upper ontologies e.g., WonderWeb foundational ontology (Masolo et al., 2003), SUMO (Niles, 2001) etc. The *middle ontology* is more specific, more detailed and thus more difficult to agree on among stakeholders. It usually defines concepts that can be shared by a single system among all domains. The *lower ontology* is the most specific one. It is usually suitable for one particular domain only. The middle ontology has to be connected with an upper ontology and likewise the lower ontology has to be connected with a middle one.

There are two details worth mentioning. First, there are special types of concepts called *data values*. These are atomic values such as strings, integers, date/time values, etc. Data values can appear only at the third position (the object) in the triplet. The relation between a concept and a data value is called *data value relation*.

The second detail is that advanced versions of languages for ontology description allow *advanced properties of relations*, such as *transitive*, *symmetric*, *functional* and other properties to be described. These properties simplify the ontology definition and enrich its expressive power but they increase the demands on the ontology reasoning engine.

There are two essential technologies commonly used in the semantic web. The *Resource Description Framework* (*RDF*) is generally used to store triplets and for data interchange. The *Web Ontology Language* (*OWL*) is a language for authoring ontologies. These technologies built around W3C consortium are intended to provide formal description of concepts, terms, and relationships within a given knowledge domain.

Lightweight Syntactic Processing

Tools for a full scale syntactic analysis or other advanced means of linguistic processing are not usually used in semantic web applications and there are good reasons for this.

Arguably the most important reason is that the input queries are often not written as complete sentences or they are not grammatically correct. Because the input is only one short sentence or just a phrase there is not enough context to perform disambiguation required for more elaborate linguistic processing.

Effectiveness and sufficiency of lightweight syntactic processing is supported by Katz and Lin (2003) by showing that full syntactic parse trees capture relations and dependencies well, but they are difficult to manipulate with.

System Architecture

Despite some minor differences, all state-of-the-art systems share a similar abstract architecture. The six steps that are usually found in every QA system exploiting semantic web technologies are discussed next.

Figure 4 shows the general principle of operation of current QA systems.

Step 1

In the first step the system accepts a user input — a question in the natural language. The input text is tokenized and preprocessed. During preprocessing, lemmatization or stemming and morphological (part-of-speech) tagging is usually performed.

Figure 5 shows the example of preprocessing consisting of morphological tagging and lemmatization. The meaning of morphological tags is explained in the Penn tree bank description – see Marcus et al. (1993).

Step 2

In the next step systems execute the NER task often with the help of *gazetteers*. A gazetteer is a large list of known words or phrases that need to be recognized in a text, these typically include various types of names, such as locations, organizations, or people and a variety of domain dependent terms — see Tablan et al. (2008). The named entities are usually connected to the "bottom entities" in the ontology.

Figure 6 depicts the example of the named entity recognition result. In the example sentence one named entity – "Africa" – was discovered. The named entity is connected to the ontology.

Step 3

The third step usually consists of some kind of lightweight syntactic processing. Common methods being used are the so called VP chunking (verb phrase chunking) or just a simple syntactic text chunking. Text chunking is a method of partial syntactic parsing. The method creates chunks that have no internal structure, in contrast to the phrases created during a full scale syntactic parsing (Tjong et al., 2000). VP chunking is used e.g., in Lopez et al. (2007).

Another method being used for lightweight linguistic processing is parsing with specially prepared context-free grammars taking advantage

Figure 4. Abstract architecture of QA systems working within the semantic web framework

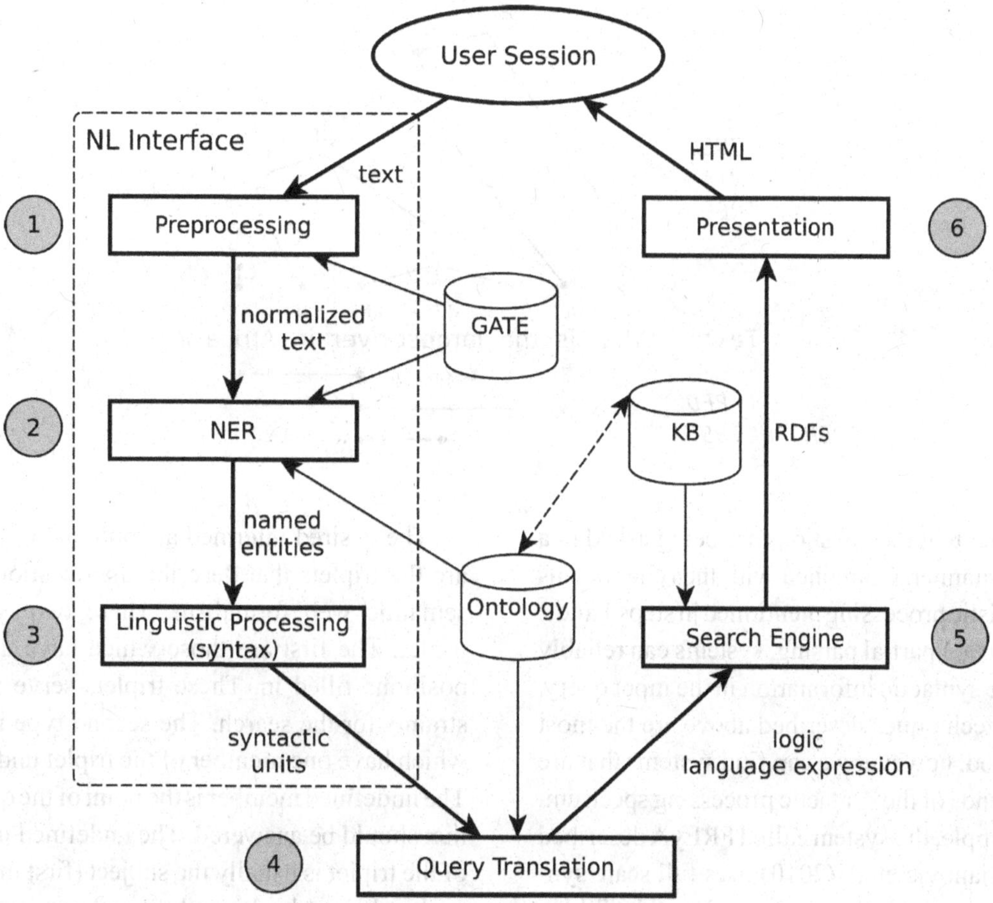

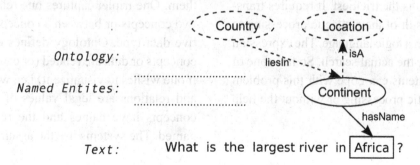

Figure 5. Step 1 illustration

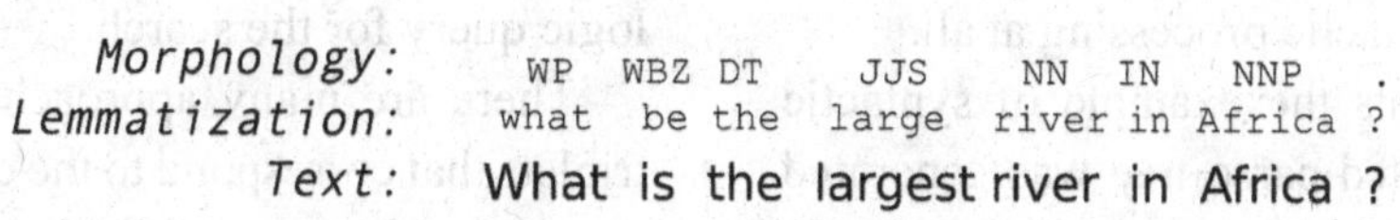

Morphology:	WP WBZ DT JJS NN IN NNP .
Lemmatization:	what be the large river in Africa ?
Text:	What is the largest river in Africa ?

Figure 6. Step 2 illustration

Ontology:

Named Entites:

Text: What is the largest river in Africa ?

Figure 7. Step 3 illustration

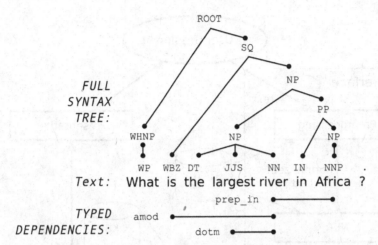

FULL SYNTAX TREE:

Text: What is the largest river in Africa ?

TYPED DEPENDENCIES:

of the fact that the questions are being asked in a similar manner. Combined with the other means of linguistic processing mentioned in steps 1 and 2 and by using partial parsing, systems can reliably annotate syntactic information in the input query.

The techniques described above are the most often used, however we can find systems that are at both ends of the syntactic processing spectrum. For example, the system called FREyA described in Damljanovic et al. (2010) uses full scale syntactic processing, while systems QuestIO (Tablan et al., 2008) and NLP-Reduce (Kaufmann et al., 2007) are at the other end of the spectrum since they do not use syntactic processing at all.

Figure 7 presents the example of syntactic parsing. The depicted parse tree was generated by the Stanford parser (Klein & Manning, 2003)

Step 4

The fourth step is the trickiest. It requires transforming the result of the syntactic processing to an expression in a logic language. The expression is then used for the actual search. So far, none of the current systems can cope with this problem without heuristic processing or without the help of the user.

The desired intermediate outputs of this step are the triplets that describe the question in the semantic web formalism. There two types of triplet. The first are those which have all three positions filled in. These triplets serve as constraints for the search. The second type is those which have one member of the triplet undefined. The undefined member is the point of the question that should be answered. The undefined member of the triplet is usually the subject (first member) or the object (third member) and very rarely the second member (predicate). When the triplets are created it is quite straightforward to build up the logic query for the search.

There are many approaches to creating the triplets that correspond to the question. Although the approaches may differ in many aspects, they share one key element – the use of ontology *and a knowledge base*. As we explained earlier, the ontology describes concepts and relations between them. One triplet captures one relation between two concepts or between a concept and a primitive data type. Ontology defines exactly which concepts or data are related (or can be connected if one wishes to visualize it) i.e., which concepts and relations are legal values of a triplet. The concepts have names and the relation is also named. The systems use the assumption that the

Figure 8. An ontology example

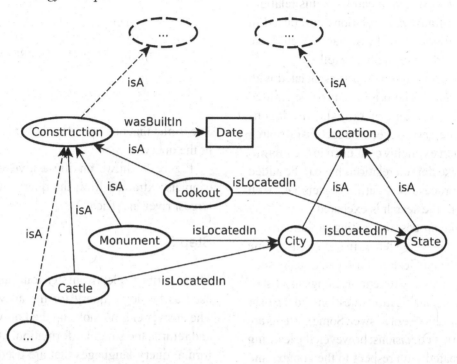

names of the concept and the relation are similar to the words used in the questions. For example, consider the following sequence of words placed in the question: "A city *is located* in a place" then the system assumes that there will be a relation named *isLocated* in the ontology that implements the link between a city (city is a concept in the ontology) and a place (also a concept). Obviously this assumption cannot be applied without an additional linguistic processing to handle an instance such as "A city *lies* somewhere" or "A city *is situated* somewhere", etc. There is a similar problem with the names of concepts. They can also be expressed in a different but synonymic expression or the name can be a compound of several words. However, this problem is more frequent in the case of relation names than in the case of concept names. To address issues with different but semantically equal expressions, systems use dictionaries of synonymic words, string similarity techniques and learning. We address these methods in a separate section "Using Ontology as the Information Source."

The problem of expressions that are differently expressed but semantically equal is not the only issue to be handled. Many times it is also necessary to carry out advanced reasoning using the ontology. Let us demonstrate it using the simple example in Figure 8. Here the concepts of *city* and *state* are connected with the relation *isLocatedIn*; however, the concepts of *monuments* and *state* are not connected. The relation though holds between those concepts as well (e.g., question "In what country lies the Statue of Liberty"). The reasoning process has to take into account that some relations have a transitive property. A similar kind of reasoning has to be done with inherited relations. If a relation holds between two superior (generic/general) concepts it also holds between two inferior (specific/concrete) concepts. For example, consider the relation *wasBuiltIn* that holds between concept *Construction* and the primitive data type *Date*. Clearly all superior concepts of the concept *Construction* can have this relation. Other types of advanced relations introduced in the section "Elements of the Semantic Web" have to be processed accordingly as well.

The last common problem is associated with *default relations*. The original query submitted by the user may contain generally known relations which are necessary to execute a successful search but that are not explicitly contained in the submitted text. These default relations have to be added during the process of creating triplets i.e., well ahead, before the search is executed.

During the process of creating triplets, an *ambiguity* may be encountered. In such a case some systems use a clarification dialogue. Usually such a dialogue presents different meanings in a list of choices or in a clarification question and the user is supposed to choose or answer. Some systems are able to learn user decisions; however, the learning has to be treated with respect to the context and the user profile. The context is necessary because the same word can have different meanings in different contexts. Also, default relations may be ambiguous and valid only for a specific context.

The *user profile* is a special kind of context. Each user may use words with different meanings and also can expect different implicit knowledge of the system (internally represented by the default relations). For example, consider the question "What is the largest river in Africa?" Here the word "largest" can mean *riverLength*, *riverWidth*, *riverBasin* or *riverDischarge*. After the user specifies that *riverLength* was meant then the search can be executed and the system learns this clarification with respect to the context and the user profile. The word *largest* itself can mean *riverBasin* for a different user. In the context of a different topic (for example, information about countries) the word can mean *stateArea* vis-à-vis for example *statePopulation*.

At this point the QA engine is ready to generate the logic query for the answer. All the triplets that have all positions defined serve as constrains.

Figure 9. Step 4 illustration

```
<?river, isLocatedIn, Continent1>
<Continent1, hasName, "Africa">
<?river, hasLength, "LARGEST">
```

The triplet that has a position left free is the topic of the query.

Figure 9 shows an illustrative example of tripplets extracted from the query "What is the largest river in Africa?"

Step 5

The resulting triplets from step four can be directly used as the logic query for the answer engine. The answer engine looks up the knowledge base and returns the sought information. Out of many formal query languages that are used to specify the search in a triplet database, two are the most often used:

- SPARQL: used in many RDF frameworks (Pellet, Jena, Redland, 3Store and others), W3C standard, used by Kaufmann et al. (2007) and (Damljanovic et al. (2010).
- SeRQL: has more SQL like syntax, used in Sesame framework, used by Tablan et al. (2008).

The results of SPARQL and SeRQL queries can be *result sets* or *RDF graphs*. The *result sets* are tables with columns representing the language's SELECT statement (see Prud'hommeaux & Seaborne, 2008; Broeskstra & Kampman, 2008). RDF graphs are oriented graphs expressed in triplets. The triplets in the result graphs have the same format as the data definition in the knowledge base.

Figure 10 shows an illustrative example of a simplified SeRQL query generated from the triplets described in the Figure YY and from an ontology.

Figure 10. Step 5 illustration

```
select c0, c1, p1, i1, p2, i2, p3
from
    {c0} rdf:type{<http://namespace.com/type#River>},
    {c1} rdf:type{<http://namespace.com/type#Continent>},
    {c0} p1 {c1},
    {c1} p2 {i1},
    {c0} p3 {i2}
where
    p1 = <http://namespace.com/relation#isLocatedIn> and
    p2 = <http://namespace.com/relation#hasName> and
    i1 = <http://namespace.com/value#Africa> and
    p3 = <http://namespace.com/relation#hasLength> and
    i2 = <http://namespace.com/quantif#LARGEST>
```

Step 6

The last step is a proper presentation of the found information. In the simplest case the information is presented as it is. Nevertheless, in more elaborate systems the information is presented within a grammatically correct sentence derived from the question. Some systems also provide an explanation of the search and inference processes to ensure the user that his or her question was correctly interpreted by the system. It also sometimes offers to browse the knowledge base for other relations.

This last step is in many aspects similar to the traditional QA systems described in the "Answer Formulation" section. It differs in how the answer can be explained and in the possibility to access the knowledge base through the ontology.

The explanation usually consists of showing the user how the logic query was constructed. Of course, it is not satisfactory to present the query in a SPARQL or SeRQL statement. It is more convenient for the user to show the triplet graph or to display the search constrains in a table (Damljanovic et al., 2010). In more elaborate systems, users can alter the constrains to obtain different or more accurate answers (Cimiano et al., 2008).

It is also possible to show the results in the context of the knowledge base. A user is allowed to browse other information related to the found answer. For example, consider the question "What is the largest river in Africa?" for which the system offers "Nile" as the correct answer. The user can then browse other related information such as average discharge, states or cities through which the river Nile flows, and so on.

Ontology as the Information Source

The main domain specific knowledge source of the QA systems operating in the semantic web environment is the ontology. In this section we show how a system automatically extracts the information from ontology in order to minimize the system customization required when deployed to another domain.

Most of the time concepts and relations have meaningful names. The names are the main part of the information that is usable for query analysis. If a system finds in a question the named entity called *city* it looks for the concept *city* in the ontology. The same principle is applied to relations. When a system finds the verb phrase *is located in* it looks for the *isLocatedIn* relation. It is obvious that this basic approach would not be very robust if applied without any further "smart" processing when deploying the system to a new domain.

One vehicle used to improve the basic approach is the use of *language lexicons*. The lexicons organize words in synonymic groups and define relations (hyponymy, meronymy, etc.) between them (Jurafsky & Martin, 2009). The use of the synonyms is obvious – since a user can use a synonymic word in a query, the exact lexical match with the word stored in the ontology would fail without the use of synonyms. Hyponymy and meronymy relations work in a similar manner. A user can use a more abstract or more specific term than exists in the ontology.

Some systems make use of existing lexicons (such as the WordNet) (Fellbaum, 1998) others rely on lexicons created dynamically by means of learning, as the system is being used. The advantage of the former is that it is available beforehand, is usually well documented and has a proven record of successful deployments. The advantage of the latter is that it provides domain specific knowledge vis-à-vis the knowledge contained in off-the-shelf lexicons likely to be much more general and therefore not valid for a particular domain.

In the ontology the names of concepts and relations are usually written in the so called *pretty name notation*. This is the form of notation where words or phrases are demarcated by big letters or dashes instead of spaces – e.g., relation name *isLocatedIn* or *is-located-in* is a phrase compounded from the words: *is*, *located*, and *in*. The algorithm that works with pretty names has to be able to provide approximate matches even when words are missing or left out.

The learning algorithm that extracts the knowledge from the ontology has to be able to get as much information as possible. A good practice when developing ontology is to provide extra description of concepts and relations. These are usually short texts that explain the details of concepts and relations that do not fit into their names. For example, the detailed description of the concept *monument* can be "Towers, statues, columns, archaeological sites and other structures of special interest". Such a description can be a rich source of useful words that extend the information contained solely in the name "monument".

Another way of providing a better match for words in questions with words in the ontology is to use string similarity metrics. The metrics can compare two strings and measure how alike they are. This is a good way of dealing with typos and slight differences in spelling. Some of the useful metrics are presented in Cohen at el. (2003).

Naturally, all the above mentioned auxiliary techniques are not perfectly reliable and some sort of scoring needs to be employed to make sure that a word that is exactly the same as the concept in the ontology is scored better than a word that is only matched by some of the techniques mentioned above.

Typical Errors and Failures

There are several levels where a QA system working within the semantic web framework can fail.

Firstly the NLP module can make an error in morphology tagging or can fail to assign a named entity. Also syntactic parsing is not perfectly reliable even if the parsing is shallow only. The error in named entity is the most significant one since named entities are the values for searching constraints. A missing relation in syntactic parsing can prevent the system to discover a relation between concepts. This can also mean a missing constrain for searching. The typical reasons for named entity recognition failure or syntactic analysis failure are misspelled words, unknown words, insufficient context, and ungrammatical expressions.

The second area of potential problems lays in the principle of using semantic web technologies to transform the NLP results to the logic query. The possible problems are too complicated questions (some systems limit a question to 2 or 3 triplets - for example the AquaLog system (Lopez et al., 2007) limits the amount of generated triplets to maximum of two), the poor descriptions in the ontology (bad names or no description of concepts and relations) or a heuristics failure (all the systems use some amount of heuristics during the transformation process and it can obviously fail). The problems can be summarized into two issues: too complicated or untypical questions and a poor ontology.

Last level of possible issues in QA is the insufficient information in the knowledge base or database or out of scope questions. The system can analyze the question correctly however the answer may not be present in the knowledge base.

Distinguished Features of Existing Systems

In this section we present several systems that use the architecture described. Apart from the way the syntactic processing is implemented, these systems differ in some peculiar details that may be small but play an important role and make them worth mentioning.

Aqualog (Lopez et al., 2007) is arguably the best known QA system that uses the architecture described above. Its distinctive feature is that it uses triplets as an intermediate representation from the syntactic processing to the logic query transformation. When facing insufficient information, Aqualog exploits the user's help to disambiguate questions and learns user's hints. Although the authors claim Aqaulog to be easily portable there are some non-trivial procedures that have to be accomplished when deploying Aqualog to a new domain. First of all it has to be specified which terms "who", "where", "when" correspond to which concepts in the ontology. A second issue faced during installation is to choose or develop a suitable plug-in that maps names in the ontology (the *pretty names*) to the names used in plain text. A positive aspect of Aqualog is that it is a mature system that has been well tested. During the performance evaluation, Aqualog scored almost 70% of correctly answered questions. The testing collection consisted of 68 queries in the

domain of information about wines. An important Aqualog feature for the research community is the fact that it is developed as an open source project (http://sourceforge.net/projects/aqualog) and has a solid user base.

NLP-Reduce (Kaufmann et al., 2007) is a QA system that tries to reduce the NL interface functionality to a minimum. It does not rely on syntactic processing at all, with the sole exception of stemming, but NLP-Reduce uses WordNet to improve the process of generating ontology triplets. The advantage of the system is its very high level of portability at the cost of its question understanding being very shallow. The reported performance measured using the F-measure varies around 70% however the results are somewhat dubious.

The Orakel QA system (Cimiano, 2008) uses *logical description grammars* that combine syntactic rules for syntactic analysis and first order predicate calculus (FOPC) for semantic analysis. Named entities are used to generalize the FOPC rules, although it is not explicitly mentioned by authors. The advantage of the system is the compositional approach to semantic analysis. This way the system is able to cope with quantification, negation and conjunction in the question. The main drawback of the system is that it can cope neither with ungrammatical input nor with unknown words. Another weakness is the limited portability of the system because of being a complicated process – the system requires a domain-specific lexicon to be manually created for each domain. To reduce the adaptation cost the graphical user interface for adaptation is offered. Interestingly, the adaptation is based on wrongly answered questions. The reported performance of the system in the F-measure metric is around 60%.

The QuestIO system (Tablan et al., 2008) is very similar to Aqualog although it lacks learning capability. Evaluation of its contribution is difficult due to the existence of a lot of hard-coded heuristic rules. Its value and distinctive feature is in putting more weight on the processing of incomplete or syntactically ill-formed questions by the extensive use of heuristics and scoring the intermediate results. The performance of the system was not given.

The FreyA (Damljanovic et al., 2010) is a follow-up research prototype based on the QuestIO system. It is one of the QA systems that exploit full syntactic processing with all the consequences mentioned in the "Lightweight Syntactic Processing" section. The system uses advanced learning from the clarification dialogues called up in case of ambiguities. The learning involves not only aligning words from questions with words in ontology but also learning alternative scoring in the transformation process from syntactic units to logical query. The reported performance of FreyA is given in MRR. The system reached the value 0.72. However, the performance was measured on a small corpus of 250 questions.

ISSUES, CONTROVERSIES AND RECOMMENDATIONS

Reference Services and Knowledge Markets

In recent years we have seen a new type of on-line service rapidly gaining in popularity: the *knowledge markets* that are also known as *question-and-answer services* (Roush, 2006) or *question-answering communities* (Gazan, 2006). In essence these systems use Web 2.0 tools to implement the reference services of traditional libraries (in a traditional library there is a service on offer where the librarian answers a client's question or points him to resources).

Current computer-based solutions still involve human beings that answer questions. However, the solutions offer several levels of automation which we address in the rest of this section.

An example of the most straightforward implementation of such a human-assisted QA is the electronic reference and on-line library collection service "Internet Public Library" (IPL) (McCrea, 2004). IPL is a non-profit organization that relies on librarian volunteers and graduate students in library science programs to answer submitted questions. Technically this is not really interesting but it is seen as the baseline for the computerized human-assisted knowledge market QA systems described in the reminder of this section.

Web-based knowledge markets can be categorized into price-based and community-based services. The former includes Google Answers, Uclue and BitWine, while the latter includes Yahoo! Answers, Knowledge-iN (KiN), Quora and Facebook Questions. In Chen et al. (2010) authors studied the effects of price, tips, and reputation of the system on the quality of answers as well as on the answerer's motivation. This study led to such observations as offering higher prices for the answer leads to significantly longer, but not better, answers, while an answerer with a higher reputation offers significantly better answers. Worth mentioning is also the approach of Facebook Questions which is based on assumption that answers of one's friends are likely to be more relevant than that of an anonymous answerer, especially answers to subjective questions (often why-questions).

A detailed description of technologies needed to implement a human-assisted QA system including *user modeling*, *reputation management*, and *answer clustering and fusion* is found in Wenyin et al. (2009). The authors deal with the problem of handling accumulated answers in the system, which (if well archived and formalized in a global knowledge database) can be reused later. The idea of reuse is based on finding a match between the question asked by a user and an older question already answered and stored in the system. The main issue to be addressed is that the questions and answers in plain text format are not easily understood by machines and therefore it is difficult to find matches between questions.

The accumulated questions and answers are usually represented and stored in a pattern-based format, which can be converted to a formal knowledge representation for efficient machine understanding, processing, and reasoning. A *pattern-based user interface* for asking and answering questions was proposed in Tianyong et al. (2008) and Wenyin et al. (2009) and named *semantic question pattern*.

In such systems the *model of user* who is answering questions typically includes

- A user's interest in the topic.
- A user's authority (capability of correctly answering the questions on a particular topic).
- A user's reputation which is a measure of how much he/she can be trusted when he/she promises something.

User reputation is derived from social network analysis where relational data is represented using a graph called a sociogram which is a directed and weighted graph (Wasserman & Faust, 1994).

An interesting aspect of the system (Hao et al., 2008) is that even though the money offered for a certain question is zero, potential answerers also have motivations to provide their answers since there are chances that their answers can be automatically reused to answer new yet similar (or even exactly the same) questions in the future and they can still earn the money offered for such new similar questions.

Commercial Sector and Business Models

In recent years several commercial QA projects have been launched. The first commercially successful search engine with QA extension was arguably the Ask Jeeves (today known as Ask. com) founded in 1996. Ask Jeeves was sold in 2005 for $1.85 billion in stock showing clearly that question answering is a commercially attractive domain. Interestingly, shortly after the acquisition the QA part of the website was abandoned in favor

of SERP but later the QA came back a today ask. com image is based on QA functionality (while also delivering SERPs for user convenience).

Since then several other QA systems have popped up. Notable projects were Yedda bought by AOL or PowerSet bought by Microsoft (Arrington, 2008). Other QA systems are being developed using venture capital worth tens of millions of dollars. A notable example is the promising prototype hakia.com (Weisenthal, 2007).

In general, little can be said about the technology used in commercial systems. For marketing reasons the description of systems and algorithms is usually boasted about, but superficial and in any case not detailed enough to verify any of the statements. Nevertheless, there are two systems that are worth commenting on.

The first service is *Wolfram Alpha* – an answer engine developed by Wolfram Research, the company behind the popular Mathematica software. Wolfram Alpha is an online service that answers factual queries directly by computing the answer from structured data collected beforehand, rather than providing the answer from text documents or Web pages. The company is said to employ over 100 people to collect information on all the major branches of science. Thanks to the use of Mathematica this system is also well suited to questions involving algebra, symbolic and numerical computation, visualization, and statistical capabilities.

The second service is *True Knowledge* – a QA engine using a database of discrete facts to comprehend posed questions by disambiguating from all possible meanings of the words in the question and to find the most likely meaning of the question being asked. The data are imported from "credible" external databases and from user submissions following a consistent format (Bradley, 2008). A distinctive feature of True Knowledge is that it offers the user not only the answer but also the facts and rules from which the answer is constructed.

A special attention needs to be paid to IBM's Watson system which recently received lots of attention from media thanks to its success in "Jeopardy!" competition. Similarly to other commercial systems little details are known about implementation of its DeepQA technology but from commercial standpoint this system may become a very important one as IBM already announced plans to deploy the system to many areas, including health care (notably clinical decision support system), financial services and other industries. Considering the position IBM has among corporate and institutional clients and how it shaped the landscape in the past, the DeepQA is definitely on of the technologies to watch.

Commercial QA systems use several rather distinct business models to make profit and/or attract users and/or investors. QA systems that require payment per answer are rare. Reputation-based systems such as Yahoo Answers create revenue from advertising.

Some QA systems provide an API for a fee (Fiveash, 2009) and via this API it delivers answers to other applications. For example Wolfram Alpha delivers to Microsoft's Bing search engine. Moreover, some companies penetrate the mobile market such as iOS and Android devices with paid applications to provide an optimized interface for mobile access.

In general, the current state of commercial sector is such that QA systems either provides reliable answers but operates only in a very strict environment (closed-domain systems that are often expert systems) or the answers are not very reliable and serves more as a convenience and supplementary feature than a single shot answer. QA capable web search engines tend to offer concise answer followed by rationale for its selection and snippet of the source information. Rest of the SERP is quite conventional ordered list of links to web pages. As of today there are no off-the-shelf products providing the QA capability without the need to invest significant amount of effort to fine tune the system to user needs.

A yet unsolved issue is the question of using the intellectual property of third parties when delivering answers to QA system users. In the future the increasing quality of QA systems may lead to scenarios where users would merely use the QA engine and, being satisfied with the answers provided, they might never go the information source web page. In this case the source information provider may lose revenues from advertising and in turn implement counter measures to prevent QA systems mining information from their web pages. A sustainable business model dealing with this problem has yet to be found.

FUTURE RESEARCH DIRECTIONS

The QA has been seen as promising technology for web search for many years without so far materializing in a reliable system that covers many different domains (some sort of The Ultimate QA System). Some researches wonder whether at all this is achievable in foreseeable future. However lots of progress has been made and authors are optimistic about the achievements yet to come.

As indicated earlier, QA is a commercially attractive domain and in all likelihood it will grow in importance in the near future. For Web-based QA there is still the issue of an unresolved business model relying on third-party information providers. It remains to be seen whether new services solutions would accelerate the QA domain even further.

Research interest in recent decades has moved from closed-domain systems to open-domain systems, namely to the Web. This shift has opened the field to new researchers resulting in never before seen investments in research both in terms of money and manpower.

The experience which the research community gathers while studying the open-domain systems may be applied back to closed-domain systems. These are traditionally perceived as a simpler problem due to limited data and the more controlled general knowledge which a system must possess to work effectively. However, with the advent of the semantic web and all its related technologies penetrating into QA, we may experience unprecedented applications of the technology developed for open-domain systems being used in their closed-domain counterparts, taking advantage of their constrained data.

As far as QA systems exploiting the semantic web technologies are concerned, the focus will be on harvesting the knowledge contained in the ontology to infer a sufficient amount of the information needed to perform the correct transformation of an input question to the logic query. By doing so, systems greatly increase their portability and reduce the difference between open-domain and closed-domain systems. With easy portability the closed-domain systems can be easily installed on another domain, thus covering more topics. In fact, some of the systems are looking into reducing the portability issues in order to be automatically able to cover all available domains in the semantic web framework. In this way the systems could achieve the properties of an open-domain system.

With the upcoming semantic web era (the so called Web 3.0), QA systems will be provided with extra possibilities for question answering. The pioneer systems working in the semantic web framework have shown the way, however many issues remain unsolved. Systems have yet to achieve the ability to work simultaneously with multiple resources (ontologies and knowledge bases). Knowledge bases with overlapping and possibly contradictory knowledge possess a special challenge.

A hot topic is also the deep understanding of questions, especially covering negations, conjunctions, quantifications, comparison, temporal information and other semantically advanced features of questions. The ultimate goal is to combine deep understanding, processing of grammatically ill-formed or incomplete questions and domain independent processing.

Quite apart from the further evolution of the methods, techniques and algorithms already in place at various levels of maturity as described in the previous sections, there are still unsolved issues in QA that remain outside the scope of the current research but, in our opinion, deserve to be covered in the near future. We offer a short of overview of what we consider to be the "next big thing" in QA.

Assessment of the quality of answers to non-factoid questions is probably the most urgent issue given the recent gain in popularity of QA systems capable of answering these questions. In the near future we expect a lot of attention to be devoted to understanding the complex semantic relationships between parts of text corpora, presumably relying on tools such as FrameNet and PropBank (Boas, 2009; Hwang, 2010).

Ideally, a QA system should deliver correct answers knowing that they are correct, i.e., it can deliver a proof of the correctness of the answers. Since the current systems can only deliver answers with a certain trustworthiness (a credibility measure of an answer), determination of answer credibility may only be estimated from the plausibility of the answer source and context using various meta information. The first QA system credibility model (QAS-CM) was proposed by Sacaleanu and Neumann (2006), but further research is needed before answer credibility is adopted by the industry, possibly complementing recent achievements in trust modeling (Netrvalova & Safarik 2008).

Research in personalized QA is still in a very early stage and a lot needs to be done at the modeling level. This means studying a user model and its attributes to represent the users of a QA system who can have very different expectations from the system due to their background knowledge (for example, a question about genetics asked by a medical student and by a child). It has already been identified as a key technology in Maybury (2002) but such a technique has not been applied to many QA systems since then, especially in open-domain QA (Komatani et al., 2003; Hickl & Harabagiu, 2006). A number of modeling issues were raised in Quarteroni (2007).

A related problem is the interactivity of a QA system and dialogue management strategy. This topic was also recently tackled in Quarteroni (2007), presenting a prototype implementation of a personalized and interactive QA system which may now serve as a baseline solution, but at the same time a number of open points were identified and called for further investigation. Commercial systems are arguably well ahead of academia in presenting the answers along with related information but the topic has not yet been rigorously studied in literature.

We expect that TREC will remain an important programmatic driver to facilitate the development of new technologies addressing specific needs as identified by the community.

CONCLUSION

This chapter covered the state-of-the-art of question answering focusing on systems, techniques and approaches that are likely to be employed in the next generation of search engines. For this reason special attention was paid to QA using World Wide Web as their data source and to QA exploiting the possibilities of Semantic Web. Later we provided considerations about the current issues and prospects for promising future research.

We have seen an enormous influx of resources – both monetary and manpower – into QA in recent years. Commitments announced by the search engine industry as well as steadily increasing activity in academia confirms that QA is an expanding research domain. We invite the reader to watch the topic carefully.

ACKNOWLEDGEMENT

This work was supported by the UWB grant SGS-2010-028 Advanced Computer and Information Systems.

REFERENCES

Ahrenberg, L., Jönsson, A., & Dahlbäck, N. (1990). Discourse representation and discourse management for a natural language dialogue system. In *Proceedings of the Second Nordic Conference on Text Comprehension in Man and Machine*, Taby, Stockholm, Sweden.

Antoniou, G., & Harmelen, F. (2008). *A Semantic Web Primer* (2nd ed.). Cambridge, MA: MIT Press.

Arrington, M. (2008). *Ok, now it's done. Microsoft to acquire Powerset*. Retreived from http://techcrunch.com/ 2008/07/01/ok-now-its-done-microsoft-to-acquire-powerset/

Arvola, P., Kekäläinen, J., & Junkkari, M. (2010). Expected reading effort in focused retrieval evaluation. *Information Retrieval*, *13*(5), 460–484. doi:10.1007/s10791-010-9133-9

Balog, K., Vries, P., Serdyukov, P., & Thomas, P. (2010). *TREC Entity 2010 guidelines*. Retrieved October 19, 2010, from http://ilps.science.uva.nl/ trec-entity/guidelines/

Beaulieu, M. M., Gatford, M., Huang, Y., Robertson, S. E., Walker, S., & Williams, P. (1997). Okapi at TREC-5. In *Proceedings of the Fifth Text REtrieval Conference on Information Technology* (pp. 143-165).

Bernhard, D. (2010). Query expansion based on pseudo relevance feedback from definition clusters. In *Proceedings of the 23rd International Conference on Computational Linguistics: Posters*, Beijing, China (pp. 54-62).

Bilotti, M. W. (2004). *Query expansion techniques for question answering* (Unpublished master's thesis). Massachusetts Institute of Technology, Cambridge, MA.

Blanke, T., & Lalmas, M. (2010). Specificity aboutness in XML retrieval. *Information Retrieval, 14*(1), 68–88. doi:10.1007/s10791-010-9144-6

Boas, H. C. (2009). Multilingual FrameNets in computational lexicography: Methods and applications. *International Journal of Lexicography, 23*(1), 105–109.

Bouma, G. (2006). Linguistic knowledge and question answering. In *Proceedings of the Workshop KRAQ on Knowledge and Reasoning for Language Processing*, Trento, Italy (pp. 2-3).

Bradley, P. (2008). *True knowledge - Questions search engine*. Retrieved from http://philbradley.typepad.com/ phil_bradleys_weblog/2008/09/true-knowledge---questions-search-engine.html

Brill, E., Lin, J., Banko, M., Dumais, S., & Ng, A. (2001). Data-intensive question answering. In *Proceedings of the Tenth Text REtrieval Conference* (pp. 393-400).

Broeskstra, J., & Kampman, A. (2008, November 13-14). SeRQL: A second generation RDF query language. In *Proceedings of the SWAD-Europe Workshop on Semantic Web Storage and Retrieval*, Amsterdam, The Netherlands.

Budiu, R., & Hielsen, J. (2009). *Usability of mobile Websites: 85 design guidelines for improving access to Web-based content and services through mobile devices*. Fremont, CA: Nielsen Norman Group.

Buscaldi, D., Rosso, P., Gómez-Soriano, J. M., & Sanchis, E. (2010). Answering questions with an n-gram based passage retrieval engine. *Journal of Intelligent Information Systems, 34*(2), 113–134.

Chen, P. P., Akoka, J., Kangassalu, H., & Thalheim, B. (Eds.). (1999). *Conceptual modeling: current issues and future directions*. Berlin, Germany: Springer-Verlag.

Chen, Y., Teck-Hua, H., & Yong-Mi, K. (2010). Knowledge market design: A field experiment at Google Answers. *Journal of Public Economic Theory, 12*(4), 641–664. doi:10.1111/j.1467-9779.2010.01468.x

Chengfei, L., Jianxin, L., Jeffrey, X. Y., & Rui, Z. (2010). Adaptive relaxation for querying heterogeneous XML data sources. *Information Systems, 35*(6), 688–707. doi:10.1016/j.is.2010.02.002

Cimiano, P., Haase, P., Heizmann, J., Mantel, M., & Studer, R. (2008). Towards portable natural language interfaces to knowledge bases - The case of the ORAKEL system. *Data & Knowledge Engineering, 65*(2), 325–354. doi:10.1016/j.datak.2007.10.007

Cohen, W. W., Ravikumar, P., & Fienberg, S. E. (2003). A comparison of string distance metrics for name-matching tasks. In *Proceedings of the International Joint Conferences of Artificial Intelligence Workshop on Information Integration* (pp. 73-78).

Comas, P., & Turmo, J. (2009). Robust question answering for speech transcripts: UPC experience in QAst 2008. In C. Peters, T. Deselaers, N. Ferro, J. Gonzalo, G. Jones, M. Kurimo, et al. (Eds.), *Proceedings of the 9th Workshop on Evaluating Systems for Multilingual and Multimodal Information Access* (LNCS 5706, pp. 492-499).

Conesa, J., Storey, V. C., & Sugumaran, V. (2008). Improving web-query processing through semantic knowledge. *Data & Knowledge Engineering, 66*(1), 18–34. doi:10.1016/j.datak.2007.07.009

Correa, S., Buscaldi, D., & Rosso, P. (2009). NLEL-MAAT at CLEF-ResPubliQA. In *Proceedings of the 10th Cross-language Evaluation Forum Conference on Multilingual Information Access Evaluation: Text Retrieval Experiments*, Corfu, Greece.

Damljanovic, D., Agatonovic, M., & Cunningham, H. (2010). Natural language interfaces to ontologies: Combining syntactic analysis and ontology-based lookup through the user interaction. In *Proceedings of the 7th Extended Semantic Web Conference*, Heraklion, Greece.

Dang, H. T., Kelly, D., & Lin, J. (2007). Overview of the TREC 2007 question answering track. In *Proceedings of the 16th Text REtreival Conference* (p. 1).

De Boni, M., & Manandhar, S. (2005). Implementing clarification dialogues in open domain question answering. *Natural Language Engineering, 11*(4), 343–361. doi:10.1017/S1351324905003682

de Rijke, M., & Webber, B. (Eds.). (2003). *Proceedings of the Workshop on Natural Language Processing for Question Answering*, Budapest, Hungary. Stroudsburg, PA: ACL.

Fellbaum, C. (1998). *WordNet - An electronic lexical database*. Cambridge, Ma: MIT Press.

Ferret, O., Grau, B., Hurault-Plantet, M., Illouz, G., & Jacquemin, C. (2001). Terminological variants for document selection and question/answer matching. In *Proceedings of the Workshop on Open-Domain Question Answering*, Toulouse, France (Vol. 12, pp. 1-8).

Ferrucci, D., Nyberg, E., Allan, J., Barker, K., Brown, E., & Chu-Carroll, J. …Zadrozny, W. (2008). *Towards the open advancement of question answering systems* (Research Report No. RC24789). Armonk, NY: IBM.

Fiveash, K. (2009). *Wolfram Alpha given keys to the Bingdom*. Retrieved from http://www.theregister.co.uk/2009/11/12/bing_wolfram_alpha_deal/

Gaizauskas, R., Greenwood, M., & Hepple, M. (2004). Proceedings of the workshop on information retrieval for question answering at SIGIR workshop. *SIGIR Forum, 38*(2), 41-44.

Gazan, R. (2006). Specialists and synthesists in a question answering community. *Proceedings of the American Society for Information Science and Technology, 43*(1), 1–10. doi:10.1002/meet.1450430171

Gloeckner, I., & Pelzer, B. (2009, September 30-October 2). The LogAnswer Project at CLEF. In *Proceedings of the Working Notes for the Cross-language Evaluation Forum Workshop*, Corfu, Greece.

Gomez, J. M., Buscaldi, D., Rosso, P., & Sanchis, E. (2007, January 4-6). JIRS language-independent passage retrieval system: A comparative study. In *Proceedings of the 5th International Conference on Natural Language Processing*, Hyderabad, India.

Hao, T. Y., Hu, D. W., Liu, W. Y., & Zeng, Q. T. (2008). Semantic patterns for user-interactive question answering. *Concurrency and Computation, 20*(7), 783–799. doi:10.1002/cpe.1273

Harabagiu, S., & Chaudhri, V. (Eds.). (2002). *Proceedings of the AAAI Spring Symposium on Mining Answers from Texts and Knowledge Bases*, Stanford, CA. Menlo Park, CA: AAAI Press.

Harabagiu, S., Hickl, A., Lehmann, J., & Moldovan, D. (2005). Experiments with interactive question-answering. In *Proceedings of the 43rd Annual Meeting on Association for Computational Linguistics*, Ann Arbor, MI (pp. 205-214).

Harabagiu, S., Pasca, M., & Maiorano, S. (2000b). Experiments with open-domain textual question answering. In *Proceedings of the 18th Annual International Conference on Computational Linguistics* (pp. 292-298).

Harabagiu, S. M., Mariorano, S. J., & Pasca, M. A. (2003). Open-domain textual question answering techniques. *Natural Language Engineering, 9*(3), 231–267. doi:10.1017/S1351324903003176

Hartrumpf, S. (2005). Question answering using sentence parsing and semantic network matching. In C. Peters, P. Clough, J. Gonzalo, G. Jones, M. Kluck, & B. Magnini (Eds.), *Proceedings of the 5th Workshop on Multilingual Information Access for Text, Speech and Images* (LNCS 3491, pp. 512-521).

Hickl, A., Lehmann, J., Williams, J., & Harabagiu, S. (2004). Experiments with interactive question answering in complex scenarios. In *Proceedings of the Human Language Technologies Annual Conference of the North American Chapter of the Association for Computational Linguistics Workshop on Pragmatics of Question Answering*, Boston, MA (pp. 60-69).

Higashinaka, R., & Isozaki, H. (2008, January). *Corpus-based question answering for why-questions*. Paper presented at the Third International Joint Conference on Natural Language Processing, Hyderabad, India.

Hori, C., Hori, T., & Furui, S. (2003). Evaluation methods for automatic speech summarization. In *Proceedings of Eurospeech* (pp. 2825-2828).

Horrocks, I., Patel-Schneider, P. F., & Harmelen, F. (2003). From SHIQ and RDF to OWL: the making of a Web ontology language. *Web Semantics: Science. Services and Agents on the World Wide Web, 1*(1), 7–26. doi:10.1016/j.websem.2003.07.001

Hovy, E. H., Hermjakob, U., & Ravichandran, D. (2002). A question/answer typology with surface text patterns. In *Proceedings of the Human Language Technology Conference*, San Diego, CA (pp. 247-251).

Hwang, J. D., Bhatia, A., Bonial, C., Mansouri, A., Vaidya, A., Xue, N., & Palmer, M. (2010). PropBank annotation of multilingual light verb constructions. In *Proceedings of the Fourth Linguistic Annotation Workshop*, Uppsala, Sweden (pp. 82-90).

Ifteen, A., Trandabat, D., Moruz, A., Pistol, I., Husarciuc, M., & Cristea, D. (2010). Question answering on English and Romanian Languages. In C. Peters, G. Nunzio, M. Kurimo, D. Mostefa, A. Penas, & G. Roda (Eds.), *Proceedings of the Workshop on Multilingual Information Access Evaluation I. Text Retrieval Experiments* (LNCS 6241, pp. 229-236).

Imiliensi, A., & Signorini, A. (2009). If you ask nicely, I will answer: Semantic search and today's search engines. In *Proceedings of the 3rd IEEE International Conference on Semantic Computing* (pp. 184-191).

Ittycheriah, A., Franz, M., Zhu, W., Ratnaparkhi, A., & Mammone, R. J. (2001). Question answering using maximum entropy components. In *Proceedings of the Second Meeting of the North American Chapter of the Association for Computational Linguistics on Language technologies*, Pittsburgh, PA (pp. 1-7).

Jiang, J. J., & Conrath, D. W. (1997). Semantic similarity based on corpus statistics and lexical taxonomy. In *Proceedings of the International Conference on Research in Computational Linguistics*, Taipei, Taiwan (pp. 19-33).

Jurafsky, D., & Martin, J. H. (2008). *Speech and language processing* (2nd ed.). Upper Saddle River, NJ: Prentice Hall.

Jurafsky, D., & Martin, J. H. (2009). *Speech and language processing: An introduction to natural language processing, computational linguistics, and speech recognition* (2nd ed., pp. 650–651). Upper Saddle River, NJ: Pearson/Prentice Hall.

Katz, B., & Lin, J. (2003). Selectively using relations to improve precision in question answering. In *Proceedings of the EACL Workshop on Natural Language Processing for Question Answering*.

Kaufmann, E., Bernstein, A., & Fischer, L. (2007). NLP-Reduce: A "naive" but domain-independent natural language interface for querying ontologies. In *Proceedings of the 4th European Semantic Web Conference*, Innsbruck, Austria.

Klein, D., & Manning, C. D. (2003). Accurate unlexicalized parsing. In *Proceedings of the 41st Meeting of the Association for Computational Linguistics* (pp. 423-430).

Konopík, M., & Rohlík, O. (2010). Question answering for not yet semantic Web. In P. Sojka, A. Horák, I. Kopecek, & K. Pala (Eds.), *Proceedings of the 13th International Conference on Text, Speech and Dialogue* (LNCS 6231, pp. 125-132).

Kosseim, L., Plamondon, L., & Guillemette, L. (2003). Answer formulation for question-answering. In Y. Xiang & B. Chaib-draa (Eds.), *Proceedings of the 16th Canadian Society for Computational Studies of Intelligence Conference on Advances in Artificial Intelligence* (LNCS 2671, pp. 24-34).

Kosseim, L., & Yousefi, J. (2008). Improving the performance of question answering with semantically equivalent answer patterns. *Data & Knowledge Engineering, 66*, 63–67. doi:10.1016/j.datak.2007.07.010

Kurata, G., Okazaki, N., & Ishizuka, M. (2004). GDQA: Graph driven question answering system - NTCIR-4 QAC2 experiments. In *Proceedings of the Working Notes of the Fourth NTCIR Workshop Meeting*, Tokyo, Japan (pp. 338-344).

Larosa, S., Penarrubia, J., Rosso, P., & Montes, M. (2005, September 26-30). Cross-language question answering: The key role of translation. In *Proceedings Avances en la Ciencia de la Computación, VI ENCuentro Int. de Computación*, Puebla, Mexico (pp. 131-135).

Laurent, D., Séguéla, P., & Negre, S. (2005). Cross lingual question answering using QRISTAL for CLEF 2005. In *Proceedings of the Working Notes of the Cross-Language Evaluation Forum* (pp 21-23).

Li, X., & Croft, W. B. (2001, March 18-20). Evaluating question answering techniques in Chinese. In *Proceedings of Human Language Technology Conference*, San Diego, CA (pp. 201-206).

Li, X., & Roth, D. (2006). Learning question classifiers: the role of semantic information. *Natural Language Engineering, 12*(3), 229–249. doi:10.1017/S1351324905003955

Llopis, F., & Vicedo, J. (2002). IR-n: A passage retrieval system at CLEF-2001. In C. Peters, M. Braschler, J. Gonzalo, & M. Kluck (Eds), *Proceedings of the Second Workshop on Evaluation of Cross-Language Information Retrieval Systems* (LNCS 2406, pp. 1211-1231).

Lopez, V., Uren, V., Motta, E., & Pasin, M. (2007). AquaLog: An ontology-driven question answering system for organizational semantic intranets. *Web Semantics: Science. Services and Agents on the World Wide Web, 5*(2), 72–105. doi:10.1016/j.websem.2007.03.003

Losada, D. (2010). Statistical query expansion for sentence retrieval and its effects on weak and strong queries. *Information Retrieval, 13*(5), 485–506. doi:10.1007/s10791-009-9122-z

Magnini, B., Speranza, M., & Kumar, V. (2009). Towards interactive question answering: An ontology-based approach. In *Proceedings of the IEEE International Conference on Semantic Computing* (pp. 612-617).

Manning, C., Raghavan, P., & Schütze, H. (2008). *Introduction to information retrieval.* Cambridge, UK: Cambridge University Press.

Marcus, M. P., Santorini, B., & Marcinkiewicz, M. A. (1993). Building a large annotated corpus of English: The Penn Treebank. *Computational Linguistics, 19*(2), 313–330.

Masolo, C., Stefano, B., Gangemi, A., Guarino, N., & Oltramari, A. (2003). *WonderWeb Deliverable D18* (Tech. Rep. ISTC-CNR). Trento, Italy: Laboratory for Applied Ontology.

Maybury, M. (2004). Question answering: An introduction. In Maybury, M. T. (Ed.), *New directions in question answering* (pp. 3–18). Palo Alto, CA: AAAI Press.

Maybury, M. (2006). New directions in question answering. In Strzalkowski, T., & Harabagiu, S. (Eds.), *Text, speech and language technology: Advances in open domain question answering* (*Vol. 32*, pp. 533–558). Berlin, Germany: Springer-Verlag. doi:10.1007/978-1-4020-4746-6_18

McCrea, R. (2004). Evaluation of two library-based and one expert reference service on the web. *Library Review, 53*(1), 11–16. doi:10.1108/00242530410514748

Moldovan, D., Pasca, M., Harabagiu, S., & Surdenau, M. (2003). Performance issues and error analysis in an open-domain question answering system. *ACM Transactions on Information Systems, 21*(2), 133–154. doi:10.1145/763693.763694

Mollá, D. (2009). *From minimal logical forms for answer extraction to logical graphs for question answering. Searching answers: Festschrift in Honour of Michael Hess on the Occasion of His 60th Birthday* (pp. 101–108). Münster, Germany: MV-Wissenschaft.

Mollá, D., & Vicedo, J. (2007). Question answering in restricted domains: An overview. *Computational Linguistics, 33*(1), 41–61. doi:10.1162/coli.2007.33.1.41

Moriceau, V., & Tannier, X. (2010). FIDJI: using syntax for validation answers in multiple documents. *Information Retrieval, 13*(5), 507–533. doi:10.1007/s10791-010-9131-y

Naughton, M., Stokes, N., & Carthy, J. (2010). Sentence-level event classification in unstructured texts. *Information Retrieval, 13*(2), 132–156. doi:10.1007/s10791-009-9113-0

Netrvalova, A., & Safařík, J. (2008). Selection of partners for co-operation based on interpersonal trust. In *Proceedings of the Conference on Human System Interaction*, Kraków, Poland.

Niles, I., & Pease, A. (2001). Towards a standard upper ontology. In *Proceedings of the 2nd International Conference on Formal Ontology in Information Systems*, Ogunquit, ME.

Ounis, I., Macdonald, C., & Soboroff, I. (2008). Overview of the TREC 2008 Blog track. In *Proceedings of the 17th Text REtrieval Conference.*

Paris, C., Wan, S., & Thomas, P. (2010). Focused and aggregated search: a perspective from natural language generation. *Information Retrieval, 13*(5), 434–459. doi:10.1007/s10791-009-9121-0

Pasca, M. A., & Harabagiu, S. M. (2001). High performance question/answering. In *Proceedings of the 24th Annual International ACM SIGIR Conference on Research and Development in Information Retrieval*, New Orleans, LA (pp. 366-374).

Paulheim, H., & Probst, F. (2010). Ontology-enhanced user interfaces: A survey. *International Journal on Semantic Web and Information Systems, 6*(2), 36–59. doi:10.4018/jswis.2010040103

Penas, A., Forner, P., Sutcliffe, R., Rodrigo, A., Forascu, C., & Alegria, I. ...Osenova, P. (2010). Overview of ResPubliQA 2009: Question answering evaluation over European legislation. In C. Peters, G. Di Nunzio, M. Kurimo, D. Mostefa, A. Penas, and G. Roda (Ed.), *Proceedings of the Workshop on Multilingual Information Access Evaluation I. Text Retrieval Experiments* (LNCS 6241, pp. 174-196).

Prud'hommeaux, E., & Seaborne, A. (2008). *SPARQL query language for RDF.* Retrieved October 15, 2010, from http://www.w3.org/ TR/ rdf-sparql-query/

Quarteroni, S. (2007). *Advanced techniques for personalized, interactive question answering* (Unpublished doctoral dissertation). Department of Computer Science, The University of York, York, UK.

Quarteroni, S., & Manandhar, S. (2008). Designing and interactive open-domain question answering system. *Natural Language Engineering, 15*(1), 73–95. doi:10.1017/S1351324908004919

Ravin, Y., Prager, J., & Harabagiu, S. (Eds.). (2001). *Proceedings of the Workshop on Open-Domain Question Answering*, Toulouse, France. Stroudsburg, PA: ACL.

Roush, W. (2006). What comes after Web 2.0? *MIT TechReview*. Retrieved October 18, 2010, from http://www.technologyreview.com/ Infotech/17845/

Roussinov, D., Fan, W., & Robles-Flores, J. (2008). Beyond keywords: Automated question answering on the Web. *Communications of the ACM, 51*(9), 60–65. doi:10.1145/1378727.1378743

Sacaleanu, B., & Neumann, G. (2006). Cross-cutting aspects of cross-language question answering systems. In *Proceedings of the Workshop on Multilingual Question Answering, Association for Computational Linguistics*, Morristown, NJ (pp. 15-22).

Sánchez, D., Batet, M., Valls, A., & Gibert, K. (2009). Ontology-driven web-based semantic similarity. *Journal of Intelligent Information Systems, 35*(3).

Santos, D., & Cabral, L. M. (2010). GikiCLEF: Expectations and lessons learned. In C. Peters, G. M. Di Nunzio, M. Kurimo, T. Mandl, D. Mostefa, A. Peñas, & G. Roda (Eds.), *Proceedings of the 10th Workshop on Multilingual Information Acess Evaluation I: Text Retrieval Experiments* (LNCS 6241, pp. 212-222).

Soricut, R., & Brill, E. (2006). Automatic question answering using the web: Beyond the factoid. *Information Retrieval, 9*(2), 191–206. doi:10.1007/s10791-006-7149-y

Soubbotin, M., & Soubbotin, S. (2001). Patterns of potential answer expression as clues to the right answers. In *Proceedings of the Tenth Text REtrieval Conference* (pp. 175-182).

Tablan, V., Damljanovic, D., & Bontcheva, K. (2008). A natural language query interface to structured information. In *Proceedings of the 5th European Semantic Web Conference on the Semantic Web: Research and Applications*, Spain (pp. 361-375).

Tannier, X., & Moriceau, V. (2010). Studying syntactic analysis in a QA system: FIDJI @ ResPubliQA'09. In C. Peters, G. Nunzio, M. Kurimo, D. Mostefa, A. Penas, & G. Roda (Eds.), *Proceedings of the 10th Workshop on Multilingual Information Access Evaluation I: Text Retrieval Experiments* (LNCS 6241, pp 237-244).

Tianyong, H., Wanpeng, S., Dawei, H., & Wenyin, L. (2008). Automatic generation of semantic patterns for user-interactive question answering. In H. Li, T. Liu, W.-Y. Ma, T. Sakai, K.-F. Wong, & G. Zhou (Eds.), *Proceedings of the 4th Asia Information Retrieval Technology Symposium* (LNCS 4993, pp. 632-637).

Tjong, E. F., Sang, K., & Buchholz, S. (2000). Introduction to the CoNLL-2000 shared task: Chunking. In *Proceedings of the 2nd Workshop on Learning Language in Logic and the 4th Conference on Computational Natural Language Learning*, Lisbon, Portugal (Vol. 7).

Trillo, R., Po, L., Ilarri, S., Bergamaschi, S., & Mena, S. (2010). Using semantic techniques to access web data. *Information Systems, 36*(2).

Trotman, A., Geva, A., Kamps, J., Lalmas, M., & Murdock, V. (2010). Current research in focused retrieval and result aggregation. *Information Retrieval, 13*(5), 407–411. doi:10.1007/s10791-010-9137-5

Usunier, N., Amini, M., & Gallinari, P. (2004). Boosting weak ranking functions to enhance passage retrieval for question answering. In *Proceedings of the Workshop on Information Retrieval for Question Answering* (pp. 1-6).

Van Schooten, B. W., Op Den Akker, R., Rosset, S., Galibert, O., Max, A., & Illouz, G. (2009). Follow-up question handling in the IMIX and Ritel systems: A comparative study. *Natural Language Engineering, 15*, 97–118. doi:10.1017/S1351324908004920

Varges, S., Weng, F., & Pon-Barry, H. (2008). Interactive question answering and constraint relaxation in spoken dialogue systems. *Natural Language Engineering, 15*(1), 9–30. doi:10.1017/S1351324908004889

Verberne, S. (2010). *In search of the why - Developing a system for answering why-questions* (Unpublished doctoral dissertation). Radboud Universiteit Nijmegen, Nijmegen-Midden, The Netherlands.

Verberne, S., Boves, L., Oostdijk, N., & Coppen, P. A. (2010). What is no in the Bag of Words for Why-QA? *Computational Linguistics, 36*(2), 229–245.

Verberne, S., Halteren, H., Theijssen, D., Raaijmakers, S., & Boves, L. (2011). Learning to rank for why-question answering. *Information Retrieval, 14*(2). doi:10.1007/s10791-010-9136-6

Verberne, S., Raaijmakers, S., Theijssen, D., & Boves, L. (2009). Learning to rank answers to why-questions. In *Proceedings of the Dutch-Belgium Information Retrieval Workshop* (pp. 34-41).

Voorhees, M. (2001a). Overview of the TREC 2001 question answering track. In *Proceedings of the Tenth Text REtrieval Conference* (pp. 42-51).

Voorhees, M. (2001b). The TREC question answering track. *Natural Language Engineering, 7*, 361–378. doi:10.1017/S1351324901002789

Voorhees, M. (2003). Overview of the TREC 2003 question answering track. In *Proceedings of the Twelfth Text REtrieval Conference* (pp. 54-68).

Wasserman, S., & Faust, K. (1994). *Social network analysis*. Cambridge, UK: Cambridge University Press.

Weisenthal, J. (2007). *Hakia raises $2 million for semantic search*. Retrieved from http://www.nytimes.com/paidcontent/PCORG_317848.html

Wenyin, L., Tianyong, H., Chen, W., & Min, F. (2009). A Web-based platform for user-interactive question-answering. *World Wide Web (Bussum), 12*(2), 107–124. doi:10.1007/s11280-008-0051-3

Zhang, D., & Lee, W. S. (2003). Question classification using support vector machines. In *Proceedings of the 26th Annual International ACM SIGIR Conference on Research and Development in Informaion Retrieval*, Toronto, ON, Canada (pp. 26-32).

Zhu, L., Ma, Q., Liu, C., Mao, G., & Yang, W. (2010). Semantic-distance based evaluation of ranking queries over relational databases. *Journal of Intelligent Information Systems, 35*(3). doi:10.1007/s10844-009-0116-5

APPENDIX

Although we have thoroughly supplemented the core sections of this chapter with references to available literature, some related issues may be of interest to the reader. Thus, we provide a list of recommended additional reading.

Additional reading related to QA in the Semantic Web environment

A historical overview of the development of the Web Ontology Language (OWL), its incentives, fundamentals and philosophy is well described in Horrocks et al. (2003).

Ontology-based QA using ontology databases, with application to two case studies in biomedicine, using ontologies and data from genetics and neuroscience can be found in LePendu and Dou (2010).

A set of semantics techniques to group the results provided by a traditional search engine into categories defined by the different meanings of the input keywords is proposed in Trillo et al. (2010). The authors claim that their proposal is different since their method considers the knowledge provided by ontologies available on the web in order to dynamically define the possible categories.

A very common problem in research areas such as natural language processing, knowledge acquisition, information retrieval or data mining is the estimation of the degree of semantic similarity/distance between concepts. Sánchez et al. (2009) analyze this issue and propose modifications of classical similarity measures.

A complex survey of ontology-enhanced user interfaces can be found in Paulheim and Probst (2010).

Additional reading related to QA and IR

The results of CLEF tasks between years 2000 and 2007 can be found at http://www.clef-campaign.org/. We can recommend this reports to readers who want to get familiar with detailed results of compeeting systems in this QA task.

Query expansion based on pseudo relevance feedback which tries to solve the problem of relevant expansion term identification using so-called definition clusters is presented in Bernhard (2010). Their experiments use the freely available Microsoft Research Question-Answering Corpus (MSRQA) which provides a fully annotated set of questions and answers retrieved from the Encarta 98 encyclopedia (it can be obtained at http://research.microsoft.com)

A comprehensive overview of QA in restricted domains including a list of existing systems is presented in Mollá and Vicedo (2007).

A comparison of multimodal interactive QA with speech recognition on the input is described in Van Schooten et al. (2009).

Sentence level classification is an important task for QA. Classification of unstructured text using SVM and language models can be found in Naughton et al. (2010).

Incorporating semantic knowledge into query processing in traditional web search engines is described in Conesa et al. (2008).

The effect of distinct statistical expansion methods on sentence retrieval is thoroughly studied and evaluated in Losada (2010).

Both focused retrieval and result aggregation provide the user with answers to their information needs, rather than just pointers to whole documents. An overview of the current research in this area is presented in Trotman et al. (2010).

Since aggregated search techniques represent an important part of the new generation of search applications, Paris et al. (2010) focuses on exploring the parallels between aggregated search and natural language generation, leading to further advances in the way search technologies can better serve the user.

An adaptation of ranking query to the relational database environment is presented in Zhu et al. (2010) where the evaluation of ranking queries is based on semantic distance.

Additional reading related to QA over structured data

A theoretical methodology to evaluate XML retrieval systems and their filters, along with the formal investigation of qualitative properties of retrieval models, is thoroughly described in Blanke and Lalmas (2010).

A study presented in Arvola et al. (2010) introduces a novel framework for evaluating passage and XML retrieval. This study seeks evaluation metrics for retrieval methods and proposes a framework, where the passages of the retrieved document are re-organized, so that the best matching passages are read first in sequential order.

XML query relaxation is necessary for searching XML data with a structured XML query, which can improve the precision of results compared with a keyword search. An adaptive relaxation approach which relaxes a query against different data sources differently based on their conformed schemas is proposed by Chengfei et al. (2010).

Chapter 15
Finding Answers to Questions, in Text Collections or Web, in Open Domain or Specialty Domains

Brigitte Grau
LIMSI-CNRS and ENSIIE, France

ABSTRACT

This chapter is dedicated to factual question answering, i.e., extracting precise and exact answers to question given in natural language from texts. A question in natural language gives more information than a bag of word query (i.e., a query made of a list of words), and provides clues for finding precise answers. The author first focuses on the presentation of the underlying problems mainly due to the existence of linguistic variations between questions and their answerable pieces of texts for selecting relevant passages and extracting reliable answers. The author first presents how to answer factual question in open domain. The author also presents answering questions in specialty domain as it requires dealing with semi-structured knowledge and specialized terminologies, and can lead to different applications, as information management in corporations for example. Searching answers on the Web constitutes another application frame and introduces specificities linked to Web redundancy or collaborative usage. Besides, the Web is also multilingual, and a challenging problem consists in searching answers in target language documents other than the source language of the question. For all these topics, this chapter presents main approaches and the remaining problems.

DOI: 10.4018/978-1-4666-0330-1.ch015

INTRODUCTION

The large number of documents currently on the Web, but also in intranets, makes it necessary to provide users intelligent assistant tools to help them finding the specific information they are searching for. Relevant information at the right time is able to help solving a particular task. Thus, purpose is to be able to access the content of texts, and not only give access to documents. The document is the means to reach the knowledge it contains, not the goal of the research. Question-answering systems address this question and their purpose is to provide a user the information she is looking for instead of documents she will have to read to find the required answer.

This topic arose since the early work in Artificial Intelligence with systems dedicated for questioning knowledge base in natural language, as BASEBALL in 1963 (Green et al., 1986) LUNAR in 1973 and LADDER in 1977 (Barr et al., 1981) for a brief description of these systems). Afterward, Lehnert with her system QUALM (Lehnert, 1977) has posed the problem of the semantic modeling of questions in order to associate them different strategies to find answers.

However, these works were based largely on manual modeling of knowledge and remained dedicated to limited domains. Thus, they have not led to realistic applications and the research for precise answers turn towards the development of database interrogation interfaces.

It is only recently that the problem has re-emerged at TREC, in 1999, with the first evaluation of question-answering systems in open domain dedicated to find answers to factual questions in texts.

As in querying database, factual questions wait for short answers that give precise information. Factual questions are those questions that ask for a short and concise answer about precise facts, as for example a person name as in *"What is the name of the managing director of Apricot Computer?"* or a date as in *"When is Bastille Day?."* However,

this time, topics are not limited and knowledge is not structured previously, since these are the texts that are its repositories. Finding answers requires analyzing texts and this is made possible thanks to mature natural language processing tools. The wide availability of texts in numeric format has allowed to model and evaluate linguistic processes and led to the distribution of tools widely applicable, such as word syntactic category taggers (also called part-of-speech (POS) taggers) or robust syntactic parsers. Word syntactic category taggers is the process of identifying which word is used in a text, and which is its grammatical category, as noun, verb, adjective. Syntactic parsers realize grammatical analysis of sentences, highlighting the different phrases (noun phrases, verbal phrases, etc.) and their relations, as subject, direct object, etc. The dissemination of knowledge sources, such as lexicons, thesauri and ontology also enables the realization of advanced text processing.

Thus, the problem of finding answers to questions is now posed differently: it consists in extracting a piece of information from a text. The texts themselves are the sources of knowledge and can be structured and enriched by automatic processes. As first systems have found applications in natural language interface for querying databases by non expert users, QA systems are an answer each time there is a great amount of documents to interrogate for precise information needs, even in professional sectors: business analysis, technologic scouting, journalistic documentation, biography, etc.

Since their beginnings in TREC, question-answering systems have known a great interest from the community, either in Information Retrieval or in Natural Language Processing. Following TREC, the task was introduced in other conferences in IR evaluations: CLEF 2 in 2003, for European languages and multi-lingual approach, NTCIR 3 for Asian languages, in 2003 too.

These researches have led to the realization of systems which differ from document retrieval systems (cf. Chapter ??).

Their first characteristic is the way to specify the information sought. When a user searches for specific information, the most explicit and easier way for her to give her request is to use her own language, without having to translate it in a query dedicated to a search engine. In fact, whatever the query language used, ranging from lists of words to more structured and constrained queries, all queries are intended to describe the type of document sought: documents that are similar to the query. In such queries, type of the expected information is not explicit, and it is not clear whether are searched all documents that refer to a subject or just a specific information or even a definition. QA systems start from a formulation in natural language and provide just the exact answer, and not documents, as a result.

This is the second characteristic of QA systems, and it is this that makes their specificity: they return as a result a set of answers, not a set of documents that the user has to read to find the information she looks for. When a classical search engine entails the need to read documents to assess their relevance, a QA system will prevent this work to the user. Thus, a QA system provides answers supported by excerpts of documents enabling the user to verify their validity. We will see that this notion of validity of an answer goes beyond the assessment of its relevance.

Depending on the application, search will be made in different resources. Technology scouting will lead to browse the Web to answer questions such as the list of companies whose turnover is down by June 2003, or companies that manufacture products X or Y. The search for technical information, such as "how to install a printer" or "what is the command to copy a file" should be made in manuals or on the Web, or will be addressed more specifically by research in FAQ. Knowing the winner of the Nobel Prize in 1965 is possible by consulting newspaper articles or the Web. With the semantic Web, it may also turn to interrogate factual or encyclopedic knowledge base, structured or semi-structured to obtain information.

We will see that different media induce different retrieval processes.

In this chapter we will first present question-answering systems whose purpose is to extract answers from documents in a fixed collection, in response to open domain questions. They will be our reference systems. We will then present QA in specialty domains, focusing on the specific approaches they required and the need for using dedicated knowledge bases. We will see after how to search the Web and what particularities it induces by examining different points: i) the Web as a source of knowledge, with its characteristics in terms of size and kind of knowledge it holds; ii) the multilingual Web as the diversity of languages makes it necessary to develop interlingual or crosslingual systems where the question is in a language and the answer is found in documents in another language; iii) finally, the collaborative Web, where the Web is the vector for providing collective answers to questions and entails new search processes to exploit these resources automatically.

QA IN OPEN DOMAIN

Question answering in open domain is the most studied domain, and has essentially focused on finding answers to factual questions. Such kinds of answer generally correspond to named entities. Named entities are multiword units that can be recognized in texts, according to surface criteria and gazetteers, and that refer to objects of the world as person, location etc. (Nadeau et al., 2007). However, answers can also be other kinds of entities, as in *"Which alphabet has only four letters, A, C, G and T?"* or in Why or How questions. Even if named-entity questions give a supplementary clue for finding the exact answer, all question types present same characteristics to account for. Thus, before describing question-answering systems, we will show the problems they have to address.

Figure 1. Lexical variations between question and passage

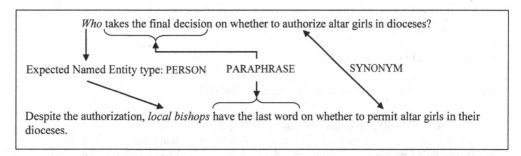

Relations between a Question and an Answer

Searching for specific answers in texts poses two major problems: finding the passage of text containing the answer and the extraction of the exact answer from this passage. Passages are the units preferred by users over documents for supporting an exact answer provided by a system. Thus, a relevant passage may be defined as a piece of text, usually one to three sentences, which contains the information given in the question and the expected answer. Very often, this information is not provided in the exact terms of the question, and there is a gap between the question wording and the text excerpt wording. So a passage will be considered as relevant if it paraphrases the question put into a declarative form and contains the answer. Often, relevant passages are not strict paraphrases of the question they answer: they may contain such a paraphrase plus other information, or they may entail the answer. Thus, our definition of paraphrase covers this larger phenomenon.

Depending on the question and texts phrasing, these paraphrases are more or less distant from the original question: either a passage contains exactly the terms and the syntactic form of the question, but it is pretty rare, or, and that is what question-answering systems have to face, there are linguistic variations in term of different wording of semantically equivalent contents.

At term level, variations involve use of:

- Synonyms or other semantic relations between terms such as hypernyms or hyponyms[1] to designate entities;
- Morphological variations, such as the transformation from verb to name as "*to meet and the meeting*" or vice versa;
- Combinations of these variations that lead to deal with paraphrases of terms.

In the example Figure 1, matching question and passage requires tying "to take final decision" with "to have last words" and "authorize" with "permit", and we can see that a Who question does not always lead to search for a person name, but a person category.

At sentence level, systems have to cope with anaphora and paraphrases, either paraphrases of subpart of question or of the whole question. Anaphora occurs when an entity of the previous discourse is referred by a personal pronoun or another name in a sentence, as Bill Clinton ..., the president ..., he ...

In example Figure 2, the passage contains almost all the question words, but they are not in the same sentence: there exists an anaphoric chain that begins with "Orville and Wilbur Wright", then continues with "the Wrights" and ends at "their" in the sentence that contains the answer. Note that the brotherhood between *Orville* and *Wilbur* is not explicit, and should be verified in another document, or in an encyclopedia to be sure. In order to select the right answer, *120 feet*, and not *852 feet*, which are both lengths, some

Figure 2. Syntactic phenomena between question and passage

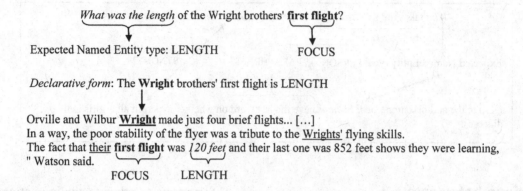

syntactic dependencies have to be checked: the subject of verb *be* is the focus *first flight*, in order to be a paraphrase of the information provided by the question.

Answering a question involves processes related to information retrieval (IR), information extraction (IE) and natural language processing (NLP) fields: NLP to analyze question, IR to search for documents or passages likely to contain the answer and IE and NLP to analyze them and extract the answer. It requires the implementation of various processes, modeling varying levels of understanding.

Components of a Question Answering System

Question-answering systems generally comprise three steps:

- Question analysis, that determines the characteristics of the answer;
- The selection and the analysis of passages, taking into account the elements identified in the analysis of questions;
- The extraction of the answer from the selected passages.

We will present the general principles implemented by the various systems for these three modules in open domain QA systems.

Question Analysis

Analysis of questions makes explicit the information sought by the user as it can then be exploited by the following modules. An important feature deals with the expected type of the answer that systems are able to recognize in texts, outside the question context. These types are associated to classical named entities such as person and organization names, places, dates, quantities, etc. but also to types specific to the QA field, as the definition of different dates (birth, death), subcategories of organizations or persons as political parties, newspapers, universities, actors, politicians, etc. and new types that regularly arise in questions, as symbols of countries, titles of films or books. The number of types varies greatly from one system to another and can range from tens to hundreds.

Thus, Prager et al. (2000) have identified 50 types of answers, the system Webclopedia (Hovy et al., 2001) 122, called qtargets, recognized by a set of rules or patterns, consisting of named entity types or semantic categories present into a knowledge base. A broad classification is further developed in Harabagiu et al. (2000) based primarily on WordNet (Fellbaum, 1998).

Table 1. Example 1 of question analysis

Question	What is the chemical formula for sulphur dioxide?
Answer type	chemical formula
Focus	sulphur dioxide
Terms	chemical formula, sulphur dioxide, plus the single terms
Category	instance

Table 2. Example 2 of question analysis

Question	What female leader succeeded Ferdinand Marcos as president of the Philippines?
Expected named entity type	PERSON
Answer type	female leader
Focus	to succeed
Terms	female leader, Ferdinand Marcos, president of the Philippines, plus the single terms
Category	event + role subject

Ittycheriah et al. (2001) make use of a statistical approach to type answers (31 types divided into 5 classes), but their performance remains limited (56% of items labeled, or 280 out of 500), and handwriting rule remains the best solution. Since, more corpus have been developed, and some work propose question type recognition by machine learning methods (for example Day et al., 2007) for Chinese and English).

Another concern of question analysis is the representation of the information given in the question. Two main trends exist then. The first class of approaches produces a comprehensive analysis of sentence, both syntactic and semantic (Moldovan et al., 2002; Hartrumpf, 2005; Bouma et al., 2006a) to find similar sentences in texts that are analyzed in the same way. The method coverage relies on the capabilities of syntactic parser to produce in depth analysis, and on the existence of semantic knowledge base for achieving semantic analysis.

The second kinds of approaches perform a surface analysis, and highlights certain features, like significant words, their POS[2] tags, the term pivot about which information is sought, called the focus in Ferret et al. (2002), Laurent, Nègre, and Séguéla (2005), and Plamondon et al. (2003),

relations between the terms of the question. In some system, the term focus corresponds to the designation of the answer type (for example *president* in *Which president*), or the focus corresponds to one or several terms of the questions (Soubbotin et al., 2001; Ittycheriah et al., 2001; Hovy et al., 2001). In particular, Hovy et al. identify the relevant question terms and expands them using WordNet, and Soubbotin and Soubbotin recognize primary words (the words which are indispensable for sentence comprehension).

Questions can also be categorized according to the type of information searched, such as a definition, a characteristic of the focus, a role in an event to determine how this information could be expressed and extracted (Ferret et al., 2002; Moldovan et al., 2002; Grau et al., 2006).

Tables 1 and 2 exhibit some examples of question analysis.

The answer will be a kind of formula, associated to the focus. We will see in the answer extraction paragraph how these characteristics guide the extraction process.

The answer will be a named entity that should correspond to the subject of the verb that designates an event.

Most QA systems develop shallow analysis that may involve use of syntactic parsers, and question analysis is usually performed by hand-made rules based on surface criteria (word order, type of words, standard expression, etc.). Some words, either nouns or verbs, play a triggering role to detect the expected named entity type and they are classified relative to this type. Thus, rules for determining this type of answer are based on the interrogative word, the class of the word it is linked to and the class of the main verb. The focus is often the subject of the main verb, except when the latter corresponds to the expected type, it is then the object. The category of the question can be determined by syntactic criteria on the form of the question.

Document and Passage Analysis

Most systems first retrieved documents with the help of a search engine, then extract relevant passages from them using a dedicated process. Queries are made of the significant question words, eventually expanded by synonyms. A first choice concerns the kind of search engine to rely on. Tellex et al. (2003) have conducted a series of experiments with a Boolean search engine on one hand (Lucene) and a vector model engine (Prise). A Boolean query is made of words related by AND, OR and NOT operators as in "president AND (USA OR American)" and relevant documents have to verify this query, e.g., contain the two words *president* and *USA* or the two words *president* and *American*. Nowadays Boolean search engines also provide an approximate verification when the query is not fully verified. A vector model search engine evaluates a similarity between a query made of a set of words and documents, represented by set of words also. They conclude that both engines produce similar results.

The methods applied for selecting passage from documents can vary widely from one system to another. Many systems develop a weighting scheme to select passages from the retrieved

documents, whose size varies from one to three sentences. Prager et al. (2000) and Clarke et al. (2001) based their QA system on passage retrieval techniques, rather than on classical IR techniques and they directly select passages from the whole corpus. However whatever the process is, the main criteria considered remain the same to score passages, only their combination differs. Thus, some systems annotate the whole collection in order to perform a fine grained collection indexing and search (Laurent, Nègre, & Séguéla, 2005; Rosset et al., 2005), while others search for passages, then annotate and weight them. Weighting schemes are based on the following criteria (Ferret et al., 2001; Magnini et al., 2002a; Ittycheriah et al., 2001):

- The number of significant words of the question, usually weighted either according to their degree of specificity in natural language or to their expected role in answer extraction (for example the focus);
- Variations of these words, in order to try to cover all formulations of the underlying concepts that can be found in answering passage;
- Expected Named Entities;
- The proximity of the question terms identified in the passage;
- Eventually syntactic relations between phrases.

All the systems annotate passages by named entity recognizers. In order to detect linguistic variations in passages, QALC (Grau et al., 2006; Chalendar de et al., 2002) analyses them with Fastr (Jacquemin, 2001), a transformational shallow parser for the recognition of term occurrences and variants. Terms, which correspond to multiword units, as "president of the USA", are transformed into grammar rules and the single words building these terms are extracted and linked to their morphological and semantic families, in order to recognize for example "American president". This term recognition shows two advantages: i) documents that contain multiword units in place of single terms are often more relevant; ii) linguistic variations computed on multiword units are more reliable as these terms are less ambiguous than single words. If we consider the example given in Table 1, the WordNet synonyms of *formula* are: *expression, recipe, convention, normal, pattern, rule. Chemical* has only one synonym, *chemic,* and the meaning involved in this question "*chemical formula*" has no synonym found in the corpus by Fastr. By the way, all synonyms of single terms can be discarded as inappropriate. Disambiguation of words is a hard task, and QA systems rarely implement such a process. Thus, synonyms involved in multiword units will be in some manner disambiguated by each term of the unit, and will lead to less noise.

Studies about passage length (Gillard et al., 2005) recommend selecting passages of three to five sentences.

Recent works developed passage reranking techniques, and are mostly evaluated on collections of pairs (Question/Answering passages) and not fully integrated in QA systems. They are based on learning methods in order to take into account lexical and syntactic similarities between passages or questions/passages, or to classify passages (Moschitti et al., 2007) (see section about Collaborative QA).

Extraction of Answers

The selection of passages is a first evaluation of the reliability of candidates by applying global criteria. For extracting the answer, more local criteria, related to its formulation, are necessary. The implementation of these criteria can be based on a parsing, syntactic or semantic, of the passage sentences. Within numerical approaches, the system relies on a measure of proximity of recognized terms with the candidate answer, selected according to its type. Gillard et al. (2005) defines a standardized mean score of compacity of the realizations of the question words in the right and left neighborhoods of candidate answer. Other researchers have developed machine learning approach in place of a weighting scheme.

Systems that develop deep analysis of sentences rely on one sentence passages and have to define a distance between the syntactic representations of the question and each candidate sentence. Bouma et al. (2006a) define similarity as the proportion of syntactic dependency relations of the question that match dependency relations of the candidate sentence. The answer is then extracted based on the knowledge of the type expected and additional criteria such as the frequency of the short answer. The determination of the answer may also result from a logical proof of candidate answers (Moldovan et al., 2003; Hartrumpf et al., 2006): sentences and questions are represented by logical formulas, and the proof relies on deduction rules that model world knowledge. However, such a prover must implement relaxing process when computing the proof to avoid silence.

The most common approach consists in applying extraction patterns to select the correct answer. In Soubbotin et al. (2001, 2002), these are regular expressions describing all types of expected answer. In Ligozat et al. (2006a), patterns correspond to local syntax rules in the formalism of SCOL (Abney, 1996), written on POS tags (Figure 3).

These rules are articulated around the focus tagged FC or FCS or the expected type, tagged TG or TGS and associated to the category of the question. They are written by the definition of two levels: the first identifies different basic noun phrases in sentences NPH, the noun phrases that contain the focus (NPFoc) and the expected type (NPTG). The second level corresponds to the patterns themselves and is based on previously identified groups.

Labels are used to sort the patterns according to their reliability. Thus the answers recognized by pattern *a* are more reliable than those recognized by pattern *b*.

Returning to example Table 1, the following sentences can be retrieved:

Figure 3. Extraction patterns written in SCOL formalism, dedicated to instance or definition questions

Level 1: Phrases
SP = "comma|parenthesis|dash";
NPFoc → DT ? RB ? (ADJ (CC ADJ) ?) ? (FC|FCS) RB ? ;
NPTG → DT ? RB ? (ADJ (CC ADJ) ?) ? (TG|TGS) RB ? ;
NPH → (DT? RB* ADJ* (NN|NNS)+ RB* ADJ* | DT ? RB* ADJ* (NP|NPS)+;

Level 2: Patterns
The answer is characterized by its type in an apposition phrase or by a modifier inside its phrase
RTsep → b= NPH SEP NPTG ;
RInTP → NPTG c=NPH;

Precision of the answer type
RDefTG → NPTG (IN NPFoc)? VB a= NPH;

The answer defines the focus (by using verb be or by an apposition)
RDefFoc → NPFoc VB a= NPH;
RAppFoc → NPFoc SEP a= NP SEP;

Legend:
DT: determinant, RB: adverb, ADJ: adjective, NP, NPS: proper noun(s), IN: preposition
FC, FCS: focus or focus variant, TG, TGS: answer type or a variant

- S1: Sulfur dioxide (also sulphur dioxide) is the chemical compound with the <u>formula</u> SO2
- S2: The structural formula of sulphur dioxide is SO2, and …
- S3: The chemical formula for sulphur dioxide is SO2
- S4: For example, sulfur dioxide (SO2) and nitric acid (HNO3) may ...

By applying pattern RDefTG on S2 or S3, the answer *SO2* is extracted, as VB stands for the verb *be*, while pattern RInTP allows to extract the answer in S1 and RAppFoc applies on S4.

After the extraction step, some systems apply a validation step, if the extraction approach itself does not entail this validation. Systems generally try to validate the answer by a confirmation coming from another source of knowledge.

Answer Validation

A first approach consists to confirm the answer based on the size and redundancy of the Web. Magnini et al. (2002b, 2002c) have tested two approaches. The first is purely statistical and is based on the number of documents returned. The Web is queried by Altavista with a query made of keywords of the question and the answer to validate, linked by Boolean and proximity operators, AND, OR or NEAR. They do not search an exact match of the question in the documents found on the Web. The validity of an answer is calculated from the number of documents returned for three queries: one is made from the only question words, the other from the answer words and the third from the previous two. The second method tested is based on the content and relevance of answers relative to questions and is evaluated by a measure based on co-occurrence of words in the snippets returned by Google. These two methods are similar in term of gains and were incorporated into their system evaluated at TREC11 that tries to validate 40 answers per question (Magnini et al., 2002a). The final weighting of answers is based on the coefficient of validity from the Web search and the reliability of the answer type. The best result is obtained with the second method and enabled them to find 38.4% of correct answers. This type of approach has been extended in Awadallah et al.

(2006), by adding more measures and applying it to the Arabic language. The test corpus consists of questions from TREC 11 and questions from the game "The Millionaire" that exists in English and Arabic. Results on the two languages are better with strategies based on co-occurrences in the extracts, although below the results of Magnini et al. (2002c), and results on Arabic are low, probably due to two main factors according to authors: the greater ambiguity of the Arabic words and fewer documents found on the Web, for which the search engines have no linguistic approximation techniques. This fact shows that the applicability of methods often depends on the analyzed language and the resources available for it.

In QALC (de Chalendar et al., 2003), a similar search is performed on the collection and the Web, and only the query formulation changes (see section QA and the Web). Then, the results of the two systems are merged, to promote same answers found in the two sources of knowledge. This strategy allows QALC to validate 106 of the 165 correct answers to 500 questions from TREC 11.

Another form of validation consists in trying to validate missing information in external source of knowledge. Indeed, when an answer is extracted from a passage, its type is not always identified. This is the case of answers whose expected type is given in the question but do not fit exactly a general named entity type but a more specific one, as with the type *female leader* and named entity type PERSON. The verification of the answer can be driven by checking its type into a knowledge base (Bouma et al., 2006a), or by exploiting external textual resources (Grappy et al., 2010; Schlobach et al., 2007), as Wikipedia and the Web to compute different criteria giving some evidence about the validity of the answer type, and combine them by a machine learning approach. Such a case occurs in the following answering passage of example in Table 2:

In 1986, **President Ferdinand_E._Marcos** *fled the* **Philippines** *after 20 years of rule in the wake of a tainted election;* {[REP] **Corazon Aquino**} *assumed the* **presidency**<.>

It has to be checked that Corazon Aquino is a female leader.

Verifying that an answer extracted from a passage answers a question may also be posed as a problem of "textual entailment" to find if a passage entails a hypothesis made of the question in a declarative form plus the candidate answer. Evaluations RTE[3] (Recognising Textual Entailments) and AVE (Answer Validation Exercise) (Peñas, Rodrigo, Sama, & Verdejo, 2008) at CLEF gave a frame to evaluate this kind of task. The RTE task consists in determining whether a passage implies a hypothesis while the AVE task whether a passage justifies the answer to a question. This last task can be resumed to the first question by considering the couple question plus answer as a hypothesis.

Systems rely mostly on machine learning approaches incorporating various criteria, most often of lexical order: terms of the hypothesis present in the passage, common named entities or similarity measures. To get a better fit when comparing terms, systems make use of external semantic knowledge such as WordNet (Fellbaum, 1998) or VerbOcean (Chklovski & Pantel, 2004). A criterion frequently used is the longest common substring between the question and the passage (Newman et al., 2005), that also may reflect linguistic variations (Herrera et al., 2006; Hickl et al., 2006; Ligozat et al., 2007). Such a criterion allows systems to take into account both syntactic and lexical similarities in a same measure, with common words and common syntactic roles, considering that if the hypothesis and the passage share an important subpart, there is a strong evidence that their topic is same. However, criteria based on syntactic dependencies can also be explicitly introduced as a criterion, and Moriceau et al. (2008) compute the number of common syntactic relations. In order to develop a comparison of sentence structures, some systems developed syntactic graph matching (Kouylekov et al., 2006; Iftene et al., 2009) or semantic graph matching (Wang, Zhang, & Neumann, 2009). As many occurring phenomena can be solved by different methods, Wang et al. (2008) combine all of them within a voting approach.

The last kinds of methods rely on logical proofs, which often lack of robustness since they depend on the completeness of the knowledge base. Thus, they are used in conjunction with the above methods (Tatu et al., 2006; Clark et al., 2009; Bensley et al., 2008). Best systems obtain an accuracy value around 70-75%.

Such paradigm supposes that the justification can be found in few consecutive sentences, and cannot allow studying justifying processes based on information found in different documents and resources.

The ultimate verification of the validity of an answer is made by the user of the system. Given the answer and the justifying passage, she can usually judge the validity of the proposal. But she may have doubts about the confidence she can give to the materials from which is extracted the answer or to the behavior of the system. To this end, Inference Web (McGuinness et al., 2004a, 2004b) is a tool able to trace the reasoning process for finding an answer and to specify from which sources it is extracted. This tool requires that the reasoning can be modeled by documents PML (Proof Markup Language). By a less formal approach, Javelin (Calais et al., 2004) and REVISE (El Ayari et al., 2010) provide an environment for storing intermediate results and source documents in a relational database, to associate them XML elements and then view the processing steps and the results of modules via a Web browser.

Evaluation

While the problematic of question answering exists since the beginning of NLP, the introduction of a dedicated task in TREC in 1999, campaign organized by NIST, has renewed the topic, by focusing on open domain factual questions whose answer can be extracted from documents (Voorhees, 2001). The success known by this task and its growing complexity has shown the vitality of the researches. The synopsis of the evaluation proposes a set of questions the systems have to answer. Human judges evaluate system results, with several judgments for a same answer. A result consists of an answer along with a document that justifies the answer. Thus an answer with a right value, but that is not warranted in the proposed document will not be considered as correct.

In the first campaign, TREC8, the organizers selected two hundred questions among a set proposed by the twenty-six participants. Systems had to return five ordered excerpts of 250 characters as answers, extracted from a corpus of 1.9 gigabytes, or 528,000 documents. The documents came from American newspapers, the Los Angeles Times, the Financial Times, FBIS and the Federal Register. At this first attempt, around 50% of answers were found by the best systems. This first campaign makes in evidence the need to use NLP approaches and semantic knowledge. The TREC9 campaign, the following year, proposed two subtasks to the participants, around 25, one still focused on the extraction of passages, the other requiring short answers (50 characters). A set of 700 questions, including 200 rewritings, were built from logs provided by search engines and selected by the organizer according to their scope (general enough) and leading to evaluable answers. The size of the collection has nearly doubled since it contained 980 000 texts of 3 gigabytes.

The TREC10 campaign in 2001 complicated the task since only short answers were allowed, and some questions had no answers in the documents. Many questions focused on definitions that have caused some problems in their assessment. Indeed, answers could be quite disparate, ranging from the proposition of a generic concept to a part of the definition. For example, the question, "What is an atom?" or "Who is Colin Powell?"

were answered by very different levels of granularity and different answer completeness. This is why such questions were deleted from TREC11 when they were not precise enough. The number of participants has stabilized around 35.

The difficulty of TREC11 focused on two points: i) to give only the exact answer and not a short passage, ii) to give only one answer per question and iii) to classify the answer according to a degree of confidence. The collection has been replaced by the corpus AQUAINT. Most systems have searched answers on the Web. Although some works developed a fine grained analysis of sentences, the broadest topping approach relies on criteria to approximate such an analysis. Apart from the LCC system (Moldovan et al., 2002) that gets more than four hundred correct answers of five hundred, the other systems, which certainly differ in their modules but all try to marry surface NLP processes, use of semantic knowledge and techniques of information retrieval, got results that could still be significantly improved.

In parallel to the main task, a track addressing answering questions by multiple answers (list questions) existed since 2000. An attempt to held chained questions was abandoned; the aim was to move towards an evaluation of successive couples of questions and answers related to each other as a simulation of dialogue. Best systems obtained an accuracy value around 70-80%.

From TREC12 (2003) to last campaigns in 2007, questions of definition were reintroduced, assuming a same context defined *a priori* for several questions. After this time, the QA track held in the Text Analysis Conference (TAC) with opinion questions in 2008, and then closed.

In Europe, the campaign CLEF created in 2003 a multilingual question answering track, whose evaluation was conducted similarly to TREC. The difference comes from questions and documents in two different languages, in addition to monolingual QA tracks. The NTCIR evaluation followed analogous specifications, but for Asian languages.

QA IN SPECIALTY DOMAIN

QA Dedicated to Ontologies on the Web

An evolution of the Web is the vision that it would allow to store and access structured semantic knowledge represented by ontologies. This view brings out new forms of interrogation and search and some research in QA explore this field. As we already said, solutions based on a logical representation of questions and documents for answering open domain factual questions have been proposed and evaluated in Moldovan et al. (2002, 2003), who developed extended WordNet for representing inference rules, and in Hartrumpf (2006), based on its ontology MultiNet interfaced with the German language through HaGenLex to build and match semantic graphs. Zajac (2001) and Lopez Garcia et al. (2006, 2005) explored the formalization of the process of finding answers in a formal ontology, but it is the work of Atzeni et al. (2004) and Calais et al. (2006) which defines the problem for the Web and explore the querying of several ontologies. The first work takes place in the multilingual project MOSES which aims at querying a federation of university websites, each in a different language. To this end, it proposes to merge the ontologies in order to relate concepts described in two different languages, based on the structure of the ontologies as well as translation of labels associated to concepts. The second work envisions the problem differently and search answers in several ontology and merge them in order to increase the completeness of the system proposition.

In a more particular context, some initiatives propose to interrogate semi-structured database (often RDF[4] triplets) build from manual or semi-manual entries (http://www.wolframalpha.com/ ; http://www.trueknowledge.com/).

However there is few works in this domain, according to its restrictive application field and more systems were developed to interrogate specialty or restrictive domains.

QA on Restrictive Domains

It is interesting to see that QA on restrictive domains (RDQA) regained an interest in the research community, and is back since the early years of AI and first QA systems, presented in the introduction section. Some examples of such domains are services of telecommunication corporation (Doan-Nguyen et al., 2006), Biomedical domain (Sang et al., 2005; Rinaldi et al., 2004; Demner-Fuschman et al., 2007), practical domains as weather information (Chung et al., 2004) or geographical domain (Ferrés et al., 2006). Information is obtained from documents, or semi-structured knowledge or databases. In this latter case, databases are built from documents, generally with offline processes.

Some particularities distinguish this field from open domain QA (Doan-Nguyen et al., 2006; Minock et al., 2005):

- Restricted domain collection, and thus scarcity of answers;
- Domain specific terminology;
- Complex questions and different types of answers than factual ones.

As the domain knowledge is better delimited, and thus can be modeled formally into a conceptual representation that supports inferences, deep analysis of text can be applied to transform documents and questions in such a representation and questions are mapped over the knowledge base (Sang et al., 2005; Rinaldi et al., 2004; Frank et al., 2007). Besides classical problem related to natural language processing, the main problem concerns the recognition of terms of the domain, as they play a pivotal role. Without having terminological resources or ontologies having a broad covering of the domain, systems performances remain low, as shown when applying a non dedicated QA system.

While open domain QA system are designed to answer factual questions, questions in restricted domain lead to different type of answers, and are often formulated in a more complex manner. Thus, developing a RDQA system requires new classifications of questions (see Yu et al., 2005) for the medical domain) and another level of granularity for answers: precise answer but also passages (Sang et al., 2005; Doan-Nguyen et al., 2006).

Thus, even if their general architecture remains the same in each domain, many processes have to be redesigned or adapted to develop a RDQA system (Minock et al., 2005; Jacquemart et al., 2003). However these systems provide new tools in information processing and management in corporations for example. The reader can report to the overview of Molla and Vicedo (2007) for more references.

QA AND THE WEB

Searching the Web or searching a much smaller collection introduces differences in query formulation and QA systems make the hypothesis that there must be at least a document on the Web, and even more documents, which provides the answer in a form closed to the question wordings. The redundancy of the Web also gives some clues to select the correct answer without having to implement complicated extraction techniques.

Searching the Web for QA

One of the first systems that allowed questions in natural language on the Web was AskJeeves. This system was looking for answers as documents in its database. One of the first QA systems designed to query the web using an existing search engine is MULDER (Kwok et al., 2001). With the creation of the QA track at TREC, many systems have early used the Web as a resource for answer validation. These systems performed a rewriting of questions to bring the relevant documents in the top, or to extract only the excerpts provided by the engine (i.e., the snippets). All of them exploit the idea that the huge size and the high redundancy of information allows to find relevant documents even with a very specific query.

Queries for Getting Precise Answers

MULDER and QALC (Berthelin et al., 2003) generate queries as specific as possible, while keeping the capability of relaxing constraints. A rewriting of questions aims at building queries close to the wording of the answers, where the verbal phrase is converted in a declarative form, clues dedicated to introduce the answer are added, and groups of words are kept. This rephrasing is realized by handmade rules and their conception relies on the same principles that guide the conception of extraction pattern. An evaluation of the contribution of these reformulations for MULDER can be found in Kwok et al. (2001). The two systems make use of Google. Hermjacob et al. (2002) generate paraphrases of the question using syntactic and semantic rules. These paraphrases are used to build Boolean queries (three paraphrases per question on average) to search the Web. Brill et al. (2001) implement simpler question reformulations by keeping the question words in their original order and moving the verb in all possible positions. They demand the search engine to make comparisons at the string level.

The last approach presented here concerns reformulation learning, related to each of the search engines used to make the query, Google and AltaVista (Agistein et al., 2001). Lexical clues that might introduce answers according to their expected types are learned. The training corpus is coming from the Web and was created from FAQ (Frequently Asked Question). The authors have restricted their work to definition questions, i.e., "Who is" and "What is" questions, and questions "how" and "where", covering a specialty domain, computer science.

Use of Redundancy

Extraction of exact answers can rely on the concept of redundancy and avoid implementing strategies based on the development of extraction patterns. Clarke, Cormack, and Lynam (2001) select answers according to their redundancy and study more particularly this factor, focusing on answers corresponding to names of person, by evaluating the impact of the number and size of the selected passages on the results.

To quantify their strategy, Dumais et al. (2002) have applied an adaptation of the approach they have developed for the Web on the TREC collection. Their system exploits primarily redundancy of the Web. This enables to rewrite questions simply (Brill et al., 2001) and implement an extraction technique as simple, since it retains the string the most frequent in the snippets returned by the search engine, after applying some filters based on the types of questions as an alternative to tagging named entities: existence of uppercase, numbers, for example. The system, applied to the Web with TREC9 questions, finds 61% of answers within the first 5 ranks. Applied to the collection AQUAINT, the system, after some modifications in the extraction of short passages, is 24% right, against 53% for the previous system applied under the same conditions. A similar technique was used on Portuguese (Costa, 2006), whose pages indexed by Google are estimated at 60.5 million. The system performs a simple rewriting of questions, eliminates noise caused by some sites that have been manually selected, select the first 100 snippets returned by Google and extract the answer based on a technique of frequent n-grams. The system found only 30% of correct answers to questions from CLEF 2004 and 2005, but these issues are dedicated to a collection dating from 1994 and maybe the answers are not all on the Web.

Another approach is to use the Web to assist a search in a reference corpus against finding answers exclusively on the Web. Clarke et al. (2001) select 40 passages among the top 200 documents returned by two Web search engines and 20 passages in their reference corpus, in which the answer is extracted, provided it belongs to the reference corpus. The Web is used here to increase the redundancy factor of candidates. This approach has improved the results of their system from 25 to 30%.

The Web can also be seen as a repository of knowledge from which information can be extracted that will populate knowledge bases. Thus, Fleischman et al. (2003) have built a large corpus of 15GB, consisting of newspaper articles and documents from the Web to extract concept-instance relationships, in order to answer questions like "Who is the Mayor of Boston "and" Who is Jennifer Capriati. ". 2,000,000 of such relationships were obtained after filtering by a classifier to eliminate noise caused by patrons of extractions. Questions were collected on the site www.askjeeves.com, available in 2003, and the evaluation was calculated on 100 questions. The base can improve the performance of QA system of 36% answers.

Crosslingual QA

The richness of the Web is also its multilinguism, and an important challenge concerns the ability to ask a question in its own language and receive an answer extracted from texts written in any language. When looking for a fact relating to a particular event in a country, it is more likely to find the answer in texts written in the language of that country. That is the purpose of crosslingual systems. They should then not only solve the problem of searching for answers in a language different from the question but also, for completeness, consider their translation. This last point is less problematic than machine translation in all its generality, see Bos et al. (2006) for example for translating answers. Currently, most QA systems that implement crosslingual solutions leave the answer in the target language. These systems, evaluated at CLEF, provide answers in English

from different question source languages, French, Italian, etc. or inversely.

Translation of Questions

Some systems make use of machine translation to translate the questions and apply a monolingual system thereafter (PER04) (Jijkoun et al., 2004; Neumann et al., 2004, 2005; Ahn et al., 2004). Perret (2004) and Jijkoun et al. (2004) have also applied their monolingual system to the same set of questions to compare results. The first, in its English-Dutch version obtained a decrease of 10.5% on its results: 91 (45.5%) to 70 (35%) correct answers, and the results of the second, in its English-French version, saw its percentage of correct answers decrease of 13.5: 49 (24.5%) to 22 (11%) answers. BiQue (Neumann et al., 2004, 2005) made use of several tools for translating German into English to get a good coverage. Alignment of translated questions provides the translation of the source words that are put together in a "bag-of-words" representation used for expanding the query. This set is completed with synonyms, after disambiguation. The disambiguation module uses EuroWordNet to find correspondences between words in the two languages (English and German) and, for each ambiguous word; it looks at which of its meaning are expressed both in the source question (in German) and its translations (in English). Their system has achieved 25.5% correct answers at CLEF 2005, and from English into German, 23%. Bouma et al. (2006b) complete the question translation by automatic translations of named entities and bi-word expressions found in Wikipedia as these types of terms are poorly processed by translators that do not contain them in their dictionaries. Their system, which in the monolingual Dutch task obtained 31% of correct answers, gets 20% in bilingual, English-Dutch.

The two major problems in using machine translations for the questions lie in the bad resolution of ambiguity of the question word and in syntactically incorrect translations. If a word

Table 3. Validation of bi-terms translations by Fastr

Total number of bi-terms formed from the questions	777	
Number of bi-terms found	307	39.5%
Number of bi-terms found only in their original form	52	17%
Number of bi-terms found only by semantic derivation	150	54%

relevant to the search of the answer is badly translated, this error cannot usually be compensated by other words of the question, because questions are often quite short, and the mistranslation of a word changes its meaning.

Translation of the Question Terms

Another solution consist in analyzing the question in the source language, extract all the useful features, i.e., the type of the expected answer, the words and phrases (nominal, verbal and prepositional), focus and question category. This information remains the same regardless of the language, so only words have to be translated. This brings out the only problem of managing multiple meanings of words. This solution has been chosen by many systems. Tanev et al. (2004), considering that the results of machine translation, especially for questions, were not quite encouraging, managed to translate the keywords of the question: after a step of removing irrelevant words, keywords are translated. To eliminate the noise inherent to such a process, they only retain the combinations of translations the most plausible, i.e., those that appear most frequently in two reference corpus (AQUAINT and TIPSTER). This type of approach was already used in Grefenstette (1999) in the context of machine translation for validating translations of noun phrases on the Web. They get a score of 45 (22.5%) correct responses in bilingual cons 56 (28%) in monolingual, so with a loss of 6% of correct answers only.

A combination of translators and the validation of translated multi-terms of the question in a corpus can be found in Sutcliffe et al. (2006) and Ligozat et al. (2006b). In Ligozat et al., instead of relying only on co-occurrences, English translations of biterms (terms made of two words) and their possible variations are sought, using Fastr (Jacquemin, 2001) (Table 3). For example, from the 777 bi-terms extracted from the questions of CLEF 2005, 39.5% are found in a subset of the collection, 54% only as variants of the given form. This means that the translation of the biterm is not found as such, and therefore does probably not fit with a correct translation, but allow to finding the correct expression. The only bi-terms found alike are often proper names, usually names of people. Each bi-term found in corpus entails to validate translations of its single words, thus relative to the context of the questions. The system found 25% of responses in 2006 in the French to English track.

Synapse (Laurent, Séguéla, & Nègre, 2005, 2006) also translates words and idioms, and their system found 44% of French answers from questions in English, while their monolingual French system is 69% correct. In the same paradigm, the crosslingual system English-Spanish BRILIW (Ferrandez et al., 2009) uses EuroWordNet and Wikipedia for translating common words and named entities, and obtains better results than by translating the questions.

Translation of Documents

The latter technique explored by Bowden et al. (2006) is quite rare as they translate the documents into the language of the question, in this case French documents translated into English. The answer is then extracted and "re-translated" by aligning documents. The system is 40% correct in the source language, translation introduces a loss of 50% of responses.

The choice of an appropriate method relies on available resources for translation from a language to another: machine translator, bilingual dictionary or none of them, using then aligned or parallel corpora to find translations. As machine translation does not provide tools able to produce always well written texts, an experiment (Lopez et al., 2006) was made with users who have to search manually for exact answers in a monolingual frame with documents written the source language (Spanish), and in a crosslingual frame with documents translated automatically from the target language (English to Spanish), using a same QA tool. The authors found that the performance of users for searching answers in the monolingual experiment was only 11.4% better, but they performed the task 40% faster on average. Given these facts for human beings, QA systems have a difficult task to achieve consisting in attaining performances of monolingual systems, even if some burden would be admitted by users. However, a more realistic task that would consists in searching different documents in different languages and merging results has not be proposed in QA, while this kind of task was proposed in information retrieval evaluation conferences.

Collaborative QA

User-generated contents become more and more popular on the Web since the last decade, and community-driven question-answering portals gain a large audience. Recent works are dedicated to provide tools for retrieving existing answers to users' questions, as Yahoo answers. In this specific context, focus is turn towards detecting questions similarities between user's question and existing ones, or similarities between the user's question and existing answers.

Similarity is often posed as a paraphrase problem detection (Agistein et al., 2008; Wang et al., 2009; Cui et al., 2005), on the intrinsic content of the compared extracts, based on lexical and syntactic information. However, links between contents and rating of them can also be considered for selecting better answers (Agistein et al., 2008), provided that content found on such sites are less trustful, and systems have to consider this kind of problems.

Dealing with paraphrases become more crucial in this context given that users' formulations of a same need vary and that questions and answers do not possess same properties as in open domain answer extraction: answers are given in response to a question, and not extracted from texts to answer questions, thus their distances in term of vocabulary and forms of sentences are greater.

Web documents present specific structures with informative content, as tables, lists, frames, etc. QA systems that want to exploit them have to recognize such structures and to develop specific analysis (Lerman et al., 2004). That is why some projects have emerged to extract information from structured Web documents. Lixto (Baumgartner et al., 2005) allows to writing wrappers dedicated to sites in order to extract information from the tree representation of the pages, wrappers that can adapt to changing sites. More specifically to answer questions, Katz et al. (2003) and Lin et al. (2003) have developed a hybrid approach to find answers, based either on simple extraction techniques exploiting the redundancy of the Web, or on the interrogation of certain sites, and then functioning as dedicated knowledge bases. Answers to questions about the characteristics of countries, elements of biography of famous people, film is sought on some sites listed and for which wrappers have been developed., Their system answers 30 questions about 42 dedicated to be solved by this technique, from the questions of TREC 2002, and 153 from 458 by a conventional extraction technique, so 16% of answers are found by the use of some sites.

CONCLUSION AND PERSPECTIVES

The evolution of processes used in the question answering field is significant of the evolution in the field of NLP. From first systems, operating on high-level conceptual representations to infer information from their knowledge base within a narrow scope, now it came to systems that can answer questions concerning any field. Differences rely on the types of questions addressed and the sources of knowledge. QA systems answer factual questions when the answer exists in a text, even in an altered form in relation to the question and terms used. Thus, current approaches are working on unstructured knowledge bases, i.e., text collection or Web, and all processes are dedicated to structure this knowledge, primarily through use of NLP. Questions and especially candidate passages are analyzed to identify named entities, noun and verbal phrases, syntactic or semantic relations. Systems often apply surface analysis allowing the identification or the approximation of such information, and approaches as closed to those used in information extraction, where the use of extraction patterns, more or less fixed, was widely chosen, leaving aside the generic analysis of sentences and texts.

However, Moldovan et al. (2002, 2003) showed that it was also possible to apply fine grained analysis, while preserving good coverage. Thus, using a version of extended WordNet, a robust parsing and a relaxed logic prover, their system is over 80% of answers. Systems that use approximate methods to treat the same phenomena are closer to 70% of answers. The great lesson we can draw is that implementing elaborated linguistic processes in order to answer factual questions is possible, even in open domain, without damaging the overall performance. When such skills are missing, another way would be to implement different strategies and to apply them dynamically according to their performance. Systems that seek answers in different sources of knowledge (structured databases, the Web, documents from the collection of reference) show important gains. Others have tried using different strategies, by using two systems with different approaches or with different sources of knowledge (de Chalendar et al., 2003) or by combining in depth analysis and surface numeric processes (Jijkoun & De Rijke, 2004) and get better results than a system or a strategy operating alone. The effectiveness of the techniques described is less tied to the type of question than the difficulty of solving the question, which depends on the sources of knowledge, the number of responses that are present and their formulation.

Monolingual QA evaluations show that the rate of correct answers for a given language is strongly related to the existence of resources, and solutions to overcome this limitation could be found in their acquisition from texts. All these approaches have found their utilization in the IBM system, WATSON (http://www-03.ibm.com/innovation/us/watson/), dedicated to participate to the American game Jeopardy, which consists in finding an answer from information related to it. WATSON is the integration of multiple search strategies and resources in a parallel environment.

A question-answering system does not represent a self content system and should depend on the application in which it operates. According to the application frame, it involves definition of user type, her degree of knowledge and expertise, the usage context of the system (why do we ask questions, what is the level of answer expected), and what are the searched knowledge bases.

Protocols of answers were little studied until now. It is often assumed there is only one correct answer to a question, or that different answers are complementary or equivalent, and thus are all correct. However, the question of the relevance of the information returned often arises. In TREC, the problem was partially solved by considering an answer in relation with a supporting document that should help to assess the veracity of the answer according to the context it provides. Thus, answers that are different depending on the period covered by the documents will be all accurate. This means that an answer cannot be considered correct by itself, without the passage that justifies it. Thus, to the question "Who married Tom Cruise?", Nicole Kidman is the correct answer in the collection AQUAINT. This raises the problem of presentation of the answer inside its justifying context and a correct answer would be "in 2001, Nicole Kidman". The problem of management of claims should be resolved as well, producing responses indicating "according to X, the answer is Y, as it is not always possible to choose among several answers. This problem will be even more crucial if searched sources do not have same reliability and this leads to the differentiation of the search for answers on the Web and in a reference collection certified as to its content.

The search for specific information on the Web has its own peculiarities and the problem is a little different than looking for specific information in a collection of smaller size. Characteristics that induce strategies dedicated to the Web are a) its size: the information sought is likely to exist in a form similar to that of the question b) its redundancy: the correct answer is probably the proposition which is found in several documents and c) its multilinguism: the answer can be found in a language different from the language question, and it would encourage under-represented languages, since the information provided in these languages would be sources of answers, regardless of the interrogation language.

Question-answering systems have thus adapted their strategies to the particularities of Web search, whether to formulate queries, which can often be very specific, or to extract answers: intensive use of redundancy to select the more probable answer. Note that QA systems usually use Google to search for documents, and very often only select the returned snippets. Indeed, criteria for selecting passages in systems are based on common words between question and passage as well as their proximity and Google implements these criteria in its selection process of documents. With such a light approach, systems can claim to answer 60% of the questions. It remains that the 40% unanswered questions require more elaborate treatments, to deal with linguistic variation, ambiguity of natural language and finding rare information.

Systems of question answering on the Web have to offer crosslingual search. Current solutions show performances less than the monolingual frame, as are added translation ambiguities and problems of lexicon coverage, particularly as regards proper names and acronyms. Currently, only the translation problems have been studied in QA systems. Other interesting possibilities would be to use multilingual sites, or to guide the research on the language depending on each question: a question about a particular culture is more likely to be found in its language.

Finally, it is important to overcome factual questions and interrogation process limited to a single exchange, to study other types of questions and especially to integrate the notion of context in the process. First, the application context: why does one perform a search, for what purpose? What level of knowledge of the user? Considering these aspects will lead to produce different answers to the same questions. Then, if the questioning process is iterative, this should lead to be able to treat more questions and give more accurate and complete answers. Users do not always perceive the implicit that exists in their own request. QA systems would become closer to dialogue systems, at least for managing the interaction (Rosset et al., 2005; Quarteroni et al., 2009). This raises the problem of the evaluation methodology of such contextual system for evaluating systems under the same conditions.

REFERENCES

Abney, S. (1996). Partial parsing via finite-state cascades. *Journal of Natural Language Engineering*, *2*(4), 337–344. doi:10.1017/S1351324997001599

Agichtein, E., Castillo, C., Donato, D., Gionis, A., & Mishne, G. (2008). Finding high-quality content in social media. In *Proceedings of the International Conference on Web Search and Web Data Mining.*

Agichtein, E., Lawrence, S., & Gravano, L. (2001). Learning search engine specific query transformations for question answering. In *Proceedings of the Conference on World Wide Web.*

Ahn, K., Alex, B., Bos, J., Dalmas, T., Leidner, J. L., & Smillie, M. B. (2004). Cross-lingual question answering with QED. In *Proceedings of the Working Notes of CLEF Cross-Language Evaluation Forum*, Bath, UK (pp. 335-342).

Atzeni, P., Basili, R., Haltrup Hansen, D., Missier, P., Paggio, P., Pazienza, M. T., & Zanzotto, F. M. (2004). Ontology-based question answering in a Federation of University Sites: The MOSES case study. In *Proceedings of the 17th International Conference on Applications of Natural Language Processing to Information Systems* (pp. 413-420).

Awadallah, R., & Rauber, A. (2006). Web-based multiple choice question answering for English and Arabic questions. In *Proceedings of the European Conference on Information Retrieval* (pp. 515-518).

Barr, A., & Feigenbaum, E. A. (Eds.). (1981). *The handbook of artificial intelligence (Vol. 1*, pp. 281–316). New York, NY: William Kaufmann.

Baumgartner, R., Frölich, O., Gottlob, G., Harz, P., Herzog, M., & Lehmann, P. (2005). Web data extraction for business intelligence: the Lixto approach. In *Proceedings of the German Database Conference Datenbanksysteme in Büro, Technik und Wissenschaft*, Karlsruhe, Germany.

Bensley, J., & Hickl, A. (2008). Application of LCC's GROUNDHOG System for RTE-4. In *Proceedings of the Text Analysis Conference*, Gaithersburg, MD.

Berthelin, J. B., de Chalendar, G., Ferret, O., Grau, B., ElKateb, F., & Hurault-Plantet, M. …Vilnat A. (2003). Trouver des réponses sur le Web et dans une collection fermée. In *Proceedings of the INFORSID Workshop Recherche d'Information: un nouveau passage à l'échelle.*

Bos, J., & Nissim, M. (2006). Cross-lingual question answering by answer translation. In *Proceedings of the Workshop of the Cross-language Evaluation Forum and the European Conference on Research and Advanced Technology for Digital Libraries Conference.*

Bouma, G., Fahmi, I., Mur, J., van Noord, G., van der Plas, L., & Tiedemann, J. (2006a). Linguistic knowledge and question. *Répondre à des questions, 46*(3).

Bouma, G., Fahmi, I., Mur, J., van Noord, G., van der Plas, L., & Tiedemann, J. (2006b). The University of Groningen at QA@CLEF 2006: Using syntactic knowledge for QA. In *Proceedings of the Workshop of the Cross-language Evaluation Forum and the European Conference on Research and Advanced Technology for Digital Libraries Conference.*

Bowden, M., Olteanu, M., Suriyentrakorn, P., Clark, J., & Moldovan, D. (2006). LCC's PowerAnswer at QA@CLEF 2006. In *Proceedings of the Workshop of the Cross-language Evaluation Forum and the European Conference on Research and Advanced Technology for Digital Libraries Conference.*

Brill, E., Lin, J., Banko, M., Dumais, S., & Ng, A. (2001). Data-intensive question answering. In *Proceedings of the Text Retrieval Conference*, Gaithersburg, MD.

Calais Pedro, V., Ko, J., Nyberg, E., & Mitamura, T. (2004). An information repository model for advanced question answering systems. In *Proceedings of the Fourth International Conference on Language Resources and Evaluation.*

Calais Pedro, V., Nyberg, E., & Carbonell, J. (2006). Federated ontology search. In *Proceedings of First International Workshop of Semantic Information Integration on Knowledge Discovery*.

Chklovski, T., & Pantel, P. (2004). VerbOcean: Mining the web for fine-grained semantic verb relations. In *Proceedings of Conference on Empirical Methods in Natural Language Processing*, Barcelona, Spain.

Chung, H., Song, Y. I., Han, K. S., Yoon, D. S., Lee, J. Y., Rim, H. C., & Kim, S. H. (2004). A practical QA system in restricted domains. In *Proceedings of the 42nd Annual Meeting of the Association for Computational Linguistics Workshop on Question Answering in Restricted Domains*.

Clark, P., & Harrison, P. (2009). An inference-based approach to recognizing entailment. In *Proceedings of the Text Analysis Conference*, Gaithersburg, MD.

Clarke, C. L. A., Cormack, G. V., & Lynam, T. R. (2001). Exploiting redundancy in question answering. In *Proceedings of the 24th Annual International ACM SIGIR Conference on Research and Development in Information Retrieval*.

Clarke, C. L. A., Cormack, G. V., Lynam, T. R., Li, C. M., & McLearn, G. L. (2001). Web reinforced question answering (multitext experiments for TREC 2001). In *Proceedings of the 10ᵗʰ Text Retrieval Conference*, Gaithersburg, MD.

Costa, L. F. (2006). A question answering system in the Web using the Web. In *Proceedings of 11th Conference of the European Chapter of the Association for Computational Linguistics*.

Cui, H., Sun, R., Li, K., Kan, M.-Y., & Chua, T.-S. (2005). Question answering passage retrieval using dependency relations. In *Proceedings of the 28th Annual International ACM SIGIR Conference on Research and Development in Information Retrieval* (pp. 400-407).

Day, M. Y., Ong, C. S., & Hsu, W. L. (2007). Question classification in English-Chinese cross-language question answering: an integrated genetic algorithm and machine learning approach. In *Proceedings of the IEEE International Conference on Information Reuse and Integration* (pp. 203-208).

de Chalendar, G., Dalmas, T., Elkateb-Gara, F., Ferret, O., Grau, B., & Hurault-Plantet, M. … Vilnat A. (2002). The question answering system QALC at LIMSI, experiments in using Web and WordNet. In *Proceedings of the 11ᵗʰ Text Retrieval Conference* (pp. 457-467).

de Chalendar, G., Ferret, O., Grau, B., ElKateb, F., Hurault-Plantet, M., & Monceaux, L. … Vilnat, A. (2003). Confronter des sources de connaissances différentes pour obtenir une réponse plus fiable. In *Proceedings of the Conference on Traitement Automatique des Langues Naturelles*, Nancy, France.

Demner-Fushman, D., & Lin, J. (2007). Answering clinical questions with knowledge-based and statistical techniques. *Computational Linguistics, 33*(1), 63–103. doi:10.1162/coli.2007.33.1.63

Doan-Nguyen, H., & Kosseim, L. (2006). Using terminology and a concept hierarchy for restricted-domain question-answering. *Research on Computing Science, 18*.

Dumais, S., Banko, M., Brill, E., Lin, J., & Ng, A. (2002). Web question answering: Is more always better? In *Proceedings of the 25th ACM/SIGIR International Conference on Research and Development in Information Retrieval*, Tampere, Finland.

El Ayari, S., Grau, B., & Ligozat, A.-L. (2010). Fine-grained linguistic evaluation of question answering systems. In *Proceedings of the International Conference on Language Resources and Evaluation*.

Fellbaum, C. (1998). *WordNet: An electronic lexical database*. Cambridge, MA: MIT Press.

Ferrandez, S., Toral, A., Ferrandez, O., Ferrandez, A., & Munoz, R. (2009). Exploiting Wikipedia and EuroWordNet to solve cross-lingual question answering. *Information Sciences, 179*(20), 3473–3488. doi:10.1016/j.ins.2009.06.031

Ferrés, D., & Rodriguez, H. (2006). Experiments adapting an open-domain question answering system to the geographical domain using scope-based resources. In *Proceedings of the Workshop on Multilingual Question Answering*.

Ferret, O., Grau, B., Hurault-Plantet, M., Illouz, G., & Jacquemin, C. (2001). Document selection refinement based on linguistic features for QALC, a question answering system. In *Proceedings of Recent Advances in Natural language Processing*, Tsigov Chark, Bulgaria.

Ferret, O., Grau, B., Hurault-Plantet, M., Illouz, G., Jacquemin, C., & Monceaux, L. (2002). How NLP can improve question answering. *Journal of Knowledge Organization, 29*(3-4), 135–155.

Fleischman, M., Echihabi, A., & Hovy, E. H. (2003). Offline strategies for online question answering: Answering questions before they are asked. In *Proceedings of the ACL Conference*, Sapporo, Japan.

Frank, A., Krieger, H. U., Xu, F., Uszkoreit, H., Crysmann, B., Jörg, B., & Schäfer, U. (2007). Question answering from structured knowledge sources. *Journal of Applied Logic, 5*(1). doi:10.1016/j.jal.2005.12.006

Gillard, L., Sitbon, L., Bellot, P., & El-Bèze, M. (2005). Dernières évolutions de SQuaLIA, le système de Questions/Réponses du LIA. *Répondre à des questions, 46*(3).

Grappy, A., & Grau, B. (2010). Answer type validation in question answering systems. In *Proceedings of the 9th RIAO Conference on Adaptivity, Personalization and Fusion of Heterogeneous Information*.

Grau, B., Ferret, O., Hurault-Plantet, M., Monceaux, L., Robba, I., Vilnat, A., & Jacquemin, C. (2006). Coping with alternate formulations of questions and answers. In Strzalkowski, T., & Harabagiu, S. (Eds.), *Advances in open-domain question-answering: Text, speech and language technology* (*Vol. 32*). Berlin, Germany: Springer-Verlag. doi:10.1007/978-1-4020-4746-6_6

Green, B., Wolf, A., Chomsky, C., & Laughery, K. (1986). BASEBALL: An automatic question answerer. In Grosz, B. J., Jones, K. S., & Webber, B. L. (Eds.), *Readings in natural language processing* (pp. 545–550). San Francisco, CA: Morgan Kaufmann.

Grefenstette, G. (1999). The World Wide Web as a resource for example-based machine translation tasks. In *Proceedings of the ASLIB Conference on Translating and the Computer*, London, UK (Vol. 21).

Harabagiu, S., Pasca, M., & Maiorano, J. (2000). Experiments with open-domain textual question answering. In *Proceedings of the 19th Annual International Conference on Computational Linguistics*, Saarbrucken, Germany.

Hartrumpf, S. (2005). University of Hagen at QA@CLEF 2005: Extending knowledge and deepening linguistic processing for question answering. In *Proceedings of the CLEF Cross-Language System Evaluation Campaign, Working Notes for the CLEF Workshop*.

Hartrumpf, S., & Leveling, J. (2006). University of Hagen at QA@CLEF 2006: Interpretation and normalization of temporal expressions. In *Proceedings of the CLEF Cross-Language System Evaluation Campaign, Working Notes for the CLEF Workshop*, Alicante, Spain.

Hermjakob, U., Echihabi, A., & Marcu, D. (2002). Natural language based reformulation resource and Web exploitation for question answering. In *Proceedings of the 11th Text Retrieval Conference*, Gaithersburg, MD.

Herrera, J., Rodrigo, A., Penas, A., & Verdejo, F. (2006). F. UNED submission to AVE 2006. In *Proceedings of the CLEF Cross-Language System Evaluation Campaign, Working Notes for the CLEF Workshop*.

Hickl, A., Williams, J., Bensley, J., Kirk Roberts, Y. S., & Rink, B. (2006). Question answering with LCC's Chaucer at TREC 2006. In *Proceedings of the Fifteenth Text Retrieval Conference*.

Hovy, E., Hermjacob, U., Lin, C.-Y., & Ravichandran, D. (2001). Towards semantics-based answer pinpointing. In *Proceedings of the DARPA Human Technology Conference*, San Diego, CA.

Iftene, A., & Moruz, A. M. (2009). UAIC Participation at RTE5. In *Proceedings of the Text Analysis Conference Workshop*.

Ittycheriah, A., Franz, M., & Roukos, S. (2001). IBM's statistical question answering system. In *Proceedings of the 10th Text Retrieval Conference*, Gaithersburg, MD.

Jacquemart, P., & Zweigenbaum, P. (2003). Towards a medical question-answering system: a feasibility study. In *Proceedings Medical Informatics Europe. Studies in Health Technology and Informatics, 95*, 463–468.

Jacquemin, C. (2001). *Spotting and discovering terms through NLP*. Cambridge, MA: MIT Press.

Jijkoun, V., & De Rijke, M. (2004). Answer selection in a multi-stream open domain question answering system. In (Eds.), (LNCS 2997, pp. 99-111).

Jijkoun, V., Mishne, G., de Rijke, M., Schlobach, S., Ahn, D., & Muller, K. (2004). The University of Amsterdam at QA@CLEF2004. In *Proceedings of the Working Notes of CLEF Cross-Language Evaluation Forum*, Bath UK (pp. 321-325).

Katz, B., Lin, J., Loreto, D., Hildebrandt, W., Bilotti, M., & Felshin, S. …Mora, F. (2003). Integrating Web-based and corpus-based techniques for question answering. In *Proceedings of the Twelfth Text Retrieval Conference*.

Kouylekov, M., Negri, M., Magnini, B., & Coppola, B. (2006). Towards entailment-based question answering: ITC-irst at CLEF 2006. In *Proceedings of the Working Notes for the CLEF Workshop*.

Kwok, C. C. T., Etzioni, O., & Weld, D. S. (2001). Scaling question answering to the Web. In *Proceedings of the Conference of World Wide Web*.

Laurent, D., Nègre, S., & Séguéla, P. (2005). QRISTAL, le QR à l'épreuve du public. *Répondre à des questions, 46*(3).

Laurent, D., Séguéla, P., & Nègre, S. (2005). Cross lingual question answering using QRISTAL for CLEF 2005. In *Proceedings of the Working Notes of CLEF Cross-Language Evaluation Forum*, Vienna, Austria.

Laurent, D., Séguéla, P., & Nègre, S. (2006). Cross lingual question answering using QRISTAL for CLEF 2006. In *Proceedings of the Working Notes of CLEF Cross-Language Evaluation Forum and the ECDL Conference*.

Lehnert, W. (1977). Human and computational question answering. *Cognitive Science, 1*, 47–63. doi:10.1207/s15516709cog0101_3

Lerman, K., Getoor, L., Minton, S., & Knoblock, C. A. (2004). Using the structure of web sites for automatic segmentation of tables. In *Proceedings of the ACM SIGMOD International Conference on Management of Data.*

Ligozat, A.-L., Grau, B., Robba, I., & Vilnat, A. (2006a). L'extraction des réponses dans un système de question-réponse. In *Proceedings of la Conférence sur le Traitement Automatique des Langues Naturelles*, Leuven, France.

Ligozat, A.-L., Grau, B., Robba, I., & Vilnat, A. (2006b). Evaluation and improvement of cross-lingual question answering strategies. In *Proceedings of the Workshop on Multilingual Question Answering* (pp. 23-30).

Ligozat, A.-L., Grau, B., Vilnat, A., Robba, I., & Grappy, A. (2007). Towards an automatic validation of answers in Question Answering. In *Proceedings of the 19th IEEE International Conference on Tools with Artificial Intelligence* (Vol. 2, pp. 444-447).

Lin, J., & Katz, B. (2003). Question answering from the Web using knowledge annotation and knowledge mining Techniques. In *Proceedings of the ACM Conference on Information and Knowledge Management.*

Lopez, V., Motta, E., & Uren, V. (2006). AquaLog: An ontology-driven question answering system to interface the semantic Web. In *Proceedings of the Human Language Technology Conference of the NAACL, Companion Volume: Demonstrations* (pp. 269-272).

Lopez, V., Pasin, M., & Motta, E. (2005). AquaLog: An ontology-portable question answering system for the semantic Web. In *Proceedings of the European Semantic Web Conference.*

Magnini, B., Negri, M., Prevete, R., & Tanev, H. (2002a). Mining knowledge from repeated co-occurrences: DIOGENE at TREC 2002. In *Proceedings of the 11ᵗʰ Text Retrieval Conference*, Gaithersburg, MD.

Magnini, B., Negri, M., Prevete, R., & Tanev, H. (2002b). Is it the right answer? Exploiting Web redundancy for answer validation. In *Proceedings of the Association of Computational Linguistics* (pp. 425-432).

Magnini, B., Negri, M., Prevete, R., & Tanev, H. (2002c). Comparing statistical and content-based techniques for answer validation on the Web. In *Proceedings du VIII Convegno AI*IA.*

McGuinness, D. L., & Pinheiro Da Silva, P. (2004a). Trusting answers on the Web. In Maybury, M. T. (Ed.), *New directions in question answering.* Palo Alto, CA: AAAI Press.

McGuinness, D. L., & Pinheiro Da Silva, P. (2004b). Explaining answers from the semantic Web: the inference Web approach. *Journal of Web Semantics*, *1*(4), 397–413. doi:10.1016/j.websem.2004.06.002

Minock, M. (2005). Where are the 'killer applications' of restricted domain question answering? In *Proceedings of the IJCAI Workshop on Knowledge Reasoning in Question Answering*, Edinburgh, UK (p. 4).

Moldovan, D., Clark, C., Harabagiu, S., & Maiorano, S. (2003). COGEX: A logic prover for question answering. In *Proceedings of Human Language Technologies: The Annual Conference of the North American Chapter of the Association for Computational Linguistics*, Edmonton, AB, Canada (pp. 87-93).

Moldovan, D., Harabagiu, S., Girju, R., Morrarescu, P., Lacatusu, F., Novishi, A., et al. (2002). LCC Tools for Question Answering. In *Proceedings of the 11ᵗʰ Text Retrieval Conference*, Gaithersburg, MD.

Mollà, D., & Vicedo, J. L. (2007). Question answering in restricted domains: An overview. *Computational Linguistics, 33*(1). doi:10.1162/coli.2007.33.1.41

Moriceau, V., Tannier, X., Grappy, A., & Grau, B. (2008). Justification of answers by verification of dependency relations – The French AVE task. In *Proceedings of the Working Notes of CLEF Workshop and the ECDL Conference.*

Moschitti, A., Quarteroni, S., Basili, R., & Manandhar, S. (2007). Exploiting syntactic and shallow semantic kernels for question answer classification. In *Proceeding of the Workshop of the Association for Computational Linguistics* (pp. 776-783).

Nadeau, D., & Sekine, S. (2007). A survey of named entity recognition and classification. *Journal of Linguisticae Investigationes, 30*(1).

Neumann, G., & Sacaleanu, B. (2004). Experiments on robust NL question interpretation and multi-layered document annotation for a cross-language question/answering system. In *Proceedings of the Working Notes of CLEF Cross-Language Evaluation Forum*, Bath, UK (pp. 311-320).

Neumann, G., & Sacaleanu, B. (2005). DFKI's LT-lab at the CLEF 2005 multiple language question answering track. In *Proceedings of the Working Notes of CLEF Cross-Language Evaluation Forum.*

Newman, E., Stokes, N., Dunnion, J., & Carthy, J. (2005). UCD IIRG approach to the textual entailment challenge. In *Proceedings of the PASCAL Challenges Workshop on Recognising Textual Entailment* (pp. 53-56).

Peñas, A., Rodrigo, A., Sama, V., & Verdejo, F. (2008). Testing the reasoning for question answering validation. *Journal of Logic and Computation, 18*(3).

Perret, L. (2004). Question answering system for the French Language. In *Proceedings of the Working Notes of CLEF Cross-Language Evaluation Forum*, Bath, UK (pp. 295-305).

Plamondon, L., Lapalme, G., & Kosseim, L. (2003). The quantum question answering system at TREC 11. In *Proceedings of the 11ᵗʰ Text Retrieval Conference.*

Prager, J., Brown, E., Radev, D. R., & Czuba, K. (2000). One search engine or two for question-answering. In *Proceedings of the 9ᵗʰ Text Retrieval Conference*, Gaithersburg, MD (pp. 235-240).

Quarteroni, S., & Manandhar, S. (2009). Designing an interactive open-domain question answering system. *Language Engineering Journal, 15*(1), 73–95. doi:10.1017/S1351324908004919

Rinaldi, F., Dowdall, J., Schneider, G., & Persidis, A. (2004). Answering questions in the genomics domain. In *Proceedings of the ACL Workshop on Question Answering in Restricted Domains.*

Rosset, S., Galibert, O., Illouz, G., & Max, A. (2005). Interaction et recherche d'information le projet RITEL. *Répondre à des questions, 46*(3).

Sang, E. T. K., Bouma, G., & de Rijke, M. (2005). Developing offline strategies for answering medical questions. In *Proceedings of the AAAI Workshop on Question Answering in Restricted Domains.*

Schlobach, S., Ahn, D., de Rijke, M., & Jijkoun, V. (2007). Data-driven type checking in open domain question answering. *Journal of Applied Logic, 5*(1). doi:10.1016/j.jal.2005.12.001

Soubbotin, M. M., & Soubbotin, S. M. (2001). Patterns of potential answer expressions as clues to the right answers. In *Proceedings of the 10ᵗʰ Text Retrieval Conference*, Gaithersburg, MD.

Soubbotin, M. M., & Soubbotin, S. M. (2002). Use of patterns for detection of likely answer strings: a systematic approach. In *Proceedings of the 11ᵗʰ Text Retrieval Conference*, Gaithersburg, MD.

Sutcliffe, R. F. E., White, K., Slattery, D., Gabbay, I., & Mulcahy, M. (2006). Cross-Language French-English question answering using the DLT system at CLEF 2006. In *Proceedings of the Working Notes of CLEF Cross-Language Evaluation Forum.*

Tanevm, H., Negrim, M., & Magninim, B. m & Kouylekovm M. (2004). The DIOGENE question answering system at CLEF-2004. In *Proceedings of the Working Notes of CLEF Cross-Language Evaluation Forum*, Bath, UK (pp. 325-333).

Tatu, M., Iles, B., Slavick, J., Novischi, A., & Moldovan, D. (2006). COGEX at the second recognizing textual entailment challenge. In *Proceedings of the PASCAL Challenges Workshop on Recognising Textual Entailment.*

Tellex, S., Katz, B., Lin, J., Fernandes, A., & Marton, G. (2003). Quantitative evaluation of passage retrieval algorithms for question answering. In *Proceedings of the 26th Annual International ACM SIGIR Conference on Research and Development in Information Retrieval*, Toronto, ON, Canada (pp. 41-47).

Voorhees, E. M. (2001). The TREC question answering track. *Journal of Natural Language Engineering, 7*(4). doi:10.1017/S1351324901002789

Wang, K., Ming, Z., & Chua, T. S. (2009). A syntactic tree matching approach to finding similar questions in community-based QA services. In *Proceedings of the 32nd International ACM SIGIR Conference on Research and Development in Information Retrieval.*

Wang, R., & Neumann, G. (2008). An accuracy-oriented divide-and-conquer strategy for recognizing textual entailment. In *Proceedings of the Text Analysis Conference.*

Wang, R., Zhang, Y., & Neumann, G. (2009). A joint syntactic-semantic representation for recognizing textual relatedness. In *Proceedings of the Text Analysis Conference on Notebook Papers and Results* (pp. 1-7).

Yu, H., Sable, C., & Zhu, H. R. (2005). Classifying medical questions based on an evidence taxonomy. In *Proceedings of the 20th National Conference on Artificial Intelligence and the Workshop on Question Answering in Restricted Domains.*

Zajac, R. (2001). Towards ontological question answering. In *Proceedings of the Workshop on Open Domain Question Answering.*

KEY TERMS AND DEFINITIONS

Question-Answering Systems: Fine-grained information retrieval; information extraction; passage retrieval; named entity recognition, syntactic and semantic matching. Question-answering systems are dedicated to extract precise answers from large collection of texts, to questions given in natural language.

Information Extraction: from texts consists in analyzing texts in order to recognize the information searched, which can be entities or relations between them.

Text Analysis: relies on different level of analysis: lexical level, to recognize words and their characteristics, syntactic level to recognize phrases of a sentence and their relationships, semantic analysis to type entities and associate conceptual information to words and sentences.

ENDNOTES

[1] Hypernym is a term that refers to a more general concept, as fruit for apple, and hyponym is the opposite

[2] POS: part-of-speech, the morphosyntactic category of a token

[3] Recent RTE challenges held at TAC: http://www.nist.gov/tac/about/index.html

[4] RDF: The Resource Description Framework (RDF) is a family of World Wide Web Consortium (W3C) specifications originally designed as a metadata data model (from Wikipedia).

Chapter 16
Context–Aware Mobile Search Engine

Jawad Berri
College of Computing and Information Sciences, King Saud University, Saudi Arabia

Rachid Benlamri
Lakehead University, Canada

ABSTRACT

Exploiting context information in a web search engine helps fine-tuning web services and applications to deliver custom-made information to end users. While context, including user and environment information, cannot be exploited efficiently in the wired Internet interaction type, it is becoming accessible with the mobile web where users have an intimate relationship with their handsets. In this type of interaction, context plays a significant role enhancing information search and therefore, allowing a search engine to detect relevant content in all digital forms and formats. This chapter proposes a context model and an architecture that promote integration of context information for individuals and social communities to add value to their interaction with the mobile web. The architecture relies on efficient knowledge management of multimedia resources for a wide range of applications and web services. The research is illustrated with a corporate case study showing how efficient context integration improves usability of a mobile search engine.

1. INTRODUCTION

The emergence of mobile handsets as new means of information exchange has naturally enticed a need for search engines capable to search and retrieve information for nomadic users. The "mobile"

trend has changed the user habits towards a more active involvement in dealing with information at hand. New services have been made available to satisfy mobile user needs in terms of information, entertainment and social networking (Loke, 2007). In this new landscape, further research work is needed to develop new search models that can make use of the various contextual elements

DOI: 10.4018/978-1-4666-0330-1.ch016

including user's social context. The new user-interaction needs to be more useful, custom-made and also entertaining.

In the last few years, much progress has been made to develop robust mobile search engines offering interesting services to users (Google, 2010; Yahoo, 2010; Taptu, 2010). Examples of such services are: (1) location-awareness where search engines offer services according to users' location, privileging relevant local businesses and providing directions to each business location (Google, 2010; Yahoo, 2010); (2) voice speech search where search engines are equipped with speech recognition capabilities that allow efficient query-entry, thus avoiding the tedious task of typing the query on the mobile phone (Google, 2010; Taptu, 2010); and (3) multimedia interface where search engines provide access to various multimedia resources such as images, videos, maps, and games (Google, 2010; Yahoo, 2010; Taptu, 2010). Although, the progress made so far is significant, mobile search engines are still limited in their capabilities, and do not offer fine-tuned services that most users want. One of the features that have not been fully exploited by existing mobile search engines is the integration of context management to offer a real customized interaction experience. Context management allows a good understanding of user's needs using their profile, current activity, interaction history, information dispensed to individuals and social communities, service adaptation to current user's identity, and device adaptation.

This chapter addresses mainly the problem of context modeling and management in mobile search engines, showing how a rigorous context model can add value to the interaction of users, as individuals or communities. The research is illustrated with a corporate case study to show how efficient context integration improves the mobile application usability for individual users and social communities.

2. RELATED WORK

The rapid growth in number of mobile Internet users creates vast business opportunities for corporations, opening potential channels of communication, sales, and marketing, and creating potential revenue drivers. According to a report published by the Institute for Prospective Technological Studies for the European Union (Gomez-Barroso et al., 2010), the mobile base will reach nearly 5,000 million subscribers worldwide by 2012. In addition, by the end of 2013, broadband mobile connections (3G, 3.5G+) will account for more than half of all connections and 40% of all subscribers will be using mobile internet (Gomez-Barroso et al., 2010). In another study (Anderson & Rainie, 2008), it was reported that mobile devices will surpass computers as the primary tool for Internet connectivity by 2020. The widespread adoption of mobile devices will lead to an explosion of mobile content and applications, which will require access to data and content in an efficient and user-friendly manner. In short, search is likely to become equally or even more critical in the mobile domain than in the wired environment (Gomez-Barroso et al., 2010; Anderson & Rainie, 2008). To meet this demand, we will need new techniques for representing, modeling, indexing, and retrieving mobile data (Tsai et al., 2010). More sophisticated mobile search engines will therefore be needed. The new search engines will have to exploit the fact that mobiles are personal devices that store and regularly capture a lot of data about the user profile, their location, user's social network, etc. This will enable context-aware search services in current and future ambient intelligent environments.

Applications on mobiles which make use of search technology can be grouped into two broad categories. First, there are those that adapt or emulate existing web search services to the mobile environment. Second, there are search services that exploit the unique features of mobile devices or the environments in which they operate. The first category can be considered a subset of existing search engines for the wired environment and are mainly based on content adaptation. Example of such systems is the Powerbrowser (Jose & Downes, 2005) that relies on real-time HTML to WML conversion, and uses Google search engine. The query is forwarded to Google by using a Java Servlet to retrieve top documents, which are downloaded, parsed, summarized and converted to WML in the background. Another system from this category is the SmartCredo (Carpineto et al., 2009) search engine that uses search-results clustering instead of traditional list-based search interface. If searched items are correctly clustered, and if the user chooses the right path from the cluster labels, these items can be accessed in logarithmic rather linear time. Both of these systems are used for efficient search and to improve the user experience which is limited by the device input mode. In the second category however, mobile search engines make effective use of contextual information (relevant data embedded in the mobile device, information in the surrounding environment, users' profiles or behavioral patterns) to improve the meaningfulness of the search results. Example of system from this category is the thesaurus-based context-aware auto-completion search engine proposed by Arias et al. (2010). To overcome the mobile device usability problems, the system can help the user in completing the desired query terms avoiding manual typing. It can also filter out non-relevant query terms based on user circumstances, the access mechanism (device and web browser) and the surrounding environment. Another system from this category is the Context Aware Browser (Coppola et al., 2010). Instead of querying the system, it is the browser who pushes data to the user based on the user's context. The browser automatically and dynamically loads Web pages, services, and applications selected according to the user's current context.

In another more detailed taxonomy, Mobile search engines have been classified into eight categories (Gomez-Barroso et al., 2010). The first category is On Device Search where software pre-installed in the terminals performs the search. The second category is On Portal Search which refers to search in closed frameworks. However, users want more and more going off-portal to explore the content and destinations they want and not the ones mobile operators have chosen or created for them. The third category is Open Search with a browser-based web site that seeks pages from the mobile internet using algorithms such as PageRank-like ones. The fourth category is Meta-Search which inquires a variety of content sources and providers and "blend" and combines a multitude of search results. This allows users to search across a number of content providers through a single interface. Meta-search engines deal with technological challenges frequently encountered in the mobile space such as heterogeneity of content, and the incompatibility of devices and systems. The fifth category is Social Network-based Search where users search for content within the proprietary database of a social network. Technologically, this kind of search is not dissimilar to web search. The data may be stored on a centralized or decentralized servers and data is enriched by users (e.g., tags, voting, reputation, etc.). The sixth category is Messaging Service-based Search where text-messages-based search services allow users to send a question to a central database (usually calling a special short number). The seventh category is Multimedia Search where different techniques are applied to audio and visual search. Finally, the eighth category, and the most important one, is Context-aware Search where the relevance of retrieved information improves the more the system is aware of the search context. Due to the changing nature of mobile environments, context-aware mobile search is most appropriate and is the one that has received most research focus. Mobiles, being personal devices, offer valuable contextual information, because the location is (usually) known and easily identified. Using information about the user's context, the search engine can perform a personalized search and offer tailored results.

Context awareness is regarded as an enabling technology with a high potential for mobile data applications, particularly in the field of mobile search. It refers to all technologies concerned with the acquisition of context (using sensors to collect information about the surroundings or environment), and the abstraction and understanding of context. One problem with context data is that context is inherently dynamic and constantly changing. Another main technical challenge in achieving seamless integration of sensory context data is interoperability. Interconnection and interoperability of sensor technology is considered a key factor for success. In addition, to build robust context-aware systems, much research in cognitive technologies is needed, as it is not well known how to perceive and blend contextual information to build knowledge for broader context understanding. One way of achieving this goal is to come up with an unambiguous representation of the context, including a framework to ease the development of context-aware applications. Based on the context model, applications can figure out which action(s) should be triggered or what data is potentially relevant to the user (Al Ali et al., 2008). Nonetheless, the heterogeneous nature of context-aware applications makes it impossible to have a universal, unique representation of the context. However, a good compromise can be achieved if context models are able to manage a set of universal properties, useful for any application, in conjunction with application-specific, custom properties (Al Ali et al., 2008).

Previous works (Benlamri et al., 2006) propose a context structure and a framework which define several abstract layers of knowledge. Such layers are ready to be mapped with the properties that actually will model the context. In addition, formal reasoning techniques can be employed to create derived properties based on those which are directly fetched. Another important issue is related to gathering all the significant context

information that can be of interest to an application. It is noteworthy that each application will be only interested in a limited subset of the context. As a result, context frameworks should provide mechanisms to allow applications to express their interest in certain context properties. Additionally, the context framework should be prepared to create bindings between context properties and the corresponding information sources. Such bindings should hide applications from the lower-level protocols or services used to actually obtain the context property values. Besides, some directly measured context properties are not suitable to use as-is; there can be properties that need a previous transformation or processing to be useful for an application. For example, an application might require GPS coordinates as input in some cases, but in others it might need the place name. As a consequence, a context framework should perform automatic context data transformations on behalf of the application.

To know each user's interest, we usually generate the user's profile. However, since users do not feel safe by submitting personal information to untrusted servers (Keenoy & Levene, 2003), other techniques to gather user profile data are needed. Collaborative filtering techniques analyze user behavior to create implicit user profiles. They take into account which links are more frequently clicked or the time spent on each one to extrapolate user interests without them even noticing. Users with similar interests can also be grouped into classes. Once the individual has been classified, assumptions about their interests can be made based on those of the whole group. This introduces the concept of social profiling, which can be valuable when a new user connects to the application for the first time and fewer details about him/her are available.

3. CASE STUDY

In this section we present a case study – *the inspector example* which will be used in the rest of the paper to show how context is managed and then exploited by a search engine to support people in organizations performing their daily tasks. Rachid is a 56 years old engineer in Sonatrach – the Algerian Petroleum and Gas Corporation. His long experience in the field of corrosion, in the different plants of the corporation, put him into a key position as a chief inspector. He is the coordinator of a group of experts in corrosion who perform regular field inspections in the different plants and elaborate inspection reports which spot equipment problems, evaluate the risk, and propose recommendations and action plans. The corrosion problem is persistent since many corporations' plants use sea water to cool various machinery which causes inevitable deterioration of equipments. The corporation realizes that this problem needs special attention and has decided to consider it among its strategic priorities. For this, it has created a research group to conduct research in the corrosion field. Rachid is a member of this research group, and his role is to feed the research group with data related to corrosion. He is also involved in the elaboration of the "Corrosion Ontology" – an ontology used by the knowledge management system to organize field data included in the inspection reports. In addition, Rachid is responsible of a group of trainees who have been hired by the corporation and who have spent one year training at the different plants before being permanently assigned to a specific plant.

Today, Rachid's task is to inspect Column 201E in GL2Z plant. While in site, he connects his tablet PC to the wireless network, logs into the system using his identity as an inspector, specifies the current activity and starts filling the inspection report. The system offers a very convenient touch screen Graphical User Interface (GUI) where Rachid writes his remarks based on his observations and equipment testing. His laptop is equipped with multimedia facilities allowing him to record audio remarks, take pictures and record videos; all collected multimedia resources are part of the inspection report. Rachid noticed an abnormal corrosive wear in location MH2 at the bottom of pipe C. He accesses the system to consult past reports in order to be able to evaluate the evolution of the defect and to follow up on maintenance done so far for this specific equipment. Rachid could not figure out the issue. He then decides to open a chat session with Ahmed, a member of the inspectors group who inspected the column last year, to consult him and to get his feedback. After a discussion, the two inspectors decide to initiate a process requiring urgent maintenance on site. Rachid reports the issues that have been noticed by writing a paragraph along with a video record, and then sends a high priority note to the maintenance department recommending an urgent action in the next week. Rachid recognizes that the current case is quite interesting for corporate training and e-learning, so using his laptop, he opens the knowledge management system and adds a description of the report using the concept hierarchy of the "Corrosion Ontology" to describe the case. The current inspection is broadcasted through the video conference system to his trainees who can interact with him on-line, but are not recommended to enter the site for security reasons. Also, the system allows users to access various LAN's applications as well as a search engine integrating the LAN and the web.

4. CONTEXT MODELING

Context-aware applications utilize contextual information; they sense the current situation and the surrounding environment of the user in order to be able to adapt displayed information to the user's current context. Context models need to include all context ingredients namely the user, the device, and the environment, in order to process information, to interpret it, and then to provide users with feedback. The context model includes the following information (Al Ali et al., 2008):

User Profile

The user profile includes information about the user; it is categorized as static and dynamic. Static information is permanent; it does not change in time such as user's personal information. This category includes but is not limited to the following: name, gender, age, preferred language, occupation, interest, preferred currency, hometown, etc. Dynamic information changes in time and is dependent on many parameters such as time (for instance the user's expertise in a game which is upgraded from beginner to expert), location (a tourist has interests that are different from his hometown' interests), and application (user preferences deduced from past interactions and experiences with an application)

Identity

The user identity is to be distinguished from his profile. It defines specific rights for a user to access data or to use some services. A user may have different identities but his profile is unchanged. He may be involved as a member in different groups with a different identity for each one. In the inspector example, Rachid has different identities; he is a member of the inspectors' group; he is also a trainer of a group of new recruits with the privilege of sharing data with them; and he is a research group member.

The user's identity is more interesting for applications and services than the user's profile. Identity holds more personalized information resulting in an adapted and fine-tuned interaction of the proposed services with the user. Figure 1 shows the relation between the profile holding the basic information about a user and his possible identities which complement his information. Each application and service in turn deals with a

Figure 1. User's profile vs. user's identities

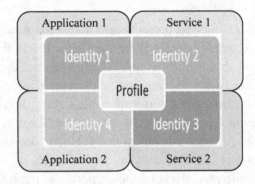

specific user's identity and a unified profile for the same user.

User's Location

The user's location is important because it correlates the user's interests with his/her surrounding environment. For example, a mobile tourist advisor might suggest to a tourist to visit a museum if the current user's location is nearby. In mobile applications, the user's current location can be known from the built-in GPS receiver or through a connection to an external GPS receiver.

Device Specifications

This context element is necessary for applications using mobile handsets. Information displayed on the user's mobile need to suit the device technical constraints. It includes a set of attributes about the device type and its capabilities, such as supported browsers, multimedia support, screen size, navigation tools, bandwidth limitations, multi-language capabilities, cookies support, caching support, memory, and processing power limitations.

Date and Time

Information related to time is relevant to adjust the content delivered to users according to the current time and date. For instance the application might

Figure 2. System architecture

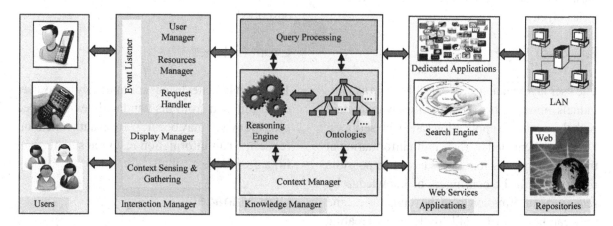

propose to a tourist at lunch time the restaurants nearby his location.

Current Event

Current event represents a specific event requiring particular consideration from the application. Events are all activities limited in time and which might interest the user to be involved in. For instance a tourist might be interested in events such as exhibitions, expositions, trade fairs, shows, and so on. Event information consists of elements to identify the event such as: event name, event type, event location, and event start date/time and duration. Event information can be retrieved from specific web services which maintain a schedule of known events.

Activity

The current activity the user is involved in can be known from the user or it can be derived from the handheld task manager. This context ingredient allows the system architecture to be aware of the current user's task and accordingly enhance semantically the interaction between the user and the system in one side and the user and his community in the other side. The activity allows

also the system to monitor and manage user tasks towards an efficient use of the mobile resources.

The context ingredients presented above are the necessary elements of information that constitute the context model used in our architecture. Having said that, we are aware that the heterogeneous nature of applications in the mobile paradigm, makes it impossible to have a universal and unique representation of the context that fits all cases. Some applications may need additional information to build knowledge for broader context understanding. For this reason, our context model can be extended to incorporate other types of information provided that they are specified in the system. Based on this specification, applications can figure out which action(s) should be triggered or what data is potentially relevant to the user for a given context instance.

5. SYSTEM ARCHITECTURE

The system architecture presented in Figure 2 sustains the information ecosystem and supports the deployment of various applications and web services for user communities. The architecture exhibits five components namely: the user layer, the interaction manager, the knowledge manager, the applications layer and the information repositories layer.

5.1. User Layer

The user layer manages all possible users as individuals or members of communities who interact with the available applications and web services. Users are identified by their login information at the start of any session. Users have two possible roles; they can be consumers of knowledge by requesting information from the repositories, and they can be producers of knowledge by creating content to be shared by other community users. The latter aspect is very interesting for many applications since users are involved actively, as individuals or communities, in the production of multimedia resources while they are in the field facing real-life situations. In the inspector example, Rachid and his peer inspectors record multimedia resources and share them among the inspectors community and also with other communities such as the trainees for learning purposes.

Retrieved information for user communities promotes the community shared information as it is contextually more relevant than information retrieved from the LAN or the Web. Therefore, any information request from a community member to the search engine favors first the community shared information. Managing community users need to be done carefully in order to preserve personal information confidentiality and privacy related to contextual user's information such as personal information. Moreover, since user content is made available to other community members, a special care is given to intellectual property related to all resources created by users.

5.2. Interaction Manager

Users interact with the Interaction Manager which handles their requests, senses the current context and manages the graphical user interface. In order to achieve the abovementioned tasks, the Interac-

tion Manager includes a set of modules that are described below.

Event Listener

The Event Listener listens continuously to any user event initiated from his handheld device. Three possible events may occur: i) a user authentication request; ii) an information resource submission; iii) a user request submission.

User Manager

The User Manager authenticates users who are requesting access to the system. At each session, it requests the user's login and password and eventually his community membership if he/she is a member of a community. The User Manager manages also user sessions by maintaining the history of sessions and retrieving the previous session on user's request.

Resources Manager

The Resources Manager handles the resources produced by users. It is activated whenever the user submits a multimedia resource to the system. The Resources Manager categorizes and labels the resource with context related information and then stores it in a specific repository. Among information associated to every resource, we mention the author of the resource and his/her affiliation to a community, the current location, the current task, and a description of the resource added by the author.

Request Handler

The Request Handler manages all the user's interactions with the application layer in order to activate a service or to retrieve information through queries submitted to the Search Engine. The Request Handler handles also all user requests to personalize the system and to update the individual settings.

Display Manager

Displayed information is tailored to the user's device by the Display Manager which manages the content displayed and adapts it to the user's current context and preferences. The Display Manager handles also issues related to the technical specifications of the user's handheld device such as the image size to fit the screen resolution and the video formats to be streamed by the available video players.

Context Sensing and Gathering

At the start of each session, Context Sensing and Gathering module creates an instance of the context model including all information gathered from the user and his environment. Personal user's information and personal preferences are set during initial registration through form-filling and are unchanged. Device specifications are sensed at each session by querying WURFL (Wireless Universal Resource File - http://wurfl.source-forge.net/) – a web service from which an XML file is downloaded to map every device with its specification. Information depending on time and location is dynamic; it is sensed and processed periodically during every session.

5.3. Knowledge Manager

Information produced by users and retrieved from repositories needs to be organized in order to be used effectively by the applications and available web services. Making efficient use of available information is a key feature of our architecture. Knowledge management sets a standard description of the concepts to be used by the different applications and web services. It is a requirement to capture, represent and interpret information resources. Context management needs also to rely

on efficient knowledge management in order to allow the system to adapt to the various situations and to be able to take the right decisions whenever a change occurs in the context.

The architecture embeds the Knowledge Manager module which is responsible of maintaining a standard conceptual description for an efficient understanding of information and how to apply it effectively. The Knowledge Manager includes the reasoning engine and specific purpose ontologies (Benlamri et al., 2006). Ontologies are used as a backbone structure to organize all concepts related to a given domain of interest. The reasoning engine queries the ontologies to satisfy the requests of the context manager and the query processing module. All submitted queries are processed by the Query Processing module which expands the query based on context information. Hence the user's identity, his location, the current event and the user's activity are context elements which are added to the query. The enhanced query is no more context free, it is tight to the current user's context and represents a fine-tune specification of the actual user's information needs. The applications layer uses the enhanced query to deal with user requests. The search engine for instance, attempts to find a match between the enhanced query and available information; results are ranked according to the best match. Section 6 presents an example that illustrates the query enhancement and the matching process.

Context Manager

The Context Manager maintains a data structure representing the context instance for a session. It receives periodic information from the Context Sensing and Gathering module, updates the context instance, requests if needed additional knowledge from the reasoning engine and takes the suitable decisions to be reflected on the system and the GUI.

Query Processing

The Query Processing module enhances queries submitted by the user by adding semantic information correlated to the query concepts and also by integrating context related information to the query. For instance the user may query the search engine about available "business centers" nearby his location. Hence, the location of the user is updated to his current location and the query is sent to the search engine. If the query returns no results, the Context Manager extends the query by requesting from the reasoning engine additional knowledge about "business center" which in turn queries specific ontologies for related concepts. An extension of the current query is done by retrieving synonyms of "business center" namely "shopping center", "commercial center". Accordingly, the initial query is expanded with the new concepts for submission to the search engine.

Ontology-based Knowledge Management

The integration of ontologies in the knowledge management process is of great value for applications which use multimedia resources available in repositories. These resources need to be described semantically according to a standard knowledge structure in order to be shared, exchanged and reused. Ontologies which are shared conceptual-knowledge structures can be used to describe formally multimedia resources (Stuckenshmidt et al., 2005). In our architecture (Figure 2) multimedia resources in the repositories layer are described with ontology concepts and become independent entities which can be used by other users and applications. For a search engine, ontologies provide efficient semantic-based retrieval capabilities of existing resources since the search uses a standard vocabulary that is controlled by the ontology concepts.

The development of ontologies is a complex task requiring time and efforts especially if the domain is very broad. In a restricted domain this process requires coordination between domain experts to represent the ontology into a formal language and then to express it into a markup language in order to be available for different user communities. In the inspector example, the ontology development is a process where researchers and engineers who are the specialists in corrosion, feed the knowledge management system, in a first step, with concepts, relationships and rules related to the corrosion body of knowledge. In a second step, the gathered information is organized and represented into the system in order to be used to describe data collected from the field. Therefore, any inspection report, document or multimedia resource (image, video, audio) related to the field of corrosion needs to be described with concepts from the ontology.

Reasoning Engine

The reasoning engine has three roles: i) Ensures ontology consistency specifically during ontology updates. For instance, an initial check consist in verifying whether any concept to be added is not already in the ontology; ii) Supports resources description by providing navigation facility through the ontology relationships and concepts in order to allow the users to describe semantically produced multimedia resources; iii) Retrieves concepts based on requests from the query processing module to extend semantically unfruitful queries. A first extension of the query consists in extending all the query terms present in the ontology with their synonyms. Another extension consists in adding all sub concepts using the semantic relationship "is-a."

5.4. Applications Layer

Applications Layer includes applications, web services and the search engine destined to a variety of user communities. Applications aim to produce information that is relevant, instructive and adaptive. Relevancy is an important criterion in order to not submerge the user with useless information that is not related to his request. The objective is to produce information that fits precisely the user needs. This is why the user query is analyzed so that concepts and semantic relationships in the query are taken into account by the reasoning engine while retrieving the response. The output is instructive in two senses: First, it is meant to inform the user about a specific topic while giving him the possibility to extend his knowledge by providing structured related information should he wish to get in-depth information. This is guaranteed by the existence of ontologies that structure output information; Second, the output make use of available multimedia web resources to promote information diversity allowing the user to consult videos, images, presentations and documents related to the same topic. The applications promote adaptivity by providing information that adapts to the user's context and therefore adjusts the delivered information content and shapes it to the user needs.

6. SCENARIO EXECUTION

Most of the existing search engines are text based using keywords extracted from the user's query as the only input to search and retrieve information. In the wired Internet, it is hard to exploit surrounding and user-contextual information to enhance the interaction and thus improving the ranking of the results and the variety of the output in terms of multimedia resources. In mobile computing, the situation is different, mobile search is operated from a device with which the user has an intimate relationship. Handheld devices are personal, for this reason user information which is available, can play a significant role to enhance information search towards detecting relevant information adapted to the user's needs (Coppola et al., 2010). Moreover, in the mobile area, the user's location which can be known form the GPS (Global Posi-

tioning System) device is valuable information to characterize the current context and consequently improve the query with additional information to be used by a mobile search engine.

In our inspector example, user personal information and location information are fully exploited with regard to the context model as described in Section 4. When the inspector logs in the system, he identifies himself whether as an individual user or as part of a group of users. Rachid who is a chief inspector logs in with his personal username and also adds his affiliation to the group of inspectors since his activity is to inspect a column. He can then access all information of the inspectors' group and can also post information to group members. He then specifies his current activity "Inspecting Column C". The location is gathered by the GPS device, then based on a perimeter calculation the system deduces GL2Z as the plant that is concerned with today's inspection. The location is periodically gathered in order to assign to any data collected during the current session its corresponding location. Figure 3 shows the context elements and an example of the multi-media results expected.

In order to make use of context elements and be able to use them for reasoning in our system, we use first order predicate logic to represent them as shown in Table 1.

The predicates are instantiated in our case with the following constants that are gathered by the context manager from the user and his environment. Figure 4 shows the actual predicate facts that are added to the system.

The concepts weld, under_pressure, stainless_steel, chlorine_solution, are chosen from the Corrosion Ontology by the inspector to describe the current inspection case. Figure 5, presents a fragment of the Corrosion Ontology from where the concepts have been taken.

The above context instance information is automatically added to describe the inspection report and also the images and videos recorded by the inspector in order to be indexed in the

Figure 3. Making use of context elements

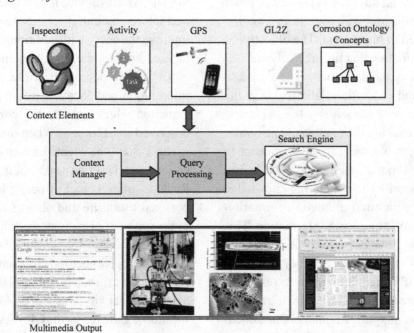

Table 1. Context predicates

Predicate	Description
user(Id, Group).	The user identifier is stored into variable Id. This will be used to retrieve all personal user information. Group is the group of interest representing the user's affiliation. During the current session, the user is able to access all private information of the mentioned group. In case the user wishes to access many groups of interest, then he needs to specify the groups at the beginning of the session.
gps(Lat, Lon).	The predicate gps stores the current GPS coordinates as gathered by the handheld GPS device: Lat for latitude and Lon for Longitude. This information is used to process the user's location.
activity(Type, Item)	Activity predicate represents the user's current activity. Variable Type specifies the type of activity and variable Item represents the current item (object, machinery, plant) under consideration by the activity.
location(Plant, Focus).	location predicate defines the place where the activity occurs. Variable Plant stores the Plant as calculated by a program which identifies the corporation's plant and then possibly finds a more precise location inside the plant represented by the variable Focus.
concept(Ontology, C).	The predicate concept represents any concept C belonging to the ontology Ontology and used in the description of the current context elements. The concepts are used to enhance the user's query and also to describe the multimedia resources authored by the user.

content management system. It is also used by the Query Processing module to enhance the user's queries during the current session. Therefore, any query submitted to the search engine is processed and enhanced with selected information from the current context predicates. When Rachid queries the search engine about the anomaly he noticed, he types the query "*column corrosion*"; the Query Processing module adds context information to the query and then submits it. Notice that the GPS information is not used in the matching process; instead we use the location which is processed from the actual GPS location and which is more significant. The top match result with the

Figure 4. Predicates representing the context elements

```
user(brachid, inspectors).
gps(35.8283914339243, -0.292510986328125).
activity(inspection, column_C).
location(GP2Z, process_zoneA).
concept(corrosion, weld).
concept(corrosion, corrosion_under_pressure).
concept(corrosion, stainless_steel).
concept(corrosion, chlorine_solution).
```

Figure 5. Fragment of the corrosion ontology

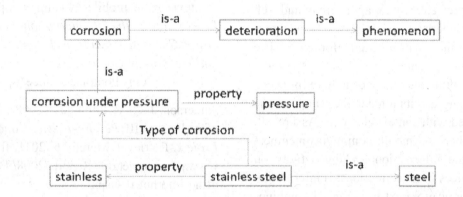

Figure 6. Matching the query with report description

Enhanced Query	Retrieved Report Description
query(column, corrosion) user(brachid, inspectors). activity(inspection, column_C). location(GP2Z, process_zoneA). concept(corrosion, weld). concept(corrosion, corrosion_under_pressure). concept(corrosion, stainless_steel). concept(corrosion, chlorine_solution)	user(rahmed, inspectors). activity(inspection, column_C). location(GP2Z, process_zoneA).

enhanced query is a report done by Ahmed, a member of the inspectors group. Figure 6 shows the enhanced query, on the left column, including keywords from the user's query and context information as in Figure 4, except the GPS related information. On the right column, we can see the description of the report which has been used to retrieve Ahmed's report. In our case the similarity is very high although Ahmed did not use a semantic description from the Corrosion Ontology as Rachid did. In our case, both inspectors are from the same group (inspectors group), and both have inspected the same column Column C which belongs to GP2Z.

Notice that at the present stage we only consider isolated ontology concepts to expand the query. This can be improved in the future by considering synonyms and ontology relationships among concepts. In doing so, the matching between the query and information available will be done using semantic relationships resulting in a better understanding of the user needs.

7. CONCLUSION

In this chapter we proposed an architecture that supports context-aware mobile search for individual users and communities. Integration of context is a key element for applications and web services to understand the user's needs and therefore provide them with relevant information. The purpose of using context is twofold. First, context describes multimedia resources authored by users. Secondly, queries submitted to the search engine are enhanced with context elements. As a result, interaction between mobile community members improves the information seeking activity on mobile devices in two directions: i) information exchanged is no more text-based only, it combines different kinds of multimedia resources to the advantage of end-users; ii) information retrieved is relevant and adapted to users, since it takes into account the user's query and the context of the interaction.

As future work, we plan to integrate into the architecture a new module to handle the matching between user requests and the semantic description of multimedia data, and to embed a ranking of the results based on context compatibility. We plan also to identify and fully exploit context and semantic information available in corporate knowledge management systems, such as in the inspector example, to develop mobile applications for mobile learning. In fact, Collective Intelligence that emerges from the collaboration of the corporate community needs to be utilized to empower the company's expertise.

Another research opportunity is to use our architecture into Web 2.0 and social networks worlds. This will allow evaluating the proposed architecture in a dynamic and interactive environment where information evolves continuously. This experience will be an opportunity to scale the architecture to deal with larger mobile user communities that produce inherent personalized and contextualized multimedia web content.

REFERENCES

Al Ali, M., Berri, J., & Zemerly, J. (2008). Context-aware mobile Muslim companion. In *Proceedings of the 5th International Conference on Soft Computing as a Transdisciplinary Science and Technology, Context Aware Mobile Learning Workshop*, Cergy Pontoise, France (pp. 553-558).

Anderson, J. Q., & Rainie, L. (2008). The future of the Internet III. *Pew Internet and American Life Project*. Retrieved March 26, 2011, from http://www.pewinternet.org/Reports/2008/The-Future-ofthe-Internet-III.aspx

Arias, M., Cantera, J. M., & Vegas, J. (2008, August 23-28). Context-based personalization for mobile Web search. In *Proceedings of the 34th International Conference on Very Large Data Bases*, Auckland, New Zealand.

Benlamri, R., Berri, J., & Atif, Y. (2006). A framework for ontology-aware instructional design and planning. *Journal of E-Learning and Knowledge Society*, *2*(1), 83–96.

Carpineto, C., Mizzaro, S., Romano, G., & Snidero, M. (2009). Mobile information retrieval with search results clustering: prototypes and evaluations. *Journal of the American Society for Information Science and Technology*, *60*(5), 877–895. doi:10.1002/asi.21036

Coppola, P., Della Mea, V., Di Gaspero, L., Menegon, D., Mischis, D., & Mizzaro, S. (2010). The context aware browser. *Intelligent Systems*, *25*(1), 38–47. doi:10.1109/MIS.2010.26

Gómez-Barroso, J. L., Compañó, R., Feijóo, C., Bacigalupo, M., Westlund, O., & Ramos, S. ... García-Jiménez, M. C. (2010). *Prospects of mobile search* (Tech. Rep. No. EUR 24148 EN, Catalogue number: LF-NA-24148-EN-C). Seville, Spain: EU Joint Research Centre, Seville: Institute for Prospective Technological Studies.

Google Inc. (2010). *Google search engine*. Retrieved April 20, 2010, from http://www.google.com/ mobile/

Jose, J. M., & Downes, S. (2005, June 7-11). Evaluation of mobile information retrieval strategies. In *Proceedings of the 5th ACM/IEEE Joint Conference on Digital Libraries*, Denver, CO (pp. 411-412).

Keenoy, K., & Levene, M. (2003). Personalisation of web search. In *Proceedings of the IJCAI Workshop on Intelligent Techniques for Web Personalization*, Acapulco, Mexico (pp. 201-228).

Loke, S. (2007). *Context-aware pervasive systems. Architectures for a new breed of applications*. Boca Raton, FL: Auerbach.

Schmidt, A. (2005). A layered model for user context management with controlled aging and imperfection handling. In *Proceedings of the Second International Workshop on Modeling and Retrieval of Context*, Edinburgh, UK (pp. 86-100).

Stuckenshmidt, H., & van Harmelen, F. (2005). *Information sharing on the semantic Web*. Berlin, Germany: Springer.

Taptu Limited. (2010). *Taptu search engine*. Retrieved April 20, 2010, from http://taptu.com/corp/

Tsai, F. S., Etoh, M. X., Lee, X. W., & Yang, Q. (2010). Introduction to mobile information retrieval. *Intelligent Systems*, *25*(1), 11–15. doi:10.1109/MIS.2010.22

Yahoo Inc. (2010). *Yahoo search engine*. Retrieved April 20, 2010, from http://mobile.yahoo.com/ search

Chapter 17
Spatio–Temporal Based Personalization for Mobile Search

Ourdia Bouidghaghen
IRIT-CNRS-University Paul Sabatier of Toulouse, France

Lynda Tamine
IRIT-CNRS-University Paul Sabatier of Toulouse, France

ABSTRACT

The explosion of the information available on the Internet has made traditional information retrieval systems, characterized by one size fits all approaches, less effective. Indeed, users are overwhelmed by the information delivered by such systems in response to their queries, particularly when the latter are ambiguous. In order to tackle this problem, the state-of-the-art reveals that there is a growing interest towards contextual information retrieval (CIR) which relies on various sources of evidence issued from the user's search background and environment, in order to improve the retrieval accuracy. This chapter focuses on mobile context, highlights challenges they present for IR, and gives an overview of CIR approaches applied in this environment. Then, the authors present an approach to personalize search results for mobile users by exploiting both cognitive and spatio-temporal contexts. The experimental evaluation undertaken in front of Yahoo search shows that the approach improves the quality of top search result lists and enhances search result precision.

DOI: 10.4018/978-1-4666-0330-1.ch017

Figure 1. The multi-dimensional concept of context in IR

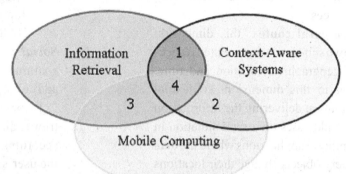

1. Contextual Information Retrieval
2. Context-Aware Mobile Systems
3. Mobile Information Retrieval
4. Contextual Mobile Information Retrieval

INTRODUCTION

Information retrieval (IR) deals with the representation, storage, and access to information according to the user's information need. The main goal of an information retrieval system (IRS) is to bring relevant documents to users in response to their queries. However, the explosion of the information available on the Internet and its heterogeneity has made traditional IRS less effective (Dervin & Nilan, 1986; Shamber, 1994). In Budzik and Hammond (2000) the authors show that the main reason is that traditional IRS do not take into account the user context in the retrieval process. Indeed, traditional retrieval models and system design are based solely on the query and the document collection which leads to providing the same set of results for different users when the same query is submitted. In order to tackle this problem, a key challenge in IR is: how to capture and how to integrate contextual information in the retrieval process in order to increase the search performance? In Allan (2002) contextual retrieval is defined as "combine search technologies and knowledge about query and user context into a single framework in order to provide the most appropriate answer for users information needs".

Thus, contextual IR aims at optimizing the retrieval accuracy by involving two related steps: appropriately defining the context of user information needs, commonly called "search context", and then adapting the search by taking it into account in the information selection process.

One of the fundamental research questions in contextual IR is: which context dimensions should be considered in the retrieval process? Several studies proposed a specification of context within and across application domains (Göker & Myrhaug, 2002; Vieira et al., 2007). Figure 1 presents a context taxonomy presented in Tamine, Boughanem, and Daoud (2009), it synthesizes five context specific dimensions listed below, that have been explored in contextual IR literature.

1. **Device**: device refers to a physical tool that gives to the user direct access to the information such as computer, mobile phone, PDA etc. Regarding this dimension, adapting retrieval consists mainly in considering the device characteristics. For instance, working with small devices implies that high level of interaction is difficult, memory resources are limited (Göker & Myrhaug, 2002); therefore, the retrieval process should avoid

using sophisticated outputs and managing huge resources.

2. **Spatio-temporal contex**: this dimension contains two sub-dimensions related respectively to geographical location and time. According to this dimension, contextual retrieval aims at delivering the information that better addresses the user's situation in spatio-temporal applications where the data and/or query objects change their locations and they are not valid over time like in tourist guide and network routing applications (Tao, Mamoulis, & Papadias, 2003; Göker & Myrhaug, 2008).

3. **User context**: user context is the central dimension in contextual IR and the most widely one addressed in the research area. This dimension contains two sub-dimensions related respectively to the personal context of the user and his social environment.

   a) *Personal context*: deals with the following sub-dimensions:

      a. **Demographic context:** personal preference attributes such as language (Google personalized, Yahoo) and gender are used in order to customize the search (Frias-Martinez et al., 2007; Hupfer & Detlor, 2006).

      b. **Psychological context:** anxiety and frustration are examples of user's affective characteristics that influence information-seeking behavior and user's relevance assessments (Bilal, 2000; Kim, 2008).

      c. **Cognitive context:** this sub-dimension is the most addressed one in the area. It refers to the user's levels of expertise (Timothy, M., Sherry, C., Robert, 2005) and user interests either short-term ones (Daoud et al., 2009; Shen, Tan, & Zhai, 2005) or long-term ones

(Sieg, Mobasher, & Burke, 2004; Tamine, Boughanem, & Zemirli, 2008).

   b) *Social context*: points on the user's community such as friends, neighbours and colleagues for instance. According to the social dimension, adapting retrieval aims at leveraging the search according to implied preferences of the user's community rather than just the individual (Lang, 1995; Smyth & Balfe, 2006).

4. **Task/problem:** this dimension refers to the basic goal or intention behind the search activity such as fact-finding vs. exploration task (Navarro-Prieto, Scaife, & Rogers, 2006), transactional, informational or navigational task in web search (Jansen, Booth, & Spink, 2007).

5. **Document context**: Two main sub-dimensions could characterize the document context. The first one concerns the document surrogates (relevant text fragments) such as form, colors, structural elements, citations, metadata (Tombros, Ruthven, & Jose, 2005). The second dimension concerns the data source characteristics and their perception by the users (Xie, 2008).

Most recent research advances in contextual IR have focused on developing models and strategies according to the user's context and task/problem. These dimensions have been addressed by research studies in personalized IR which could be considered as a sub-field of contextual IR, supporting explicit/implicit representations of the user himself involved in the retrieval framework (Anand & Mobasher, 2007). However, the continuous evolution of wireless technologies and the spread of internet enabled mobile devices, has made access to huge and heterogeneous collection of documents on the web, possible anywhere and anytime. This new and extremely challenging search environment accentuate the need and the necessity of considering more contextual factors in order to offer mobile search systems the capability to adapt their search results to the inherently changing context of the mobile user.

In this chapter, we intend to exploit other sources of evidence beyond the cognitive context to better encompass the specific needs of the mobile user. For that purpose, we aim at enhancing the search context by some spatio-temporal annotations, notably the location of the user and the time during his search activity. Our contribution consists in abstracting from sensor data some semantic information to characterize situations in which a user submits a query to the IR system. The idea is to build for every identified situation, a profile grouping the user interests learnt on the basis of past search activities occurred in this situation. Personalizing search results is achieved via a case based reasoning approach in order to dynamically select the most appropriate profile for a given situation. In the absence of a standard evaluation framework for mobile search, we propose a novel evaluation scenario based on diary study entries.

The chapter is organized as follows. First we outline motivation and challenges of mobile IR and reviews a state-of-the-art related works. Next we present our spatio-temporal based approach for personalization of mobile search. We present our experimental evaluation, discussion and obtained results. The last section presents our conclusion and points out possible directions for future work.

MOBILE INFORMATION RETRIEVAL: BACKGROUND AND MOTIVATIONS

The proliferation of mobile technologies such as (PDAs and mobile phones, etc) has made access to huge and heterogeneous collections of documents on the web, possible anywhere and anytime. Search technologies are starting to play an important role in the mobile space.

However, constraints and technical features of mobile devices, such as difficulties of query input and limited display zone, yield to search practices which are different from that of the traditional desk queries. Indeed, studies on logs of mobile Internet user queries (Kamvar & Baluja, 2007a) show that user queries are shorter (thus more ambiguous), that there are fewer requests by session and fewer users who consult farther than the first page of the results list. This brings big challenges for researches in the information retrieval domain. This includes the need to provide information tailored to the resource constraints of mobile devices and for the specific requesting user on the one hand. And on the other hand, taking into account contextual factors influencing the user perception of what is relevant information. In the rest of this section, we firstly discuss context dependency of information needs in mobile environment, and secondly outline the main research works on contextual search applied to mobile environments.

Mobile Queries: Context Dependency

People often need information while mobile. They are likely to be interested in locating different types of content. Sometimes the information required is essential to the task at hand, such as *"finding a hotel for the night"*. Other times, the need is associated with a question prompted by a conversation or a nearby object e.g., "a billboard". In particular, changing contexts such as location, time, activity and social interactions are likely to impact on the types of information needs that arise. Understanding mobile information needs and associated interaction challenges is thus fundamental to improve search results accuracy for mobile users.

There have been a number of recent studies that examine mobile information needs (Sohn et al., 2008; Church & Smyth, 2009; Bierig & Göker, 2006). These studies are important because they provide insights into what mobile users look for and how they search for information online. One important finding that emerged ahead from these studies is the importance of context. In particular, according to (Sohn et al., 2008), 72% of the information needs of mobile users are related to contextual factors such as users' interests, location, time and near persons. Furthermore, the results highlighted the importance of the personal context; in Bierig and Göker (2006) users' interests were identified to have a strongest effect on the users' perception of usefulness.

Based on this finding, we have attempted to distinguish different types of query context dependency, noting that some queries may be related to multiple aspects of context:

1. **Interests-based query**: is dependent on the user's current interests. For example, a computer science engineer may be interested on: programming languages, internet security, web technology, while he is at work, and issues queries like: "*java*", "*trojan horse*", etc. When at home, he may be interested on: art, culture, travel and issues queries like: "*da vinci code*", "*trojan war*", etc. In order to better answer such queries the IR system has to personalize the search results by taking into account the user's dynamic interests.

2. **Location-based query**: is dependent on its issuer's current geographic location such as geographic coordinates, address or place-names. For example for queries such as: "*nearby shops*", "*restaurants*", "*route guidance*", "*train connections check*", "*weather reports*", it is clear that the user's location may be taken into account to return accurate search results.

3. **Time-based query**: is dependent on its issuer's current time, for example answering the following search queries: "*find a bar*", "*find a hamburger*", "*movies in theatre*" and so forth, is different when it is morning, afternoon or midnight. The system may en-

hance the search results accuracy by taking into account the user current time.

4. **Situation-based query**: is dependent on the situation (the activity) the issuer is now. For example if the user issued the query "*first-aid instruction*", search results may be adapted whether the user is in vacation in a mountain or at the beach.

5. **Conversation-based query**: is dependent on any phone or in-person conversation the issuer is involved in. For example: "*apple software*", "*nicotine poisoning*", and so forth. When answering such queries, the system may take into account the user's social context to adapt the search results, which may be different whether the user is with his son or with his friend.

In all this cases, taking the user's context in the retrieval IR seems to be of most importance in order to meet better answer users' information needs. In the following, we give an insight into recent work in IR that attempt to respond to such mobile search information specificities by taking into account different context elements, and situate our work.

Contextual IR in Mobile Environment

Most traditional search engines do not consider the search context in the retrieval process and are not tuned to mobile environments. Recent works in IR community (Göker & Myrhaug, 2008; Jones & Brown, 2004) attempt to improve the search accuracy in this environment. This research works can be grouped under the field of "Contextual Mobile Information Retrieval" (CMIR) which can be viewed as an inter-disciplinary research field among IR, context-aware systems and mobile computing, as shown in Figure 2. CMIR aims to tackle the problem of information overload by providing appropriate results according to the resource constraints in one hand and users' location, time and interests on the other hand.

Figure 2. Research components constituting our research domain

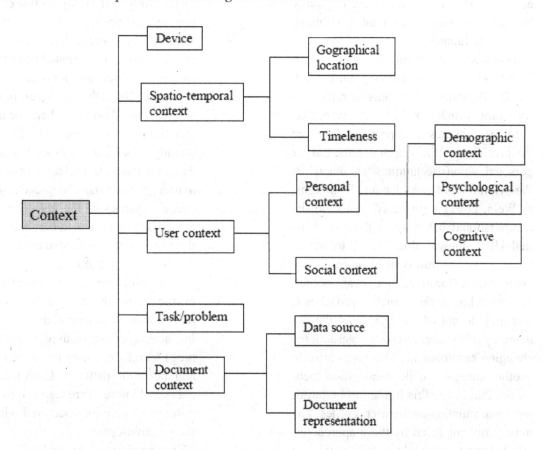

Contextual retrieval is achieved by exploiting the mobile context during query reformulation and document re-ranking steps. Below we give an overview of some significant approaches in this domain which we can categorize into three main categories: device-based adaptation approaches, location-based adaptation approaches and user-based adaptation approaches.

- **Device-based adaptation:** the related works have addressed issues concerning the limited functionality of mobile devices. Their main objectives are: 1) to facilitate query input through automatic query prediction and auto-completion techniques (Kamvar & Baluja, 2007b), and spoken query based search techniques (Schofield

& Kubin, 2002), 2) to improve the search results visualization quality: typical approaches applied clustering algorithms (August, Hansen & Shriver, 2002), and summarization techniques (Sweeney & Crestani, 2006) on the search results.

- **Location-based adaptation:** this category of works classified under the commonly known location-based IR works (Asadi et al., 2007), has exploited the ability of mobile devices to be aware of their physical location, in the sense that they are capable of determining and transmitting their current geographical coordinates. While some works propose to filter information based on proximity to user physical locations (Mountain & MacFarlane, 2007; Bouvin et al., 2003), others reformulate the query by including the location context (Hattori, Tezuka, & Tanaka, 2007).

- **User-based adaptation:** this category of works aims at personalizing the search results. Personalization aims to return information which matches the user preferences and interests, improving therefore the precision of the search results. Earlier personalization techniques (Samaras & Panayiotou, 2002; Anderson, Domingos, & Weld, 2001) were based solely on the computational behavior of the user (visited URL, viewed documents) to model his interests regardless of his surrounding environment (location, time, near people). The main limitation of such approaches is that they do not take into account the dynamicity of the user interests regarding his changing environment. This gives arise to another category of personalization techniques that tackle this limitation by building some situation-aware user profiles. The main problems faced by these approaches are: 1) How to model the user situation and its related interests? 2) How to represent the relation between situation and interests? And 3) How to personalize the search results? In what follows, we review some key points answering these questions.

  ○ Regarding situation-aware user profile modeling, in Yau et al. (2003) the authors propose to model user situations by different physical attributes such as location, time, light, etc, and/ or actions (navigation, reading, etc), and user interests by keywords profiles represented by the most frequent words extracted from documents viewed in the identified situations. In Panayiotou and Samaras (2006) the authors propose a temporal-based profile, where the user situation is represented by temporal zones learnt

by the study of the daily routine of the user and his activities. The user preferences and interests learnt from his past activities are weighted according to the identified temporal zones. In Bila et al. (2008) the authors propose a location-based profile, where the user situations are represented by the frequently visited locations by the user. The user interests are learnt based on a user questionnaire approach with specific queries to the user (e.g., to ask what kinds of activities the user does in a given frequented region). In Bellotti et al. (2008) the authors propose to build an activity-based user profile where the user situations are represented by leisure activities (eating, seeing, doing, reading, and shopping) learnt from user time, location and behavior patterns. User preferences and interests are learnt from the past search activities occurred within these activities.

  ○ The second problem deals with the representation schema proposed to model the relation between the user situations and interests. While Yau et al. (2003) propose a relation-entity representation, Panayiotou and Samaras (2006) exploit metadata mechanism, Bila et al. (2008) use a tree-based representation, and Bellotti (2008) exploit activity patterns.

  ○ The third problem concerns the strategy adopted for search personalization. It is performed by means of query refinement in Yau et al. (2003), query-document matching in Panayiotou and Samaras (2006), and a combination of query-document matching and filtering techniques in Bila et al. (2008) and Bellotti et al. (2008).

Our work presented in this chapter belongs to this last category. We propose a context-aware personalization approach that can be used to adapt search results according to users' information needs expressed by their query in a specific situation. Unlike previously related works, our approach for personalizing mobile search has several new features:

1. Regarding the representation of the context-aware profile: first, we propose to build a four level semantic representation of the user search situations as concepts from location and time ontologies, while in Yau et al. (2003) the user situation is represented by low level data. Second, our approach is implicit and automatic; no efforts are needed from the user, while in Panayiotou and Samaras (2006) and Bila et al. (2008) the user is solicited in the process of building his profile. Third, our approach does not take any restriction on user's situations or population, while in Bellotti et al. (2008) the proposed approach is devoted to some specific situations and specific populations.

2. We propose to use a CBR approach to model the relation between a situation and its related interests. The main advantage of this approach is the flexibility it offers to separately model the user interests, location and time from external ontologies, allowing thus to compute an ontology based similarity between situations.

3. Our strategy adopted for search personalization is based on a re-ranking approach that combines the initial score of a document and its personalized score.

PERSONALIZING MOBILE SEARCH USING A SPATIO-TEMPORAL USER PROFILE

Motivation and General Approach

In mobile IR, the computing environment is continuously changing due to the inherent mobility framework. More specifically, users' interests may change anytime due to change in their environment (location, time, near persons, etc.). Just for example, assume that a person being at a "*museum*" submits the query "*Water lilies*", knowing that he is interested both in "*art*" and "*gardens*", we can improve search results by taking into account his interests for "*art*" and not for "*gardens*" given that he is at a "*museum*" and not in a "garden". Static approaches for building the user profile are therefore poorly useful, so we rather focus on more dynamic techniques, any time capable of adjusting the user interests to the current search situation. Our general approach for search personalization relies on building and selecting the most appropriate user profile in a particular search situation. In fact, while a user can have many profiles, one of these profiles is the one primarily corresponding to the current users' query and situation. In order to select the most adequate user profile to be used for personalization, we compare the similarity between a new search situation and the past ones. Comparing past user experiences is referred to in the literature as case-based reasoning (CBR) (Aamodt & Plaza, 1994). In CBR a problem is solved based on solutions of past similar problems. A case is described by a pair tuple <*premise, value*>. *Premise* is the description of the case which contains its characteristics, while the *value* is the result of the reasoning based on the premise. The *premise* part of a case referred in our situation similarity computing seating, is a specific search situation S of a mobile user, while the *value* part of a case is the user profile G to be used for the personalization of the search results. Each case from our case base represents then a specific ele-

Figure 3. General approach

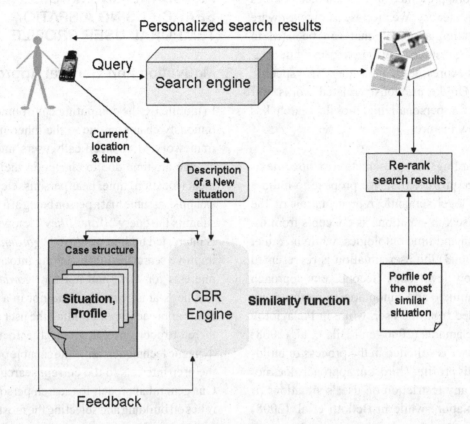

ment from *U*, denoted: *Case = (S, G)*. Figure 3, gives a general view of our approach. For each new submitted query, we build a new semantic situation, by modeling its associated time and location contexts. A situation based similarity measure is set up and allows selecting the most similar situation, from the past ones from the case base. When the computed similarity is above a threshold value, we re-rank the search results of the query using the user profile associated to the most similar situation. After the user clicks or views interesting documents, the user feedback is used to maintain the case base.

With respect to this general view, we address in the remainder of this chapter the following research questions: How to model the user search situations? How to build and maintain a graph-based user profile in a specific search situation?

How to select the adequate user profile and how to personalize the search results?

Situation Modeling

In our, approach we propose to model the user situation on the basis of two context elements: location and time. The motivation behind our choice is twofold: first, our intuition is that mobile user's information needs are related to his current activity. Knowing that each human activity is dependent or evolves within time and location space, we assume that these latter are sufficient for our purpose to describe the relation between user's interests and his environment. The second reason is typically technical; it considers the fact that these contextual elements can easily be acquired in an automatic way.

Our challenge when building this situation-aware profile is to use sensory data to identify a user situation. We propose to associate low level information directly acquired from sensors to semantic concepts extracted from temporal and spatial ontologies. Hence, instead of knowing that a user is at location "48.7818034, 2.2183314" and time "Tue Aug 3 12:10:00 CEST 2008" we derive that he is "at beach, summer, holiday, midday". Our situation model is then represented by an aggregation of four dimensions:

- **Location type**: refers to class name (such as beach, school…) extracted from a classification category of location types (like ADL feature type thesaurus) (University of California, Santa Barbara, 2001).
- **Season**: refers to one of the year's seasons.
- **Day of the week**: refers either to workday, weekend or holiday.
- **Time of the day**: refers to time zone of a day such as morning, night …

More specifically, a situation S can be represented as a vector whose features X are the values assigned to each dimension: $S = (X_l, X_u, X_v, X_w)$; where X_l (resp. X_u, X_v, X_w) is the value of the location type (resp. season, day of the week and time of the day) dimension. We give an outline of the location and time models on which the situation model relies.

Location Modeling

Location represents the point in space, where the user of the application is located. As discussed in Dobson (2005), there are different plausible and correct ways to answer the question: *where is the user located?* and consequently different ways to characterize a location. As returned by location sensor systems (like GPS), location is an absolute position in some geographic coordinates systems. However, user behavior is unlikely to be conditioned by coordinates per se, but rather

by what (else) is at these coordinates. Thus, we consider, in our work, a location class label (or named class) as relevant for our purpose of characterizing a situation of search. Such named classes are generally functional (like "yellow pages" naming), more importantly, a label directly represents the place's demographic (*school*), environmental (*beach*), historic (*monument*), personal (*residence*) or commercial (*shop*) significance and is the desired abstraction for our situation identification task. Simple automated place labeling is already commercialized (Google map, Yahoo local, Map-Point), it consists of merging web data such as postal addresses with maps enabling thus Nearest-X services. Also, manual place classification is practiced in most geographic information systems like the Alexandria Digital Library (http://www.alexandria.ucsb.edu/) and GeoNames (http://www.geonames.org/) servers. To insure the connection between the location coordinates and its semantic classification, a conceptual model is necessary to represent and reason about location. As in the SPIRIT project (Jones, 2007), we use a spatial data base (as geo service) and a spatial thesaurus for representing and reasoning on geographic information. Figure 4, shows a simplified model for representing spatial information.

Geographic places are related by different spatial relations such as: *contains, part-of, near,* etc. For example the geographical place "*Eiffel Tower*" is near the geographical place "*Champ de Mars*", and the two are part of the geographical place "*Paris*". Moreover, the mapping between the concrete class "Footprint", which represents the geographic coordinates, and the abstract class "Geographic Place", allows us to relate pure geographic coordinates to semantic places represented by their name and type or class label. For example, if we get from the user GPS device, that he is at coordinate "*48.861073°, 2.335784°*", we can infer from this mapping that the user is at the geographical place "*Le Louvre*" which is of type "*museum*". In our work, we rely on this mapping to automatically transform the physical locations

Figure 4. A simple schema of the location model

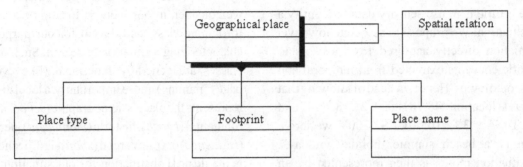

of the user to more semantical representations, generally expressed as "reverse geo-coding operation". This particularly allows us to group together places of the same type, for example if the user is now in another geographical coordinate given by "40.779447°, -73.96311°", we can infer that the user is in a similar situation "*museum*", although he is not in the same physical place.

Time Modeling

The temporal information is complex; it is continuous and can be represented at different levels of granularity. Many works within geographical IR (Pustejovsky et al., 2010; Le Parc-Lacayrelle et al., 2007), has addressed issues on extracting, representing and exploiting temporal aspects of time for computing some temporal relevancy between documents and users' queries. In our work, we exploit time information to decline the users' interests within time context. So, to define the temporal aspects characterizing the situation a user is in while submitting a query, we suggest abstracting the continuum time into some specific and significant periods (abstract time classes), which we expect having an effect on the user behavior (e.g., *morning, weekend, winter*). To allow a good representation of the temporal information and its manipulation, we propose to use OWL-Time ontology (Pan, 2007) and to extend it with some special classes of time: *time of day, day of week and season*. The time ontology abstracts a

time point to a set of significant time intervals of our daily life, the mapping between the two is implemented by axioms and predicates. For the *time of day* class we define five periods: *morning, midday, afternoon, evening, night*. For the *day of week* class we distinguish workdays (*Mon, Tue, Thu, Wed, Fry*), and rest-days composed of weekends (*Sat, Sun*) and holidays (*any day on which work is suspended by law or custom*).

User Profile Modeling

Below, we give an overview of the graph-based ontological representation of the user profile detailed in our previous work (Daoud et al., 2009). This type of representation allows us to entirely benefit from all the semantic relations within the general ontology to better model the users' interests. This representation is based on users' search activity, namely: submitted queries and clicked URLs, viewed document from the retrieved search results list, to model users' interests. A user profile is then built at the end of each search activity, based on three main steps: (1) initializing the query context as a set of keywords extracted from the users' documents of interest in a search activity, (2) mapping the keyword user profile on the reference ontology to build an initial weighted concept set, and (3) inferring the graph-based query profile using a score propagation strategy applied on the initial weighted concept set. These steps are detailed in the next section.

Query Context Initialization

We assume that the user profile could be inferred across similar search situations using the user's documents of interest. Our goal here is to create the query context that holds the user interest as the most relevant terms occurring in the relevant documents judged by the user. Let q^s be the query submitted by a specific user at time s. Let D^s be the set of relevant documents returned with respect to the query q^s, which is represented as a single term vector using the *tf.idf* weighting scheme. The keyword user profile K^s is a single term vector that represents the centroid of the documents in D^s, where the weight of a term t is computed as follows:

$$K^s(t) = \frac{1}{|D^s|} \sum_{d \in D^s} w_{td} \qquad (2)$$

Where w_{td} is the weight of term t in document d. In order to enhance the flat representation of the keyword user profile, a concept-based user profile is built by mapping it on reference ontology.

Mapping the Keyword User Profile on the Ontology

The keyword user profile K^s is mapped on the ODP (http://www.dmoz.org) ontology in order to extract a set of concepts that reflect semantically the user interest. Each concept of the ODP is related to other concepts with different relations (e.g., "is-a", "symbolic", "related") and is associated to a set of web pages classified under that concept. Each concept is presented by a single term vector $\vec{c}_j$ extracted from all individual web pages classified under that concept as well as all of its sub concepts. Strategy involved briefly consists of creating a super-document Sd_j for each concept c_j by concatenating the first 60 titles and descriptions associated to the web pages classified

under that concept. Then stop words are removed and porter stemming algorithm is applied on the collection of super-documents. Finally, each concept c_j is represented as a single term vector $\vec{c}_j$ where each term's weight w_i is computed using *tf.idf* weighting scheme. Specifically, *tf* is the total term frequency in the superdocument Sd_j as well as in the superdocuments associated to its sub-concepts. Given a concept c_j of the ODP, represented by the term vector $\vec{c}_j$, its similarity weight $sw(c_j)$ with $\vec{K}^s$ is computed as follows:

$$sw(c_j) = \cos(\vec{c}_j, \vec{K}^s) \qquad (3)$$

The result of mapping the keyword query context on the ontology is an initial set containing the top-50 weighted concepts, called $\theta^s = \{(c_1, score(c1)), ..., (c_j, score(c_j))\}$. For experimental purpose, we used the top-50 concepts matched with the query context and assume that this number is sufficient to include concepts of interest to the user. Based on this set, we attempt to build a graph of semantically related concepts of ontology using a score propagation detailed in the next section.

Inferring the Graph-Based Query Profile Using Score Propagation

We infer the graph-based representation of the query profile using one-hop score propagation applied on the concept set θ^s. We distinguish the role of different edges in activating linked concepts in the score propagation. Indeed, we re-use the edge weight setting adopted in Maguitman et al. (2005) in our score propagation as follows: $w_{ij} = \alpha_S$ for $e_{ij} \square S \cup T$, $w_{ij} = \alpha_R$ for $e_{ij} \square R$, where e_{ij} is the edge linking concept i to concept j. We set $\alpha_S = 1$ because symbolic links seem to be treated as first-class link "is-a" in the ODP web interface, and we set $\alpha_R = 0.5$ because related links are treated differently on the ODP web interface, labeled as "see also" topics. We did not consider "is-a" links in score propagation because we assume that concepts linked by "is-a" relations are activated in the initial concept set, as specific concepts have common terms with their general concepts and they are both matched with the query terms. The process of inferring the graph-based query profile takes θ^s as the initial set of weighted concepts of the ODP ontology. Each concept $c_i \in \theta^s$ propagates its weight to all its linked concepts c_k (made of "is-a", "related" and "symbolic" edges) according to the ontology. When a concept is activated by multiple concepts, its score is recomputed by accumulating its weight with the propagated one. Interrelated concepts are grouped together in order to create a single or disconnected weighted graphs G_i. The weight $w(G_i)$ of the graph G_i is computed by summing the scores of its concept nodes. As the score is propagated at one hop from an initially weighted concept set θ^s, created graphs may have common concepts. So we proceed by combining these graphs together in a single one by merging the node and edge sets as well as their weights. Finally, the ontological query profile G^s_q is represented by the highly weighted graph among the created ones. The user profile is initialized by the query profile G^s_q if the query is the first one submitted in the search situation S.

Case-Based Reasoning Approach for Personalization

Our CBR approach is involved across four steps process: (1) identifying the current case, (2) retrieving the most similar case, (3) reusing the case, (4) revising the proposed solution and/or retaining the case.

Identifying the Current Case: For a current query q^* submitted to the search engine, a current case denoted: $Case^* = (S^*, ?)$ is built. In order to represent the current situation S^*, sensory data related to the query q^* are gathered from GPS sensor and system clock and then abstracted from the time and location ontologies. We obtain then a semantic representation of S^*:

$$S^* = (X_l^*, X_u^*, X_v^*, X_w^*)$$

$Case^*$ is then sent to the case base to complete its value part.

Retrieve the Most Similar Case: To determine the expected user profile in the current case $Case^*$, the current situation S^* is compared to the past ones. Let $PS = \{S^1, ..., S^n\}$ be the set of past situations, we select the situation S^{opt} that satisfies:

$$S^{opt} = \underset{S^i \in PS}{\arg\max} \left(\sum_j a_j \times sim_j(X_j^*, X_j^i) \right). \quad (4)$$

Where X_j^* (resp. X_j^i) is the value of the jth feature of the situation vector S^* (resp. S^i), sim_j is the similarity metric related to the jth feature of a situation vector and α_j its associated weight.

These metrics are based on concepts proximity in the ontology used to represent the time or location dimensions of the situation model. For any new situation S^* *and any situation* $S^i \in PS$, the similarity between two features X_j^* (of S^*) and X_j^i (of S^i) depends on how closely they are related in the taxonomy. For example, the similarity between the location type *museum* and *theater* is greater than the similarity between *museum* and *hospital*. We use a similarity measure like in Wu and Palmer (1994) which is defined by:

$$sim_{location}(X_j^*, X_j^i) = \frac{2 * depth(lcs)}{depth(X_j^*) + depth(X_j^i)}. \quad (5)$$

where *lcs* is the Least Common Subsumer of X_j^* and X_j^i, and *depth* is the number of nodes on the path from a node to the root in the ontology.

Reuse the Case: Re-Rank Search Results: In order to insure a better precision of the search results, the personalization phase takes place only if the following condition is satisfied:

$$sim(S^*, S^{opt}) \geq \beta \; ; \text{ where } \beta \text{ is a threshold value.}$$

The corresponding user's profile G^{opt} is used to re-rank the search results returned by the search engine with respect to the current query q^*. The search results are re-ranked by combining for each retrieved document d_k, the original score returned by the system $score_o(q^*, d_k)$ and a personalized score $score_p(d_k, G^{opt})$ leading to a final $score_f(d_k)$ as follows:

$$score_f(dk) = (1 - \gamma) * score_o(q^*, d_k) + \gamma * score_p(d_k, G^{opt}) \tag{6}$$

Where γ ranges from 0 to 1. Both personalized and original scores could be bounded by varying the values of γ. The personalized score $score_p(d_k, G^{opt})$ is computed using the cosine similarity measure between the result d_k and the top ranked concepts of the user profile G^{opt} as follows:

$$score_p(d_k, G^{opt}) = \sum_{c_j \in G^{opt}} sw(c_j) * \cos(\vec{d_k}, \vec{c_j}). \tag{7}$$

Where $sw(c_j)$ is the similarity weight of the concept c_j in the user profile G^{opt}.

4. **Revise the Proposed Solution and/or Retain the Case**: The case base is updated based on the user feedback which is used to learn the user profile G^* for the search activity related to the current query q^*. Depending on the similarity value between the current situation S^* and the most similar one S^{opt}, two scenarios are plausible:
   a. $sim(S^*, S^{opt}) \neq 1$: a new case is added to the case base which is composed of the current situation S^* with its learned profile G^*.

$sim(S^*, S^{opt}) = 1$: the case containing the situation S^{opt} is updated. Let G^{opt} and G^* be the user profiles for the search activities related to the same situation S^{opt}. The updating method is based on the following principles: (1) enhance the weight of possible common concepts that can appear in two profiles related to the same S^{opt}, (2) alter the weight of non-common concepts using a decay factor η. The new weight of a concept c_j in the user profile G^{opt} is computed as follows:

$$sw_{G^{opt}}(c_j) = \begin{cases} \eta * sw_{G^{opt}}(c_j) + (1 - \eta) * sw_{G^*}(c_j) & \text{if } c_j \text{ in } G^{opt} \\ \eta * sw_{G^*}(c_j) & \text{otherwise} \end{cases} \tag{8}$$

where $sw_{G^{opt}}(c_j)$ is the weight of concept c_j in the profile G^{opt} and $sw_{G^*}(c_j)$ is the weight of concept c_j in the profile G^*.

EXPERIMENTAL EVALUATION

In the development of an IR system for mobile environments, evaluation plays an important role, as it allows to measure the effectiveness of the system and to better understand problems from both the system and the user interaction point of view. It is commonly accepted that the traditional evaluation methodologies used in TREC, CLEF and INEX campaigns are not always suitable for considering the contextual dimensions in the information access process. Indeed, laboratory-based or system oriented evaluation is challenged by the presence of contextual dimensions such as the user profile or the environment which significantly impact on the relevance judgments or usefulness ratings made by the end user (Tamine, Boughanem, & Daoud, 2009). Contextual evaluation methodologies have been proposed (Göker & Myrhaug, 2008) to integrate the user context in the evaluation scenario. However, evaluation remains challenging because of the main following reasons (Kjeldskov & Graham, 2003):

1) environmental data should be available and several usage scenarios should be evaluated across them, 2) evaluation, if present, concerns a specific application (e.g., tourist guide), generalization to a wide range of information access applications is difficult.

In the absence of a standard evaluation framework for mobile IR, we will give in this section, a brief overview of evaluation methodologies proposed in this domain and then detail our own evaluation framework supported by experimental results analysis.

Overview of Contextual Evaluation Methodologies in Mobile IR

We can classify evaluation methodologies within mobile contextual IR, to two main types: evaluation by context simulations and evaluation by user studies.

The first kind of evaluation simulates users and interactions by means of well defined retrieval scenarios (hypothesis). Contextual simulation frameworks allow systems to be evaluated, according to a formative view, with less regard for constraints that arise from using sensor technologies, low-level system functionalities and several social and personal differences of users in interaction with the system. The contextual simulation framework proposed in Bouidghaghen, Tamine, and Boughanem (2009) is based on hypothetic user search context and queries. User context is represented by a set of possible locations, users' interests are integrated in the evaluation strategy according to a simulation algorithm that generates them using hypothetic user interactions for each query. In Mizzaro, Nazzi, and Vassena (2008), authors propose a contextual simulation framework based on a set of simulated context descriptors that include location, time and user activities. User's queries are automatically formulated from the context descriptors using different techniques. Context simulation based evaluation method is worthwhile since it is less time consuming and

costly than experiments with real users. However, the method has still areas of uncertainty, for example the choice of assumptions underlying the major scenarios is open to criticism for its lack of realism.

The evaluation by user studies is carried out with real users, called participants, to test the system performance through real users' interactions with the system. To evaluate the performance of contextualized search, each participant is required to issue a certain number of test queries and determine whether each result is relevant in its context. There are two types of user studies adopted in the domain. The first one (Göker & Myrhaug, 2008; Panayiotou & Samaras, 2006) is based on the evaluation framework proposed in Borlund and Ingwersen (1998) which makes use of "simulated work task situations", where users are assigned a set of predefined tasks to perform in predefined situations. This kind of user studies is criticized because it still rely on artificial information needs and may be confounded by inter-subject and order effects. The second kind of contextual evaluation by user studies (Cheverst et al., 2000; Mountain & MacFarlane, 2007; Bellotti et al., 2008) is carried out in realistic use settings, where users are free to use the system as they would wish to use it and for only as long as they want, submitting their own queries arising from their natural information needs within real and natural situations, rather than asking them to perform some predefined series of tasks. The advantage of user studies based evaluation is that they are conducted with real users and thus the relevance can be explicitly specified by them. The main limitation they introduce is that: they may be of little use if the system is not fully developed, they induce extra costs and the experiments are not repeatable.

We propose in this chapter, an evaluation framework based on a diary study as a tool to integrate real user queries and contexts into the Cranfield paradigm. Our evaluation framework integrates the benefits of the state-of-the-art evalu-

Table 1. An example of some diary entries

User	Date	houre	place	query
2	27-févr	11h10	périphérique	"Parking relais Bordeaux
6	16-févr	16h30	musée	"exposition beaubourg artistes"
7	02-mars	19h40	Station bus	"Tisseo Horaire bus 2"

ation approaches, by allowing evaluation with real users and real contexts without requiring that the system be fully developed.

Diary Study Based Evaluation Framework

The main problem we faced to evaluate our approach, is the absence of a standard evaluation benchmark and dataset for evaluating context-aware approaches for mobile search. We propose an evaluation framework that is based on a diary study approach. In what follows, we describe our evaluation methodology and the different datasets we build.

Evaluation Methodology: A Diary Study

We conducted a diary study, where mobile users were asked to record the date, the time, their current location, and the query they have while they are mobile. Seven volunteers participated to our study (3 female and 4 male), ages ranged from 21 to 36. All the participants already have experience with using search engines on the web, using a PC or a mobile phone. The diary study lasted for 4 weeks and it generated 79 diary entries, with an average of 11.28 entries per person (min=3, max=35, standard deviation=10.8). Table 1 illustrates an example of such diary entries; each diary entry represents a userid, a user situation (time, date and place) and the user query.

Query Set

From the diary study entries, we obtained a total of 79 queries expressed principally in the French language. Query length varies between 1 and 5, with an average of 2,99 and a standard deviation of 0.99. The user intent behind these queries is mostly informational *"velo hauteur selle"* or transactional *"paris hotel cardinal"* (query language is French). We represent each query by a three tuple <query, description, narrative>.

Situation Set

From the diary study entries, we extract time and location information associated with each query. While the location information is already expressed in semantic concepts, the time entries are not. Thus we transform each date time on a semantic period of the day or the week. We totally obtained 36 groups of similar situations, with an average of 5 groups by user (min=2, max=12) and an average of 3 (min=1, max=8) queries within a same situation group. All the obtained situation groups are used to test the accuracy of the CBR technique to identify similar situations.

Ground Truth

A second problem we face to while building our evaluation framework is to construct a document collection together with relevance judgments according to the collected user queries and their context. To answer this problem, we build our document collection by collecting the top 100 results retrieved from the publicly available Yahoo boss search API (http://developer.yahoo.com/search/boss/) for each query. In our evaluation setting, only the top 50 retrieved documents are used for re-ranking the search results using the user profile. The relevance assessments for the queries were given through an assessment tool available on line. To do, each user who submitted a query (in the diary study), was asked to judge whether a document from the set of top 50 results retrieved from Yahoo as response to his query was relevant or not according to his query and its context. Relevance judgments have been made using a three level relevance scale: relevant, partially relevant, or not relevant.

Experimental Results and Analysis

In this experimental evaluation, we have conducted two set of experiments to evaluate the accuracy of our proposed CBR technique to select an appropriate situation and to evaluate the personalized search effectiveness.

Evaluating the Accuracy of the CBR Technique to Select the Most Similar Situation

In order to evaluate the accuracy of the CBR technique to identify similar situations and particularly to set out the threshold similarity value, we propose to use a manual classification as a baseline and compare it with the results obtained by the CBR technique. So, we manually classify the initial user contexts into groups of similar situations, the weight α_j of the similarity metrics in equation 4, are fixed according to the user's feedback from the diary study. We compare the manual constructed groups to the results obtained by our similarity algorithm in formula 4, with different β threshold values in the interval [0 1]. Our measure of accuracy is based on the precision and recall measures defined as follows:

$$\mathrm{Pr}\,ecision = \frac{CAG}{AG}\,; \qquad \mathrm{Re}\,call = \frac{CAG}{MG}$$

where AG is the total number of automatically constructed groups of similar situations by our algorithm, MG is the total number of the manually constructed groups of similar situations and CAG is the number of correctly automatically constructed groups of similar situations according to the manually ones. Figure 5 shows the effect of varying the threshold situation similarity parameter β in the interval [0 1] on the overall precision and recall. Results show that the best performance is obtained when the threshold value $\beta = 0.6$ achieving a high accuracy of 0.97 recall and 0.98 precision.

Evaluating the Personalized Search Effectiveness

We evaluated the personalized search effectiveness based on a k-fold cross validation protocol over a set of similar situations of a user using the optimal threshold value identified above ($\beta = 0.6$). The protocol is explained as follows:

- For each group of similar situations of a user, divide the query set into k equally sized subsets, and using k-1 training subsets for learning the user interests and the remaining subset as a test set,
- For each query in the training set, generate the associated profile based on its top n relevant documents listed in the relevance judgments file,
- Update user profile concept weights across the queries in the training set, like described in formula 11, and use it for re-ranking the search results of the queries in the test set,
- Evaluate the personalized retrieval effectiveness for each testing query using

Figure 5. Effect of the parameter Beta on the situations similarity accuracy

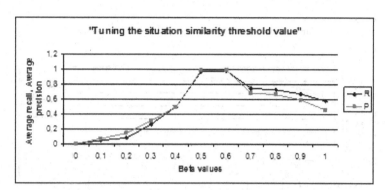

the user profile compared to the baseline search performed by Yahoo boss search using only the testing query,

- Pool together the queries and judgments of all the 7 users, so that the evaluation result will be an average over the whole testing queries.

As Evaluation measures we used the *precision* (*P*) and the *Normalized Discounted Cumulative Gain (nDCG)* measures, computed at different cut-off points (*x*), they are defined as follows:

Precision at rank x (Px): measures the proportion of relevant document within the Top x ranked list of search results documents list, it is computed as follows: $Px = \dfrac{Re\,lDoc_x}{x}$; where $RelDoc_x$ is the number of relevant documents that appear within the top *x* search results,

Normalized Discounted Cumulative Gain (nDCG): is the normalized form of the *discounted cumulative gain (DCG)* (Jarvelin & Kekalainen, 2002). It is a rank-position oriented measure devoted for the estimation of overall relevance gained by a user when observing the top ranked documents. It is computed as follows:

$$nDCGx = \frac{DCGx}{IDCGx}$$

Where *DCGx* is *discounted cumulative gain* at position *x*, computed by:

$$DCGx = rel_1 + \sum_{i=2}^{x} \frac{rel_i}{\log_2 i}$$

Where rel_i is the graded relevance of the document at position *i* in the search results list.

And *IDCGx* is the ideal rank at position *x*, obtained by sorting documents of a result list by relevance, producing an ideal *DCG*.

For these two measures we used the cut-off points of 5, 10, and 20. The rationale behind this decision is the fact that the majority of search result click activity (89.8%) happens on the first page of search results (Spink et al., 2006), that is, users only consider the first 10 (20) documents. The *Px* and *nDCGx* values for all queries and all users are finally averaged to obtain a measure of the average performance.

In this experiment, we study in a first time, the effect of combining the original document's rank of Yahoo (corresponding to the original document score in formula 9) and the personalized document rank obtained according to our approach, on the retrieval effectiveness. Figure 6 and Figure 7 show the improvement of our personalized search in terms of P5, P10 and P20 (respect. in terms of nDCG5, nDCG10 and nDCG20) with varying the combination parameter γ in the interval [0 1].

Figure 6. Effect of the parameter gamma on Precision in the combined rank

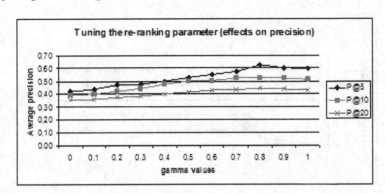

Figure 7. Effect of the parameter gamma on nDCG in the combined rank

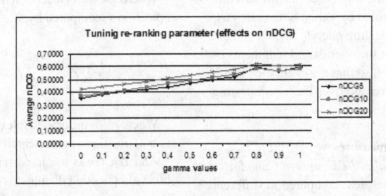

Table 2. Average Top-n precision and nDCG comparison between our personalized search and Yahoo boss over all queries

	Average precision			Average nDCG		
	P5	P10	P20	nDCG5	nDCG10	nDCG20
Yahoo boss	0.42	0.39	0.36	0.35	0.37	0.42
Our approach	0.60	0.52	0.43	0.59	0.58	0.61
Improvement	43.03%	32.14%	19.58%	66.65%	55.84%	44.48%

Results show that the best performance is obtained when γ is 0.8. This is likely due to the fact that all the results on the top 50 match the query well and thus the distinguishing feature is how well they match the user profile.

In a second time, we compare our personalized retrieval effectiveness to the baseline search. Table 2 shows the improvement of our personal-

ized search in terms of P5, P10, P20, nDCG5, nDCG10 and nDCG20 over all the tested queries.

As we can observe in Table 2, results prove that personalized search achieves higher retrieval precision of almost the queries. We also observe that in general, our approach enhances the initial nDCG5, nDCG10 and nDCG20 obtained by the standard search and improve thus the quality of the top search results lists. Best performance is achieved by the personalized search in terms of average precision at different cut-off points achieving an improvement of 43.03% at P5, 32.14% at P10, and 19.58% at P20, and in terms of accumulated gain achieving an improvement of 66.65% at nDCG5, 55.84% at nDCG10 and 44.48% at nDCG20 comparatively to Yahoo boss. In order to verify if this improvement is statistically significant, we have also conducted a t-test between the means obtained on P5, P10, P20, nDCG5, nDCG10 and nDCG20, by the baseline search performed by Yahoo boss and our personalizing approach. We assume that the difference between ranking is significant if $p < 0.05$ (noted * in Table 1). As shown in Table 1, our proposed approach has shown significant p-value according to the t-test at P5, P10, P20, nDCG5, nDCG10 and nDCG20.

CONCLUSION AND FUTURE WORK

This chapter gives an overview of a number of representative state-of-the-art contextual IR techniques in the mobile environment and describes our spatio-temporal based personalization approach for mobile search. Our approach for personalizing mobile search consists of three basic steps: (1) inferring semantic situations from low level location and time data, (2) learning and maintaining user interests based on his search history related to the identified situations, (3) selecting a profile to use for personalization given a new situation by exploiting a CBR technique. We have presented a novel evaluation framework based on a diary study approach devoted for a context-aware personalization approach for mobile search. We evaluated our approach according to the proposed evaluation framework and show that it is effective. In future work, we plan to extend this protocol by using real user data provided from a search engine log file. Extending the protocol aims at testing the effectiveness of the personalized search based on

real mobile search contexts and click-through data available in the log file.

REFERENCES

Aamodt, A., & Plaza, E. (1994). Case-based reasoning: Foundational issues, methodological variations, and system approaches. *AI Communications, 7*(1).

Allan, J. (Ed.). (2002). Challenges in information retrieval and langage modelling. In *Proceedings of the Report of a Workshop held at the Center for Intelligent Information Retrieval*, Amherst, MA.

Anand, S. S., & Mobasher, B. (2007). Introduction to intelligent techniques for web personalization. *ACM Transactions on Internet Technology, 7*(4), 18. doi:10.1145/1278366.1278367

Anderson, C. R., Domingos, P., & Weld, D. S. (2001). Personalizing Web sites for mobile users. In *Proceedings of the 10th International Conference on World Wide Web* (pp. 565-575).

Asadi, S., Zhou, X., Jamali, H. R., & Mofrad, H. V. (2007). Location-based search engines tasks and capabilities: A comparative study. *Webology, 4*(4), 48.

August, K. G., Hansen, M. H., & Shriver, E. (2002). Mobile Web searching. *Bell Labs Technical Journal, 6*(2).

Bellotti, V., Begole, B., Chi, E. H., Ducheneaut, N., Fang, J., & Isaacs, E. …Walendowski, A. (2008). Activity-based serendipitous recommendations with the Magitti mobile leisure guide. In *Proceedings of the Twenty-Sixth Annual SIGCHI Conference on Human Factors in Computing Systems.*

Bierig, R., & Göker, A. (2006). Time, location and interest: an empirical and user-centred study. In *Proceedings of the 1st International Conference on Information Interaction in Context* (pp. 79-87).

Bila, N., Cao, J., Dinoff, R., Ho, T. K., Hull, R., Kumar, B., & Santos, P. (2008). Mobile user profile acquisition through network observables and explicit user queries. In *Proceedings of the 9th International conference on Mobile Data Management* (pp. 98-107).

Bilal, D. (2000). Children's use of the yahooligans! Web search engine: cognitive, physical, and affective behavior on fact-based search tasks. *Journal of the American Society for Information Science American Society for Information Science, 51*(7), 646–665. doi:10.1002/(SICI)1097-4571(2000)51:7<646::AID-ASI7>3.0.CO;2-A

Borlund, P., & Ingwersen, P. (1998). Measures of relative relevance and ranked half-life. In *Proceedings of the 21st Annual International ACM SIGIR Conference on Research and Development in Information Retrieval* (pp. 324-331).

Bouidghaghen, O., Tamine, L., & Boughanem, M. (2010). Contextual evaluation of mobile search. In *Proceedings of the Second Workshop on Contextual Information Access, Seeking and Retrieval Evaluation*, Milton Keynes, UK (Vol. 569).

Bouvin, N. O., Christensen, B. G., Grønbaek, K., & Hansen, F. A. (2003). HyCon: a framework for context-aware mobile hypermedia. *New Review of Hypermedia and Multimedia, 9*, 59–88. doi:10.1080/13614560410001725310

Budzik, J., & Hammond, K. (2000). User interactions with every day applications as context for just-in-time information access. In *Proceedings of the 5th International Conference on Intelligent User Interfaces* (pp. 44-51).

Cheverst, K., Davies, N., Mitchell, K., Friday, A., & Efstratiou, C. (2000). Developing a context-aware electronic tourist guide: Some issues and experiences. In *Proceedings of SIGCHI Conference on Human Factors in Computing Systems* (pp. 17-24).

Church, K., & Smyth, B. (2009). Understanding the intent behind mobile information needs. In *Proceedings of the 13th International Conference on Intelligent User Interfaces* (pp. 247-256).

Daoud, M., Tamine, L., Boughanem, M., & Chebaro, B. (2009). A session based personalized search using an ontological user profile. In *Proceedings of the ACM Symposium on Applied Computing* (pp. 1031-1035).

Dervin, B., & Nilan, M. (1986). Information needs and uses. *Annual Review of Information Science & Technology, ▪▪▪*, 3–33.

Dobson, S. (2005). Leveraging the subtleties of location. In *Proceedings of the Conference on Smart Objects and Ambient Intelligence* (pp. 189-193).

Frias-Martinez, E., Chen, S. Y., Macredie, R. D., & Liu, X. (2007). The role of human factors in stereotyping behavior and perception of digital library users: a robust clustering approach. *User Modeling and User-Adapted Interaction, 17*(3), 1573–1391. doi:10.1007/s11257-007-9028-7

Göker, A., & Myrhaug, H. (2002). User context and personalization. In *Proceedings of the EC-CBR Workshop on Case Based Reasoning and Personalization*, Aberdeen, UK.

Göker, A., & Myrhaug, H. (2008). Evaluation of a mobile information system in context. *Information Processing & Management, 44*(1), 39–65. doi:10.1016/j.ipm.2007.03.011

Hattori, S., Tezuka, T., & Tanaka, K. (2007). Context-aware query refinement for mobile web search. In *Proceedings of the International Symposium on Applications and the Internet Workshops*.

Hupfer, M. E., & Detlor, B. (2006). Gender and Web information seeking: A self-concept orientation model. *Journal of the American Society for Information Science and Technology, 57*(8), 1105–1115. doi:10.1002/asi.20379

Jansen, B., Booth, D., & Spink, A. (2007). Determining the user intent of Web search engine queries. In *Proceedings of the 16ᵗʰ International Conference on World Wide Web* (pp. 1149-1150).

Jones, C. B. (2007). *Spatially-aware information retrieval on the Internet*. Retrieved from http://www.geo-spirit.org/ index

Jones, G. J. F., & Brown, P. J. (2004). Context-aware retrieval for ubiquitous computing environments. In F. Crestani, M. Dunlap, & S. Mizzaro (Eds.), *Proceedings of the International Workshop on Mobile and Ubiquitous Information Access* (LNCS 2954, pp. 371-374).

Kamvar, M., & Baluja, S. (2007a). Deciphering trends in mobile search. *Computer, 40*(8), 58–62. doi:10.1109/MC.2007.270

Kamvar, M., & Baluja, S. (2007b). The role of context in query input: Using contextual signals to complete queries on mobile devices. In *Proceedings of the 9ᵗʰ International Conference on Human Computer Interaction with Mobile Devices and Services* (pp. 405-412).

Kim, K. (2008). Effects of emotion control and task on web searching behavior. *Information Processing & Management, 44*(1), 373–385. doi:10.1016/j.ipm.2006.11.008

Kjeldskov, J., & Graham, C. (2003). A review of mobile HCI research method. In *Proceedings of the 5ᵗʰ International Symposium Human Computer Interaction with Mobile Devices and Services* (pp. 317-335).

Lang, K. (1995). NewsWeeder: learning to filter Netnews. In *Proceedings of the 12ᵗʰ International Conference on Machine Learning* (pp. 331-339).

Le Parc-Lacayrelle, A., Gaio, M., & Sallaberry, C. (2007). La composante temps dans l'information géographique textuelle Extraction et recherche d'information dans des fonds documentaires patrimoniaux numérisés. *Document Numérique, 10,* 129–148. doi:10.3166/dn.10.2.129-148

Maguitman, A., Menczer, F., Roinestad, H., & Vespignani, A. (2005). Algorithmic detection of semantic similarity. In *Proceedings of the 14ᵗʰ International Conference on World Wide Web* (pp. 107-116).

Mizzaro, S., Nazzi, E., & Vassena, L. (2008). Retrieval of context-aware applications on mobile devices: How to evaluate? In *Proceedings of the Second International Symposium on Information Interaction in Context* (pp. 65-71).

Mountain, D., & MacFarlane, A. (2007). Geographic information retrieval in a mobile environment: evaluating the needs of mobile individual. *Journal of Information Science, 33*(5), 515–530. doi:10.1177/0165551506075333

Navarro-Prieto, R., Scaife, M., & Rogers, Y. (1999). Cognitive strategies in web searching. In *Proceedings of the 5ᵗʰ Conference on Human Factors & the Web*.

Pan, F. (2007). *Representing complex temporal phenomena for the semantic web and natural language* (Unpublished doctoral dissertation). University of Southern California, Los Angeles, CA.

Panayiotou, C., & Samaras, G. (2006). Mobile user personalization with dynamic profiles: Time and activity. In R. Meersman, Z. Tari, & P. Herraro (Eds.), *Proceedings of Doctoral Consortium of On the Move to Meaningful Internet Systems* (LNCS 4278, pp. 1295-1304).

Pustejovsky, J., Lee, K., Bunt, H., & Romary, L. (2010). ISO-TimeML: An international standard for semantic annotation. In *Proceedings of the International Conference on Language Resources and Evaluation*.

Samaras, G., & Panayiotou, C. (2002). *Personalized portals for the wireless user based on mobile agents*. In *Proceedings of the 2ⁿᵈ International Workshop on Mobile Commerce* (pp. 70-74).

Schofield, E., & Kubin, G. (2002). On interfaces for mobile information retrieval. In F. Paternó (Eds.), *Proceedings of the 4th International Symposium on Human Computer Interaction with Mobile Devices* (LNCS 2411, pp. 383-387).

Shamber, L. (1994). Relevance and information behavior. *Annual Review of Information Science & Technology, 29,* 3–48.

Shen, X., Tan, B., & Zhai, C. (2005). Context-sensitive information retrieval using implicit feedback. In *Proceedings of the 28th Annual International ACM SIGIR Conference on Research and Development in Information Retrieval* (pp. 43-50).

Sieg, A., Mobasher, B., & Burke, R. (2004). User's information context: Integrating user profiles and concept hierarchies. In *Proceedings of the Meeting of the International Federation of Classification Societies* (Vol. 1, pp. 28-40).

Smyth, B., & Balfe, E. (2006). Anonymous personalization in collaborative web search. *Information Retrieval, 9*(2), 165–190. doi:10.1007/s10791-006-7148-z

Sohn, T., Li, K. A., Griswold, W. G., & Hollan, J. D. (2008). A diary study of mobile information needs. In *Proceedings of the 26th Annual SIGCHI Conference on Human Factors in Computing Systems* (pp. 433-442).

Spink, S., Jansen, B., Blakely, C., & Koshman, S. (2006). A study of results overlap and uniqueness among major web search engines. *Information Processing & Management, 42*(5), 1379–1391. doi:10.1016/j.ipm.2005.11.001

Sweeney, S., & Crestani, F. (2006). Effective search results summary size and device screen size: Is there a relationship? *Information Processing & Management, 42*(4), 1056–1074. doi:10.1016/j.ipm.2005.06.007

Tamine, L., Boughanem, M., & Zemirli, N. (2008). Personalized document ranking: Exploiting evidence from multiple user interests for profiling and retrieval. *Journal of Digital Information Management, 6*(5), 354–365.

Tamine-Lechani, L., Boughanem, M., & Daoud, M. (2009). Evaluation of contextual information retrieval effectiveness: Overview of issues and research. *Knowledge and Information Systems Journal, 24*(1), 1–34. doi:10.1007/s10115-009-0231-1

Tao, Y., Mamoulis, N., & Papadias, D. (2003). Validity information retrieval for spatiotemporal queries. In T. Hadzilacos, Y. Manolopoulos, J. Roddick, & Y. Theodoridis (Eds.), *Proceedings of the 8th International Symposium on Advances in Spatial and Temporal Databases* (LNCS 2750, pp. 159-178).

Timothy, M., Sherry, C., & Robert, M. (2005). Hypermedia learning and prior knowledge: domain expertise vs. system expertise. *Journal of Computer Assisted Learning, 21*(12), 53–64.

Tombros, A., Ruthven, I., & Jose, J. M. (2005). How users assess web pages for information seeking. *Journal of the American Society for Information Science and Technology, 56*(4), 327–344. doi:10.1002/asi.20106

University of California. Santa Barbara. (2001). *Alexandria digital library feature type thesaurus.* Retrieved from http://www.alexandria.ucsb.edu/gazetteer/FeatureTypes/ver100301/

Vieira, V., Tedesco, P., Salgado, A. C., & Brzillon, P. (2007). Investigating the specifics of contextual elements management: The Cemantika approach. In *Proceedings of the 6th International and Interdisciplinary Conference on Modeling and Using Context* (pp. 493-506).

Wu, Z., & Palmer, M. (1994). Verb semantics and lexical selection. In *Proceedings of the 32nd Annual Meeting of the Association for Computational Linguistics*.

Xie, H. (2008). Users' evaluation of digital libraries (DLs): Their uses, their criteria, and their assessment. *Information Processing & Management, 44*(3), 1346–1373. doi:10.1016/j. ipm.2007.10.003

Yau, S. S., Liu, H., Huang, D., & Yao, Y. (2003). Situation-aware personalized information retrieval for mobile Internet. In *Proceedings of the 27th Annual International Computer Software and Applications* Conference (pp. 638-645).

Section 4
Evaluation

Chapter 18
Studying Web Search Engines from a User Perspective:
Key Concepts and Main Approaches

Stéphane Chaudiron
University of Lille 3, France

Madjid Ihadjadene
University of Paris 8, France

ABSTRACT

This chapter shows that the wider use of Web search engines, reconsidering the theoretical and methodological frameworks to grasp new information practices. Beginning with an overview of the recent challenges implied by the dynamic nature of the Web, this chapter then traces the information behavior related concepts in order to present the different approaches from the user perspective. The authors pay special attention to the concept of "information practice" and other related concepts such as "use", "activity", and "behavior" largely used in the literature but not always strictly defined. The authors provide an overview of user-oriented studies that are meaningful to understand the different contexts of use of electronic information access systems, focusing on five approaches: the system-oriented approaches, the theories of information seeking, the cognitive and psychological approaches, the management science approaches, and the marketing approaches. Future directions of work are then shaped, including social searching and the ethical, cultural, and political dimensions of Web search engines. The authors conclude considering the importance of Critical theory to better understand the role of Web Search engines in our modern society.

DOI: 10.4018/978-1-4666-0330-1.ch018

INTRODUCTION

A simple technical definition of a Web search refers to an information retrieval system (IRS) which allows keywords searches in textual and multimedia distributed pieces of content over the Web. But when asking people what a search engine is, they more likely answer that it is the first step to enter the Web to find the useful and relevant information they look for, to check an already known but forgotten information, to verify the spelling of some complicated words or even to point out the major interest trends through search streams. These definitions, both on the technical and the user sides, show that studying search engines and, more generally, online information searching systems refers to several academic fields, in particular information science, cognitive psychology, linguistics, computer science and artificial intelligence.

The number and diversity of studies focusing on Web searching give valuable insights regarding the importance of this activity. An overview of these results is presented in various review articles (Su, 2003; Spink & Jansen, 2004; Bar-Ilan, 2004; Martzoukou, 2005; Ihadjadene & Chaudiron, 2008; Waller, 2011). Interesting findings of these studies include topic trends in Web searching, structure of the Web queries, multilingual searching, video and image searching, categorization and visualization of the results, query reformulation, search tactics and strategies, mobile, real time and social searching, use of search engine by various populations, etc. But beyond the functional aspects, Web searching has become a large socio-economic, political and cultural phenomenon. Web search engines (now WSE) play a central role in the evolution of users' information behavior as they are not any more used only in professional contexts but in everyday life contexts for different purposes such as looking for a hotel, having a good price for a trip, finding a doctor or a babysitter. WSE still allow people to access information but they also drive search traffic towards particular sites

(Search Engine Optimization), influence marketing strategies and consumer behaviors (*Google AdWords*), inform about people interests with *Google Trends*, and they even may be considered as a new media.

The rapidly changing nature of Web searching brings scholars to reconsider the theoretical and methodological frameworks to grasp new information practices. On one hand, WSE are designed with new searching and browsing functionalities and deal with different digital collections (textual, music and video corpora, bibliographic records, etc) and new information channels and sources (blogs, chats, social networks...). As a consequence, they tend to change very quickly and are more and more integrated in wider devices such as commercial websites. On the other hand, the advent of the Internet has created a diversity of small digital interconnected worlds, allowing millions of users to produce, navigate and search for information. These users have various backgrounds with different levels of ability and knowledge. The growing place of digital environments brings major changes on Information Retrieval (IR) systems, on user behaviors and on information practices. One major issue for researchers is to understand how they really use these technical devices, how they adapt themselves to the technical constraints, what kind of knowledge they mobilize during search sessions, etc.

The aim of this chapter is to present an overview of the theoretical and practical models which are used by scholars to study Web searching practices. To achieve this goal, we first rapidly shape recent challenges in search engine evolution pointing out the major current issues which impact searching behavior. In the second section, we introduce the main concepts in user-oriented approaches with a special attention to the concepts of "information practice", "use" and "behavior" which are used with different meanings. The goal of this section is to provide a conceptual questioning as an attempt to clarify how scholars and practitioners use these terms in their studies. In the third section, based on the previous clarification, we present four types of studies, classified according to the role of the user and his environment. With different goals and methodologies, they all have in common to capture the user's behavior at different levels, search tasks and strategies, personal information infrastructure, cognitive or social-organizational contexts.

1. RECENT CHALLENGES IN SEARCH ENGINE EVOLUTION

Far from being a mere and isolated technical artifact, search engine has progressively become the "keystone of digital culture". Like most other technologies, studying search engines requires to take into account the changing context in which they are used. This first section rapidly points out the main technical evolutions which impact users' Web searching behavior.

1.1. Online Information Retrieval Systems and Web Search Engines

Time is far when, within the first half of the 1960s, the prototypes of several innovative IR systems were developed and used for experimentation. Systems were extremely primitive by our standards: query input was via a stack of cards or a roll of punched paper tape and output was often data on teletypewriters printers. During the 1970s, the systems became more powerful with new advanced features such as online thesauri, ranked output, Boolean logic, truncation, cited-reference searching, automatic inclusion of synonyms in the search formulations and natural language searching. From the 1990s, Internet drastically modified the world of automatic document processing and IRS by increasing the number of information resources available to people in their everyday life. The expansion and variety of information retrieval systems has lead to a multiplication and a diversification of users and a growing heteroge-

neousness of information. This double evolution has not, however, modified the fundamental objective of information retrieval: locating relevant information with maximum precision.

Even if the widespread use of Web search engines could let us think that they are the only tools for information access, it is important to underline the diversity of electronic information access systems and their complementary nature, such as online commercial databases, online public access catalogs (OPAC), open access repositories, digital libraries, syndication and aggregation tools, social networks and collaborative search tools, etc. Web search engines can be themselves distinguished in four types:

*   Web directories with hierarchically organized indexes
*   General search engines and meta-search engines
*   Specialized (or vertical) search engines
*   Social (or community) search engines.

The ever more user-friendly functionalities and the plethoric amount of information on the Web create the illusion that users can easily and very quickly find the information they need. Studies (Markey, 2007) have found that Web users show very different patterns of searching from those in traditional IR systems, such as commercial online databases and OPACs. Results (e.g., Spink & Jansen, 2004) show in particular that Web users don't enter many queries per search session, don't use Boolean operators frequently and that each query is shorter. The environment for information retrieval on the Web differs from that of other electronic information access systems in a number of fundamental ways. The collection of data is very large and changes continually, with pages being created, added, modified and deleted. Web documents are much more heterogeneous than typical electronic document collection, with variability between the size, type, structure, format, quality and usefulness of documents. The variety of document types includes texts, images and videos, audio and scripts as well as multilingual documents. Duplication of documents and sites is common and the dynamic nature of the Web in terms of growth and changes constitutes a major difference with traditional online electronic resources.

All these characteristics deeply influence users' searching and information behavior. On one hand, the new generation of Web users expects other IR systems to have the same design and features as Web search engines. On the other hand, experienced online searchers who are accustomed to traditional online databases with a certain level of search sophistication are unsatisfied with the inefficiency of Web-based IR systems. But the general trend is that the Web search culture signifies the emergence of the end-users time. Searching for information on the Web today is not anymore the privilege of information professionals and of scientists but has also become that of scholars, consumers, citizens, tourists… Ordinary people become end-users.

1.2. Specialized Search Engines

Web search engines have recently experienced new developments. First, there is a trend to develop specialized searching tools on the Web according to different directions: the development of personalized search functions, multilingual information retrieval, question-answering techniques, images and videos retrieval, information visualization techniques for presenting the results, the development of vertical *versus* horizontal search engines, and the emergence of social search engines.

1.2.1. Personalizing Search Engines

As stated by Notess (2006) and Halavais (2009), personalizing search engines is one of the main issues in the development of the Internet. From spelling functionality that helps correctly spell the words in the queries to adaptive search engines

which are able to better meet the information needs of a user or a community of users; search engines are also more adaptive to different contexts of use. In particular, some of them can automatically adjust themselves to the specific user information needs using different means such as query refinement and personalized search algorithms. Sometimes, users can modify the interface in order to customize the way the search engine appears and works. Personalized search engines also offer features such as saving URLs, archiving pages, organizing saved results into folders, blocking specific sites, and recording a search history. In particular, search history has been for decades one of the major features of professional online databases and was first introduced in 2004 by the *Amazon* search engine. Several search engines now offer the search history feature as *Google* and *Yahoo!* But search engine personalization also allows people to use their mobile devices for mobile searching instead of desktop searching. Due to the specific physical constraints (in particular smaller screens), they use adapted style sheets to present themselves differently on a small mobile device than they do on a bigger one. They also use the geospatial positioning function of smartphones to locate relevant places or items in response to the user needs. GPS-enabled devices are considerably changing the way people interact with the Web and search engines and mobile search engines may now combine both content relevant and geographical relevant criteria prior to propose a list of answers to users.

1.2.2. Multilingual Searching

Another important issue in the development of specialized search engines is the multilingual information retrieval functionalities. Although online, CD-ROM and OPAC systems collect multilingual information, the need for multilingual information retrieval in those environments does not appear as strong as in the Web environment. While the coverage of multilingual documents is highly selective in those systems, the Internet is a global network naturally carrying much more multilingual information. In June 2010, the Internet World Stats survey (2010) established that the Top Ten Internet Languages (i.e., the number of Internet users) were: English (27.3% of total internet users), Chinese (22.6%), Spanish (7.8%), Japanese (5.0%), Portuguese (4.2%), German (3.8%), Arabic (3.3%), French (3.0%), Russian (3.0%), and Korean (2.0%). These data estimate that 72.7% of the almost 2 billion people who use the Internet are non-English speakers, and that 36% speak a non-Latin alphabet language. The survey gives valuable facts to appreciate the boom of multilingual information on the Internet and the need for multilingual searching functions such as translation facilities and cross-language information retrieval (CLIR) tools.

Multilingual searching can be accomplished in different ways. One is to conduct the search using a Web search engine specifically built for a particular language (e.g., Google in France) with search queries in that language. Another type of multilingual searching is to restrict the search results to a specific language by selecting the chosen language on the home page of an engine. The search query remains in French, for example, but the results will be in the language specified (e.g., English). Retrieval of this kind should be considered as cross-language information retrieval. In addition, multilingual access can also be obtained by means of an automatic translation software which can be plugged in the search engines or used separately (see the *Systran* or the *Reverso* companies).

1.2.3. Question-Answering

Question answering (QA) is a long-standing goal in information retrieval. This feature is not yet widely implemented in Web search engines but represents a big challenge as a solution to overcome the increasing amount of information available on the Web. QA techniques involve the retrieval of information and knowledge from the texts of documents. They are developed in order to give a direct answer to a question instead of presenting a list of documents the user needs to go through. A user presents a query to the system in natural language and receives a specific piece of text that contains the answer rather than a pointer to a document.

1.2.4. Images and Videos Searching

Another important trend concerning information searching on the Web is images and videos retrieval. As the Web carries more multimedia information, the need for locating and obtaining such information is also steadily increasing. Numerous methods have been developed to retrieve multimedia information but they basically fall into two broad categories: the description-based approach and content-based approach. The first one employs keywords, metadata (such as title, author, artist) and other descriptions assigned to the documents. Both keywords and controlled vocabularies are adopted in retrieving images or videos. Keywords are mostly derived from captions or other textual information accompanying the documents. Controlled vocabularies are also used in image retrieval, such as the *Art and Architecture Thesaurus* (Paul Getty's Museum, Los Angeles). On the other hand, the content-based approach refers to techniques based on automatic processing of multimedia information itself (Kondekar, Kolkure, & Kore, 2010). Unlike keywords-based system, visual features for content-based system are extracted from the image itself. Images attributes specified in the query are features such as color, texture and shape. A variety of techniques are used to measure similarity between the query and stored images. Content-based image retrieval allows users to enter images as queries in order to find similar content in the collection.

1.2.5. Information Visualization Techniques

Information visualization techniques show considerable interest for searching and exploiting the Web. Visualizations can be useful at many different levels. Visual representations of documents can help the searcher by graphically representing some information about the content of the document. Visualization of multiple documents or pages can be useful in representing relationships among objects, grouping together images with similar colors or shapes, or linking the content of multiple Web sites through shared concepts (Enser, 2008). These techniques permit to detect and visualize large-scale hierarchical structures and help users to explore unstructured information, such as text documents, Web pages, or e-mail messages.

According to Zhu and Chen (2005, p. 161), "Web visualization aims to provide a more effective way to access and maintain the Web". The authors point out two types of Web visualization: visualization of a single Web site and visualization of a collection of Web sites. Most existing visualization systems for a single Web site apply a tree representation and use visual cues to describe each page, relying on users to identify patterns. Even if the metaphor of the tree seems to be natural to most users, the problem is to see how a very large-scale tree can be displayed on a computer screen in an understandable way. Different techniques are used to visualize collections of Web sites or pages, "based on content analysis and applying the output of self-organizing map to project categories" or "based on the link structure" (Zhu & Chen, 2005, p. 163). As with browsing techniques, the strength of visualization allows users to identify relevant relationships or useful information rather than having to scroll large lists of results or to recall pertinent keywords as in the querying approaches.

1.2.6. Vertical vs. Horizontal Search Engines

Another trend is the recent rise of vertical search engines, in opposition to the general search engines such as *Google* or *Ask*. In recent years, specialized search engines which intend to seek to index, not the whole Web but some parts of it, have emerged. These search engines are referred to as "vertical search engines" and they are specialized in a particular type of content or in a knowledge sub-domain, as opposed to "horizontal search engines" which are of general purpose. Scientific publishers and databases were among the first to provide this kind of search engines to make scientific literature available for web users, but general engines such as *Google* (with *Google Scholar*) also provide articles and citation index from scholarly journals.

Other examples are domain based search engines such as *Truevert* (an environmental vertical search engine), *MedlinePlus* (a service of the U.S. National Library of Medicine), *Pickanews*, (a French vertical search engine dedicated to medias online), or *TinEye* (an image search engine using image identification technology rather than keywords, metadata or watermarks).

1.2.7. Social Searching and Collaborative Filtering

With the emergence of the Web 2.0 techniques, social searching has become a major issue of Web searching. It suggests that Internet users want to be part of large communities to produce, ask for and share information about common interests. Switching from the traditional IRS perspective, social searching considers assigning relevance to information by considering the user's perspective rather than Web-masters' or the content producers' point of view. Current social searching technologies tend to rely on explicit human recommendations and mine user behavior patterns to produce search results directly pertinent to the needs of an individual user. They analyze explicit user actions such as browsing, voting, annotating. Finding information in the social networks mainly depends on social (or collaborative) tagging which may be defined as the process where a user assigns a tag to an object (image, document, Website…).

Made popular by *Delicious*, *Flickr* and other Web 2.0 Web sites in the mid-2000s, social or collaborative tagging is a good example of the *crowdsourcing* process where users assign tags to resources shared with other users. Besides hierarchical classifications such as thesauri or taxonomies which depend on a top-down knowledge organization approach, social tagging is based on a user-generated classification which emerges through a bottom-up consensus in a decentralized way to tag Web site content. This practice of collaborative categorization using freely chosen keywords by a group of people cooperating spontaneously within a community of interests has been named Folksonomy. Advocates of Folksonomies consider that "their advantage over traditional top-down classification is their capability of matching users' real needs and language" (Gupta et al., 2010, 59) and they are a cheaper solution than traditional expert top-down categorization.

Some Search engines are explicitly based on social tags, votes and reviews by individuals who share interests to offer collaborative filtering techniques. Rather than rely on the opinion of a few Web-content editors, collaborative searching filters like *Digg* aggregate opinions of thousands of users to decide which stories to promote to the front page. Filters (*Reddit*, *StumbleUpon*, *Furl*, *CiteULike*…) offer slightly different operating processes but they all serve the same goal to discover documents, information or sites people didn't know they were looking for. By tracking the votes received by newly submitted stories over time, collaborative filtering offers a new paradigm for interacting with information.

2. KEY CONCEPTS RELATED TO WEB INFORMATION SEARCHING

Studies in information searching and browsing are related to various fields and disciplines and researchers dealing with search engines use a very diverse and polysemic terminology depending on their scientific backgrounds. Information searching and browsing is part of a more general process usually referred to as information seeking and use behavior which "focus on how people seek, manage, give and use information, both purposefully and passively, in the varied roles that comprises their everyday lives" (Fisher & Julien, 2009, p. 317). Information seeking and use behavior, also commonly known in the literature as just information behavior, is a broad field of interest that in its widest interpretation may include any research that deals with information and people (Case, 2006).

The goal of this section is to delimitate the conceptual nature of "information seeking and use behavior" and clarify some key concepts, such as the difference between "information searching" *versus* "information seeking", "behavior", "use", and "practice", which are commonly used by scholars and practitioners in different ways. The practical interest of this discussion is to define a conceptual framework in order to classify the studies we present in section three.

2.1. Information Searching vs. Information Seeking

Information searching on the Web is one of the specific facets of information retrieval whose central problem is how to access information which is supposed to be stored in a distant database. Information retrieval refers to two different processes. According to Wilson (2000), *information-seeking* refers to purposive behavior involving users' interactions with any kind of information sources (computer-based systems, libraries, documentation centers…) and *information-searching* refers to the process of interacting with information systems. Information-seeking behavior may also be labeled as information accessing.

If *information-searching* mainly focuses on the query formulation task, *information-seeking* is used to designate the process of selecting any potential information source of interest. Information searching explicitly designates the context of information retrieval using an IRS and even focuses on the query formulation. At this stage of the "retrieval" process, the system (for instance the Web search engine) has been identified and the user is engaged in the task of elaborating the query while taking into account the functional features of the system: selecting the appropriate keywords, using or not Boolean operators and the engine's specific features (exact wording, unwanted words, language, file type, domain search…), etc.

On the contrary, "information seeking" may be defined as the process of attempting to obtain information in both human and technological contexts. For a user, it refers to the situation of identifying the relevant information sources or channels in order to satisfy his/her information need. The potentially relevant information "device" may be a library and he/she will then choose to browse the catalog, or to look on the shelves or even ask the librarian; it may be a phone call to ask colleagues or acquaintances or an information system such as a Web search engine.

This distinction permits to consider wider information practices such as navigating or browsing the web and finding useful, relevant documents, without having researched them, by accident. This way of accessing information has been referred to as "serendipity" for a few years and designates a mode of "retrieval" of information that is not guided by the goal. While information searching emphasizes the user's interaction with the system, information seeking pays more attention to the social and cultural environment of the user.

2.2. The Concept of Use

The difference between seeking and searching leads us to examine the concept of "use" which may have two different meanings: one referring to the individual context of use, and the other referring to the social environment of use. This distinction which is very clear in French (between the two words "*utilisation*" and "*usage*") is not so evident in English but refers to two different concepts. The term "*utilisation*" (that we roughly translate by *utilization*) is synonymous with practical use when the term "usage" has a more general meaning. It is the action, the way of making something useful to a specific goal.

The term "utilization" refers to the interaction between a person and a device and to the way an individual uses a device, such as a search engine, according to his/her own skills, cognitive style, habits, etc. It denotes the way a "particular user", in his/her own singularity, discovers, grasps and operates a technical device such as a search engine. It doesn't mean that this concept doesn't take into account the user's environment (private, professional, social, symbolic etc.) but that the studies dedicated to individual users focus more on the interactive dimension than on the social and cultural ones. It is for example the case of studies carried out in the cognitive ergonomics and psycho-cognition approaches.

On the opposite, the concept of "social user" has a wider meaning. Breton and Proulx (2006) state that this concept refers to a sociological perspective and describes the social context of the interactions between a user and a device. As specified by Rieffel (2005), the first works focusing on "user-oriented" aspects of information and communication technologies (ICT) appeared in the early 1980s, switching from "utilization" to "usage". This difference implied a shift of perspective and theoretical framework. Works on the "social user" no longer focused only on the cognitive dimension of the person-system interaction but on the social, cultural and symbolic dimensions.

In this approach, studies cannot be consistent if they don't pay attention to interactions between users (who are historically, socially and cognitively situated) and devices. These interactions are organized within the framework of a "communication contract" resulting, on one hand, from the ergonomic features of the device (position of texts and images on the screen, size and type of characters, etc.) and, on the other hand, the social habits of the user. As a result, uses are viewed as the expression of a process made of complex interactions relating an individual and a device which may or may not be a technical artifact (a printed book for example). Another characteristic of use (as "usage") is its stability or at least its relative stability, diachronic and synchronic at the same time. Diachronic since the use is anchored in a socio-technical reference framework (Flichy, 1995) and synchronic because it is collectively observable. From this perspective, one may speak of the uses of the Internet or the uses of a public library or the uses of a scientific museum. This ties up with Perriault (1989, p. 205) who states that a "usage" is a "stabilized utilization of an object, tool, to obtain an effect."

2.3. The Concept of Information Behavior

Although the difference between behavior, use and practice is still not clearly established in social sciences, these concepts need to be clarified as much as possible.

The concept of "information behavior" mainly focuses on people's information needs and how they seek, search, manage and use information. The field of information needs, seek and use, shortened as information behavior, presents a large array of studies, topics, populations, examples, theories and methods. Reviews of these approaches have been published successively by Case (2006), and Fisher and Julien (2009) in the *Annual Review of Information Science and Technology* (*ARIST*).

For Wilson (2000, p. 49), information behavior is "the totality of human behavior in relation to sources and channels of information, including both active and passive information seeking and information use". Seen this way, information behavior includes all kinds of information access (i.e., information searching and browsing, and serendipitous encountering); and the different types of information use (filtering, sharing, giving). This definition assumes that a central aspect of information behavior is the interaction between the user's information needs and the potential sources or channels of information. Following this assumption, information behavior is very closely related to the process of discovering information in order to satisfy one's needs.

In his review, Case (2006, p. 295) stresses the seeking dimension of information behavior pointing out four areas to categorize the literature dedicated to this field: "the information seekers by occupation (e.g., scientists, managers), the information seekers by role (e.g., patient or student), the information seekers by demographics (e.g., by age or ethnic group), and the theories, models and methods used to study information seekers." This categorization brings the idea that researchers pay less attention to other aspects of information behavior even if Donald Case notes that information behavior has a broadening scope in particular due to the plethora of Web searching studies. As a consequence, the concept of information behavior first suggests that information seekers are motivated by an explicit need for information which is doubtfulness. It is assumed that people have information needs to satisfy or "anomalous states of knowledge" that arise from professional or every-day contexts.

Moreover, studies in Library and Information Science (LIS) dedicated to information use seem scarce, as if this aspect of information behavior was at the boarder of the scope despite the definitions of information behavior by Wilson (2000), Case (2006), and Fisher and Julien (2009) which formally include this dimension. On the contrary, theories and studies developed in communication science and journalism or in the field of management seem to be aware of this aspect and explore other sides of information behavior such as gatekeeping. The concept of gatekeeping refers broadly to the process of controlling information such as selecting and filtering news, mediating between information sources and end-users, brokering expert information. In this perspective, gatekeeping is part of information behavior and more specifically part of information use, but very rarely identified as such within LIS studies.

The concept of information behavior also assumes a face-to-face interaction between the information seeker and information sources and systems, as well as the passive reception of information, without any intention of acting on the information given. At such a micro-level, information behavior focuses on the specific ways in which an individual's cognitive structures change when she/he seeks and retrieves information. In this approach, attention may also be devoted to the emotional or affective changes that can be identified in the user's information processing.

Lastly, following Savolainen (2008, p. 22), "one of the problems encountered in the use of the concept of "behavior" is that it often reminds one of behaviorism, the mechanistic psychological paradigm." In that sense, behavior seems to denote a passive attitude as if individuals just reacted to stimuli. Even if information behavior researchers don't believe that the explanation of users' behavior cannot omit to pay attention to the context (Fisher & Julien, 2009) and mental representations of the world, the term behavior is suspiciously considered, mainly in social sciences.

2.4. The Concept of Information Practice

As Savolainen quotes (2008, p. 37), "the concept of information practice appears randomly in the information-seeking literature as early as the 1960s and 1970s. However, a more detailed discussion on the nature of this concept was only started recently and major articles on this topic began appearing in the early 2000s." And Savolainen adds that the discussion about the concept of practice took place in order to find an alternative to the dominating concept of information behavior.

While the concept of behavior is based on a psychologist viewpoint on information use, the concept of practice draws on a more sociological and contextual perspective. McKenzie (2003, p. 24) states that "a focus on practices rather than on behavior shifts the analysis from cognitive to social and is consistent with the study of information seekers within their social context". She suggests studying information use as a continuum of information practices, from actively seeking out a known source or planning a questioning strategy, to serendipitously being contacted by a previously unknown source or being given unasked-for advice. Using empirical studies conducted in the early 2000s, she developed a model of information practice which presents four modes: active seeking, active scanning, nondirected scanning and obtaining information by proxy (McKenzie, 2003, pp. 26-27). The main idea of the model is that people may use different modes of information practice depending on the context, the environment and the needs.

Following McKenzie, Savolainen (2008) insists on the social dimension of information practice. Based on a socio-phenomenological perspective, Savolainen's model of everyday information practices refers to "the totality of experiences (individually perceived life world) and the shared context of intersubjective action that is determined by social, cultural, and economic factors" (2008, p. 64). Thus, the concept of information practice may be first understood as a shift towards the necessity to both include social, cultural and also symbolic aspects of the information seeking and use process.

Secondly, the concept of information practice includes other dimensions of information processing such as producing, publishing, sharing, and

Table 1. Criteria for classifying WSE studies

WSE as a:	Focus on:	Types of Studies
"Tool"	Technical features	System-oriented approach: A simplified User model
System	Functional features	Information (searching) behavior
Device	Social features	Information practice

recycling information. These various dimensions of information processing, including information seeking, searching and use, are embedded in work-related and non work-related contexts and cannot be anymore considered as separated from everyday social practices.

Information practices are formal and non-formal, visible and invisible; they are related to a composite set of conscious and unconscious actions and habits. The studies related to information practices focus on human aspects (whether individual or collective) to analyze their behaviors, habits, representations and attitudes. Analyzing "information practices" therefore requires to consider human action as a complex process resulting from many aspects: the individual stock of knowledge, abilities and cognitive skills which can be mobilized in order to act, the ways and desires of "doing things", the habitus (a term used in Bourdieu's theory of practice (Bourdieu, 1990) to roughly designate the relatively stable system of dispositions by which individuals integrate their experiences and evaluate the importance of different choices.

The concept of "information practice" is therefore used to consider the ways people effectively meet with devices and artifacts, formal and informal information sources, needs, habits, etc; in the different situations of production, sharing, research and information processing. Information practices may be understood as a set of socially and culturally established ways to identify, seek, use, share, communicate and produce available information.

2.5. Criteria for Classifying Web Search Engine Studies

Following the previous definitions, we identify three different groups of studies focusing on Web search engines. This classification (Table 1) is based on three series of criteria: the perception of WSE as a "tool", a system or a device which implies to focus respectively on technical, functional and social features. Accordingly, we consider three levels of use: the simplified user model which is implemented in system-oriented evaluation, the information user behavior and the wider approach of information practices.

A first group of studies considers WSE as merely technical "tools" and focuses on their technical features (basically the matching and ranking processes), mainly in order to process comparative evaluation. In this approach, the evaluation protocol is based on a very simplified model of the user.

A second group of studies aims to study the users' information searching behavior and the way they use (or not) functional features as part of a whole system. Studies pay a particular attention to the different functionalities such as query formulation (number and length of queries per search session, Boolean operators...), use of specific features such as visualization or clusters functionalities, etc.

The third group of studies enlarges the scope of the analysis and considers the global environment in which WSEs are used. They are not anymore studied for their searching functionalities but for their role in the modern digital culture. New questions arise such as social, political, cultural issues concerning how people deal with Web search engines. Legacy and ethical considerations are also included in the scope of this type of studies.

Table 1 highlights the different criteria which permit to classify the studies we present in Section 3.

3. MODELS FOR WEB SEARCHING ANALYSIS

Studies related to information retrieval systems date from the 1950s. They first focused on the technical features of the systems and then were progressively interested in the user's seeking behavior, mainly on the cognitive, affective and communicational dimensions. However, they rarely took into account the social and economical environments such as the cultural and linguistic stakes, the digital gap, the payment for referencing the web sites, the online advertising, etc., which are now decisive factors in the use of Internet search engines.

These aspects are now strictly related to the information access global environment because they both influence and depend on the users' information behavior. Many approaches exist to study information access systems which may be classified according to the role they give to the user and his or her environment. The next sections give an overview of five main approaches which have played, and still play for some of them, a dominant role in the comprehension of the information seeking process.

3.1. The System-oriented Approach

The first studies in IRS focused on the functional analysis of the systems (structuring and organizing the data collection, indexation, matching, formulation and reformulation of queries, etc.), with the goal of improving their global performance. In the "system-oriented" approach, particular attention is paid to the features of queries and documents that can be represented, how they can most accurately and adequately be represented, and how those representations can be manipulated to produce the desired results.

According to Ellis (1992), the system-oriented approach (or physical paradigm) emerged in reaction to conventional information retrieval established by library science and documentation. While these disciplines were developing extensive and logical systems of description, classification, and organization of information, there were no evidence of retrieval effectiveness of these systems. In order to solve this problem, Cyril Cleverdon organized the first Cranfield (United Kingdom) experiments in the mid-1950s (Spärck Jones, 1981) which aimed to establish information retrieval research as an empirical discipline. These tests were based on the idea that the effectiveness of IRS could only be assessed by using quantitative measures of information system retrieval performance. The explicit purpose of the Cranfield experiments was to compare different means of representing texts in order to determine which of them performed best when retrieving texts in response to test queries. In order to achieve this goal, relevance-based quantitative measures to assess retrieval performance were defined and used to compare the systems. Cleverdon and his colleagues stated that the efficiency of a system could be measured by using the *recall* and *precision* metrics. Emphasis is put on the improvement and the evaluation of the information processing according to a linear model of the information retrieval process that has been described, among others, by Ellis (1984) and Saracevic (1996).

The system-oriented approach has therefore constituted, for over five decades, the dominant paradigm in the information retrieval field. Although it was initiated in the 1960s, this approach still is a major model in information retrieval, in particular with the TREC (Text REtrieval Conferences) (http://trec.nist.gov) evaluation campaigns which started in 1992 and the TREC-like campaigns such as the NTCIR Japanese program (http://research.nii.ac.jp/ntcir/) or the European Cross-Language Evaluation Form (CLEF) program (http://www.clef-campaign.org). Throughout the years, and despite the criticisms, the TREC methodology has become the reference methodology. Besides its indisputable interest, the TREC methodology raises some questions concerning both the protocol and the metrics, as well as some theoretical questions. Chaudiron (2004a, 2004b) presents an in-depth review of the theoretical and methodological limits addressed to the approach which is posed by the implicit model of information-seeking behavior assumed by the TREC approach to evaluation. This approach implies certain reductions of users' information behavior in order to be able to apply a quantitative method to evaluate IRS. Central problems are identified, in particular:

- Users of IRS don't always have explicit recognized information needs and, when they do so, the representation of these needs are too mechanical (queries are imperfect representations of information needs),
- The absence of the users in the evaluation process (in particular in his/her interaction with the system),
- Since the definitions of recall and precision (and related metrics) are operational, they are built on a very narrow conception of the users' satisfaction,
- The over-simplification of the concept of "relevance" specifically when discrete judgments regarding the retrieved documents need to be done.

As soon as 1968, researchers like Taylor (1968) showed that the notion of information need was much more complex than the definition commonly accepted by IRS designers, and that different levels of information need existed. Following these ideas, the questions of "information need," "queries formulation," and "relevance" became

important issues as well as the necessity to integrate the user as a major element in the information retrieval process. Based on these ideas, the user-oriented evaluation considers that attention must be paid to the users' real expectations in respect with the system he/she operates and with his/her environment. Although the initial interest concerning the user was an attempt to incorporate some behavioral characteristics to improve the performance of the systems, it gradually became a separate research domain whose specific issues were, and still are, to better understand the users' information behavior.

The basic difference between the two approaches is that the first focuses on the information sources and the way they are organized and structured while the latter focuses on its destination. Information scientists and practitioners working under the guidance of the user-oriented approach are thus less interested in how well a system retrieves information than in how well it informs. They state that improvements in IRS not merely come from more sophisticated indexing methods and matching algorithms, but also from a better understanding of how and why human beings need and use information.

Under the generic term of "user-oriented approach", different areas of research may be identified which present a large spectrum of methodological and theoretical backgrounds. These studies share the same goal to better understand the users' information (searching) behavior.

3.2. Studying Information (Seeking or Searching) Behavior

3.2.1. Theories in Information Seeking

According to Case (2002, p. 6), "systematic research on information seeking dates back nearly a century" but it was not until the 1970s that researchers begin to shift away from the "system-oriented approach" toward the user. From this time, investigations began to consider a wide range of people, situations and contexts. A key development in this shift was raised in the early 1970s by several scholars, among which Marcia Bates and Brenda Dervin.

Case (2002), Fisher (2005), and Xie (2008) among others provided a comprehensive overview of the various models used to study information behavior and practices. While Case (2002) highlights five of the general models of information seeking, Fischer (2005) presents more than 70 of them or considered as such which were suggested over the last three decades to take into consideration the information behavior of users including tasks, activities, affective, social and even cognitive dimensions.

Among the first attempts to understand the information-searching user's behavior was Marcia Bates who was interested, by the end of the 1970s, in the decomposition of users' research strategies in an initially pedagogical perspective. In the context of "information specialists", Bates introduced the concept of information search tactic as "a move made to further a search" and argued that "search tactics are intended to be practically useful in information searching" (Bates, 1979, p. 205). She thus identified 29 tactics organized in four types:

- **Monitoring tactics:** are tactics to keep the search on track and efficient.
- **File structure tactics:** are techniques for threading one's way through the file structure of the information facility to desired file, source, or information within source.
- **Search formulation tactics:** are tactics to aid in the process of designing or redesigning the search formulation. (These tactics are not restricted to computer search formulations.)
- **Term tactics:** are tactics to aid in the selection and revision of specific terms within the search formulation.

Later in the 1980s, Bates (1989) proposed the Berry Picking model which can be considered as one of the first approaches suggesting the inclusion of navigation in the information retrieval process. Following this model, Ellis and Haugan (1997) and Leckie, Pettigrew, and Sylvain (1996) suggested more detailed models describing the different stages of an information seeking process. For example, the Leckie model depicts information seeking behavior in the context of professionals (such as doctors, lawyers, engineers...) and gives emphasis on the work roles, the tasks to be accomplished, the characteristics of information needs, the sources of information.

Researchers such as Taylor (1968) focused on the notion of information need that was subsequently been studied by Nicholas Belkin in his ASK model (Belkin, 1980) and Dervin (1992) in the Sense Making model. These models were then enriched by Khulthau (1993) who included the affective dimension of information retrieval.

Another trend does not consider the user as an isolated individual confronted with a device but takes into account his/her social, cultural, and linguistic context, and focuses on the interpersonal and social forces between individuals during the information seeking process. This trend may be illustrated by Tom Wilson's model (Wilson, 1996), Brenda Dervin's Sense-Making Model (Dervin, 1992), Elfreda Chatman (Chatman, 1999), and more recently Reijo Savolainen's Everyday Life Model (Savolainen, 1995).

Wilson's model (1996) relies on works originating from other disciplines in order to take into consideration certain particular aspects of behavior. The central point of the model is made up of two activating mechanisms corresponding to the "lacks" that take place between the initial situation (or the individual in his/her specific context) and information retrieval. Tom Wilson suggests the presence of diverse sources of motivation for information retrieval:

- "Stress/coping theory", which offers the possibility to explain why some needs do not necessarily imply the implementation of an effective retrieval strategy,
- The "risk/reward theory", which helps us understand why some sources of information are used and others not,
- And the social learning theory, which introduces the self-efficacy concept (i.e., one can constantly adapt his behavior to meet the expected result).

In Wilson's opinion, information seeking is part of the human communication processes. He proposes to take into account the contextual factors which modify the information behavior, including the general social environment: historical, geographical, politico-economic context; the demographic context: impact of demographic variables that are age, sex, socio-professional category, level of education, socio-linguistic characteristics; the social position of the user; the micro-sociological or organizational context, and the physical and material context. Consequently, Tom Wilson puts forward the multidimensional aspect of the informative process by drawing attention on the user and his/her context.

Other scholars also based some of their studies on the cognitive approach to information seeking introduced by De Mey (1980). This approach was then popularized by different conceptual frameworks such as Nicholas Belkin's ASK framework (Belkin, 1980), Bryce Allen's analysis of cognitive skills, processes and styles (Allen, 1991) and finally Peter Ingwersen's poly-representation model (1996). Ingwersen and Järvelin (2005), for example, pointed out the necessity to switch from an individual to a holistic cognitive viewpoint and presented a cognitive framework for information seeking and retrieval representing relations of information objects, information technology systems, interfaces and cognitive actors in context (organizational, social, cultural context). These perspectives are different from

the psycho-cognitive approaches described later as they try to enlarge the cognitive dimension of the user to other contextual and social aspects.

3.2.2. Cognitive and Psychological Processes in Information Searching

The cognitive approach is based on the assumption that information processing (such as information seeking and searching) and communication are necessarily mediated by systems of conceptual categories which model the user's informational practice. The users' cognitive model structures facts, perceptions, and values related to his or her informational environment. For example, not all the information accessed during the search process is noticed or, if noticed, treated with the same attention. Information can be selected or rejected, but it must be assessed and classified according to various criteria which constitute the cognitive filter of the users. One major criterion is the user's perception of relevance which is cognitively and psychologically situated.

Selective perception, cognitive assessment and the condition of being open or narrow-minded are examples of phenomena which depend on the individual cognitive model of the world. The successful retrieval of information from the Web (textual documents, images, paintings or pieces of music) may occur only because this information has been first structured and organized for use by systems of conceptual categories in order to match with the users' cognitive frameworks. Understanding how and why these structures impact information searching and use is central to the cognitive approach.

Thus, information searching cannot be separated from the context within which information is retrieved and used. For example, Denecker and Kolmayer (2006) state that, in cognitive psychology, information searching must be considered as a secondary task serving the purpose of more strategic activities such as decision-making, problem solving, teaching, etc. In this approach, the term "information searching" refers to the task of information identifying and gathering, textual exploration, content extraction and filtering and information analysis, etc.

There are several attempts to characterize hypermedia and Web access in cognitive terms. Existing theories such as Information Foraging (Pirolli, 2007) and Construction-Integration (Kintsch, 1998) and models such as ESP (Rouet & Tricot, 1998) or CoLiDeS (Kitajima, Blackmon, & Polson, 2000) are concerned with the general cognitive processes that take place when reading a hypermedia/Web document.

Proposed by Peter Pirolli, the Information Foraging theory assumes for example that people have strategies to maximize information gain and minimize the cost (effort) associated with that gain. Based on the text comprehension theory of Kintsch (1998), the CoLiDeS model (Comprehension-based Linked model of Deliberate Search) explains how users parse and understand the content and the meaning of a webpage for then selecting the action to perform next. On their part, Rouet and Tricot (1998) have developed a cyclic model of cognitive steps (ESP model) which relies on the hypothesis that every information retrieval process is based on three basic stages: Evaluation, Selection and Processing. Three cognitive management mechanisms represent the interaction between the ESP phases: planning, control, and regulation.

From a methodological point of view, the psycho-cognitive approaches in information retrieval have most of the times considered the user as an isolated individual, neglecting his social and cultural dimension. One limitation of these models is the relatively narrow conceptualization and modeling of the information seeking concept.

3.2.3. Information Searching and Management

Another approach is to study information searching within organizations (company, institution, etc) from the management science viewpoint. In this approach, studies focus on two particular contexts: during the socialization process of a new incomer and the managerial decision-making.

Organizational socialization is the process through which individuals acquire knowledge about their work context and adjust to it (Ashforth, Sluss, & Saks, 2007). The socialization process has often been considered as either socialization tactics (formalized ways for socializing individuals) or newcomer proactive behavior (individual-driven or informal ways of "self-socializing"). Different studies have shown that new incomers in organizations change their tactics according to the type of information they are trying to obtain (Griffin, Colella, & Goparaju, 2000). They use various strategies for information acquisition. Three types of information seeking behavior have been identified: monitoring, observing by seeking signals that can be derived from an event or the behavior of others, inquiring (asking people for information) and consulting written materials. Miller and Jablin's model (1991) focuses on newcomers' pro-active search for information in order to reduce the uncertainty associated with organizational socialization. On her side, Morrison (1993, 2002) investigated several types of information that newcomers seek: referent, social, feedback, technical, normative information as it relates to the behavioral and attitudinal expectations of the organization.

The domain of strategic scanning and business intelligence is one of the most challenging concerning the problem of information access, specifically for the decision makers. Different models scan the information processes, such as Francis Aguilar's strategic scanning process (Aguilar, 1967) or Richard Daft's chief scanning behavior (Daft, Sormune, & Parks, 1988). Other models in information management, in particular the one suggested by Robert Taylor then revisited by Howard Rosenbaum, quoted by Choo, Detlor, and Turbull (2000), aim to articulate information seeking and decision making process. Two examples may illustrate this trend: the environment scanning model suggested by Choo, Detlor, and Turbull (1999), the informational ecology model of Davenport and Prusak (1997) and the model of "Web information behaviors of organizational workers" proposed by Detlor (2004).

Choo et al. (1999) place the emphasis on the individual and on the group at the same time. This is the reason why they refer to the information process within the organization. Combining Aguilar's modes of scanning and Ellis's seeking behaviors, the authors propose an integrated model (Human Information Seeking: an Integrated Model). The model identifies four main modes of information seeking on the Web: undirected viewing, conditioned viewing, informal search, and formal search. For each mode, the model indicates which information seeking activities or moves are likely to occur frequently: Starting, Chaining, Browsing, Differentiating, Monitoring, and Extracting. To validate the model, the scholars involved 34 participants from seven companies to discover how knowledge workers used the Web to seek external information as part of their daily work. All of the users primarily utilized the Web for business purposes as an integral part of their work responsibilities and activities.

The information ecology model proposed by Davenport and Prusak (1997) aims to represent the organization's information environment and the numerous interacting interdependent social, cultural and political subsystems that shape the creation, flow and use of information in the organization. The model identifies six elements in the information environment of organizations: the definition of an information strategy, the information governance, the information culture and behavior, the information professionals' network, the information processes, and the architecture of information. In the information ecology model, Daveport and Prusak (1997) state that managers need to switch their attention from systems and architectures to the behavioral and cultural changes in order to create an environment where knowledge is produced and freely shared with others.

Detlor (2004) proposed the model of Web information behaviors of organizational workers to explain how these workers use various Web-based information systems, such as company portals and Web sites or the WWW for knowledge creation, diffusion and use. Based on Choo's general model of information use and Taylor's value-added approach, Detlor's model aims to show how organizational workers use Web-based systems in order to solve work-related problems. The model basically stresses on a cyclic three-step process: the awareness of information needs, the information seeking step where users turn to a Web-based system, and the information use which starts when the user has completed a scan of the information sources available from the Web-based system. The iterative cycle illustrates the dynamic nature of organizational information environments.

For these authors, business strategic management requires to consider information not as an object, but more as the result of a subjective construction in which the cognitive, affective and situational factors play a decisive role.

3.2.4. The Consumer and Marketing Approaches

The consumers' buying behavior has always been a popular marketing topic, extensively studied and debated over the last decades. As the Web became a major source for all kinds of commerce related information, including business, e-commerce, travel, employment and economics, scholars paid more attention to the online consumer information behaviour as part of the whole buying behavior. More and more customers now use the Web as a transaction channel for products identifications and comparisons, e-commerce purchases and commerce related information access. The use of the Web search engines may now be considered as the primary Internet application (Rainie, 2005), and Spink and Jansen (2007) state that commerce related queries currently represent between 28% and 30% of Web queries.

Web search engines and social networks have become an important issue in the understanding of consumer behavior. Researchers in this field have long been studying how consumers search for information about products as they claim that information search behavior is the prerequisite of decision making (Kotle, Filiatrault, & Turner, 2000). Researchers insist on the twofold dimensions of the commercial information searching: a pragmatic dimension in order to do the best choice before buying, and a leisure dimension which refers to pleasure and satisfaction (Babin, Darden, & Griffin, 1994).

The proliferation of online stores has given rise to a number of studies that look at the consumer's intention to purchase online. An example is the study conducted by Marable (2003). Based on 15 major search and navigation sites, the study used an ethnographic approach that allowed researchers to observe experienced Web searchers in their natural surroundings. The major findings were that most of the Web searchers have little understanding of how search engines retrieve, rank, or prioritize links on the results page; and that the majority of participants never clicked beyond the first page of search results. Constantinides (2004) analyses the factors which affect the online consumer's behavior and examines how e-marketers can influence the outcome of the virtual interaction and buying process. He also provides a contribution to the theoretical debate about the factors influencing the online consumer's behavior and outlines some noticeable similarities and differences between the traditional and virtual consumers. He clearly shows that functionality factors such as site navigation and search facilities are key issues to expect easy site navigation and easily accessible information.

More specific researches deal with the effect of sponsored links on e-commerce information seeking on the Web. Jansen and Resnick (2006) investigated the relationship between searching self-efficacy, searching experience, types of e-commerce information needs, and the order of links on the viewing of sponsored links. The results of the study indicate that there is a strong preference for non-sponsored links, with searchers viewing these results first more than 82% of the time.

Kulviwat, Guo, and Engchanil (2004) suggested a conceptual model that allows studying different determinants of information retrieval on the Internet. According to these authors, it is necessary to enlarge the scope of the study and to take into consideration the various components (usability, efficiency, risk perception, consumer satisfaction, user knowledge, level of education) to explain the user behavior. While some researchers in marketing do not see any fundamental differences between the traditional and online buying behavior, it is more and more frequently argued that a new step has been added to the online buying process: the step of building trust or confidence. And the way consumers trust their search engines is a major issue for e-marketers.

More recently, researchers investigate how e-commerce companies try to support the customers' decision making process by introducing personalized Web systems. Collaborative filtering systems provide personalized recommendations based on purchase history, past ratings' profile and votes. They are integrated in many e-commerce websites (restaurants, books, music, etc.). Kim and Srivastava (2007) present an overview of the impact of social influence in e-commerce decision making and discuss how captured data about social influence can be used by e-commerce websites to aid users' decision making process.

Jansen et al. (2010) provide an analysis of information seeking and sharing behaviors of teenagers and young adults in the e-commerce domain on four social networking sites (*Facebook*, *MySpace*, *myYearbook*, and *Twitter*). Research results show that the majority of them have accounts on multiple social networking sites, with more than 40% having profiles on three social networking sites and an additional 20% have four social networking accounts. They also investigate the motivations for using different social media sites, showing that the reasons for engaging differ among sites, indicating continued use of multiple social networking services. Implications are that companies and organizations interested in marketing to this demographic cannot cluster social networking users for more personalized targeting of advertisements and other information.

Consumers want detailed product descriptions that include specifications and information on how the product works but they also look for ratings, comments and recommendations from other consumers. This quite recent phenomenon, called social commerce, has deeply changed the e-commerce, on the vendors' side and on the e-consumers' side, and particularly impacts the consumer's information seeking behavior.

4. FUTURE DIRECTIONS

Web search has changed dramatically in the last decade with the emergence of social searching which impacts information seeking behavior in multiple ways. The term social search refers broadly to the process of finding information online with the assistance of social resources, such as by asking friends, librarians, or unknown persons online for assistance. From a machine-mediated Web searching, individuals now experiment a human-mediated Web searching based on votes, comments and recommendations. Even if the process labeled by "social search" isn't new (asking a librarian or a colleague may be considered as a "social search"), the term has been applied widely in the field of Web 2.0 to describe searches that take place in social and expertise networks using collective intelligence to improve the search process. Evans and Chi (2010, p. 2) define social search as "an umbrella term used to describe search acts that make use of social interactions with others. These interactions may be explicit or implicit, co-located or remote, synchronous or asynchronous". On their side, Morris et al. (2010a) define the term social searching as "the use of social mechanisms to find information online. Social search can involve the use of search engines, if the engine indexes social media (e.g., public *Twitter* posts) or uses community members, actions to rank results (e.g., *Heystaks*, *Groupization*). Social search engines can also be devised using the output of social tagging systems such as delicious (delicious.com)".

Combining traditional WSE-technology with online collaborative filtering techniques to produce personalized results, social search engines represent one of the most important challenges as the social Web will become more central to search. A few social search engines depend only on online communities but most of them are based both on traditional searches and on distributed approaches. Depending on the features of a particular search engine, the results to a particular query may then be saved and added to community search results, improving the relevance of results for future searches of that query.

Many issues emerge from social searching. Social approaches to tagging and categorizing texts, pictures or videos are now a very important source of metadata in addition to the expert description of documents. The combination of professional classifications (such as classification systems, controlled vocabularies, taxonomies and thesauri) and folksonomies or social tagging shapes a new information organization system. While professional systems and folksonomies share a number of properties, the two approaches often do not intersect, and more work is needed to understand their similarities and differences. Another major issue is to understand what kind of information needs and topics people turn to a social network and a social search engine, rather than a traditional search engine. What are their motivations to do so and how do they operate the complementary functionalities of both search engine and social search engine? Some studies already try to answer these questions: Morris et al.

(2010b) examine how people fulfill information needs using general-purpose social tools by using status messages to ask questions. They conducted a survey on 624 people using social networking services like *Facebook* and *Twitter* in order to analyse the motivations people have for asking and answering questions on social networks rather than using a Web search engine. The survey found that many people are turning to social networking tools because they are specifically designed to help users satisfy their information needs by facilitating social connectedness and awareness rather than information-seeking. Other findings suggest there are several factors differentiating information seeking using "traditional" online sources versus social networks: the strength of social networks seems to be in their ability to provide answers to questions concerning opinions and recommendation questions.

Another study (Evans & Chi, 2010) analysing critical-incident survey of 150 users on *Amazon's Mechanical Turk* service suggests that social interactions play an important role throughout the search process. The results show that the social interactions between individuals before, during, and after the search episodes, together with the degree of coordination, vary from case to case. Some searches may require collaboration before search, but neither during nor after search, while others may include only post-search coordination. Highly coordinated information-seeking tasks may in fact include coordination during all three phases of the search process. These results show that the human mediation is the nexus of the whole process. Social searching means reintroducing the human component during the information seeking behavior and illustrates the fact that these devices are clearly human-mediated artifacts. Quoting Horowitz and Kamvar (2010), we may consider that Web search engines and social information retrieval represent the library *versus* the village paradigms of knowledge acquisition by users: "In a library, people use keywords to search; the knowledge base is created by a small number of content publishers before the questions are asked, and trust is based on authority. In a village, by contrast, people use natural language to ask questions, answers are generated in real-time by anyone in the community, and trust is based on intimacy."

Another future direction of studies requires considering the role of Web search engines as the keystone of the attention economy in the Internet ecology. As the amount of information available on the Web exceeds the users' capacity to digest that information, Web-content managers and producers develop a whole set of "technologies of attention". They try to improve the visibility of the Web pages by using different techniques of search engine optimization (SEO): visible or invisible keywords, "cloaked" sites, spams, "bombings", etc. Between the millions of Web pages and the millions of users, there are a small number of search engines which try to connect the content with the searchers. On one hand, search engines are crucial to retrieve information on the Web but, at the same time, information which cannot be identified (because not indexed or bad ranked), even if existing somewhere, does not exist for the user. A non-retrieved document or website cannot be found unless the user knows the specific URL. In that way, Search engines may also be considered as potential barriers in the retrieval system. On the other hand, Web search engines "represent the screens through which we view the content of the web, screens that allow us to inflict our own desires on the "giant mass of the web" (Halavais, 2009, p. 2). Accordingly, Web search statistics can be used to predict human behavior. Existing research using search queries has shown that search volume is predictive, which means it can be used to accurately track results such as the unemployment rate, sales car and home, the development of tourism, consumer preferences or the prevalence of the disease in near real time (Choi & Varian, 2009; Goel et al., 2010).

With the development of cultural and commercial contents on the Internet, the existence of "neutral" search engines is crucial for the users, and specifically for "naïve" or "disable" users. The line between relevant information, spamdexing and "commercials" is very fuzzy and implies from users to be very attentive as long as the engines modify the rules of "authority" and "equity" on the Web. As most people cannot make any difference between a paid result page and a non-sponsored page, some organizations may try to control the mediation process by purchasing search terms. Marketers can change the content of the results through paid keywords in the index, or paid inclusion on the results page. The collaborative nature of the search engines also affects the "transparency" of the mediation process. Considering that links between Web pages are more than just connections but votes of interest, *Google* and others consider the hyperlink structure of the Web as a source of relevant information to include in the ranking algorithms. As a result, some selections proposed by the ranking algorithm are not the "best" but may appear in the first-ranked pages. This issue of identifying relevant information deals with the wider problem of information literacy which may be defined as the ability to recognize the extent and nature of an information need, then to locate, evaluate, and effectively use the needed information.

Because Search engines present centralizing tendencies, the question of knowledge is another issue. The cultural dimension of search engines has been recently amplified with *Google*'s efforts to digitize major libraries. If *Google* comes to be the most easily accessed source of knowledge, the ranking of various books in their collections may have consequences on the diffusion of the various local cultures. Because the US dominate the search market at a global level and regional initiatives rarely have a significant use outside the different countries (except the *Baidu* Chinese search engine), US search engines and sites have more "authority" (in term of *PageRank*). Even if he use a French or German version of *Google News* or *Yahoo News*, a French or a German is

likely to be exposed to new sources in English and published in the US. The over-representation of this content by search engines implies that they may ignore the rich diversity of content that is available on the Web.

Another issue is the capacity of surveillance and control of search engines. The surveillance of the citizens is not only about practices of authoritarian regimes but is as old as the modern States. The illusion that the scientific and technical progress would give protection against all the risks from the beginning to the end of the life leads to accept limitations of personal freedom and to allow some reduction of privacy. Several recent cases have showed the capacities of censorship of the internet by using search engines. Major search engines proposed censored versions of their services and content. If China and Singapore are the most cited examples, some democratic countries (as France and Germany) also ask search engines to remove racist or anti-Semitic sites from the page results in accordance with the local laws (Meiss & Menczer, 2008). Search engines' treatment of privacy, censorship and copyright are important issues to discuss because they can store data on individuals for a long period of time (Zimmer, 2008).

5. CONCLUSION

In this chapter, we tried to delineate the field of Web searching from a user perspective. The objective of the chapter has first been to shape some recent challenges in search engine evolution that modify the users' information behavior. In particular, adaptive interaction, mobile searching, multilingual functionalities, visualization techniques, question-answering, thematic (or vertical) search engines and social searching deeply transform the whole context of Web searching and require users to apply multiple information-seeking strategies. To understand the role of this new digital environment on the information practices, we then defined the core concepts related to information behavior on the Web. By providing this discussion, the chapter contributes to give some cues to better understand the user studies. In the third section, we shaped the major models that study Web search engines in a user-oriented perspective. After having rapidly presented the system-oriented approach, we identified four major trends in the "user-oriented approach" that focus respectively on strategies and tactics, the cognitive and psychological approaches, the management and the consumer and marketing approaches. Nevertheless, the dynamics and the nature of interaction between Web searching and users are not fully understood, and other aspects need to be considered. Section 4 tried to delineate future directions about Web searching including the growing role of social networks and social searching in information seeking, search engine optimization, ethics, cultural and political issues.

As a socio-technical device, a Web search engine must be studied as a "mediator" between content and users in its social and technical dimensions. It means that, beyond the technical and the cognitive aspects of information-seeking, we need to pay attention to the political, the economic, the social and the cultural dimensions of Web search engines use. These issues imply to explore other dimensions of the Web search engines than the technical or the tasks-based information behavior. Integrating Critical theory with traditional "user-oriented" approaches could contribute to study Web search engines from a user perspective. Based in particular on the theoretical model of Proulx (2005), we argue that exploring the information practices on the Web implies to consider several levels. The information use is only one of them and Proulx suggests adding four other levels: the social practice, the innovation, the community mediation and the political representation as parts of the "appropriation" process.

REFERENCES

Aguilar, F. J. (1967). *Scanning the business environment*. New York, NY: Macmillan.

Allen, B. (1991). Cognitive research in information science: Implications for design. *Annual Review of Information Science & Technology, 26*, 3–37.

Ashforth, B. E., Sluss, D. M., & Saks, A. M. (2007). Socialization tactics, proactive behavior, and newcomer learning: Integrating socialization models. *Journal of Vocational Behavior, 70*, 447–462. doi:10.1016/j.jvb.2007.02.001

Babin, B. J., Darden, W. R., & Griffin, M. (1994). Work and fun: measuring hedonic and utilitarian shopping value. *The Journal of Consumer Research, 20*(4), 127–140. doi:10.1086/209376

Bar-Ilan, J. (2004). The use of Web search engines in information science research. *Annual Review of Information Science & Technology, 38*, 231–288. doi:10.1002/aris.1440380106

Bates, M. J. (1979). Information search tactics. *Journal of the American Society for Information Science American Society for Information Science, 30*(4), 205–214. doi:10.1002/asi.4630300406

Bates, M. J. (1989). The design of browsing and berrypicking techniques for the online search interface. *Online Review, 13*, 407–424. doi:10.1108/eb024320

Belkin, N. J. (1980). Anomalous states of knowledge as a basis for information retrieval. *The Canadian Journal of Information Science, 5*, 133–143.

Bourdieu, P. (1990). *The logic of practice*. Cambridge, UK: Polity Press.

Breton, P., & Proulx, S. (2006). *L'Explosion de la Communication. Introduction aux Théories et aux Pratiques de la Communication*. Paris, France: La Découverte.

Case, D. (2002). *Looking for information: A survey of research on information seeking, needs, and behaviour*. San Diego, New York: Academic Press/Elsevier Science.

Case, D. (2006). Information behavior. *Annual Review of Information Science & Technology*, *40*, 293–327. doi:10.1002/aris.1440400114

Chatman, E. (1999). A theory of life in the round. *Journal of the American Society for Information Science American Society for Information Science*, *50*(3), 207–217. doi:10.1002/(SICI)1097-4571(1999)50:3<207::AID-ASI3>3.0.CO;2-8

Chaudiron, S. (2004a). L'évaluation des systèmes de recherche d'informations. In Ihadjadene, M. (Ed.), *Les Systèmes de Recherche d'Informations: Modèles Conceptuels* (pp. 185–207). London, UK: Hermès.

Chaudiron, S. (2004b). La place de l'usager dans l'évaluation des systèmes de recherche d'informations. In Chaudiron, S. (Ed.), *Evaluation des Systèmes de Traitement de l'Information* (pp. 287–310). London, UK: Hermès.

Choi, H., & Varian, H. (2009). *Predicting the present with Google trends*. Retrieved June 8, 2011, from http://googleresearch.blogspot.com/2009/04/predicting-present-with-google-trends.html

Choo, C., Detlor, B., & Turbull, D. (1999). Information seeking on the Web. An integrated model of browsing and searching. In *Proceedings of the ASIS Annual Seminar and Exhibits*, Dallas, TX. Retrieved June 8, 2011, from http://choo.fis.utoronto.ca/fis/respub/asis99/

Choo, C., Detlor, B., & Turbull, D. (2000). *Web work: Information seeking and knowledge work on the World Wide Web*. Norwell, MA: Kluwer Academic.

Constantinides, E. (2004). Influencing the online consumer's behavior: The Web experience. *Internet Research*, *14*(2), 111–126. doi:10.1108/10662240410530835

Daft, R. L., Sormune, J., & Parks, O. (1988). Chief executive scanning, environmental characteristics and company performance: an empirical study. *Strategic Management Journal*, *9*, 123–139. doi:10.1002/smj.4250090204

Davenport, T. H., & Prusak, L. (1997). *Information ecology: Mastering the information and knowledge environment*. New York, NY: Oxford University Press.

De Mey, M. (1980). The relevance of the cognitive paradigm for information science. In Harbo, O. (Ed.), *Theory and application of information research* (pp. 48–61). London, UK: Mansell.

Denecker, C., & Kolmayer, E. (2006). *Eléments de Psychologie Cognitive pour les Sciences de l'Information*. Villeurbanne, France: Presses de l'ENSSIB.

Dervin, B. (1992). From the mind's eye of the user: The sense-making qualitative-quantitative methodology. In Glazier, D. J., & Powell, R. R. (Eds.), *Qualitative research in information management* (pp. 61–84). Englewood, CO: Libraries Unlimited.

Detlor, B. (2004). *Towards knowledge portals: From human issues to intelligent agents*. Dordrecht, The Netherlands: Kluwer Academic.

Ellis, D. (1984). Theory and explanation in information retrieval research. *Journal of Information Science*, *8*(1), 25–38. doi:10.1177/016555158400800105

Ellis, D. (1992). The physical and cognitive paradigms in information retrieval research. *The Journal of Documentation*, *48*(1), 45–64. doi:10.1108/eb026889

Ellis, D., & Haugan, M. (1997). Modelling the information seeking patterns of engineers and research scientists in an industrial environment. *The Journal of Documentation, 53*(4), 384–403. doi:10.1108/EUM0000000007204

Enser, P. (2008). Visual image retrieval. *Annual Review of Information Science & Technology, 42*, 3–42.

Evans, B. M., & Chi, E. H. (2010). An elaborated model of social search. *Information Processing & Management, 46*(6), 656–678. doi:10.1016/j.ipm.2009.10.012

Fiedler, A. M., Lash, P. B., Wong, R. M., & Tiainen, T. (2009). *The impact of individual employee difference on information seeking in today's information rich Information-Seeking Behaviors environment.* Paper presented at the International Consortium for Electronic Business (ICEB) Conference. Retrieved August 16, 2010, from http://www.ebrc.fi/kuvat/Fiedler_Lash_Wong_Tiainen.pdf

Fisher, K., Erdelez, S., & McKechnie, L. (Eds.). (2005). *Theories of information behavior.* Medford, NJ: Information Today.

Fisher, K., & Julien, H. (2009). Information behavior. *Annual Review of Information Science & Technology, 43*, 317–358. doi:10.1002/aris.2009.1440430114

Flichy, P. (1995). *L'Innovation Technique. Récents Développements en Sciences Sociales. Vers une Nouvelle Théorie de l'Innovation.* Paris, France: La Découverte.

Goel, S., Hofman, J. M., Lahaie, S., Pennock, D. M., & Watts, D. J. (2010). Predicting consumer behavior with Web search. *Proceedings of the National Academy of Sciences of the United States of America, 107*(41), 17486–17490. doi:10.1073/pnas.1005962107

Griffin, A., Colella, A., & Goparaju, S. (2000). Newcomer and organizational socialization tactics: An interactionist perspective. *Human Resource Management Review, 10*(4), 453–474. doi:10.1016/S1053-4822(00)00036-X

Gupta, M., Li, R., Yin, Z., & Han, J. (2010). Survey on social tagging techniques. *ACM SIGKDD Explorations, 12*(1), 58–72. doi:10.1145/1882471.1882480

Halavais, A. (2009). *Search engine society.* Cambridge, UK: Polity Press.

Horowitz, D., & Kamvar, S. (2010, April 26-30). The anatomy of a large scale social search engine. In *Proceedings of the 19th International World Wide Web Conference*, Raleigh, NC (pp. 431-440).

Ihadjadene, M., & Chaudiron, S. (2008). Quelle analyse de l'usage des moteurs de recherche? Quelques questions méthodologiques. *Questions de Communication, 14*, 17–32.

Ingwersen, P. (1996). Cognitive perspectives of information-retrieval interaction - elements of a cognitive IR theory. *The Journal of Documentation, 52*(1), 3–50. doi:10.1108/eb026960

Ingwersen, P., & Jarvelin, K. (2005). *The turn: Integration of information seeking and retrieval in context.* New York, NY: Springer.

Internet World Stats. (2010). *Internet world users by language.* Retrieved August 30, 2010, from http://www.internetworldstats.com/ stats7.htm

Jansen, B., & Resnick, M. (2006). An examination of searcher's perceptions of nonsponsored and sponsored links during ecommerce Web searching. *Journal of the American Society for Information Science and Technology, 57*(14), 1949–1961. doi:10.1002/asi.20425

Jansen, B., Sobel, K., & Cook, G. (2010). Classifying ecommerce information sharing behaviour by youths on social networking sites. *Journal of Information Science, 20*(10), 1–20.

Khulthau, C. (1993). *Seeking meaning: a process approach to library and information services.* Norwood, MA: Ablex.

Kim, Y. A., & Srivastava, J. (2007, August 19-22). Impact of social influence in e-commerce decision making. In *Proceedings of the 9th International Conference on Electronic Commerce* (pp. 293-301).

Kintsch, W. (1998). *Comprehension: A paradigm for cognition.* New York, NY: Cambridge University Press.

Kitajima, M., Blackmon, H., & Polson, P. (2000). A comprehension-based model of Web navigation and its application to Web usability analysis. In *Proceedings of the 15th Conference on People and Computers - Usability or Else!* (pp. 337-57).

Kondekar, V. H., Kolkure, V. S., & Kore, S. N. (2010). Image retrieval techniques based on image features: A state of art approach for CBIR. *International Journal of Computer Science and Information Security, 7*(1), 69–76.

Kotle, P., Filiatrault, P., & Turner, R. (2000). *Marketing management.* Montréal, QC, Canada: Edition Gaëtan Morin.

Kulviwat, S., Gu, C., & Engchanil, N. (2004). Determinants of online information search: a critical review and assessment. *Internet Research, 14*(3), 245–253. doi:10.1108/10662240410542670

Leckie, G. J., Pettigrew, K. E., & Sylvain, C. (1996). Modelling the information seeking of professionals: a general model derived from research on engineers, health care professionals, and lawyers. *The Library Quarterly, 66*(2), 161–193. doi:10.1086/602864

Marable, L. (2003). False oracles: Consumer reaction to learning the truth about how search engines work, results of an ethnographic study. *Consumer WebWatch*, 1-66.

Markey, K. (2007). Twenty-five years of end-user searching, Part 1: Research findings. *Journal of the American Society for Information Science and Technology, 58*(8), 1071–1081. doi:10.1002/asi.20462

Martzoukou, K. (2005). A review of Web information seeking research: considerations of method and foci of interest. *Information Research, 10*(2), 215. Retrieved June 8, 2011, from http://InformationR.net/ ir/10-2/paper215.html

McKenzie, P. (2003). A model of information practices in accounts of everyday life information seeking. *The Journal of Documentation, 59*(1), 19–40. doi:10.1108/00220410310457993

Meiss, M., & Menczer, F. (2008). Visual comparison of search results: A censorship case study. *First Monday, 13*(7). Retrieved June 8, 2011 from http://firstmonday.org htbin/cgiwrap/bin/ojs/ index.php/fm/rt/ printerFriendly/2019/1988

Miller, V. D., & Jablin, F. M. (1991). Information seeking during organizational entry: influences, tactics, and a model of the process. *Academy of Management Review, 16*(1), 92–120.

Morris, M. R., Teevan, J., & Panovich, K. (2010a). A comparison of information seeking using search engines and social networks. In *Proceedings of the Fourth International AAAI Conference on Weblogs and Social Media*, Washington, DC.

Morris, M. R., Teevan, J., & Panovich, K. (2010b). What do people ask their social networks, and why? A survey study of status message Q&A behavior. In *Proceedings of the 28th International Conference on Human Factors in Computing Systems*

Morrison, E. W. (1993). Longitudinal study of the effects of information seeking on newcomer socialization. *The Journal of Applied Psychology, 78*(2), 173–183. doi:10.1037/0021-9010.78.2.173

Morrison, E. W. (2002). Information seeking within organizations. *Human Communication Research, 28*(2), 229–242. doi:10.1111/j.1468-2958.2002.tb00805.x

Notess, G. R. (2006). Tracking your search history. *Online, 30*(2), 41–43.

Perriault, J. (1989). *La Logique de l'Usage. Essai sur les Machines à Communiquer*. Paris, France: Flammarion.

Pirolli, P. (2007). *Information foraging theory: Adaptive interaction with information*. New York, NY: Oxford University Press. doi:10.1093/acpro f:oso/9780195173321.001.0001

Proulx, S. (2005). Penser les usages des technologies de l'information et de la communication aujourd'hui: enjeux – modèles – tendances. In Veira, L., & Pinède, N. (Eds.), *Enjeux et usages des TIC: aspects sociaux et culturels* (pp. 7–20). Bordeaux, France: Presses Universitaires de Bordeaux.

Rainie, L. (2005). Search Engine use shoots up in the past year and edges towards email as the primary Internet application. *Pew Internet and American Life Project*. Retrieved from http://www.pewInternet.org/ PPF/r/167/report_display.asp

Rieffel, R. (2005). *Sociologie des Médias*. Paris, France: Ellipses Marketing.

Rouet, J.-F., & Tricot, A. (1998). Chercher de l'information dans un hypertexte: vers un modèle des processus cognitifs. In Tricot, A., & Rouet, J.-F. (Eds.), *Les Hypermédias: Approches Cognitives et Ergonomiques* (pp. 57–74). Paris, France: Hermès.

Saracevic, T. (1996). Modeling interaction in information retrieval (IR): A review and proposal. In *Proceedings of the Annual Meeting of the American Society for Information Science, 33*, 3-9.

Savolainen, R. (1995). Everyday life information seeking: approaching information seeking in the context of way of life. *Library & Information Science Research, 17*(3), 259–294. doi:10.1016/0740-8188(95)90048-9

Savolainen, R. (2008). *Everyday information practices: A social phenomenological perspective*. Lanham, MD: The Scarecrow Press.

Solomon, M., Bamossy, G., & Askegaard, S. (1999). *Consumer behaviour – A European perspective* (4th ed.). London, UK: Prentice Hall Europe.

Sparck Jones, K. (1981). The Cranfield tests. In Sparck Jones, K. (Ed.), *Information retrieval experiment* (pp. 256–284). London, UK: Butterworth-Heinemann.

Spink, A., & Jansen, B. J. (2004). *Web search: Public searching of the Web*. Berlin, Germany: Springer-Verlag.

Spink, A., & Jansen, B. J. (2007, December 7). Commerce related Web search: Current trends. In *Proceedings of the 18th Australasian Conference on Information Systems*, Toowoomba, Australia. Retrieved from http://www.acis2007.usq.edu.au/assets/papers/10.pdf

Su, L. (2003). A comprehensive and systematic model of user evaluation of Web search engines: I. theory and background. *Journal of the American Society for Information Science and Technology, 54*(13), 1175–1192. doi:10.1002/asi.10303

Taylor, R. (1968). Question negociation and information seeking in libraries. *College & Research Libraries, 29*, 178–194.

Waller, V. (2011). Not just information: Who searches for what on the search engine Google? *Journal of the American Society for Information Science and Technology, 62*(4), 761–777. doi:10.1002/asi.21492

Wilson, T. (1996). *Information behaviour: an interdisciplinary perspective. A report to the British Library Research and Innovation Centre*. London, UK: British Library Research and Innovation Centre. Retrieved August 16, 2010, from http://informationr.net /tdw/publ/infbehav/chap7.html

Wilson, T. (2000). Human information behaviour. *Informing Science, 3*(2), 49–56.

Xie, I. (2008). *Interactive information retrieval in digital environments*. Hershey, PA: IGI Global. doi:10.4018/978-1-59904-240-4

Zhu, B., & Chen, H. (2005). Information visualization. *Annual Review of Information Science & Technology, 39*, 139–177. doi:10.1002/aris.1440390111

Chapter 19
Artificial Intelligence Enabled Search Engines (AIESE) and the Implications

Faruk Karaman
Gedik University, Turkey

ABSTRACT

Search engines are the major means of information retrieval over the Internet. People's dependence on them increases over time as SEs introduce new and sophisticated technologies. The developments in the Artificial Intelligence (AI) will transform the current search engines Artificial Intelligence Enabled Search Engines (AIESE). Search engines already play a critical role in classifying, sorting and delivering the information over the Internet. However, as Internet's mainstream role becomes more apparent and AI technology increases the sophistication of the tools of the SEs, their roles will become much more critical. Since, the future of search engines are examined, the technological singularity concept is analyzed in detail. Second and third order indirect side effects are analyzed. A four-stage evolution-model is suggested.

INTRODUCTION

Undoubtedly, search engines are among the major enablers of the Internet (http://en.wikipedia.org/wiki/Web_search_engine). Without them, the Internet revolution would not exist (Hartman,

DOI: 10.4018/978-1-4666-0330-1.ch019

Sifonis, & Kador, 1999). Search engines classify and order the online information. The source of the indexed information has so far been the human intelligence. However, increasingly human being uses non-biological intelligence including computers (Kurzweil, 1999).

In the future, the exponential growth will even accelerate, since non-biological intelligence will

Figure 2. Different singularity points of different observers

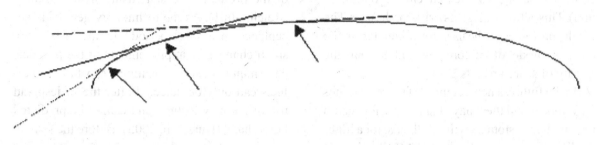

catch up the human intelligence (Kurzweil, 2005). Therefore, search engines will be forced to deal with much more information. Most probably, new search algorithms and approaches will be requires.

The search engine of the future will utilize artificial intelligence (AI) technologies, so they can be called artificial intelligence enabled search engines (AIESE). AI is already in use by the search engines. However, the AI itself will develop, and the SEs will be among the first to benefit from (Richards, 2002).

In the future, SE customization and personalization is likely to reach to such a point that, almost every customer delivered unique results. Although, this helps the user in reaching the results desired, this will also mean different views of the world by different Internet users (Figure 2).

The most catastrophic consequence may be disintegration of knowledge since the Internet is becoming the mainstream information distribution medium. This will also mean that the search engine companies will have the power to control the information delivery and may even deliver different search results for the same search keyword combination. The risk is really high and the necessary precautions should be taken now.

In less democratic countries, government-affiliated AI-enabled national search engines can be introduced and these engines can control the access to the information at the individual level. Assume that person A is critical of the government at that country and the national AIESE will limit his/her access to the information. In the information age,

limiting the access to the information is almost equivalent of limiting the physical freedom of a person. His/her power will be diminished by the delivery of limited information. Worse than that, the government can even use the national AIESE as a powerful tool of disinformation.

A more subtle risk is a philosophical one. Even in the case the all AIESEs national or global level do not distract the knowledge and just filter and organize it, they indeed change the original information since the classification of knowledge is itself a knowledge. If AIESEs apply different filtering and classification for different persons, they each person will see only a part of the whole information and each see the meta-information the AIESE delivered. A careful reader may point that there is already disintegration of knowledge among individuals each having different backgrounds. However, delivering AI-enabled customized search results will deepen the disintegration.

Even at the current level of AI, the search engine companies play a significant role over the access to the Information. They can choose not see a particular content and they do not add it to their search results very few people will access it. For the time being, there seems to be little concern about their power even in the academia. However, as the AI advances, their power may become a more serious problem.

Another related issue is the business model of the search engines. Most of the popular search engines are free. Their revenue is from ads search-engine optimization (SEO) tools (http://

en.wikipedia.org/wiki/Search_engine_optimization). This actually presents a risk for the user. The results presented to the user are affected from the business model of the company and this puts the quality of search results at risk.

In the future, a new segment of search engines may appear and they may charge a fee for search results. The customers will pay the fee for a high-quality search result. Fee-based AIESEs can use the AI technology to improve the search results. The definition of "high-quality content" is open to debate but there is apparent low-quality content in the results of current search engines. These consume precious user time. AI technology may act like human intelligence to filter these.

In this study, the "technological singularity" concept plays a key role, since the aim is making some predictions about the near future. Technological developments reached such a point that, it impossible to analyze the future of any technology without singularity.

TECHNOLOGY AND SOCIAL CHANGE

It is widely known that legal institutions and protective mechanisms of the society are slow in front of the technological change (Ohmae, 1999). It becomes harder and harder for the society to absorb the full effects of the technological change (McClellan III & Dorn, 2006).

Before the society absorbs a technology a new wave appears. Even worse, new technologies appear more and more frequently (Christensen, 1997). Generation gaps occur only in a few years; it is not necessary to wait for a full biological generation. Technological knowledge is also short-lived and becomes obsolete in a short time (Kurzweil, 2005). Even professions are under threat one cannot depend on a single profession (Yamamoto & Karaman, 2006b).

Ordinary people just obey what the technological change dictates, purchase the latest versions of the products and start using it immediately (Reich, 2001). As the technology gets wide acceptance in a short period of time, even very small changes or improvements of the products have major social implications. Most of such effects can only be detected after the widespread use of the new feature, and cannot be predicted beforehand (Kurzweil, 2005). Before the society passes the new regulations, new versions appear and regulations become obsolete almost instantly.

The problem with any particular technology is that while a certain problem is solved, other unforeseen problems appear (Karaman & Yamamoto, 2007). Companies developing the commercial technology are under the competitive pressures to shorten time-to-market i.e., the time passes from idea to the final product sold in the market (Nesheim, 2000). Under such circumstances almost no company can deal with the intricate second or third-order side effects of the technology. They have no motivation or obligation to do so. There is no international body enforcing limitations to the companies to keep the unexpected side effects under control.

Environmentalist movements and some religious groups are trying to put a control over the pace and extend of the technological change. However, since the technology is considered to be synonymous with advancement, civilization and better life frequently such criticisms are considered to be merely reactionary and unproductive (Pacey, 1991).

The technology cannot be seen as the mere extension of science. Technology is fed by science and vice versa. However, technology can follow a different path than science and technology's priorities may be different than that of science. This is due to the shortsightedness and result-oriented nature of the technology (Arthur, 2009).

The efforts to control or to regulate technology should include international cooperation (Singer, 2009). At least all technology generating countries should be included in this alliance. A spectacular example is the cooperation to prevent the spread of the nuclear weapons. That is a unique successful example to control technology and to limit its side effects.

It is easy to see the destroying power of the nuclear weapons (http://en.wikipedia.org/wiki/Atomic_bombings_of_Hiroshima_and_Nagasaki) after the disasters of Hiroshima and Nagasaki. However, for ICT, Internet, wireless, search engines, it is very hard to see the bad side of the technology. This is because their side effects are much more indirect and occur over time.

A closer assessment will mean a slower pace of technological improvement. This may translate into moderated technology company profits. However, for the sake of humanity, the quest for the control of technology should never stop even though some scholars and philosophers including Martin Heidegger (http://en.wikipedia.org/wiki/Philosophy_of_technology) reject the idea of controlling technology.

Technology can be used in controlling the pace of technology. AI technologies can generate powerful tools. However even AI cannot address the essence of the problems brought by technology and may even be the largest part of the problem as explained in the next section.

When technology is concerned, the ease of use shades the complexity. Ironically, the easiest use means the most complex technology. However, complex communities may be unable to manage the ever-increasing complexity of the environment (Tainter, 1988).

Technology is the product of human being and its accrued civilization, however technology can get such a complexity that human being cannot understand it. The accumulation of human efforts can result in a product that cannot be comprehended by human being (Kurzweil, 2005).

Technological changes are mainly adopted by young generations and older people stick with the older technology they are comfortable with. Even the technology companies have difficulty in assessing the importance new, disruptive technologies (Christensen, 1997). This pattern is es-

pecially visible in emerging countries like Turkey (Yamamoto & Karaman, 2007b). As the young generations become older, the next generation assumes the role to adopt the latest technology. This is why generation gaps widen and cultural differences between generations deepen.

For young generations, the latest technology is also a means to their independent identity against the older people. Being able to use the latest technology and learning the technical details give the young people a high status that cannot be acquired by anything else. It is not surprising that the majority of people misusing technology are young.

Such crimes are also means to demonstrate themselves and proving that they can overcome the control mechanisms of the society even though they are very young. They are like young priests of the latest technology who think they hold the ultimate truth that will illuminate the whole society. Since the latest technology is the source of their status, for them it is hard to think about the dark side of technology.

MOORE'S LAW AND ARTIFICIAL INTELLIGENCE (AI)

Moore's law is well known in the ICT community (Kurzweil, 1999). It states that roughly, the processor speed doubles every 1.5 years. This is an exponential improvement in speed and makes computers possible to perform more and more sophisticated tasks much before than the general public predicts. Moore's Law proponents found similar patterns in many areas of technology and proved that technological change has an exponential nature.

Moore's law is important in that ICT is the enabler of nearly all other technologies (Kurzweil, 1999). ICT technologies' power, primarily depend on the processor speed. As the computers come with more CPU speed, more sophisticated software is possible as they can solve more problems at a specific period of time. Another consequence of Moore's law is that technology gets cheaper over time and in fact there is deflation of prices when it comes to ICT-related technology. This makes it possible a much more widespread use of technology and the specific technology's impact over the society deepens.

There are some physical limits to Moore's law and it became increasingly difficult to install more transistors to the same area. However, by means of optimization of the chip architecture and by utilizing multi-kernel technology, the chip producers try to extend the life of Moore's law. All predictions about its end have proven wrong so far and Moore's law persisted (Kurzweil, 2005).

This law is at the center of the singularity concept analyzed in the next section. In a world without Moore's Law, AI could not advance and technological singularity will not be an issue. If chip-makers hit a wall in designing faster chips, all predictions about singularity will have to be revised (Kurzweil, 2005).

In other words, quantum and sub-atomic physics became the servant of the chip technology other than being a subject of theoretical physics studied in ivory towers of science. This is another example of how seemingly unrelated fields of science and technology are becoming closely tied in a complex and hard-to-understand manner (Arthur, 2009).

TECHNOLOGICAL SINGULARITY

Technological Singularity can be defined as a point of uncertainty due to the accumulated affects of fast technological change (Kurzweil, 1999). Technological improvements lead to a pattern of exponential increase. New technologies appear before people can adapt to the old ones. The renowned philosopher Heidegger asked the question that whether technology controls the society or society controls technology. He concluded that the technology couldn't be controlled by the society (O'Brien, 2004).

Experts of singularity predict that it will occur in the 21st century and after that point humanity will have no control over the technology and will not be able to understand and analyze it. In fact, technology has always been a phenomenon too complex to complex to analyze (Richards, 2002).

Although, humans still seem to have control over the events, there seems to be no power to stop the acceleration or exponential change brought by the technology. Today, human being use technology to produce more advanced technology. In the near future, AI-enabled technologies will be so advanced that they will not need human skills and intelligence to develop even more advanced AI-based technologies. This will be the point where humans and human intelligence will be needless (Gardner, 2007).

These ideas are discussed among AI professionals and singularity experts. The majority of them accept the view that there is a risk of singularity. However, the most dangerous aspect of singularity is that since it means the rise of super-human intelligence, it is very hard for humans to understand actually when it occurs. Singularity is depicted in Figure 1.

Some singularity experts expect a sudden and remarkable change at the point of singularity. However, most probably the point of singularity will not be a certain date and hour; rather it will be a continuum and a process that cannot be understood by human-level intelligence (Kurzweil, 2005). Super-human intelligences can use such indirect ways to do their duties and manage the process so seamlessly that the exact point of singularity cannot be detected.

Even the super-human intelligences don't try their presence at first, since they are much more intelligent than humans, they will find very indirect paths human mind cannot detect. Only after a significant time passes, human being may understand the occurrence of singularity and super-intelligent AI can easily prove the opposite.

The predictions about the future may occur earlier than expected. That is because' linear

Figure 1. Singularity Chart

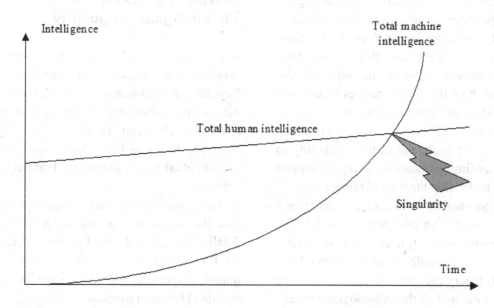

extrapolation is used in predicting the future. However, technological change is exponential (Kurzweil, 2005). In other words, it is very slow at the beginning, after a while the change is visible, and then it takes off and affects and transforms all aspects of life. Artificial intelligence (AI) is no exception. Computers seem to lack some aspects of human mind but their matching our brains will take much less time than we think (Gardner, 2007).

In the future, due to the developments in quantum computing, nanotechnology, biotechnology and nano-biotechnology, cheap commercial and small versions of human-equivalent computers can be produced. After that point super-human computers will follow and there is no force to stop this process.

The danger is about non-human intelligences and even to understand the nature of this danger a high level of intelligence and knowledge is required. Put differently, only the most intelligent and highly educated people can understand and accept the existence of such a danger. For the rest, the issue is a topic of science fiction books and films and humans will always maintain their status of the most intelligent beings over the world.

In fact, the first use of singularity is the point actually it occurs. Singularity experts defined the term to tell their inability to forecast the future after a certain point of time. After the most intelligent humans lose their full insight into the future, it is the singularity. The point is that, since society cannot stop the technological developments, technological singularity seems inevitable.

Is Singularity Exaggerated?

Singularity fears are similar to the Year-2000 (Y2K) (http://en.wikipedia.org/wiki/Year_2000_problem) discussions in some respects. Y2K expectations did not materialize and Y2K-proponents explained this due to the successful efforts to make the ICT technology Year-2000 compliant. Singularity may be another version of Y2K but it is true that, humans have difficulty in analyzing technology. There will always be an uncertainty related to the future. Singularity is the ultimate level of uncertainty. After the path of the technology became certain, uncertainty may diminish and singularity may disappear.

The market forces fuel the technological change since there is no visible and undeniable side effect for advanced technology. Even if there are some proven side effects, they do not attract enough attention from the media and academia. The debate about the mobile phones is one such example. There are many academic studies about the side effects of mobile phones over human brain. However, such studies have difficulty in finding financing compared to the capital amount dedicated to develop these hand phones.

Although singularity is a very sophisticated concept, it is also an easy way to explain the technological complexity ahead of humanity. It is acceptance of our inability to analyze technology. Singularity theory explains nothing other than the impossibility to analyze the technological process.

Advanced technology builds a chaotic universe, which may still be deterministic but hard to model (Pacey, 1991). That means chaos theory or quantum theory may find applications in analyzing the possibility of a technological singularity and in describing the essence of it. Singularity exists in weather predictions. However, with more sophisticated mathematical models it became possible to predict the weather for next several days. The prediction horizon is limited.

A similar analysis can be made for the future of technology. It is almost impossible to make predictions after a certain point in the future. There is a horizon for predictions. However, as time passes that uncertain point become more predictable and a new unpredictable point is set.

Therefore, the definition of "near future" will change as technology develops. As seen in Figure 2, different scholars can make different predictions about the point of singularity.

The inability to describe the post-singularity era stems from our lack of proper terminology to define the phenomena in that period. A new name should be coined just to describe that era. It is even hard to imagine a suitable name since the pre-singularity era concepts are in use.

Search Engines and the Technological Singularity

The Internet can be defined as the network of the networks (http://en.wikipedia.org/wiki/Internet). Beyond its technical definition the Internet acts as the medium connecting the intellectual abilities of its users (Tapscott, Ticoll, & Lowy, 2000). In other words it acts like a huge brain consisted of individual brains just like a brain consist of neurons.

Individuals make chat, write on forums or join the social media http://tech-strategy.org/Analiz/Gruplar-Nedir-Ne-Degildir.pdf, retrieved on 10/11/2010. All of their activities are like transfer of synapses (http://en.wikipedia.org/wiki/Synapse) between neurons.

Before the Internet the minds of the human being were not connected to such an extent. Both the number of connections and the number of connected people increase (Bovet & Martha, 2000). The Internet is not just a bulk information medium but rather it is a mega intelligence that can decide the direction humanity advances. There has always been a collective thinking in the history of human being but not to the extent that Internet made possible (Shapiro & Varian, 1999).

Using the mega-intelligence metaphor for the Internet may seem odd and somewhat mystic. However, anything less will be too simple to model the highly complex nature of the Internet (Tompkins, 2000). What makes the Internet powerful are the brains of the individuals, not the hardware or software. The AI technology is heavily used throughout the Internet architecture but they are comparable to human intelligence yet. No one has an AI chat partner or no forum site has AI-based member which can discuss the recent news on the media.

According to those who emphasize the role of computer hardware as the most critical factor, the technological singularity is seen as a direct consequence of Moore's law (Kurzweil, 1999). The mega-intelligence of the Internet is often neglected. Today, a great majority of the knowledgeable people spends some time over the Internet.

Internet's efficiencies are not without its own costs. To facilitate, companies should invest in infrastructure, both in terms of hardware and software (Kalakota & Robinson, 1999). All initial investments by the Internet companies were for the sake of the future benefits and no profits had been posted initially (Schiller, 2001).

As with many other contemporary technology, the Internet speeds up the occurrence of the events due to the efficiencies it provides (Evans & Wurster, 2000). Both speed and the mega intelligence pave the way for the technological singularity. Moreover, the emergence an widespread use of the Internet can itself be considered the technological singularity given that Internet's mega intelligence take control of all intellectual activities of human being.

That does not mean that the pre-Internet era should be restored. Even the critics of technology use the Internet to find the material they need. However, the main problem with any technology and the Internet is that as people use them more they become more dependent on them (Aldrich, 1999). After a point, one finds out that we cannot live without that particular technology but after it is too late.

The Internet's mega intelligence is at the core of the society. It transforms values, culture, and civilization (Kotkin, 2000). Today, this mega intelligence is dominated by human intelligence. But, as the AI technology matures, AI's share will increase and the Internet is likely to be the major medium for the AI's future dominance all over the world. Whether there will be a technological singularity or not is open to debate.

However, if singularity occurs, the Internet will be the key technology to control all aspects of daily life. Technological singularity is impossible without a widespread network such as the Internet. The singularity discussion should be made with the sophistication of the Internet in mind.

Just like Internet is the key to control all other technologies, the search engines are key to control the Internet. Therefore, the search engines possess one of the most critical and strategic technologies in the world. Search engines control people's access to information and the ever-increasing information is so clear. Search engines cannot be analyzed without analyzing the Internet, since SEs are the kernel and core of the Internet. Without search engines, Internet would collapse.

Although social media are also useful for the control, most of the search engines are very closely integrated with the social media. They can use their search engine technology the content produced in the social media.

The fastest growing parts of the Internet are open and include social media or so-called Web2.0 sites (http://en.wikipedia.org/wiki/Web_2.0). The stock market financing favors such areas and then crashes occur (Schiller, 2001). All of the private content in these sites are actually not as private as they first seem. There is a danger of intrusion to the private information of the Internet users. Apart from that, these private data can be easily searched.

The open structure of the Internet is maintained in new versions of the underlying technology and users cannot hide their data whatever method or technology they use (Cohan, 1999). Even the non-users of the Internet are under the control of the Internet activity and they are not immune to the control of Internet's mega intelligence. Such people are among elderly or live at the poor regions of the world and their number shrink over time (Patel & McCarthy, 2000). Therefore, no sector and no company can disregard Internet's trade and community-building potential (Haylock & Muscarella, 1999).

Nearly all of the people in the industrialized or developing countries are forced to use the Internet for their official transactions. Governments force their citizens to use the Internet to gather the information in an easy-to-analyze format. B2B transactions quickly moved to the Internet as companies saw the opportunities (Kuglin & Rosenbaum, 2001). Many big company force their offline suppliers or customers to use their online transaction environment (Giunipero & Sawchuk, 2000).

In other words, the share of the offline activity will diminish over time and the Internet will enjoy a more powerful control over the daily life of the individual in direct and some very indirect ways (Raisch, 2001). The ultimate level of this control is exactly what the technological singularity means.

Without the concept of singularity, an analysis about the SEs will be incomplete and would lead misleading results. In today's complex world, nearly all of the technological developments became interrelated and isolated analyses and specialized views cannot capture the essence of technology. The technology of SEs is only a subset of that greater problem.

Since, SEs operate in a key sector controlling the access to information, AI-based SEs can easily be the tools to shape the ideas of the society or individuals. The oligopolistic structure in the sector is problematic and no governmental or inter-governmental institution addresses this issue.

Due to the nature of their business, SEs use the most advanced AI technologies and invest heavily in them. They are at the forefront of the technology of non-human intelligence. They use AI in optimizing their search results and in delivering services like translation. The most advanced commercial use of the AI technology is by SEs.

The Internet can be seen as a map of the intellectual life over the world (Shapiro & Varian, 1999). People's bodies still live in the classical world but much of our information and communication is over the Internet. The Internet is becoming the mainstream medium of idea exchange and we consume others' ideas over the Internet (Ohmae, 1999). To sum up, the Internet has a control on ideas as the leading medium. Thus, SEs have the potential to be one of the key elements of the singularity.

At the point of singularity, seemingly unrelated technologies will merge and their control will be taken over by super-human intelligence. Since people cannot understand very complex second-order, third-order effects of the merging technologies they will lose their ability to analyze and understand the full effects of the technology.

They will simply assume that more and more advanced technology will be better for the humanity; they will give technology almost a religious status. In fact, the current situation is very close to this worst case and the question that when the singularity will occur lost its meaning.

SEs will use more and more advanced AI and they will introduce advanced services. The majority of these services will try to automate tasks accomplished by human brain and will cause significant unemployment since the service of many professionals will be taken over by AI. The best example is the translation services. The AI may not be as good as expert translators, however, for basic needs the service of the AI is acceptable for many people. As the software and hardware develops and computational problems solved even the expert translators will lose their jobs.

Other than the loss of the control to the technology, a more apparent danger is certainly the unemployment (Arthur, 2009). Technology improves exponentially and replaces first basic then advanced jobs. It is beyond human capability to adapt such changes and earn new profession every time a new technology introduced.

If the current trend persists, in the near future, the skills and knowledge of the majority of people will be obsolete and one of the major reasons behind the recent global economic crisis seems to be the exponential growth in the technological innovations. Rules and legislations cannot follow the pace of the technology and the unemployment problem cannot be solved although we have the advanced technologies capable of making every individually wealthy.

SEs attack the last parcels of land owned by the human intelligence. People no longer need to learn anything. The only thing that one should learn is to go to the home page of a browser. The question need not be grammatically correct. The user may prefer the communication style of a little child.

SEs try to give the best service to their online customers. They develop themselves employing more and more advanced technologies and innovations based on them (Porter, 1998). In doing so, they make a very deep impact all over the world. They transform how people live, think and organize their ideas. This is inevitable. However, one should accept that, their perfect service of delivering the desired information is not without some unintended side effects. For example, they threaten the jobs of many knowledge workers via advancing their engines.

EPISTEMOLOGICAL DIMENSIONS OF SEARCH ENGINES (SEs)

The use of SEs are simple, however, the role of SEs is not as simple as it seems first. They do not only help people in finding the relevant knowledge they also re-shape the hierarchy and map of the knowledge in people's minds deliberately or not.

Search engines use a ranking mechanism to sort all kinds of knowledge available over the Internet. Many users do not look the pages after the first several ones although some searches results in millions of hits. Therefore, being on the first page is highly critical for any web page. Some SEs charge web sites for appearing at the top and this is part of their business model.

Currently, SEs use some sophisticated criteria to be able to sort pages and these criteria is not publicly available to avoid churning and misuse. However, the lack of openness hides these mechanisms and the public cannot judge the suitability of knowledge ranking mechanism. As the Internet becomes the mainstream media to produce, distribute and classify the information; SEs become the key actors in reshaping the map of

the knowledge humanity possesses. SEs can even judge that some online content can be classified as information or not. Thus a critical function of human intelligence is transferred to technology.

Even though, there is some control and supervision over the search results, this is largely an automated process. Humans' role in search engines is limited to the development of the search criteria and SE software. AIESE technology is likely to limit the role of humans even further and much more dynamic event-based SE criteria can be developed by the AIESE software.

The ordinary person may have no worry about the re-shaping of the knowledge map and fast delivery of the relevant piece of information may be enough for his/her daily needs. The knowledge map, meta-knowledge, hierarchy of knowledge, or epistemology is the concern of the philosopher or the intellectual. A piece of information by itself does not have any meaning. In order to fully understand it, one needs to know the context it produced and its linkages to other pieces of information.

As seen in Figure 3, consider a set of information consisting of A, B, C and D. Alternatively, assume that there is a second set of information consisting of A, B, C. The information A in the first set is understood differently than information A in the set B. In other words, SEs change the meaning and the interpretation of the information by changing their ranks in the search results. The way they deliver and present information reshapes the knowledge maps of individuals. When individuals are transformed, the knowledge of humanity transformed.

SEs currently do not have the technology to elegantly manage the transformation process so as to implant the desired worldviews to individual users. However AIESE's will have the technological ability to change individuals' ideas, beliefs and even political opinions, ideologies and religions by delivering them the desired pieces of information in the desired order, format and combination.

Figure 3. Different sets of information and worldview

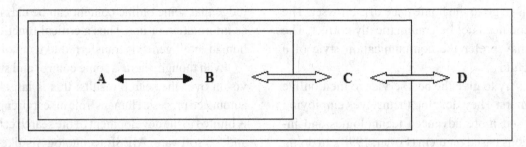

Customization or Disintegration

Customization is presented as one of the virtues of technology. Personalized services give people the sense that they are important. However, when the intellectual services of SEs are concerned, personalization means a distorted, engineered, filtered view of the universe. Given that, each person will be delivered different set of knowledge, each will have a different view of the universe. People will have less in common and there will be as many ideology and philosophy as the number of people since each have their own map of knowledge.

Currently, it is true that, the services of the SEs are not personalized to that extent. However, AIESEs will have advanced customization and personalization capabilities and they will use them under the pressure of market forces. The competition in the market will force the SEs to deliver more and more individualized service. SEs cannot disregard the competition and possible entrants (Porter, 1998).

Disintegration of knowledge can be lessened by a formal education with a generalist approach. However the over specialization brought by the Industrial Revolution has already caused disintegration. Over-specialization damages and transforms information by breaking its links to the broader topics and changing its content.

Customization of the information services is the ultimate form of specialization making each individual specialist in a field not known by anyone else. Therefore, customization breaks the links with the rest of the society.

Over-customized AIESEs are likely change humans to disintegrated individuals unable to find a meaning to the universe other than the meaning delivered by AIESEs. Without AIESEs, they will not be able to analyze and interpret a new piece of knowledge. They will have outsources such advanced functions of brain to AIESEs. So, AIESEs will cause loss of brainpower among individuals similar to loss of calculation capabilities after heavy use of calculators. These fears are likely to become more widespread among scholars in the near future.

Stages of Search Engine Evolution:

To clarify, the ideas developed in this chapter, the evolution of the search engines can be analyzed in stages as in Figure 4.

Stage 1: SSEs (Simple Search Engines or Initial Search Engines)

These SE's arose at the start of the Internet and they were simply the lists of classified web pages. The search results were poor and search algorithms were rather simple. There were little multimedia features.

Stage 2: ASEs (Advanced Search Engines or Current Search Engines)

These are the current search engines. There are more advanced and their search results are

Figure 4. Stages of search engine evolution

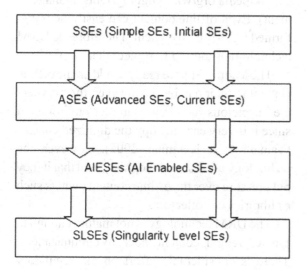

better. They interact with the social media and Web2.0 companies. Search engines are clever and understand the users intends to some extent.

Stage 3: AIESEs (Artificial Intelligence Enabled Search Engines)

AIESEs are analyzed extensively in this chapter. They are evolved search engines which will use much more advanced AI technologies to give an extremely personalized search technology.

Stage 4: SLSEs (Singularity Level Search Engines)

Such a search engine will appear at the time of technological singularity. It will utilize an ultimately advanced AI technology and very advanced user interfaces. Its AI is so advanced that, it may reshape, destroy information in subtle ways.

SEs AND DANGER OF CENSURE

A single bit of information which is unlisted by SEs, cannot be reached by other people and it is practically nonexistent. The great majority of

people will not be aware of even the existence of that information. SEs may claim that they use a fair criterion to filter and sort the information over the web. However, such a power and authority can be easily misused and be used for ideological and political purposes (Yamamoto & Karaman, 2006a). SE technology gives governments such a power.

This is a much more sophisticated way of censure compared to previous methods of banning books or newspapers in that it is hard to detect and understand even the existence of a censure. As the technology becomes more advanced, it becomes impossible for the ordinary people to understand the full affects of it. AIESEs will include advanced AI technology, which is practically the most advanced and sophisticated type of technology. Even the AI scholars or the cleverest people cannot fully comprehend the full aspects of improvements in the AI technology.

To sum up, AIESE technology can make it possible the use of new and sophisticated ways of censure. It is even very hard to prove that there is a censure. People, cannot react to a hidden censure. This is even true for highly educated and intellectual segments of the society. In other words, SEs can be the key tools of censure in the coming decades (Yamamoto & Karaman, 2007a).

SEs and Libraries

For centuries, libraries functioned as the main places to store and retrieve information. Libraries with large number volumes were the spiritual places for scholars, writers and the like. After the Internet, the status of the library is under threat and even for the academic studies the Internet and the online services are sufficient in many fields of study (Shapiro & Varian, 1999).

In role of librarians are taken over by the SEs. So, this is one of the professions threatened by the never-ending waves of the technology. At first, the Internet-based information was considered to be unreliable but that view is altered over the time.

Also, publishers increasingly come up with new e-book titles and their doubts seem to be dissipated.

Even the greatest offline library cannot deliver the services of a medium-level SE. In addition, establishing libraries are much more expensive than establishing data centers for SEs. It can be easily predicted the majority of the libraries will disappear in the future as the digital technology advances and digital rights management (DRM) regulation and practice matures (Yamamoto & Karaman, 2005).

Classical books may survive in some limited form but libraries will definitely be online especially AI-based technologies to a certain-level. However, it is a mistake to claim the end of classical libraries. This is another example of human's increasing dependence over the technology.

Technology presents easier and more efficient ways to access the relevant information, however humans' understanding of the delivery mechanism is largely diminished. If one day the SEs technology is lost due to a huge natural disaster this will be equivalent of the loss of the books in the Library of Alexandria. It will be impossible to restore the information lost. The digitization of information should have some limits and classical methods should not be left over night (Yamamoto & Karaman, 2005).

Technology is not the ultimate cure for all problems and advanced technology does not always mean more prosperity and a sign of an advanced civilization (Tainter, 1988). In today's society, the technology gained such a sacred position that even the anti-technology ideas seem surprising for the ordinary people. For the earlier and relatively simple technologies this could be understandable. However, as the more advanced technologies merges with each other, technology lost its innocent status.

SEs and the DRM Technology

The developers of the Digital Rights Management (DRM) tools try to protect online content (http://

en.wikipedia.org/wiki/Digital_rights_management). Even offline content can easily be transformed into a digital content. Therefore the DRM technology is aiming to protect them too.

The leading SEs are ready to add all the offline content to their database. However, their owners are suspicious about the Internet environment since it is very easy to copy the digitized content (Yamamoto & Karaman, 2005). However, the technology of SEs are so sophisticated that it they put pressure over the offline content owners such as libraries or collectors.

The DRM technology is not mature enough to protect precious content under any circumstances. There is considerable effort on the regulatory part; however, the legislation cannot be applied fully in practice. That is because the fact that the owners of the classical content cannot fully visualize how technology changed the scene and their understanding of content is a classical and even old-fashioned way.

In today's environment, people consume much more content than they consumed previously and therefore they want the content to be free or at least cheap. Even so, it is seen that the publishers for example, put the same price over their books' digital copies although the cost of digital publishing is much less. They do not pass this cost advantage to the readers and see the high price as a mechanism to protect them against the theft of content.

On the contrary, the Internet does not reward the jealously protected information or content (Patel & McCarthy). Free and high-quality content reach masses through personal recommendations. The owner of the content is rewarded by fame and in many times by some financial return. Money, however, is not earned directly from content, but from the network acquired by giving away the free content.

The owners of high-quality content have difficulty in seeing the power of free or cheap content. Most of the time information loses its value over time. The young generations prefer online technologies to produce and disseminate content. There the high-quality offline content stay as the products of older generations and the value of that content is lost over time. At a point, the legal protection over them will be lost and they will be freely available online and will be indexed by SEs.

As time passes, the share of offline content in the total amount of content will diminish. The quality and value of online content will rise, while that of offline content will drop. This is mostly true for text-based content. However, multimedia content is likely to follow a similar path.

DRM technology will speed up this process and at a point in the future, it is most likely that all available content will have digital copy and will be indexed by SEs. It is naïve to assume that SEs will deliver all available content free of charge. They will start charging for some of their services. However, DRM tools should mature, before online content can be charged.

After, all offline content become digital and online and SEs indexes them, digital-only content will explode, as they are cheaper to produce, deliver and maintain. Thus, it can be safely assumed that offline content will shrink and this will increase our dependence over the digital technology and SEs in particular. If the digital technology is lost by a major disaster nearly all content accumulated by human being will be lost and it will be impossible to recover them.

OLIGOPOLISTIC STRUCTURE OF THE SE MARKET

It is a widely known fact that the SE market is oligopolistic globally. Local SEs could not survive in the face of the competition from the global giants since they introduced multi-language versions of their products. The necessary investment for the establishment of a search engine is huge and this is an entry barrier for the competitors (Porter, 1998). Another factor is the online habits of the users.

Internet users do not change their habits easily. So, the leading SEs stay as the leaders unless a new competitor with the disrupting technology appears.

Given the highly critical role of SEs in governing the Internet, the dominance of some countries should also be examined. SEs will be seen as part of the national defense in the coming years and national or local SEs will need to be developed.

One of the entry barriers is the high initial investments and long payback periods in the SE market (Porter, 1998). In fact, although the oligopolistic structure can be criticized, there is no place for hundreds of global SEs. Even so, an international body should regulate the SE sector more closely. Humanity cannot leave the control over the information to few hands and their over-complicated AI technology. Information processing cannot be the task and duty of the SEs alone.

SEs and the Citation Indices

Academic world is slow in adapting technological change when it comes to publishing. Long-held traditions cannot be left over night. However, the waves of changes fueled by the Internet transforms the academic publishing. Citation indices (http://en.wikipedia.org/wiki/Citation_index) have long been the major tools to assess the productivity of academicians.

The technology of SEs can replace the classical citation indices in that SEs can scan much more content in a shorter time. Major search engines introduced academic services and they are likely to be more respected in the future. SEs can measure the full impact of a writer in very sophisticated ways and this process can be much more automated than the offline databases.

SEs heavily invest in their technologies and they are expert in analyzing and classifying any kind of content. They can produce many new statistics that can judge the efficiency of academicians or academic institutions. Moreover, they can update these statistics almost instantly. To sum up, SEs and their successors AIESEs will gain prestige in academic circles and classical offline services are likely to lose their business to SEs how prestigious they are. The reason is that they don't have the financial power and the technology of SEs.

This is just another example of how SEs will become the major powers in controlling the classification of delivery of content. Even academic content cannot escape from this trend. More advanced technology of SEs will rule out older technologies known as citation indices. Some criticisms will be resolved but SEs will bring new problems to the world of academia.

CONCLUSION

Search engines became integral parts of our lives and it is hard to imagine life without them. However, as one enjoys the convenience of SEs, s/he adapts the worldview delivered by SEs. SEs' selection, sort and presentation criteria act as a digitally designed philosophy. Such a philosophy takes more and more active role in governing the intellectual and academic life of humanity. The worst is that the majority of people is unaware of the deep, second or third order control of SEs.

Search engines have already used Artificial Intelligence (AI) technology. But after the AI technology mature, SEs will reach a new stage and we call them Artificial Intelligence Enabled Search Engines (AIESEs). They will augment the problems and threats posed by SEs and the indirect controls and affects of SEs will be much more invisible. It will become harder to persuade people about the negative aspects of SEs. Ultimately a single system of Sigularity Level Search Engine (SLSE) may arise.

The technological singularity is very important in understanding the future evolution of the search engines. Almost any technology will be affected by the accelerating merging developments in other technologies. However, the search engine technology will be affected in more direct ways as it heavily uses AI technologies.

The oligopolistic nature of the industry should especially be addressed and the competitive environment should be protected. Since, the Internet unites all individual local markets, the competitive structure of the SE market, can only be addressed by global institutions. Although, the Internet is a very dynamic medium, regulators should interfere when required. Even if an anti-trust case is filed, it takes too long and the competitive environment changes radically in the meantime.

REFERENCES

Aldrich, D. F. (1999). *Mastering the digital marketplace*. New York, NY: John Wiley & Sons.

Arthur, W. B. (2009). *The nature of technology: What it is and how it evolves*. New York, NY: Free Press.

Bovet, D., & Martha, J. (2000). *Value Nets: Breaking the supply chain to unlock hidden profits*. New York, NY: John Wiley & Sons.

Christensen, C. M. (1997). *The innovator's dilemma: When new technologies cause great firms to fail*. Boston, MA: Harvard Business School Press.

Cohan, P. S. (1999). *Net profit*. San Francisco, CA: Jossey-Bass.

Evans, P., & Wurster, T. S. (2000). *Blown to bits: How the new economics of information transforms strategy*. Boston, MA: Harvard Business School Press.

Gardner, J. (2007). *The intelligent universe: AI, ET, and the emerging mind of the cosmos*. Pompton Plains, NJ: New Page Books.

Giunipero, L. C., & Sawchuk, C. (2000). *e-Purchasing plus changing the way corporations buy*. Mantua, NJ: JGC Enterprises.

Hartman, A., Sifonis, J., & Kador, J. (2000). *Net-ready: Strategies for success in the e-conomy.* New York, NY: McGraw-Hill.

Haylock, C. F., & Muscarella, L. (1999). *Net success.* Holbrook, NY: Adams Media.

Kalakota, D. R., & Robinson, M. (1999). *e-Business: Roadmap for success.* Reading, MA: Addison-Wesley.

Karaman, F., & Yamamoto, G. T. (2007). Controlling the pace and direction of technological change. *E-Business Review, 7.*

Kotkin, J. (2000). *The new geography: How the digital revolution is reshaping the American landscape.* New York, NY: Random House.

Kuglin, F. A., & Rosenbaum, B. A. (2001). *The supply chain network @ Internet speed: Preparing your company for the e-commerce revolution.* New York, NY: Amacom, American Management Association.

Kurzweil, R. (1999). *The age of spiritual machines: When computers exceed human intelligence.* New York, NY: Penguin Books.

Kurzweil, R. (2005). *The singularity is near: When humans transcend biology.* New York, NY: Penguin Books.

McClellan, J. E. III, & Dorn, H. (2006). *Science and technology in world history: An introduction* (2nd ed.). Baltimore, MD: The John Hopkins University Press.

Nesheim, J. L. (2000). *High tech start up: Complete handbook for creating successful new high tech companies.* New York, NY: Free Press.

O'Brien, M. (2004). Commentary on Heidegger's "The Question Concerning Technology". In *Proceedings of the IWM Junior Fellows' Winter Conference on Thinking Together* (Vol. 16).

Ohmae, K. (1999). *The invisible continent: Four strategic imperatives of the new economy.* New York, NY: HarperBusiness.

Pacey, A. (1991). *Technology in world civilization.* Cambridge, MA: MIT Press.

Patel, K., & McCarthy, M. P. (2000). *The essentials of e-business leadership: Digital transformation.* New York, NY: McGraw-Hill.

Porter, M. E. (1998). *On competition.* Boston, MA: Harvard Business School Press.

Raisch, W. D. (2001). *The eMarketplace: Strategies for success in B2B eCommerce.* New York, NY: McGraw-Hill.

Reich, R. B. (2001). *The future of success.* New York, NY: Alfred A. Knopf.

Richards, J. W. (Ed.). (2002). *Are we spiritual machines?* Seattle, WA: Discovery Institute.

Schiller, R. J. (2001). *Irrational exuberance.* New York, NY: Broadway Books.

Shapiro, C., & Varian, H. R. (1999). *Information rules: A strategic guide to the network economy.* Boston, MA: Harvard Business School Press.

Singer, P. W. (2009). *Wired for war: The robotics revolution and conflict in the 21st century.* New York, NY: The Penguin Press.

Tainter, J. A. (1988). *The collapse of complex societies.* Cambridge, UK: Cambridge University Press.

Tapscott, D., Ticoll, D., & Lowy, A. (2000). *Digital capital: Harnessing the power of business Webs.* Boston, MA: Harvard Business School Press.

Tompkins, J. A. (2000). *No boundaries: Moving beyond supply chain management.* Raleigh, NC: Tompkins Press.

Yamamoto, G. T., & Karaman, F. (2005). A road-map for the development of the content protecting technologies (CPT) for the content based e-business models. *E-Business Review*, 5, 226–232.

Yamamoto, G. T., & Karaman, F. (2006a). User rating system for the Internet (URSI) and Central Authority for Internet Security (CAIS). *The Journal of Business*, 5(2).

Yamamoto, G. T., & Karaman, F. (2006b). ICT, new working elite, and social implications. *E-Business Review, 6*.

Yamamoto, G. T., & Karaman, F. (2007a). Technologies collecting user data and privacy issues. In *Proceedings of the 7th Annual Conference of the International Academy of E-Business 7th Annual Conference*, Vancouver, BC, Canada.

Yamamoto, G. T., & Karaman, F. (2007b). Business ethics and technology in Turkey: An emerging country at the crossroad of civilizations. In Nemati, H. (Ed.), *Information security and ethics: Concepts, methodologies, tools and applications*. Hershey, PA: Information Science Reference. doi:10.4018/978-1-59904-937-3.ch131

APPENDIX

Terms and Abbreviations

AI: Artificial Intelligence

AIESE: Artificial Intelligence Enabled Search Engine

ASE: Advanced Search Engine

CPU: Central Processing Unit

DRM: Digital Rights Management

ICT: Information and Communication Technologies

IT: Information Technology

Mega Intelligence: The synergistic whole of people's interconnected intelligences.

Moore's Law: The law stating that the speed of microprocessors' double every 18 months. That implies an exponential growth in speed.

Disintegration of knowledge: A peculiar view of the universe due to the unique set of AI-delivered information to each individual and loss of a common view among humans.

SE: Search Engine

SSE: Simple Search Engine

SEO: Search Engine Optimization

Singularity: Technological singularity means loss of human control over thedevelopment and direction of the technology after the complex whole of the advanced technologies become too sophisticated to be analyzed by human mind.

SLSE: Singularity Level Search Engine

Web 2.0: Includes highly interactive web sites and is used almost interchangeably with "social media"

Chapter 20
A Framework for Evaluating the Retrieval Effectiveness of Search Engines

Dirk Lewandowski
Hamburg University of Applied Sciences, Germany

ABSTRACT

This chapter presents a theoretical framework for evaluating next generation search engines. The author focuses on search engines whose results presentation is enriched with additional information and does not merely present the usual list of "10 blue links," that is, of ten links to results, accompanied by a short description. While Web search is used as an example here, the framework can easily be applied to search engines in any other area. The framework not only addresses the results presentation, but also takes into account an extension of the general design of retrieval effectiveness tests. The chapter examines the ways in which this design might influence the results of such studies and how a reliable test is best designed.

INTRODUCTION

Information retrieval systems in general and specific search engines need to be evaluated during the development process, as well as when the system is running. A main objective of the evaluations is to improve the quality of the search results, although other reasons for evaluating search engines do exist (Lewandowski & Höchstötter, 2008). A variety of quality factors can be applied to search engines. These can be grouped into four major areas (Lewandowski & Höchstötter, 2008):

- Index Quality: This area of quality measurement indicates the important role that search engines' databases play in retrieving relevant and comprehensive results. Areas of interest include Web coverage

DOI: 10.4018/978-1-4666-0330-1.ch020

(e.g., Gulli & Signorini, 2005), country bias (e.g., Liwen, Vaughan, & Thelwall, 2004; Liwen, Vaughan, & Zhang, 2007), and freshness (e.g., Lewandowski, 2008a; Lewandowski, Wahlig, & Meyer-Bautor, 2006).

- Quality of the results: Derivates of classic retrieval tests are applied here. However, which measures should be applied and whether or not new measures are needed to satisfy the unique character of the search engines and their users should be considered (Lewandowski, 2008d).
- Quality of search features: A sufficient set of search features and a sophisticated query language should be offered and should function reliably (e.g., Lewandowski, 2004, 2008b).
- Search engine usability: The question is whether it is possible for users to interact with search engines in an efficient and effective way.

While all the areas mentioned are of great importance, this chapter will focus on ways in which to measure the quality of the search results, a central aspect of search engine evaluation. Nonetheless, it is imperative to realize that a search engine that offers perfect results may still not be accepted by its users, due, for example, to usability failures.

This chapter will describe a framework for evaluating next generation search engines, whether they are Web search engines or more specific applications. A search engine in the context of this chapter refers to an information retrieval system that searches a considerably large database of unstructured or semi-structured data (as opposed to a general information retrieval system that searches a structured database). A *next-generation search engine* is a search engine that does not present its results as a simple list, but makes use of advanced forms of results presentation; that is to say, they enrich the list-based results presentation with ad-

ditional information or the results are presented in a different style. Thus, the results are unequally presented in terms of *screen real estate*, that is, in terms of the area on the results screen that each results description is granted.

While the term "search engine" is often equated with "Web search engine," in this chapter, all types of search engines are considered, although points regarding Web search engines are particularly emphasized, as they constitute the major area of our research.

The remainder of this chapter is organized as follows: First, a certain amount of background information on information retrieval evaluation is presented; next, the relevant literature related to such areas of interest as search engine retrieval effectiveness tests, click-through analysis, search engine user behavior, and results presentation. Then, a framework for search engine retrieval effectiveness evaluation, which will be described in detail, is presented. The chapter concludes by alluding to future research directions and with a set of concluding remarks.

BACKGROUND

Evaluation has always been an important aspect (and an important research area) of information retrieval. Most studies follow (at least to a certain degree) the Cranfield paradigm, using a set of ad-hoc queries for evaluation and calculating effectiveness measures such as precision and recall. While the Cranfield paradigm has often been criticized, it is not without merit and is used in large evaluation initiatives such as TREC and CLEF, which were designed to evaluate search results. Most search engine evaluations today are "TREC-style,"[1] as they follow the approach used in these tests.

They use, however, a somewhat limited understanding of a user's behavior. As will become apparent in the literature review section, user results are determinant upon selection behavior, which is influenced by many factors. However, TREC-style evaluations focus on a "dedicated searcher," i.e., someone who is willing to examine every result given by the search engine and follow the exact order in which the results are presented (Harman & Voorhees, 2006, p. 117). Additionally, these evaluations assume that a user is interested in a high recall, as well as in a high level of precision of the results. Finally, the user is willing to consider a large number of documents for his query (Harman & Voorhees, 2006, p. 117). It can be easily seen that these assumptions may not hold true for each use scenario; for example, in Web searches, users usually only examine a few results presented at the top of the results screen, and not necessarily in the order in which they are presented. Web search engine users are usually interested in a few good-quality documents (a high precision, at least on the first few results positions) and not interested in a complete set of all relevant results (a high recall).

However, even if the kind of searching behavior assumed in TREC-style evaluations were once accurate in other contexts than Web search, now it is no longer applicable. As Web search engines largely influence user behavior in all searching contexts, there is a need for new models for evaluating all types of search engines.

LITERATURE REVIEW

In this section, we review the literature on retrieval effectiveness tests with a focus on Web search engines. We will see that most of the problems that occur in the evaluation of Web search engines also occur when the subject of evaluation is an entirely different kind of search engine. In addition, we will briefly review the literature on search engine user behavior and on results presentation in search engines. From the literature review, we will derive the major points that will be implemented in our search engine evaluation framework, presented later.

Retrieval Effectiveness Tests

Retrieval effectiveness tests should focus on only one query type (either informational, navigational, or transactional queries – for a detailed discussion on query types, see below). While for informational queries, a results *set* can be considered, navigational queries are usually satisfied with only one result. For the satisfaction of transactional queries, a certain degree of interaction is needed. To measure the performance of a search engine on such queries, these interactions must be modeled. Therefore, simple retrieval effectiveness tests are not sufficient; one should use a combined user- and effectiveness study.

In our review, only studies using informational queries (cf. Broder, 2002) will be considered. While there are some existing studies on the performance of Web search engines on navigational queries (Hawking & Craswell, 2005; Lewandowski, 2011a), these should be considered separately because of the very different information needs being considered. However, there are some "mixed studies" (for example, Griesbaum, 2004) that use query sets consisting of informational as well as navigational queries. These studies are flawed because, in contrast to informational queries, the expected result for a navigational query is just one result. When a greater number of results are considered, even a search engine that found the desired page and placed it in the first position would receive bad precision values. Therefore, informational and navigational queries should be strictly separated.

In general, retrieval effectiveness tests rely on methods derived from the design of information retrieval tests (Tague-Sucliffe, 1992) and on advice that focuses more on Web search engines (Gordon & Pathak, 1999; Hawking, Craswell, Bailey, & Griffiths, 2001). However, there are some remarkable differences in study design, which are reviewed in the following paragraphs.

First, the number of queries used in the studies varies greatly. The oldest studies, especially

(Chu & Rosenthal, 1996; Ding & Marchionini, 1996; Leighton & Srivastava, 1999), use only a few queries (5 to 15) and are, therefore, of limited use (for a discussion of the minimum number of queries that should be used in such tests, see Buckley & Voorhees, 2000). Newer studies use a minimum of 25 queries, some 50 or more.

In older studies, queries are usually taken from reference questions or commercial online systems, while newer studies focus more on the general users' interests or combine both types of questions. There are studies that deal with a special set of query topics (for example, business) (Gordon & Pathak, 1999), but a trend is observable in focusing on the general user in search engine testing (cf. Lewandowski, 2008d).

Regarding the number of results taken into account, most investigations consider only the first 10 or 20 results. This is due not only to the amount of work required for the evaluators but also to the general behavior of search engine users. These users only seldom view more than the first results page. While these results pages typically consist of 10 results (the infamous "ten blue links"), search engines now tend to add additional results (from news or video databases, for example), so that the total number of results, especially on the first results page, is often considerably higher (Höchstötter & Lewandowski, 2009).

Furthermore, researchers found that general Web search engine users heavily focus on the first few results (Cutrell & Guan, 2007; Granka, Hembrooke, & Gay, 2005; Hotchkiss, 2007; Joachims, Granka, Pan, Hembrooke, & Gay, 2005), which are shown in the so-called "visible area" (Höchstötter & Lewandowski, 2009)—that is, the section of the first search engine results page (SERP) that is visible without scrolling down. Keeping these findings in mind, a cut-off value of 10 in search engine retrieval effectiveness tests seems reasonable.

An important question is how the results should be judged. Most studies use relevance scales (with three to six points). Griesbaum's studies (Gries-

baum, 2004; Griesbaum, Rittberger, & Bekavac, 2002) use binary relevance judgments with one exception: results can also be judged as "pointing to a relevant document" (for example, the page itself is not relevant but contains a hyperlink to a relevant page). This is so as to take into account the special nature of the Web. However, it seems problematic to judge these pages as somewhat relevant, as pages may contain dozens or even hundreds of links, and a user would then (in bad circumstances) have to follow a number of links to access the relevant document.

Two particularly important points in the evaluation of search engine results are whether the source of the results is made anonymous (i.e., the jurors do not know which search engine delivered a certain result) and whether the results lists are randomized. Randomization is important in order to avoid learning effects. While most of the newer studies anonymize the results (as far as which search engine produced the results), only three studies were found that randomized the results lists (Gordon & Pathak, 1999; Lewandowski, 2008d; Véronis, 2006).

Most studies make use of students as jurors. This comes as no surprise, as most researchers teach courses where they have access to students that can serve as jurors. In some cases (again, mainly older studies), the researchers themselves are the ones to judge the documents (Chu & Rosenthal, 1996; Ding & Marchionini, 1996; Dresel et al., 2001; Griesbaum, 2004; Griesbaum et al., 2002; Leighton & Srivastava, 1999).

To our knowledge, no study regarding the effectiveness of search engine retrieval utilizes multiple jurors, a fact that may result in flawed results, as different jurors may not agree on the relevance of individual results.

While retrieval effectiveness tests that make use of jurors are time-consuming and thus expensive, a cheaper approach involves using click-through data to determine the relevance of certain results. The quality of a result is determined by the number of times it was selected on the results page,

Table 1. Typical elements presented on Web search engine results pages (Höchstötter & Lewandowski, 2009)

Name	Description	Position
Organic	Results from Web crawl. "Objective hits" not influenced by direct payments.	Central on results page.
Sponsored	Paid results, separated from the organic results list.	Above or below organic results, on the right-hand side of the results list.
Shortcuts	Emphasized results, pointing to results from a special collection.	Above organic results, within organic results list.
Primary search result	Extended result that highlights different collections and is accompanied by an image as well as further information.	Above organic results, often within organic results.
Prefetch	Results from a preferred source, emphasized in the results set.	Above or within organic results.
Snippet	Regular organic result, for which the result description is extended by additional navigational links.	Within organic results list (usually only in first position).
Child	Second result from the same server, with a link to further results from the same server.	Within organic results list; indented.

the length of time users spent reading the result ("dwell time"), and the number of times a user directly returned to the results screen after screening the results clicked ("bounce rate"). While such studies have the advantage of considering a large number of queries and results (e.g., Joachims et al., 2005), one significant disadvantage is that only results that users actually clicked can be considered. As discussed in the following section, users only view a small portion of the results list, and click-through data is only available for this portion. Utilizing click-through data to improve the performance of a search engine may lead to a "rich get richer" effect, as results presented at the top of the results list are clicked more often than those positioned lower on the list.

Lewandowski (2008d) provides an overview of the major Web search engine retrieval effectiveness tests conducted between 1996 and 2007. For an overview of older tests, see Gordon and Pathak (1999, p. 148).

Results Presentation

Results presentation in Web search engines has dramatically changed from a list presentation of "10 blue links", that is, ten results, each equally presented with a title, description, and URL, to individual descriptions (containing additional information for certain results), different sizes, and graphically supported presentations of certain results. While findings regarding the composition of search engine results pages with a focus on Web search engines are presented here, similar results presentations can also be found in other contexts. It seems likely that even more results pages composed from different sources ("Universal Search") will make an appearance in the future, as users' expectations are largely guided by what they see in their daily use of Web search engines.

Table 1 provides an overview of the different types of results that can be presented on search engine results pages. An example of an extended presentation of search engine results is given in Figure 1.

While search engines usually return thousands of results, users are not willing to view more than

Figure 1. Results presentation (complete SERP) in the Google search engine (Höchstötter & Lewandowski, 2009, p. 1798)

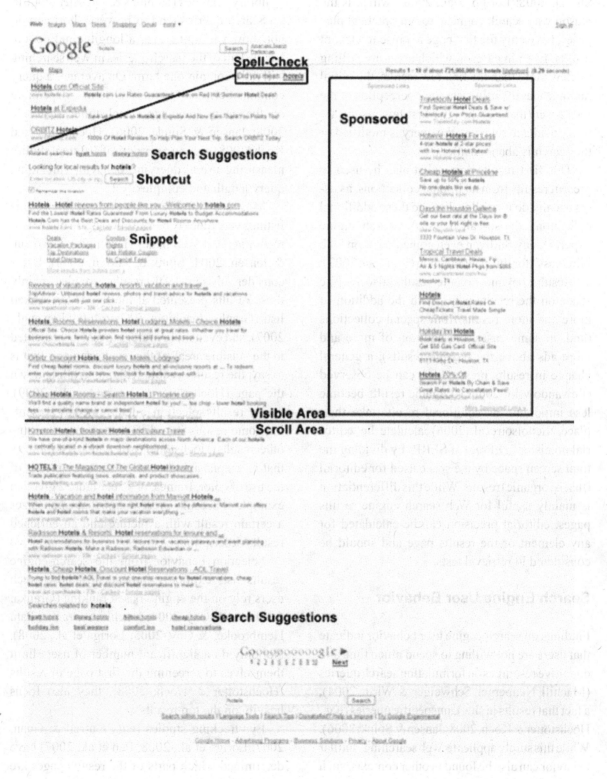

a few (Jansen & Spink, 2006; Keane, O'Brien, & Smyth, 2008; Lorigo et al., 2008), which is the reason why search engines, for all practical purposes, have only the first page to present relevant results. Even in cases in which users are willing to view more than the first few results, the initial ranking heavily influences their perception of the results set (that is, when the first few results are not considered relevant, the query is modified or the search is abandoned).

This first results page must also be used to present results from additional collections, as users usually do not follow links to these additional collections, the so-called "tabs". Search engine expert Danny Sullivan even coined the term "tab blindness" for this phenomenon (Sullivan, 2003).

Results beyond organic results also require space on the results page. With the addition of more and more results from special collections (and, in some cases, the addition of more and more ads above the organic results), a general change in results presentation can be observed (Lewandowski, 2008c). Organic results become less important, as additional results take their place. Nicholson et al. (2006) calculate the "editorial precision" (EPrec) of SERPs by dividing the total screen space by the space used for editorial (that is, organic) results. While this differentiation is mainly useful for Web search engine results pages, editorial precision can be calculated for any element of the results page and should be considered in retrieval tests.

Search Engine User Behavior

Findings on search engine user behavior indicate that users are not willing to spend much time and cognitive resources on formulating search queries (Machill, Neuberger, Schweiger, & Wirth, 2004), a fact that results in short, unspecific queries (e.g., Höchstötter & Koch, 2008; Jansen & Spink, 2006). While this surely applies to Web searching, similar behavior can also be found in other contexts, such

as in scientific searching (Rowlands et al., 2008) or library searches (Hennies & Dressler, 2006).

Search queries tend to be very short and do not show variations over a longitudinal period. Nearly half of the search queries in Web searching still only contain one term. On average, a query contains between 1.6 and 3.3 terms, depending on the query language (Höchstötter & Koch, 2008; Jansen & Spink, 2006). Höchstötter and Koch (2008) give an overview of different studies measuring users' querying behavior (including query length and complexity).

Most searching persons evaluate the results listings very quickly before clicking on one or two recommended Web pages (Hotchkiss, Garrison, & Jensen, 2004; Spink & Jansen, 2004). Users consider only some of the results provided, mainly those results presented at the top of the ranked lists (Granka, Joachims, & Gay, 2004; Pan et al., 2007), and even more prefer the results presented in the "visible area" of the results screens, that is to say, the results visible without scrolling down the page (Höchstötter & Lewandowski, 2009). Lastly, results selection is determined by presenting some results in a different manner than the other results (Höchstötter & Lewandowski, 2009), that is, emphasizing certain results by means of the use of color, frames, or size. Figure 2 gives an example of a results presentation that emphasizes a certain result with a picture and an enriched results description.

Selection behavior from the search-engine results lists explicitly indicate just how much users rely on the engine-based ranking (Granka, Joachims, & Gay, 2004; Joachims, Granka, Pan, Hembrooke, & Gay, 2005; Loriga et al., 2008). Not only do a significant number of users limit themselves to screening the first page of results (Höchstötter & Koch, 2008), they also focus heavily on the top results.

Eye-tracking studies (e.g., Cutrell & Guan, 2007; Lorigo et al., 2008; Pan et al., 2007) have determined which parts of the results pages are perceived by the users. Typical viewing patterns

Figure 2. Results presentation (clipping from a Yahoo results list), emphasizing a certain result by using a picture

Angela **Merkel** - Startseite
Die persönliche Internetseite der Vorsitzenden der CDU Deutschlands, Angela **Merkel**. ...
Deutschland auf dem richtigen Weg ist", erklärte Bundeskanzlerin Angela **Merkel**. ...
www.angela-merkel.de - Im Cache

Angela **Merkel** – Wikipedia
Werdegang | Politische... | Öffentlichkei... | Familiäres
Angela Dorothea **Merkel** ist eine deutsche Politikerin. Seit dem 10.
April 2000 ist sie Bundesvorsitzende der CDU und seit dem
22. November 2005 deutsche Bundeskanzlerin.
de.wikipedia.org/wiki/Angela_Merkel - 186k - Im Cache

Merkel: Deutsch
Merkel RX.HELIX. Besuchen Sie die Helix Seite und erfahren Sie mehr über die
Weltneuheit ... **Merkel** lädt zur Helix-Challenge 2010 ...
www.merkel-die-jagd.de - Im Cache

Merkel Freudenberg - Spezialist für innovative Dichtsysteme - www ...
Merkel Freudenberg Fluidtechnic, Ein Unternehmen der weltweiten Freudenberg Gruppe ...
Flyer **Merkel** Counter Surface Parameters. Flyer Bergbau. Prospekt Bergbau ...
www.merkel-freudenberg.de - Im Cache

(such as the "golden triangle") have been determined and can be used to improve results presentation. Hotchkiss (2007) discussed the Google triangle, which clearly indicates users' focus on the upper left corner. However, this only holds true for a list-based results presentation, in which all results are presented equally. For unequal results presentations, quite different viewing patterns are found (Figure 3).

A FRAMEWORK FOR EVALUATING THE RETRIEVAL EFFECTIVENESS OF SEARCH ENGINES

In the following sections, a framework for evaluating the retrieval effectiveness of search engines is presented. The framework consists of five parts, namely queries selection, results collection, results weighting, results judgment, and data analysis. While different choices regarding the individual stages of the test design are made for different tests, guidance for designing such tests is given.

In the section pertaining to query selection, the kinds of queries that should be utilized when evaluating search engines are discussed. In the section on results collection, the information collected in addition to the URLS of the results are detailed. The results weighting section deals with the positions and the higher visibility of certain results, due to an emphasized presentation. The section on results judgment addresses who should make relevance judgments, what scales should be used, and how click-through data can support retrieval effectiveness tests. In the last portion of the framework (data analysis), appropriate measures that go beyond the traditional metrics of *recall* and *precision* are discussed. The framework, including all of the elements described below, is depicted in Figure 4.

Query Selection

This section of the framework deals with selecting appropriate queries to evaluate. This selection is of great importance, as, due to limited resources,

Figure 3. Viewing pattern on a results page, revealing an unequal results presentation (heatmap from an eye-tracking study of 50 testing persons, in which the stimulus was displayed for 5 seconds)

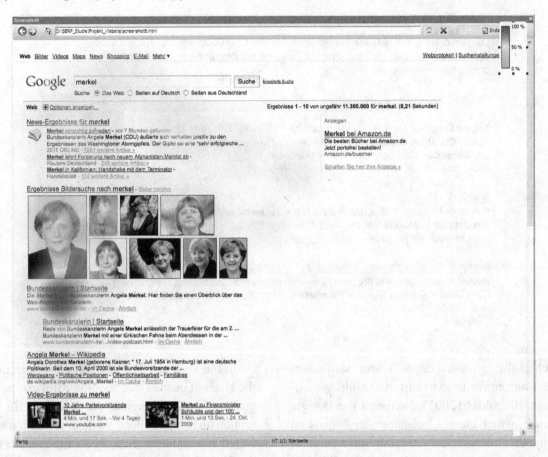

such tests must rely on a relatively small selection of queries. The use of queries with certain intent, query topics, how query descriptions (that is, descriptions of the underlying information needs) can be generated, how different aspects of a query can be taken into account, and how query properties can be used in evaluations are discussed below.

Query Intent

As already mentioned in the literature review section, queries used in testing should be separated according to type. In information science, a differentiation is made between a Concrete Information Need (CIN) and a Problem-Oriented Information Need (POIN) (Frants, Shapiro, & Voiskunskii, 1997). A CIN asks for factual information, and is satisfied with only one factum. In the case of document retrieval, this may mean satisfaction with only one document containing the required factum. In contrast, a POIN requires a smaller or larger number of documents for satisfaction.

Broder (2002) differentiates between three different types of intentions in terms of querying Web search engines: informational, navigational, and transactional. Navigational queries aim at a Web page that is already known to the user or to one which the user assumes exists (for example, the homepages of companies such as Ebay or people such as John von Neumann). Such queries normally terminate in one correct result. The

Figure 4. Framework for the evaluation of the effectiveness of search engines

Framework for Evaluating the Retrieval Effectiveness of Search Engines

QUERY SELECTION	RESULTS COLLECTION	RESULTS PRESENTATION	RESULTS JUDGEMENT	DATA ANALYSIS
Intents	Descriptions	Position of result description in SERP	Selection of jurors	Relevance of the results
Topics	Results		Jurors per query	Results descriptions
Generating descriptions	Other elements (ads, one-box results)	Screen real estate of description	Scales	Diversity
Generating query/topic aspects	(Results classification)	Graphical elements		Other analysis (based on results classification)
Query properties (demographic etc.)				

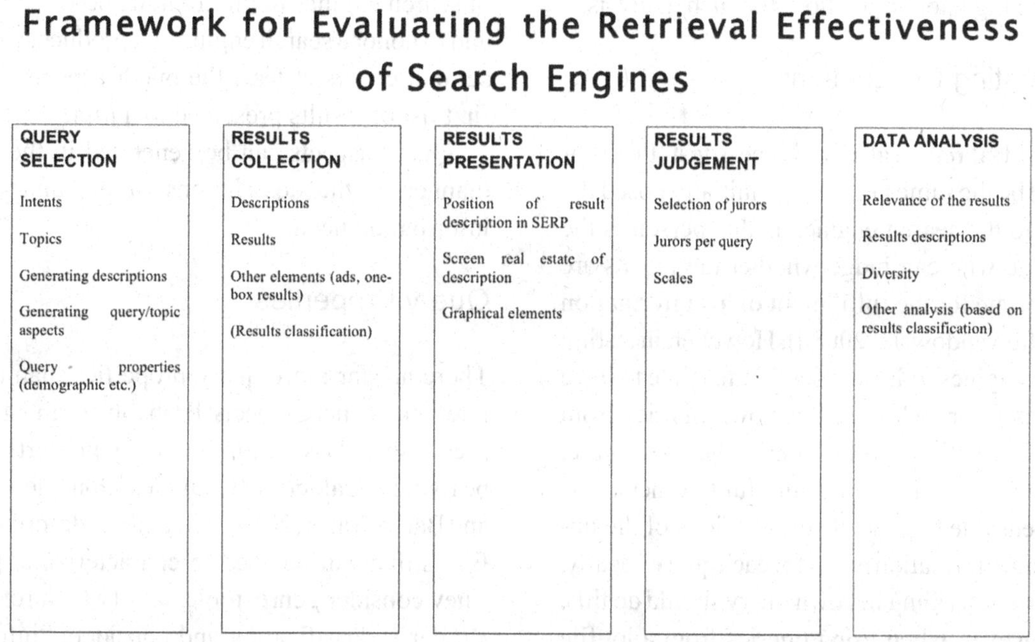

information need is satisfied when the requested page is found.

In contrast, informational queries require more than one document (POIN). The user wishes to become informed about a topic and therefore intends to read several documents. Informational queries aim at static documents to acquire the desired information, which makes further interaction with the Web page unnecessary.

Transactional queries, however, aim at Web pages offering the possibility of a subsequent transaction such as the purchase of a product, the downloading of data, or the searching of a database.

Broders's taxonomy was used as a starting point by researchers who refined and amended it. Kang and Kim (2003) use classes very similar to Broder's, but use different notations ("topic relevance task" refers to an informational query, "homepage finding task" to a navigational query, and "service finding task" to a transactional query).

In terms of the evaluation of search engines, the different types must be considered separately (Lewandowski, 2008d, 2011a). Current studies

mainly use informational queries or mix different query types. In tests using "real-life queries," the intent could (at least to some degree) be determined by using click-through data (Joachims, 2002). The evaluation of search systems should always be oriented towards the queries that are put to this special type of search system.

It should be kept in mind that when a search engine's performance for two or more *different* query types is to be evaluated, the researcher must build distinct collections of queries and apply different metrics in the data analysis.

Query Topics

Topics should reflect users' needs in the search engine under investigation. To achieve a statistically valid sample of queries according to their topics, one can classify a sample from the logfiles of the search engine under investigation (cf. Lewandowski, 2006).

It is important to use a variety of topics. However, when one wants to know how the search engine performs with different topics, sample sizes must be big enough to allow for such analysis.

Generating Descriptions

For an ideal retrieval effectiveness test, the juror should be the same person who initially posed the query to the search engine, as this person is the only one who can judge whether the results are appropriate for the fulfillment of his information need (Lewandowski, 2008d). However, in testing search engines, it is only seldom feasible to have users as jurors who use their own queries from real-life situations. As the queries themselves are, for the most part, not meaningful to others, it is indispensable to generate descriptions of the underlying information needs for each query. Ideally, a person describing her own query should do this.

However, when using queries from a logfile (which has the advantage that one can differentiate between popular and rare queries or even weight the queries by frequency), other methods must be used. One such method is to have different people describe what they think the underlying information need for a query is. Then, the different information needs are compared and similar information needs are synthesized. This leads to a basic set of information needs that can be used for the test. This method was used in Huffman and Hochster (2007), and produced good results.

Generating Query Aspects

While the generation of query descriptions may reveal a variety of completely different information needs underlying the same query, documents answering the same query may cover more than one aspect of a query. For example, the query "James Bond" may involve aspects such as films, books, character biographies, actors who played the character, and so forth. While certain documents may contain general information about the topic and therefore cover many or even all aspects in brief, some documents may cover one or more aspects in depth. It is important in the evaluation of search engines to differentiate between topics and to honor a search engine that produces a result set that covers at least the major aspects on the first list of results presented to a user.

Query aspects can be generated in the same manner as the descriptions of the underlying information need.

Query Properties

There are far more query properties than query intents and query aspects. Probably the most comprehensive classification of query properties can be found in Calderon-Benavides, Gonzalez-Caro, and Baeza-Yates (2010). The authors describe nine facets that can be used to characterize a query. They consider genre, topic, task (which refers to Broder's classification and considers "informational," "not informational," and "both"), objective (where "action" is an indication of a commercial intent, and "resource" refers to a non-commercial intent), specificity, scope, authority sensitivity, spatial sensitivity, and time sensitivity.

Even demographic data can be obtained for the queries. Demographics Prediction, a free tool from Microsoft (http://adlab.msn.com/Demographics-Prediction/), allows one to see whether a query is generally male- or female-oriented and what age groups pose this query at what frequency. While the data is for Web search, it can also be used for queries from other search engines. However, one should keep in mind that the demographics might be quite different between individual search tools.

Query descriptions, query aspects, and other query properties can be generated in one combined step. One can use jurors for generating these query properties or use a combined approach with jurors and the specific person who actually posed the query to the search engine (if this person is available).

Results Collection

The second pillar of the proposed framework deals with the collection of the results and additional information pertaining to the results from the search engines under investigation. Such additional information may include the results description, information on the type of result (direct answer vs. organic result description leading to a document), the position on the results screen, or the space a certain result obtains on the results screen.

Results Descriptions

The results descriptions are of great importance because they help a user to decide whether or not to select a particular result (Lewandowski, 2008d). However, the descriptions are not considered in the vast majority of evaluation studies. This distorts the results of retrieval effectiveness studies, in that results that would not have been clicked are considered. Research has shown that descriptions can be misleading. The titles and the descriptions of recommended Web pages are very important for users to evaluate the results lists (Machill, Neuberger, Schweiger, & Wirth, 2003; Machill et al., 2004). Descriptions should be collected in the same manner as the results themselves and should be considered in the results judgment, as well as in the data analysis phase.

Capturing Organic Results

How results from a search engine should be captured depends on the nature of the engine(s) under investigation. If one is dealing with a system that searches a static database (for example, a test collection built for evaluating the search engine), there is no need to save the results, as they will not vary within the testing period. However, when using search engines not under the control of the investigator (whether because the search engine's database is not static or because changes may occur at any time during the testing period),

all results must be saved in their entirety. While in the first case it may be enough to capture the results' URLs, in the second case the complete results must be saved.

The position of each individual result must also be captured. When comparing different search engines, the name of the search engine that produced an individual result must be captured.

Capturing other Elements of the Results Pages

When results are not presented equally, the type of result should be captured, as different result types may be perceived differently by the user. For example, the results page shown in Figure 1 depicts results of organic, advertisement, shortcut, and extended snippet types (i.e., for an organic result, additional links are shown within the description). Figure 2 shows a results description with an added picture.

Results Classification

Not only queries can be further classified, but also the results presented by a search engine. In Web searches, results may come from blogs, news sites, government agencies, and other types of pages. If the database searched by a search engine is not quality-controlled in a strict sense (that is, generally all types of documents from (a part of) the free Web are accepted for inclusion in the index), it may be useful to provide a good mix of results of different types.

In Web search, it may also be useful to classify results according to their commercial intent, as top results may be heavily influenced by search engine optimization (SEO) techniques (Lewandowski, 2011b).

Results classification may reveal biases in results sets that were not intended in the design of a search engine. Additionally, different search engines may follow different approaches in mixing results of different types, which may affect the relevance of the *results set*, while pure relevance judgments may not provide an indication as to why a certain results set is considered of low relevance in its entirety.

Results Weighting

In this section, we consider results weighting, which involves weighting the relevance of results according to position and design. As we know from eye-tracking research and click-through analysis, results are not perceived equally. However, this is not considered in traditional retrieval effectiveness studies.

Results weighting can provide a weighting score for each results description, either according to its position on the search engine results page (SERP), the space it uses on the SERP, or the graphical accentuation it receives. For example, when considering the results list shown in Figure 2, the result with the picture could receive a higher weighting score, as a user is more likely to perceive (and therefore, click) this result than the others that are simply presented on a text-basis.

Position of the Result Descriptions within the SERP

While traditional retrieval effectiveness tests consider the results position (see also the section on data analysis), this may not be enough when the results presentation is either (1) not list-based or (2) a list with more than one column. Consider the results presentation depicted in Figure 1: the right-hand column presents context-based advertisements, which should also be considered as results, although they are surely, of a different type. However, as can be seen from eye-tracking research and click-through analysis, these results are not perceived as strongly as the organic results in the "main column" of the results page. When results are collected for a retrieval effectiveness test, the position of the individual result within a result *list* should be captured, as well as its position within the results *page*.

Screen Real Estate

"Screen real estate" is a term introduced by Nielsen and Tahir (2002) to measure the amount of space taken up by a Web page that is filled with content (vs. the part that is left blank). Nicholson et al. (2006) use screen real estate to calculate the space that search engines grant organic results vs. paid results on the first results screen shown to the user. While this is a specific application in the context given, screen real estate can be calculated for every result presented by a search engine. The use of screen real estate may seem obvious when results are presented in different formats; however, it can also be used for list-based results presentation, when not all results are equally presented. Figure 1 demonstrates that the first organic result is given far more real estate than the other results. Consequently, the first result should be given more weight when measuring retrieval effectiveness.

Graphic Elements

Search engine results pages do not necessarily consist of text-based results descriptions alone. Some results may be presented with additional pictures (Figure 3) or may be emphasized by the use of color. For example, the context-based ads depicted in Figure 1 (above the organic results list) are highlighted in yellow. Users thus perceive these results more, giving them a higher probability of being clicked.[2] While such results could be weighted utilizing their screen real estate, it seems reasonable to ascribe even more weight to them due to their high influence on user behavior.

Results Judgment

This section discusses how jurors should be selected, how many queries a juror should be given to evaluate, and what scales should be used for relevance judgments. As these elements can influence the validity of retrieval effectiveness tests, choices should be made wisely.

Selection of Jurors

In most retrieval effectiveness studies, students are selected as jurors (see the literature review above), as they are easy to recruit and are usually willing to judge large numbers of documents, when relevance judgments are included as part of their coursework. However, while students may be good judges for general-purpose queries (as those used in Web search studies), they may not be good judges in other contexts in which more background knowledge is needed. Consider, for example, a search engine for pharmaceutical information from the Web. Students (with the exception of students majoring in pharmacy) simply lack the background knowledge to evaluate the results appropriately. Studies using the "wrong" jurors are flawed; clearly, the effort of conducting a study should be avoided, when it is obvious that the results will be of limited use. Jurors should always be chosen according to the topic and target group of the search engine.

Another approach entails using a convenience sample of users to judge the results. This approach seems reasonable, as long as the target group of the search engine is homogeneous. When different user groups are targeted, more judgments per query should be selected.

Jurors should clearly be selected with great care, as only a relatively small number of jurors can be recruited, due to the cost and effort retrieval effectiveness studies require.

Jurors per Query

Assuming that each juror reviews all of the results produced for a given query, we refer to "jurors per query" instead of "jurors per document." Although the latter terminology may seem more precise, it has the potential of leading to the false assumption that documents resulting from a single query are judged by different persons, that is to say, that a juror may judge only a part of the documents returned for an individual query.

Ideally, a large number of jurors per query should be used in a test so as to ensure that even when people judge results differently, these differences would be represented in the test. However, due to limited resources, most retrieval effectiveness studies utilize only one juror per query. When experimenting with a crowdsourcing-approach that allowed results to be judged by multiple jurors, it was determined that differences in results judgments are low and can therefore be neglected in a context that is familiar to the vast majority of users (Web search) and for more general queries,. In other contexts, on the other hand, more jurors per query should be used. Unfortunately, only a limited amount of research has been done on inter-rater agreement in relevance judgments (Schaer, Mayr, & Mutschke, 2010). Therefore, a clear recommendation regarding the ideal number of jurors cannot yet be made. However, when a search engine targets different user groups, jurors from each group should judge the same documents, where applicable.

Scales

When asking jurors to give their relevance judgments, it must be decided whether these judgments should be binary (relevant or not relevant) or collected using scales. While the first approach allows for ease in collecting data and computing precision scores (see "data analysis"), the results may be flawed, as it is often not too difficult for a search engine to produce results that are *somehow* relevant, but can prove considerably more challenging to produce results that are *highly* relevant. Consequently, a more differentiated collection of relevance judgments seems preferential, although simple (e.g., 5-point) scales are to be preferred over, for example, more complex percent scales.

Data Analysis

In this section, the ways in which the data gathered in retrieval effectiveness tests can be analyzed are discussed, alongside the major measures used in such tests. Recommendations on what measures to use are also given.

Relevance of the Results

The foremost goal of retrieval tests is to measure the relevance of the results provided by the search engines under investigation. However, as relevance is a concept not clearly defined (Borlund, 2003; Hjorland, 2010; Mizzaro, 1997; Saracevic, 2007), an overwhelming number of relevance measures exist (for an overview, see Demartini & Mizzaro, 2006). In the remainder of this section, the "classic" relevance measures will be presented, as well as certain newer measures that seem promising for search engine evaluation purposes.

Retrieval performance of the IR system is usually measured by the "two classics," precision and recall. *Precision* measures the ability of an IR system to produce only relevant results. Precision is the ratio between the number of relevant documents retrieved by the system and the total number of documents retrieved. An ideal system would produce a precision score of 1; that is to say, every document retrieved by the system would be deemed relevant.

The other classic measure, *recall*, measures the ability of an IR system to find the complete set of relevant results from within a collection of documents. Recall refers to the ratio of the number of relevant documents retrieved by the system to the total number of relevant documents for the given query. As the total number of relevant documents must be known for each query within the database, recall is quite difficult to measure. Apart from retrieval effectiveness studies using test collections, recall cannot be calculated. A proposed solution to this problem is the method of pooling results from different engines and then measuring the relative recall of each engine.

Precision and recall are not mathematically dependent upon one another, but as a rule of thumb, the higher the precision of a results set, the lower the recall, and vice versa. For example, a system only retrieving one relevant result receives a precision score of 1, but usually scores a low recall. Another system that returns the complete database as a result (perhaps thousands or even millions of documents) will earn the highest recall but a very low precision.

Other "classic" retrieval measures include fallout and generality (for a good overview of retrieval measures see Korfhage, 1997). Newer approaches to measuring the quality of search results are as follows:

- *Median Measure* (Greisdorf & Spink, 2001), which takes into account the total number of results retrieved. Median measure measures not only how positive the given results are, but also how positive they are in relation to all negative results.
- *Importance of completeness of search results* and *Importance of precision of the search to the user* (Su, 1998). These two measures attempt to integrate typical user needs into the evaluation process. Whether the user requires a few precise results or a complete result set (while accepting a lower precision rate) is taken into account. These two measures seem highly promising for search engine evaluation purposes that focus on the user.
- *Value of Search Results as a Whole* (Su, 1998) is a measure that seems to correlate well with other retrieval measures that are regarded as important. Therefore, it can be used to shorten the evaluation process, making it less time-consuming and less costly.
- *Salience* refers to the sum of ratings for all hits for each service out of the sum of rat-

ings for all services investigated (Ding & Marchionini, 1996). This measure takes into account how well all search engines studied perform on a certain query.

- *Relevance concentration* measures the number of items with ratings of 4 or 5 [on a five-point relevance scale] in the first 10 or 20 hits (Ding & Marchionini, 1996).

- *CBC ratio* (MacCall & Cleveland, 1999) measures the number of content-bearing clicks (CBC) in relation to the number of other clicks in the search process. A CBC can be defined as "any hypertext click that is used to retrieve possibly relevant information, as opposed to a hypertext click that is used for other reasons, such as the 'search' click that begins a database search or a 'navigation' click that is used to traverse a WWW-based information resource" (p. 764).

- *Quality of result ranking* takes into account the correlation between search engine ranking and human ranking (Vaughan, 2004, p. 681).

- *Ability to retrieve top ranked pages* combines the results retrieved by all search engines considered and lets them be ranked by humans. The "ability to retrieve top ranked pages" then measures the ratio of the top 75 percent of documents in the results list of a certain search engine (Vaughan, 2004).

As can be seen, retrieval measures vary considerably. Since the measure(s) chosen can strongly influence the results, the measures that are to be applied should be carefully selected, according to the goal of the search engine(s) under investigation. Results from analysis using different measures should be weighted against each other. As most of the retrieval measures proposed could be calculated from data collected by means of traditional retrieval measures, it is

unproblematic to choose additional measures in the analysis of the data.

Results Descriptions

Results descriptions play an important role, as the user makes a judgment about whether or not to select a result based on the description. Since descriptions can sometimes be deceptive, they should be taken into account in all retrieval effectiveness tests. Even the best results are of no use to the user if he ignores them because of bad descriptions.

To clarify the underlying problem, an overview of the possible description/result pairs follows:

- *Relevant description → relevant result*: This is the ideal solution and should be provided for every result.

- *Relevant description → irrelevant result*: In this case, the user assumes from the description that the result is relevant and clicks on the results link, which leads the user to an irrelevant result. In most cases, the user returns to the search engine results page, but is frustrated to a certain degree.

- *Irrelevant description → irrelevant result*: The user generally does not click on the results link because of the irrelevant description and, therefore, does not examine the irrelevant result. One could say that such results descriptions are useful in that they at least warn the user not to click on the irrelevant results. However, these results descriptions really should not be presented on the results pages in the first place.

- *Irrelevant description → relevant result*: In this case, the user is unlikely to consider the result due to its misleading description. The user thus misses a relevant result on account of the poor description.

To measure the ability of search engines to produce consistent description/result pairs, we introduced specific measures (Lewandowski, 2008d):

- *Description-result precision* measures the ratio of results in which the description as well as the result itself were judged relevant. This measure can be regarded as measuring a kind of "super-precision;" every search engine should aim to provide only such results.
- *Description-result conformance* takes into account all pairs for which the description and result are judged the same (either both are deemed relevant or both are deemed irrelevant).
- *Description fallout* measures the ratio of results missed by a searcher due to a description that appears to point to an irrelevant result (that is, the description is judged irrelevant, while the actual result was judged relevant).
- *Description deception* measures in how many cases a user is led to an irrelevant result due to a description that appears to lead to a relevant result. Description deception can result in frustrated users and should be avoided by search engines.

Diversity

Depending on the context, a diversity of sources is essential to obtaining a good result set. However, diversity within the result set may not be enough, as diversity should really be presented on the first result screen in order to give users an overview of different sources that have information on a particular topic. Consider, for example, a user seeking out information regarding minimum wage discussions. The first result screen should already present information from different sources. The user may be interested in the position of political parties, as well as the positions of the employers' federation and trade unions. Diversity of sources is relatively simple to measure, as the higher the

number of sources presented on the first result screen, the better.

However, diversity of sources does not measure whether the query results cover all aspects of the underlying information need. When aspects are collected in the results collection phase, these aspects can be extracted from the documents found and compared to the former. Thereafter, the number of results a user must view in a certain search engine until all aspects of the topic are displayed can be measured. Even if this appears to be too strict of an approach and it can be argued that users rarely require access to information on *all* different aspects of a topic, measuring aspects can be a good way of identifying search engines that produce relevant results, but where these results are too similar to each other.

Other Analysis (based on Results Classification)

If results classification was applied in the results collection step, further analysis can reveal whether certain types of results are more useful to the user than others. Consider, for example, results sets that feature results from weblogs. While in certain contexts (such as Web searches), these results may prove useful, in other contexts (for example, a search engine for trustworthy news), jurors may judge them as less useful. Separately calculating precision scores (or other retrieval measures) for the different kinds of results can reveal certain of these types to be more useful than others.

CONCLUSIONS AND FUTURE RESEARCH DIRECTIONS

In this chapter, a new framework was presented for measuring the retrieval effectiveness of search engines. It is hoped that the framework proves useful in designing retrieval effectiveness tests.

While the work presented in this chapter is theoretical in nature, we plan to conduct extensive empirical studies using the framework. In the past, it has been difficult to utilize all of the elements of the framework for retrieval effectiveness tests, due to the great number of elements considered and the considerable effort that would result from employing them all. However, we have since developed a software tool meant to assist such tests, which makes it possible to conduct tests using the complete framework without inappropriate effort.

A major shortcoming of the proposed framework is that it fails to take user interaction into account. Information searching is more complex than the "query-response paradigm" (used in the framework) suggests (Marchionini, 2006). Search sessions are often quite a bit longer and include query modifications. Therefore, retrieval effectiveness studies would do well to consider search sessions as well, rather than merely focusing on isolated queries (Singer, Norbisrath, Vainikko, Kikkas, & Lewandowski, 2011). While considering search sessions could over-complicate such studies, the relationship of queries and sessions should at least be modeled (Huffman & Hochster, 2007).

REFERENCES

Borlund, P. (2003). The concept of relevance in IR. *Journal of the American Society for Information Science and Technology, 54*(10), 913–925. doi:10.1002/asi.10286

Broder, A. (2002). A taxonomy of web search. *SIGIR Forum, 36*(2), 3–10. doi:10.1145/792550.792552

Buckley, C., & Voorhees, E. M. (2000). Evaluating evaluation measure stability. In *Proceedings of the 23rd Annual International ACM SIGIR Conference on Research and Development in Information Retrieval* (pp. 33-40).

Calderon-Benavides, L., Gonzalez-Caro, C., & Baeza-Yates, R. (2010). Towards a deeper understanding of the user's query intent. In *Proceedings of the SIGIR Workshop on Query Representation and Understanding*, Geneva, Switzerland (pp. 21-24).

Chu, H., & Rosenthal, M. (1996). Search engines for the World Wide Web: A comparative study and evaluation methodology. In *Proceedings of the ASIS Annual Meeting* (pp. 127-135).

Cutrell, E., & Guan, Z. (2007). *Eye tracking in MSN Search: Investigating snippet length, target position and task types.* Retrieved October 19, 2010, from http://research.microsoft.com/pubs/70395/tr-2007-01.pdf

Demartini, G., & Mizzaro, S. (2006). A classification of IR effectiveness metrics. In *Proceedings of the European Conference on Information Retrieval Research* (pp. 488-491).

Ding, W., & Marchionini, G. (1996). A comparative study of web search service performance. In *Proceedings of the 59th American Society for Information Science Annual Meeting on Learned Information* (pp. 136-142).

Dresel, R., Hörnig, D., Kaluza, H., Peter, A., Roßmann, N., & Sieber, W. (2001). Evaluation deutscher Web-Suchwerkzeuge. *Nachrichten für Dokumentation, 52*(7), 381–392.

Gordon, M., & Pathak, P. (1999). Finding information on the World Wide Web: the retrieval effectiveness of search engines. *Information Processing & Management, 35*(2), 141–180. doi:10.1016/S0306-4573(98)00041-7

Granka, L., Hembrooke, H., & Gay, G. (2005). *Location location location: Viewing patterns on WWW pages.* Paper presented at the Eye Tracking Research and Applications Symposium (ETRA).

Granka, L. A., Joachims, T., & Gay, G. (2004). Eye-tracking analysis of user behavior in WWW search. In *Proceedings of the Twenty-Seventh Annual International ACM SIGIR Conference on Research and Development in Information Retrieval* (pp. 478-479).

Greisdorf, H., & Spink, A. (2001). Median measure: an approach to IR systems evaluation. *Information Processing & Management, 37*(6), 843–857. doi:10.1016/S0306-4573(00)00064-9

Griesbaum, J. (2004). Evaluation of three German search engines: Altavista.de, Google.de and Lycos. de. *Information Research, 9*(4).

Griesbaum, J., Rittberger, M., & Bekavac, B. (2002). Deutsche Suchmaschinen im Vergleich: AltaVista.de, Fireball.de, Google.de und Lycos. de In *Proceedings of the 8th Internationales Symposium für Informationswissenschaft Information und Mobilität. Optimierung und Vermeidung von Mobilität durch Information* (pp. 201-223).

Gulli, A., & Signorini, A. (2005). The indexable Web is more than 11.5 billion pages. In *Proceedings of the Special Interest Tracks and Posters of the 14th International Conference on World Wide Web*, Chiba, Japan (pp. 902-903).

Harman, D. K., & Voorhees, E. M. (2006). TREC: An overview. *Annual Review of Information Science & Technology, 40*.

Hawking, D., & Craswell, N. (2005). The very large collection and Web tracks. In Voorhees, E. M., & Harman, D. K. (Eds.), *TREC experiment and evaluation in information retrieval* (pp. 199–231). Cambridge, MA: MIT Press.

Hawking, D., Craswell, N., Bailey, P., & Griffiths, K. (2001). Measuring search engine quality. *Information Retrieval, 4*(1), 33–59. doi:10.1023/A:1011468107287

Hennies, M., & Dressler, J. (2006). Clients information seeking behaviour: An OPAC transaction log analysis. In *Proceedings of the Australian Library and Information Association Biennial Conference*.

Hjorland, B. (2010). The foundation of the concept of relevance. *Journal of the American Society for Information Science and Technology, 61*(2), 217–237.

Höchstötter, N., & Koch, M. (2008). Standard parameters for searching behaviour in search engines and their empirical evaluation. *Journal of Information Science, 34*(1), 45–65. doi:10.1177/0165551508091311

Höchstötter, N., & Lewandowski, D. (2009). What users see – Structures in search engine results pages. *Information Sciences, 179*(12), 1796–1812. doi:10.1016/j.ins.2009.01.028

Hotchkiss, G. (2007). *Search in the year 2010*. Retrieved October 19, 2010, from http://search-engineland.com/search-in-the-year-2010-11917

Hotchkiss, G., Garrison, M., & Jensen, S. (2004). Search engine usage in North America. *A Research Initiative by Enquiro*. Retrieved March 16, 2006, from http://www.enquiro.com

Huffman, S. B., & Hochster, M. (2007). How well does result relevance predict session satisfaction? In *Proceedings of the 30th Annual International ACM SIGIR Conference on Research and Development in Information Retrieval* (pp. 567-573).

Jansen, B. J., & Spink, A. (2006). How are we searching the World Wide Web? A comparison of nine search engine transaction logs. *Information Processing & Management, 42*(1), 248–263. doi:10.1016/j.ipm.2004.10.007

Joachims, T. (2002). Optimizing search engines using Clickthrough data. In *Proceedings of the Eighth ACM SIGKDD International Conference on Knowledge Discovery and Data Mining* (pp. 133-142).

Joachims, T., Granka, L., Pan, B., Hembrooke, H., & Gay, G. (2005). In accurately interpreting Clickthrough data as implicit feedback. In *Proceedings of the Conference on Research and Development in Information Retrieval*, Salvador, Brazil (pp. 154-161).

Kang, I. H., & Kim, G. (2003). Query type classification for Web document retrieval. In *Proceedings of the ACM SIGIR Forum Information Retrieval* (pp. 64-71).

Keane, M. T., O'Brien, M., & Smyth, B. (2008). Are people biased in their use of search engines? *Communications of the ACM, 51*(2), 49–52. doi:10.1145/1314215.1340914

Korfhage, R. R. (1997). *Information storage and retrieval*. New York, NY: John Wiley & Sons.

Leighton, H. V., & Srivastava, J. (1999). First 20 precision among World Wide Web search services (search engines). *Journal of the American Society for Information Science American Society for Information Science, 50*(10), 870–881. doi:10.1002/(SICI)1097-4571(1999)50:10<870::AID-ASI4>3.0.CO;2-G

Lewandowski, D. (2004). Date-restricted queries in web search engines. *Online Information Review, 28*(6), 420–427. doi:10.1108/14684520410570544

Lewandowski, D. (2006). Query types and search topics of German Web search engine users. *Information Services & Use, 26*(4), 261–269.

Lewandowski, D. (2008a). A three-year study on the freshness of Web search engine databases. *Journal of Information Science, 34*(6), 817–831. doi:10.1177/0165551508089396

Lewandowski, D. (2008b). Problems with the use of Web search engines to find results in foreign languages. *Online Information Review, 32*(5), 668–672. doi:10.1108/14684520810914034

Lewandowski, D. (2008c). Search engine user behaviour: How can users be guided to quality content? *Information Services & Use, 28*(3-4), 261–268.

Lewandowski, D. (2008d). The retrieval effectiveness of Web search engines: Considering results descriptions. *The Journal of Documentation, 64*(6), 915–937. doi:10.1108/00220410810912451

Lewandowski, D. (2011a). The retrieval effectiveness of search engines on navigational queries. *Aslib Proceedings, 63*(4), 354–363. doi:10.1108/00012531111148949

Lewandowski, D. (2011b). The influence of commercial intent of search results on their perceived relevance. In *Proceedings of the ACM iConference* (pp. 452-458).

Lewandowski, D., & Höchstötter, N. (2008). Web searching: A quality measurement perspective. In Spink, A., & Zimmer, M. (Eds.), *Web search: Multidisciplinary perspectives* (pp. 309–340). Berlin, Germany: Springer-Verlag.

Lewandowski, D., Wahlig, H., & Meyer-Bautor, G. (2006). The freshness of Web search engine databases. *Journal of Information Science, 32*(2), 133–150. doi:10.1177/0165551506062326

Lorigo, L., Haridasan, M., Brynjarsdóttir, H., Xia, L., Joachims, T., & Gay, G. (2008). Eye tracking and online search: Lessons learned and challenges ahead. *Journal of the American Society for Information Science and Technology, 59*(7), 1041–1052. doi:10.1002/asi.20794

MacCall, S. L., & Cleveland, A. D. (1999). A relevance-based quantitative measure for Internet information retrieval evaluation. In *Proceedings of the American Society for Information Science Annual Meeting* (pp. 763-768).

Machill, M., Neuberger, C., Schweiger, W., & Wirth, W. (2003). Wegweiser im Netz: Qualität und Nutzung von Suchmaschinen. In Machill, M., & Welp, C. (Eds.), *Wegweiser im Netz* (pp. 13–490). Gütersloh, Germany: Bertelsmann Stiftung.

Machill, M., Neuberger, C., Schweiger, W., & Wirth, W. (2004). Navigating the Internet: A study of German-language search engines. *European Journal of Communication, 19*(3), 321–347. doi:10.1177/0267323104045258

Marchionini, G. (2006). Exploratory search: From finding to understanding. *Communications of the ACM, 49*(4), 41–46. doi:10.1145/1121949.1121979

Mizzaro, S. (1997). Relevance: The whole history. *Journal of the American Society for Information Science American Society for Information Science, 48*(9), 810–832. doi:10.1002/(SICI)1097-4571(199709)48:9<810::AID-ASI6>3.0.CO;2-U

Nicholson, S., Sierra, T., Eseryel, U. Y., Park, J.-H., Barkow, P., & Pozo, E. J. (2006). How much of it is real? Analysis of paid placement in Web search engine results. *Journal of the American Society for Information Science and Technology, 57*(4), 448–461. doi:10.1002/asi.20318

Nielsen, J., & Tahir, M. (2002). *Homepage usability: 50 websites deconstructed*. Indianapolis, IN: New Riders.

Pan, B., Hembrooke, H., Joachims, T., Lorigo, L., Gay, G., & Granka, L. (2007). In Google we trust: Users' decisions on rank, position, and relevance. *Journal of Computer-Mediated Communication, 12*(3), 801–823. doi:10.1111/j.1083-6101.2007.00351.x

Rowlands, I., Nicholas, D., Williams, P., Huntington, P., Fieldhouse, M., & Gunter, B. (2008). The Google generation: The information behaviour of the researcher of the future. *Aslib Proceedings: New Information Perspectives, 60*(4), 290–310.

Saracevic, T. (2007). Relevance: a review of the literature and a framework for thinking on the notion in Information Science. Part III: behavior and effects of relevance. *Journal of the American Society for Information Science and Technology, 58*(13), 2126–2144. doi:10.1002/asi.20681

Schaer, P., Mayr, P., & Mutschke, P. (2010, October 4-6). *Implications of inter-rater agreement on a student information retrieval evaluation*. Paper presented at the Lernen, Wissen, Adaptivität Workshop, Kassel, Germany.

Singer, G., Norbisrath, U., Vainikko, E., Kikkas, H., & Lewandowski, D. (2011). Search-logger -- Tool support for exploratory search task studies. In *Proceedings of the 26th ACM Symposium on Applied Computing*, TaiChung, Taiwan.

Spink, A., & Jansen, B. J. (2004). *Web search: Public searching of the Web* (*Vol. 6*). Dordrecht, The Netherlands: Kluwer Academic.

Su, L. T. (1998). Value of search results as a whole as the best single measure of information retrieval performance. *Information Processing & Management, 34*(5), 557–579. doi:10.1016/S0306-4573(98)00023-5

Sullivan, D. (2003). Searching with invisible tabs. *Search Engine Watch*. Retrieved October 19, 2010, from http://searchenginewatch.com/3115131

Tague-Sucliffe, J. (1992). The pragmatics of information retrieval experimentation, revisited. *Information Processing & Management, 28*(4), 467–490. doi:10.1016/0306-4573(92)90005-K

Vaughan, L. (2004). New measurements for search engine evaluation proposed and tested. *Information Processing & Management, 40*(4), 677–691. doi:10.1016/S0306-4573(03)00043-8

Vaughan, L., & Thelwall, M. (2004). Search engine coverage bias: Evidence and possible causes. *Information Processing & Management, 40*(4), 693–707. doi:10.1016/S0306-4573(03)00063-3

Vaughan, L., & Zhang, Y. (2007). Equal representation by search engines? A comparison of websites across countries and domains. *Journal of Computer-Mediated Communication, 12*(3), 7. doi:10.1111/j.1083-6101.2007.00355.x

Véronis, J. (2006). *A comparative study of six search engines.* Retrieved October 19, 2010, from http://www.up.univ-mrs.fr/veronis/pdf/2006-comparative-study.pdf

ADDITIONAL READING

Agrawal, R., Gollapudui, S., Halverson, A., & Ieong, S. (2009). Diversifying search results. In *Proceedings of the Second ACM International Conference on Web Search and Data Mining*, Barcelona, Spain (Vol. 10, pp. 5-14).

Ashkan, A., & Clarke, C. L. A. (2009). Characterizing commercial intent. In *Proceedings of the 18th ACM International Conference on Information and Knowledge Management* (pp. 67-76).

Baeza-Yates, R., Calderon-Benavides, L., & Gonzalez-Caro, C. (2006). The intention behind web queries. In F. Crestani, P. Ferragina, & M. Sanderson (Eds.), *Proceedings of the 13th International Conference on String Processing and Information Retrieval* (LNCS 4209, pp. 98-109).

Bailey, P., Thomas, P., & Hawking, D. (2007). *Does brandname influence perceived search result quality? Yahoo! Google, and WebKumara.* Paper presented at the 12th Australasian Document Computing Symposium, Melbourne, Australia.

Bar-Ilan, J., Keenoy, K., Yaari, E., & Levene, M. (2007). User rankings of search engine results. *Journal of the American Society for Information Science and Technology, 58*(9), 1254–1266. doi:10.1002/asi.20608

Beitzel, S. M., Jensen, E. C., Lewis, D. D., Chowdhury, A., & Frieder, O. (2007). Automatic classification of Web queries using very large unlabeled query logs. *ACM Transactions on Information Systems, 25*(2). doi:10.1145/1229179.1229183

Brooks, T. A. (2003). Web search: how the Web has changed information retrieval. *Information Research, 8*(3).

Carterette, B., Allan, J., & Ramesh, S. (2006). Minimal test collections for retrieval evaluation. In *Proceedings of the 29th Annual International ACM SIGIR Conference on Research and Development in Information Retrieval*, Seattle, WA (pp. 268-275).

Chu, H. (2005). *Information representation and retrieval in the digital age.* Medford, NJ: Information Today.

Couvering, E. V. (2007). Is relevance relevant? Market, science, and war: Discourses of search engine quality. *Journal of Computer-Mediated Communication, 12*(3), 866–887. doi:10.1111/j.1083-6101.2007.00354.x

Della Mea, V., Demartini, G., & Mizzaro, S. (2006). Measuring retrieval effectiveness with Average Distance Measure (ADM). *Information Wissenschaft und Praxis, 57*(8), 433–443.

Dou, Z., Song, R., Yuan, X., & Wen, J.-R. (2008). Are click-through data adequate for learning Web search rankings? In *Proceedings of the 17th ACM Conference on Information and Knowledge Management*, Napa Valley, CA (pp. 73-82).

Downey, D., Dumais, S., Liebling, D., & Horvitz, E. (2008). Understanding the relationship between searchers' queries and information goals. In *Proceeding of the 17th ACM Conference on Information and Knowledge Management* (pp. 449-458).

Greisdorf, H. (2000). Relevance: an interdisciplinary and information science perspective. *Informing Science, 3*(2), 67–71.

Lancaster, F. W., & Gale, V. (2003). Pertinence and relevance. In Drake, M. A. (Ed.), *Encyclopedia of library and information science* (pp. 2307–2316). New York, NY: Dekker.

Lewandowski, D. (2005). Web searching, search engines and information retrieval. *Information Services & Use, 18*(3), 137–147.

Losee, R. M. (2007). Percent perfect performance (PPP). *Information Processing & Management, 43*(4), 1020–1029. doi:10.1016/j.ipm.2006.08.009

MacFarlane, A. (2007). Evaluation of web search for the information practitioner. *Aslib Proceedings: New Information Perspectives, 59*(4-5), 352–366.

Mandl, T. (2008). Recent development in the evaluation of information retrieval systems: Moving towards diversity and practical relevance. *Informatica, 32*, 27–28.

Raban, D. R. (2007). User-centered evaluation of information: a research challenge. *Internet Research, 17*(3), 306–322. doi:10.1108/10662240710758948

Radlinski, F., Kurup, M., & Joachims, T. (2008). How does Clickthrough data reflect retrieval quality? In *Proceedings of the 17th ACM Conference on Information and Knowledge Management*, Napa Valley, CA (pp. 43-52).

Robertson, S. (2008). On the history of evaluation in IR. *Journal of Information Science, 34*(4), 439–456. doi:10.1177/0165551507086989

Sakai, T. (2003). Average gain ratio: A simple retrieval performance measure for evaluation with multiple relevance levels. In *Proceedings of the 26th Annual International ACM SIGIR Conference on Research and Development in Information Retrieval* (pp. 417-418).

Saracevic, T. (1995). Evaluation of evaluation in information retrieval. In *Proceedings of the Annual International ACM SIGIR Conference on Research and Development in Information Retrieval*, Seattle, WA (pp. 138-146).

Soboroff, I. (2006). Dynamic test collections: measuring search effectiveness on the Live Web. In *Proceedings of the Annual International ACM SIGIR Conference on Research and Development in Information Retrieval*, Seattle, WA (pp. 276-283).

Stock, W. G. (2006). On relevance distributions. *Journal of the American Society for Information Science and Technology, 57*(8), 1126–1129. doi:10.1002/asi.20359

Su, L. T. (1994). The relevance of recall and precision in user evaluation. *Journal of the American Society for Information Science American Society for Information Science, 45*(3), 207–217. doi:10.1002/(SICI)1097-4571(199404)45:3<207::AID-ASI10>3.0.CO;2-1

Turpin, A., & Scholer, F. (2006). User performance versus precision measures for simple search tasks In *Proceedings of the Annual International ACM SIGIR Conference on Research and Development in Information Retrieval*, Seattle, WA (pp. 11-18).

KEY TERMS AND DEFINITIONS

Query Description: As queries themselves are often ambiguous and/or can mislead jurors, they must be further explained if the person judging the documents in a retrieval effectiveness test is not the same person who initially posed the query. Therefore, short descriptions of the queries used in the study are generated. The aim of the query description is to describe the underlying information need.

Query Type: Queries posed to search engines can be divided into certain query types. The most popular means of distinction is Andrei Broder's classification into informational, navigational, and transactional queries, where informational queries target a results set, navigational queries target a certain (known) item, and transactional queries target an interaction on the result.

Results Screen: A results screen refers to the portion of a search engine results page (SERP) that is visible to the user without scrolling. The size of the results screen can differ from one user to the next due to monitor and/or window size.

Retrieval Measure: A retrieval measure is used to quantify a certain aspect of the performance of a search engine. Most measures used in retrieval effectiveness studies deal with the perceived relevance of the documents presented by a certain search engine. However, some retrieval measures properties of the results presented (such as the ratio of a certain document type) into account.

Screen Real Estate: The screen real estate refers to the area on the results screen that is given a certain element (e.g., a result description). When results are presented unequally, screen real estate can be used to measure the relative importance of a certain result within the search engine results page or the results screen.

Search Engine Results Page (SERP): A search engine results page is a complete presentation of search engine results; that is, it presents a certain number of results (determined by the search engine). To obtain more results, a user must select the "further results" button, which leads to another SERP.

ENDNOTES

[1] "TREC-style" refers to the test design used in the TREC ad-hoc tracks.

[2] This does not consider that a certain number of Web search engine users developed a pattern of ignoring the ads because they know that these results are advertisements. The example can be regarded as an illustration of how user perception can be directed by emphasizing certain results.

Compilation of References

Aamodt, A., & Plaza, E. (1994). Case-based reasoning: Foundational issues, methodological variations, and system approaches. *AI Communications, 7*(1).

Abney, S. (1996). Partial parsing via finite-state cascades. *Journal of Natural Language Engineering, 2*(4), 337–344. doi:10.1017/S1351324997001599

Agichtein, E., Castillo, C., Donato, D., Gionis, A., & Mishne, G. (2008). Finding high-quality content in social media. In *Proceedings of the International Conference on Web Search and Web Data Mining*.

Agichtein, E., Lawrence, S., & Gravano, L. (2001). Learning search engine specific query transformations for question answering. In *Proceedings of the Conference on World Wide Web*.

Agrawal, R., & Srikant, R. (1994). Fast algorithms for mining association rules in large databases. In *Proceedings of the 20th International Conference on Very Large Data Bases*, Santiago, Chile (pp. 487-499).

Agrawal, R., Imielinski, T., & Swami, A. (1993). Mining association rules between sets of items in large databases. In *Proceedings of the ACM SIGMOD International Conference on Management of Data*, Washington, DC (pp. 207-216).

Aguilar, F. J. (1967). *Scanning the business environment*. New York, NY: Macmillan.

Ahn, K., Alex, B., Bos, J., Dalmas, T., Leidner, J. L., & Smillie, M. B. (2004). Cross-lingual question answering with QED. In *Proceedings of the Working Notes of CLEF Cross-Language Evaluation Forum*, Bath, UK (pp. 335-342).

Ahrenberg, L., Jönsson, A., & Dahlbäck, N. (1990). Discourse representation and discourse management for a natural language dialogue system. In *Proceedings of the Second Nordic Conference on Text Comprehension in Man and Machine*, Taby, Stockholm, Sweden.

Ailamaki, A., Kantere, V., & Dash, D. (2010). Managing scientific data. *Communications of the ACM, 53*(6), 68–78. doi:10.1145/1743546.1743568

Al Ali, M., Berri, J., & Zemerly, J. (2008). Context-aware mobile Muslim companion. In *Proceedings of the 5th International Conference on Soft Computing as a Transdisciplinary Science and Technology, Context Aware Mobile Learning Workshop*, Cergy Pontoise, France (pp. 553-558).

Albert, R., & Barabási, A.-L. (2002). Statistical mechanics of complex networks. *Reviews of Modern Physics, 74*(1), 47–97. doi:10.1103/RevModPhys.74.47

Aldrich, D. F. (1999). *Mastering the digital marketplace*. New York, NY: John Wiley & Sons.

Allan, J. (Ed.). (2002). Challenges in information retrieval and langage modelling. In *Proceedings of the Report of a Workshop held at the Center for Intelligent Information Retrieval*, Amherst, MA.

Allen, B. (1991). Cognitive research in information science: Implications for design. *Annual Review of Information Science & Technology, 26*, 3–37.

Alpert, J., & Hajaj, N. (2008). *We knew the web was big...* Retrieved October 13, 2010, from http://googleblog.blogspot.com/ 2008/07/we-knew-web-was-big.html

Alrahabi, M. (2010). *EXCOM2: Plate-forme d'annotation automatique de catégories sémantiques: Conception, modélisation et réalisation informatique. Applications à la catégorisation des citations en arabe et en français* (Unpublished doctoral dissertation). University of Paris-Sorbonne, Paris, France.

Alrahabi, M., & Desclés, J.-P. (2008, August 25-27). Automatic annotation of direct reported speech in Arabic and French, according to semantic map of enunciative modalities. In *Proceedings of the 6th International Conference on Natural Language Processing*, Gothenburg, Sweden (pp. 41-51).

Amir, A., & Aumann, Y. (2005). *Maximal association rules: a tool for mining association in text*. Boston, MA: Kluwer Academic.

Anand, S. S., & Mobasher, B. (2007). Introduction to intelligent techniques for web personalization. *ACM Transactions on Internet Technology*, *7*(4), 18. doi:10.1145/1278366.1278367

Ananiadou, S., Kell, D. B., & Tsujii, J. (2006). Text mining and its potential applications in systems biology. *Trends in Biotechnology*, *24*(12). doi:10.1016/j.tibtech.2006.10.002

Anderson, C. R., Domingos, P., & Weld, D. S. (2001). Personalizing Web sites for mobile users. In *Proceedings of the 10th International Conference on World Wide Web* (pp. 565-575).

Anderson, J. Q., & Rainie, L. (2008). The future of the Internet III. *Pew Internet and American Life Project*. Retrieved March 26, 2011, from http://www.pewinternet.org/ Reports/2008/ The-Future-ofthe-Internet-III.aspx

Anh, V., & Moffat, A. (2005). Inverted index compression using word-aligned binary codes. *Information Retrieval*, *8*(1), 151–166. doi:10.1023/B:INRT.0000048490.99518.5c

Anthonisse, J. (1971). *The rush in a directed graph* (Tech. Rep. No. BN9/71). Amsterdam, The Netherlands: Stichting Mahtematisch Centrum.

Antoniou, G., & Harmelen, F. (2008). *A Semantic Web Primer* (2nd ed.). Cambridge, MA: MIT Press.

Apple Inc. (2010a, June 7). *Apple Releases Safari 5*. Retrieved April 4, 2011, from http://www.apple.com/uk/pr/library/2010/06/07safari.html

Apple Inc. (2010b). *What is Safari?* Retrieved September 20, 2010, from http://www.apple.com/safari/what-is.html

Arias, M., Cantera, J. M., & Vegas, J. (2008, August 23-28). Context-based personalization for mobile Web search. In *Proceedings of the 34th International Conference on Very Large Data Bases*, Auckland, New Zealand.

Arrington, M. (2008). *Cuil exits stealth mode with a massive search engine*. Retrieved October 13, 2010, from http://techcrunch.com/ 2008/07/27/cuill-launches-a-massive-search-engine/

Arrington, M. (2008). *Ok, now it's done. Microsoft to acquire Powerset*. Retreived from http://techcrunch.com/ 2008/07/01/ok-now-its-done-microsoft-to-acquire-powerset/

Arthur, W. B. (2009). *The nature of technology: What it is and how it evolves*. New York, NY: Free Press.

Arvola, P., Kekäläinen, J., & Junkkari, M. (2010). Expected reading effort in focused retrieval evaluation. *Information Retrieval*, *13*(5), 460–484. doi:10.1007/s10791-010-9133-9

Asadi, S., Zhou, X., Jamali, H. R., & Mofrad, H. V. (2007). Location-based search engines tasks and capabilities: A comparative study. *Webology*, *4*(4), 48.

Asanovic, K., Bodik, R., Demmel, J., Keaveny, T., Keutzer, K., & Kubiatowicz, J. …Yelick, K. (2008). *The Parallel Computing Laboratory at U.C. Berkeley: A research agenda based on the Berkeley View* (Tech. Rep.). Berkeley, CA: UC Berkeley.

Asher, N., Benamara, F., & Mathieu, Y. Y. (2009). Appraisal of opinion expressions in discourse. *Lingvisticae Investigationes*, *32*(2), 279–292. doi:10.1075/li.32.2.10ash

Ashforth, B. E., Sluss, D. M., & Saks, A. M. (2007). Socialization tactics, proactive behavior, and newcomer learning: Integrating socialization models. *Journal of Vocational Behavior*, *70*, 447–462. doi:10.1016/j.jvb.2007.02.001

Atzeni, P., Basili, R., Haltrup Hansen, D., Missier, P., Paggio, P., Pazienza, M. T., & Zanzotto, F. M. (2004). Ontology-based question answering in a Federation of University Sites: The MOSES case study. In *Proceedings of the 17th International Conference on Applications of Natural Language Processing to Information Systems* (pp. 413-420).

August, K. G., Hansen, M. H., & Shriver, E. (2002). Mobile Web searching. *Bell Labs Technical Journal, 6*(2).

Awadallah, R., & Rauber, A. (2006). Web-based multiple choice question answering for English and Arabic questions. In *Proceedings of the European Conference on Information Retrieval* (pp. 515-518).

Babin, B. J., Darden, W. R., & Griffin, M. (1994). Work and fun: measuring hedonic and utilitarian shopping value. *The Journal of Consumer Research, 20*(4), 127–140. doi:10.1086/209376

Baeza-Yates, R. A., & Ribeiro-Neto, B. (1999). *Modern information retrieval*. Boston, MA: Addison-Wesley.

Baeza-Yates, R., & Ribeiro-Neto, B. (2004). *Modern information retrieval*. Reading, MA: Addison-Wesley.

Baeza-Yates, R., & Ribeiro-Neto, B. (2011). *Modern information retrieval: The concepts and terminology behind search* (2nd ed.). Reading, MA: Addison-Wesley.

Balasubramanian, K., Kim, J., Puretskiy, A., Berry, M. W., & Park, H. (2010, May). A fast algorithm for nonnegative tensor factorization using block coordinate descent and an active-set-type method. In *Proceedings of the Text Mining Workshop held in conjunction with the Tenth SIAM International Conference on Data Mining*, Columbus, OH.

Baldonado, M. Q. W., Woodruff, A., & Kuchinsky, A. (2000). Guidelines for using multiple views in information visualization. In *Proceedings of the ACM Advanced Visual Interfaces Conference* (pp. 110-119). New York, NY: ACM

Balog, K., Vries, P., Serdyukov, P., & Thomas, P. (2010). *TREC Entity 2010 guidelines*. Retrieved October 19, 2010, from http://ilps.science.uva.nl/ trec-entity/guidelines/

Barabási, A.-L. (2009). Scale-free networks: A decade and beyond. *Science, 325*, 412–413. doi:10.1126/science.1173299

Bar-Ilan, J. (2004). The use of Web search engines in information science research. *Annual Review of Information Science & Technology, 38*, 231–288. doi:10.1002/aris.1440380106

Barlow, N. (2010, October). Prompt processing of LHC collision data with the ATLAS reconstruction. In *Proceedings of the Software International Conferences on Computing in High Energy and Nuclear Physics*, Taipei, Taiwan.

Barnum, C. M. (2001). *Usability testing and research*. London, UK: Longman.

Barr, A., & Feigenbaum, E. A. (Eds.). (1981). *The handbook of artificial intelligence* (*Vol. 1*, pp. 281–316). New York, NY: William Kaufmann.

Bates, M. J. (1979). Information search tactics. *Journal of the American Society for Information Science American Society for Information Science, 30*(4), 205–214. doi:10.1002/asi.4630300406

Bates, M. J. (1989). The design of browsing and berrypicking techniques for the online search interface. *Online Review, 13*, 407–424. doi:10.1108/eb024320

Baumgartner, R., Frölich, O., Gottlob, G., Harz, P., Herzog, M., & Lehmann, P. (2005). Web data extraction for business intelligence: the Lixto approach. In *Proceedings of the German Database Conference Datenbanksysteme in Büro, Technik und Wissenschaft*, Karlsruhe, Germany.

Bawa, M., Manku, G. S., & Raghavan, P. (2003). Sets: search enhanced by topic segmentation. In *Proceedings of the 26th Annual International ACM SIGIR Conference on Research and Development in Information Retrieval* (pp. 306-313). New York, NY: ACM.

Beal, A. (2004). *Web 2.0 - Exclusive demonstration of clustering from Google*. Retrieved December 9, 2009, from http://www.searchenginelowdown.com/ 2004/10/ web-20-exclusive-demonstration-of.html

Beaulieu, M. M., Gatford, M., Huang, Y., Robertson, S. E., Walker, S., & Williams, P. (1997). Okapi at TREC-5. In *Proceedings of the Fifth Text REtrieval Conference on Information Technology* (pp. 143-165).

Belkin, N. J. (1980). Anomalous states of knowledge as a basis for information retrieval. *The Canadian Journal of Information Science, 5*, 133–143.

Bellegarda, J. R. (2007). *Latent semantic mapping* (p. 27). San Francisco, CA: Morgan & Claypool.

Bellotti, V., Begole, B., Chi, E. H., Ducheneaut, N., Fang, J., & Isaacs, E. ... Walendowski, A. (2008). Activity-based serendipitous recommendations with the Magitti mobile leisure guide. In *Proceedings of the Twenty-Sixth Annual SIGCHI Conference on Human Factors in Computing Systems.*

Bender, M., Michel, S., Triantafillou, P., Weikum, G., & Zimmer, C. (2005). Improving collection selection with overlap awareness in p2p search engines. In *Proceedings of the 28th Annual International ACM SIGIR Conference on Research and Development in Information Retrieval* (pp. 67-74). New York, NY: ACM.

Benlamri, R., Berri, J., & Atif, Y. (2006). A framework for ontology-aware instructional design and planning. *Journal of E-Learning and Knowledge Society, 2*(1), 83–96.

Bensley, J., & Hickl, A. (2008). Application of LCC's GROUNDHOG System for RTE-4. In *Proceedings of the Text Analysis Conference*, Gaithersburg, MD.

Bernhard, D. (2010). Query expansion based on pseudo relevance feedback from definition clusters. In *Proceedings of the 23rd International Conference on Computational Linguistics: Posters*, Beijing, China (pp. 54-62).

Berry, M. W. (2009). *Exploiting nonnegative tensor factorization for scenario and plot discovery in large document sets.* Retrieved September 1, 2010, from http://www.catalystsecure.com/images/crs/articles/UVA/October/berry-presentation-4up.pdf

Berry, M. W. (2004). *Survey of text mining: clustering, classification, and retrieval.* New York, NY: Springer.

Berry, M. W., Drmac, Z., & Jessup, E. (1999). Matrices, vector spaces, and information retrieval. *SIAM Review, 41*, 335–362. doi:10.1137/S0036144598347035

Berthelin, J. B., de Chalendar, G., Ferret, O., Grau, B., ElKateb, F., & Hurault-Plantet, M. ... Vilnat A. (2003). Trouver des réponses sur le Web et dans une collection fermée. In *Proceedings of the INFORSID Workshop Recherche d'Information: un nouveau passage à l'échelle.*

Besançon, R., Ferret, O., & Fluhr, C. (2004). *Integrating new languages in à multilingual search system based on a deep linguistic analysis.* In C. Peters, P. Clough, J. Gonzalo, G. J. F. Jones, M. Kluck, & B. Magnini (Eds.), *Proceedings of the 5th Workshop of the Cross-Language Evaluation Forum on Multilingual Information Access for Text, Speech and Images* (LNCS 3491, pp. 83-89).

Besançon, R., Hède, P., Moëllic, P.-A., & Fluhr, C. (2004). *Cross-media feedback strategies: Merging text and image information to improve image retrieval.* In C. Peters, P. Clough, J. Gonzalo, G. J. F. Jones, M. Kluck, & B. Magnini (Eds.), *Proceedings of the 5th Workshop of the Cross-Language Evaluation Forum on Multilingual Information Access for Text, Speech and Images* (LNCS 3491, pp. 709-717).

Bharat, K., & Broder, A. (1998). A technique for measuring the relative size and overlap of public web search engines. In *Proceedings of the 7th International World Wide Web Conference*, Brisbane, Australia (pp. 379-388).

Bhavnani, S. K., & Bates, M. J. (2002). Separating the knowledge layers: Cognitive analysis of search knowledge through hierarchical goal decompositions. *Proceedings of the American Society for Information Science and Technology, 39*(1), 204–213. doi:10.1002/meet.1450390122

Bierig, R., & Göker, A. (2006). Time, location and interest: an empirical and user-centred study. In *Proceedings of the 1st International Conference on Information Interaction in Context* (pp. 79-87).

Bila, N., Cao, J., Dinoff, R., Ho, T. K., Hull, R., Kumar, B., & Santos, P. (2008). Mobile user profile acquisition through network observables and explicit user queries. In *Proceedings of the 9th International conference on Mobile Data Management* (pp. 98-107).

Bilal, D. (2000). Children's use of the yahooligans! Web search engine: cognitive, physical, and affective behavior on fact-based search tasks. *Journal of the American Society for Information Science American Society for Information Science, 51*(7), 646–665. doi:10.1002/(SICI)1097-4571(2000)51:7<646::AID-ASI7>3.0.CO;2-A

Bilotti, M. W. (2004). *Query expansion techniques for question answering* (Unpublished master's thesis). Massachusetts Institute of Technology, Cambridge, MA.

Birukov, A., Blanzieri, E., & Giorgini, P. (2005). Implicit: an agent-based recommendation system for web search. In *Proceedings of the Fourth International Joint Conference on Autonomous Agents and Multiagent Systems* (pp. 618-624). New York, NY: ACM.

Bishop, C. (2006). *Pattern recognition and machine learning*. New York, NY: Springer.

Blanke, T., & Lalmas, M. (2010). Specificity aboutness in XML retrieval. *Information Retrieval, 14*(1), 68–88. doi:10.1007/s10791-010-9144-6

Blei, D. M., Ng, A. Y., & Jordan, M. I. (2003). Latent Dirichlet allocation. *Journal of Machine Learning Research, 3*, 993–1022.

Boas, H. C. (2009). Multilingual FrameNets in computational lexicography: Methods and applications. *International Journal of Lexicography, 23*(1), 105–109.

Bobillo, F., & Straccia, S. (2008, May). Towards a crisp representation of fuzzy description logics under Łukasiewicz Semantics. In A. An, S. Matwin, Z. W. Raś, & D. Ślęzak (Eds.), *Proceedings of the 17th International Conference on Foundations of Intelligent Systems* (LNCS 4994, pp. 309-318).

Bobillo, F., Delgado, M., & Gomez-Romero, J. (2007). Optimizing the crisp representation of the fuzzy description logic SROIQ. In P. C. da Costa, C. d'Amato, N. Fanizzi, K. B. Laskey, K. J. Laskey, T. Lukasiewicz, M. Nickles, & M. Pool (Eds.), *Proceedings of the 3rd International Workshop on Uncertainty Reasoning for the Semantic Web* (LNCS 5327, pp. 189-206).

Boguñá, M., Krioukov, D., & Claffy, K. C. (2009). Navigability of complex networks. *Nature Physics, 5*(1), 74–80. doi:10.1038/nphys1130

Borlund, P., & Ingwersen, P. (1998). Measures of relative relevance and ranked half-life. In *Proceedings of the 21st Annual International ACM SIGIR Conference on Research and Development in Information Retrieval* (pp. 324-331).

Borlund, P. (2003). The concept of relevance in IR. *Journal of the American Society for Information Science and Technology, 54*(10), 913–925. doi:10.1002/asi.10286

Bos, J., & Nissim, M. (2006). Cross-lingual question answering by answer translation. In *Proceedings of the Workshop of the Cross-language Evaluation Forum and the European Conference on Research and Advanced Technology for Digital Libraries Conference*.

Boucon, D., Moreno, R., Heulet, D., Kopp, P., Duplaa, M., & Larroque, M. (2009). *SERAD (CNES Service for data referencing and archiving) ensuring long-term preservation and adding value to scientific and technical data*. Madrid, Spain: European Space Astronomy Centre (ESAC) ESA, Villafranca del Castillo.

Boughanem, M., & Savoy, J. (2008). *Recherche d'information: états des lieux et perspectives*. Paris, France: Éditions Hermès/Lavoisier.

Bouidghaghen, O., Tamine, L., & Boughanem, M. (2010). Contextual evaluation of mobile search. In *Proceedings of the Second Workshop on Contextual Information Access, Seeking and Retrieval Evaluation*, Milton Keynes, UK (Vol. 569).

Bouma, G. (2006). Linguistic knowledge and question answering. In *Proceedings of the Workshop KRAQ on Knowledge and Reasoning for Language Processing*, Trento, Italy (pp. 2-3).

Bouma, G., Fahmi, I., Mur, J., van Noord, G., van der Plas, L., & Tiedemann, J. (2006b). The University of Groningen at QA@CLEF 2006: Using syntactic knowledge for QA. In *Proceedings of the Workshop of the Cross-language Evaluation Forum and the European Conference on Research and Advanced Technology for Digital Libraries Conference*.

Bourdieu, P. (1990). *The logic of practice*. Cambridge, UK: Polity Press.

Bouvin, N. O., Christensen, B. G., Grønbaek, K., & Hansen, F. A. (2003). HyCon: a framework for context-aware mobile hypermedia. *New Review of Hypermedia and Multimedia, 9*, 59–88. doi:10.1080/13614560410001725310

Bovet, D., & Martha, J. (2000). *Value Nets: Breaking the supply chain to unlock hidden profits*. New York, NY: John Wiley & Sons.

Bowden, M., Olteanu, M., Suriyentrakorn, P., Clark, J., & Moldovan, D. (2006). LCC's PowerAnswer at QA@ CLEF 2006. In *Proceedings of the Workshop of the Cross-language Evaluation Forum and the European Conference on Research and Advanced Technology for Digital Libraries Conference*.

Bradley, P. (2008). *True knowledge - Questions search engine*. Retrieved from http://philbradley.typepad.com/phil_bradleys_weblog/2008/09/true-knowledge---questions-search-engine.html

Brandes, U. (2001). A faster algorithm for betweenness centrality. *The Journal of Mathematical Sociology, 25*(2), 163–177. doi:10.1080/0022250X.2001.9990249

Braschler, M., & Harman, D. (2010, September 20-23). Introduction. In *Proceedings of the Conference on Multilingual and Multimodal Information Access Evaluation*, Padua, Italy.

Brazma, A., Hingamp, P., Quackenbush, J., Sherlock, G., Spellman, P., & Stoeckert, C. (2001). Minimum information about a microarray experiment (MIAME)-toward standards for microarray data. *Nature Genetics, 29*(4), 365–371. doi:10.1038/ng1201-365

Brazma, A., Parkinson, H., Sarkans, U., Shojatalab, M., Vilo, J., & Abeygunawardena, N. (2003). ArrayExpress--a public repository for microarray gene expression data at the EBI. *Nucleic Acids Research, 31*(1), 68–71. doi:10.1093/nar/gkg091

Breton, P., & Proulx, S. (2006). *L'Explosion de la Communication. Introduction aux Théories et aux Pratiques de la Communication*. Paris, France: La Découverte.

Brill, E., Lin, J., Banko, M., Dumais, S., & Ng, A. (2001). Data-intensive question answering. In *Proceedings of the Tenth Text REtrieval Conference* (pp. 393-400).

Brin, S., & Page, L. (1998). The anatomy of a large-scale hypertextual Web search engine. In *Proceedings of the 7th International World Wide Web Conference*, Brisbane, Australia (pp. 107-117).

Bringay, S., Laurent, A., Poncelet, P., Roche, M., & Teisseire, M. (2010). Bien cube, les données textuelles peuvent s'agréger! In S. B. Yahia & J.-M. Petit (Eds.), *10èmes journées d'extraction et gestion des connaissances* (pp. 585-596). Hammamet, Tunisia: Cépaduès-Éditions.

Broder, A. (2002). A taxonomy of Web search. *ACM SIGIR Forum, 36*(2), 3–10. doi:10.1145/792550.792552

Broekstra, J., Klein, M., Decker, S., Fensel, D., Harmelen, F., & Horrocks, I. (2001). Enabling knowledge representation on the web by extending RDF schema. In *Proceedings of the 10th International Conference on World Wide Web*, Hong Kong (pp. 467-478).

Broeskstra, J., & Kampman, A. (2008, November 13-14). SeRQL: A second generation RDF query language. In *Proceedings of the SWAD-Europe Workshop on Semantic Web Storage and Retrieval*, Amsterdam, The Netherlands.

Broklova, Z. (2004). *Simulations of ATLAS silicon strip detector modules in Athena framework* (Unpublished master's thesis). Charles University, Prague, Czech Republic.

Brun, C., Campedel, M., Dessaigne, N., Gaillard, B., Guillemin-Lanne, S., & Hoogstoel, P. (2011). L'analyse sémantique au profit de la nouvelle génération de moteurs de recherche multimédia. In Campedel, M., & Hoogstoel, P. (Eds.), *Sémantique et multimodalité en analyse de l'information*. Paris, France: Hermès.

Buckley, C., & Voorhees, E. M. (2000). Evaluating evaluation measure stability. In *Proceedings of the 23rd Annual International ACM SIGIR Conference on Research and Development in Information Retrieval* (pp. 33-40).

Budiu, R., & Hielsen, J. (2009). *Usability of mobile Websites: 85 design guidelines for improving access to Web-based content and services through mobile devices*. Fremont, CA: Nielsen Norman Group.

Budzik, J., & Hammond, K. (2000). User interactions with every day applications as context for just-in-time information access. In *Proceedings of the 5th International Conference on Intelligent User Interfaces* (pp. 44-51).

Buscaldi, D., Rosso, P., Gómez-Soriano, J. M., & Sanchis, E. (2010). Answering questions with an n-gram based passage retrieval engine. *Journal of Intelligent Information Systems, 34*(2), 113–134.

Büttcher, S., Clarke, C. L. A., & Lushman, B. (2006, August 6-11). Term proximity scoring for ad-hoc retrieval on very large text collections. In *Proceedings of the 29th Annual International ACM SIGIR Conference on Research and Development in Information Retrieval*, Seattle, WA.

Calafiura, P., Leggett, C. G., Quarrie, D. R., Ma, H., & Rajagopalan, S. (2003). *The StoreGate: a data model for the Atlas software architecture*. La Jolla, CA: Computing in High Energy and Nuclear Physics.

Calais Pedro, V., Ko, J., Nyberg, E., & Mitamura, T. (2004). An information repository model for advanced question answering systems. In *Proceedings of the Fourth International Conference on Language Resources and Evaluation*.

Calais Pedro, V., Nyberg, E., & Carbonell, J. (2006). Federated ontology search. In *Proceedings of First International Workshop of Semantic Information Integration on Knowledge Discovery*.

Calderon-Benavides, L., Gonzalez-Caro, C., & Baeza-Yates, R. (2010). Towards a deeper understanding of the user's query intent. In *Proceedings of the SIGIR Workshop on Query Representation and Understanding*, Geneva, Switzerland (pp. 21-24).

Calegari, S., & Ciucci, D. (2007). Fuzzy ontologies, fuzzy description logic and fuzzy-OWL. In *Proceedings of the 7th International Workshop on Fuzzy Logic and Applications: Applications of Fuzzy Sets Theory*, Camogli, Italy (pp. 118-126).

Callan, J. (2000). Distributed information retrieval. In *Proceedings of the International Conference on Advances in Information Retrieval* (pp. 127-150). New York, NY: Springer.

Card, S. K., Mackinlay, J. D., & Shneiderman, B. (1999). *Readings in information visualization: Using vision to think*. San Francisco, CA: Morgan Kaufmann.

Carpineto, C., Mizzaro, S., Romano, G., & Snidero, M. (2009). Mobile information retrieval with search results clustering: prototypes and evaluations. *Journal of the American Society for Information Science and Technology, 60*(5), 877–895. doi:10.1002/asi.21036

Carpineto, C., Osinski, S., Romano, G., & Weiss, D. (2009). A survey of Web clustering engines. *ACM Computing Surveys, 41*(3). doi:10.1145/1541880.1541884

Carpineto, C., & Romano, G. (2004). Exploiting the potential of concept lattices for information retrieval with CREDO. *Journal of Universal Computer Science, 10*(8), 985–1013.

Carrot Search. (2010). *Circle: Interactive cluster visualization*. Retrieved September 22, 2010 from http://carrotsearch.com/ circles-overview.html

Case, D. (2002). *Looking for information: A survey of research on information seeking, needs, and behaviour*. San Diego, New York: Academic Press/Elsevier Science.

Case, D. (2006). Information behavior. *Annual Review of Information Science & Technology, 40*, 293–327. doi:10.1002/aris.1440400114

Cassidy, M., & Kulick, M. (2011). *An update to Google social search*. Retrieved from March 17, 2011, from http://googleblog.blogspot.com/ 2011/02/update-to-google-social-search.html

Caubet, A., & Verger, C. (2009). Dangers du bruit en milieu professionnel. *Réseau pédagogique de l'Université Médicale Virtuelle Francophone*. Retrieved from http://www.med.univrennes1.fr/ wkf/stock/RENNES-20090319042208molacBRUIT_module_7.pdf

Chatman, E. (1999). A theory of life in the round. *Journal of the American Society for Information Science American Society for Information Science, 50*(3), 207–217. doi:10.1002/(SICI)1097-4571(1999)50:3<207::AID-ASI3>3.0.CO;2-8

Chaudiron, S. (2004a). L'évaluation des systèmes de recherche d'informations. In Ihadjadene, M. (Ed.), *Les Systèmes de Recherche d'Informations: Modèles Conceptuels* (pp. 185–207). London, UK: Hermès.

Chaudiron, S. (2004b). La place de l'usager dans l'évaluation des systèmes de recherche d'informations. In Chaudiron, S. (Ed.), *Evaluation des Systèmes de Traitement de l'Information* (pp. 287–310). London, UK: Hermès.

Chen, C., Ibekwe-sanjuan, F., Sanjuan, E., & Weaver, C. (2006). Visual analysis of conflicting opinions. In *Proceedings of the IEEE Symposium on Visual Analytics Science and Technology* (pp. 59-66).

Chen, L.-C. (2010). Using a two-stage technique to design a keyword suggestion system. *Information Research: An International Electronic Journal, 15*(1). Retrieved from http://informationr.net/ ir/15-1/paper425.html

Chen, X., & Huang, L. (2009). The research of personalized search engine based on users' access interest. In *Proceedings of the Asia-Pacific Conference on Computational Intelligence and Industrial Applications* (pp. 337-340). Washington, DC: IEEE Computer Society.

Cheng, D., Kannan, R., Vempala, S., & Wang, G. (2006). A divide-and-merge methodology for clustering. *ACM Transactions on Database Systems, 31*(4), 1499–1525. doi:10.1145/1189769.1189779

Chengfei, L., Jianxin, L., Jeffrey, X. Y., & Rui, Z. (2010). Adaptive relaxation for querying heterogeneous XML data sources. *Information Systems, 35*(6), 688–707. doi:10.1016/j.is.2010.02.002

Chen, P. P., Akoka, J., Kangassalu, H., & Thalheim, B. (Eds.). (1999). *Conceptual modeling: current issues and future directions*. Berlin, Germany: Springer-Verlag.

Chen, Y., Teck-Hua, H., & Yong-Mi, K. (2010). Knowledge market design: A field experiment at Google Answers. *Journal of Public Economic Theory, 12*(4), 641–664. doi:10.1111/j.1467-9779.2010.01468.x

Cherfi, H., & Napoli, A. (2005). Deux méthodologies de classification de règles d'association pour la fouille de textes. In *Revue des nouvelles technologies de l'information.*

Cherfi, H., & Toussaint, Y. (2002). Adéquation d'indices statistiques à l'interprétation de règles d'association. In *Proceedings of Actes des 6èmes Journées internationales d'Analyse statistique des Données Textuelles*, Saint-Malo, France.

Cheverst, K., Davies, N., Mitchell, K., Friday, A., & Efstratiou, C. (2000). Developing a context-aware electronic tourist guide: Some issues and experiences. In *Proceedings of SIGCHI Conference on Human Factors in Computing Systems* (pp. 17-24).

Chiang, T., Chang, J., Lin, M., & Su, K. (1992). Statistical models for word segmentation and unknown resolution. In *Proceedings of the Conference on Computational Linguistics and Speech Processing* (pp. 121-146).

Chirita, P. A., Firan, C., & Nejdl, W. (2006). Summarizing local context to personalize global Web search. In *Proceedings of the ACM Conference on Information and Knowledge Management* (pp. 287-296). New York, NY: ACM

Chklovski, T., & Pantel, P. (2004). VerbOcean: Mining the web for fine-grained semantic verb relations. In *Proceedings of Conference on Empirical Methods in Natural Language Processing*, Barcelona, Spain.

Choi, H., & Varian, H. (2009). *Predicting the present with Google trends*. Retrieved June 8, 2011, from http://googleresearch.blogspot.com/ 2009/04/predicting-present-with-google-trends.html

Cho, J., & Garcia-Molina, H. (2003). Estimating frequency of change. *ACM Transactions on Internet Technology, 3*(3), 256–290. doi:10.1145/857166.857170

Choo, C., Detlor, B., & Turbull, D. (1999). Information seeking on the Web. An integrated model of browsing and searching. In *Proceedings of the ASIS Annual Seminar and Exhibits*, Dallas, TX. Retrieved June 8, 2011, from http://choo.fis.utoronto.ca/ fis/respub/asis99/

Choo, C., Detlor, B., & Turbull, D. (2000). *Web work: Information seeking and knowledge work on the World Wide Web*. Norwell, MA: Kluwer Academic.

Choosing a web browser. (2009, December 3). *Pandia Search Engine News*. Retrieved March 28, 2011, from http://www.pandia.com/sew/2335-choosing-a-web-browser.html?utm_source=feedburner&utm_medium=feed&utm_campaign=Feed%3A+pandia%2Fvfbc+%28Pandia+Search+Engine+News%29&utm_content=Google+Reader

Christensen, C. M. (1997). *The innovator's dilemma: When new technologies cause great firms to fail*. Boston, MA: Harvard Business School Press.

Chu, H., & Rosenthal, M. (1996). Search engines for the World Wide Web: A comparative study and evaluation methodology. In *Proceedings of the ASIS Annual Meeting* (pp. 127-135).

Chung, H., Song, Y. I., Han, K. S., Yoon, D. S., Lee, J. Y., Rim, H. C., & Kim, S. H. (2004). A practical QA system in restricted domains. In *Proceedings of the 42nd Annual Meeting of the Association for Computational Linguistics Workshop on Question Answering in Restricted Domains*.

Church, K., & Smyth, B. (2009). Understanding the intent behind mobile information needs. In *Proceedings of the 13th International Conference on Intelligent User Interfaces* (pp. 247-256).

Cilibrasi, R. L., & Vitányi, P. M. B. (2007). The Google similarity distance. *IEEE Transactions on Knowledge and Data Engineering, 19*(3), 370–383. doi:10.1109/TKDE.2007.48

Cimiano, P. (Ed.). (2006). *Ontology learning and population from text*. New York, NY: Springer.

Cimiano, P., Haase, P., Heizmann, J., Mantel, M., & Studer, R. (2008). Towards portable natural language interfaces to knowledge bases - The case of the ORAKEL system. *Data & Knowledge Engineering, 65*(2), 325–354. doi:10.1016/j.datak.2007.10.007

Clark & Parsia. (2004). *Pellet OWL 2 reasoner for Java*. Retrieved from http://clarkparsia.com/pellet

Clark, P., & Harrison, P. (2009). An inference-based approach to recognizing entailment. In *Proceedings of the Text Analysis Conference*, Gaithersburg, MD.

Clarke, C. L. A., & Cormack, G. V. (1997, June). Relevance ranking for one-to-three-term queries. In *Proceedings of the 5th Recherche d'Information Assistee par Ordinateur sur Internet*, Montreal, QC, Canada.

Clarke, C. L. A., Cormack, G. V., & Lynam, T. R. (2001). Exploiting redundancy in question answering. In *Proceedings of the 24th Annual International ACM SIGIR Conference on Research and Development in Information Retrieval*.

Clarke, C. L. A., Cormack, G. V., Lynam, T. R., Li, C. M., & McLearn, G. L. (2001). Web reinforced question answering (multitext experiments for TREC 2001). In *Proceedings of the 10th Text Retrieval Conference*, Gaithersburg, MD.

Clearinghhouse. (2006). *The American Heritage Dictionary of the English Language* (4th ed.). New York, NY: Houghton Mifflin.

Coady, A. (2002). *U. S. Patent No. 6,751,628: Process and system for sparse vector and matrix representation of document indexing and retrieval*. Washington, DC: United States Patent and Trademark Office.

Cochrane, G. R., & Galperin, M. Y. (2011). The 2011 nucleic acids research database issue and the online molecular biology database collection. *Nucleic Acids Research, 39*(1), 1–6.

Cohan, P. S. (1999). *Net profit*. San Francisco, CA: Jossey-Bass.

Cohen, W. W., Ravikumar, P., & Fienberg, S. E. (2003). A comparison of string distance metrics for name-matching tasks. In *Proceedings of the International Joint Conferences of Artificial Intelligence Workshop on Information Integration* (pp. 73-78).

Collaud, G. (2007, September 3). Firefox campus edition. *Le blog du Centre NTE*. Retrieved January 13, 2011, from http://nte.unifr.ch/blog/2007/09/03/firefox-campus-edition

Comas, P., & Turmo, J. (2009). Robust question answering for speech transcripts: UPC experience in QAst 2008. In C. Peters, T. Deselaers, N. Ferro, J. Gonzalo, G. Jones, M. Kurimo, et al. (Eds.), *Proceedings of the 9th Workshop on Evaluating Systems for Multilingual and Multimodal Information Access* (LNCS 5706, pp. 492-499).

Conesa, J., Storey, V. C., & Sugumaran, V. (2008). Improving web-query processing through semantic knowledge. *Data & Knowledge Engineering, 66*(1), 18–34. doi:10.1016/j.datak.2007.07.009

Constantinides, E. (2004). Influencing the online consumer's behavior: The Web experience. *Internet Research, 14*(2), 111–126. doi:10.1108/10662240410530835

Coppola, P., Della Mea, V., Di Gaspero, L., Menegon, D., Mischis, D., & Mizzaro, S. (2010). The context aware browser. *Intelligent Systems, 25*(1), 38–47. doi:10.1109/MIS.2010.26

Correa, S., Buscaldi, D., & Rosso, P. (2009). NLEL-MAAT at CLEF-ResPubliQA. In *Proceedings of the 10th Cross-language Evaluation Forum Conference on Multilingual Information Access Evaluation: Text Retrieval Experiments*, Corfu, Greece.

Costa, L. F. (2006). A question answering system in the Web using the Web. In *Proceedings of 11th Conference of the European Chapter of the Association for Computational Linguistics*.

Courtois, B. (1990). Un système de dictionnaires électroniques pour les mots simples du français. *Langue Française*, 87(1), 11–22. doi:10.3406/lfr.1990.6323

Crespo, A., & Garcia-Molina, H. (2005). Semantic overlay networks for p2p systems. In *Proceedings of the Third International Workshop on Agents and Peer-to-Peer Computing* (pp. 1-13). New York, NY: Springer.

Cristianini, N., & Shawe-Taylor, J. (2000). *An introduction to support vector machines and other kernel-based learning methods*. Cambridge, UK: Cambridge University Press.

Croft, W. B., & Harper, D. J. (1979). Using probabilistic models of document retrieval without relevance information. *The Journal of Documentation*, 35(4), 285–295. doi:10.1108/eb026683

Cui, H., Sun, R., Li, K., Kan, M.-Y., & Chua, T.-S. (2005). Question answering passage retrieval using dependency relations. In *Proceedings of the 28th Annual International ACM SIGIR Conference on Research and Development in Information Retrieval* (pp. 400-407).

Cunningham, H., Maynard, D., Bontcheva, K., & Tablan, V. (2002, July). GATE: A framework and graphical development environment for robust NLP tools and applications. In *Proceedings of the 40th Anniversary Meeting of the Association for Computational Linguistics*, Philadelphia, PA.

Cutrell, E., & Guan, Z. (2007). *Eye tracking in MSN Search: Investigating snippet length, target position and task types*. Retrieved October 19, 2010, from http://research.microsoft.com/pubs/70395/tr-2007-01.pdf

Cutting, D. R., & Pedersen, J. O. (1997, June). Space optimizations for total ranking. In *Proceedings of the Computer-Assisted Information Searching on Internet*, Montreal, QC, Canada (pp. 401-412).

Cutting, D. R., Karger, D. R., Pedersen, J. O., & Tukey, J. W. (1992, June 21-24). Scatter/Gather: A cluster-based approach to browsing large document collections. In *Proceedings of the 15th Annual International ACM SIGIR Conference on Research and Development in Information Retrieval*, Copenhagen, Denmark.

Cutting, D. R., Karger, D., Pedersen, J. O., & Tukey, J. W. (1992). Scatter/Gather: A cluster-based approach to browsing large document collections. In *Proceedings of the 15th Annual International ACM SIGIR Conference on Research and Development in Information Retrieval* (pp. 318-329). New York, NY: ACM.

Cutts, M. (2006, February 2). *Confirming a penalty*. Retrieved October 13, 2010, from http://www.mattcutts.com/ blog/confirming-a-penalty/

Daft, R. L., Sormune, J., & Parks, O. (1988). Chief executive scanning, environmental characteristics and company performance: an empirical study. *Strategic Management Journal*, 9, 123–139. doi:10.1002/smj.4250090204

Damashek, M. (1995). Gauging similarity with n-grams: Language-independent categorization of text. *Science*, 267, 843–848. doi:10.1126/science.267.5199.843

Damljanovic, D., Agatonovic, M., & Cunningham, H. (2010). Natural language interfaces to ontologies: Combining syntactic analysis and ontology-based lookup through the user interaction. In *Proceedings of the 7th Extended Semantic Web Conference*, Heraklion, Greece.

Dang, H. T., Kelly, D., & Lin, J. (2007). Overview of the TREC 2007 question answering track. In *Proceedings of the 16th Text REtreival Conference* (p. 1).

Daoud, M., Tamine, L., Boughanem, M., & Chebaro, B. (2009). A session based personalized search using an ontological user profile. In *Proceedings of the ACM Symposium on Applied Computing* (pp. 1031-1035).

Davenport, T. H., & Prusak, L. (1997). *Information ecology: Mastering the information and knowledge environment*. New York, NY: Oxford University Press.

Davis, F. D. (1989). Perceived usefulness, perceived ease of use, and user acceptance of information technology. *Management Information Systems Quarterly*, 13(3), 319–340. doi:10.2307/249008

Davison, B. D., Gerasoulis, A., Kleisouris, K., Lu, Y., Seo, H., Wang, W., & Wu, B. (1999, May). DiscoWeb: Applying link analysis to Web search. In *Proceedings of the Eighth International World Wide Web Conference*, Toronto, ON, Canada.

Day, M. Y., Ong, C. S., & Hsu, W. L. (2007). Question classification in English-Chinese cross-language question answering: an integrated genetic algorithm and machine learning approach. In *Proceedings of the IEEE International Conference on Information Reuse and Integration* (pp. 203-208).

De Boni, M., & Manandhar, S. (2005). Implementing clarification dialogues in open domain question answering. *Natural Language Engineering*, *11*(4), 343–361. doi:10.1017/S1351324905003682

de Chalendar, G., Dalmas, T., Elkateb-Gara, F., Ferret, O., Grau, B., & Hurault-Plantet, M. …Vilnat A. (2002). The question answering system QALC at LIMSI, experiments in using Web and WordNet. In *Proceedings of the 11ᵗʰ Text Retrieval Conference* (pp. 457-467).

de Chalendar, G., Ferret, O., Grau, B., ElKateb, F., Hurault-Plantet, M., & Monceaux, L. …Vilnat, A. (2003). Confronter des sources de connaissances différentes pour obtenir une réponse plus fiable. In *Proceedings of the Conference on Traitement Automatique des Langues Naturelles*, Nancy, France.

De Mey, M. (1980). The relevance of the cognitive paradigm for information science. In Harbo, O. (Ed.), *Theory and application of information research* (pp. 48–61). London, UK: Mansell.

de Rijke, M., & Webber, B. (Eds.). (2003). *Proceedings of the Workshop on Natural Language Processing for Question Answering*, Budapest, Hungary. Stroudsburg, PA: ACL.

de Saussure, F. (1913). *Cours de linguistique générale*. Paris, France: Payot.

Dean, J., & Ghemawat, S. (2004). *U. S. Patent No. 7,650,331: System and method for efficient large-scale data processing*. Washington, DC: United States Patent and Trademark Office.

Dean, J., & Ghemawat, S. (2004, December). MapReduce: Simplified data processing on large clusters. In *Proceedings of the Sixth Symposium on Operating System Design and Implementation*, San Francisco, CA. Retrieved October 13, 2010, from http://labs.google.com/ papers/ mapreduce.html

Demartini, G., & Mizzaro, S. (2006). A classification of IR effectiveness metrics. In *Proceedings of the European Conference on Information Retrieval Research* (pp. 488-491).

Demartini, G., & Siersdorfer, S. (2010). Dear search engine: what's your opinion about...? In *Proceedings of the 3rd International Semantic Search Workshop* (pp. 1-7). New York, NY: ACM.

Demner-Fushman, D., & Lin, J. (2007). Answering clinical questions with knowledge-based and statistical techniques. *Computational Linguistics*, *33*(1), 63–103. doi:10.1162/coli.2007.33.1.63

Denecker, C., & Kolmayer, E. (2006). *Eléments de Psychologie Cognitive pour les Sciences de l'Information*. Villeurbanne, France: Presses de l'ENSSIB.

Dervin, B. (1992). From the mind's eye of the user: The sense-making qualitative-quantitative methodology. In Glazier, D. J., & Powell, R. R. (Eds.), *Qualitative research in information management* (pp. 61–84). Englewood, CO: Libraries Unlimited.

Dervin, B., & Nilan, M. (1986). Information needs and uses. *Annual Review of Information Science & Technology*, •••, 3–33.

Desclés, J.-P. (2008). Towards a bridge between cognitive linguistics and formal ontology. In *Proceedings of the Twenty First International Florida Artificial Intelligence Research Society Conference*, Coconut Grove, FL (pp. 18-20).

Desclés, J. P., & Djioua, B. (2009). La recherche d'information par accès aux contenus sémantiques. In Desclés, J.-P. (Ed.), *Annotations automatiques et recherche d'informations*. Le Priol Florence, Hermes: Traite IC2 -- serie Cognition et Traitement de l'information.

Desclés, J.-P. (1997). Systèmes d'exploration contextuelle. In Guimier, C. (Ed.), *Co-texte et calcul du sens* (pp. 215–232). Caen, France: Presses Universitaires de Caen.

Detlor, B. (2004). *Towards knowledge portals: From human issues to intelligent agents*. Dordrecht, The Netherlands: Kluwer Academic.

Detyniecki, M. (2002). *Mathematical aggregation operators and their application to video querying* (Unpublished doctoral dissertation). Université Pierre et Marie Curie, Paris, France.

Ding, W., & Marchionini, G. (1996). A comparative study of web search service performance. In *Proceedings of the 59th American Society for Information Science Annual Meeting on Learned Information* (pp. 136-142).

Diop, C. T., & Lo, M. (2007). Intégration de règles d'association pour améliorer la recherche d'informations XML. In *Proceedings of Actes de la Quatrième conférence francophone en Recherche d'Information et Applications*, Saint-Étienne, France.

Djioua, B., & Desclés, J.-P. (2007). Indexing documents by discourse and semantic contents from automatic annotations of texts. In *Proceedings of the International Florida Artificial Intelligence Research Society Conference Special Talk "Automatic Annotation and Information Retrieval: New Perspectives."*

Djioua, B., García Flores, J. J., Blais, A., Desclés, J.-P., Guibert, G., & Jackiewicz, A. ...Sauzay, B. (2006). EXCOM: an automatic annotation engine for semantic information. In *Proceedings of the International Florida Artificial Intelligence Research Society Conference* (pp. 285-290).

Do you know how massive Google is? (2010). *99c Blog*. Retrieved October 13, 2010, from http://www.99cblog.com/ 4739/do-you-know-how-massive-is-google-size-infographic

Doan-Nguyen, H., & Kosseim, L. (2006). Using terminology and a concept hierarchy for restricted-domain question-answering. *Research on Computing Science, 18*.

Dobson, S. (2005). Leveraging the subtleties of location. In *Proceedings of the Conference on Smart Objects and Ambient Intelligence* (pp. 189-193).

Dörk, M., Carpendale, S., Collins, C., & Williamson, C. (2008). VisGets: Coordinated visualizations of Web-based information exploration and discovery. *IEEE Transactions on Visualization and Computer Graphics, 14*(6), 1205–1212. doi:10.1109/TVCG.2008.175

Dosseto, A., Turner, S. P., & van Orman, J. A. (2010). *Timescales of magmatic processes*. Oxford, UK: Wiley-Blackwell. doi:10.1002/9781444328509

Doulkeridis, C., Norvag, K., & Vazirgiannis, M. (2008). Peer-to-peer similarity search over widely distributed document collections. In *Proceedings of the ACM Workshop on Large-Scale Distributed Systems for Information Retrieval* (pp. 35-42). New York, NY: ACM.

Doyle, T., & Hammond, J. L. (2006). Net cred: evaluating the internet as a research source. *RSR. Reference Services Review, 34*(1), 56–70. doi:10.1108/00907320610648761

Dresel, R., Hörnig, D., Kaluza, H., Peter, A., Roßmann, N., & Sieber, W. (2001). Evaluation deutscher Web-Suchwerkzeuge. *Nachrichten für Dokumentation, 52*(7), 381–392.

Drucker, P. F. (1999a). *L'Avenir du management*. Paris, France: Ed. Village mondial.

Drucker, P. F. (1999b). *Management challenges for the 21st century*. Oxford, UK: Butterworth-Heinemann.

Dubois, D., & Prade, H. (1979). Fuzzy real algebra: Some results. *Fuzzy Sets and Systems, 2*(4), 327–348. doi:10.1016/0165-0114(79)90005-8

Dubois, J., & Dubois-Charlier, F. (1997). *Les verbes français. Expressions*. Paris, France: Larousse-Bordas.

Duff, T. (2006, April 25). A New IE Add-on Site. *IEBlog*. Retrieved April 4, 2011, from http://blogs.msdn.com/b/ie/archive/2006/04/25/583369.aspx

Dumais, S., Banko, M., Brill, E., Lin, J., & Ng, A. (2002). Web question answering: Is more always better? In *Proceedings of the 25th ACM/SIGIR International Conference on Research and Development in Information Retrieval*, Tampere, Finland.

Edgar, R., Domrachev, M., & Lash, A. E. (2002). Gene expression omnibus: NCBI gene expression and hybridization array data repository. *Nucleic Acids Research, 30*(1), 207–210. doi:10.1093/nar/30.1.207

El Amrani, M. Y., Delisle, S., & Biskri, I. (2004). Agents personnels d'aide à la recherche sur le Web. In *Proceedings of Actes de la 11ème conférence de Traitement automatique des langues naturelles*. Rabat, Morocco: GEWEB.

El Ayari, S., Grau, B., & Ligozat, A.-L. (2010). Fine-grained linguistic evaluation of question answering systems. In *Proceedings of the International Conference on Language Resources and Evaluation*.

Elias, P. (1975). Universal code word sets and representations of the integers. *IEEE Transactions on Information Theory, 21*(2), 194–203. doi:10.1109/TIT.1975.1055349

Ellis, D. (1984). Theory and explanation in information retrieval research. *Journal of Information Science, 8*(1), 25–38. doi:10.1177/016555158400800105

Ellis, D. (1992). The physical and cognitive paradigms in information retrieval research. *The Journal of Documentation, 48*(1), 45–64. doi:10.1108/eb026889

Ellis, D., & Haugan, M. (1997). Modelling the information seeking patterns of engineers and research scientists in an industrial environment. *The Journal of Documentation, 53*(4), 384–403. doi:10.1108/EUM0000000007204

Enser, P. (2008). Visual image retrieval. *Annual Review of Information Science & Technology, 42*, 3–42.

Ertöz, L., Steinbach, M., & Kumar, V. (2001). *Finding topics in collections of documents: A shared nearest neighbor approach*. Paper presented at the Actes de Text Mine Workshop of the 1st SIAM International Conference on Data Mining.

Essex, D. (2005). *Ride dolphin through Web waters*. Retrieved June 27, 2010, from http://www.pcworld.com/article/16602/ride_dolphin_through_web_waters.html

Esuli, A., & Sebastiani, F. (2006). SENTIWORDNET: a publicly available lexical resource for opinion mining. In *Proceedings of the 5th Conference on Language Resources and Evaluation*, Genoa, Italy (pp. 417-422).

Eude, V. (1998). *Modélisation de données imprécises et incomplètes dans le domaine du renseignement militaire* (Unpublished doctoral dissertation). Université Pierre et Marie Curie, Paris, France.

Evans, B. M., & Chi, E. H. (2010). An elaborated model of social search. *Information Processing & Management, 46*(6), 656–678. doi:10.1016/j.ipm.2009.10.012

Evans, P., & Wurster, T. S. (2000). *Blown to bits: How the new economics of information transforms strategy*. Boston, MA: Harvard Business School Press.

Fellbaum, C. (1998). *WordNet: an electronic lexical database (Language, speech and communication)*. Cambridge, MA: MIT Press.

Feng, S., Wang, D., Yu, G., Yang, C., & Yan, N. (2009). Sentiment clustering: A novel method to explore in the blogosphere. In Q. Li, L. Feng, J. Pei, S. X. Wang, X. Zhou, & Q.-M. Zhu (Eds.), *Proceedings of the Joint International Conference on Advances in Data and Web Management* (LNCS 5446, pp. 332-344).

Ferragina, P., & Guli, A. (2008). A personalized search engine based on Web-snippet hierarchical clustering. *Software, Practice & Experience, 38*(1), 189–225. doi:10.1002/spe.829

Ferrandez, S., Toral, A., Ferrandez, O., Ferrandez, A., & Munoz, R. (2009). Exploiting Wikipedia and Euro-WordNet to solve cross-lingual question answering. *Information Sciences, 179*(20), 3473–3488. doi:10.1016/j.ins.2009.06.031

Ferrés, D., & Rodriguez, H. (2006). Experiments adapting an open-domain question answering system to the geographical domain using scope-based resources. In *Proceedings of the Workshop on Multilingual Question Answering*.

Ferret, O., Grau, B., Hurault-Plantet, M., Illouz, G., & Jacquemin, C. (2001). Document selection refinement based on linguistic features for QALC, a question answering system. In *Proceedings of Recent Advances in Natural language Processing*, Tsigov Chark, Bulgaria.

Ferret, O., Grau, B., Hurault-Plantet, M., Illouz, G., & Jacquemin, C. (2001). Terminological variants for document selection and question/answer matching. In *Proceedings of the Workshop on Open-Domain Question Answering*, Toulouse, France (Vol. 12, pp. 1-8).

Ferret, O., Grau, B., Hurault-Plantet, M., Illouz, G., Jacquemin, C., & Monceaux, L. (2002). How NLP can improve question answering. *Journal of Knowledge Organization, 29*(3-4), 135–155.

Ferrucci, D., Nyberg, E., Allan, J., Barker, K., Brown, E., & Chu-Carroll, J. ...Zadrozny, W. (2008). *Towards the open advancement of question answering systems* (Research Report No. RC24789). Armonk, NY: IBM.

Ferrucci, D., & Lally, A. (2004). UIMA: an architectural approach to unstructured information processing in the corporate research environment. *Natural Language Engineering Archive, 10*(3-4), 327–348. doi:10.1017/S1351324904003523

Fiedler, A. M., Lash, P. B., Wong, R. M., & Tiainen, T. (2009). *The impact of individual employee difference on information seeking in today's information rich Information-Seeking Behaviors environment.* Paper presented at the International Consortium for Electronic Business (ICEB) Conference. Retrieved August 16, 2010, from http://www.ebrc.fi /kuvat/Fiedler_Lash_Wong_Tiainen.pdf

Field, H., Allan, J., & Jones, R. (2010). Predicting searcher frustration. In *Proceedings of the ACM SIGIR Conference on Research and Development in Information Retrieval* (pp. 34-41). New York, NY: ACM.

Field, D., Garrity, G., Gray, T., Morrison, N., Selengut, J., & Sterk, P. (2008). The minimum information about a genome sequence (MIGS) specification. *Nature Biotechnology, 26*(5), 541–547. doi:10.1038/nbt1360

Fischer, G., & Nurzenski, A. (2005). Towards scatter/gather browsing in a hierarchical peer-to-peer network. In *Proceedings of the ACM Workshop on Information Retrieval in Peer-to-Peer Networks* (pp. 25-32). New York, NY: ACM.

Fisher, K., Erdelez, S., & McKechnie, L. (Eds.). (2005). *Theories of information behavior.* Medford, NJ: Information Today.

Fisher, K., & Julien, H. (2009). Information behavior. *Annual Review of Information Science & Technology, 43,* 317–358. doi:10.1002/aris.2009.1440430114

Fiveash, K. (2009). *Wolfram Alpha given keys to the Bingdom.* Retrieved from http://www.theregister.co.uk/2009/11/12/bing_wolfram_alpha_deal/

Fleischman, M., Echihabi, A., & Hovy, E. H. (2003). Offline strategies for online question answering: Answering questions before they are asked. In *Proceedings of the ACL Conference*, Sapporo, Japan.

Flichy, P. (1995). *L'Innovation Technique. Récents Développements en Sciences Sociales. Vers une Nouvelle Théorie de l'Innovation.* Paris, France: La Découverte.

Flock Inc. (2010, September 17). Flock Browser—About Us. *Flock.* Retrieved September 20, 2010, from http://beta.flock.com/about

Fluhr, C., & Moellic, P.-A. (2006). *Usage-oriented multimedia information retrieval technological evaluation.* Santa Barbara, CA: MIR.

Fluhr, C., Schmit, D., Ortet, P., Elkateb, F., Gurtner, K., & Radwan, K. (1998). Distributed cross-lingual information retrieval. In Grefenstette, G. (Ed.), *Cross-language information retrieval.* Boston, MA: Kluwer Academic.

Foley, C. (2008). *Division of labour and sharing of knowledge for synchronous collaborative information retrieval* (Unpublished doctoral dissertation). Dublin City University School of Computing, Dublin, UK.

Foster, I., & Kesselman, C. (1997). Globus: A metacomputing infrastructure toolkit. *The International Journal of Supercomputer Applications, 11*(2), 115–128. doi:10.1177/109434209701100205

Fox, C. (1989). A stop list for general text. *ACM SIGIR Forum, 24*(1-2), 19–35. doi:10.1145/378881.378888

Frank, A., Krieger, H. U., Xu, F., Uszkoreit, H., Crysmann, B., Jörg, B., & Schäfer, U. (2007). Question answering from structured knowledge sources. *Journal of Applied Logic, 5*(1). doi:10.1016/j.jal.2005.12.006

Freeman, L. (1977). A set of measuring centrality based on betweenness. *Sociometry, 40,* 35–41. doi:10.2307/3033543

Frias-Martinez, E., Chen, S. Y., Macredie, R. D., & Liu, X. (2007). The role of human factors in stereotyping behavior and perception of digital library users: a robust clustering approach. *User Modeling and User-Adapted Interaction, 17*(3), 1573–1391. doi:10.1007/s11257-007-9028-7

Frost, C. O., Taylor, B., Noakes, A., Markel, S., Torres, D., & Drabenstott, K. M. (2000). Browse and search patterns in a digital image database. *Information Retrieval, 1*(4), 287–313. doi:10.1023/A:1009979200555

Fukuhara, T., Nakagawa, H., & Nishida, T. (2007). Understanding sentiment of people from news articles: Temporal sentiment analysis of social events. In *Proceedings of the International Conference on Weblogs and Social Media*, Boulder, CO. Menlo Park, CA: AAAI Press.

Fung, B. C. M., Wang, K., & Ester, M. (2003, May 1-3). Hierarchical document clustering using frequent itemsets. In *Proceedings of the Third SIAM International Conference on Data Mining*, San Francisco, CA.

Funt, P. (1998). Extracting key terms from Chinese and Japanese texts. *International Journal of Computer Processing of Oriental Languages*, 99-121.

Furuse, O., Hiroshima, N., Yamada, S., & Kataoka, R. (2007). Opinion sentence search engine on open-domain blog. In *Proceedings of the 20th International Joint Conference on Artificial Intelligence* (pp. 2760-2765). San Francisco, CA: Morgan Kaufmann.

Gaizauskas, R., Greenwood, M., & Hepple, M. (2004). Proceedings of the workshop on information retrieval for question answering at SIGIR workshop. *SIGIR Forum, 38*(2), 41-44.

Gangemi, A., Guarino, N., Masolo, C., Oltramari, A., & Schneider, L. (2002). Sweetening ontologies with DOLCE. In *Proceedings of the 13th International Conference on Knowledge Engineering and Knowledge Management. Ontologies and the Semantic Web* (pp. 166-181).

Gardner, J. (2007). *The intelligent universe: AI, ET, and the emerging mind of the cosmos*. Pompton Plains, NJ: New Page Books.

Gaudet, P., Bairoch, A., Field, D., Sansone, S. A., Taylor, C., & Attwood, T. K. (2011). BioDBCore working group. Towards BioDBcore: a community-defined information specification for biological databases. *Nucleic Acids Research, 39*(1), 7–10. doi:10.1093/nar/gkq1173

Gazan, R. (2006). Specialists and synthesists in a question answering community. *Proceedings of the American Society for Information Science and Technology, 43*(1), 1–10. doi:10.1002/meet.1450430171

Germain, M. (2010). Usager numérique et entreprise 2.0. In L. Calderan, B. Hidoine, & J. Millet (Eds.), *L'usager numérique: séminaire INRIA, 27 septembre-1er octobre 2010, Anglet*, Sciences et techniques de l'information (pp. 89-115). Paris, France: ADBS éditions.

Ghemawat, S., Gobioff, H., & Leung, S. (2003, October). The Google file system. In *Proceedings of the 19th ACM Symposium on Operating Systems Principles*, Lake George, NY. Retrieved October 13, 2010, from http://labs.google.com/ papers/gfs.html

Ghorbel, H., Bahri, A., & Bouaziz, B. (2010). Fuzzy ontologies model for semantic Web. In *Proceedings of the International Conference on Information and Knowledge Management*, St. Maarten, The Netherlands.

Ghorbel, H., Bahri, A., & Bouaziz, R. (2008, December). A framework for fuzzy ontology models. In *Proceedings of the Conference Journées Francophones sur les Ontologies*, Lyon, France (pp. 21-30).

Ghorbel, H., Bahri, A., & Bouaziz, R. (2008, March). Les Langages de Description des Ontologies: RDF & OWL. In *Proceedings of the Conference Génie électrique et informatique*, Sousse, Tunisie (pp. 597-606).

Ghorbel, H., Bahri, A., & Bouaziz, R. (2010, July) Fuzzy ontologies building method: Fuzzy ontomethodology. In *Proceedings of the Meeting of the North American Fuzzy Information Processing Society's Conference*, Toronto, ON, Canada (pp. 1-8).

Ghorbel, H., Bahri, A., & Bouaziz, R. (2010, June). *UML – Fuzzy ontologies: Towards a language for the representation of fuzzy ontologies.* Paper presented at the Meeting of Ontose, Hammamet, Tunisie.

Giacomo, E. D., Didimo, W., Grilli, L., & Liotta, G. (2007). Graph visualization techniques for Web clustering engines. *IEEE Transactions on Visualization and Computer Graphics, 13*(2), 294–304. doi:10.1109/TVCG.2007.40

Giannotti, F., Nanni, M., Pedreschi, D., & Samaritani, F. (2003, June 24-27). WebCat: Automatic categorization of Web search results. In *Proceedings of the 11th Italian Symposium on Advanced Database Systems*, Cosenza, Italy.

Gillard, L., Sitbon, L., Bellot, P., & El-Bèze, M. (2005). Dernières évolutions de SQuaLIA, le système de Questions/Réponses du LIA. *Répondre à des questions, 46*(3).

Girvan, M., & Newman, M. E. J. (2002). Community structure in social and biological networks. *Proceedings of the National Academy of Sciences of the United States of America*, *99*(12), 7821–7826. doi:10.1073/pnas.122653799

Giunipero, L. C., & Sawchuk, C. (2000). *e-Purchasing plus changing the way corporations buy*. Mantua, NJ: JGC Enterprises.

Gloeckner, I., & Pelzer, B. (2009, September 30-October 2). The LogAnswer Project at CLEF. In *Proceedings of the Working Notes for the Cross-language Evaluation Forum Workshop*, Corfu, Greece.

Gluster, F. S. (2010). *Gluster file system*. Retrieved October 13, 2010, from http://www.gluster.org

Goel, S., Hofman, J. M., Lahaie, S., Pennock, D. M., & Watts, D. J. (2010). Predicting consumer behavior with Web search. *Proceedings of the National Academy of Sciences of the United States of America*, *107*(41), 17486–17490. doi:10.1073/pnas.1005962107

Göker, A., & Myrhaug, H. (2002). User context and personalization. In *Proceedings of the ECCBR Workshop on Case Based Reasoning and Personalization*, Aberdeen, UK.

Göker, A., & Myrhaug, H. (2008). Evaluation of a mobile information system in context. *Information Processing & Management*, *44*(1), 39–65. doi:10.1016/j.ipm.2007.03.011

Golomb, S. W. (1966). Run-length encodings. *IEEE Transactions on Information Theory*, *12*(3), 399–401. doi:10.1109/TIT.1966.1053907

Gomez, J. M., Buscaldi, D., Rosso, P., & Sanchis, E. (2007, January 4-6). JIRS language-independent passage retrieval system: A comparative study. In *Proceedings of the 5th International Conference on Natural Language Processing*, Hyderabad, India.

Gómez-Barroso, J. L., Companó, R., Feijóo, C., Bacigalupo, M., Westlund, O., & Ramos, S. …García-Jiménez, M. C. (2010). *Prospects of mobile search* (Tech. Rep. No. EUR 24148 EN, Catalogue number: LF-NA-24148-EN-C). Seville, Spain: EU Joint Research Centre, Seville: Institute for Prospective Technological Studies.

Gomez-Pérez, A., Fernandez-Lopez, M., & Corcho, O. (2004). Ontology development methods and methodologies. *International Journal of Ontological Engineering*, 113-153.

Google Inc. (2010). *Google search engine*. Retrieved April 20, 2010, from http://www.google.com/ mobile/

Google Inc. (2010, January 25). Extensions, bookmark sync and more for Google Chrome. *The Official Google Blog*. Retrieved April 4, 2011, from http://googleblog.blogspot.com/2010/01/extensions-bookmark-sync-and-more-for.html

Google. (2010). *Google news*. Retrieved September 22, 2010, from http://news.google.com

Google. (2010). *Google: Zeitgeist 2009*. Retrieved July 1, 2010, from http://www.google.com/ intl/en_us/press/zeitgeist2009/overview.html

Gordon, M., & Pathak, P. (1999). Finding information on the World Wide Web: the retrieval effectiveness of search engines. *Information Processing & Management*, *35*(2), 141–180. doi:10.1016/S0306-4573(98)00041-7

Goto, N., Kurokawa, K., & Yasunaga, T. (2007). Analysis of invariant sequences in 266 complete genomes. *Gene*, *401*(1-2), 172–180. doi:10.1016/j.gene.2007.07.017

Gottgtroy, P., Kasabov, N., & MacDonell, S. (2006). Evolving ontologies for intelligent decision support. In Sanchez, E. (Ed.), *Fuzzy logic and the semantic Web, capturing intelligence* (pp. 415–440). Amsterdam, The Netherlands: Elsevier. doi:10.1016/S1574-9576(06)80023-7

Granka, L. A., Joachims, T., & Gay, G. (2004). Eye-tracking analysis of user behavior in WWW search. In *Proceedings of the Twenty-Seventh Annual International ACM SIGIR Conference on Research and Development in Information Retrieval* (pp. 478-479).

Granka, L., Hembrooke, H., & Gay, G. (2005). *Location location location: Viewing patterns on WWW pages*. Paper presented at the Eye Tracking Research and Applications Symposium (ETRA).

Granovetter, M. S. (1973). The strength of weak ties. *American Journal of Sociology*, *78*(6), 1360–1380. doi:10.1086/225469

Grappy, A., & Grau, B. (2010). Answer type validation in question answering systems. In *Proceedings of the 9th RIAO Conference on Adaptivity, Personalization and Fusion of Heterogeneous Information.*

Grau, B., Ferret, O., Hurault-Plantet, M., Monceaux, L., Robba, I., Vilnat, A., & Jacquemin, C. (2006). Coping with alternate formulations of questions and answers. In Strzalkowski, T., & Harabagiu, S. (Eds.), *Advances in open-domain question-answering: Text, speech and language technology (Vol. 32).* Berlin, Germany: Springer-Verlag. doi:10.1007/978-1-4020-4746-6_6

Green, B., Wolf, A., Chomsky, C., & Laughery, K. (1986). BASEBALL: An automatic question answerer. In Grosz, B. J., Jones, K. S., & Webber, B. L. (Eds.), *Readings in natural language processing* (pp. 545–550). San Francisco, CA: Morgan Kaufmann.

Grefenstette, G. (1999). The World Wide Web as a resource for example-based machine translation tasks. In *Proceedings of the ASLIB Conference on Translating and the Computer*, London, UK (Vol. 21).

Grefenstette, G., Qu, Y., Shanahan, J. G., & Evans, D. A. (2004). Coupling niche browsers and affect analysis for an opinion mining. In *Proceedings of the Recherche d'Informations Assistée par Ordinateur conference* (pp. 186 -194).

Greffenstette, G. (1995). Comparing two language identification schemes. In *Proceedings of Actes des 3èmes Journées internationales d'Analyse statistique des Données Textuelles*, Rome, Italy.

Gregory, M. L., Payne, D., Mccolgin, D., Cramer, N., & Love, D. (2007). Visual analysis of weblog content. In *Proceedings of the International Conference on Weblogs and Social Media*, Boulder, CO. Menlo Park, CA: AAAI Press.

Greiff, W. R. (1998). A theory of term weighting based on exploratory data analysis. In *Proceedings of the 21st Annual International ACM SIGIR Conference on Research and Development in Information Retrieval* (pp. 11-19).

Greisdorf, H., & Spink, A. (2001). Median measure: an approach to IR systems evaluation. *Information Processing & Management, 37*(6), 843–857. doi:10.1016/S0306-4573(00)00064-9

Griesbaum, J. (2004). Evaluation of three German search engines: Altavista.de, Google.de and Lycos.de. *Information Research, 9*(4).

Griesbaum, J., Rittberger, M., & Bekavac, B. (2002). Deutsche Suchmaschinen im Vergleich: AltaVista.de, Fireball.de, Google.de und Lycos.de In *Proceedings of the 8th Internationales Symposium für Informationswissenschaft Information und Mobilität. Optimierung und Vermeidung von Mobilität durch Information* (pp. 201-223).

Griffin, A., Colella, A., & Goparaju, S. (2000). Newcomer and organizational socialization tactics: An interactionist perspective. *Human Resource Management Review, 10*(4), 453–474. doi:10.1016/S1053-4822(00)00036-X

Griffith, C. (1996). Summation blaze: Litigation support at the touch of a key. *Corporate Legal Times, 61*, 12.

Griffiths, T. L., & Steyvers, M. (2004). Finding scientific topics. *Proceedings of the National Academy of Sciences of the United States of America, 101*(1), 5228–5235. doi:10.1073/pnas.0307752101

Gritsenko, V. (2011). *Daily statistics*. Retrieved March 24, 2011, from The Apache XML Project website: http://people.apache.org/ ~vgritsenko/stats/daily.html

Gross, M. (1975). Méthodes en syntaxe: régime des constructions complétives. In Schwartz, L. (Ed.), *Actualités scientifiques et industrielles (Vol. 1).* Paris, France: Hermann.

Gross, M. (1994). Constructing lexicon-grammars. In Atkins, B. T. S., & Zampolli, A. (Eds.), *Computational approaches to the lexicon* (pp. 213–263). Oxford, UK: Oxford University Press.

Gross, M. (1995). Une grammaire locale de l'expression des sentiments. *Langue Française, 105*(1), 70–87. doi:10.3406/lfr.1995.5294

Grossman, L. (2010). How computers know what we want – before we do. *Time, Inc.* Retrieved May 28, 2010, from http://www.time.com/ time/magazine/article/0,9171,1992403,00.html

Grossmann, F., & Tutin, A. (2004). Joie profonde, affreuse tristesse, parfait bonheur. Sur la predicativité des adjectifs intensifiant certains noms d'émotion. *Cahiers de lexicologie: Revue internationale de lexicologie et lexicographie*, (86), 179-196.

Gulli, A., & Signorini, A. (2005, May 10-14). The indexable web is more than 11.5 billion pages. In *Proceedings of the International World Wide Web Conference*, Chiba, Japan.

Gupta, M., Li, R., Yin, Z., & Han, J. (2010). Survey on social tagging techniques. *ACM SIGKDD Explorations*, *12*(1), 58–72. doi:10.1145/1882471.1882480

Gusfield, D. (1997). *Algorithms on strings, trees and sequences: Computer science and computational biology*. Cambridge, UK: Cambridge University Press. doi:10.1017/CBO9780511574931

Hajek, P., Havel, I., & Chytil, M. (1966). The GUHA method of automatic hypotheses determination. *Computing*, *1*(4), 293–308. doi:10.1007/BF02345483

Halavais, A. (2009). *Search engine society*. Cambridge, UK: Polity Press.

Hamon, T., & Nazarenko, A. (2001). Exploitation de l'expertise humaine dans un processus de constitution de terminologie. In *Proceedings of the International Conference on Traitement Automatique des Langues Naturelles*, Tours, France (pp. 213-222).

Hao, T. Y., Hu, D. W., Liu, W. Y., & Zeng, Q. T. (2008). Semantic patterns for user-interactive question answering. *Concurrency and Computation*, *20*(7), 783–799. doi:10.1002/cpe.1273

Harabagiu, S., & Chaudhri, V. (Eds.). (2002). *Proceedings of the AAAI Spring Symposium on Mining Answers from Texts and Knowledge Bases*, Stanford, CA. Menlo Park, CA: AAAI Press.

Harabagiu, S., Hickl, A., Lehmann, J., & Moldovan, D. (2005). Experiments with interactive question-answering. In *Proceedings of the 43rd Annual Meeting on Association for Computational Linguistics*, Ann Arbor, MI (pp. 205-214).

Harabagiu, S., Pasca, M., & Maiorano, J. (2000). Experiments with open-domain textual question answering. In *Proceedings of the 19th Annual International Conference on Computational Linguistics*, Saarbrucken, Germany.

Harabagiu, S., Pasca, M., & Maiorano, S. (2000b). Experiments with open-domain textual question answering. In *Proceedings of the 18th Annual International Conference on Computational Linguistics* (pp. 292-298).

Harabagiu, S. M., Mariorano, S. J., & Pasca, M. A. (2003). Open-domain textual question answering techniques. *Natural Language Engineering*, *9*(3), 231–267. doi:10.1017/S1351324903003176

Harb, A., Dray, G., Plantié, M., Poncelet, P., Roche, M., & Trousset, F. (2008). Détection d'opinion: Apprenons les bons adjectifs! In *Proceedings of Informatique des Organisations et Systèmes d'Information et de Décision*, Fontainebleau, France (pp. 59-66).

Harman, D. K., & Voorhees, E. M. (2006). TREC: An overview. *Annual Review of Information Science & Technology*, 40.

Hartman, A., Sifonis, J., & Kador, J. (2000). *Net-ready: Strategies for success in the e-conomy*. New York, NY: McGraw-Hill.

Hartrumpf, S. (2005). Question answering using sentence parsing and semantic network matching. In C. Peters, P. Clough, J. Gonzalo, G. Jones, M. Kluck, & B. Magnini (Eds.), *Proceedings of the 5th Workshop on Multilingual Information Access for Text, Speech and Images* (LNCS 3491, pp. 512-521).

Hartrumpf, S. (2005). University of Hagen at QA@CLEF 2005: Extending knowledge and deepening linguistic processing for question answering. In *Proceedings of the CLEF Cross-Language System Evaluation Campaign, Working Notes for the CLEF Workshop*.

Hartrumpf, S., & Leveling, J. (2006). University of Hagen at QA@CLEF 2006: Interpretation and normalization of temporal expressions. In *Proceedings of the CLEF Cross-Language System Evaluation Campaign, Working Notes for the CLEF Workshop*, Alicante, Spain.

Hattori, S., Tezuka, T., & Tanaka, K. (2007). Context-aware query refinement for mobile web search. In *Proceedings of the International Symposium on Applications and the Internet Workshops*.

Hawking, D., & Craswell, N. (2005). The very large collection and Web tracks. In Voorhees, E. M., & Harman, D. K. (Eds.), *TREC experiment and evaluation in information retrieval* (pp. 199–231). Cambridge, MA: MIT Press.

Hawking, D., Craswell, N., Bailey, P., & Griffiths, K. (2001). Measuring search engine quality. *Information Retrieval*, *4*(1), 33–59. doi:10.1023/A:1011468107287

Haylock, C. F., & Muscarella, L. (1999). *Net success.* Holbrook, NY: Adams Media.

Hazel, P. (2009). *PCRE - Perl Compatible Regular Expressions.* Retrieved July 1, 2010, from http://www.pcre.org/

Hearst, M. (1995). TileBars: Visualization of term distribution information in full text information access. In *Proceedings of the ACM Conference on Human Factors in Computing Systems* (pp. 59-66). New York, NY: ACM.

Hearst, M. A., & Pedersen, J. O. (1996). Reexamining the cluster hypothesis: Scatter/Gather on retrieval results. In *Proceedings of the 19th Annual International ACM SIGIR Conference on Research and Development in Information Retrieval* (pp. 76-84). New York, NY: ACM.

He, B., Patel, M., Zhang, Z., & Chang, K. C.-C. (2007). Accessing the deep web. *Communications of the ACM,* *50*(5), 94–101. doi:10.1145/1230819.1241670

Helft, M. (2007, September 2). In a search refinement, a chance to rival. *The New York Times.* Retrieved November 15, 2010, from http://www.nytimes.com/ 2007/02/09/technology/09license.html

Hennies, M., & Dressler, J. (2006). Clients information seeking behaviour: An OPAC transaction log analysis. In *Proceedings of the Australian Library and Information Association Biennial Conference.*

Hermjakob, U., Echihabi, A., & Marcu, D. (2002). Natural language based reformulation resource and Web exploitation for question answering. In *Proceedings of the 11ᵗʰ Text Retrieval Conference*, Gaithersburg, MD.

Herper, M. (2000). *Dolphin search's knowledge box, trawls networks.* Retrieved June 28, 2010, from http://www.forbes.com/ 2000/10/17/1017dolphin.html

Herrera, J., Rodrigo, A., Penas, A., & Verdejo, F. (2006). F. UNED submission to AVE 2006. In *Proceedings of the CLEF Cross-Language System Evaluation Campaign, Working Notes for the CLEF Workshop.*

Hey, T., & Trefethen, A. E. (2002). The UK e-science core program and the grid. In *Proceedings of the International Conference on Computational Science-Part I* (pp. 3-21).

Hey, T., Tansley, S., & Tolle, K. (2009). *The fourth paradigm: Data-intensive scientific discovery.* Redmond, WA: Microsoft Research.

Hey, T., & Trefethen, A. (2003). The data deluge: An e-science perspective. In Berman, F., Fox, G., & Hey, A. J. G. (Eds.), *Grid computing – Making the global infrastructure a reality.* New York, NY: Wiley.

Hickl, A., Lehmann, J., Williams, J., & Harabagiu, S. (2004). Experiments with interactive question answering in complex scenarios. In *Proceedings of the Human Language Technologies Annual Conference of the North American Chapter of the Association for Computational Linguistics Workshop on Pragmatics of Question Answering*, Boston, MA (pp. 60-69).

Hickl, A., Williams, J., Bensley, J., Kirk Roberts, Y. S., & Rink, B. (2006). Question answering with LCC's Chaucer at TREC 2006. In *Proceedings of the Fifteenth Text Retrieval Conference.*

Hiemstra, D. (2000). A probabilistic justification for using tf.idf term weighting in information retrieval. *International Journal on Digital Libraries, 3*(2), 131–139. doi:10.1007/s007999900025

Higashinaka, R., & Isozaki, H. (2008, January). *Corpus-based question answering for why-questions.* Paper presented at the Third International Joint Conference on Natural Language Processing, Hyderabad, India.

Hjorland, B. (2010). The foundation of the concept of relevance. *Journal of the American Society for Information Science and Technology, 61*(2), 217–237.

Hobbs, J. R., & Gordon, A. S. (2005). Toward a large-scale formal theory of commonsense psychology for metacognition. In *Proceedings of the AAAI Spring Symposium on Metacognition in Computation*, Stanford, CA (pp. 49-54).

Höchstötter, N., & Koch, M. (2008). Standard parameters for searching behaviour in search engines and their empirical evaluation. *Journal of Information Science, 34*(1), 45–65. doi:10.1177/0165551508091311

Höchstötter, N., & Lewandowski, D. (2009). What users see – Structures in search engine results pages. *Information Sciences, 179*(12), 1796–1812. doi:10.1016/j.ins.2009.01.028

Hoeber, O. (2008). Web information retrieval support systems: The future of Web search. In *Proceedings of the IEEE/WIC/ACM International Conference on Web Intelligence – Workshops (International Workshop on Web Information Retrieval Support Systems)* (pp. 29-32). Washington, DC: IEEE Computer Society.

Hoeber, O. (2009). User evaluation methods for visual Web search interfaces. In *Proceedings of the International Conference on Information Visualization* (pp. 139-145). Washington, DC: IEEE Computer Society.

Hoeber, O., & Gorner, J. (2009). BrowseLine: 2D timeline visualization of web browsing histories. In *Proceedings of the International Conference on Information Visualization* (pp. 156-161). Washington, DC: IEEE Computer Society.

Hoeber, O., & Liu, H. (2010). Comparing tag clouds, term histograms, and term lists for enhancing personalized Web search. In *Proceedings of the IEEE/WIC/ACM International Conference on Web Intelligence – Workshops (International Workshop on Web Information Retrieval Support Systems)* (pp. 309-313). Washington, DC: IEEE Computer Society.

Hoeber, O., & Massie, C. (2009). Automatic topic learning for personalized re-ordering of Web search results. In *Proceedings of the Atlantic Web Intelligence Conference* (pp. 105-116). Berlin, Germany: Springer-Verlag.

Hoeber, O., Brooks, M., Schroeder, D., & Yang, X. D. (2008). TheHotMap.com: Enabling flexible interaction in next-generation Web search interfaces. In *Proceedings of the IEEE/WIC/ACM International Conference on Web Intelligence* (pp. 730-734). Washington, DC: IEEE Computer Society.

Hoeber, O., Schroeder, D., & Brooks, M. (2009). Real-world user evaluations of a visual and interactive Web search interface. In *Proceedings of the International Conference on Information Visualization* (pp. 119-126). Washington, DC: IEEE Computer Society.

Hoeber, O., & Yang, X. D. (2008). Evaluating WordBars in exploratory Web search scenarios. *Information Processing & Management, 44*(2), 485–510. doi:10.1016/j.ipm.2007.07.003

Hoeber, O., & Yang, X. D. (2009). HotMap: Supporting visual explorations of Web search results. *Journal of the American Society for Information Science and Technology, 60*(1), 90–110. doi:10.1002/asi.20957

Hofmann, T. (1999). Probabilistic latent semantic analysis. In *Proceedings of the Uncertainty in Artificial Intelligence* (pp. 289-296).

Hori, C., Hori, T., & Furui, S. (2003). Evaluation methods for automatic speech summarization. In *Proceedings of Eurospeech* (pp. 2825-2828).

Horowitz, D., & Kamvar, S. (2010, April 26-30). The anatomy of a large scale social search engine. In *Proceedings of the 19th International World Wide Web Conference*, Raleigh, NC (pp. 431-440).

Horrocks, I., Patel-Schneider, P. F., & Harmelen, F. (2003). From SHIQ and RDF to OWL: the making of a Web ontology language. *Web Semantics: Science. Services and Agents on the World Wide Web, 1*(1), 7–26. doi:10.1016/j.websem.2003.07.001

Hotchkiss, G. (2007). *Search in the year 2010*. Retrieved October 19, 2010, from http://searchengineland.com/search-in-the-year-2010-11917

Hotchkiss, G., Garrison, M., & Jensen, S. (2004). Search engine usage in North America. *A Research Initiative by Enquiro*. Retrieved March 16, 2006, from http://www.enquiro.com

HotMap. (2010). *HotMap Web search: An interactive and visual way to explore your search results!* Retrieved September 23, 2010, from http://www.thehotmap.com

Hovy, E. H., Hermjakob, U., & Ravichandran, D. (2002). A question/answer typology with surface text patterns. In *Proceedings of the Human Language Technology Conference*, San Diego, CA (pp. 247-251).

Hovy, E., Hermjacob, U., Lin, C.-Y., & Ravichandran, D. (2001). Towards semantics-based answer pinpointing. In *Proceedings of the DARPA Human Technology Conference*, San Diego, CA.

Howie, J., & Potters, M. (2009). Industry consolidation. *Association of Litigation Support Professionals*. Retrieved August 1, 2010, from http://www.howieconsulting.com/articles/IndustryConsolidation.html

Hu, M., & Liu, B. (2004). Mining opinion features in customer reviews. In *Proceedings of the 19th National Conference on Artificial Intelligence* (pp. 755-760). Menlo Park, CA: AAAI Press.

Huffman, S. B., & Hochster, M. (2007). How well does result relevance predict session satisfaction? In *Proceedings of the 30th Annual International ACM SIGIR Conference on Research and Development in Information Retrieval* (pp. 567-573).

Hupfer, M. E., & Detlor, B. (2006). Gender and Web information seeking: A self-concept orientation model. *Journal of the American Society for Information Science and Technology, 57*(8), 1105–1115. doi:10.1002/asi.20379

Hurt, R. L., Gauthier, A., Christensen, L. L., & Wyatt, R. (2009). Astronomy Visuallization Metadata (AVM) in action. In *Proceedings of the American Astronomical Society Meeting* (Serial No. 213).

Hwang, J. D., Bhatia, A., Bonial, C., Mansouri, A., Vaidya, A., Xue, N., & Palmer, M. (2010). PropBank annotation of multilingual light verb constructions. In *Proceedings of the Fourth Linguistic Annotation Workshop*, Uppsala, Sweden (pp. 82-90).

Ifteen, A., Trandabat, D., Moruz, A., Pistol, I., Husarciuc, M., & Cristea, D. (2010). Question answering on English and Romanian Languages. In C. Peters, G. Nunzio, M. Kurimo, D. Mostefa, A. Penas, & G. Roda (Eds.), *Proceedings of the Workshop on Multilingual Information Access Evaluation I. Text Retrieval Experiments* (LNCS 6241, pp. 229-236).

Iftene, A., & Moruz, A. M. (2009). UAIC Participation at RTE5. In *Proceedings of the Text Analysis Conference Workshop*.

Ihadjadene, M., & Chaudiron, S. (2008). Quelle analyse de l'usage des moteurs de recherche? Quelques questions méthodologiques. *Questions de Communication, 14*, 17–32.

Imiliensi, A., & Signorini, A. (2009). If you ask nicely, I will answer: Semantic search and today's search engines. In *Proceedings of the 3rd IEEE International Conference on Semantic Computing* (pp. 184-191).

Ingwersen, P. (1996). Cognitive perspectives of information-retrieval interaction - elements of a cognitive IR theory. *The Journal of Documentation, 52*(1), 3–50. doi:10.1108/eb026960

Ingwersen, P., & Jarvelin, K. (2005). *The turn: Integration of information seeking and retrieval in context*. New York, NY: Springer.

Institut national des techniques de la documentation (Paris, France). (2004). Recherche d'information. In A. Boulogne (Ed.), *Vocabulaire de la documentation* (3rd ed.). Paris, France: ADBS éditions. Retrieved September 1, 2010, from http://www.adbs.fr/recherche-d-information-18313.htm?RH=OUTILS_VOC

Internet World Stats. (2010). *Internet world users by language*. Retrieved August 30, 2010, from http://www.internetworldstats.com/ stats7.htm

Ittycheriah, A., Franz, M., & Roukos, S. (2001). IBM's statistical question answering system. In *Proceedings of the 10th Text Retrieval Conference*, Gaithersburg, MD.

Ittycheriah, A., Franz, M., Zhu, W., Ratnaparkhi, A., & Mammone, R. J. (2001). Question answering using maximum entropy components. In *Proceedings of the Second Meeting of the North American Chapter of the Association for Computational Linguistics on Language technologies*, Pittsburgh, PA (pp. 1-7).

Jacquemart, P., & Zweigenbaum, P. (2003). Towards a medical question-answering system: a feasibility study. In *Proceedings Medical Informatics Europe. Studies in Health Technology and Informatics, 95*, 463–468.

Jacquemin, C. (2001). *Spotting and discovering terms through NLP*. Cambridge, MA: MIT Press.

Jansen, B. J., Booth, D. L., & Spink, A. (2007). Determining the user intent of Web search engine queries. In *Proceedings of the International World Wide Web Conference* (pp. 1149-1150). New York, NY: ACM.

Jansen, B. J., & Pooch, U. (2001). A review of Web searching studies and a framework for future research. *Journal of the American Society for Information Science and Technology, 52*(3), 235–246. doi:10.1002/1097-4571(2000)9999:9999<::AID-ASI1607>3.0.CO;2-F

Jansen, B. J., & Spink, A. (2006). How are we searching the World Wide Web? A comparison of nine search engine transaction logs. *Information Processing & Management, 42*(1), 248–263. doi:10.1016/j.ipm.2004.10.007

Jansen, B., & Resnick, M. (2006). An examination of searcher's perceptions of nonsponsored and sponsored links during ecommerce Web searching. *Journal of the American Society for Information Science and Technology, 57*(14), 1949–1961. doi:10.1002/asi.20425

Jansen, B., Sobel, K., & Cook, G. (2010). Classifying ecommerce information sharing behaviour by youths on social networking sites. *Journal of Information Science, 20*(10), 1–20.

Jansen, M. B. J., Spink, A., Bateman, J., & Saracevic, T. (1998). Real life information retrieval: A study of user queries on the Web. *ACM SIGIR Forum, 32*(1), 5–17. doi:10.1145/281250.281253

Jiang, J. J., & Conrath, D. W. (1997). Semantic similarity based on corpus statistics and lexical taxonomy. In *Proceedings of the International Conference on Research in Computational Linguistics*, Taipei, Taiwan (pp. 19-33).

Jijkoun, V., & De Rijke, M. (2004). Answer selection in a multi-stream open domain question answering system. In (Eds.), (LNCS 2997, pp. 99-111).

Jijkoun, V., Mishne, G., de Rijke, M., Schlobach, S., Ahn, D., & Muller, K. (2004). The University of Amsterdam at QA@CLEF2004. In *Proceedings of the Working Notes of CLEF Cross-Language Evaluation Forum*, Bath UK (pp. 321-325).

Jin, T. (2011, February 15). *China economic watch: Regional GDB, inflation, search market, rate hike.* Retrieved March 17, 2011, from http://www.thechinaperspective.com/ articles/chinaeconomicwatchregionalgdpinflation-searchmarketratehike8181/index.html

Joachims, T. (2002). Optimizing search engines using Clickthrough data. In *Proceedings of the Eighth ACM SIGKDD International Conference on Knowledge Discovery and Data Mining* (pp. 133-142).

Joachims, T., Granka, L., Pan, B., Hembrooke, H., & Gay, G. (2005). In accurately interpreting Clickthrough data as implicit feedback. In *Proceedings of the Conference on Research and Development in Information Retrieval*, Salvador, Brazil (pp. 154-161).

Johnson, L. (2004). *Contextual search capabilities.* Retrieved June 28, 2010, from http://www.litigation-support.org/ viewtopic.php?t=8799

Joint, M., Moellic, P.-A., Hede, P., & Adam, P. (2004). PIRIA: a general tool for indexing, search, and retrieval of multimedia content. *Proceedings of the Society for Photo-Instrumentation Engineers, 5298*, 116.

Jones, C. B. (2007). *Spatially-aware information retrieval on the Internet.* Retrieved from http://www.geo-spirit.org/ index

Jones, G. J. F., & Brown, P. J. (2004). Context-aware retrieval for ubiquitous computing environments. In F. Crestani, M. Dunlap, & S. Mizzaro (Eds.), *Proceedings of the International Workshop on Mobile and Ubiquitous Information Access* (LNCS 2954, pp. 371-374).

Jose, J. M., & Downes, S. (2005, June 7-11). Evaluation of mobile information retrieval strategies. In *Proceedings of the 5th ACM/IEEE Joint Conference on Digital Libraries*, Denver, CO (pp. 411-412).

Joshi, A., & Rambow, O. (2003). A formalism for dependency grammar based on tree adjoining grammar. In *Proceedings of the 1st International Conference on Meaning-Text Theory.*

Joshi, A., & Jiang, Z. (2002). Retriever improving web search engine results using clustering. In Gangopadhyay, A. (Ed.), *Managing business with electronic commerce: Issues and trends.* Hershey, PA: Idea Group.

Jurafsky, D., & Martin, J. H. (2008). *Speech and language processing* (2nd ed.). Upper Saddle River, NJ: Prentice Hall.

Jurafsky, D., & Martin, J. H. (2009). *Speech and language processing: An introduction to natural language processing, computational linguistics, and speech recognition* (2nd ed., pp. 650–651). Upper Saddle River, NJ: Pearson/Prentice Hall.

Kahane, S. (2001). Grammaires de dépendance formelles et théorie Sens-Text. In *Proceedings of the Tutoriel Actes Traitement Automatique des Langues Naturelles* (Vol. 2).

Kalakota, D. R., & Robinson, M. (1999). *e-Business: Roadmap for success*. Reading, MA: Addison-Wesley.

Kamps, J., Marx, M., Mokken, R., & de Rijke, M. (2004). Using WordNet to measure semantic orientation of adjectives. In *Proceedings of the 4th International Conference on Language Resources and Evaluation*, Biarritz, France (pp. 174-181).

Kamvar, M., & Baluja, S. (2007b). The role of context in query input: Using contextual signals to complete queries on mobile devices. In *Proceedings of the 9th International Conference on Human Computer Interaction with Mobile Devices and Services* (pp. 405-412).

Kamvar, M., & Baluja, S. (2007a). Deciphering trends in mobile search. *Computer, 40*(8), 58–62. doi:10.1109/MC.2007.270

Kang, I. H., & Kim, G. (2003). Query type classification for Web document retrieval. In *Proceedings of the ACM SIGIR Forum Information Retrieval* (pp. 64-71).

Kanungo, T., Mount, D., Netanyahu, N., Piatko, C., Silverman, R., & Wu, A. (2002). An efficient k-means clustering algorithm: Analysis and implementation. *IEEE Transactions on Pattern Analysis and Machine Intelligence, 24*, 881–892. doi:10.1109/TPAMI.2002.1017616

Kapur, S., Parikh, J., & Joshi, D. (2004). *U. S. Patent Application No. 20050080795: Systems and methods for search processing using superunits*. Washington, DC: Untied States Patent and Trademark Office.

Karaman, F., & Yamamoto, G. T. (2007). Controlling the pace and direction of technological change. *E-Business Review, 7*.

Katz, B., & Lin, J. (2003). Selectively using relations to improve precision in question answering. In *Proceedings of the EACL Workshop on Natural Language Processing for Question Answering*.

Katz, B., Lin, J., Loreto, D., Hildebrandt, W., Bilotti, M., & Felshin, S. …Mora, F. (2003). Integrating Web-based and corpus-based techniques for question answering. In *Proceedings of the Twelfth Text Retrieval Conference*.

Kaufmann, E., Bernstein, A., & Fischer, L. (2007). NLP-Reduce: A "naive" but domain-independent natural language interface for querying ontologies. In *Proceedings of the 4th European Semantic Web Conference*, Innsbruck, Austria.

Ke, W. (2010). *Scalability of findability: Decentralized search and retrieval in large information networks* (Unpublished master's thesis). School of Information and Library Science, The University of North Carolina, Chapel Hill, NC.

Ke, W., & Mostafa, J. (2009). Strong ties vs. weak ties: Studying the clustering paradox for decentralized search. In *Proceedings of the 7th Workshop on Large-Scale Distributed Systems for Information Retrieval, in conjunction with the 32nd Annual International ACM SIGIR Conference on Research and Development in Information Retrieval*, Boston, MA (pp. 49-56). New York, NY: ACM.

Ke, W., & Mostafa, J. (2010). Scalability of findability: effective and efficient IR operations in large information networks. In *Proceeding of the 33rd International ACM SIGIR Conference on Research and Development in Information Retrieval* (pp. 74-81). New York, NY: ACM.

Ke, W., Sugimoto, C. R., & Mostafa, J. (2009). Dynamicity vs. effectiveness: Studying online clustering for Scatter/Gather. In *Proceedings of the 32th Annual International ACM SIGIR Conference on Research and Development in Information Retrieval*, Boston, MA (pp. 19-26). New York, NY: ACM.

Keane, M. T., O'Brien, M., & Smyth, B. (2008). Are people biased in their use of search engines? *Communications of the ACM, 51*(2), 49–52. doi:10.1145/1314215.1340914

Keenoy, K., & Levene, M. (2003). Personalisation of web search. In *Proceedings of the IJCAI Workshop on Intelligent Techniques for Web Personalization*, Acapulco, Mexico (pp. 201-228).

Kerbrat-Orecchioni, C. (1980). *L'Énonciation - De la subjectivité dans le langage*. Paris, France: Armand Colin.

Kesmodel, D. (2005, September 22). Sites get dropped by search engines after trying to 'optimize' rankings. *Wall Street Journal*. Retrieved October 13, 2010, from http://online.wsj.com/ article/SB112714166978744925.html

Khulthau, C. (1993). *Seeking meaning: a process approach to library and information services*. Norwood, MA: Ablex.

Kim, S., & Hovy, E. (2006). Extracting opinions, opinion holders, and topics expressed in online news media text. In *Proceedings of the Coling-ACL Workshop on Sentiment and Subjectivity in Text*, Sydney, Australia (pp. 1-8).

Kim, Y. A., & Srivastava, J. (2007, August 19-22). Impact of social influence in e-commerce decision making. In *Proceedings of the 9th International Conference on Electronic Commerce* (pp. 293-301).

Kim, K. (2008). Effects of emotion control and task on web searching behavior. *Information Processing & Management, 44*(1), 373–385. doi:10.1016/j.ipm.2006.11.008

King, A. (2008). *The average Web page*. Retrieved March 17, 2011, from http://www.optimizationweek.com/ reviews/average-web-page/

Kintsch, W. (1998). *Comprehension: A paradigm for cognition*. New York, NY: Cambridge University Press.

Kiryakov, A., Popov, B., Terziev, I., Manov, D., & Ognyanoff, D. (2004). Semantic annotation, indexing and retrieval. *Journal of Web Semantics: Science. Services and Agents on the World Wide Web, 2*, 49–79. doi:10.1016/j.websem.2004.07.005

Kitajima, M., Blackmon, H., & Polson, P. (2000). A comprehension-based model of Web navigation and its application to Web usability analysis. In *Proceedings of the 15th Conference on People and Computers - Usability or Else!* (pp. 337-57).

Kjeldskov, J., & Graham, C. (2003). A review of mobile HCI research method. In *Proceedings of the 5th International Symposium Human Computer Interaction with Mobile Devices and Services* (pp. 317-335).

Klein, D., & Manning, C. D. (2003). Accurate unlexicalized parsing. In *Proceedings of the 41st Meeting of the Association for Computational Linguistics* (pp. 423-430).

Kleinberg, J. M. (2006). Social networks, incentives, and search. In *Proceedings of the 29th Annual International ACM SIGIR Conference on Research and Development in Information Retrieval* (pp. 210-211). New York, NY: ACM.

Kleinberg, J. (1999). Authoritative sources in a hyperlinked environment. *Journal of the ACM, 46*(5), 604–632. doi:10.1145/324133.324140

Kleinberg, J. M. (2000). Navigation in a small world. *Nature, 406*(6798). doi:10.1038/35022643

Koenig, P., & Melançon, G. (2008). Dagmap: exploration interactive de relations d'héritage. *Revue d'Intelligence Artificielle, 22*(1), 353–368. doi:10.3166/ria.22.353-368

Kokinov, B., & French, R. M. (2003). Computational models of analogy making. In Nadel, L. (Ed.), *Encyclopedia of conginitve science* (Vol. 1, pp. 113–118). London, UK: Nature Publishing.

Konchady, M. (2008). *Building search applications. A practical guide to building search applications using open source software*. UK: Mustru.

Kondekar, V. H., Kolkure, V. S., & Kore, S. N. (2010). Image retrieval techniques based on image features: A state of art approach for CBIR. *International Journal of Computer Science and Information Security, 7*(1), 69–76.

Konopík, M., & Rohlík, O. (2010). Question answering for not yet semantic Web. In P. Sojka, A. Horák, I. Kopecek, & K. Pala (Eds.), *Proceedings of the 13th International Conference on Text, Speech and Dialogue* (LNCS 6231, pp. 125-132).

Korfhage, R. R. (1997). *Information storage and retrieval*. New York, NY: John Wiley & Sons.

Kosseim, L., Plamondon, L., & Guillemette, L. (2003). Answer formulation for question-answering. In Y. Xiang & B. Chaib-draa (Eds.), *Proceedings of the 16th Canadian Society for Computational Studies of Intelligence Conference on Advances in Artificial Intelligence* (LNCS 2671, pp. 24-34).

Kosseim, L., & Yousefi, J. (2008). Improving the performance of question answering with semantically equivalent answer patterns. *Data & Knowledge Engineering, 66*, 63–67. doi:10.1016/j.datak.2007.07.010

Kotkin, J. (2000). *The new geography: How the digital revolution is reshaping the American landscape*. New York, NY: Random House.

Kotle, P., Filiatrault, P., & Turner, R. (2000). *Marketing management*. Montréal, QC, Canada: Edition Gaëtan Morin.

Kouylekov, M., Negri, M., Magnini, B., & Coppola, B. (2006). Towards entailment-based question answering: ITC-irst at CLEF 2006. In *Proceedings of the Working Notes for the CLEF Workshop*.

Kuglin, F. A., & Rosenbaum, B. A. (2001). *The supply chain network @ Internet speed: Preparing your company for the e-commerce revolution*. New York, NY: Amacom, American Management Association.

Kules, B., Kustanowitz, J., & Shneiderman, B. (2006). Categorizing Web search results into meaningful and stable categories using fast-feature techniques. In *Proceedings of the ACM/IEEE-CS Joint Conference on Digital Libraries* (pp. 210-219). New York, NY: ACM.

Kulviwat, S., Gu, C., & Engchanil, N. (2004). Determinants of online information search: a critical review and assessment. *Internet Research*, *14*(3), 245–253. doi:10.1108/10662240410542670

Kurata, G., Okazaki, N., & Ishizuka, M. (2004). GDQA: Graph driven question answering system - NTCIR-4 QAC2 experiments. In *Proceedings of the Working Notes of the Fourth NTCIR Workshop Meeting*, Tokyo, Japan (pp. 338-344).

Kurauskas, V., & Šileikis, M. (2006). *Wrapping persistent ROOT framework objects in an object-oriented mediator system* (Unpublished master's thesis). University of Uppsala, Uppsala, Sweden.

Kurzweil, R. (1999). *The age of spiritual machines: When computers exceed human intelligence*. New York, NY: Penguin Books.

Kurzweil, R. (2005). *The singularity is near: When humans transcend biology*. New York, NY: Penguin Books.

Kwok, C. C. T., Etzioni, O., & Weld, D. S. (2001). Scaling question answering to the Web. In *Proceedings of the Conference of World Wide Web*.

Lallich, S., & Teytaud, O. (2003). Évaluation et validation de l'intérêt des règles d'association. In *Revue des nouvelles Technologies de l'information*.

Landauer, T., Foltz, P. W., & Laham, D. (1998). Introduction to latent semantic analysis. *Discourse Processes*, *25*, 259–284. doi:10.1080/01638539809545028

Landauer, T., McNamara, D., Dennis, S., & Kintsch, W. (Eds.). (2007). *Handbook of latent semantic analysis*. Mahwah, NJ: Lawrence Erlbaum.

Lang, K. (1995). NewsWeeder: learning to filter Netnews. In *Proceedings of the 12th International Conference on Machine Learning* (pp. 331-339).

Langville, A. N., & Meyer, C. D. (2006). *Google's PageRank and beyond: The science of search engine rankings*. Princeton, NJ: Princeton University Press.

Laouamer, L., Biskri, I., & Houmadi, B. (2005). Towards an automatic classification of images: Approach by the n-grams. In *Proceedings of the World Multiconference on Systemics, Cybernetics and Informatics*, Orlando, FL.

Lari, K., & Young, S. J. (1990). The estimation of stochastic context-free grammars using the inside-outside algorithm. *Computer Speech & Language*, *4*, 35–56. doi:10.1016/0885-2308(90)90022-X

Lari, K., & Young, S. J. (1991). Applications of stochastic context-free grammars using the inside-outside algorithm. *Computer Speech & Language*, *5*, 237–257. doi:10.1016/0885-2308(91)90009-F

Larosa, S., Penarrubia, J., Rosso, P., & Montes, M. (2005, September 26-30). Cross-language question answering: The key role of translation. In *Proceedings Avances en la Ciencia de la Computación, VI ENCuentro Int. de Computación*, Puebla, Mexico (pp. 131-135).

Lassalle, E. (2011). Acquisition Automatique de Terminologie à partir de Corpus de Texte. In *Proceedings of the Tutoriel Actes Traitement Automatique des Langues Naturelles*.

Laurent, D., Nègre, S., & Séguéla, P. (2005). QRISTAL, le QR à l'épreuve du public. *Répondre à des questions, 46*(3).

Laurent, D., Séguéla, P., & Nègre, S. (2005). Cross lingual question answering using QRISTAL for CLEF 2005. In *Proceedings of the Working Notes of CLEF Cross-Language Evaluation Forum*, Vienna, Austria.

Lawrence, S., & Giles, C. L. (1999). Accessibility of information on the web. *Nature, 400,* 107–109. doi:10.1038/21987

Le Deuff, O. (2006, November 23). Autorité et pertinence vs popularité et influence: réseaux sociaux sur Internet et mutations institutionnelles (Popularity takes the place of authority, whereas influence replaces relevance). *HAL: Hyper Articles en Ligne.* Retrieved April 3, 2011, from http://hal.archives-ouvertes.fr/sic_00122603

Le Novère, N., Bornstein, B., Broicher, A., Courtot, M., Donizelli, M., & Dharuri, H. (2006). BioModels database: a free, centralized database of curated, published, quantitative kinetic models of biochemical and cellular systems. *Nucleic Acids Research, 34*(1), 689–691. doi:10.1093/nar/gkj092

Le Parc-Lacayrelle, A., Gaio, M., & Sallaberry, C. (2007). La composante temps dans l'information géographique textuelle Extraction et recherche d'information dans des fonds documentaires patrimoniaux numérisés. *Document Numérique, 10,* 129–148. doi:10.3166/dn.10.2.129-148

Leckie, G. J., Pettigrew, K. E., & Sylvain, C. (1996). Modelling the information seeking of professionals: a general model derived from research on engineers, health care professionals, and lawyers. *The Library Quarterly, 66*(2), 161–193. doi:10.1086/602864

Lee, D. D., & Seung, H. S. (2001). Algorithms for non-negative matrix factorization. In *Proceedings of the Conference on Advances in Neural Information Processing Systems.* Kontostathis, A., Moulding, E., & Spiteri, R. J. (2010, May). EDLSI with PSVD updating. In *Proceedings of the Text Mining Workshop held in conjunction with the Tenth SIAM International Conference on Data Mining,* Columbus, OH.

Lee, H., Ferguson, P., O'Hare, N., Gurrin, C., & Smeaton, A. F. (2010). Integrating interactivity into visualizing sentiment analysis of blogs. In *Proceedings of the First International Workshop on Intelligent Visual Interfaces for Text Analysis,* Honk Kong, China (pp. 17-20). New York, NY: ACM.

Lee, D., & Seung, H. S. (1999). Learning the parts of objects by non-negative matrix factorization. *Nature, 401,* 788–791. doi:10.1038/44565

Lee, S., & Choi, K.-S. (1999). *A reestimation algorithm for probabilistic dependency grammars.* Cambridge, UK: Cambridge University Press.

Lehmann, F. (Ed.). (1992). *Semantic networks.* Oxford, UK: Pergamon Press.

Lehnert, W. (1977). Human and computational question answering. *Cognitive Science, 1,* 47–63. doi:10.1207/s15516709cog0101_3

Leidner, J. L. (2003). Current issues in software engineering for natural language processing. In *Proceedings of the HLT-NAACL Workshop on Software Engineering and Architecture of Language Technology Systems,* Edmonton, AB, Canada (pp. 45-50).

Leighton, H. V., & Srivastava, J. (1999). First 20 precision among World Wide Web search services (search engines). *Journal of the American Society for Information Science American Society for Information Science, 50*(10), 870–881. doi:10.1002/(SICI)1097-4571(1999)50:10<870::AID-ASI4>3.0.CO;2-G

Lenat, D., & Guha, R. V. (1990). *Building large knowledge-based systems: Representation and inference in the Cyc Project.* Reading, MA: Addison-Wesley.

Lerman, K., Getoor, L., Minton, S., & Knoblock, C. A. (2004). Using the structure of web sites for automatic segmentation of tables. In *Proceedings of the ACM SIGMOD International Conference on Management of Data.*

Lewandowski, D. (2011b). The influence of commercial intent of search results on their perceived relevance. In *Proceedings of the ACM iConference* (pp. 452-458).

Lewandowski, D. (2004). Date-restricted queries in web search engines. *Online Information Review, 28*(6), 420–427. doi:10.1108/14684520410570544

Lewandowski, D. (2006). Query types and search topics of German Web search engine users. *Information Services & Use, 26*(4), 261–269.

Lewandowski, D. (2008a). A three-year study on the freshness of Web search engine databases. *Journal of Information Science, 34*(6), 817–831. doi:10.1177/0165551508089396

Lewandowski, D. (2008b). Problems with the use of Web search engines to find results in foreign languages. *Online Information Review*, *32*(5), 668–672. doi:10.1108/14684520810914034

Lewandowski, D. (2008c). Search engine user behaviour: How can users be guided to quality content? *Information Services & Use*, *28*(3-4), 261–268.

Lewandowski, D. (2008d). The retrieval effectiveness of Web search engines: Considering results descriptions. *The Journal of Documentation*, *64*(6), 915–937. doi:10.1108/00220410810912451

Lewandowski, D. (2011a). The retrieval effectiveness of search engines on navigational queries. *Aslib Proceedings*, *63*(4), 354–363. doi:10.1108/00012531111148949

Lewandowski, D., & Höchstötter, N. (2008). Web searching: A quality measurement perspective. In Spink, A., & Zimmer, M. (Eds.), *Web search: Multidisciplinary perspectives* (pp. 309–340). Berlin, Germany: Springer-Verlag.

Lewandowski, D., Wahlig, H., & Meyer-Bautor, G. (2006). The freshness of Web search engine databases. *Journal of Information Science*, *32*(2), 133–150. doi:10.1177/0165551506062326

Li, X., & Croft, W. B. (2001, March 18-20). Evaluating question answering techniques in Chinese. In *Proceedings of Human Language Technology Conference*, San Diego, CA (pp. 201-206).

Liben-Nowell, D., Novak, J., Kumar, R., Raghavan, P., & Tomkins, A. (2005). Geographic routing in social networks. *Proceedings of the National Academy of Sciences of the United States of America*, *102*(33), 11623–11628. doi:10.1073/pnas.0503018102

Ligozat, A.-L., Grau, B., Robba, I., & Vilnat, A. (2006a). L'extraction des réponses dans un système de question-réponse. In *Proceedings of la Conférence sur le Traitement Automatique des Langues Naturelles*, Leuven, France.

Ligozat, A.-L., Grau, B., Robba, I., & Vilnat, A. (2006b). Evaluation and improvement of cross-lingual question answering strategies. In *Proceedings of the Workshop on Multilingual Question Answering* (pp. 23-30).

Ligozat, A.-L., Grau, B., Vilnat, A., Robba, I., & Grappy, A. (2007). Towards an automatic validation of answers in Question Answering. In *Proceedings of the 19th IEEE International Conference on Tools with Artificial Intelligence* (Vol. 2, pp. 444-447).

Lin, C. X., Ding, B., Han, J., Zhu, F., & Zhao, B. (2008). Text cube: Computing IR measures for multidimensional text database analysis. In *Proceedings of the IEEE International Conference on Data Mining* (pp. 905-910). Washington, DC: IEEE Computer Society.

Lin, J., & Katz, B. (2003). Question answering from the Web using knowledge annotation and knowledge mining Techniques. In *Proceedings of the ACM Conference on Information and Knowledge Management.*

Liu, B., Hu, M., & Cheng, J. (2005). Opinion observer: analyzing and comparing opinions on the Web. In *Proceedings of the 14th International Conference on World Wide Web*, Chiba, Japan (pp. 342-351). New York, NY: ACM.

Li, X., & Roth, D. (2006). Learning question classifiers: the role of semantic information. *Natural Language Engineering*, *12*(3), 229–249. doi:10.1017/S1351324905003955

Llopis, F., & Vicedo, J. (2002). IR-n: A passage retrieval system at CLEF-2001. In C. Peters, M. Braschler, J. Gonzalo, & M. Kluck (Eds), *Proceedings of the Second Workshop on Evaluation of Cross-Language Information Retrieval Systems* (LNCS 2406, pp. 1211-1231).

Loke, S. (2007). *Context-aware pervasive systems. Architectures for a new breed of applications*. Boca Raton, FL: Auerbach.

Lopez, V., Motta, E., & Uren, V. (2006). AquaLog: An ontology-driven question answering system to interface the semantic Web. In *Proceedings of the Human Language Technology Conference of the NAACL, Companion Volume: Demonstrations* (pp. 269-272).

Lopez, V., Pasin, M., & Motta, E. (2005). AquaLog: An ontology-portable question answering system for the semantic Web. In *Proceedings of the European Semantic Web Conference.*

Lopez, V., Uren, V., Motta, E., & Pasin, M. (2007). Aqua-Log: An ontology-driven question answering system for organizational semantic intranets. *Web Semantics: Science. Services and Agents on the World Wide Web, 5*(2), 72–105. doi:10.1016/j.websem.2007.03.003

Lorigo, L., Haridasan, M., Brynjarsdóttir, H., Xia, L., Joachims, T., & Gay, G. (2008). Eye tracking and online search: Lessons learned and challenges ahead. *Journal of the American Society for Information Science and Technology, 59*(7), 1041–1052. doi:10.1002/asi.20794

Losada, D. (2010). Statistical query expansion for sentence retrieval and its effects on weak and strong queries. *Information Retrieval, 13*(5), 485–506. doi:10.1007/s10791-009-9122-z

Lu, J., & Callan, J. (2003). Content-based retrieval in hybrid peer-to-peer networks. In *Proceedings of the Twelfth International Conference on Information and Knowledge Management* (pp. 199-206). New York, NY: ACM.

Lu, J., & Callan, J. (2006). User modeling for full-text federated search in peer-to-peer networks. In *Proceedings of the 29th Annual International ACM SIGIR Conference on Research and Development in Information Retrieval* (pp. 332-339). New York, NY: ACM.

Lua, E. K., Crowcroft, J., Pias, M., Sharma, R., & Lim, S. (2005). A survey and comparison of peer-to-peer overlay network schemes. *IEEE Communications Surveys and Tutorials, 7*, 72–93. doi:10.1109/COMST.2005.1610546

Lu, J. (2007). Full-text federated search in peer-to-peer networks. *SIGIR Forum, 41*(1), 121–121. doi:10.1145/1273221.1273233

Lunt, C., Galbreath, N., & Winner, J. (2004). *U. S. Patent No. 10/967,609: Ranking search results based on the frequency of clicks on the search results by members of a social network who are within a predetermined degree of separation.* Washington, DC: United States Patent and Trademark Office.

Luu, T., Klemm, F., Podnar, I., Rajman, M., & Aberer, K. (2006). Alvis peers: a scalable full-text peer-to-peer retrieval engine. In *Proceedings of the International Workshop on Information Retrieval in Peer-to-Peer Networks* (pp. 41-48). New York, NY: ACM.

Maalej, S., Ghorbel, H., Bahri, A., & Bouaziz, R. (2010). Construction des composants ontologiques flous à partir de corpus de données sémantiques floues. In *Proceedings of Actes du XXVIIIème Congrès INFORSID*, Marseille, France (pp. 361-376).

Maarek, Y. S., Fagin, R., Ben-Shaul, I. Z., & Pelleg, D. (2000). *Ephemeral document clustering for Web applications (No. RJ 10186).* Armonk, NY: IBM.

MacCall, S. L., & Cleveland, A. D. (1999). A relevance-based quantitative measure for Internet information retrieval evaluation. In *Proceedings of the American Society for Information Science Annual Meeting* (pp. 763-768).

Machill, M., Neuberger, C., Schweiger, W., & Wirth, W. (2003). Wegweiser im Netz: Qualität und Nutzung von Suchmaschinen. In Machill, M., & Welp, C. (Eds.), *Wegweiser im Netz* (pp. 13–490). Gütersloh, Germany: Bertelsmann Stiftung.

Machill, M., Neuberger, C., Schweiger, W., & Wirth, W. (2004). Navigating the Internet: A study of German-language search engines. *European Journal of Communication, 19*(3), 321–347. doi:10.1177/0267323104045258

Magnini, B., Negri, M., Prevete, R., & Tanev, H. (2002a). Mining knowledge from repeated co-occurrences: DIOGENE at TREC 2002. In *Proceedings of the 11th Text Retrieval Conference*, Gaithersburg, MD.

Magnini, B., Negri, M., Prevete, R., & Tanev, H. (2002b). Is it the right answer? Exploiting Web redundancy for answer validation. In *Proceedings of the Association of Computational Linguistics* (pp. 425-432).

Magnini, B., Negri, M., Prevete, R., & Tanev, H. (2002c). Comparing statistical and content-based techniques for answer validation on the Web. In *Proceedings du VIII Convegno AI*IA*.

Magnini, B., Speranza, M., & Kumar, V. (2009). Towards interactive question answering: An ontology-based approach. In *Proceedings of the IEEE International Conference on Semantic Computing* (pp. 612-617).

Maguitman, A., Menczer, F., Roinestad, H., & Vespignani, A. (2005). Algorithmic detection of semantic similarity. In *Proceedings of the 14th International Conference on World Wide Web* (pp. 107-116).

Manning, C. D., Prabhakar, R., & Hinrich, S. (2008). *Introduction to information retrieval.* Cambridge, UK: Cambridge University Press.

Manning, C., Raghavan, P., & Schütze, H. (2008). *Introduction to information retrieval.* Cambridge, UK: Cambridge University Press.

Marable, L. (2003). False oracles: Consumer reaction to learning the truth about how search engines work, results of an ethnographic study. *Consumer WebWatch*, 1-66.

Marchionini, G. (1992). Interfaces for end-user information seeking. *Journal of the American Society for Information Science American Society for Information Science, 43*(2), 156–163. doi:10.1002/(SICI)1097-4571(199203)43:2<156::AID-ASI8>3.0.CO;2-U

Marchionini, G. (1995). *Information seeking in electronic environments.* Cambridge, UK: Cambridge University Press. doi:10.1017/CBO9780511626388

Marchionini, G. (2006). Exploratory search: From finding to understanding. *Communications of the ACM, 49*(4), 41–46. doi:10.1145/1121949.1121979

Marchisio, G., Dhillon, N., Liang, J., Tusk, C., Koperski, K., & Nguyen, T. (2007). A case study in natural language based Web search. In Kao, A., & Poteet, S. R. (Eds.), *Natural language processing and text mining* (pp. 69–90). New York, NY: Springer. doi:10.1007/978-1-84628-754-1_5

Marcus, M. P., Santorini, B., & Marcinkiewicz, M. A. (1993). Building a large annotated corpus of English: The Penn Treebank. *Computational Linguistics, 19*(2), 313–330.

Markey, K. (2007). Twenty-five years of end-user searching, Part 1: Research findings. *Journal of the American Society for Information Science and Technology, 58*(8), 1071–1081. doi:10.1002/asi.20462

Markkula, M., & Sormunen, E. (2000). End-user searching challenges indexing practices in the digital photograph archive. *Information Retrieval, 1*(4), 259–285. doi:10.1023/A:1009995816485

Martin, J. R., & White, P. R. R. (2005). *The language of evaluation: appraisal in English.* Basingstoke, UK: Palgrave Macmillan.

Martzoukou, K. (2005). A review of Web information seeking research: considerations of method and foci of interest. *Information Research, 10*(2), 215. Retrieved June 8, 2011, from http://InformationR.net/ ir/10-2/paper215.html

Masolo, C., Stefano, B., Gangemi, A., Guarino, N., & Oltramari, A. (2003). *WonderWeb Deliverable D18* (Tech. Rep. ISTC-CNR). Trento, Italy: Laboratory for Applied Ontology.

Mathieu, B., Besançon, R., & Fluhr, C. (2004, April 26-28). Multilingual document clusters discovery. In *Proceedings of the 21st International Conference on Computational Linguistics and the 44th Annual Meeting of the Association for Computational Linguistics*, Avignon, France.

Mathieu, Y. Y. (2006). A computational semantic lexicon of French verbs of emotion. In J. G. Shanahan, Y. Qu, & J. Wiebe (Eds.), *Computing attitude and affect in text: Vol. 20. Theory and applications* (pp. 109-124). Berlin, Germany: Springer-Verlag.

Maybury, M. (2004). Question answering: An introduction. In Maybury, M. T. (Ed.), *New directions in question answering* (pp. 3–18). Palo Alto, CA: AAAI Press.

Maybury, M. (2006). New directions in question answering. In Strzalkowski, T., & Harabagiu, S. (Eds.), *Text, speech and language technology: Advances in open domain question answering* (*Vol. 32*, pp. 533–558). Berlin, Germany: Springer-Verlag. doi:10.1007/978-1-4020-4746-6_18

Mazza, R., & Berré, A. (2007). Focus group methodology for evaluating information visualization techniques and tools. In *Proceedings of the International Conference on Information Visualization* (pp. 74-80). Washington, DC: IEEE Computer Society.

McClellan, J. E. III, & Dorn, H. (2006). *Science and technology in world history: An introduction* (2nd ed.). Baltimore, MD: The John Hopkins University Press.

McCrea, R. (2004). Evaluation of two library-based and one expert reference service on the web. *Library Review, 53*(1), 11–16. doi:10.1108/00242530410514748

McGuinness, D. L., & Pinheiro Da Silva, P. (2004a). Trusting answers on the Web. In Maybury, M. T. (Ed.), *New directions in question answering*. Palo Alto, CA: AAAI Press.

McGuinness, D. L., & Pinheiro Da Silva, P. (2004b). Explaining answers from the semantic Web: the inference Web approach. *Journal of Web Semantics, 1*(4), 397–413. doi:10.1016/j.websem.2004.06.002

McKenzie, P. (2003). A model of information practices in accounts of everyday life information seeking. *The Journal of Documentation, 59*(1), 19–40. doi:10.1108/00220410310457993

Meiss, M., & Menczer, F. (2008). Visual comparison of search results: A censorship case study. *First Monday, 13*(7). Retrieved June 8, 2011 from http://firstmonday.org htbin/cgiwrap/bin/ojs/ index.php/fm/rt/ printer-Friendly/2019/1988

Mel'čuk, I. A. (1997). *Vers une linguistique Sens-Texte. Leçon inaugurale*. Paris, France: Collège de France, Chaire internationale.

Meunier, J. G., Biskri, I., Nault, G., & Nyongwa, M. (1997). Exploration de classifieurs connexionnistes pour l'analyse terminologique. In *Proceedings of Actes de la conférence Recherche d'Informations Assistée par Ordinateur*, Montréal, QC, Canada.

Miao, Q., Li, Q., & Dai, R. (2009). AMAZING: A sentiment mining and retrieval system. *Expert Systems with Applications, 36*(3), 7192–7198. doi:10.1016/j.eswa.2008.09.035

Microsoft. (2011, April). Téléchargements des différentes versions d'Internet Explorer 8, Internet Explorer 9, Internet Explorer 7, Internet Explorer 6. *Windows Internet Explorer*. Retrieved March 30, 2011, from http://www.microsoft.com/france/windows/internet-explorer/telechargement-versions-internet-explorer.aspx

Middleton, C., & Baeza-Yates, R. (2007). *A comparison of open source search engines*. Retrieved March 24, 2011, from http://wrg.upf.edu/ WRG/dctos/Middleton-Baeza.pdf

Miller, C. C. (2010, October 31). A new search engine, where less is more. *The New York Times*. Retrieved November 15, 2010, from http://www.nytimes.com/2010/11/01/technology/01search.html

Miller, V. D., & Jablin, F. M. (1991). Information seeking during organizational entry: influences, tactics, and a model of the process. *Academy of Management Review, 16*(1), 92–120.

Minka, T., & Lafferty, J. (2002). Expectation-propagation for the generative aspect model. In *Proceedings of the 18th Conference on Uncertainty in Artificial Intelligence*.

Minock, M. (2005). Where are the 'killer applications' of restricted domain question answering? In *Proceedings of the IJCAI Workshop on Knowledge Reasoning in Question Answering*, Edinburgh, UK (p. 4).

Mishne, G., Balog, K., Rijke, M., & Ernsting, B. (2007). MoodViews: Tracking and searching mood-annotated blog posts. In *Proceedings of the International Conference on Weblogs and Social Media*, Boulder, CO (pp. 323-324). Menlo Park, CA: AAAI Press.

Mizzaro, S., Nazzi, E., & Vassena, L. (2008). Retrieval of context-aware applications on mobile devices: How to evaluate? In *Proceedings of the Second International Symposium on Information Interaction in Context* (pp. 65-71).

Mizzaro, S. (1997). Relevance: The whole history. *Journal of the American Society for Information Science American Society for Information Science, 48*(9), 810–832. doi:10.1002/(SICI)1097-4571(199709)48:9<810::AID-ASI6>3.0.CO;2-U

Moffat, A., & Zobel, J. (1996). Self-indexing inverted files for fast text retrieval. *ACM Transactions on Information Systems, 14*(4), 349–379. doi:10.1145/237496.237497

Moldovan, D., Clark, C., Harabagiu, S., & Maiorano, S. (2003). COGEX: A logic prover for question answering. In *Proceedings of Human Language Technologies: The Annual Conference of the North American Chapter of the Association for Computational Linguistics*, Edmonton, AB, Canada (pp. 87-93).

Moldovan, D., Harabagiu, S., Girju, R., Morrarescu, P., Lacatusu, F., Novishi, A., et al. (2002). LCC Tools for Question Answering. In *Proceedings of the 11ᵗʰ Text Retrieval Conference*, Gaithersburg, MD.

Moldovan, D., Pasca, M., Harabagiu, S., & Surdenau, M. (2003). Performance issues and error analysis in an open-domain question answering system. *ACM Transactions on Information Systems, 21*(2), 133–154. doi:10.1145/763693.763694

Mollá, D. (2009). *From minimal logical forms for answer extraction to logical graphs for question answering. Searching answers: Festschrift in Honour of Michael Hess on the Occasion of His 60th Birthday* (pp. 101–108). Münster, Germany: MV-Wissenschaft.

Mollá, D., & Vicedo, J. (2007). Question answering in restricted domains: An overview. *Computational Linguistics, 33*(1), 41–61. doi:10.1162/coli.2007.33.1.41

Mook, N. (2005). *Microsoft tests search clustering*. Retrieved April 2, 2010, from http://www.eweek.com/ c/a/ Windows/Microsoft-Tests-Search-Clustering/

Moose, F. S. (2010). *Moose file system*. Retrieved October 13, 2010, from http://www.moosefs.org

Moriceau, V., Tannier, X., Grappy, A., & Grau, B. (2008). Justification of answers by verification of dependency relations – The French AVE task. In *Proceedings of the Working Notes of CLEF Workshop and the ECDL Conference.*

Moriceau, V., & Tannier, X. (2010). FIDJI: using syntax for validation answers in multiple documents. *Information Retrieval, 13*(5), 507–533. doi:10.1007/s10791-010-9131-y

Morris, M. R., & Horvitz, E. (2007). SearchTogether: An interface for collaborative Web search. In *Proceedings of the ACM Symposium on User Interface Software and Technology* (pp. 3-12). New York, NY: ACM.

Morris, M. R., Teevan, J., & Panovich, K. (2010a). A comparison of information seeking using search engines and social networks. In *Proceedings of the Fourth International AAAI Conference on Weblogs and Social Media*, Washington, DC.

Morris, M. R., Teevan, J., & Panovich, K. (2010b). What do people ask their social networks, and why? A survey study of status message Q&A behavior. In *Proceedings of the 28th International Conference on Human Factors in Computing Systems*

Morrison, E. W. (1993). Longitudinal study of the effects of information seeking on newcomer socialization. *The Journal of Applied Psychology, 78*(2), 173–183. doi:10.1037/0021-9010.78.2.173

Morrison, E. W. (2002). Information seeking within organizations. *Human Communication Research, 28*(2), 229–242. doi:10.1111/j.1468-2958.2002.tb00805.x

Moschitti, A., Quarteroni, S., Basili, R., & Manandhar, S. (2007). Exploiting syntactic and shallow semantic kernels for question answer classification. In *Proceeding of the Workshop of the Association for Computational Linguistics* (pp. 776-783).

Mostafa, J. (2005). Seeking better web searches. *Scientific American, 292*(2), 66–73. doi:10.1038/scientificamerican0205-66

Motzkin, D. (1994). On high performance of updates within an efficient document retrieval system. *Information Processing & Management, 30*(1), 93–118. doi:10.1016/0306-4573(94)90026-4

Mountain, D., & MacFarlane, A. (2007). Geographic information retrieval in a mobile environment: evaluating the needs of mobile individual. *Journal of Information Science, 33*(5), 515–530. doi:10.1177/0165551506075333

Mozilla. (2004, November 9). Mozilla Firefox 1.0 Release Notes. *Mozilla Firefox*. Retrieved April 4, 2011, from http://www.mozilla.com/en-US/firefox/releases/1.0.html

Mozilla. (2011, April 7). Add-on collector. *Add-ons for Firefox*. Retrieved April 7, 2011, from https://addons.mozilla.org/en-US/firefox/addon/11950

Na, A., & Priest, M. (2007). *Sensor Observation Service: Version 1.0.0* (Report No. OGC 06-009r6). Wayland, MA: Open Geospatial Consortium. Retrieved from http://portal.opengeospatial.org/ files/?artifact_id=26667

Nadeau, D., & Sekine, S. (2007). A survey of named entity recognition and classification. *Journal of Linguisticae Investigationes, 30*(1).

Nadella, S. (2010, October 13). *New signals in search: The Bing social layer*. Retrieved October 13, 2010 from http://www.bing.com/ community/blogs/search/ archive/2010/10/13/ new-signals-in-search-the-bing-social-layer.aspx

Naughton, M., Stokes, N., & Carthy, J. (2010). Sentence-level event classification in unstructured texts. *Information Retrieval*, *13*(2), 132–156. doi:10.1007/s10791-009-9113-0

Navarro-Prieto, R., Scaife, M., & Rogers, Y. (1999). Cognitive strategies in web searching. In *Proceedings of the 5th Conference on Human Factors & the Web*.

Neilsen, J. (1994). Enhancing the explanatory power of usability heuristics. In *Proceedings of the ACM Conference on Human Factors in Computing Systems* (pp. 152-158). New York, NY: ACM.

Neilsen, J., & Mack, R. L. (1994). *Usability inspection methods*. New York, NY: John Wiley & Sons.

Nesheim, J. L. (2000). *High tech start up: Complete handbook for creating successful new high tech companies*. New York, NY: Free Press.

Netrvalova, A., & Safařík, J. (2008). Selection of partners for co-operation based on interpersonal trust. In *Proceedings of the Conference on Human System Interaction*, Kraków, Poland.

Neumann, G., & Sacaleanu, B. (2004). Experiments on robust NL question interpretation and multi-layered document annotation for a cross-language question / answering system. In *Proceedings of the Working Notes of CLEF Cross-Language Evaluation Forum*, Bath, UK (pp. 311-320).

Neumann, G., & Sacaleanu, B. (2005). DFKI's LT-lab at the CLEF 2005 multiple language question answering track. In *Proceedings of the Working Notes of CLEF Cross-Language Evaluation Forum*.

Newman, E., Stokes, N., Dunnion, J., & Carthy, J. (2005). UCD IIRG approach to the textual entailment challenge. In *Proceedings of the PASCAL Challenges Workshop on Recognising Textual Entailment* (pp. 53-56).

Nicholson, S., Sierra, T., Eseryel, U. Y., Park, J.-H., Barkow, P., & Pozo, E. J. (2006). How much of it is real? Analysis of paid placement in Web search engine results. *Journal of the American Society for Information Science and Technology*, *57*(4), 448–461. doi:10.1002/asi.20318

Nielsen, J., & Tahir, M. (2002). *Homepage usability: 50 websites deconstructed*. Indianapolis, IN: New Riders.

Niles, I., & Pease, A. (2001). Towards a standard upper ontology. In *Proceedings of the 2nd International Conference on Formal Ontology in Information Systems*, Ogunquit, ME.

Noël, E. (2008). Veille et nouveaux outils d'information. In J. Dinet (Ed.), *Usages, usagers et compétences informationnelles au 21e siècle, Traité des Sciences et Techniques de l'Information* (pp. 257-284). Paris, France: Hermès science publications; Lavoisier

Notess, G. R. (2006). Tracking your search history. *Online*, *30*(2), 41–43.

O'Brien, M. (2004). Commentary on Heidegger's "The Question Concerning Technology". In *Proceedings of the IWM Junior Fellows' Winter Conference on Thinking Together* (Vol. 16).

Oelke, D., Hao, M., Rohrdantz, C., Keim, D., Dayal, U., Haug, L.-E., & Janetzko, H. (2009). Visual opinion analysis of customer feedback data. In *Proceedings of the IEEE Symposium on Visual Analytics Science and Technology*, Atlantic City, NJ (pp. 187-194). Washington, DC: IEEE Computer Society.

Ohmae, K. (1999). *The invisible continent: Four strategic imperatives of the new economy*. New York, NY: HarperBusiness.

Ölund, G., Lindqvist, P., & Litton, J.-E. (2007). BIMS: An information management system for biobanking in the 21st century international business machines. *IBM Systems Journal*, *46*(1), 171–182. doi:10.1147/sj.461.0171

OMG. (2006). *Documents associated with object constraint language, version 2.0*. Retrieved from http://www.omg.org/ spec/OCL/2.0/

Opera Software ASA. (2010, December 16). Are you ready for Opera 11? *Opera Software*. Retrieved April 4, 2011, from http://www.opera.com/press/releases/2010/12/16

Opera Software ASA. (2011). Opera business solutions: TV & device OEMs. *Opera Software*. Retrieved April 12, 2011, from http://www.opera.com/business/devices

Oppen, D. C., & Dalal, Y. K. (1983). The Clearinghouse: A decentralized agent for locating named objects in a distributed environment. *ACM Transactions on Information Systems*, *1*(3), 230–253. doi:10.1145/357436.357439

Osinski, S., & Weiss, D. (2005). A concept-driven algorithm for clustering search results. *IEEE Intelligent Systems*, *20*(3), 48–54. doi:10.1109/MIS.2005.38

Osiński, S., & Weiss, D. (2005). A concept-driven algorithm for clustering search results. *IEEE Transactions on Intelligent Systems*, *20*(3), 48–54. doi:10.1109/MIS.2005.38

Ounis, I., Macdonald, C., & Soboroff, I. (2008). Overview of the TREC 2008 Blog track. In *Proceedings of the 17th Text REtrieval Conference*.

Owens, T. (2007, August 30). Firefox Campus edition preloaded with Zotero. *Zotero: The Next-Generation Research Tool*. Retrieved January 13, 2011, from http://www.zotero.org/blog/firefox-campus-edition-preloaded-with-zotero

Pacey, A. (1991). *Technology in world civilization*. Cambridge, MA: MIT Press.

Pan, F. (2007). *Representing complex temporal phenomena for the semantic web and natural language* (Unpublished doctoral dissertation). University of Southern California, Los Angeles, CA.

Panayiotou, C., & Samaras, G. (2006). Mobile user personalization with dynamic profiles: Time and activity. In R. Meersman, Z. Tari, & P. Herraro (Eds.), *Proceedings of Doctoral Consortium of On the Move to Meaningful Internet Systems* (LNCS 4278, pp. 1295-1304).

Pan, B., Hembrooke, H., Joachims, T., Lorigo, L., Gay, G., & Granka, L. (2007). In Google we trust: Users' decisions on rank, position, and relevance. *Journal of Computer-Mediated Communication*, *12*(3), 801–823. doi:10.1111/j.1083-6101.2007.00351.x

Pang, B., & Lee, L. (2008). Opinion mining and sentiment analysis. *Foundations and Trends in Information Retrieval*, *2*(1-2), 1–135. doi:10.1561/1500000011

Paris, C., Wan, S., & Thomas, P. (2010). Focused and aggregated search: a perspective from natural language generation. *Information Retrieval*, *13*(5), 434–459. doi:10.1007/s10791-009-9121-0

Paroubek, P., Pak, A., & Mostefa, D. (2010). Annotations for opinion mining evaluation in the industrial context of the DoXa project. In *Proceedings of the Language Resources and Evaluation Conference*, Malta.

Pasca, M. A., & Harabagiu, S. M. (2001). High performance question/answering. In *Proceedings of the 24th Annual International ACM SIGIR Conference on Research and Development in Information Retrieval*, New Orleans, LA (pp. 366-374).

Patel, N., & Mundur, P. (2005). An N-gram based approach to finding the repeating patterns in musical. In *Proceedings of the European Conference on Internet and Multimedia Systems and Applications*, Grindelwald, Switzerland.

Patel, K., & McCarthy, M. P. (2000). *The essentials of e-business leadership: Digital transformation*. New York, NY: McGraw-Hill.

Patterson, A. L. (2004). *U.S. Patent No. 20060031195: Phrase-based searching in an information retrieval system*. Washington, DC: United States Patent and Trademark Office.

Patterson, A. L. (2005). *We wanted something special for our birthday...* Retrieved October 13, 2010, from http://googleblog.blogspot.com/ 2005/09/we-wanted-something-special-for-our.html

Paulheim, H., & Probst, F. (2010). Ontology-enhanced user interfaces: A survey. *International Journal on Semantic Web and Information Systems*, *6*(2), 36–59. doi:10.4018/jswis.2010040103

Paumier, S. (2008). *Unitex manual*. Retrieved December 9, 2010, from http://www-igm.univ-mlv.fr/~unitex/index.php?page=4

Penas, A., Forner, P., Sutcliffe, R., Rodrigo, A., Forascu, C., & Alegria, I. ...Osenova, P. (2010). Overview of ResPubliQA 2009: Question answering evaluation over European legislation. In C. Peters, G. Di Nunzio, M. Kurimo, D. Mostefa, A. Penas, and G. Roda (Ed.), *Proceedings of the Workshop on Multilingual Information Access Evaluation I. Text Retrieval Experiments* (LNCS 6241, pp. 174-196).

Peñas, A., Rodrigo, A., Sama, V., & Verdejo, F. (2008). Testing the reasoning for question answering validation. *Journal of Logic and Computation, 18*(3).

Pereira, R., Ricarte, I., & Gomide, F. (2006). Fuzzy relational ontological model in information search systems. In Sanchez, E. (Ed.), *Fuzzy logic and the semantic Web, capturing intelligence* (pp. 395–412). Amsterdam, The Netherlands: Elsevier. doi:10.1016/S1574-9576(06)80022-5

Perret, L. (2004). Question answering system for the French Language. In *Proceedings of the Working Notes of CLEF Cross-Language Evaluation Forum*, Bath, UK (pp. 295-305).

Perriault, J. (1989). *La Logique de l'Usage. Essai sur les Machines à Communiquer*. Paris, France: Flammarion.

Pickens, J. (2008). *Communicating about collaboration: Depth of mediation*. Retrieved September 1, 2010, from http://palblog.fxpal.com/ ?p=274

Pickens, J., Golovchinsky, G., Shah, C., Ovarfordt, P., & Back, M. (2008, July 20-24). Algorithmic mediation for collaborative exploratory search. In *Proceedings of the ACM SIGIR Conference on Information Retrieval*, Singapore (pp. 315-322).

Piolat, A., & Bannour, R. (2009). EMOTAIX: un scénario de Tropes pour l'identification automatisée du lexique émotionnel et affectif. *L'Année Psychologique, 109*(4), 655–698. doi:10.4074/S0003503309004047

Pirolli, P. (2007). *Information foraging theory: Adaptive interaction with information*. New York, NY: Oxford University Press. doi:10.1093/acprof:o so/9780195173321.001.0001

Plaisant, C. (2004). The challenge of information visualization evaluation. In *Proceedings of the Working Conference on Advanced Visual Interfaces* (pp. 109-116). New York, NY: ACM.

Plamondon, L., Lapalme, G., & Kosseim, L. (2003). The quantum question answering system at TREC 11. In *Proceedings of the 11th Text Retrieval Conference.*

Ploux, S., & Manguin, J.-L. (1998). *Le dictionnaire électronique des synonymes du CRISCO*. Retrieved November 9, 2010, from http://www.crisco.unicaen.fr/ cgi-bin/cherches.cgi

Ponte, J. M., & Croft, W. B. (1998). A language modeling approach to information retrieval. In *Proceedings of the 21st Annual International ACM SIGIR Conference on Research and Development in Information Retrieval* (pp. 275-281).

Popescu, A., Grefenstette, G., & Moëllic, P.-A. (2006, December 4-5). Using semantic commonsense resources in image retrieval. In *Proceedings of the International Workshop on Semantic Media Adaptation and Personalization*, Athens, Greece (pp. 31-36).

Popescu, A., Tsikrika, T., & Kludas, J. (2010, September 20-23). Overview of the Wikipedia Retrieval Task. In *Proceedings of the Conference on Multilingual and Multimodal Information Access Evaluation*, Padua, Italy.

Popescu, A.-M., & Etzioni, O. (2005). Extracting product features and opinions from reviews. In *Proceedings of the Conference on Human Language Technology and Empirical Methods in Natural Language Processing*, Vancouver, BC, Canada (pp. 339-346). Stroudsburg, PA: ACL.

Portele, C. (2007). *OpenGIS Geography Markup Language (GML) Encoding Standard. Version 3.2.1.* (Report No. OGC 07-036). Retrieved from http://portal.opengeospatial.org/ files/?artifact_id=20509

Porter, M. E. (1998). *On competition*. Boston, MA: Harvard Business School Press.

Porter, M. F. (1980). An algorithm for suffix stripping. *Program, 14*(3), 130–137. doi:10.1108/eb046814

Porter, M. F. (1997). *Readings in information retrieval: An algorithm for suffix stripping*. San Francisco, CA: Morgan Kaufmann.

Prado, H. A. d., & Ferneda, E. (2007). *Emerging technologies of text mining: Techniques and applications*. Hershey, PA: Idea Group. doi:10.4018/978-1-59904-373-9

Prager, J., Brown, E., Radev, D. R., & Czuba, K. (2000). One search engine or two for question-answering. In *Proceedings of the 9ᵗʰ Text Retrieval Conference*, Gaithersburg, MD (pp. 235-240).

Proulx, S. (2005). Penser les usages des technologies de l'information et de la communication aujourd'hui: enjeux – modèles – tendances. In Veira, L., & Pinède, N. (Eds.), *Enjeux et usages des TIC: aspects sociaux et culturels* (pp. 7–20). Bordeaux, France: Presses Universitaires de Bordeaux.

Prud'hommeaux, E., & Seaborne, A. (2008). *SPARQL query language for RDF.* Retrieved October 15, 2010, from http://www.w3.org/ TR/rdf-sparql-query/

Pugh, W. (1990). Skip lists: A probabilistic alternative to balanced trees. *Communications of the ACM, 33*(6), 668–676. doi:10.1145/78973.78977

Pustejovsky, J., Lee, K., Bunt, H., & Romary, L. (2010). ISO-TimeML: An international standard for semantic annotation. In *Proceedings of the International Conference on Language Resources and Evaluation.*

Quan, T. T. Hui1, S. C., & Cao, T. H. (2004). FOGA: A fuzzy ontology generation framework for scholarly semantic Web. In *Proceedings of the Knowledge Discovery and Ontologies Workshop at ECML/PKDD* (pp. 37-48).

Quarteroni, S. (2007). *Advanced techniques for personalized, interactive question answering* (Unpublished doctoral dissertation). Department of Computer Science, The University of York, York, UK.

Quarteroni, S., & Manandhar, S. (2008). Designing and interactive open-domain question answering system. *Natural Language Engineering, 15*(1), 73–95. doi:10.1017/S1351324908004919

Quarteroni, S., & Manandhar, S. (2009). Designing an interactive open-domain question answering system. *Language Engineering Journal, 15*(1), 73–95. doi:10.1017/S1351324908004919

Raftopoulou, P., & Petrakis, E. G. (2008). A measure for cluster cohesion in semantic overlay networks. In *Proceeding of the ACM Workshop on Large-Scale Distributed Systems for Information Retrieval* (pp. 59-66). New York, NY: ACM.

Rainie, L. (2005). Search Engine use shoots up in the past year and edges towards email as the primary Internet application. *Pew Internet and American Life Project.* Retrieved from http://www.pewInternet.org/ PPF/r/167/report_display.asp

Raisch, W. D. (2001). *The eMarketplace: Strategies for success in B2B eCommerce.* New York, NY: McGraw-Hill.

Ramachandran, S. (2010, May 26). *Web metrics: Size and number of resources.* Retrieved March 17, 2011, from http://code.google.com/ speed/articles/web-metrics.html

Rao, L. (2010, October 13). *Facebook now has klout.* Retrieved October 13, 2010, from http://techcrunch.com/ 2010/10/13/facebook-now-has-klout/

Rao, L. (2010, September 14). *Twitter seeing 90 million tweets per day, 25 percent contain links.* Retrieved October 13, 2010, from http://techcrunch.com/ 2010/09/14/twitter-seeing-90-million-tweets-per-day

Rasmussen, E. M. (2003). Indexing and retrieval for the Web. *Annual Review of Information Science & Technology, 37*(1), 91–124. doi:10.1002/aris.1440370104

Ratnasamy, S., Francis, P., Handley, M., Karp, R., & Schenker, S. (2001). A scalable content-addressable network. In *Proceedings of the Conference on Applications, Technologies, Architectures, and Protocols for Computer Communications* (pp. 161-172). New York, NY: ACM.

Ravat, F., Teste, O., & Tournier, R. (2007). OLAP aggregation function for textual data warehouse. In *Proceedings of the 9th International Conference on Enterprise Information Systems* (pp. 151-156).

Ravin, Y., Prager, J., & Harabagiu, S. (Eds.). (2001). *Proceedings of the Workshop on Open-Domain Question Answering*, Toulouse, France. Stroudsburg, PA: ACL.

Reich, R. B. (2001). *The future of success.* New York, NY: Alfred A. Knopf.

Rice, R. F. (1979). *Some practical universal noiseless coding techniques* (Tech. Rep. No. 79-22). Pasadena, CA: Jet Propulsion Laboratory.

Richards, J. W. (Ed.). (2002). *Are we spiritual machines?* Seattle, WA: Discovery Institute.

Rieffel, R. (2005). *Sociologie des Médias*. Paris, France: Ellipses Marketing.

Rinaldi, F., Dowdall, J., Schneider, G., & Persidis, A. (2004). Answering questions in the genomics domain. In *Proceedings of the ACL Workshop on Question Answering in Restricted Domains*.

Ripley, B. D. (1996). *Pattern recognition and neural networks*. Cambridge, UK: Cambridge University Press.

Robertson, S. E., van Rijsbergen, C. J., & Porter, M. F. (1981). Probabilistic models of indexing and searching. In *Proceedings of the 3rd Annual ACM Conference on Research and Development in Information Retrieval* (pp. 35-56).

Robertson, S. E., & Saragoza, H. (2009). The probabilistic relevance framework: BM25 and beyond. *Foundation and Trends in Information Retrieval*, *3*(4), 333–389. doi:10.1561/1500000019

Robertson, S. E., & Spärck Jones, K. (1977). Relevance weighting of search terms. *Journal of the American Society for Information Science American Society for Information Science*, *27*, 129–146. doi:10.1002/asi.4630270302

Rocca-Serra, P., Brandizi, M., Maguire, E., Sklyar, N., Taylor, C., & Begley, K. (2010). ISA software suite: supporting standards-compliant experimental annotation and enabling curation at the community level. *Bioinformatics (Oxford, England)*, *26*(18), 2354–2356. doi:10.1093/bioinformatics/btq415

Roitblat, H. L. (1999). *U. S. Patent No. 6,189,002: Process and system for retrieval of documents using context-relevant semantic profiles*. Washington, DC: United States Patent and Trademark Office.

Rompré, L., Biskri, I., & Meunier, F. (2008). Text classification: A preferred tool for audio file classification. In *Proceedings of the 6th ACS/IEEE International Conference on Computer Systems and Applications*, Doha, Qatar (pp. 834-839).

Rosenblatt, S. (2010, June 16). New Flock divorces Firefox, snuggles up to. *cnet Downloads*. Retrieved September 20, 2010, from http://download.cnet.com/8301-2007_4-20007842-12.html

Rosset, S., Galibert, O., Illouz, G., & Max, A. (2005). Interaction et recherche d'information le projet RITEL. *Répondre à des questions*, *46*(3).

Rouet, J.-F., & Tricot, A. (1998). Chercher de l'information dans un hypertexte: vers un modèle des processus cognitifs. In Tricot, A., & Rouet, J.-F. (Eds.), *Les Hypermédias: Approches Cognitives et Ergonomiques* (pp. 57–74). Paris, France: Hermès.

Roush, W. (2006). What comes after Web 2.0? *MIT TechReview*. Retrieved October 18, 2010, from http://www.technologyreview.com/ Infotech/17845/

Roussinov, D., Fan, W., & Robles-Flores, J. (2008). Beyond keywords: Automated question answering on the Web. *Communications of the ACM*, *51*(9), 60–65. doi:10.1145/1378727.1378743

Rowlands, I., Nicholas, D., Williams, P., Huntington, P., Fieldhouse, M., & Gunter, B. (2008). The Google generation: The information behaviour of the researcher of the future. *Aslib Proceedings: New Information Perspectives*, *60*(4), 290–310.

Rozenknop, A. (2009). *Cours de recherche et extraction d'information*. Paris, France: Université de Paris 13. Retrieved from http://www-lipn.univ-paris13.fr/~rozenknop/Cours/MICR_REI/

Russel-Rose, T., & Stevenson, M. (2009). The role of natural language processing in information retrieval: Searching for meaning and structure. In Göker, A., & Davis, J. (Eds.), *Information retrieval, searching in the 21st century* (pp. 215–227). New York, NY: John Wiley & Sons. doi:10.1002/9780470033647.ch10

Rutledge, G. K., Alpert, J., & Ebuisaki, W. (2006). NOMADS: A climate and weather model archive at the National Oceanic and Atmospheric Administration. *Bulletin of the American Meteorological Society*, *87*, 327–341. doi:10.1175/BAMS-87-3-327

Sacaleanu, B., & Neumann, G. (2006). Cross-cutting aspects of cross-language question answering systems. In *Proceedings of the Workshop on Multilingual Question Answering, Association for Computational Linguistics*, Morristown, NJ (pp. 15-22).

Salton, G. (1962). *The use of citations as an aid to automatic content analysis* (Tech. Rep. No. ISR-2, Section III). Cambridge, MA: Harvard Computation Laboratory.

Salton, G., & McGill, M. J. (1983). *Introduction to modern information retrieval*. New York, NY: McGraw-Hill.

Salton, G., Wong, A., & Wang, C. S. (1975). A vector space model for automatic indexing. *Communications of the ACM, 18*(11), 613–620. doi:10.1145/361219.361220

Samaras, G., & Panayiotou, C. (2002). *Personalized portals for the wireless user based on mobile agents*. In *Proceedings of the 2nd International Workshop on Mobile Commerce* (pp. 70-74).

Sánchez, D., Batet, M., Valls, A., & Gibert, K. (2009). Ontology-driven web-based semantic similarity. *Journal of Intelligent Information Systems, 35*(3).

Sang, E. T. K., Bouma, G., & de Rijke, M. (2005). Developing offline strategies for answering medical questions. In *Proceedings of the AAAI Workshop on Question Answering in Restricted Domains*.

Sansone, S. A., Rocca-Serra, P., Brandizi, M., Brazma, A., Field, D., & Fostel, J. (2008). The first RSBI (ISA-TAB) workshop: can a simple format work for complex studies? *OMICS: A Journal of Integrative Biology, 12*(2), 143–149. doi:10.1089/omi.2008.0019

Santos, D., & Cabral, L. M. (2010). GikiCLEF: Expectations and lessons learned. In C. Peters, G. M. Di Nunzio, M. Kurimo, T. Mandl, D. Mostefa, A. Peñas, & G. Roda (Eds.), *Proceedings of the 10th Workshop on Multilingual Information Acess Evaluation I: Text Retrieval Experiments* (LNCS 6241, pp. 212-222).

Saracevic, T. (1996). Modeling interaction in information retrieval (IR): A review and proposal. In *Proceedings of the Annual Meeting of the American Society for Information Science, 33*, 3-9.

Saracevic, T. (2007). Relevance: a review of the literature and a framework for thinking on the notion in Information Science. Part III: behavior and effects of relevance. *Journal of the American Society for Information Science and Technology, 58*(13), 2126–2144. doi:10.1002/asi.20681

Savolainen, R. (1995). Everyday life information seeking: approaching information seeking in the context of way of life. *Library & Information Science Research, 17*(3), 259–294. doi:10.1016/0740-8188(95)90048-9

Savolainen, R. (2008). *Everyday information practices: A social phenomenological perspective*. Lanham, MD: The Scarecrow Press.

Schaer, P., Mayr, P., & Mutschke, P. (2010, October 4-6). *Implications of inter-rater agreement on a student information retrieval evaluation*. Paper presented at the Lernen, Wissen, Adaptivität Workshop, Kassel, Germany.

Schiller, R. J. (2001). *Irrational exuberance*. New York, NY: Broadway Books.

Schlobach, S., Ahn, D., de Rijke, M., & Jijkoun, V. (2007). Data-driven type checking in open domain question answering. *Journal of Applied Logic, 5*(1). doi:10.1016/j.jal.2005.12.001

Schmidt, A. (2005). A layered model for user context management with controlled aging and imperfection handling. In *Proceedings of the Second International Workshop on Modeling and Retrieval of Context*, Edinburgh, UK (pp. 86-100).

Schofield, E., & Kubin, G. (2002). On interfaces for mobile information retrieval. In F. Paternó (Eds.), *Proceedings of the 4th International Symposium on Human Computer Interaction with Mobile Devices* (LNCS 2411, pp. 383-387).

Scholer, F., Williams, H., Yiannis, J., & Zobel, J. (2002). Compression of inverted indexes for fast query evaluation. In *Proceedings of the 25th Annual International ACM SIGIR Conference on Research and Development in Information Retrieval* (pp. 222-229).

Sebe, N. (2010). Human-centered computing. In Nakashima, H., Aghajan, H., & Augusto, J. C. (Eds.), *Handbook of ambient intelligence and smart environments* (pp. 349–370). New York, NY: Springer. doi:10.1007/978-0-387-93808-0_13

Selberg, E. (1999). *Towards comprehensive Web search* (Unpublished doctoral dissertation). University of Washington, Seattle, WA.

Shamber, L. (1994). Relevance and information behavior. *Annual Review of Information Science & Technology, 29*, 3–48.

Shankaranarayanan, G., & Even, A. (2006). The metadata enigma. *Communications of the ACM, 49*(2), 88–94. doi:10.1145/1113034.1113035

Shapiro, C., & Varian, H. R. (1999). *Information rules: A strategic guide to the network economy.* Boston, MA: Harvard Business School Press.

Sharman, N., Alpdemir, N., Ferris, J., Greenwood, M., Li, P., & Wroe, C. (2004, August). *The myGrid information model.* Paper presented at the UK e-Science All Hands Meeting, Nottingham, UK.

Shen, D., Sun, J.-T., Yang, Q., & Chen, Z. (2006, December 18-22). Latent friend mining from blog data. In *Proceedings of the Sixth International Conference on Data Mining*, Hong Kong.

Shen, X., Tan, B., & Zhai, C. (2005). Context-sensitive information retrieval using implicit feedback. In *Proceedings of the 28th Annual International ACM SIGIR Conference on Research and Development in Information Retrieval* (pp. 43-50).

Sherman, C. (2004). *4th Annual Search Engine Awards.* Retrieved April 2, 2010, from http://searchenginewatch.com/ 3309841

Sherman, C. (2005). *Metacrawlers and metasearch engines - Search Engine Watch (SEW).* Retrieved April 2, 2010, from http://searchenginewatch.com/ 2156241

Shnier, C. F. (2000). Web-based document repositories. *Law Technology News.* Retrieved August 1, 2010, from http://ltn-archive.hotresponse.com/ august00/litigation_support_p39.html

Sieg, A., Mobasher, B., & Burke, R. (2004). User's information context: Integrating user profiles and concept hierarchies. In *Proceedings of the Meeting of the International Federation of Classification Societies* (Vol. 1, pp. 28-40).

Silberschatz, G. (1994). Distributed file systems. In Silberschatz, A., Galvin, P. B., & Gagne, G. (Eds.), *Operating system concepts.* Reading, MA: Addison-Wesley.

Silberztein, M., & Tutin, A. (2005). Nooj, un outil TAL pour l'enseignement des langues. Application pour l'étude de la morphologie lexicale en FLE. *International Journal of Apprentissage des langues et systèmes d'information et de communication, 8*, 123-134.

Silverstein, C., Henzinger, M., Marais, H., & Moricz, M. (1998). *Analysis of a very large AltaVista query log.* Retrieved July 1, 2010, from http://www.hpl.hp.com/ techreports/Compaq-DEC/SRC-TN-1998-014.pdf

Silverstein, C., Henzinger, M., Marais, H., & Moricz, M. (1999). Analysis of a very large web search engine query log. *SIGIR Forum, 33*(1), 6–12. doi:10.1145/331403.331405

Simsek, O., & Jensen, D. (2008). Navigating networks by using homophily and degree. *Proceedings of the National Academy of Sciences of the United States of America, 105*(35), 12758–12762. doi:10.1073/pnas.0800497105

Singer, G., Norbisrath, U., Vainikko, E., Kikkas, H., & Lewandowski, D. (2011). Search-logger -- Tool support for exploratory search task studies. In *Proceedings of the 26th ACM Symposium on Applied Computing*, TaiChung, Taiwan.

Singer, P. W. (2009). *Wired for war: The robotics revolution and conflict in the 21st century.* New York, NY: The Penguin Press.

Singh, G., Bharathi, S., Chervenak, A., Deelman, E., Kesselman, C., Manohar, M., et al. (2003, November). A metadata catalog service for data intensive applications. In *Proceedings of the ACM/IEEE Conference on Supercomputing*, Phoenix, AZ (p. 33).

Singhal, A., Buckley, C., & Mitra, M. (1996). Pivoted document length normalization. In *Proceedings of the 19th Annual International ACM SIGIR Conference on Research and Development in Information Retrieval*, Zurich, Switzerland (pp. 21-29).

Singh, M. P., Yu, B., & Venkatraman, M. (2001). Community-based service location. *Communications of the ACM, 44*(4), 49–54. doi:10.1145/367211.367255

Skobeltsyn, G., Luu, T., Zarko, I. P., Rajman, M., & Aberer, K. (2007). Web text retrieval with a p2p query-driven index. In *Proceedings of the 30th Annual International ACM SIGIR Conference on Research and Development in Information Retrieval* (pp. 679-686). New York, NY: ACM.

Smedley, D., Schofield, P., Chen, C. K., Aidinis, V., Ainali, C., & Bard, J. (2010). Finding and sharing: new approaches to registries of databases and services for the biomedical sciences. *Database*, (n.d.), 2010.

Smeulders, A., Worring, M., Santini, S., Gupta, A., & Jain, R. (2000). Content-based image retrieval at the end of the early years. *IEEE Transactions on Pattern Analysis and Machine Intelligence, 22*(12). doi:10.1109/34.895972

Smith, A. J. (1985). Disk cache—miss ratio analysis and design considerations. *ACM Transactions on Computer Systems, 3*(3), 161–203. doi:10.1145/3959.3961

Smyth, B., & Balfe, E. (2006). Anonymous personalization in collaborative web search. *Information Retrieval, 9*(2), 165–190. doi:10.1007/s10791-006-7148-z

Sohn, T., Li, K. A., Griswold, W. G., & Hollan, J. D. (2008). A diary study of mobile information needs. In *Proceedings of the 26th Annual SIGCHI Conference on Human Factors in Computing Systems* (pp. 433-442).

Solomon, M., Bamossy, G., & Askegaard, S. (1999). *Consumer behaviour – A European perspective* (4th ed.). London, UK: Prentice Hall Europe.

Soricut, R., & Brill, E. (2006). Automatic question answering using the web: Beyond the factoid. *Information Retrieval, 9*(2), 191–206. doi:10.1007/s10791-006-7149-y

Soubbotin, M. M., & Soubbotin, S. M. (2001). Patterns of potential answer expressions as clues to the right answers. In *Proceedings of the 10th Text Retrieval Conference*, Gaithersburg, MD.

Soubbotin, M. M., & Soubbotin, S. M. (2002). Use of patterns for detection of likely answer strings: a systematic approach. In *Proceedings of the 11th Text Retrieval Conference*, Gaithersburg, MD.

Spärck Jones, K., Walker, S., & Robertson, S. E. (2000). A probabilistic model of information retrieval: Development and comparative experiments. *Information Processing & Management: an International Journal, 36*(6), 779-808, 809-840.

Sparck Jones, K. (1981). The Cranfield tests. In Sparck Jones, K. (Ed.), *Information retrieval experiment* (pp. 256–284). London, UK: Butterworth-Heinemann.

Speretta, M., & Gauch, S. (2005). Personalized search based on user search histories. In *Proceedings of the IEEE/WIC/ACM International Conference on Web Intelligence* (pp. 622-628). Washington, DC: IEEE Computer Society.

Spink, A., & Jansen, B. J. (2007, December 7). Commerce related Web search: Current trends. In *Proceedings of the 18th Australasian Conference on Information Systems*, Toowoomba, Australia. Retrieved from http://www.acis2007.usq.edu.au/ assets/papers/10.pdf

Spink, A. (2002). A user-centered approach to evaluating human interaction with Web search engines: an exploratory study. *Information Processing & Management, 38*(3), 401–426. doi:10.1016/S0306-4573(01)00036-X

Spink, A., & Jansen, B. J. (2004). *Web search: Public searching of the Web (Vol. 6)*. Dordrecht, The Netherlands: Kluwer Academic.

Spink, A., & Jansen, B. J. (2004). *Web search: Public searching of the Web*. Berlin, Germany: Springer-Verlag.

Spink, A., Wolfram, D., Jansen, B. J., & Saracevic, T. (2001). Searching the web: the public and their queries. *Journal of the American Society for Information Science and Technology, 52*(3), 226–234. doi:10.1002/1097-4571(2000)9999:9999<::AID-ASI1591>3.0.CO;2-R

Spink, S., Jansen, B., Blakely, C., & Koshman, S. (2006). A study of results overlap and uniqueness among major web search engines. *Information Processing & Management, 42*(5), 1379–1391. doi:10.1016/j.ipm.2005.11.001

StatCounter. (2011, March 21). Top 12 browser versions on Mar 11. *StatCounter Global Stats*. Retrieved March 21, 2011, from http://gs.statcounter.com/#browser_version-ww-monthly-201103-201103-bar

Steedman, M. (1987). Combinatory grammars and parasitic gaps. *Natural Language and Linguistic Theory, 5*, 403–439. doi:10.1007/BF00134555

Stoesser, G., Baker, W., van den Broek, A., Camon, E., Garcia-Pastor, M., & Kanz, C. (2002). The EMBL nucleotide sequence database. *Nucleic Acids Research, 30*(1), 21–26. doi:10.1093/nar/30.1.21

Stoica, I., Morris, R., Karger, D., Kaashoek, M. F., & Balakrishnan, H. (2001). Chord: A scalable peer-to-peer lookup service for internet applications. In *Proceedings of the Conference on Applications, Technologies, Architectures, and Protocols for Computer Communications* (pp. 149-160). New York, NY: ACM.

Stoilos, G., Simou, N., Stamou, G., & Kollias, S. (2006). Uncertainty and the semantic Web. *International Journal of IEEE Intelligent Systems, 21*(5), 84–87. doi:10.1109/MIS.2006.105

Stoyanov, V., & Cardie, C. (2008). Topic identification for fine-grained opinion analysis. In *Proceedings of the 22nd International Conference on Computational Linguistics* (pp. 817-824). Stroudsburg, PA: ACL.

Straccia, U. (2006). A fuzzy description logic for the semantic Web. In Sanchez, E. (Ed.), *Fuzzy logic and the semantic Web, capturing intelligence* (pp. 73–90). Amsterdam, The Netherlands: Elsevier. doi:10.1016/S1574-9576(06)80006-7

Strapparava, C., & Valitutti, A. (2004). WordNet-Affect: an affective extension of WordNet. In *Proceedings of the 4th International Conference on Language Resources and Evaluation*, Lisboa, Portugal (pp. 1083-1086).

Stuckenshmidt, H., & van Harmelen, F. (2005). *Information sharing on the semantic Web*. Berlin, Germany: Springer.

Sufi, B., Matthews, K., & van Dam, K. (2003, September). *An interdisciplinary model for the representation of scientific studies and associated data holdings*. Paper presented at the UK e-Science All Hands Meeting, Nottingham, UK.

Sugiyama, K., Hatano, K., & Yoshikawa, M. (2004). Adaptive Web search based on user profile construction without any effort from users. In *Proceedings of the World Wide Web Conference* (pp. 675-684). Washington, DC: IEEE Computer Society.

Su, L. (2003). A comprehensive and systematic model of user evaluation of Web search engines: I. theory and background. *Journal of the American Society for Information Science and Technology, 54*(13), 1175–1192. doi:10.1002/asi.10303

Su, L. T. (1998). Value of search results as a whole as the best single measure of information retrieval performance. *Information Processing & Management, 34*(5), 557–579. doi:10.1016/S0306-4573(98)00023-5

Sullivan, D. (2003). Searching with invisible tabs. *Search Engine Watch*. Retrieved October 19, 2010, from http://searchenginewatch.com/3115131

Sutcliffe, R. F. E., White, K., Slattery, D., Gabbay, I., & Mulcahy, M. (2006). Cross-Language French-English question answering using the DLT system at CLEF 2006. In *Proceedings of the Working Notes of CLEF Cross-Language Evaluation Forum*.

Sweeney, S., & Crestani, F. (2006). Effective search results summary size and device screen size: Is there a relationship? *Information Processing & Management, 42*(4), 1056–1074. doi:10.1016/j.ipm.2005.06.007

Tablan, V., Damljanovic, D., & Bontcheva, K. (2008). A natural language query interface to structured information. In *Proceedings of the 5th European Semantic Web Conference on the Semantic Web: Research and Applications*, Spain (pp. 361-375).

Tague-Sucliffe, J. (1992). The pragmatics of information retrieval experimentation, revisited. *Information Processing & Management, 28*(4), 467–490. doi:10.1016/0306-4573(92)90005-K

Tainter, J. A. (1988). *The collapse of complex societies*. Cambridge, UK: Cambridge University Press.

Tamine, L., Boughanem, M., & Zemirli, N. (2008). Personalized document ranking: Exploiting evidence from multiple user interests for profiling and retrieval. *Journal of Digital Information Management, 6*(5), 354–365.

Tamine-Lechani, L., Boughanem, M., & Daoud, M. (2009). Evaluation of contextual information retrieval effectiveness: Overview of issues and research. *Knowledge and Information Systems Journal, 24*(1), 1–34. doi:10.1007/s10115-009-0231-1

Tanevm, H., Negrim, M., & Magninim, B. m & Kouylekovm M. (2004). The DIOGENE question answering system at CLEF-2004. In *Proceedings of the Working Notes of CLEF Cross-Language Evaluation Forum*, Bath, UK (pp. 325-333).

Tang, C., Xu, Z., & Dwarkadas, S. (2003). Peer-to-peer information retrieval using self-organizing semantic overlay networks. In *Proceedings of the Conference on Applications, Technologies, Architectures, and Protocols for Computer Communications* (pp. 175-186). New York, NY: ACM.

Tannier, X., & Moriceau, V. (2010). Studying syntactic analysis in a QA system: FIDJI @ ResPubliQA'09. In C. Peters, G. Nunzio, M. Kurimo, D. Mostefa, A. Penas, & G. Roda (Eds.), *Proceedings of the 10th Workshop on Multilingual Information Access Evaluation I: Text Retrieval Experiments* (LNCS 6241, pp 237-244).

Tao, Y., Mamoulis, N., & Papadias, D. (2003). Validity information retrieval for spatiotemporal queries. In T. Hadzilacos, Y. Manolopoulos, J. Roddick, & Y. Theodoridis (Eds.), *Proceedings of the 8th International Symposium on Advances in Spatial and Temporal Databases* (LNCS 2750, pp. 159-178).

Tapscott, D., Ticoll, D., & Lowy, A. (2000). *Digital capital: Harnessing the power of business Webs*. Boston, MA: Harvard Business School Press.

Taptu Limited. (2010). *Taptu search engine*. Retrieved April 20, 2010, from http://taptu.com/corp/

Tashian, C. (2009). *Bytes and Pixes (Web Page Sizes)*. Retrieved March 17, 2011, from http://tashian.com/htmlguide/sizes.html

Tatu, M., Iles, B., Slavick, J., Novischi, A., & Moldovan, D. (2006). COGEX at the second recognizing textual entailment challenge. In *Proceedings of the PASCAL Challenges Workshop on Recognising Textual Entailment*.

Taylor, C. F., Field, D., Sansone, S. A., Aerts, J., Apweiler, R., & Ashburner, M. (2008). Promoting coherent minimum reporting guidelines for biological and biomedical investigations: the MIBBI project. *Nature Biotechnology*, *26*(8), 889–896. doi:10.1038/nbt.1411

Taylor, C. F., Paton, N. W., Lilley, K. S., Binz, P. A., Julian, R. K. Jr, & Jones, A. R. (2007). The minimum information about a proteomics experiment (MIAPE). *Nature Biotechnology*, *25*(8), 887–893. doi:10.1038/nbt1329

Taylor, R. (1968). Question negociation and information seeking in libraries. *College & Research Libraries*, *29*, 178–194.

TechTarget. (1999, February 24). What is knowledge worker? - Definition from Whatis.com. *SearchCRM.com*. Retrieved April 7, 2011, from http://searchcrm.techtarget.com/definition/knowledge-worker

Teissedre, C., Djioua, B., & Desclés, J.-P. (2008). Automatic retrieval of definitions in texts, in accordance with a general linguistic ontology. In *Proceedings of the 21st International Florida Artificial Intelligence, Research Society Conference* (pp. 518-523).

Tellex, S., Katz, B., Lin, J., Fernandes, A., & Marton, G. (2003). Quantitative evaluation of passage retrieval algorithms for question answering. In *Proceedings of the 26th Annual International ACM SIGIR Conference on Research and Development in Information Retrieval*, Toronto, ON, Canada (pp. 41-47).

Terrasse, M. N., & Roux, M. (2010). Metamodelling architectures for complex data integration in systems biology. *International Journal of Biomedical Engineering and Technology*, *3*(1-2), 22–42. doi:10.1504/IJBET.2010.029650

The Global Earth Observation System of Systems (GEOSS). (2005). *10-year implementation plan*. Retrieved from http://www.earthobservations.org

The Open Source Census. (2011). *Census summary report*. Retrieved March 24, 2011, from https://www.osscensus.org/ summary-report-public.php

Tianyong, H., Wanpeng, S., Dawei, H., & Wenyin, L. (2008). Automatic generation of semantic patterns for user-interactive question answering. In H. Li, T. Liu, W.-Y. Ma, T. Sakai, K.-F. Wong, & G. Zhou (Eds.), *Proceedings of the 4th Asia Information Retrieval Technology Symposium* (LNCS 4993, pp. 632-637).

Timothy, M., Sherry, C., & Robert, M. (2005). Hypermedia learning and prior knowledge: domain expertise vs. system expertise. *Journal of Computer Assisted Learning, 21*(12), 53–64.

Tjong, E. F., Sang, K., & Buchholz, S. (2000). Introduction to the CoNLL-2000 shared task: Chunking. In *Proceedings of the 2nd Workshop on Learning Language in Logic and the 4th Conference on Computational Natural Language Learning*, Lisbon, Portugal (Vol. 7).

Tombros, A., Ruthven, I., & Jose, J. M. (2005). How users assess web pages for information seeking. *Journal of the American Society for Information Science and Technology, 56*(4), 327–344. doi:10.1002/asi.20106

Tompkins, J. A. (2000). *No boundaries: Moving beyond supply chain management*. Raleigh, NC: Tompkins Press.

Trillo, R., Po, L., Ilarri, S., Bergamaschi, S., & Mena, S. (2010). Using semantic techniques to access web data. *Information Systems, 36*(2).

Troncy, T., & Isaac, A. (2002, June). *Semantic commitment for designing ontologies: A tool proposal*. Poster presented at the Meeting of the International Semantic Web Conference, Sardinia, Italia.

Trotman, A. (2003). Compressing inverted files. *Information Retrieval, 6*(1), 5–19. doi:10.1023/A:1022949613039

Trotman, A., Geva, A., Kamps, J., Lalmas, M., & Murdock, V. (2010). Current research in focused retrieval and result aggregation. *Information Retrieval, 13*(5), 407–411. doi:10.1007/s10791-010-9137-5

Tsai, F. S., Etoh, M. X., Lee, X. W., & Yang, Q. (2010). Introduction to mobile information retrieval. *Intelligent Systems, 25*(1), 11–15. doi:10.1109/MIS.2010.22

Tseng, F., & Chou, A. (2004). The concept of document warehousing and its applications on managing enterprise business intelligence. In *Proceedings of Pacific Asia Conference on Information Systems*, Shanghai, China.

Tsyganov, S., Mallón Amérigo, S., Petit, T., Pettersson, A., & Suwalska, A. (2008). A search engine for the engineering and equipment or data management system (EDMS) at CERN. *Journal of Physics: Conference Series, 119*(4), 20–29. doi:10.1088/1742-6596/119/4/042029

Tsyganov, S., Petit, T., & Suwalska, A. (2009). Oracle Text at the CERN engineering and equipment data management system search engine. *Swiss Oracle User Group Newsletter, 1-2*, 28–35.

Turenne, N. (2000). *Apprentissage statistique pour l'extraction de concepts à partir de textes (Application au filtrage d'informations textuelles)* (Unpublished doctoral dissertation). Université Louis-Pasteur, Strasbourg, France.

Turney, P. D. (2002). Thumbs up or thumbs down? Semantic orientation applied to unsupervised classification of reviews. In *Proceedings of the 40th Annual Meeting on Association for Computational Linguistics*, Philadelphia, PA.

Ukkonen, E. (1995). On-line construction of suffix trees. *Algorithmica, 14*(3), 249–260. doi:10.1007/BF01206331

University of California. Santa Barbara. (2001). *Alexandria digital library feature type thesaurus*. Retrieved from http://www.alexandria.ucsb.edu/gazetteer/FeatureTypes/ver100301/

Usunier, N., Amini, M., & Gallinari, P. (2004). Boosting weak ranking functions to enhance passage retrieval for question answering. In *Proceedings of the Workshop on Information Retrieval for Question Answering* (pp. 1-6).

Vaillant, B., & Meyer, P. (2006). Mesurer l'intérêt des règles d'association. *Revue des Nouvelles Technologies de l'Information (Extraction et gestion des connaissances: État et perspectives)*.

Van Gemmeren, P., & Malon, D. (2010, October). Supporting high-performance I/O at the petascale: the event data store for ATLAS at the LHC. In *Proceedings of the IEEE International Conference on Cluster Computing*, Heraklion, Crete, Greece.

van Rijsbergen, C. J. (1979). *Information retrieval* (2nd ed.). Oxford, UK: Butterworth-Heinemann.

Van Schooten, B. W., Op Den Akker, R., Rosset, S., Galibert, O., Max, A., & Illouz, G. (2009). Follow-up question handling in the IMIX and Ritel systems: A comparative study. *Natural Language Engineering, 15*, 97–118. doi:10.1017/S1351324908004920

Varges, S., Weng, F., & Pon-Barry, H. (2008). Interactive question answering and constraint relaxation in spoken dialogue systems. *Natural Language Engineering*, *15*(1), 9–30. doi:10.1017/S1351324908004889

Vaughan, L. (2004). New measurements for search engine evaluation proposed and tested. *Information Processing & Management*, *40*(4), 677–691. doi:10.1016/S0306-4573(03)00043-8

Vaughan, L., & Thelwall, M. (2004). Search engine coverage bias: Evidence and possible causes. *Information Processing & Management*, *40*(4), 693–707. doi:10.1016/S0306-4573(03)00063-3

Vaughan, L., & Zhang, Y. (2007). Equal representation by search engines? A comparison of websites across countries and domains. *Journal of Computer-Mediated Communication*, *12*(3), 7. doi:10.1111/j.1083-6101.2007.00355.x

Vechtomova, O. (2010). Facet-based opinion retrieval from blogs. *Information Processing & Management*, *46*(1), 71–88. doi:10.1016/j.ipm.2009.06.005

Verberne, S. (2010). *In search of the why - Developing a system for answering why-questions* (Unpublished doctoral dissertation). Radboud Universiteit Nijmegen, Nijmegen-Midden, The Netherlands.

Verberne, S., Raaijmakers, S., Theijssen, D., & Boves, L. (2009). Learning to rank answers to why-questions. In *Proceedings of the Dutch-Belgium Information Retrieval Workshop* (pp. 34-41).

Verberne, S., Boves, L., Oostdijk, N., & Coppen, P. A. (2010). What is no in the Bag of Words for Why-QA? *Computational Linguistics*, *36*(2), 229–245.

Verberne, S., Halteren, H., Theijssen, D., Raaijmakers, S., & Boves, L. (2011). Learning to rank for why-question answering. *Information Retrieval*, *14*(2). doi:10.1007/s10791-010-9136-6

Véronis, J. (2006). *A comparative study of six search engines*. Retrieved October 19, 2010, from http://www.up.univ-mrs.fr/veronis/pdf/2006-comparative-study.pdf

Vieira, V., Tedesco, P., Salgado, A. C., & Brzillon, P. (2007). Investigating the specifics of contextual elements management: The Cemantika approach. In *Proceedings of the 6th International and Interdisciplinary Conference on Modeling and Using Context* (pp. 493-506).

Vizcaíno, J. A., Côté, R., Reisinger, F., Foster, J. M., Mueller, M., & Rameseder, J. (2009). A guide to the proteomics identifications database proteomics data repository. *Proteomics*, *9*(18), 4276–4283. doi:10.1002/pmic.200900402

Voorhees, M. (2001a). Overview of the TREC 2001 question answering track. In *Proceedings of the Tenth Text REtrieval Conference* (pp. 42-51).

Voorhees, M. (2003). Overview of the TREC 2003 question answering track. In *Proceedings of the Twelfth Text REtrieval Conference* (pp. 54-68).

Voorhees, E. M. (2001). The TREC question answering track. *Journal of Natural Language Engineering*, *7*(4). doi:10.1017/S1351324901002789

Voorhees, M. (2001b). The TREC question answering track. *Natural Language Engineering*, *7*, 361–378. doi:10.1017/S1351324901002789

Vouros, G. A. (2008). Searching and sharing information in networks of heterogeneous agents. In *Proceedings of the 7th International Joint Conference on Autonomous Agents and Multiagent Systems* (pp. 1525-1528). Richland, SC: International Foundation for Autonomous Agents and Multiagent Systems.

Waller, V. (2011). Not just information: Who searches for what on the search engine Google? *Journal of the American Society for Information Science and Technology*, *62*(4), 761–777. doi:10.1002/asi.21492

Wan, X. (2009). Combining content and context similarities for image retrieval. In M. Boughanem, C. Berrut, J. Mothe, & C. Soule-Dupuy (Eds.), *Proceedings of the 31st European Conference on Advances in Information Retrieval* (LNCS 5478, pp. 749-754).

Wang, K., Ming, Z., & Chua, T. S. (2009). A syntactic tree matching approach to finding similar questions in community-based QA services. In *Proceedings of the 32nd International ACM SIGIR Conference on Research and Development in Information Retrieval*.

Wang, R., & Neumann, G. (2008). An accuracy-oriented divide-and-conquer strategy for recognizing textual entailment. In *Proceedings of the Text Analysis Conference*.

Wang, R., Zhang, Y., & Neumann, G. (2009). A joint syntactic-semantic representation for recognizing textual relatedness. In *Proceedings of the Text Analysis Conference on Notebook Papers and Results* (pp. 1-7).

Wardrip-Fruin, N., & Montfort, N. (Eds.). (2003). *The new media reader (Sec. 54)*. Cambridge, MA: MIT Press.

Ware, C. (2004). *Information visualization: Perception for design* (2nd ed.). San Francisco, CA: Morgan Kaufmann.

Wasserman, S., & Faust, K. (1994). *Social network analysis*. Cambridge, UK: Cambridge University Press.

Watts, D. J., Dodds, P. S., & Newman, M. E. J. (2002). Identity and search in social networks. *Science*, *296*(5571), 1302–1305. doi:10.1126/science.1070120

Watts, D. J., & Strogatz, S. H. (1998). Collective dynamics of 'small-world' networks. *Nature*, *393*(6684). doi:10.1038/30918

Weisenthal, J. (2007). *Hakia raises $2 million for semantic search*. Retrieved from http://www.nytimes.com/paidcontent/PCORG_317848.html

Weiss, D., & Stefanowski, J. (2003, June 2-5). Web search results clustering in Poish: Experimental evaluation of Carrot. In *Proceedings of the New Trends in Intelligent Information Processing and Web Mining Conference*, Zakopane, Poland.

Wenyin, L., Tianyong, H., Chen, W., & Min, F. (2009). A Web-based platform for user-interactive question-answering. *World Wide Web (Bussum)*, *12*(2), 107–124. doi:10.1007/s11280-008-0051-3

White, R. W., Kules, B., Drucker, S. M., & Schraefel, M. C. (2006). Supporting exploratory search. *Communications of the ACM*, *49*(4), 37–39.

Wiebe, J., & Riloff, E. (2005). Creating subjective and objective sentence classifiers from unannotated texts. In A. Gelbukh (Eds.), *Proceedings of the 6th International Conference on Computational Linguistics and Intelligent Text Processing* (LNCS 3406, pp. 486-497).

Wiebe, J., & Cardie, C. (2005). Annotating expressions of opinions and emotions in language. *Language Resources and Evaluation*, *39*(2-3), 165–210. doi:10.1007/s10579-005-7880-9

Wielinga, B., Schreiber, A., Wielemaker, Q., & Sandberg, J. (2001, October 22-23). From thesaurus to ontology. In *Proceedings of the 1st International Conference on Knowledge Capture*, Victoria, BC, Canada.

Wikipedia. (2011). *Lucene*. Retrieved March 16, 2011, from http://en.wikipedia.org/wiki/Lucene

Wikipedia. (2011). *Yandex*. Retrieved March 16, 2011, from http://en.wikipedia.org/wiki/Yandex

Wilson, T. (1996). *Information behaviour: an interdisciplinary perspective. A report to the British Library Research and Innovation Centre*. London, UK: British Library Research and Innovation Centre. Retrieved August 16, 2010, from http://informationr.net/tdw/publ/infbehav/chap7.html

Wilson, T., Hoffmann, P., Somasundaran, S., Kessler, J., Wiebe, J., Choi, Y., et al. (2005). OpinionFinder. In *Proceedings of the Human Language Technology Conference Conference on Empirical Methods in Natural Language Processing on Interactive Demonstrations*, Vancouver, BC, Canada (pp. 34-35).

Wilson, T. (2000). Human information behaviour. *Informing Science*, *3*(2), 49–56.

Wilson, T., Wiebe, J., & Hoffmann, P. (2009). Recognizing contextual polarity: An exploration of features for phrase-level sentiment analysis. *Computational Linguistics*, *35*(3), 399–433. doi:10.1162/coli.08-012-R1-06-90

Wise, J. A., Thomas, J. J., Pennock, K., Lantrip, D., Pottier, M., Schur, A., et al. (1995). Visualizing the non-visual: Spatial analysis and interaction with information from text documents. In *Proceedings of IEEE Symposium on Information Visualization* (pp. 51-58). Washington, DC: IEEE Computer Society.

Witten, A. H., Moffat, A., & Bell, T. C. (1999). *Managing gigabytes: Compressing and indexing documents and images* (2nd ed.). San Francisco, CA: Morgan Kaufmann.

World Meteorological Organization. (2010). *Core metadata profile version 1.2. Guidelines on the use of metadata for WIS*. Retrieved from http://www.wmo.int/

Wright, A. (2009, August 23). Mining the Web for feelings, not facts. *The New York Times*. Retrieved October 13, 2010, from http://www.nytimes.com/2009/08/24/technology/internet/24emotion.html

Wu, Y.-F. B., Rakthin, C., & Li, C. (2002, August 9-11). Summarizing search results with automatic tables of contents. In *Proceedings of the 8th Americas Conference on Information Systems.*

Wu, Y.-F. B., Shankar, L., & Chen, X. (2003, November 2-8). Finding more useful information faster from Web search results. In *Proceedings of the ACM CIKM International Conference on Information and Knowledge Management,* New Orleans, LA.

Wu, Z., & Palmer, M. (1994). Verb semantics and lexical selection. In *Proceedings of the 32nd Annual Meeting of the Association for Computational Linguistics.*

Wu, C. H., Yeh, L. S., Huang, H., Arminski, L., Castro-Alvear, J., & Chen, Y. (2003). The protein information resource. *Nucleic Acids Research, 31*(1), 345–347. doi:10.1093/nar/gkg040

Xie, H. (2008). Users' evaluation of digital libraries (DLs): Their uses, their criteria, and their assessment. *Information Processing & Management, 44*(3), 1346–1373. doi:10.1016/j.ipm.2007.10.003

Xie, I. (2008). *Interactive information retrieval in digital environments.* Hershey, PA: IGI Global. doi:10.4018/978-1-59904-240-4

Yahoo Inc. (2010). *Yahoo search engine.* Retrieved April 20, 2010, from http://mobile.yahoo.com/ search

Yahoo. (2009). *Yahoo! Year in Review 2009 - Top 10 searches.* Retrieved July 1, 2010, from http://yearinreview.yahoo.com/ 2009/top10

Yahoo. (2010). *The history of Yahoo! How it all started...* Retrieved October 13, 2010, from http://docs.yahoo.com/info/misc/history.html

Yamamoto, G. T., & Karaman, F. (2006b). ICT, new working elite, and social implications. *E-Business Review, 6.*

Yamamoto, G. T., & Karaman, F. (2007a). Technologies collecting user data and privacy issues. In *Proceedings of the 7th Annual Conference of the International Academy of E-Business 7th Annual Conference,* Vancouver, BC, Canada.

Yamamoto, G. T., & Karaman, F. (2005). A road-map for the development of the content protecting technologies (CPT) for the content based e-business models. *E-Business Review, 5,* 226–232.

Yamamoto, G. T., & Karaman, F. (2006a). User rating system for the Internet (URSI) and Central Authority for Internet Security (CAIS). *The Journal of Business, 5*(2).

Yamamoto, G. T., & Karaman, F. (2007b). Business ethics and technology in Turkey: An emerging country at the crossroad of civilizations. In Nemati, H. (Ed.), *Information security and ethics: Concepts, methodologies, tools and applications.* Hershey, PA: Information Science Reference. doi:10.4018/978-1-59904-937-3.ch131

Yao, Y. (2002). Information retrieval support systems. In *Proceedings of the IEEE International Conference on Fuzzy Systems* (pp. 1092-1097). Washington, DC: IEEE Computer Society.

Yau, S. S., Liu, H., Huang, D., & Yao, Y. (2003). Situation-aware personalized information retrieval for mobile Internet. In *Proceedings of the 27th Annual International Computer Software and Applications* Conference (pp. 638-645).

Yee, K.-P., Swearingen, K., Li, K., & Hearst, M. (2003). Faceted metadata for image search and browsing. In *Proceedings for the ACM Conference on Human Factors in Computing Systems* (pp. 401-408). New York, NY: ACM.

Yi, J., Nasukawa, T., Bunescu, R., & Niblack, W. (2003). Sentiment analyzer: Extracting sentiments about a given topic using natural language processing techniques. In *Proceedings of the IEEE International Conference on Data Mining,* Melbourne, FL. Washington, DC: IEEE Computer Society.

Yippy, Inc. (2010). *Yippy – Welcome to the cloud.* Retrieved September 23, 2010, from http://search.yippy.com

Yu, B., & Singh, M. P. (2003). Searching social networks. In *Proceedings of the Second International Joint Conference on Autonomous Agents and Multiagent Systems* (pp. 65-72). New York, NY: ACM.

Yu, H., & Hatzivassiloglou, V. (2003). Towards answering opinion questions: Separating facts from opinions and identifying the polarity of opinion sentences. In *Proceedings of the Conference on Empirical Methods in Natural Language Process,* Sapporo, Japan (pp. 129-136).

Yu, H., Sable, C., & Zhu, H. R. (2005). Classifying medical questions based on an evidence taxonomy. In *Proceedings of the 20th National Conference on Artificial Intelligence and the Workshop on Question Answering in Restricted Domains.*

Yuncheng, J., Yong, T., Ju, W., & Suqin, T. (2010). Representation and reasoning of context-dependant knowledge in distributed fuzzy ontologies. *International Journal of Expert Systems with Applications, 37*(8), 6052–6060. doi:10.1016/j.eswa.2010.02.122

Zadeh, L. (1965). Fuzzy sets. *Information and Control, 8*(3), 338–353. doi:10.1016/S0019-9958(65)90241-X

Zadeh, L. (1975). The concept of a linguistic variable and its application to approximate reasoning. *International Journal of Information Science, 4*(4), 301–357.

Zajac, R. (2001). Towards ontological question answering. In *Proceedings of the Workshop on Open Domain Question Answering.*

Zamir, O., & Etzioni, O. (1999). Grouper: A dynamic clustering interface to Web search results. *Computer Networks, 31*(11-16), 1361-1374.

Zarko, I. P., & Silvestri, F. (2007). The CIKM 2006 workshop on information retrieval in peer-to-peer networks. *SIGIR Forum, 41*(1), 101-103.

Zeng, H.-J., He, Q.-C., Chen, Z., Ma, W.-Y., & Ma, J. (2004, July 25-29). Learning to cluster Web search results. In *Proceedings of the 27th Annual International ACM SIGIR Conference on Research and Development in Information Retrieval,* Sheffield, UK.

Zha, H. (1999). On updating problems in latent semantic indexing. *SIAM Journal on Scientific Computing, 21*(2), 782–791. doi:10.1137/S1064827597329266

Zhang, D., & Dong, Y. (2004). Semantic, hierarchical, online clustering of Web search results. In J. X. Yu, X. Lin, H. Lu, & Y. Zhang (Eds.), *Proceedings of the 6th Asia-Pacific Conference on Advanced Web Technologies and Applications* (LNCS 3007, pp. 69-78).

Zhang, D., & Lee, W. S. (2003). Question classification using support vector machines. In *Proceedings of the 26th Annual International ACM SIGIR Conference on Research and Development in Informaion Retrieval,* Toronto, ON, Canada (pp. 26-32).

Zhang, H., & Lesser, V. (2006). Multi-agent based peer-to-peer information retrieval systems with concurrent search sessions. In *Proceedings of the Fifth International Joint Conference on Autonomous Agents and Multiagent Systems* (pp. 305-312). New York, NY: ACM.

Zhang, H., & Lesser, V. (2007). A reinforcement learning based distributed search algorithm for hierarchical peer-to-peer information retrieval systems. In *Proceedings of the 6th International Joint Conference on Autonomous Agents and Multiagent Systems* (pp. 1-8). New York, NY: ACM.

Zhang, H., Croft, W. B., Levine, B., & Lesser, V. (2004). A multi-agent approach for peer-to-peer based information retrieval system. In *Proceedings of the Third International Joint Conference on Autonomous Agents and Multiagent Systems* (pp. 456-463). Washington, DC: IEEE Computer Society.

Zhang, J., Long, X., & Suel, T. (2007). Performance of compressed inverted list caching in search engines. In *Proceedings of the 17th International Conference on World Wide Web* (pp. 387-396).

Zhang, Q. (2011). *Engineering the ATLAS TAG Browser* (Tech. Rep. No. ATL-SOFT-PROC-2011-034). Retrieved from http://cdsweb.cern.ch/ record/1322654

Zhang, W., Yu, C., & Meng, W. (2007). Opinion retrieval from blogs. In *Proceedings of the Sixteenth ACM Conference on Conference on Information and Knowledge Management,* Lisbon, Portugal. New York, NY: ACM.

Zhang, D., Zhai, C., Han, J., Srivastava, A., & Oza, N. (2009). Topic modeling for OLAP on multidimensional text databases: topic cube and its applications. *Statistical Analysis and Data Mining, 2*(5-6), 378–395. doi:10.1002/sam.10059

Zhu, B., & Chen, H. (2005). Information visualization. *Annual Review of Information Science & Technology, 39,* 139–177. doi:10.1002/aris.1440390111

Zhu, L., Ma, Q., Liu, C., Mao, G., & Yang, W. (2010). Semantic-distance based evaluation of ranking queries over relational databases. *Journal of Intelligent Information Systems, 35*(3). doi:10.1007/s10844-009-0116-5

Zobel, J., & Moffat, A. (2006). Inverted files for text search engines. *ACM Computing Surveys, 38*(2). doi:10.1145/1132956.1132959

Zuckerberg, M. (2008, December 4). Facebook across the Web. *The Facebook Blog.* Retrieved October 13, 2010, from http://blog.facebook.com/ blog.php?post=41735647130

Zuckerberg, M. (2010, July 21). 500 million stories. *The Facebook Blog.* Retrieved October 13, 2010, from http://blog.facebook.com/ blog.php?post=409753352130

Zuk, T., Schlesier, L., Neumann, P., Hancock, M., & Carpendale, S. (2006). Heuristics for information visualization evaluation. In *Proceedings of the AVI Workshop on Beyond Time and Errors: Novel Evaluation Methods for Information Visualization* (pp. 1-6). New York, NY: ACM.

About the Contributors

Christophe Jouis is assistant professor at the University Paris Sorbonne Nouvelle, France. He received a PhD in Applied Mathematics at the "Ecole des Hautes Etudes en Sciences Sociales" (EHESS); and CAMS ("Centre d'Analyse et de Mathématiques Sociales"), OPTION: Science, Logic, Linguistics. From 2000 to 2004 he was associate professor in the Department of Computer Science at the University of Quebec at Trois-Rivieres (Canada), under the direction of Professor Ismail Biskri. In 2005, he joined the LIP6 ("Laboratoire d'Informatique de Paris 6), affiliated with the University Pierre et Marie Curie (UMPC) and the CNRS (France). Within the LIP6, he is currently a member of the research team ACASA ("Cognitive Agents and Automated Symbolic Learning"), led by Professor Jean-Gabriel Ganascia. His research interests are in natural language processing (NLP), cognitive sciences, ontology, typicality, data mining and information retrieval.

Ismaïl Biskri is full professor in computational linguistics and artificial intelligence at the computer science department of the University of Quebec at Trois-Rivières. He is also associate professor at the computer science department of the University of Quebec at Montreal. He is a researcher at the LAMIA Laboratory. His research interests concern aspects of fundamental research on the syntactic and functional semantic analysis of natural languages with using models of Categorial Grammars and combinatory logic. He also works on specific issues in text-mining, information retrieval and terminology. His research is funded by the Canadian granting agencies FQRSC, SSHRC, NSERC.

Jean-Gabriel Ganascia is presently Professor of computer science at Paris University Pierre et Marie Curie (Paris VI) and researcher at the computer science laboratory of Paris VI University (LIP6) where he leads the ACASA ("Cognitive Agents and Automated Symbolic Learning") team. He originally worked on symbolic machine learning and knowledge engineering. His "thèse d'état", defended in 1987, was a pioneering work on the algebraic framework on which the association rule extraction techniques are based. Today, his main scientific interests cover different areas of artificial intelligence: scientific discovery, cognitive modeling, data-mining and digital humanities. He has published more than 350 scientific papers in conference proceedings, journals and books. In the past, Jean-Gabriel Ganascia was also program leader in the CNRS executive from 1988 to 1992 before moving to direct the Cognitive Science Coordinated Research Program and head the Cognition Sciences Scientific Interest Group from 1993 until 2000.

Magali Roux is a CNRS Research Director involved in the development and administration of programs and courses in e-Biology. Her research interests span a wide range with domains centered on knowledge organization and data management in Medical Biology, Molecular Biology and, recently, in Systems Biology in the context of e-Sciences. After obtaining her PhD in Biochemistry from the University of the Mediterranean in 1979, she started as assistant-professor at the Marseille University Hospital before being offered a post-doctoral position at Harvard University in the Pr. J. Strominger laboratory, where she provided one of the first bioinformatics analyses performed on DNA data. Since that, she has produced leading contributions in the fields of Immunology and Cancer. In the early 2000s, she moved from Experimental to Digital Biology to promote interoperability, data sharing and re-use. Dr. Roux serves on numerous study panels and is currently active in a number of scientific societies.

* * *

Motasem Alrahabi received his Ph.D degree in computational linguistics from the University of Paris-Sorbonne in 2010. He is currently a lecturer at Paris-Sorbonne University Abu Dhabi and his researches interests in the LaLIC laboratory include computational linguistics analysis of the reported quotation and semantic annotation of texts in French and Arabic.

Michael W. Berry holds the title of Full Professor and Associate Department Head in the Department of Electrical Engineering and Computer Science at the University of Tennessee, Knoxville. He received the BS degree in Mathematics from the University of Georgia in 1981, the MS degree in Applied Mathematics from North Carolina State University in 1983, and the PhD degree in Computer Science from the University of Illinois at Urbana-Champaign. He has organized numerous workshops on Text Mining and was Conference Co-Chair of the 2003 SIAM Third International Conference on Data Mining (May 1-3) in San Francisco, CA and was Program Co-Chair of the 2004 SIAM Fourth International Conference on Data Mining (April 22-24) in Orlando, FL. He is a member of SIAM, ACM, MAA, and the IEEE Computer Society. His research interests include information retrieval, data and text mining, computational science, bioinformatics, and parallel computing.

Rachid Benlamri is a Professor and the Chair of the Software Engineering Department at Lakehead University – Canada. He obtained a Master degree and PhD in Computer Science from the University of Manchester – UK in 1987 and 1990 respectively. He recently served as the General Chair for the 5th IEEE International Conference on Digital Information Management (ICDIM'2010). He is a senior member of the IEEE. His research interests are in the area of Semantic Web, ubiquitous computing, mobile learning, and semantic video analysis. He has over sixty publications in referred international journals and conference proceedings.

Jawad Berri is an assistant professor at King Saud University – Saudi Arabia. He received his Ph.D. in Computer Science from Paris-Sorbonne University in France in 1996. Jawad's research interests focus on context-aware web systems, learning technologies and natural language processing. He has been involved in many projects related to mobile learning, semantic web, automatic summarization, web information filtering and mobile agents for web information discovery. His contributions in research projects in the industry and academia led to the publication of papers in numerous journals and conferences. Jawad is a senior member of the IEEE.

Ivan Bigorgne is a cognitive ergonomist specialized in the study of new technologies practices. He has been working for three years in the LUTIN Laboratory (Laboratoire des Usages en Technologie de l'Information Numérique). He has a M.D. in Cognitive Sciences and Cognitive Ergonomy and has a background in automatic language processing data mining, text mining and in databases. He is also specialized in using oculometric devices in the aim of studying visual path during visual exploration.

Ismaïl Biskri is full professor in computational linguistics and artificial intelligence at the Computer science department of the University of Quebec at Trois-Rivières. His research interests concern aspects of fundamental research on the syntactic and functional semantic analysis of natural languages with using models of Categorial Grammars and combinatory logic. He also works on specific issues in text-mining. His research is funded by the canadian granting agencies FQRSC, SSHRC, NSERC.

Yacine El Bouhairi is a statistical engineer specialized in data mining and application development. He has been working for one year in Thales Communications. Through different research projects, he is working on extending OLAP concepts to multimodal information and adding data mining results to business intelligence applications. He has a background in statistics and data analysis and is interested in several technologies related to information analysis: data bases, text and web mining, data and knowledge representation.

Ourdia Bouidghaghen is currently a Ph.D. student at the Laboratory of Computer Science IRIT (France). She has received a M.Sc. degree in computer science from the University of Boumerdes, Algeria in 2007 and an engineer degree in computer science from the University of Tizi-Ouzou, Algeria, in 2004. Her research interests are in contextual information retrieval and personalization in mobile environment, user profiling and semantic data mining. She is involved in the IR Quaero project (http://www.quaero.org).

Stéphanie Brizard a graduate in interpretation and translation from the Université Catholique de l'Ouest (UCO, Angers, France), Stéphanie Brizard worked for seven years as a liaison interpreter in English, Spanish and occasionnally German. She then changed tracks in 2007 and studied natural language processing at the Institut des Langues et des Civilisations Orientales (Inalco, Paris, France) from which she graduated in October 2008. Ever since, she has been working as NLP linguist at Arisem where she can rely on her former professional experience to produce linguistic resources (electronic dictionaries, local grammars, ontologies or thesauri) for automatic information extraction, in French as well as in three foreign languages.

Stéphane Chaudiron is Professor of Information Science and currently director of the GERiiCO Laboratory at the University of Lille (France). His research interests include evaluation of effective and usable information access and processing systems, knowledge organization, information practices and information science theory. This involves active lines of research on people's use of information and communication systems (search engines, information foraging and text mining tools, social networks, new medias...). He has led a number of research projects in related areas, including evaluation of multilingual information filtering systems, the role of individual differences in information seeking, information practices in competitive intelligence context. After a Ph.D in Computational linguistics on machine translation, his career has included different management positions as Project Officer in charge of the language technology and the business intelligence sectors (French Ministry of Research – ICT Unit) and Head of the Technolangue program (the French National Program in Language Technologies).

Lin-Chih Chen is an associate professor in the Department of Information Management at National Dong Hwa University, Taiwan. His research interests include Web Intelligent and Web Technology. He develops many Web Intelligent systems include *Cayley Search Engine, VLDP_KRG term suggestion system, Cayley Digital Content system, iClubs Community, Language Agent, and Web Snippet Clustering system*. He is also a leader of Cayley Group.

Abhishek Das is a Google software engineer who works on enhancing their web search experience. He holds a PhD from Stanford University where he focussed on developing a scalable and platform independent optimization framework for multiprocessor programming systems. He received his B.Tech in Computer Science from Indian Institute of Technology (IIT) Kharagpur in 2001 and his MS from Stanford University in 2003. Abhishek has had first hand experience in building a web search engine from scratch at Cuil (a venture backed startup), contributing to the core indexing and ranking components, as well as designing their real time search engine. Currently he is exploring new frontiers in web search for Google. He holds patents, and has published and spoken at various conferences.

Jean-Pierre Desclés is a professor in computer science and linguistics at the University of Paris-Sorbonne, where he teaches computational linguistics, theoretical linguistics, logic and language engineering by conducting research in these areas. He has published numerous articles and several books on Cognitive Semantic, Logic and Enunciation, including "Natural languages, languages and applications cognition", Hermes, Paris, 1990. He founded the *Applicative and Cognitive Grammar (GA&C)* and the laboratory LaLIC (Language, Logic, Computer Science and Cognition) at Paris-Sorbonne. He is also a member of "*Académie Internationale de Philosophie des Sciences*" (Bruxelles). During the early 80s he was an invited professor at Penn State University, U.S.A; and as Postdoc student at University of YALE, U.S.A.

Brahim Djioua is assistant professor in computational linguistics at the University of Paris-Sorbonne, where he teaches computer science and logic applied linguistics. His researches interests in the LaLIC laboratory are oriented primarily to a fundamental research on lexical semantics by using typed combinatory logic, and secondly to semantic annotation and indexation of texts for information retrieval. He has 15 years' experience in computational linguistics, focusing for last years on information retrieval technology and text mining. He is behind the semantic and discourse annotation framework Excom and he has been implementing semantic annotation and indexation systems for almost 8 years. He earned his M.S. in computer science from the University of Jussieu at Paris and a Ph.D. in computational linguistics from the University of Paris-Sorbonne, Paris.

Reed Esau serves as an architect and developer at Catalyst Repository Systems, developing a scalable and secure API around their next generation platform. Since 1994 he has designed and developed software in a variety of industries, including high-end printing, device control, transaction processing, and most recently in the legal industry when he joined Catalyst in 2003. He likes cats.

Bénédicte Goujon defended a PhD thesis on the information extraction from patent texts for technological watch in 2000. Now she works in Thales Research & Technology since eleven years. She is a (co-)author of several publications related to relation extraction and knowledge extraction from texts using natural language technologies in International and French conferences. She has also participated to several French project (Outilex, WebContent, Cahors…) related to textual information management. The SemPlus tool, dedicated to the extraction of relation between named entities from texts, was one of her main research subject. More recently she has also worked on opinion mining, and more specifically on the detection of opinion target using linguistic patterns and on the anaphora solving. Moreover, Bénédicte Goujon has given courses related to applied linguistic in Paris Universities for five years.

Brigitte Grau is Professor of Computer Sciences at the Ecole Nationale Supérieiure d'Informatique pour l'Industrie et l'Entreprise (ENSIIE), an engineering school on computer science, and does her research at LIMSI, a CNRS laboratory. She works on question answering on open domain since 1999, and regularly participated to TREC and CLEF evaluations. She also works on information extraction, and especially on relation extraction from bio-medical texts, and on text analysis.

Ivan Habernal recieved his master degree in computer science with special focus on natural language processing and semantic analysis at the University of West Bohemia, Czech Republic in 2007. He had also professional experiences with Java platform, especially J2EE application development. Currently he is finishing his Ph.D. studies and his thesis deals with statistical models of natural language interfaces to Semantic Web. He is a fan of modern Java-based dynamic languages, incl. Groovy and Grails.

Orland Hoeber is an Assistant Professor in the Department of Computer Science at the Memorial University of Newfoundland (Canada). He received his Ph.D. from the University of Regina (Canada) in 2007. His primary research interests include information visualization, Web search interfaces, Web search personalization, human-computer interaction, and geo-visual analytics. Since its inception four years ago, Dr. Hoeber has been the co-organizer of the International Workshop on Web Information Retrieval Support Systems, held in conjunction with the IEEE/WIC/ACM International Conferences on Web Intelligence and Intelligent Agent Technology. As a principle researcher in the User Experience Lab at Memorial University, Dr. Hoeber is actively involved in research and graduate student supervision on projects related to the human element of computing.

Madjíd Ihadjadene is Professor of Information Science at the university of Paris 8 in France and director of Index-paragraphe laboratory. His teaching experience includes courses on information retireval, digital libraries, design and development of web ressources and theories of information and communication science His current research focuses on user studies and information behaviour. Since 1998, he has published several research papers about information retrieval system, knowledge organization system, competitive intelligence and the evaluation of search engines.

Ankit Jain received his BS in Electrical Engineering and Computer Science from UC Berkeley in 2007 and his MS in Computer Science with a focus on Parallel and Distributed Computing from UC Berkeley in 2008. He received a Certificate in Management of Technology from the Walter A. Haas School of Business at UC Berkeley in 2008. Ankit helped build several parts of a web search engine from scratch at Cuil, Inc. (a venture backed startup), contributing to the indexing and serving components. While at Cuil, he also helped design and implement their real time search engine. Ankit currently works at Google developing the next generation of search and discovery technologies for mobile devices in the Android Group. Ankit is a speaker at several conferences on a variety of search related topics.

Faruk Karaman was born in 1971 in Sarkisla-Sivas of Turkey. He holds a B.S. in Electrical and Electronics Engineering from Bosphorus University, Istanbul/Turkey. He then pursued MBA and Ph.D. in management degrees at Marmara University, Istanbul/Turkey. He worked at several financial institutions as an investment banker and gave e-Business, e-CRM, e-SCM and IT Ethics lectures at several universities in Turkey. His research interests span MIS, e-business, technology strategy, ICT strategy, technological singularity, ethical use of technology and the interactions of science and technology. He has numerous academic publications in these topics. He is also founder and many of numerous Internet discussion groups in related areas.

Weimao Ke is an assistant professor in the College of Information Science and Technology at Drexel University. His research is centered around information retrieval, particularly the investigation of intelligent systems that support better connection and interaction between people and information. His recent focus is on decentralized search engines that can adapt and scale in continuously growing and increasingly interconnected information spaces. His broad interests also include complex networks, text mining, information visualization, bibliometrics, machine learning, multi-agent systems, and the notion of information. He received his Ph.D. in Information Science from the University of North Carolina at Chapel Hill, a Master of Information Science from Indiana University Bloomington, and a Bachelor of Engineering from East China University of Science and Technology. He worked in the IT industry for many years as an information systems developer, technical leader, and project manager.

Bruce Kiefer directs Catalyst's Research and Development Group, helping to develop the next generation of their technology, and is vice president of the Hosting Applications Division. He has worked in IT for many years, helping to build, deploy, manage, scale and repair networks and systems that solve problems. Before joining Catalyst, he was vice president of operations for Viawest Internet Services. During Bruce's tenure at Viawest, he built many of the internal tools, grew the network to four states, and took over product management for Viawest's managed hosting offering. In addition to his IT expertise, Bruce has a master's degree in business administration. He joined Catalyst in 2005, where he combines his knowledge of technology and business to help drive product development and build out operations.

Miloslav Konopik graduated with honours from the University of West Bohemia in computer science in Czech Republic in 2004 and obtained the Ph.D. at the same University in 2009. He has been working as a researcher at University of West Bohemia since 2005 as a member of the LICS team. Miloslav is an author or co-author of more than twenty scientific publications. His research is aimed at automatic semantic analysis of spoken and written data. He is also interested in the semantic web ideas.

Edmond Lassalle is Senior Researcher at Orange Labs (France Télécom Group) and Chief Engineer of the Corps of Mines. His research interests include Natural Language Processing, Machine Learning and Information Retrieval. He is the author of 10 patents on large data processing applied to Information Retrieval.

Emmanuel Lassalle studied Computer Science at École Normale Supérieure de Lyon. After working briefly in Information Retrieval, he is now PhD candidate at Université de Paris 7 in Computational Linguistics. His current work concerns unsupervised acquisition of lexical data and bridging resolution.

Dirk Lewandowski is a professor of information research and information retrieval at the Hamburg University of Applied Sciences. Prior to that, he worked as an independent consultant and as a part-time lecturer at the Heinrich-Heine-University Düsseldorf. He is author of more than 50 research papers, one monograph and several edited volumes.

Stéphane Lorin is specialized in data representation and data analysis. He has worked for ten years in IBM where he has participated to the development of the data-mining solution DB2 Intelligent Miner for Data. He works now in Thales Communications in the CeNTAI entity (Center of new technologies for information analysis) as an architect for analysis information solutions. His area of interest covers a large scope on data representation and data analysis: statistics, data warehouses, queries (OLAP and OLAP-mining and Text-OLAP), data-mining, text-mining and knowledge representation (semantic nets). The application domains cover opinion analysis and fraud and cyber-criminality. He is also an expert for the Cap Digital national business cluster for digital content.

Claude Martineau holds a PhD in Computer Science in the field of word-based text compression. In 2001 he has joined the team of Liguistic Informatics of the LIGM (Laboratoire d'Informatique Gaspard-Monge) at Université Paris-Est Marne-la-Vallée, France. Since then, he has been working on NLP (Natural Language Processing), automatic information and named entities extraction. He has a dedicated interest in producing linguistic resources (electronic dictionaries, local grammars), inflection tools (for both simple and compound words) for several languages (English, French, Greek). All these resources can be used within Unitex, a multi platform and multilingual corpus processing system developed at LIGM that can handle numerous languages including non-space languages (like Thai), Semitic and Asiatic ones.

Loïs Rigouste is a research and development engineer. He holds a PhD from Telecom ParisTech in statistical natural language processing about document thematic clustering. He has been working at Pertimm on topics such as linguistic and semantic search, interoperability and corpus cleaning.

Ondrej Rohlik, born in 1976 in the Czech Republic, obtained his master degree in computer science and engineering from the University of West Bohemia in Pilsen (1999) and since then he has worked on many projects in artificial intelligence and information retrieval. In particular he explored the use of itemsets to categorize documents in large collections. His dissertation (2004) focused on signal processing and classification of multi dimensional data applied to biometrics. During his postdoc period at ETH Zurich he concentrated on development of high-integrity on-board systems which are reliable by design. Since 2007 dr. Rohlik is a part-time faculty at his alma mater pursing his passion in human-machine interaction in areas like question answering for accessible web or plausible behaviour of virtual human-like software agents. Since 2008 dr. Rohlík is advising the government and represents it at various international forums on technology development issues and industrial policy matters.

Louis Rompré is a Ph.D. student in cognitive science at the University of Quebec at Montreal. He conducts his researches under the supervision of Professor Ismaïl Biskri.

Magali Roux, PhD, is a CNRS Research Scientist involved in the development and administration of programs and courses in e-Biology. Her research interests span a wide range with domains centered on knowledge organization and data management in Medical Biology, Molecular Biology and, recently, in Systems Biology in the context of e-Sciences. After obtaining her PhD in Biochemistry from the University of Méditerranée in 1979, she started as assistant-professor at the Marseille University Hospital before being offered a post-doctoral position at Harvard University in the Pr. J. Strominger'laboratory, where she provided one of the first bioinformatics analyses performed on DNA data. Since that, she has produced leading contributions in the fields of Immunology and Cancer. In the early 2000s, she moved from Experimental to Digital Biology to promote interoperability, data sharing and re-use. Dr. Roux is serving on numerous study panels and is currently active in a number of scientific societies.

Leeley Daio Pires dos Santos is a research engineer in the department of commercial innovation and market analysis at EDF (Électricité de France) R&D. Leeley received his M.D. in Computer Sciences in 2009 from the French INSA de Lyon ("Grande Ecole"). His research concerns CRM data management, modeling and storage using traditional relational solutions and NoSQL approaches. Leeley is currently working on massif electric load curve storage and processing.

Mona Sleem-Amer is a project manager/engineer and part of the research and development team at Pertimm S.A.. Following a graduate degree in information management at the University of applied sciences in Hamburg, Germany, she moved to France and received a Master's degree in natural language processing at the Paris 10 University, Nanterre in 2008. Apart from the DoXa project, she is currently working on an e-reading research project focusing on semantic search for mobile reading devices. Her fields of interest are information retrieval, knowledge representation and human machine interfaces.

Lynda Tamine-Lechani is Assistant Professor at SIG/RI team in the Laboratory of Computer Science IRIT (France). She received her Ph.D. in computer science from the University of Toulouse (France) in 2000, and a M.Sc. in computer science from the same University in 2008. Her research interests are in theoretical models, experimental evaluation and applications design in IR and focus around contextual IR and flexible IR. She has been involved in projects on IR such as Quaero (http://www.quaero.org), ANR-AMPD (http://apmd.prism.uvsq.fr) and she has regularly been invited as a PC member of conferences on IR (SAC, ECIR, FQAS, CORIA).

Lidia Varga holds a PhD in Linguistics (Paris 13 University, France, 2007), a Master's degree in French language and literature teaching (Budapest, Hungary, 1986) as well as a Bachelor's degree in electronic and automation engineering (Budapest, 1979). She is a temporary researcher in the computational linguistics group of the Gaspard-Monge computer science research laboratory (Paris-Est, Marne-la-Vallée University). Her recent activities focus on linguistic resources creation such as electronic dictionaries, local grammars; semantic modelization of the Hungarian motion predicates for Natural Language Processing (NLP), opinion mining and consulting for the development of linguistic NLP environments.

Sarah Vert, holder of a Research Masters in Information and Communication Sciences, currently works as an information officer at the CVCE. She has a particular interest in personal knowledge management and is working to develop a digital methodology for knowledge workers.

Index